D1046957

T. W. Schultz

GROWTH AND EQUITY IN AGRICULTURAL DEVELOPMENT

# GROWTH AND EQUITY IN AGRICULTURAL DEVELOPMENT

PROCEEDINGS

EIGHTEENTH
INTERNATIONAL CONFERENCE
OF AGRICULTURAL ECONOMISTS

*Held at Jakarta, Indonesia*
24th AUGUST – 2nd SEPTEMBER 1982

Edited by
Allen Maunder, Institute of Agricultural Economics,
University of Oxford, England
and
Kazushi Ohkawa, International Development Centre
of Japan, Tokyo

INTERNATIONAL ASSOCIATION OF AGRICULTURAL ECONOMISTS
INSTITUTE OF AGRICULTURAL ECONOMICS
OXFORD

1983

Gower

© The International Association of Agricultural Economists 1983

All rights reserved. No part of this publication may be reproduced, stored in a retrieval system, or transmitted in any form or by any means, electronic, mechanical, photocopying, recording, or otherwise without the prior permission of Gower Publishing Company Limited.

Published by Gower Publishing Company Limited,
Gower House, Croft Road,
Aldershot, Hampshire GU11 3HR, England

British Library Cataloguing in Publication Data

International Conference of Agricultural Economists *(18th : 1982 : Jakarta)*
Growth and equity in agricultural developmtn. 1. Agriculture — Economic aspects — Congresses I. Title II. Maunder, Allen II. Ohkawa, Kazushi IV. International Association of Agricultural Economists V. University of Oxford. Institute of Agricultural Economists
338.1 HD1405

ISBN 0-566-00636-7

CONTENTS

## SECTION II – CONCEPTS AND METHODOLOGY – ANALYTICAL ASPECTS

## SECTION III – STRUCTURE AND PATTERNS OF AGRICULTURAL GROWTH

# PREFACE

This collection of the main papers and reports presented at the Eighteenth International Conference of Agricultural Economists represents the beginning of the second half century of the International Association of Agricultural Economists. The Eighteenth Conference of the IAAE was held from August 24 to September 2, 1982 at Jakarta, Indonesia.

The contributed papers presented also at this conference, which were selected by an international jury, will be published in the *Occasional Papers* series of the IAAE.

The Association gratefully acknowledges the welcome-reception at the State Palace of all participating IAAE members by His Excellency President Soeharto: and the continuous support for the Conference by the Governor of Jakarta, Mr. Tjokropranolo, and by the Minister of Agriculture, Professor Soedarsono Hadisapoetro. The IAAE wishes to express its appreciation for the assistance of the Government of Indonesia in ensuring the success of the 18th Conference.

The Association owes sincere gratitude to Dr. A.T. Birowo, Chairman of the Indonesian National Committee of the IAAE, who was responsible for the local organization of the Conference. This tribute also includes all members of the National Organizing Committee as well as the organizing staff headed by Mr. Husin Anang.

The Jakarta Conference programme was prepared by Professor Kazushi Ohkawa of Tokyo, Japan. He selected and grouped the papers around the main topic "Growth and Equity in Agricultural Development" with great academic care and a strong personal commitment. Vice President Programme Ohkawa succeeded in designing a unique conference programme which proved to be an academic and personal challenge to all participants.

Since its inauguration in 1976, the Leonard Elmhirst Memorial Lecture has become an integral part of the IAAE tradition. At Jakarta, Elmhirst Lecturer Keith O. Campbell addressed the Conference with an outstanding paper on "Agricultural Economists and World Conservation Strategy". In a time where there seems to exist a trade-off between economy and ecology, Professor Campbell's guiding remarks proved to be of immense theoretical and practical value.

The International Association of Agricultural Economists is grateful to its Editor, Mr. Allen Maunder of the Institute of Agricultural Economics, Oxford University, for the immense amount of work which he devoted in preparing this volume, and, last but not least, to Mrs. Pearl Maunder for the support she gave.

THEODOR DAMS<br>
*President,*<br>
*International Association of*<br>
*Agricultural Economists*

# INTRODUCTION

This "proceedings" volume contains the major portion of the formal papers and discussion at the Eighteenth International Conference of Agricultural Economists held at Jakarta, Indonesia, from August 24th to September 2nd, 1982. These were the invited papers delivered at the plenary and special sessions of the conference.

The theme of the conference, *Growth & Equity in Agricultural Development,* is not a new topic for discussion by the IAAE but this is the first time it has been adopted as the theme and examined in a comprehensive manner. The problem – "who benefits from economic development" – is one of the most challenging for economists today and is both complex and profound. Section I examines the problem in general and from different view points. Section II is concerned with conceptual and methodological problems. Sections III and IV concentrate, respectively, on either growth or equity but in the context of the other. Section V looks at the theme from an action-orientated stance and is concerned with policy approaches to the problems already presented. Finally, in Section VI are discussed the international aspects of the topic and their bearing on problems of growth and equity at national or regional levels.

The editors wish to express their thanks to the authors, openers and rapporteurs of the various papers, particularly those who turned in their contributions on time and of the correct length, and to the editorial staff without whose unstinting help this volume could not have been prepared.

The contributed papers presented at the conference, together with summaries of discussion, will appear as *IAAE Occasional Papers III.* The reports of the meetings of Discussion Groups will appear in an *IAAE Members Bulletin.* The views expressed in this book are not necessarily those of the IAAE nor those of the institutions with which the various authors are connected.

ALLEN MAUNDER
*Editor, International Association of Agricultural Economists*

KAZUSHI OHKAWA
*Vice-President-Programme*

## ABBREVIATIONS

| | |
|---|---|
| ASEAN | Association of South East Asian Nations |
| CATIE | Tropical Agriculture Research and Training Centre |
| CEPE | Comisión Económica para Europa |
| CIMMYT | International Maize and Wheat Improvement Centre |
| CMEA | Council for Mutual Economic Assistance |
| ECLA | Economic Commission for Latin America |
| EEC | European Economic Community |
| FAO | Food and Agriculture Organization |
| FAP | Food and Agriculture Program |
| HYV | high yielding variety |
| IAAE | International Association of Agricultural Economists |
| IBRD | International Bank for Reconstruction and Development (World Bank) |
| ICRISAT | International Crops Research Institute for the Semi-Arid Tropics |
| IFPRI | International Food Policy Research Institute |
| IIASA | International Institute for Applied Systems Analysis |
| ILO | International Labour Organization |
| IMF | International Monetary Fund |
| IRRI | International Rice Research Institute |
| IUCN | International Union for Conserv. & Nat. Res. |
| LDC | less developed country |
| MEG | modern economic growth |
| MV | modern varieties (of crops) |
| N/C | newly industrializing country |
| NGO | non government organization |
| OPEC | Organization of the Petroleum Exporting Countries |
| UNEP | UN Environmental Programme |
| USDA | United States Department of Agriculture |
| WCARRD | World Conference on Agrarian Reform and Rural Development |
| WWF | World Wildlife Fund |

# OFFICIAL OPENING

OFFICIAL OPENING
The State Palace, Jakarta

From left to right:
Professor S. Hadispoetro, Minister of Agriculture, Republic of Indonesia
Professor T. Dams, President, International Association of Agricultural Economists
H.E. Soeharto, President of the Republic of Indonesia

# ADDRESS BY THE PRESIDENT OF THE REPUBLIC OF INDONESIA HIS EXCELLENCY SOEHARTO AT THE OPENING OF THE EIGHTEENTH INTERNATIONAL CONFERENCE OF AGRICULTURAL ECONOMISTS

Distinguished Chairman of the International Association of Agricultural Economists,
Distinguished Delegates,
Ladies and Gentlemen,

I attach great importance to the conference that you are holding at present. First of all, because it is attended by prominent agricultural economists from all over the world, whose ideas and experiences are extremely useful for the development of society, particularly development in the agricultural field. Secondly, because problems to be discussed during this conference are precisely related to a field which becomes one of the focuses of attention of Indonesia's development. This is the reason, therefore, that we are eager to take the utmost benefit from the current conference.

Meanwhile, this conference takes place at a time when the world requires more efforts towards conciliating ideas and harmonising interests of different countries and regions, which are quite often contradictory.

This is the reason, I believe, that international meetings which are technical and scientific in nature such as this conference are highly significant. Through this way we probably would be more successful in fostering better mutual understanding between fellow human beings and amongst nations. Motivated by such mutual understanding, it will be easier for us to promote closer co-operation.

One of the principle problems faced by mankind today is the problem of agriculture. Until this last decade, for example, various regions in the world are still suffering from scarcity of foodstuffs, and even famine, which have caused sufferings to millions of people: both men and women, young and old, as well as children. Scarcity of foodstuffs and famine are due not only to the limited natural resources available locally, but also to other factors such as the restricted funds, the low level of education and knowledge, the inefficient production methods, the low technological level and so forth.

These are the great challenges for all of us, and we have no other choice but to overcome them for the sake of the dignity of man and mankind. The success or failure of the efforts to overcome these challenges depend, in part, on all of you, agricultural economists.

Ladies and Gentlemen,

As an agrarian country which is engaged in developing itself, Indonesia places the development in the agricultural fields as one of the focuses of the development struggle. By placing the agricultural field as the focus of the development struggle, we hope that the agricultural field will become the foundation and the motivator of development in other sectors. Agriculture will continue to be the primary attention in our long-term development endeavours, because the livelihood of the majority of our people depends on the agricultural sector. By developing agriculture, we want to raise the income and living standard of tens of millions of farmers, to be self-sufficient in food, to promote the export of agricultural commodities in the broadest term. This is the reason, therefore, that we are developing agriculture integrally and we are putting it in the greater context of the national development.

In the long run, we are trying to strike a better balance of our economic structure, namely an economic structure which possesses strong industry and sustained by a solid agriculture, because it is only with such an economic structure that we will be able to attain our independence ideals, namely an advanced and prosperous society imbued with social justice.

In implementing development in this agricultural field – in which we are grateful because we have achieved encouraging results – there have been quite considerable difficulties and problems that we had to overcome. This is understandable, because in general our farmers have limited resources, both technically and scientifically, as well as their land ownership and their financial capabilities.

It is in overcoming these limitations and various problems that we are rich indeed with experience. These experiences can certainly serve as materials for the exchanges of views and experience during this conference. We are also eager to listen to and to learn from your other experiences. Thus, our meeting is more useful, because, on the one hand, we can avoid the errors that we have probably committed and, on the other hand, we can proceed with what we have done well.

I know that Indonesian agricultural economists who belong to the Indonesian Association of Agricultural Economists, who according with their profession, are hosting this conference, have already compiled as completely as possible all the materials related to this subject, in order to be discussed and to find solutions to their problems by the best experts from all over the world who are gathered here for this conference. I hope also that during your stay in Indonesia you will have the opportunity to see the rural and agricultural areas that are so varied and which at the same time also reflect the variety of problems we are facing.

We all hope that the results of discussions in this conference and your observations on the agricultural areas later on will produce conclusions from which we can all benefit, in order to improve the development policies in the agricultural field.

With these hopes, in concluding, I hereby declare the Eighteenth International Conference of Agricultural Economists officially opened.

May God Almighty bless us all.

Thank you.

# OPENING SESSION

# ELMHIRST MEMORIAL LECTURE

KEITH O. CAMPBELL

## *Agricultural Economists and World Conservation Strategy*

It is a daunting honour to follow in the footsteps of the illustrious men who have delivered the Elmhirst Lectures at previous conferences. At the same time, I am pleased to have been invited to undertake this task because it was my privilege to have been associated with Leonard Elmhirst (albeit in a minor capacity) in the running of this Association over a span of two decades. Though we were geographically separated by half the globe and consequently met infrequently, I came to admire his dedication to 'the improvement of economic and social conditions relating to agriculture and rural life', to use the phraseology of the Association's first constitution.

In my antipodean eyes, Leonard Elmhirst was the epitome of an 'English gentleman' – always courteous in his dealing with other people but firm in his belief in the importance of exercising leadership when he deemed the situation demanded it. He also seemed to have the true Englishman's belief that the rules of the game of cricket provide an indispensable guide to one's proper conduct in affairs, both public and private! The pressure to participate in games as a means of promoting international understanding was very great in the Association's early days. Indeed Elmhirst's fellow countryman, A. W. Ashby, felt constrained to record in the proceedings of the Second Conference that 'I may not play cricket but I certainly shall not play baseball'.[1]

Examination of Leonard Elmhirst's writings and his addresses at the thirteen conferences in which he participated between 1929 and 1967 clearly reveals his strongly-held belief that education and research could work miracles in improving the lot of farmers both in advanced as well as in less developed countries. His periods of service in India and his reconstruction of the Dartington estate in Devon (both of which were achieved with his wife's encouragement and assistance) exemplify his conviction that significant strides towards the enhancement of human welfare could be made at the village level. Elmhirst was equally convinced that 'man does not live by bread alone' – that religious values have a role in human endeavour[2] and that it is important to cultivate the arts – music, dance, drama, poetry and painting 'in order', as he said, 'to enrich our lives, to liven our aspirations, to inspire our leisure and to increase our delights in every kind of artistic expression'.[3]

Leonard Elmhirst knew his way through the corridors of power (at least in the British scene) but there is recurring evidence of an impatience with the deviousness of the machinery of government and the ineptitude of some civil servants. In a light-hearted vote of thanks to his former wartime chief, Lord Casey, at the opening of the Thirteenth Conference in Sydney, he recalled with relish the propensity of Casey to cut through bureaucratic entanglements during the years of their association together.[4] Urgent problems of food production and distribution called, in Elmhirst's view, for understanding and action rather than masterly inactivity. If agricultural economists could tear themselves away from their predeliction for the theoretical rather than the applied problem and their fetishism with computers, they could, in his opinion, provide an integrative role in applying science and engineering to improving the lot of farmers and, incidentally, the malnourished.[5]

Allied with Elmhirst's impatience with incompetent authorities was a deep-seated attachment to the intrinsic importance of the pursuit of excellence. Though his courtesy and his commitment to the promotion of international goodwill often constrained him in applying this principle in his personal relationships, he felt no such inhibition when making decisions about his superb 35-acre gardens at Dartington Hall. In describing his planting policy to me during a stroll through these gardens in 1968, he told me his guiding rule was not to 'retain any plant that does not earn its keep'. Edward Hyams in his classic work on English gardens makes the same point as an independent observer. 'One of the most striking features of the gardens [at Dartington Hall]', he wrote, 'is what one might call a negative one: there are no poor plants in it; or, stated positively, only the most distinguished varieties and species have been planted.'[6]

Those of you who were involved in the organization of the Association's meetings prior to the Fourteenth Conference in Minsk, know of Elmhirst's desire that the Association should meet away from what he initially called 'the distractions of the great cities'.[7] I have participated in some discussions as to what kind of distractions Elmhirst had in mind, but can give no definitive indication as to what they were. I can, however, attest to the fact that some conference participants have found distractions even when conferences have been held in rural areas! Eventually the sheer logistics of large meetings and the need for accessibility meant that the Association had to come to terms with the necessity to hold meetings in urban locations. In his final address to the 1967 conference, Elmhirst decried the urban sprawl and found himself in agreement with Father de Farcy's 'appeal for . . . more quiet places of beauty, for clearer air and purer water, for peace and the delights of being alone'.[8] Thus long before the conservation movement reached its present crusading proportions, Elmhirst was conscious of the importance of environmental issues.

## THE WORLD CONSERVATION STRATEGY

It is to some environmental and related issues that I wish to direct your attention today. In March 1980 under the title, *World Conservation Strategy,* there appeared a statement of considerable international significance. This document was commissioned by the United Nations Environmental Programme (UNEP), which together with the World Wildlife Fund (WWF) provided the financial support for its preparation. Its production was essentially the responsibility of the International Union for Conservation and Natural Resources (IUCN), whose views and approaches it is stated to reflect.

According to the Director-General of that scientific union:

> it is intended that the Strategy represent a consensus of policy on conservation efforts in the context of world development. . . . The final draft was submitted to the Food and Agriculture Organization of the United Nations (FAO) and the United Nations Educational Scientific and Cultural Organization (UNESCO) as well as to UNEP and WWF, and all four organizations carefully reviewed it and made significant contributions to it.[9]

In addition, the draft was reviewed by 450 government agencies and conservation organizations in over 100 countries as well as by more than 700 scientists and other experts who are members of IUCN's Commissions on ecology, threatened species, protected areas, environmental planning, environmental policy, law and administration and environmental education.[10]

I have cited the document's pedigree in some detail in order to indicate the degree of consultation and consensus that lies behind its production. The report recommends that every country prepare national and subnational conservation strategies 'to provide a means of focusing and coordinating the efforts of government agencies together with nongovernmental conservation organizations to implement the World Conservation Strategy within countries'.[11] Some countries, including my own, already have action of this kind under way.[12]

In a foreword to the paperback version of the Strategy, Sir Peter Scott, the chairman of the World Wildlife Fund, declares that the Strategy was 'the first time that development has been suggested as a major means of achieving conservation instead of being viewed as an obstruction to it'.[13] David Munro, the Director-General of the International Union for Conservation and Natural Resources, in the preface to the same volume similarly claims that the 'Strategy shows that development . . . depends upon conservation and that conservation depends equally upon development'.[14] In a sense, then, the Strategy does represent the antithesis of the anti-growth and stationary-state prescriptions of some economists[15] whose views many ecologists and environmentalists had supported with crusading zeal in the 1970s.[16] Economists such as myself, who have continued to believe that economic growth is an indispensable prerequisite to improving the lot of mankind, may be inclined to regard this reversal of direction as a welcome return to rationality.

Unfortunately, however, the Strategy itself contains a curious *pot-pourri* of exaggeration, *quasi*-facts and economic disorientation which should be enough to raise the hackles of even the most sympathetic agricultural economist. For instance the compiler and editor of the Strategy in the opening paragraph of the paperback version makes the remarkable assertion that 'Everywhere fertile soil is either built on or flushed into the sea; otherwise renewable resources are exploited beyond recovery and pollutants are thrown like wrenches into the machinery of climate'.[17] The Strategy says that 'if current rates of land degradation continue, close to one third of the world's arable land will be destroyed in the next 20 years'.[18] This prognosis is strikingly at variance with the FAO estimates published in *Agriculture: Toward 2000.*[19] Clearly the authors of the Strategy documents would have profited from reading Theodore Schultz's 1951 article on 'The Declining Economic Importance of Agricultural Land'[20] or Jack Lewis's counterpart address at the 1964 Conference of this Association.[21]

## SOME ECOLOGICAL CHALLENGES FOR AGRICULTURAL ECONOMISTS

The *World Conservation Strategy* in my view represents a challenge to agricultural economists to make a more positive input into discussions on conservation. The Strategy epitomises the virtual total disregard by the environmental movement not only for facts about land use and conservation but also for the relevant economic principles. Forty years ago ecology was a respectable field of biological science. In latter years it has become a religion rather than a science, but it still claims the authority normally accorded to the results of scientific investigation. This makes the task of bringing more objectivity to discussions about conservation issues the more difficult but I do believe that agricultural economists should not put the job in the 'too hard' basket.

Forty years ago, the agricultural economics profession was deeply involved in a field then called land economics. The leaders of the profession wrote on important land policy issues including the economics of soil and rangeland conservation. Today the land economists of yore have either gone to their reward or else been transmuted into resource economists who, with a few exceptions, spend their time in airy disputations about externalities, shadow prices and the choice of appropriate discount rates to be applied to future benefits.

Agricultural economists have been too ready to let the environmental movement of the 1960s and 1970s flood over them. They have talked of a change in community values and have tended to leave environmental economics to general economists who, as Leontief and others have pointed out, have less of a penchant than agricultural economists for dealing with applied issues.[22] Environmental economics receives a one-page treatment in the American Agricultural Economics Association's *Survey of Agricultural Economics Literature* on the grounds that 'the field of environmental economics has emerged as an area of specialization in its own right'.[23] In contrast with this nonchalant attitude I would assert that the implications for agriculture of an unfettered environmental movement are so serious and the consequences for world food supplies so enormous that agricultural economists should get back into land and conservation economics without delay and try to bring some economic light to bear on some of the major policy discussions.

Let me spend a little time focusing on some major contemporary environmentally related issues which demand attention by agricultural economists. The UN Strategy statement is an appropriate point of departure. Constraints of space and time preclude my mentioning all the issues raised by the Strategy.

*(a) Criteria for determining priorities in conservation policy*

To economists the choice criteria which conservationists use in making decisions should be of especial interest. Fortunately the criteria for determining what are called 'priority requirements' and for resolving conflicts are set out in some detail in the Strategy. I quote these so that you will appreciate the nature of the many-headed Hydra with which we have to deal.

> Three criteria have been adopted for deciding whether a requirement is a priority: significance; urgency; irreversibility.
>
> *Significance* is determined by asking such questions as:
> how important is this requirement in relation to others for achieving the objective concerned?
> what proportions of the global, regional, national population depend on this requirement being met?
> how important is the requirement to the people most affected?
> how much of a particular resource will be conserved if the requirement is met?
>
> *Urgency* is a function of the rate at which a significant problem will get worse if the requirement is not met and of the time required to meet the requirement
>
> *Irreversibility* is the key criterion: highest priority is given to significant, urgent requirements to prevent further irreversible damage to living resources – notably the extinction of species, the extinction of varieties of useful plants and animals, the loss of essential life-support systems and severe soil degradation.[24]

The task of adhering to such a cacophony of vague undefinable criteria defies the imagination. All sorts of further questions spring to mind. How, for instance, is one supposed to make judgements about the importance of one requirement relative to others? How does one ascertain the importance the people affected attach to any particular requirement without any resort to the price mechanism? How does one anticipate the rate at which a problem will get worse? I could go on but let me move on to some specific agricultural matters.

*(b) Land use and the primacy of agricultural land*

I have already referred to the document's concern about the need to reserve 'prime quality cropland for crops' rather than let it be 'drowned by dams or lost to airports, roads, factories or housing. Such conflict', the document says, 'should be anticipated and where possible avoided. Since it is not possible to resite high quality cropland but it is possible to be flexible about the siting of buildings, roads and other structures, agriculture as a general rule should have precedence'.[25]

Such statements attribute a unique, inflexible and scarce quality to agricultural land which is not only contrary to the facts but also disregards completely the complications of interregional and international competition. The possibility of economic investment as well as of economic disinvestment in land over time is ignored.[26] It is enough to make Sherman Johnson (Elmhirst's successor in the presidency) turn in his grave.[27]

Reservation of prime cropland for agriculture, the document says, 'will reduce the pressure on ecologically fragile marginal lands which tend to degrade rapidly if exploited beyond their productive capacities'.[28] One would have thought that the concept of marginal rural land defined in climatic or biological terms passed into the limbo of forgotten things forty years ago.[29] Though the document gives specific attention to the problem of desertification it does not really come to grips with the problem of semi-arid range management. 'In arid regions where rainfall and plant growth are erratic,' the report counsels, 'stocking densities must be more conservative than where annual productivity is more consistent.'[30] A more rational strategy would be one which varied the intensity of grazing pressure depending on changing pasture conditions from season to season or year to year.

*(c) Anti-technology bias*

The Strategy advocates organic farming and biogas production mainly on the questionable arguments of 'the growing cost of oil' and the fact that '113 million tonnes of plant nutrients are potentially available to developing countries from human and livestock wastes and from crop residues'.[31] Traditional cropping systems in developing countries are lauded because it has been demonstrated, so the report says, that 'many of these systems bring high yields, conserve nutrients and moisture and suppress pests'.[32] Achievement of these characteristics, of course, does not of itself ensure an economically-sustainable farming system. I am sure Dr Borlaug and his colleagues in the American foundations would be surprised to learn that the original strategy of the 'Green Revolution' was to replace multiple cropping with temperate-style monocultures.[33]

### *(d) Control of pollution*

In contrast with conservation documents of the sixties and seventies the Strategy recognises the need for continued use of chemical fertilizers and pesticides. As might be expected the use of direct controls to regulate the discharge of pollutants and use of pesticides is strongly advocated.[34] Even so, there is evidence of the typical desire of conservationists to procrastinate on the introduction of new technology on the grounds of inadequate knowledge or unrealistic yearning for zero risk.[35] Accordingly the adequacy of testing facilities for pesticides is questioned.

Only transitory reference is made to the use of tax policy as a means of controlling environmental impact. In passing I might add that I believe agricultural economists have been negligent in their failure to point out how the application of the nearly universally advocated 'user pays' principle in a rural context works almost always to the financial detriment of the farmer. This follows if one recognises that a substantial part of the pollution caused by agricultural activities occurs in the processing sector (for example effluents from abattoirs and cheese factories) and notes the economic circumstances which typically assist such processors to pass their added costs back to the producer.[36]

### *(e) Endangered species*

Adoption of the regulatory policies advocated in the Strategy for the preservation of endangered species, a topic of paramount interest to conservationists, can also adversely affect agriculture particularly if implemented in ignorance. There are, for instance, a few endangered species of kangaroo but the major species of kangaroos are increasing in numbers and are a threat to the environment as well as a major pest of Australian pastoralists. Well-intentioned but basically inappropriate bans on trade in kangaroo skins, such as those enforced by the US Government between 1974 and 1981 in line with principles now advocated in the Strategy,[37] are counterproductive to the conservation cause.

The allied problem of animal welfare, though not mentioned in the Strategy, is another case where evangelical fervour is outrunning reason to the detriment of agricultural production. Intensive but low-cost pig and poultry production has been in jeopardy for some time because of the activities of such proselytes. International trade in live animals has likewise become a hot political issue in Australia as a result of an incongruous alliance between animal liberationists and trade unionists employed in abattoirs. Agricultural economists if they are concerned about the economics of production and trade cannot remain aloof from such issues.

### *(f) Preservation of genetic diversity*

The last ten years have seen a tremendous upsurge in the concern of biologists about the need to maintain genetic resources particularly with respect to economic plants. This has been prompted by various things. One is the increasing reliance of farmers on a limited number of varieties. Another is the recurrent tendency of particular varieties to lose their resistance to pathogens and of pests to lose their vulnerability to specific insecticides. Whatever the arguments for maintaining genetic diversity (including the so-called ethical principle that 'we are morally obliged – to our descendants and to other creatures – to act prudently'[38]), it is hard to believe that resources should be diverted as profligately to that end as the Strategy contends. Surely the costs of such a policy should be related in some way to the benefits, particularly when the benefits are highly speculative and extremely uncertain.

The Strategy comes out squarely against plant breeders' (varietal) rights. This is an issue which is currently a centre of political controversy in my own country. 'Unfortunately', says the Strategy document,

> commercial plant breeders and seed suppliers increasingly are patenting varieties and demanding royalties on their use even though the varieties are as much products of freely obtained genetic diversity as they are of commercial investment.... Plant breeders' rights and the standardization of plant varieties should be so limited that neither has the effect of restricting the free exchange and use of genetic materials or of reducing genetic diversity.[39]

This is an issue which agricultural economists should not leave to a three-cornered struggle between the World Council of Churches, multinational agribusiness corporations and professional plant breeders to thrash out. They should be making a more positive input than they currently are,[40] particularly following the 1980 US Supreme Court decision in *Diamond v Chakrobarty* which allows the patenting of the products of the burgeoning genetic engineering industry.[41] The problem of the consistent treatment of genetic advances which are developed in universities and other public institutions as against those that emerge from commercial firms cries out for analysis. The allied question of the use and abuse of monopoly power in this area also demands attention.

## CONCLUSION

Recent assessments by the FAO and the World Bank indicate a more optimistic view of the future world food situation than has been their wont.[42] Nevertheless governments in the next 25 years are going to be increasingly pressed to make trade-offs between the use of modern technologies to boost food production and the avoidance of damage to the environment. But they cannot afford to accede in an irresponsible way to the wishes of urban-based environmentalists or the scientifically illiterate. As is stated in the 1981 FAO report, *Agriculture: Toward 2000,* 'ecological considerations should not always take precedence over those of increased production'.[43]

If the absolutists of the environmental movement are to be prevented from getting their way, farmers and their representative organizations are going to need substantial assistance from trained agricultural professionals.

An example of what can be done in this area is provided by the multi-disciplinary Council for Agricultural Science and Technology in the United States which is committed 'to advance the understanding and use of food and agricultural science and technology in the public interest'. I believe agricultural economists in particular, should not be backward in participating in the inevitable confrontations, even if they only go as far as pointing out the adverse economic consequences of the policies of the extreme fringe of ecologists.

Even though we are approaching the fiftieth anniversary of the publication of Lord Robbins's *Essay on the Nature and Significance of Economic Science,*[44] I still share the conviction of some of our forebears in the profession that politicians need some guidance and leadership when matters of the kind I have been discussing today are at stake. I quote the final words from the address which Henry Wallace, later to become a distinguished US Secretary of Agriculture, delivered at the first Conference of this Association held at Dartington Hall in 1929.

> I sometimes feel that our economists in order to affect society in a desirable way should have a modern adaptation of the motives which moved the Hebrew prophets and John Knox to cry aloud. People of this sort change the social scheme of things . . . . I hope that agricultural economists will recognize both strong social feeling and sound economic analysis as essential to making the world a better place to live in.[45]

At the 1967 conference in Sydney, Leonard Elmhirst, the man we honour today, spoke in a similar vein and found reason to question whether, and I quote his words, we are 'seeing our role as economists in large enough terms'.[46]

## NOTES

[1] A. W. Ashby, 'Response to address of welcome', *Proceedings of the Second International Conference of Agricultural Economists,* Menasha, Wisconsin: George Banta Publishing Company, 1930, p. 16.

[2] L. K. Elmhirst, 'Stocktaking', *Proceedings of the Thirteenth Conference of Agricultural Economists,* London: Oxford University Press, 1969, p. 444.

[3] L. K. Elmhirst, 'The Foundations of Sriniketan' in Rabindranath Tagore and L. K. Elmhirst, *Rabindranath Tagore – Pioneer in Education,* London: John Murray, 1961, p. 43. See also 'Stocktaking', p. 447.

[4] L. K. Elmhirst, *Proceedings of the Thirteenth Conference,* pp. 4, 445.

[5] Ibid., pp. 444, 447; *Proceedings of the Fifteenth Conference,* Oxford: Agricultural Economics Institute, 1974, p. 16.

[6] Edward Hyams, *The English Garden,* London: Thames and Hudson, 1964, p. 242.

[7] L. K. Elmhirst, 'Statement', *Proceedings of the First Conference of Agricultural Economists,* Menasha: George Banta Publishing Company, 1929, p. viii.

[8] L. K. Elmhirst, 'Stocktaking', op. cit., p. 447.

[9] IUCN, *World Conservation Strategy,* Gland, Switzerland, 1980, p. II.

[10] Ibid., p. III.

[11] Ibid., Section 8, para. 2.

[12] Commonwealth of Australia, Department of Home Affairs and Environment, *Towards a*

*National Conservation Strategy:* A Discussion Paper, Canberra, 1982.

[13] Robert Allen, *How to Save the World,* London: Kogan Page, 1980, p. 7; see also *World Conservation Strategy,* Section 1, para. 9.

[14] Ibid, para. 9.

[15] E.g. J. S. Mill, *Principles of Political Economy,* Vol. 2, London: J. W. Parker, 1857, pp. 320–6; H.E. Daly, *Towards a Steady State Economy,* San Francisco: W. H. Freeman, 1973.

[16] E.g. Charles Birch, *Confronting the Future,* Harmondsworth: Penguin, 1975, pp. 13–58.

[17] Allen, *How to Save the World,* p. 11.

[18] *World Conservation Strategy,* Section I. The source of this remarkable assertion is said to be the United Nations, *United Nations Conference on Desertification: Round-up, Plan of Action and Resolutions,* New York: United Nations, 1978.

[19] Food and Agriculture Organization, *Agriculture: Toward 2000,* Rome, 1981.

[20] Theodore W. Schultz, 'The Declining Economic Importance of Agricultural Land', *Economic Journal,* Vol. XLI, No. 244, December 1951, pp. 720–40.

[21] J. N. Lewis, 'The Changing Importance of Land as a Factor of Production in Farming', *Proceedings of the Twelfth International Conference of Agricultural Economists,* London: Oxford University Press, 1966, pp. 420–7.

[22] W. Leontief, 'Theoretical Assumptions and Nonobserved Facts', *American Economic Review,* Vol. 69, No. 1, March 1971, pp. 1–7.

[23] Emery N. Castle *et al.,* 'Natural Resource Economics, 1946–75' in Lee R. Martin (ed.), *A Survey of Agricultural Economics Literature,* Vol. 3, Minneapolis: University of Minnesota Press, 1981, p. 451.

[24] *World Conservation Strategy,* Section 5.

[25] Ibid., Section 5, para. 1.

[26] Charles E. Kellogg and Carleton P. Barnes, 'Farm Land Resources of the United States' in J. F. Timmons and W. G. Murray, *Land Problems and Policies,* Ames: Iowa State College Press, 1950, pp. 53–4.

[27] See, for instance, Sherman E. Johnson, 'Farming Systems in relation to Soil Conservation', *Proceedings of the United Nations Scientific Conference on the Conservation and Utilization of Resources,* Vol. VI, Lake Success, 1949, pp. 79–85.

[28] *World Conservation Strategy,* Section 5, para. 1.

[29] J. D. Black, 'Notes on "Poor Land" and "Submarginal Land"', *Journal of Farm Economics,* Vol. 27, No. 2, May 1945, pp. 345–74.

[30] *World Conservation Strategy,* Section 7, para. 11.

[31] Ibid., Section 5, para. 4.

[32] Ibid., Section 14, para. 11.

[33] Ibid.

[34] Ibid., Section 5, para. 8.

[35] Ibid., Section 12, para. 4, on this question see Keith Campbell, 'The Risks of New Technology and their Agricultural Implications' in Glenn Johnson and Allen Maunder (eds), *Rural Change,* Farnborough: Gower Publishing Company, 1981, pp. 261–70 and Keith Campbell, 'The Benefits and Risks of Advanced Agricultural Technology', *Australian Quarterly,* Vol. 54, No. 2, Winter 1982, pp. 100–108.

[36] Keith O. Campbell and Brian S. Fisher, *Agricultural Marketing and Prices* (Second Edition), Melbourne: Longman Cheshire, 1982, p. 57 or B.S. Fisher, 'The Impact of Changing Marketing Margins on Farm Prices', *American Journal of Agricultural Economics,* Vol. 63, No. 2, May 1981, pp. 261–3.

[37] *World Conservation Strategy,* Section 7, para. 8, and Section 15, paras. 7–8.

[38] Ibid., Section 3, para. 2.

[39] Ibid., Section 17, para. 12.

[40] A. P. Ockwell, *Plant Variety Rights – A Review of Issues,* Bureau of Agricultural Economics, Occasional Paper No. 65, Canberra: Australian Government Publishing Service, 1982.

[41] *Diamond v Chakrobarty,* 447 US 301 (1980).

[42] FAO, *Agriculture;* World Bank, *World Development Report,* New York: Oxford University Press, 1981.

[43] FAO, *Agriculture,* p. 130.

[44] Lionel Robbins, *An Essay on the Nature and Significance of Economic Science,* London: Macmillan, 1932.
[45] H.A. Wallace, 'Relation of the Tariff to Farm Relief in the United States', *Proceedings of the First International Conference of Agricultural Economists,* p. 180.
[46] L. K. Elmhirst, 'Stocktaking', op. cit., p. 444.

# PRESIDENTIAL ADDRESS

THEODOR J. DAMS

## *Challenges for Agricultural Economics in the Eighties*

## SOME HISTORICAL FACTS

This is the eighteenth Conference of the International Association of Agricultural Economists since 1929. It is literally a bridge between two half centuries. In 1979 at Banff, Canada, we celebrated the 'Golden Jubilee' of our Association. It was a propitious moment for agricultural economics when in 1929 Leonard K. Elmhirst, our founder President, together with leading economists of his time, explained their motives: 'to bring together agricultural economists and research methods that were of common interest, to discuss national and international problems in the field of agricultural economics and to promote a more effective and more rapid exchange of agricultural economics information'. Three years ago Denis K. Britton, President for the 1976–79 period, convincingly scrutinized the 'responses' agricultural economists have given in the fifty years that went by since L.K. Elmhirst had described the 'challenges' in 1929: 'Fifty years of Agricultural Economics – And What Next?'.

This Conference, which is held – so to speak – at the door to the second half century, is concerned with the 'and what next'. This 'what next?' has two dimensions:

1) We need favourable *institutional* conditions so that *our institution* – the IAAE – can develop and flourish in the future. Many of you may remember the last sentence of my 'Synoptic View' at the Banff Conference: *'Vivat, Floreat, Crescat'.* To this, something else must be added.
2) We need a clear-cut view of what are the main challenges for agricultural economists in the next decade. Perhaps the IAAE is the proper forum in which to come up with adequate responses. This is the *functional* aspect.

Let me turn to the first point – the institutional aspect. The challenge which faces us is not simply that we should maintain and develop the status of agricultural economics as an academic discipline or as an analytical tool for the use of policy-makers, although these are highly important. There is also a challenge for us to strengthen our institution – the IAAE – of which we are all members. This certainly requires that we perform new styles and initiate new activities, while at the same time ensuring that the intentions of our founders and predecessors are safeguarded.

For an open and mutually trusting discussion it is absolutely essential, and for all members of the IAAE it is an inalienable right, for members to be able to speak their own minds as individuals and not as a political pressure group. Everybody is granted free access to this international fraternity, no matter where in the world we meet and wherever we might come from. In organizing Conferences, it has always been the strong desire and intention of our Association to ensure that every individual member of the IAAE can participate in our activities without any hindrance whatsoever. Generally, our host countries have respected this principle; but unfortunately we have not yet been able to achieve complete observance. It is for this reason that I have to report to you that today our assembly is incomplete. (There have been similar circumstance in Canada and Kenya before.) At this moment we are still waiting for the arrival of individual members who happen to carry Israeli or South-African passports.

Your Executive Committee, including myself, is deeply concerned about this matter, and we have done, and we shall continue to do, everything possible at the diplomatic level in order to change this situation. We are firmly determined to continue to demand acceptance of this principle here.

Let me now turn to the *second* dimension. I repeat: we need a clear-cut view of what are the main challenges for agricultural economists in the next decade. It is not my intention here to make prophecies. I would rather like, from my personal point of view, to discuss some basic issues and problems which I think will be of great importance to our work as agricultural economists in the next decade or so. It is possible that some answers can already be given at our Conference here in Jakarta. For a deeper understanding of what I think are some of the pressing issues in our profession, and of possible problem-solving approaches, it seems necessary first to reiterate the historical stages of the 'philosophy' of the IAAE:

a) The agricultural sector is closely linked with the economy as a whole. This is an analytical and strategic cornerstone.
b) Political, social and economic systems of any given society are interrelated. In conjunction they determine agricultural development and agricultural policy options.
c) Rural development, more so perhaps than other areas, is subject to 'spiritual, moral and social dimensions'. Such aspects often lead to 'Country Life Policies' (Sir Horace Plunkett, 1929) tied to a wide range of contrasting values. Agricultural economists must face this situation *vis-à-vis* their own individual values.

## THE CONFERENCE TOPIC

You all have lying in front of you a copy of the carefully prepared Conference-Programme on *Growth and Equity in Agricultural Development.* Since Dr Ohkawa, our Vice President Programme, will present the outline in detail, following my 'Presidential Address', I should only like to take up some general aspects which I consider important: (a) changing conditions for agricultural growth and equity in the 1980s, (b) political and social dimensions of agricultural development, (c) the great challenge for mankind: the increase of absolute poverty, (d) the widening gap between economic theory and economic policy, (e) agricultural social policy, and (f) environmental aspects.

### *(a) Changing conditions for development*

In the three years since our last Conference, both domestic and international economic conditions for growth and equity in rural development have changed significantly. This situation is not without precedence for the IAAE as an academic institution, as the economic depression of the 1930s clearly demonstrated. It is useful in this context to have recourse to the Annals of our IAAE.

Max Sering, the 'Nestor' of German agricultural economics and, along with G. F. Warren, one of the then Vice-Presidents of the IAAE, concluded in 1930 and 1934 at Cornell and at Bad Eilsen, respectively, that 'the whole situation was changed abruptly after the middle of 1929 .... the industrial boom which had developed almost in a straight line ... came to a natural end .... but the industrial crisis would have carried with it its own remedy if it had not coincided with the outbreak of the most serious agrarian and raw material crisis in history'. And quoting M. Sering: 'I consider it to be one of the most essential tasks ... to awaken the consciousness of a common destiny and of international solidarity'. Finally, the changing conditions can be seen in the light of Sir Arthur Lewis's brilliant analysis of the world economy in his Elmhirst Lecture of 1979. In the meantime it appears to me, though, that we have moved from a 'limping world economy' to a 'world economy on crutches'.

Now, what have been the most important changes? (i) The world-wide recession, sometimes regarded the worst since the 1930s, has stricken industrialized countries as well as semi-industrialized and developing nations. An upswing can nowhere be detected. (ii) The world-wide recession exerts a tremendous impact on the extent of rural change and its direction. (iii) In some parts of the world, particularly in sub-Saharan Africa, agricultural production *per caput* is stagnating or at least is not sufficient for food security. Or, in the words of Günter Grass: 'Here the stork is faster again than the plough.' A decade ago, this was different. (iv) The indebtedness of the developing countries has increased drastically. This also applies to some industrialized countries. Debt service has become the most serious problem for many developing nations – interest payments alone are in the region of $50 billion. This reduces the investable surplus and subsequently also the rate of growth. The western industrialized countries face severe economic problems domestically. Their debt ratios have also risen and interest payments exhibit the highest growth rates in terms of their share in the national budgets. Most of these countries find it increasingly difficult to meet their targets for development aid. Thus the Third World faces a two-pronged pressure. (v) Rising energy costs and low prices for many primary exports directly affect agricultural development in Less Developed Countries (LDCs). The pressure on structural change, agricultural production and rural living conditions is stronger now than ever since World War II.

The main topic of our Conference is *Growth and Equity in Agricultural Development.* As agricultural economists we have learned what contributions the agricultural sector can make toward economic growth and how overall economic conditions affect agriculture. We have considerable evidence, drawn from extensive empirical research, that fast economic growth adversely affects the distribution of agricultural incomes. But we clearly lack the necessary insight into what the differential impact of a lasting economic slump is on agricultural incomes and agrarian structures.

In 1920, our academic 'ancestors' devoted their Cornell Conference exclusively to 'Depression and Agriculture'. I am certainly no pessimist, yet I think it is opportune now for us agricultural economists seriously to consider: (i) what implications growth rates close to zero have for production and equity in agriculture and for the future of rural areas in the world, and (ii) whether alternative definitions of 'growth', which include quality and environmental aspects, might not provide more useful concepts for agricultural development. It appears to me that we may have to move away from some of our sophisticated theoretical models in order for agricultural economic research to come closer to reality.

*(b) Political and social dimensions of agricultural development*

One often hears the charge against economists that their models are so 'pure' that they cannot make a direct contribution to solving problems which exist in reality. This may be true for the relation between pûre theory and real policy, and possibly more so for the intricate relationships between economic, social and political factors. Generally, we derive models by leaving political and social factors out, we treat them (unrealistically) as given. It is, however, methodologically unacceptable to base planning methods on preconditions that depend on magnitudes contained in the objective function. With such questionable procedures we arrive at conclusions, for example that factor prices (or the rates of interest) determine the choice of technique. That is not enough. The real determinants of growth and equity that lie behind this are obscured from us. There is no such thing as a 'purely economic' problem that can be settled by pure economic logic.

Political interests and political prejudice are definitely involved here. There are quite a number of political constraints which impede social and economic progress among rural people and which prevent a just distribution of income. We should make this point explicitly clear. Ill-distributed economic and social power is so apparent in some countries that fear and repression instead of spontaneity and action govern the lives of large segments of the population.

A vital precondition for rural development 'from below' to become effective is that human rights are guaranteed for every member of the society. Human rights include the right to self-fulfilment, the protection of life, political freedom, satisfaction of basic needs, and participation in the social and political decision-making process.

Such considerations are by no means theoretical, for – as Joan Robinson put it – 'independent economists ought to be speaking up on the side of humanity'. Reality shows us that peasant revolutions and rural uprisings often occurred because ruling classes denied the material guarantee of formal human rights. In other words, the violation of human rights paves the road for radicalism. In an environment where human rights are not observed, the prospects for agricultural growth and for improving rural living conditions are unfavourable. This means that every rural development policy must also incorporate human rights elements.

*(c) Rural poverty – the great challenge*

In my 'Synoptic View' of the 1979 Banff Conference I underlined two points in this context: (i) in tackling the problem of absolute poverty in rural areas of the Third World we are doing so in line with the history of our Association. We should recall that in 1921 L. K. Elmhirst undertook 'one of the earliest attempts at community development' which 'soon dispelled any doubts that disease and lack of technical knowledge, leading to proverty, lay at the root of the decay of Indian village life' (J. R. Currie, 1964): (ii) Because of generally unfavourable conditions for development, malnutrition and poverty have spread further since our last gathering in 1979. According to the latest World Development Report 'the outlook for reducing poverty has worsened along with the prospects for the poor countries'. In 1980 750 million people lived in absolute poverty. If no favourable changes occur, this number will have risen to 850 million by the end of this century, half of whom will be suffering from starvation. This situation is not only an economic problem. It should also be seen in its ethical dimensions.

What then should agricultural economists focus their work on?

1 We must design realistic strategies for agricultural production and rural development. Neither wishful thinking in Utopian concepts nor stumbling ahead in incremental, non goal-oriented changes is adequate in any way. Nor is it sufficient for development and progress merely to meet the minimum conditions for the whole economic system to survive. For a better solution of the pressing problems, agricultural economists should rather turn to concepts that could be labelled 'mixed scanning' (A. Etzioni). Such an approach combines both step by step improvements and far-reaching changes of decisive elements of a given economic system. In this way the disadvantages of the other strategies mentioned can be avoided

without being overambitious.

2 The dilemma in rural development is obvious: on the one hand, overall agricultural growth does not benefit the poor masses. On the other hand, strictly poverty-oriented projects are very expensive and generally of limited effectiveness. Budget constraints force us to tie our tool packages carefully. Several critical areas of priority can be identified. We must:

(a) eliminate the constraints which in the past have prevented economic growth from trickling down to the lowest strata of society;
(b) apply measures which combine growth with equity elements in favour of the rural poor;
(c) apply basic needs strategies only after options (a) and (b) have been exhausted and only if capital accumulation will not be adversely affected.

3 Despite some opposite opinion, I think that the concept of Integrated Rural Regional Development should seriously be considered a candidate for effective approaches, as it is a strategy of the mixed-scanning type I mentioned earlier on. IRRD is a demanding approach in that it requires truly interdisciplinary research and implementation. It clearly focuses on the participation of target groups and views project activities as the basis for creating a 'movement' and establishing autonomous local institutions in support of a 'development from below'. Adequate decision-making 'from above' can help create a climate favourable to such changes. In my opinion 'Redesigning Rural Development' should be analyzed in this light.

4 The extent of poverty in the world should not discourage agricultural economists. Neither should the complexity of the problem. Since WCARRD in Rome, 1979, virtually all countries have officially subscribed to a concept that is practically equivalent to integrated rural development. It is now up to us to work out alternatives for a successful application of this strategy. However, this also requires a political commitment which thus far has been lacking in many cases. Lack of political commitment on the part of the recipient countries has also led to increasingly critical assessments of the current system of development aid. Gunnar Myrdal, formerly an active supporter of development aid, has in recent years become increasingly critical of the present form of aid. The Nobel Prize Winner presents 'Relief Aid instead of Development Aid' as a new line of aid policy.

We agricultural economists must now demonstrate that rural development is economically and socially efficient at the grass roots. Gunnar Myrdal's judgement on the impact of conventional aid policies may be justified – in any case it also declares economic research and policies toward international development bankrupt.

### *(d) Shortcomings in economic theory*

It is very difficult in economic theory to 'formulate answerable questions about reality', but this also saves us, on the other hand, from formulating questions that cannot be answered. A typical example can be drawn from the area of 'growth and equity in rural development'. Economic theory has a lot to say about the determinants of growth and about how growth affects the sectoral, regional and size distribution of income. The reverse functional relationship, however, as to how the distribution of income affects growth, has received far less attention in economic reasoning. This to me is one of the big unfinished problems on the way toward more rational agricultural and rural development policies. It would be too simplistic and also too dangerous to state with welfare economics that interpersonal comparisons with respect to income distribution are not possible.

A redistribution from upper to lower wealth groups may well lead to positive growth effects by way of intensified production as well as effects from the demand side. Such theoretical findings directly affect policy decisions with respect to, say, relationships of the Kuznets curve type. We should keep in mind, however, that especially in developing countries the distribution of income may become more uneven because the availability of modern techniques and the incentives for their application are also distributed unevenly (World Bank, 1980). Thus the Kuznets curve is no 'iron law', but a challenge for economists and policy makers to minimize negative repercussions in the course of development, particularly in the case of small farmers in traditional agriculture.

There exists a theoretical argument that a highly skewed distribution of income may be necessary for economic reasons because it helps – through higher capital accumulation – to create additional employment. Such an argument is totally unacceptable, not only for social reasons but also for its dubious economic reasoning, in the case that a highly unequal distribution of power exists.

*(e) Social aspects*

Growth and equity in rural development is closely connected with social policy. During the last two decades or so both capitalist and socialist industrial countries have put great emphasis on their social policies in favour of agriculture. Social policy has become an integral part of agricultural policy, that is there are government transfer payments that improve the living conditions of rural families. Such non-market incomes are also important in their impact on structural adjustment processes in agriculture.

In many developing nations modernization policies for the agricultural sector increasingly threaten to destroy traditional forms of social security without there being new modern institutions to replace them. Today we still lack hard empirical evidence on the impact of alternative systems of social security on agricultural development.

*(f) Agriculture and ecology*

Similar comments can be made on the relationship between agriculture and the environment. Keith Campbell, our third Elmhirst Memorial Lecturer, has just pointed out that this complex set of problems should not be left exclusively to non-economists and that there is a tendency in this area to exaggerate things. Theodore W. Schultz, the first Elmhirst Memorial

Lecturer (1976), also convincingly argued, in a speech delivered to the US Agricultural Council this year, that soil erosion has declined in recent years because of higher unit yields that have prompted a reduction in the area cultivated.

This of course is only one side of the coin. There are many case studies from other parts of the world indicating that the opposite holds true. Rising energy prices and diminishing supplies of traditional energy sources have resulted in increased soil erosion in many developing countries. Also in many developed nations, the deterioration of the quality of water and other negative ecological phenomena are largely attributed to the intensive use of chemical inputs and sophisticated machinery. Such developments are induced by the high support prices for agricultural products which characterize agricultural policies in much of the western world. These examples demonstrate how widely ecological problems can differ under the broad spectrum of environmental conditions that exist. What surprises me most about the ecological discussion is that many politicians, but also some economists, do not seem to be aware of what A. C. Pigou had to say about growth, equity and ecology in his *Economics of Welfare* of 1912. Exactly seventy years ago he presented a theory of social and private gains in which he distinguished between the marginal private product and the marginal social product. Pigou also analyzed the spatial and time dimensions of external economies and diseconomies. Forty years later William Kapp, in his classic analysis, *Social Costs of Private Enterprise,* gave an assessment of what he called 'an economy of unpaid bills'. Kapp's analysis indirectly illustrates the complexity of the interrelationship between agriculture and ecology.

In my view, therefore, there are strong indications that these methodological concepts of welfare economics should be reapplied in agricultural economics. Perhaps we will have to rediscover Pigou's thoughts on growth and equity for agricultural development.

## CONCLUDING REMARKS

In preparing for this Conference and reading through the papers to be presented, I felt encouraged to include in my Presidential Address some topics which are not explicitly on the agenda. Our Vice President Programme, Professor Ohkawa, has prepared with great care an impressive conference concept and Dr Birowo, Chairman of the Indonesian National Organizing Committee, will present the Conference Theme with special reference to the host country's interests. The Conference documents also include some notes on the history of the Association. What is not included is the *'codex de bonne conduite'* for the participants, which a conference President usually phrases in his own peculiar way. I have a few examples for you.

In 1929 at Dartington Hall, his estate in Devon, Leonard Elmhirst greeted his guests by saying 'we are gathering together as a family party rather than as a group of specialists'. In 1934 Max Sering said 'we have here no other duty than to seek for truth and with all frankness to express what we have – after conscientious examination and self-criticism – found to be true; there is only one obvious limit which we must set ourselves, proceeding immediately from the respect due to the individuality of every people'. Elmhirst said in 1929 that 'our members are all individual members entitled to speak their own mind'. And D. K. Britton in 1981 said that 'the IAAE is neither a pressure group nor an action group. We have not come to Banff to pass resolutions, nor to organize some dramatic piece of world-wide collective activity'. I have nothing to add to these statements.

The most important ingredient for our 'highly sophisticated' discussions during this our family party will be an atmosphere of good will, so that an earnest crossing over of ideas can take place and so that all members will carry away with them a stimulation of mind and emotion and of friendship. Since the very beginning of our association such an atmosphere has been the key to success. In 1929 Elmhirst told his guests: 'For the time being make Dartington your home.' I am sure that the hospitality extended to us here will create a similar atmosphere. So I feel inclined to say that for the time being 'make Indonesia your home'.

In the many discussions that I am sure will come up during these ten days, I hope that all of you will bear in mind a word ascribed to John Maynard Keynes: 'Nobody knows how wrong one can be, thinking only by oneself.' With this in mind I am positive that the Eighteenth Conference here in Jakarta will be a milestone in the history of agricultural economics.

I wish you all a successful conference.

# SECTION I

*The Overall Problem*

GUSTAV RANIS

# *Growth and Equity in Development: An Overview*

## INTRODUCTION

Given the well-known proclivity of 'dismal scientists', agricultural economists included, to accentuate the negative, it is necessary to remind ourselves at the outset that the actual performance of the so-called developing countries (LDCs) over the more than three decades of post-war growth has indeed surpassed all predictions. Even the major negative 'break' in the international economic environment in 1973 (reinforced in 1979) has not had the predicted cataclysmic consequences. While global stagflation and two major oil shocks have taken their toll of growth rates everywhere, LDC performance has been generally less affected than that of the advanced countries and has, in fact, helped ease the latter's own task of adjustment.

It is, of course, true that once we disaggregate – as we must – growth in the upper income tier of LDCs, that is among the so-called newly industrializing countries (NICs) of East Asia and Latin America, has proceeded at 5 per cent annually in recent years and is seen to have increasingly out-distanced that in the really poor countries with annual rates slightly in excess of 1 per cent. It is, moreover, true that the ability of many LDCs to avoid having to adjust their growth rates radically downward, in the face of largely external shocks, has been closely related to the spurt of commercial bank lending *via* recycled OPEC surpluses, leading to a substantial increase in LDC debt as well as unprecedentedly high levels of commercial bank LDC exposure. The current outlet for our inveterate pessimism is therefore focused heavily on the possibility of widespread LDC defaults and the possible breakdown of the whole OPEC recycling *cum* international monetary mechanism. We have clearly witnessed greater flexibility and responsiveness to adversity in the international economic system than we had any right to expect.

Our main purpose here, however, is not to provide a 'pollyannish' antidote to the guild of international gloom-and-doom sayers. Rather, we accept the general premise that the unprecedented expansion of the world economy during the 1950–75 quarter century will not soon recur and want to pose the more sensible question dealing with the contemporary LDCs' ability to maintain respectable development performance in the face of a predictably less friendly future environment.

What further complicates matters, of course, is that development performance is itself increasingly being assessed as at least two-dimensional, with equity along with growth a central concern; second, disaggregation forces us to distinguish at least three groups of developing countries: the already more or less full fledged NICs of East Asia, the NICs of Latin America, and an emerging or as yet only 'potential' group of new NICs located principally in other parts of Asia and Latin America. It is in this overall context that the experience of the recent past provides a potentially valuable input into our improved understanding of the future.

Almost by definition, the East Asian and Latin American NICs together represent the best LDC growth performers of the past; but what is less well understood is that their growth performance was itself very differently generated and associated with very different levels of equity – a difference which may turn out to be crucial for the future performance of other LDCs and, indirectly, for the rich countries as well. We believe this because different growth strategies, in the first place, yield large differences in LDC employment and distributional outcomes; and in the second, because they lead to differences in exposure to the vagaries of the inevitable future shocks to the international system.

Much recent discussion, and some development literature, especially that emanating from the national and international aid agencies, has focused on the greater satisfaction of basic needs and/or the achievement of greater distributional equity as an important but neglected objective which needs now to be 'dusted off' for humanitarian and/or socio-political reasons, even if at the cost of some foregone growth. Without for a moment denying the reasonableness and, in some cases, even the urgency of such a possible broadening of traditional development objectives, the approach in this paper is somewhat different. In our view, greater efficiency in resource use will help on both counts, that is *ceteris paribus* a more equitable growth path is likely to yield *higher* growth rates, as well as *less* vulnerability to the exogenous shocks of various kinds which must clearly be anticipated.

Card-carrying members of our dismal science instinctively distrust the possibility of the existence of such 'bargains', that is the relative absence of painful trade-offs. Thus, more employment and greater equity today are usually viewed as possibly desirable but certainly not costless welfare objectives which must be weighed against the desirability of more growth now. What seems to have changed, in the minds of many, is the recognition that existing conflicts might well legitimately be resolved in favour of 'welfare' objectives; much less frequently is it as yet recognized that you can, in fact, very often have your cake (greater equity) and eat it too (more growth). If correct, this may be an ever more important finding for the more constrained decades of the 1980s and 1990s.

This view, then, that even LDCs firmly committed to the importance of growth relative to welfare or social objectives are well advised to consider a more egalitarian growth path, is based on an examination of comparative NIC performance over the past three decades of transition. While admittedly there exists no 'typical' LDC, no 'typical' African LDC, and no 'typical' Latin American or East Asian NIC, we shall, nevertheless, assume that careful generalizations from individual country performance over time are permissible and instructive, certainly superior to a historical multi-country cross-sectional analysis. We have selected the Taiwan area of China as a proto-typical East Asian NIC, Colombia as a Latin American NIC and the Philippines as a potential 'other Asian' NIC in order to examine the past and illuminate options for the future.

In Section II we will briefly analyze the post-war performance of the 'typical' East Asian NIC, including its response to the exogenous shocks of the post-1973 era, and contrast it with its 'typical' Latin American counterpart. Section III is devoted to generalizing the comparison to other 'potential' NICs and to presenting conclusions and related reflections on the nature and impact of available strategy choices in the years ahead.

## GROWTH WITH EQUITY AMONG THE POST-WAR NICs

The East Asian NICs, Taiwan area as proto-type, are relatively small, heavily labour surplus, relatively poor in natural resource endowments, and relatively rich in human resources. Of particular interest to a group of economists focusing on the role of the agricultural sector is that these systems' colonial experience generally featured heavy attention paid to the rural sector and to the extraction of food crops as 'the' colonial raw material. In contrast, the family affinity among the so-called Latin American NICs, Colombia as proto-type, may be summarized in terms of their Iberian raw material export-oriented colonial heritage, a relatively earlier start for their post-colonial transition growth effort, their somewhat larger size, an endowment which is relatively more rich in natural resources, with intermediate levels of entrepreneurial capacity, but nevertheless characterized by substantial pockets of unskilled labour surplus. The Philippine case closely parallels that of Colombia.

Other relevant differences in initial conditions include a more equally distributed asset structure, especially of land, on Taiwan, thanks to two reforms, one during the early years of Japanese control and one in the post-war period, which stands in contrast to a virtually unimplemented land reform effort in Colombia and partial reform in the Philippines. As one consequence, the land ownership Gini stands in the neighbourhood of 0.6 on Taiwan and 0.8 in Colombia. More difficult to assess is the importance of higher initial literacy rates, traditionally stronger saving habits, and greater merit-based access to educational opportunities in the case of the Taiwan area.

Given these differences at the starting gate, the East Asian, the Latin American and other NICs, as virtually all LDCs, initiated their transition growth effort by moving into what is often called primary import substitution during their respective post-independence periods; this meant a heavy focus on using traditional natural resource exports to finance the growth of a new industrial sector producing non-durable consumer goods – previously imported – for the domestic market. The Latin Americans began this process somewhat earlier, the Asians in the early 1950s. Moreover, as Table I, lines 1 and 2, indicates, the overall performance of the Taiwan area, Colombia, and the Philippines during this first subphase of transition was not all that different, at least not on the surface. Income growth rates *per caput* were certainly more than respectable in all three cases, with the shift of the centre of gravity *via* a gradual reallocation of the labour force from agriculture to non-agriculture proceeding rapidly. All three economies, even the somewhat smaller one of the Taiwan area, remained basically inward-oriented, as the well-known interventionist package of protectionist industrial and foreign exchange policies during import substitution trended the system towards the domestic market. Growth rates were more or less equivalent (lower, in the Philippines), savings rates (see line 3) more than respectable by LDC standards. Distributional indicators, it should be emphasized, whether we use the Gini coefficient (line 4) or possible alternatives (line 5), were generally highly unsatisfactory – in terms of international comparative standards – in all three cases during the import substituting 1950s.

On closer examination we may note, however, the existence of some differences between the Taiwan area of China and the other NICs, even during this common, essentially protectionist and inward looking, subphase of development, which may have relevance for the issues under discussion. One has to do with the relatively better performance of food producing agriculture, both in terms of initial yields and changes over time, in the Taiwan case. This resulted not only from her more favourable initial conditions of rural infrastructure – given better luck with her colonial antecedents – but also her relative non-neglect of agriculture during this early period of post-colonial independent development. For instance, while agriculture's terms of trade are frequently permitted to deteriorate during this phase as an additional assistance to the new industrialist class, this was not the case in the Taiwan area. A related point, if not fully documentable (line 11), is that the level of effective protection of industry was lower in the Taiwan area than in Colombia or the Philippines throughout, making its contribution to a somewhat less 'heated' industrial environment. While the infant industry conversion of a traditional land-based group into non-traditional industrial entrepreneurs requires a reasonable level of protection and profit transfers, the real difference in these two cases in the 1950s must be found in the severity and the length of time over which such policies were pursued, and, consequently, in whether or not they ultimately discouraged or encouraged the maturation process.

From the very beginning, the balanced quality of rural development in the Taiwan area had no equivalent in Colombia or the Philippines. Agricultural activity supplementary to the basic food crops on Taiwan

TABLE 1 *Comparative NIC Performance* Taiwan (China)

| | 1950 | 1960 | 1965 | 1970 | 1973 | 1974 | 1975 | 1976 | 1977 | 1978 | 1979 | 1980 |
|---|---|---|---|---|---|---|---|---|---|---|---|---|
| 1 Annual real GDP *per caput* growth rate (%) | 4.1 (55–60) | 6.1 | 6.5 | 10.7 | -.8 | 2.8 | 11.2 | 7.8 | 11.3 | 5.6 | - | - |
| 2 Non-agricultural labour as % of total | 37.3 | 43.9 | 46.3 | 63.3 | 69.5 | 69.0 | 70.1 | 70.9 | 72.9 | 75.1 | 78.5 | - |
| 3 Savings/GDP | 9.6 (55) | 11.4 | 14.5 | 18.8 | 27.5 | 25.0 | 19.8 | 25.0 | 25.0 | 27.0 | 26.1 | - |
| 4 Gini coefficient | 0.56 | 0.44 (59) | - | - | 0.29 (72) | - | - | - | - | - | - | - |
| 5 Income % of bottom 20% | 2.9 (53) | 5.6 | 7.8 (64) | - | 8.8 (72) | - | - | - | - | - | - | - |
| 6 Total exports/GDP | 8.3 (55) | 11.3 | 18.7 | 29.7 | 46.8 | 43.7 | 40.0 | 47.3 | 49.2 | 53.1 | 53.9 | - |
| 7 Agricultural exports as % of total exports | - | 51.7 (62) | 57.9 | 22.5 | 15.8 | 15.5 | 17.5 | 13.6 | 13.4 | 10.1 | 9.8 | - |
| 8 Non-agricultural income as % of total farm household income | - | - | 34.0 (66) | - | 54.8 (71) | - | - | - | - | - | - | - |
| 9 Wage share in urban non-agriculture | - | - | 62.7 (64) | - | 79.8 (72) | - | - | - | - | - | 65.8 | - |
| 10 Wage share in rural non-agriculture | - | 64.1 | - | - | - | - | 68.0 | - | - | - | 69.9 | - |
| 11 Effective rate of protection | - | - | 59.6 (66) | - | - | - | - | - | - | - | - | - |

Notes – Table I
Taiwan (China):
1. *Taiwan Statistical Databook, 1976 (TSD); Statistical Yearbook of the Republic of China,* 1980 (SYRC); 2. SYRC; 3. SYRC; 4. Fei, Ranis, Kuo, *Growth With Equity: The Taiwan Case,* Oxford University Press, 1979; 5. Jain, S., *Size Distribution of Income,* World Bank, 1975; 6. SYRC; 7. TSD; SYRC; 8. DGBAS, *National Income of the Republic of China,* Household Surveys; 9. DGBAS, National Income of the Republic of China, Household Surveys; SYRC; 10. Same as (9); 11. Galenson, W., *Economic Growth and Structural Change in Taiwan,* Cornell, 1979.

Columbia

| | | 1950 | 1960 | 1965 | 1970 | 1973 | 1974 | 1975 | 1976 | 1977 | 1978 | 1979 | 1980 |
|---|---|---|---|---|---|---|---|---|---|---|---|---|---|
| 1 | Annual real GDP *per caput* growth rate (%) | 4.6 (53–60) | 1.4 | 3.1 | 3.6 | 3.9 | 1.7 | 2.3 | 2.6 | 6.4 | - | - | |
| 2 | Non-agricultural labour as % of total | 46.1 | - | 55.5 | 62.1 | - | - | 67.8 | 68.8 | 69.8 | 70.8 | 71.1 | 73.6 |
| 3 | Savings/GDP | 8.1 (53) | 9.5 | 9.0 | 10.2 | 9.4 | 11.6 | 29 | 12.6 | 17.5 | 15.0 | - | - |
| 4 | Gini coefficient | - | 0.53 (62) | 0.60 (64) | 0.56 | - | - | - | - | - | - | - | - |
| 5 | Income % of bottom 20% | - | 4.1 (62) | 4.3 (64) | 3.5 | - | - | - | - | - | - | - | - |
| 6 | Total exports/GDP | 15.0 (53) | 15.6 | 11.4 | 14.2 | 14.9 | 14.2 | 15.1 | 16.5 | 17.4 | 17.8 | - | - |
| 7 | Agricultural exports as % of total exports | 83.1 (51) | 78.9 | 75.3 | 81.2 | 68.0 | 63.1 | 71.7 | 73.7 | 76.9 | 84.2 | - | - |
| 8 | Non-agricultural income as % of total farm household income | 14.3 (50–52) | 12.7 (59–61) | - | 9.0 (68–70) | - | - | - | - | - | - | - | - |
| 9 | Wage share in urban non-agriculture | 37.9 | 31.8 | - | - | - | 34.1 | - | - | - | - | - | - |
| 10 | Wage share in rural non-agriculture | 34.8 | 39.2 | - | - | - | 40.5 | - | - | - | - | - | - |
| 11 | Effective rate of protection | - | - | - | - | - | - | - | - | - | - | - | - |

Colombia: 1. Real GDP, *UN Yearbook of National Accounts Statistics* (UNYNAS); Population, *UN Demographic Yearbook* (UNDY); *World Table* 1980 of the World Bank (WT); 2. FAO Production Yearbook (FAOPY); 3. UNYNAS; 4. Ranis, G., 'Income Distribution and Growth in Colombia', *(Distribución del Ingreso y Crecimiento en Colombia', Desarrolloy Sociedad,* No. 3 CEDE, January 1980); 5. Same as (4); 6. UNYNAS; 7. FAO Trade Yearbook (FAOTY); 8. Berry A. and Tenjo, Jaime, *'Datos Económicos de los Sectores Agropecuarios y no Agropecuarios',* mimeo, September 1972; 9. *National Accounts* of Colombia; 10. Same as (9); 11. Ranis, G., *Sharing in Development: A Programme of Employment, Equity and Growth for the Philippines,* ILO, Geneva, 1974.

Philippines

| | | 1950 | 1960 | 1965 | 1970 | 1973 | 1974 | 1975 | 1976 | 1977 | 1978 | 1979 | 1980 |
|---|---|---|---|---|---|---|---|---|---|---|---|---|---|
| 1 | Annual real GDP *per caput* growth rate (%) | | 1.4 (55–60) | 2.2 | 1.4 | 3.1 | 2.3 | 4.6 | 2.2 | 3.7 | 2.9 | - | - |
| 2 | Non-agricultural labour as % of total | - | - | 42.9 | 46.8 | - | - | 50.4 | 51.1 | 57.8 | 52.5 | 53.2 | 54.0 |
| 3 | Savings/GDP | 4.2 | 10.9 | 14.3 | 12.0 | 17.6 | 17.1 | 16.0 | 15.1 | 16.2 | 15.9 | - | - |
| 4 | Gini coefficient | - | - | - | 0.49 (71) | - | - | - | - | - | - | - | - |
| 5 | Income % of bottom 20% | - | 4.6 (61) | - | 3.6 (71) | - | - | 5.5 | - | - | - | - | - |
| 6 | Total exports/GDP | 14.2 | 10.6 | 17.2 | 19.1 | 21.4 | 22.3 | 18.6 | 17.5 | 19.0 | 18.8 | - | - |
| 7 | Agricultural exports as % of total exports | - | - | 61.6 | 43.5 | 42.9 | 57.8 | 55.4 | 49.1 | 50.1 | 42.0 | - | - |
| 8 | Non-agricultural income as % of total farm household income | - | - | - | - | - | - | - | - | - | - | - | - |
| 9 | Wage share in urban non-agriculture | - | - | - | - | - | - | - | - | - | - | - | - |
| 10 | Wage share in rural non-agriculture | - | - | - | - | - | - | - | - | - | - | - | - |
| 11 | Effective rate of protection | - | - | 85.0 | - | - | - | - | - | - | - | - | - |

Philippines: 1. Real GDP, *UN Yearbook of National Accounts Statistics* (UNYNAS); Population, *UN Demographic Yearbook* (UNDY); *World Table 1980* of the World Bank (WT). 2. *FAO Production Yearbook* (FAOPY); 3. UNYNAS; 4. *Philippines Yearbook,* 1978 of National Census and Statistics Office; 5. Same as (4); 6. UNYNAS; 7. FAO Trade Yearbook (FAOTY); 11. Ranis, G., *Sharing in Development: A Programme of Employment, Equity and Growth for the Philippines,* ILO, Geneva, 1974.

was labour using, in terms of permitting increased multiple-cropping, as well as focusing on new, higher valued and more labour intensive food crops, that is the shift from rice and sugar to vegetables, mushrooms and asparagus; what is even more interesting is that it was apparently the poorer farmers who participated more than proportionately in the expansion of these new more labour intensive agricultural products. This helps explain in large measure the improvements in the equity indices in the course of the 1950s and early 1960s (see lines 4 and 5 of Table I).

Our analysis, moreover, indicates the importance of non-agricultural activities being spatially dispersed, thus permitting the poorest rural, including landless, workers to find alternative employment opportunities outside agriculture but still 'close to home', that is without the necessity of expensive migration to distant industrial activities. Such decentralized industrialization and evidence of much capillary action between agriculture and non-agriculture in the rural areas was not only a by-product of East Asian colonial emphasis on rural expansion, but also the object of conscious post-war government policy, including concentration on rural roads, irrigation and electrification, the construction of dispersed industrial estates, bonded factories, export processing zones and so on, all within daily reach of the rural household. The maintenance of a policy of equal power and fuel rates in rural and urban areas stands in sharp contrast to the signals which make for concentration and agglomeration in the typical Latin American or other Asian NIC. The most dramatic demonstration of this phenomenon is the fact that the average countribution of non-agricultural income to total farm household income was as high as 30 per cent in Taiwan in 1964, rising to a remarkable 52 per cent level by 1972, in contrast with a decline from 14 per cent to 9 per cent in Columbia during the same period (see Table I, line 8).

We all know that this non-durable consumer goods or primary import substitution phase must come to an end as domestic markets are saturated; it did so in Colombia, the Philippines and Taiwan at about the same time, that is around the end of the 1950s. At this point further industrialization has to slow to the pace of population plus *per caput* income growth. Faced with a reduction in industrial growth and the threat of price wars, both the East Asian and the Latin American proto-type had to devise a way out of the threatened *cul de sac.*

In fact, the choice as to the new growth path to follow made at this point may be most important in explaining the more recent divergence in the performance of the two types. The Taiwan area of China moved into primary export substitution, that is the export of the same non-durable industrial consumer goods previously produced for the domestic market into world markets, while the more typical Latin American NIC continued with her import substitution policies, but now of the secondary or consumer durable, raw materials processing, and capital goods type. This choice makes a marked difference with respect to a number of dimensions in which we are interested.

There can be little doubt, for example, that over the past quarter century of development rapid growth in East Asia has been accompanied by a high level of employment creation and the improvement of equity, whether measured by an increasingly favourable (lower) Gini or some alternative distributional and/or proverty index. By changing its policy environment in the direction of lower levels of protection and more workably competitive conditions in the domestic market, associated with more realistic relative prices, it was possible for the Taiwan area not only to embark on a rapid rural balanced growth process, that is enhanced interaction between decentralized rural industry and agriculture, but also in terms of an export orientation permitting a rapid absorption of her underemployed and unemployed in the form of labour intensive goods for international markets. The contrast in the labour intensity of technology choice and in the non-agricultural output mix is demonstrated by the level and trend of labour's relative share. This was relatively high in East Asia and rising, lower in Latin America and falling, in both rural and urban industry and services (see Table I, lines 9 and 10). As a consequence, in spite of the low wages being generally maintained during this period, the wage share could rise markedly in the East Asian case, as poor families had more of their members in a position to find employment, working more hours per week.

The contribution made by the rapid growth of labour intensive industrial exports in East Asia is documented by the dramatic change in both the overall export orientation (see Table I, line 6) and the equally dramatic shift in the composition of those exports, as captured in line 7. Meanwhile, the agricultural sector continued to make its crucial contribution, as evidenced by both continued productivity increase and near-constancy in the inter-sectoral terms of trade in East Asia, while the Latin American NIC typically maintained a more pronounced cheap urban food policy, often by increasing her food imports.

We may thus conclude that the East Asian NICs as represented by the Taiwan area of China increasingly followed a two-bladed development strategy. One blade is represented by balanced rural growth of the labour intensive variety, encouraged by the allocation of a substantial volume of infra-structure to the rural areas, both in the pre and post independence periods; the second blade is represented by the rapid deployment of a labour intensive technology embedded in output mixes directed towards external markets. The pursuit of such a twin-bladed, employment sensitive growth path was immeasurably aided by the underlying strategy of small-scale rural oriented industrialization combined with rapid agricultural productivity growth. It yielded not only rapid rates of increase in income *per caput* but also good and improving income distribution performance, long before the labour surplus in the economy could be mopped up and long before real wages began to rise in earnest, that is by the early 1970s.

Once this 'turning point' had occurred, Taiwan's comparative advantage in labour intensive manufactured goods gradually began to disappear; her industrial output mix shifted towards more skilled labour, technology and capital intensive goods, both for domestic and export markets. This may be called entering the secondary import *cum* secondary export substitution phase, reinforcing, of course, elements already present in the earlier subphases as we move along the product cycle in continuing response to gradual changes in the endowment. Capital goods and consumer durables, for example, are now produced in the Taiwan area for the home market as well as for exports, as is the longer term objective of every developing country. An accompanying phenomenon becomes the gradual atrophying of the domestic agricultural sector in which the East Asian NIC basically poor in natural resources does not have a long run comparative advantage. As a consequence, one may observe that food imports are becoming increasingly necessary in Taiwan. But it should also be noted that this is *after* the food producing agricultural sector has performed its historical role of providing a surplus in the form of both savings and released labour – while avoiding massive food imports – in the course of more than two decades of rapid and balanced development.

In the cases of Colombia and the Philippines, in contrast, once primary import substitution ends, the system tries to move directly into a secondary import substitution subphase, meaning the establishment of a more skilled labour, capital, and technology intensive industry mix. This means a continuing industrial orientation towards the domestic market, focusing now on previously imported consumer durables, capital goods, and the processing of raw materials, and necessitating an increase in the severity of the protectionist, controls-oriented policy structure inherited from the prior primary import substitution subphase. Notice the dramatic difference in the evolving levels of export orientation in the 1960s and 1970s (line 6).

While the level of total effective protection declined in the East Asian NICs during the 1960s, it generally remained high or rose elsewhere. Aside from essentially short-lived experiments in the mid-1960s neither in their foreign exchange nor capital markets did the Latin American or other Asian NICs adopt major shifts towards the more liberalized economy of the kind that the East Asian NICs undertook in the early 1960s. Instead, both Colombia and the Philippines essentially continued their relatively heavy reliance on natural resource exports, supplementing traditional ones by new crops wherever possible. To the extent that such raw materials were not only plentiful but enjoyed favourable international terms of trade – the extreme case, of course, being oil – a secondary import substitution strategy can continue to be followed indefinitely even if it becomes more expensive in terms of possibly increasing deviations from efficient industrial output and technology mixes.

A comparative look at Table I, lines 6 and 7, indicates that the contrast in the composition of exports is marked but less severe than the contrast in the extent of overall export orientation, that is the much larger role of international trade in the East Asian case. This is because the desirability of industrial exports is now universally recognized even in the Latin American and Philippine cases. Secondary import substitution regimes have thus been modified to include something which we may call export promotion which, in contrast to export substitution, may be defined as the selective encouragement of particular industries, even firms, to 'push out' exports in the absence of a general change in the structure of protection or market liberalization. Sometimes such subsidization is carried out *via* direct tax incentives or subsidies, for example public sector fiscal transfers, interest rate differentials, tariff rebates and so on, sometimes by encouraging private sector cross-subsidization, for example assuring companies of a continuation of high windfall profits in protected domestic markets in exchange for improved export performance. In other words, in the typical Latin American NIC, domestic content and export targets are often superimposed on an essentially unchanged industrial structure, with the protection of intermediate inputs and the distortion of relative prices governing the use of labour, capital and imports basically left intact. New industrial exports can grow substantially as a result of special government incentives rather than in response to the increasingly endowment sensitive production and export structure accompanying the trend towards market liberalization.

Increases in industrial exports generated in this fashion may thus have precious little to do with the product cycle type of evolution consistent with enhanced entrepreneurial maturation but result mainly from new incentives planted 'on top of' an existing import substitution structure. All NICs are responsive to the fact that industrial exports, unlike in the early days of ECLA, are now considered a 'good thing' – even if it means moving into the simultaneous domestic production and export of commodities 'up' the technology and capital intensive ladder, as, for example, in the case of automobile assembly where increased domestic component requirements and increased export quotas are frequently linked to continued guaranteed exclusivity in domestic markets.

One consequence of this contrast, already noted, is that the Colombia/Philippines NIC development path has been much less export-oriented overall and evidences a much lower participation of manufactured exports than the Taiwan/East Asia case. One may also note that the proportion of the population shifting from agricultural to non-agricultural activities is somewhat higher in the East Asian case than in the other NIC cases, in spite of the latter's higher initial level of industrialization. The relative neglect of food producing agriculture in Latin America, already noted during the primary import substitution subphase, is likely to be exacerbated in the context of a possibly sharpening protectionist régime. While net food imports thus become an increasingly important factor in the relatively natural resources rich Latin American or other Asian NICs over time, this phenomenon does not occur until much later in the East Asian case.

We should note also that Latin America's export cash crops, favoured by the allocation of public sector research as well as by the distortion of relative prices *via* government intervention, are generally substantially less labour intensive than the domestic food crops. Yet it is the cash crops which are required, along with the inflow of foreign capital, to fuel the continued growth of the import substituting industries. Finally, we should note that unskilled industrial real wages are likely to increase more in the Latin American type of situation, partly as a consequence of the greater rise in the relative price of the scarce agricultural wage good and partly as the result of the trend towards more 'invisible handshakes' between large-scale capitalists and an élite labour force. More unionization, stronger minimum wage and other welfare legislation typically accompany prolonged import substitution. In the context of the more market-oriented East Asian NIC, on the other hand, real wages do not rise markedly until after the labour surplus is, in fact, exhausted. Consequently, the Taiwan area did not begin to shift towards a more capital-intensive domestic industrial production and export structure until the early 1970s.

Even in the more difficult post-1973 years the East Asian NICs have been able to maintain a healthy export growth rate from an already high base, in spite of the advent of energy price rises, global inflation, recession, and some increase in DC protectionism which have combined to make continuation of growth difficult for non-oil LDCs generally. Overall performance has been maintained at high rates while dangerous levels of indebtedness resulting from too much reliance on foreign capital have generally been avoided.

Moreover, a lot of resilience was demonstrated in reaction to increased non-tariff barriers and other evidence of the 'New Protectionism' in the industrially advanced countries. Contrary to a widely held view, the typical East Asian NIC has had no special advantage in securing access for her labour intensive industrial exports in US and other Western markets during this post-1973 era; in fact, there is ample evidence that success, accompanied by major penetration of 'sick industry' markets in advanced countries, led to the rather rapid imposition or negotiation of voluntary quota arrangements, while less successful or laggard developing countries remained relatively exempt. In summary, I think it is fair to say that, once a country has moved on to an export substitution growth path, with all that connotes for the improvment of employment, income distribution and growth, it has also achieved greater entrepreneurial flexibility which permits it to overcome and 'work around' admittedly noxious defensive measures the advanced countries may resort to. As line 1, in Table I, indicates, the more open and exposed economy of the Taiwan area rebounded much better than either Colombia or the Philippines to resume high levels of growth after the brief post-1973 setback.

## CONCLUSIONS AND PROSPECTS

Our analysis thus indicates that the 'typical' NICs of the Third World tried to 'skip' the labour intensive primary export substitution phase and, as a consequence, were unable effectively to mobilize their plentiful unskilled labour *en route* to economic maturity. Moreover, it was essentially their relative abundance of land based raw materials which permitted them not only to move directly into the production and export of more technology and capital intensive industrial products but also afforded them the relative luxury of neglecting their domestic food producing agricultural sectors and instead importing food in order to try to keep wage goods prices from rising unduly.

The availability of plentiful natural resources and/or foreign capital which can be called upon permits this path to be followed and respectable growth rates to be maintained, as they were in most of the NICs over the past two decades. This is in marked contrast to the East Asian cases which at the end of their primary import substitution subphase could not afford to pay for the prolongation of import substitution but were instead forced to turn from a land intensive to a human resources intensive development path.

In theory, of course, a system could be better, not worse, off, *ceteris paribus,* if it has access either to a natural resources bonanza or to additional foreign capital in terms of the buffering of difficult problems of policy adjustment; but it is not difficult to see why, in fact, such bonanzas are often used to put off, or even entirely avoid, difficult decisions, that is in this case to 'skip' the labour intensive export substitution phase coupled with the mobilization of an always stubborn agricultural sector. In most developing countries, especially the Latin American NIC proto-type discussed here, many decades of import substitution growth have led to deeply entrenched habits, with strong vested interest groups, especially in the protected industrial sectors, able to resist reforms or even less radical marginal policy change. A good natural resources base may not only render the system's underlying exchange rate too 'strong', thus effectively discouraging labour intensive exports, but it also provides a psychological cushion or opiate which makes it possible for the system to 'afford' continued import substituting protectionism as it moves into ever more 'expensive' or capital intensive areas of production and export.

But the essential point is that a growth path complementary with an improvement in the distribution of income still represents a feasible development strategy for the future, as it has in the minority of developing country cases in the past. Such a strategy probably requires a somewhat heavier emphasis on the domestic balanced growth blade relative to its complement, the labour intensive export-oriented industrialization blade, in the years ahead. This is partly because of the generally 'larger than Taiwan' size of most LDCs but mainly because growth in the developed world is likely to be less buoyant in the years ahead than it was in the halcyon days of 1950–73. This requires a fuller mobilization of the rural sector, both agricultural and non-agricultural, which has so often suffered from decades – if not centuries – of neglect, but as a reward it also makes the LDCs somewhat less susceptible to exogenous shocks from abroad, and without resort to costly autarchic measures. Even though the East Asian NICs have a much higher export or trade orientation, their ability to integrate the export enclave with the workings of the domestic economy in a balanced triangular fashion is crucial to the system's ability to adjust flexibly to adversity, whether it be foreign or domestic in origin.

The availability of additional natural resources and/or access to foreign capital can, of course, be helpful in easing the transition from one policy régime to another. But unfortunately, human affairs being what they are, such availability can also be, and often has been, used to avoid what for some interest groups represent inevitably unpleasant policy changes, for example, the need for industrialists to shift from windfall profits in protected low volume domestic markets to earned profits in high volume low margin export markets and/or to domestic balanced growth activities.

In a very real sense, natural resources poor Japan and the current East Asian NICs did not have the easy alternative and thus were forced to seek their long run comparative advantage *via* a mobilization of their systems' human resources, first unskilled, then skilled. It perhaps takes a bit more statesmanship to undo the skipping of the labour intensive phase and pay increasing attention to the rural sector when one is not 'up against it' in the same way. While such 'skipping' of the primary export substitution phase in Latin America may thus be viewed as a politically convenient decision, rather than as the simple consequence of resource allocation and exchange rates, it is also true that many policies such as neglect of agricultural productivity, selective industrial export subsidies and so on can be reversed, and currently existing substantial pockets of unskilled surplus labour productively absorbed. Temporary natural resource bonanzas and the 'Kuwait Effect' can be controlled by running a surplus in trying to sterilize the inflows, and minimum wages plus the power of unions can be made to lag until the labour surplus has been exhausted at its base. Most importantly, the rural sector can be given more attention in terms of both infrastructure and the reduction of paternalism with which local government and local talent in the private sector are customarily viewed.

It is true, of course, that the East Asian NICs had certain initial advantages. But, aside from the choice of colonial antecedents, dimensions such as land reform, educational preparedness, even rural infrastructural heritage, are, of course, amenable to policies at the margin, just as differences in political constraints are amenable to continuous review and reappraisal. Differences in societal decisions are undoubtedly as much a function of political necessity, for example, the inability to overcome the strength of vested interests as long as the system is not 'up against it', as of a lack of adequate wisdom or realization of the technical alternatives available. The basic point here is not that any potential NIC is in a position to imitate the Taiwan case, even on technical grounds, but that there are usually good and sufficient reasons why countries persist with particular policy régimes. Sensitivity to the alternatives available in the difficult last two decades of the twentieth century is about as far as anyone would want to go in this type of comparative analysis of the historical record.

In the real world, of course, economies move in ambiguous, uncertain and non-monotonic paths, lurching forward in one direction, often sideways, partially retracing their steps; moreover, they are too complicated as systems to be as neatly packaged into well-defined typologies or transition phases as we have tried to do here, mainly for reasons of expositional emphasis. At the same time, this very array of real world subtle shades of grey can be viewed as a source of flexibility and strength for any given system at any point in time. There are indeed no inevitable sequences or unbreakable straitjackets – a point well illustrated by noting that some representatives of the East Asian family, for example South Korea, have considerably more in common with some representatives of the Latin American family, for example, Brazil. There is a good deal of export promotion along with the dominant export substitution pattern in the South Korean situation, especially since the early 1970s when export targets were set, combined with a substantial amount of arm twisting and implied government threats for individual firms. Korea's relative early neglect of agriculture, which was reversed only recently, also meant that foreign capital had to be relied on much more heavily – almost ten times as much as in the Taiwan area – both to support rapid industrial expansion as well as to finance larger food imports. On the other hand, Brazil's performance contains substantial elements of export substitution along with the dominance of secondary import substitution *cum* export promotion, yielding an occasional burst in labour intensive shoe and textile production and exports. There are also strong indications that Brazil is now turning seriously towards the activation of the domestic balanced growth blade in her development strategy, with the crucial help of the mobilization of her domestic food producing agricultural sector.

A brief look at other potential or emerging NICs, typified by the Philippines, is also useful here in assessing the potential reversibility of an LDC transition growth pattern which has a general tendency to attempt to skip the primary export substitution phase. Malaysia, Indonesia, Thailand, plus the Philippines in Asia, as well as Peru, Chile and Venezuela in Latin America have ample natural resource endowments, as well as other characteristics which place them at not too great a distance from the current core group of East Asian and Latin American NICs. Their performance with respect to growth and equity over the last three decades has also been generally somewhat intermediate, with Malaysia performing perhaps the best in Asia and Venezuela the worst in Latin America. In general these systems are to date probably coming closer to following the Colombia/Philippine NIC transition growth sequence, moving from a colonial pattern after World War II, to primary import substitution in the 1950s, and to secondary import substitution since. Some, for example Malaysia, which has had a much less severe primary import substitution régime, and Chile, which has recently undergone a wholesale policy reform, may now be in a position to step into the labour intensive export niche being vacated by the previously most successful East Asian NICs, the so called 'Gang of Four', which, having exhausted their unskilled labour surplus some years ago, are now well into their secondary import *cum* export substitution subphase. Indonesia currently seems to be doing somewhat less well than earlier, partly due to the impact of the oil bonanza-related 'Kuwait Effect', while the Philippines has recently effected some commercial policy and interest rate reforms but is probably still not yet ready for the really substantial shifts in policy required.

India, Pakistan and the mainland area of China, among others, are, of course, also standing in the wings ready to exercise potential flexibility in terms of policy initiatives, with India in particular currently showing substantial signs of a redirection of strategy. These LDCs, of course, are much larger countries, and have a somewhat poorer natural resources endowment. Hence we can expect of them, and other South Asian countries later on, a greater relative emphasis on the rural balanced growth blade of development strategy and a smaller relative emphasis on its export oriented labour intensive blade.

We have purposely emphasized, in the course of this *tour d'horizon,* that, while growth *cum* equity objectives may be widely shared, along with a substantial unemployment or labour surplus condition, there also exists a wide variety of individual country situations, even if we continue to leave the least developed cases entirely out of consideration. In fact, as the international agencies have been discovering, the number of required categories, or typologies, even to begin to encompass all these differences halfway intelligently, is uncomfortably large. Nevertheless, the need for scientific progress forces some attempt at generalization; and all we are claiming is that, at least for LDCs with substantial agricultural sectors still suffering from a substantial volume of underemployment, a foray through the historical laboratory of the last three decades permits the discovery of certain divergent patterns which give one some confidence about a limited number of carefully circumscribed generalizations. What we are *not* saying is that every LDC, regardless of resource endowment, income level and wage structure, must somehow pass through a light manufactured exports phase on its way to a diversified mature growth régime. What we *are* indeed saying is that past performance among the NICs with a labour surplus initially has demonstrated rather convincingly that more growth can be achieved *via* – rather than in spite of – a more equitable, labour intensive growth path; also that the achievement of such a pattern requires the adoption of a two-bladed development strategy, as described, with each blade given relatively more weight depending on such factors as country size, geography, transport cost, and so on.

The ability of LDCs to fill the various niches of labour intensive manufactured goods in world trade, of course, includes the possibility of increased trade among the developing countries themselves, both in internationally specified and in modified, more 'appropriate', goods, using more 'appropriate' processes. The possibilities of an expanding LDC domestic balanced growth process can thus be extended from considerations internal to any one country to groups of developing countries – with or without resort to regional common market arrangements. In fact, if one talks of the South-South trade potential, the two blades of a strategy enhancing growth *via* a more rural and a more export oriented development strategy begin to merge into each other.

We are certainly not advocating a turning inward or a delinking of the South from the North, nor accepting a continued deterioration of the international environment, either *via* some combination of exogenous shocks of the kind that have been experienced over the last decade or *via* the fuller blossoming of the 'New Protectionism' in the industrial countries. But, with DC growth rates themselves likely to be lower, *ceteris paribus,* in the future than in the past, and with, at best, no major reduction in protectionism on the part of the developed world, the South really has two main options. One is to continue the search for new natural resource or foreign capital inflow bonanzas which would permit a prolongation of the import substitution subphase on a country by country basis; the second, less spectacular, but more dependable, alternative would be to recognise that the attempt to capture more labour intensive industrial export markets must be combined with a broadened participation by food producers as well as medium and small-scale industrialists in both rural and urban areas within a balanced domestic growth context. Such a strategy would yield faster growth along with better distribution and employment outcomes. A 'trickle down' strategy was not reliable for the long term when respectable overall growth rates on a narrow base were still feasible, as in the pre-1973 period; it makes even less sense in the environment the developing world is very likely to be facing over the next two decades.

The advanced industrial countries, of course, also have some options. They can keep the LDCs on their back burners or recognize the increasing importance for the global economy of maintaining respectable LDC growth rates. This, in turn, will require in many, though by no means all, situations a change in the way in which LDC growth is generated. Effecting the necessary policy changes is, as we have seen, often politically as well as administratively difficult and well-deserving of international co-operation. Such co-operation is relevant not only with respect to the maintenance of market access to accommodate the labour intensive export blade of development; but also to the possible ballooning of aid – and improved access to other forms of foreign capital – in step with the easing of the political and resources pain of required LDC policy reforms in the first place.

## DISCUSSION OPENING I – WILHELM HENRICHSMEYER

Professor Ranis has presented to us a broad view on various aspects of development performance and strategies. The general line of his argument and the general conclusions drawn seem to me so balanced and so cautiously formulated that they are rather immune to critical comments.

Therefore I will focus on certain aspects of his analysis and will select a number of issues, which might be fruitful for further discussion. I will *not* comment on the performance of the specific countries, which have been chosen as examples, and will not discuss the question as to what extent the mentioned countries fit into the suggested typology. That might be better done by colleagues from these countries.

1 One of the main points of Professor Ranis's argument is that it is beneficial and rewarding for a country to pursue already in the rather early stages of development an export orientated policy and to expose the economy to international competition. He stresses especially the importance of exports in a phase before a policy of import-substitution for more advanced goods (durable, capital goods) is started.

The advantages of such a strategy are obvious: besides the immediate increase of export earnings it has widespread economic and political consequences:

- Entrepreneurs and policy-makers develop from the beginning a more outward-looking attitude;
- product quality and efficiency are seen under the viewpoint of international competition;
- lower levels of protection lead to less distorted price ratios, so that allocative incentives are given, which tend to adjust the production structures according to comparative advantages;
- and further, such a strategy tends to reduce positions of vested interests and to induce behavioural and institutional changes.

Professor Ranis has explained all that, and there will be hardly any economist who would not support such a strategy *in principle.* But the questions on which I would like to encourage further discussion are:

(a) Is the suggested strategy of primary export development feasible for *all* countries or is it only a chance for some with specific conditions, like the Taiwan area of China?

The question is, whether the market niches of the type discovered in Taiwan are large and numerous enough to allow a similar export strategy in large countries like India, or by a larger group of smaller countries. The danger is that increased supply on narrow markets will lead to a pressure on prices for this type of product.

This question has to be judged especially with the background of stagnating growth in the developing countries and only a slow increase in international trade since the middle of the 1970s. Arthur Lewis – in his Elmhirst Lecture three years ago at this Conference – has pointed out the negative effects on the developing countries if these trends continue.

The second question which we should discuss is therefore:

(b) Do past experiences and future expectations about economic growth in the developed countries suggest (or even make it necessary) to have a change of emphasis from more export orientated strategies to strategies which are more orientated to the growth of internal demand?

Professor Ranis has shown on this point that export-orientated areas, like Taiwan, have done better in this respect during the last years than most other countries. But I think that this question has to be analysed in a wider context, taking into account the causal interrelations between the different determining factors.

2 Here the more general question emerges as to whether the main orientation for the outline of a development strategy, which Professor Ranis has derived from the trade side (the necessity of import-substitution for export expansion) should not be developed more from the resource and production side, including the institutional factors. The starting point for the elaboration of a development strategy would then be:

- an assessment of the country's production potential and of the

obstacles which hinder development, thereby giving emphasis on agriculture, small scale industries and rural areas;
- a specific trade performance would then be the result, not the aim of the development strategy. Some branches would be characterized by import-substitution, others by export-expansion and still others by production for internal demand.

This approach would not be in contradiction with what has been proposed but it would be a change in viewpoint and emphasis.

3 The question of equity – the central theme of this Conference – enters Professor Ranis's argument only through the back door. The idea of the proposed development strategy seems to be that on the path of export-orientated and labour intensive development the labour surplus can gradually be absorbed and the quality of labour can be improved through learning by doing – both contributing to 'social equity'.

This leads to the central conclusion that everything that improves the use of resources and, by that, increases economic growth, also improves the employment situation and income distribution. Economic growth and equity are therefore – according to this view – only two sides of the same coin. In this context a number of questions have to be considered, which will be taken up partly in the following sessions. I will suggest only the following for further discussion:

(a) What do we understand by equity? Professor Ranis gives only an implicit definition, according to which equity improves with increased employment and growth of income per head. Many other interpretations are possible. This question should be cleared at the beginning to have a reference for the discussion.

(b) Even if one takes Professor Ranis' definition, many examples show that income distribution can be worsened in the process of economic growth, for example if the application of new technological knowledge is restricted to a subgroup of well educated and trained people.

(c) Further, it may be questioned that one can be sure whether labour intensive production processes even with low wages are competitive enough to assure an elastic absorption of labour. This is especially the problem of small-scale industries.

(d) Finally, it will need to be discussed whether this proposed strategy is sufficient for the group of the least developed countries with very unfavourable growth conditions, especially those in Africa.

All these points open up a wide field for discussion, which will be taken further in the following sessions. I have brought them up now in this first plenary session to avoid us starting out with too simple a structured answer to the complex set of questions which are related to the problem of growth and equity.

## DISCUSSION OPENING II – PER PINSTRUP ANDERSEN

Professor Ranis has prepared a most interesting paper. In line with the request by the programme chairman I shall try to draw attention to some of the issues raised by the Professor which may be further discussed later this session.

Although, as Professor Ranis pointed out, generalizations may have limited validity the three country cases nevertheless add a great deal to our understanding of the development process and how equity is influenced by the choice of growth path.

Furthermore, the paper presents interesting hypotheses regarding the influence of the resource endowment and external capital availability on the choice of development policies and growth path.

Finally, the analysis presented illustrates the role of the agricultural sector under alternative development strategies and offers guidelines for the design of agricultural policies to facilitate growth with equity.

The paper deals exclusively with the newly industrialized countries. Countries at earlier stages of development are completely ignored. Yet these – the poorest of the developing countries – have showed a very limited growth performance during the recent past. While many of these countries may not present serious equity problems, they suffer from mass proverty and the related ills such as malnutrition. These countries are faced with policy decisions and development choices which are likely to influence greatly the extent to which growth and equity goals are simultaneously achieved in the future.

What are the lessons which these countries may draw from the experiences of the newly industrialized countries in order to pursue growth with equity?

Professor Ranis argues, and I agree, that there need not be a conflict between the achievement of growth and equity goals. The difficult trade-offs between the two, which are often mentioned, may not have to be faced if the right development path is chosen.

Keeping in mind that humans are a resource as well as a beneficiary of the development process, a successful growth with equity strategy is likely to include three critical factors. First, underemployed and unemployed human resources must be drawn into the development process. Second, the productivity of human resource must be increased, and third, the control and/or ownership of land and capital resources must be distributed widely.

The importance of all three of these factors is clearly shown in the case of the Taiwan area and one could hypothesize that the absence of emphasis on these factors has contributed significantly to a less successful marriage between growth and equity in Colombia and the Philippines.

The importance of the first factor, that is drawing unused or underused human resources into production, is, I belive, rather clear. Similarly, the very high pay-off, both private and public, to human capital improving efforts such as education has been widely documented.

But just how important is the third factor, that is the resource ownership distribution? Will a growth with equity strategy only be successful if it is based on an equitable distribution of ownership of productive resources, particularly land? Would the results of the development process in Taiwan have been radically different if the land ownership had been distributed like it was and is in Colombia?

In my opinion, these are critical questions. If equitable distribution of land ownership is a necessary condition for the simultaneous achievement of growth and equity goals, then there are very few countries where a growth with equity strategy is likely to be successful.

Closely related to the question of asset distribution is the political environment within which development strategies and policies are established. The existing power structure will clearly favour a development path which produces the greatest benefits to the ruling classes. Yet such development may not result in maximum resource efficiency and – given the skewness of the distribution of political power in most developing countries – is unlikely to assure an equitable income distribution.

Let me finish by drawing your attention to Professor Ranis's suggestions that the availability of external capital and aid be linked with required policy changes in the recipient countries. This is a suggestion which may deserve some further discussion.

V. S. VYAS

# *Growth and Equity in Asian Agriculture: a Synoptic View*

Growth of agricultural production in south and south-east Asia[1] during the past decade or so has been quite satisfactory. In most countries of this region agricultural production outstripped population growth; in a number of countries the rate of growth in production was higher than that of the growth in domestic demand; the food self-sufficiency ratio for the region and for the majority of countries improved; the growth of agricultural exports outpaced the growth of agricultural imports; some of the countries where agriculture had stagnated in the 1960s turned the corner, and others could maintain the high tempo of the previous decade. This presents a sharp contrast to other developing regions such as the Middle East or Africa. In a continent of Asia's size and diversity, there are bound to be major inter-country differences in pace and pattern of growth. What is remarkable is the all-pervasive picture of buoyant agriculture with only a few notable exceptions.

An equally remarkable feature of development during the past decade is that it made very little impact on the extent of poverty in this region. Barring a few very fast growing economies like Malaysia where the problem in any case was not very acute, there is hardly any country in Asia where a remarkable dent in this problem could be made during the course of a decade of sustained growth. There were marginal gains in a few countries, but there were no dramatic changes. This is in regard to the absolute poverty. When it comes to relative inequality as expressed in terms of skewness in income distribution, with few exceptions the countries of Asia, fast growing as much as slow growing, did not show any improvement. There are problems in definition, in reliability of data, and in methodologies to process and interpret the information. There are legitimate differences among the specialists on all these counts. However, the facts of poverty and income inequality are too robust to be explained away by subtleties of definition and measurement.

On this occasion I will be addressing myself to the problems of absolute poverty, that is the problems of the households who do not have an adequate intake of calories, who cannot afford adequate clothing and shelter, whose opportunity cost of sending their children to school is prohibitive and who in all matters of social and political significance are at the periphery. A large majority of these households, as the large majority of the total population, are located in rural areas. The main groups comprising the rural poor are the households of landless labourers, rural artisans, and marginal, non-viable farmers. There is no evidence to suggest that the dependence of these households on agriculture has declined. The occupational diversification in the rural areas, even in the fast growing economies, has been slow. The basic questions to be asked, therefore, are (a) Why could not the rural poor have an equitable share in agricultural growth? (b) Why could not more employment opportunities be provided for the rural poor in non-agricultural occupations?

To answer these questions we will have to understand the sources of growth in agriculture in Asia. It is not only the rate of growth but also the pattern which determines the distribution of gains among various factor owners and factor users. During the decade of the 1970s the main source of growth was the HYV technology centering around high-yielding varieties of seeds and fertilizers. This technology spread rapidly in regions where adequate and controlled availability of water could be ensured.

Apart from sizable gains in productivity per hectare, this technology claimed three distinct advantages. In the first place, it was suggested that this technology was, by and large, a labour intensive technology, in any case it was not a labour displacing technology like, say, mechanization. It depended on larger labour disposition as complementary to larger doses of non-labour inputs, it favoured more labour intensive agronomic practices, and post-harvest labour content was distinctly higher because of larger yields. From all available evidence the per hectare labour absorption in the areas covered by this technology was high. However, it should be remembered that the new technology was not extended over all the arable area. By the end of the 1970s, in the wheat growing regions the coverage was around 60 per cent, while in the case of rice growing regions the proportion was less than half. The area under other crops had hardly any comparable labour intensive high yielding technology. For the major countries of Asia till the end of 1970s coverage under HYV was between one-third and one-half of the cropped area. Adequate investment in infrastructure, particularly irrigation, and availability of delivery outlets, conditioned the spread of the new technology. Since in large regions these prerequisites were not available in sufficient measure, the limits to the spread of HYV were soon reached.

More importantly, the labour intensiveness of agricultural production was over-estimated. The figures of labour coefficient in agricultural production in Asia vary from 0.75 to 0.40 depending on the extent of irrigation and the nature of technology. However, the most common figure used is 0.5. This means that even if agricultural production is rising at the rate of 4 per cent per annum – a rather optimistic rate for most of the Asian countries – and the rural labour force is growing at the rate of 2 per cent – a figure closer to reality – no dent will be made in the overall rate of unemployment and underemployment. For wage paid agricultural labour, therefore, there was no hope for fuller employment if sole reliance was to be placed on agriculture. We shall comment presently on the reasons for the lack of diversification of the rural economy.

Another advantage claimed for the HYV centered technology was that due to their short-maturing characteristics these varieties facilitate introduction of multiple cropping. This advantage was not reaped to the full in most of the countries of Asia as is evidenced by the fact that the index of multiple cropping has not improved in a significant way. In any event, it lagged behind the index of irrigation. Sometimes blame is put on the dearth of draft power to complete the post-harvest and pre-sowing operations between two cropping seasons in time, and a plea is made for the introduction of mechanization on this ground. The results from several studies in this region have questioned the need for mechanization of agricultural operations as a prerequisite for extension of the area under multiple cropping. In fact, multiple cropping and mechanization of agricultural operations have progressed independently. The major bottle-neck in the expansion of multiple cropping is proper water management and investment in the complementary infra-structure (that is in land shaping, drainage and so on).

The third main advantage claimed in favour of the new technology was its scale neutral characteristic. However, this was of little avail for the marginal farmers who constitute the large bulk of rural producers in most of the densely populated large countries of this region. Very substantial increase in productivity would be needed if their miniscule holdings were to yield enough surplus for sustaining a tolerable standard of living. It is estimated, for example, that in the case of India, if the agricultural production rises at the rate of 3.4 per cent per annum and if the share of the small farmers in total production is increased substantially, from their present contribution of 10 per cent to, say, 15 per cent, still at the end of the year AD 2000, nearly 30 per cent of the rural households will remain below the poverty line. The situation in other Asian countries is not likely to be qualitatively different.

There is, however, a class of small farmers which can be termed as potentially viable farmers, who with application of modern technology can raise productivity to a level which will permit them to cross the poverty line. The new technology can, presumably, assist this group. But the scale neutrality of technology does not mean resource neutrality. For the small farmers access to modern inputs (fertilizers, irrigation, improved seeds) is not easy. Their handicaps in respect of these inputs may be less severe, as compared to the handicaps in relation to land input. Yet whether it is a transaction relating to the purchase of inputs or sale of marketable surplus, or availing of extension or credit facilities, present institutions are biased against the small farmers. For example, credit availability is made difficult because of the requirements of land as the security. On paper a number of countries have dispensed with land as a collateral and are prepared to advance crop-loans, but in practice this rarely happens. In the matter of input supply and output marketing this group of producers is discriminated against because of the small, inconsequential lots which they demand or supply. The extension agencies do not pay particular attention to these groups as their contribution, even if enhanced, will remain marginal to total production.

A number of studies have shown that the small farmers growing wheat and rice have also adopted high yielding varieties in these crops, although after a time lag. These studies have also shown that the small farmers do not use a package of practices and the productivity of HYV crops on these farms is low. One can infer from these findings that the HYV had led to larger employment and higher yields and to that extent had a positive impact on the small farmers as well as on the landless labourers. But their gains were marginal when looking at the immensity of their problem. By itself improvement in agricultural productivity has not yielded any measurable results for this disadvantaged section. It should be admitted, however, that the direction of the technological change because of the scale neutral character was in favour of the poor. However, the supporting institutions of extension, credit, and marketing did not play their role.

If the main thrust of technology was neutral between large and small farmers, the posture adopted by most of the countries in Asia in regard to institutional change was distinctly pro-poor. The legislation enacted in different countries concerning the relationships in land illustrates this point. In virtually every country there were enactments imposing ceilings on land, and ensuring security of tenure and a fair share of produce to the tillers. Barring centrally planned countries including China, and countries where conquering powers, for reasons of their own, had implemented radical land reforms, that is South Korea, Taiwan (China) and Japan, no other country in Asia has had a very creditable record of implementation of land legislation. But in a number of countries the process of enlargement of holdings by the big farmers was halted. This, coupled with technological factors favouring intensive rather than extensive farming and demographic pressure on land, led to a weakening of the hegemony of large farmers and emergence of capitalist type of medium-range holdings in a number of Asian countries.

The loosening of the grip of large farmers did not help the small farmers. Growing population pressure could not be contained by marginal growth in productivity or slight improvements in employment opportunities in irrigated agricultural regions. In countries where dispossession of land of the small farmers became difficult, it led to impoverishment of the peasantry; where land market was not frozen, there was a growing army of landless labourers. The choice before a sizable section of rural producers was between pauperization and proletarianization.

Barring two city states of Singapore and Hong Kong, the only country of the Far East which entered the club of newly industrialized nations in the 1970s – Taiwan (China) and South Korea had made the grade in the 1960s – was Malaysia, which had very special features; the most distinct being abundant mineral and natural wealth and low pressure of population on land. Other countries in the ASEAN region also seem to have been doing well in terms of industrial growth during the past 3 – 4 years. It is too early to predict the course of development. The reason why countries of Asia, in general, could not experience an export-led growth as was experienced by South Korea, would include large and rapidly growing populations, lack of investment in social and physical infrastructure, and inequitable distribution of purchasing power.

The slow growth of industrial production in a majority of the countries can be traced to lack of effective domestic demand, particularly from the rural areas. This statement needs to be elaborated. Concentration of assets in a few hands meant concentration of purchasing power in a relatively small number of households. The demand pattern of these households, both rural and urban, was oriented towards high capital and skill intensive goods and services. Because of the weak backward and forward employment linkages it could not provide employment opportunities for a large number of rural artisans and craftsmen. As a consequence, rural artisans who had lost their market swelled the ranks of agricultural workers or floated to urban areas to constitute a significant proportion of the urban poor. This also acted as a brake to the rise of real wages in the countryside, further weakening the demand for goods and services from the large mass of rural poor.

An indication of the capital and skill intensive demand generated in an inegalitarian society is the changes in the product-mix in the consumer goods industry. One could see it reflected in the growth of superior varieties of clothes at the expense of coarse clothes, machine-made shoes at the expense of village cobblers' products, hydrogenated oil in place of oil expelled in the village expellers. The examples can be multiplied. The new products which entered into the consumer basket of the rural and urban well-to-do sections were hardly labour intensive. Thus, the type of development which has been witnessed in a large number of Asian countries has not done anything to break the essentially dualistic nature of these societies. True, in the rural areas a viable group of middle peasantry has emerged. These are co-opted in what has come to be known as the U class. But there is hardly any evidence to suggest that the plight of the bottom two or three deciles has improved in a remarkable way.

This led in a few countries to specific, target-group orientated, programmes, for example programmes for landless labourers, and marginal and small farmers. Where the poor were concentrated in a geographical area, mainly the areas which had severe physical handicaps (for example arid areas), the programmes were made area specific. The main thrust of these programmes was to generate employment opportunities by public works or to increase productivity on the small landholdings of the poor by introducing modern technology. In the latter case, apart from more concentrated extension efforts, major reliance was placed on subsidizing modern inputs like fertilizers. There is enough evidence to suggest that these programmes proved to be socially costly and the advantages were pre-empted by the non-poor.

It is tempting to put blame for the failure of these and similar poor-orientated programmes on defects in the designs of the programmes, and/or on the inadequacy of the implementing agencies. Both explanations are substantially true. For example, when designing these programmes the poor were considered as a homogeneous mass. That there were differences in the groups of disadvantaged households based on asset holding, skills, social and cultural milieu, physical location and so on, were seldom taken note of when identifying and formulating the projects. The programmes were translated in terms of 'schemes' with a more or less uniform format. Evidently the utility of such schemes in varied and dissimilar circumstances was severely limited.

In all these countries bureaucracy is the main implementing agency for development programmes. The role of voluntary action of people's own initiative is marginal. Bureaucracy, by its social background and culture, would have inherent limitations in implementing programmes for the poor. There have been exceptions among the bureaucrats and a few could fully identify themselves with the interests of the poor. But this has not been the common trait.

While all these negative experiences cannot be wished away, there are certain positive features in the current situation which also merit recognition. The first and foremost is the nature of technology. In HYVs we have a technology which is labour intensive, land augmenting and scale neutral. The failure of other institutions to supply basic wherewithals to support this technology has already been indicated. But the technology cannot be faulted. The major cause of worry is not the nature of the technology but the fact that the HYVs are available only for a few crops (mainly cereal crops) and that too for irrigated areas. There is a need to pay greater attention to the dry areas and to non-cereal crops. Efforts in these directions by the national agricultural systems and by the international agricultural research centres can make a significant contribution.

Barring a few notable exceptions the countries of Asia have failed in their efforts to implement redistributive types of land reforms. With growing land values and a better organized kulak class the prospects for introducing such reforms are becoming bleak. At the same time it ought to be realised that as agriculture modernizes, the importance of non-land inputs grows and that of land as an input declines. The capacity of the modern states in Asia to orientate the distribution of non-land inputs in favour of the poor is pronouncedly better than their capacity in redistributing land. Given all the limitations in the input programmes to which attention was drawn earlier, skewness in distribution of credit, fertilizers or irrigation was less acute than the skewness in landholding.

Major difficulties, then, are in the field of organization. The delivery systems, as they exist today, are adequate to meet the requirements of the medium to large farmers. But they fail when it comes to small farmers or landless workers. Apart from the class bias of those who man these institutions, the very large number of the recipients in the latter category make the task of the existing systems very difficult. One way to cope with the problem is to design delivery systems which can serve the numerous small recipients meaningfully. For certain types of enterprise (for example dairy) or for certain commercial crops (for example sugar, cotton), there are examples of successful co-operative efforts which are able to serve even the small producers effectively. But such organizations are too few and obtain in special circumstances, notably when producers or beneficiaries belong to the same asset group. The real test of such organizations comes when they have to operate in a milieu in which large producers of a commodity are members of the organization along with numerous small-scale producers. Invariably in such circumstances the organisation tilts in favour of the rich.

The crux of the problem is the mobilization of the poor to exert the pressure of their numbers on the delivery systems so that the latter may meet their requirements. Our understanding of the mobilization efforts and group action is extremely limited. Organizations for collective action like co-operatives or trade unions have not yielded the desired results. It is in this area that the countries of South and South-East Asia may learn useful lessons from the countries of East Asia. Small groups of producers having a common social background, with a more or less equal asset base and a common interest in a specific economic activity, provide the base for building the micro-level rural producers' groups in these countries. These primary groups, in turn, can protect the interest of small producers in secondary organizations. As the conditions in various countries differ, the social scientists in these countries will have to give serious thought in evolving the guidelines for group action among the poor. More likely, they will have to work with the activists to understand the dynamics of social organization.

Finally, so far as agricultural policies are concerned, particularly those pertaining to prices and subsidies, since the beginning of the 1970s the countries of Asia have been pursuing a sane policy package. The earlier notion of using the price mechanism to transfer resources to the non-agricultural sector was dispelled in the light of the actual performance of the agricultural sector which, under the régime of unfavourable prices along with technological and institutional handicaps, stagnated and thus made the countries concerned spend their scarce foreign exchange resources in importing food and other essential commodities. The price policies pursued since then do provide a favourable climate for agricultural investment without making them too adverse for rural and urban consumers. There are still problems in the area of agricultural policies, particularly those pertaining to risk and uncertainty, in the structure of inter-commodity prices and in the area of taxes and subsidies. But, by and large, the basic policy thrusts have been in the right direction and have contributed to favourable results in agriculture as witnessed during the last decade.

There is a danger, however, that, under the influence of the new orthodoxy which favours 'high' agricultural prices as a panacea, the pendulum may swing to the other extreme and may result not only in hardship for the rural and urban consumers of foodgrains, but may eventually tell upon the state's capacity to invest in agricultural infrastructure as more resources get diverted to meet the demand of wage earners to compensate them for high foodgrain prices. It should be remembered that public investment in agricultural research, extension, and infrastructure has played a major role in the agricultural progress of the 1970s, and that in a régime of an organized, or in any case vocal, urban work force, the same resources can easily get diverted to neutralize inflationary trends, set in motion by high agricultural prices. There is no reason to upset the precarious but welcome balance existing between agricultural and non-agricultural prices.

To sum up, during the last decade agricultural growth in Asian countries was not only satisfactory in itself, but it changed the picture of stagnation obtaining in most of the countries during the decade of the 1960s. The change can primarily be attributed to the spread of HYVs in irrigated areas. The emergence of medium-sized farmers who carried the main burden of agricultural growth was a result partly of the professed institutional changes and partly due to the nature of technology which favoured intensive efforts. The policy package was by and large complementary to these changes and stimulated growth; it certainly did not inhibit the process. However, the pattern of growth did not favour the small farmers and landless labourers who continued to be marginal as producers and consumers. The process of polarization could not be stopped, and the lowest deciles of rural households could not participate in the process of agricultural growth or share its benefits to any remarkable extent. At the same time the factors such as the availability of size-neutral technology and the not too discouraging record in the distribution of non-land inputs suggest that it should be possible to bring the disadvantaged sections to the mainstream of agricultural development. The key areas of action seem to be (a) introduction of size neutral technology for more and more crops and regions; (b) investment in rural infrastructure, both social and physical; and (c) organization of the rural poor in such a manner that they can have a meaningful interaction with the delivery systems. A number of countries have progressed in all these directions in a limited way, while some have performed quite satisfactorily in one or other of these prerequisites of a socially desirably pattern of growth. And in this lies the hope.

## NOTES

1 Throughout this discussion Developing Market Economies of South and South-East Asia are referred to as Asian countries.

## DISCUSSION OPENING – YANG BOO CHOE

I am very much honoured to be one of the discussion openers for the overall problems of growth and equity in agricultural development in the Third World context.

Since this very first session is assigned to identify problems which are considered to be important, and, therefore, to be discussed throughout the

Conference period, I am obliged to raise certain key questions in a very simple way. Most of my remarks are inspired by the oustanding paper just presented by Dr V. S. Vyas.

Before I left my country I met one of my closest friends, and I told him about my first trip to Indonesia, the Eighteenth Conference, and the main theme of growth and equity in agricultural development. He asked, 'World agricultural economists are going to get together to discuss the growth and equity problems of the rural poor in Bali? Why don't you make a trip to a rural village, spend some time with rural poor, and discuss their equity problems?' I said, 'No, I am not going to Bali, I am going to Jakarta.' But he replied 'Well, anyway, have fun in Bali. Don't miss the beach girls.'

Distinguished participants, the issue of growth and equity is one of the classical problems facing the agricultural economics profession from its beginning. Depressed conditions of rural peoples and small family farms have drawn a lot of intellectual minds which eventually formed this scientific community of agricultural economists. Yet, as stated in the opening addresses, today we are not adequately equipped to solve the problem of growth and equity with satisfaction. The flagrant reality of the disparities in income and quality of life existing between urban and rural peoples, and between the rich and the poor within the rural economy reminds us of the limitations of what we agricultural economists can do about the problem of growth and equity in theory and in practice. Also, the ever widening rural-urban disparities simply suggest that our past theoretical as well as practical attempts have been far less than successful.

This uneasiness and dissatisfaction with the present status of our profession in dealing with the growth and equity problem inevitably prompts us to ask: what was wrong with our theoretical efforts to explain the sources, structure, mechanism of the rural-urban disparities?

As clearly stated by Dr Vyas in his paper, we do not yet have clear answers to such questions as:

- Why could not the rural poor have an equitable share in agricultural growth?
- Why could not more employment opportunities be provided for the rural poor in non-agricultural occupations?

May I add a few more questions?

- Why is it unavoidable to sacrifice small rural family farms in the process of economic growth?
- Why could not agricultural productivity be increased without constantly dislocating the farm population?
- If the introduction of new agricultural technology is the force generating disequilibrium in the agricultural economy, why are small family farms in a constant need of new technology including HYV even under the condition of market distortion?

These are only some examples where our profession has failed to provide clear answers. In this problematic situation, one of the critical questions about the theoretical front of our profession is: What are the theoretical frameworks upon which we are discussing in vain the equity and growth problem today?

If we turn our attention to the practical front, we can easily find a long list of policy recommendations which should be carried out by the policy makers for the improvement of the welfare of rural peoples. Dr Vyas suggests three key areas of action in the conclusion of his paper: introduction of size-neutral technology, investment in rural infrastructure, and organization of the rural poor.

I am quite sure that all the participants can easily agree with him. Nevertheless, all the participants may also have their own lists and priorities. The real problem is not a shortage of brand new policy instruments, but a lack of action. If this is the case, then, one critical question to ask is: Why does such a list of policy recommendations for the improvement of rural peoples seldom take the form of concrete action in many Third World countries of Asia, Africa and Latin America? Why does such a highly desirable action programme often become a political rhetoric without action? This reality also leads us to the question: What was wrong with our practical policy suggestions and action programmes?

If you kindly agree with me that the theoretical framework provides a basis upon which we formulate a set of practical policy recommendations, then, I may say that probably our theories about the structure, mechanism, and function of the agricultural economy may not be successful at least in Asian, African and Latin American countries. Those theoretical frameworks that I am talking about are the Neoclassical-Keynsian as well as the Marxian economic theories. They created a myth that the small family farm economy is the very source of the growth and equity problems. They recommended that the small family farm economy should be replaced by a large-scale, mechanized, capitalistic farm-firm on the one hand, and by a large-scale, mechanized socialistic state (collective) farm on the other. Under these dominant theoretical frameworks, the general case of the small family farm economy in Asia, Africa and Latin America became the special case. Nevertheless, under the name of the universality of economic theory, these hypothetical and unrealistic theoretic frameworks are taken for granted and shared by most agricultural economists in the Third World countries. However, the reality of the rural poor and small family farms struggling for survival in these Third World countries suggests that we may need to take a fresh look at all our taken-for-granted theoretical frameworks applied to the small family farm economy. We must ask to what extent the neoclassical as well as the Marxian framework is valid, practical, relevant and workable? If they are limited in theory and in practice, we may need an alternative theoretical framework upon which we can deal with the small family farm's growth and equity problem with satisfaction. In this context I would like to ask whether the so-called dependency hypothesis has something to offer for our understanding and solution of the growth and equity problem in agriculture.

Let me conclude my observations by quoting the statement made by

Henry C. Taylor, the founding father of agricultural economics in America, in 1929. His statement still has many insights for the present status of our profession. He said, 'There are . . . many false doctrines which clear thinking will shatter. At the present time some of these false doctrines are being used to keep the farm from securing a fair share of the national income . . . . Agricultural economists should test every hypothesis, stated or unstated, which lies behind every theory which is paraded in public.'

DHARAM GHAI

# *Stagnation and Inequality in African Agriculture*[1]

## INTRODUCTION

The purpose of this paper is to analyze agricultural development in sub-Sahara Africa since 1960 from the point of view of growth and distribution. It should be mentioned at the outset that an attempt of this sort is severely constrained by the availability of data and literature on the subject. There are relatively few works which attempt a quantitative, macro analysis of growth and distribution in the rural economy, either at the level of the country or group of countries. A recent World Bank publication has examined agricultural growth and policies in sub-Sahara Africa as part of a more general study but it has very little to say on distribution of benefits from growth (World Bank, 1981). A publication by the International Labour Office has sought to fill this gap through studies of rural poverty and agrarian policies in nine African countries but it does not contain a systematic analysis of the growth experience (Ghai and Radwan, 1982). This paper draws on these and other publications to sketch an overview of the salient features of growth and distribution in sub-Saharan agriculture.

## THE GROWTH EXPERIENCE

The overall growth as well as the agricultural growth in sub-Sahara Africa over the past two decades has been lower than in other developing countries. Furthermore, there was a significant deceleration of growth in the 1970s as compared with the 1960s. In certain respects, the performance has been so poor that it is not too much of an exaggeration to speak of an agrarian crisis in the 1970s.

The average GDP growth rate came down from 3.9 in the 1960s to 2.9 in the 1970s; the decline being sharper – from 4.1 to 1.6 – if Nigeria is excluded from these figures. The performance of the agricultural sector was even poorer. The annual growth rate of agricultural production declined from 2.5 per cent in 1960–70 to 1.8 per cent in 1970–79 (World Bank, 1981). The seriousness of the situation may be illustrated by a few figures relating to the 1970s. Between 1969–71 and 1977–79, out of 39 sub-Sahara countries, no less than thirty experienced declines in per caput agricultural production and twenty-seven experienced falls in per caput food production (as shown in Table 1). The decline is spread across a wide range of countries, covering low income as well as middle income and oil-exporting no less than oil-importing countries. There does not appear to be any correlation between performance in food and export crop production. There are countries like Swaziland, Malawi and Kenya which have done well in both food and non-food production. Likewise countries such as Guinea, Ghana, Togo, Gambia have performed poorly in both respects. On the other hand countries like Sudan and Benin while doing relatively well on food have fared poorly with respect to export crops. The opposite picture emerges in countries such as Chad, Mali and Congo.

The picture of agricultural stagnation in sub-Sahara Africa is confirmed by figures on the production of major crops, and on agricultural exports and imports (FAO, 1980 and World Bank, 1981). There was a marked decline in growth of output of most food crops between the 1960s and the 1970s: for instance, the rate of growth of maize fell from 5.2 to 1.3 per cent per annum, rice from 4.0 to 2.9, pulses from 3.3 to 1.1, roots and tubers from 2.0 to 1.8 and sugar from 6.3 to 2.5, while the production of wheat, groundnuts, palm kernels and seed cotton fell in absolute terms. There was a worsening of performance for all agricultural exports except for tobacco. What is even more striking is that there was an absolute decline in the volume of exports of no less than sixteen commodities, including such important crops as cocoa, coffee, maize, cotton, groundnuts, oil seed cake, bananas and rubber. Consequently the African share in exports from developing countries has fallen sharply for most commodities between 1961–63 and 1977–79, the major exceptions to this being tea, coffee and cotton. On the other hand, imports of many agricultural commodities grew extremely rapidly in the period since 1961, their total value rising by nearly six-fold between 1961–63 and 1977–79.

A fully satisfactory explanation of deteriorating agricultural performance would require a detailed analysis of the specific factors that have been operative at the level of an individual country – a task that cannot be undertaken here. Yet the experience has been sufficiently widespread to warrant the conclusion that there must have been some common elements at play. The major factors which appear to have been responsible for agricultural stagnation may be classified under three broad headings – a deterioration in the quality of the productive forces, disincentives to agriculture and certain exogenous factors. We discuss each of these in turn.

*Deterioration in quality of land and agricultural labour force*

For a number of reasons there has been a decline in the quality of the two main productive forces – the land and the labour force, resulting in a decline in yields and labour productivity. The traditional African agricultural system was characterized by low population/land ratios and shifting cultivation and livestock rearing. The period of cultivation and grazing varied with the fertility of the soil but everywhere the fallowing of the land permitted the agricultural land and pastures to return to their original state. This system was disrupted by the onset of colonialism in two main ways: through the alienation of vast stretches of land for farms and plantations for European settlers and companies, primarily in Eastern and Southern African countries and the cultivation of cash, particularly perennial, crops by African peasant farmers. The process of commercialization of agriculture spread rapidly, gaining new momentum after independence, especially in countries in Eastern and Southern Africa where African agriculture and livestock had been held back during the colonial period by a variety of discriminatory policies. This process in turn led to increasing concentration of land ownership which further restricted the scope for shifting cultivation. The rapid growth in population has also been an important factor in undermining the traditional agricultural system.

These developments have resulted in declining soil fertility and yields through shortening or elimination of fallow periods, overgrazing by livestock and movement of the population to less fertile and more fragile areas. While most areas have been affected in varying degrees by this process, its most spectacular manifestation has been in the Sahelian countries and in some livestock-dominated economies like Lesotho and Botswana. The creeping desertification and the growing incidence of droughts have also been attributed to the collapse of the equilibrium between the size of population and livestock on the one hand and the 'carrying capacity' of the natural resources on the other (Van Apeldoorn, 1981 and Konczacki, 1978).

While there are few studies which rigorously establish the link between falling production, declining soil yields and changes in agricultural system, a wide variety of writers have attributed poor agricultural performance to an intensification of this process (Rene Dumont, 1978 and 1980, and Johnston, 1978). The decline between 1969–71 and 1977–79 in the yield of some important crops such as cocoa, coffee, maize, millet, wheat and seed cotton provides some evidence in favour of this thesis, although soil fertility is only one of the determinants of yields. On the other hand, it may be argued that the forces making for the deterioration of the natural resources have been underway for some time and it is not clear why its impact should be felt in such a dramatic manner only in the 1970s. While the choice of any year such as 1970 is obviously arbitrary, it would appear that the deterioration of natural resources and its impact on yields and production is a gradual and cumulative process, subject to offsetting or reinforcing influences. Some of these influences are discussed below but it may be speculated here that the reinforcing influences have tended to predominate in the 1970s.

In many regions the impact of the decline in the quality of land has been reinforced by a deterioration in the quality of the agricultural labour force. The latter is due principally to the continuing large migration flows from rural to urban areas within and across countries. The majority of the migrants are male within the 16 to 44 age-group and increasingly with

TABLE 1 *Growth of agriculture*

| | Average annual growth rate of volume of production 1969–71 to 1977–79 | | | Average annual growth rate of total production per caput 1969–71 to 1977–79 | | |
|---|---|---|---|---|---|---|
| | Food | Non-food | Total | Food | Non-food | Total |
| Low-income countries | | | 0.9 | | | −1.7 |
| Low-income semi-arid | | | 1.1 | | | −1.2 |
| 1 Chad | 1.0 | 2.0 | 1.1 | −1.0 | 0.0 | −0.9 |
| 2 Somalia | 0.6 | −0.8 | 0.6 | −1.7 | −3.1 | −1.7 |
| 3 Mali | 1.0 | 9.8 | 1.4 | −1.6 | 7.2 | −1.2 |
| 4 Upper Volta | 2.0 | 7.2 | 2.1 | 0.4 | 5.6 | 0.5 |
| 5 Gambia | 0.1 | – | 0.1 | −2.9 | – | −2.9 |
| 6 Niger | 1.3 | −7.8 | 1.3 | −1.5 | −10.6 | −1.5 |
| 7 Mauritania | −1.3 | – | −1.3 | −4.0 | – | −4.0 |
| Low-income other | | | 0.8 | | | −1.8 |
| 8 Ethiopia | 0.4 | 1.3 | 0.4 | −1.7 | −0.8 | −1.7 |
| 9 Guinea-Bissau | 1.4 | 0.0 | 1.4 | −0.2 | −1.6 | −0.2 |
| 10 Burundi | 2.7 | 1.8 | 2.6 | 0.7 | −0.2 | 0.6 |
| 11 Malawi | 3.1 | 8.6 | 4.0 | 0.3 | 5.8 | 1.2 |
| 12 Rwanda | 3.9 | 4.7 | 3.9 | 1.1 | 1.9 | 1.1 |
| 13 Benin | 2.5 | −5.2 | 2.3 | −0.4 | −8.1 | −0.6 |
| 14 Mozambique | −0.6 | −4.7 | −1.0 | −3.1 | −7.2 | −3.5 |
| 15 Sierra Leone | 1.4 | 4.9 | 1.7 | −1.1 | 2.4 | −0.8 |
| 16 Tanzania | 1.9 | −0.5 | 1.4 | −1.5 | −3.9 | −2.0 |
| 17 Zaire | 1.3 | −0.6 | 1.2 | −1.4 | −3.3 | −1.5 |
| 18 Guinea | 0.5 | −11.7 | 0.2 | −2.4 | −14.6 | −2.7 |

| | | | | | | | |
|---|---|---|---|---|---|---|---|
| 19 | Central African Republic | 2.4 | 1.5 | 2.2 | 0.2 | −0.7 | 0.0 |
| 20 | Madagascar | 1.8 | 0.7 | 1.7 | −0.7 | −1.8 | −0.8 |
| 21 | Uganda | 1.7 | −8.3 | −0.5 | −1.3 | −11.3 | −3.5 |
| 22 | Lesotho | 2.4 | −7.0 | 1.4 | 0.1 | −9.3 | −0.9 |
| 23 | Togo | −0.2 | −4.2 | −0.4 | −2.6 | −6.6 | −2.8 |
| 24 | Sudan | 3.1 | −3.9 | 1.8 | 0.5 | −6.5 | −0.8 |
| Middle-income oil importers | | | | 2.2 | | | −1.1 |
| 25 | Kenya | 2.9 | 7.5 | 4.0 | −0.5 | 4.1 | 0.6 |
| 26 | Ghana | −0.1 | −4.5 | −0.1 | −3.1 | −7.5 | −3.1 |
| 27 | Senegal | 1.0 | 11.3 | 1.1 | −1.6 | 8.7 | −1.5 |
| 28 | Zimbabwe | 2.6 | 3.8 | 2.9 | −0.7 | 0.5 | −0.4 |
| 29 | Liberia | 3.5 | 0.2 | 2.7 | 0.2 | −3.1 | −0.6 |
| 30 | Zambia | 3.0 | −0.9 | 2.8 | 0.0 | −3.9 | −0.2 |
| 31 | Cameroon | 3.3 | 1.8 | 3.1 | 1.1 | −0.4 | 0.9 |
| 32 | Swaziland | 3.7 | 14.6 | 4.6 | 1.2 | 12.1 | 2.1 |
| 33 | Botswana | 1.1 | 2.0 | 1.1 | −1.1 | −0.2 | −1.1 |
| 34 | Mauritius | 1.9 | 3.9 | 1.9 | 0.6 | 2.6 | 0.6 |
| 35 | Ivory Coast | 4.6 | 1.8 | 3.8 | −0.9 | −3.7 | −1.7 |
| Middle-income oil exporters | | | | 1.1 | | | −1.4 |
| 36 | Angola | 0.2 | −13.3 | −3.3 | −2.1 | −15.6 | −5.6 |
| 37 | Congo | −0.1 | 1.9 | −0.1 | −2.6 | −0.6 | −2.6 |
| 38 | Nigeria | 1.7 | −1.3 | 1.7 | −0.8 | −3.8 | −0.8 |
| 39 | Gabon | 0.1 | −13.3 | 0.1 | −1.1 | −14.5 | −1.1 |
| Sub-Saharan Africa | | | | 1.3 | | | −1.4 |

*Source:* *Accelerated Development in Sub-Saharan Africa – An Agenda for Action* (The World Bank, Washington DC, 1981).

TABLE 2 *Domestic terms of trade of export crops for selected countries*

| | 1971 | 1972 | 1973 | 1974 | 1975 | 1976 | 1977 | 1978 | 1979 |
|---|---|---|---|---|---|---|---|---|---|
| | (1970 = 100 unless otherwise specified) | | | | | | | | |
| Cameroon | | | | | | | | | |
| Barter terms of trade | 98.2 | 90.5 | 85.2 | 81.2 | 74.5 | 73.4 | 77.5 | 88.2 | – |
| income terms of trade | 89.8 | 96.9 | 84.0 | 81.8 | 81.1 | 66.4 | 67.2 | 91.7 | – |
| (cocoa, coffee, cotton) | | | | | | | | | |
| Ghana | | | | | | | | | |
| Barter terms of trade | 91.2 | 82.8 | 88.0 | 89.4 | 86.0 | 58.8 | 34.0 | 35.8 | 46.3 |
| Income terms of trade (cocoa) | 85.9 | 92.4 | 88.4 | 75.2 | 78.0 | 56.1 | 26.0 | 22.6 | 27.7 |
| Ivory Coast | | | | | | | | | |
| Barter terms of trade | 111.2 | 109.3 | 97.8 | 99.7 | 126.5 | 111.8 | 97.3 | 119.3 | 101.6 |
| Income terms of trade | 113.4 | 134.1 | 111.6 | 134.3 | 171.5 | 178.0 | 144.3 | 170.6 | 131.2 |
| (cocoa, coffee, cotton, palmoil) | | | | | | | | | |
| Kenya | | | | | | | | | |
| Barter terms of trade | 98.3 | 93.1 | 79.3 | 83.9 | 123.4 | 93.6 | 55.0 | 49.5 | 58.8 |
| income terms of trade | 129.2 | 157.0 | 177.9 | 198.5 | 170.1 | 280.0 | 449.6 | 263.5 | 218.0 |
| (coffee, tea, pyrethrum, cotton, maize, wheat, sisal) | | | | | | | | | |
| Malawi | | | | | | | | | |
| Barter terms of trade | 105.9 | 129.1 | 123.0 | 100.1 | 94.3 | 115.4 | 119.0 | 116.7 | – |
| Income terms of trade | 108.3 | 122.2 | 139.4 | 104.5 | 104.6 | 98.6 | 120.5 | 124.6 | – |
| (tobacco, groundnuts, cotton, maize) | | | | | | | | | |
| Mali | | | | | | | | | |
| Barter terms of trade | 81.2 | 80.6 | 69.0 | 61.2 | 83.1 | 79.4 | 65.3 | 60.0 | 50.0 |
| Income terms of trade (cotton, groundnuts) | 99.2 | 98.8 | 76.8 | 55.7 | 94.1 | 135.8 | 123.5 | 90.1 | 76.4 |

| | | | | | | | | | |
|---|---|---|---|---|---|---|---|---|---|
| Nigeria | | | | | | | | | |
| Barter terms of trade | – | – | 96.5 | 119.2 | 125.2 | 95.9 | 119.1 | 93.0 | 109.0 |
| Income terms of trade | – | – | 75.0 | 102.5 | 104.6 | 79.4 | 80.0 | 43.6 | 58.1 |
| (cocoa, cotton, palm kernels) | | | | | | | | | |
| Senegal | | | | | | | | | |
| Barter terms of trade | 97.3 | 111.9 | 104.2 | 114.1 | 120.6 | 115.1 | 103.4 | 101.5 | 91.3 |
| Income terms of trade | 77.3 | 146.1 | 81.4 | 84.5 | 141.1 | 204.2 | 148.7 | 72.2 | 104.7 |
| (groundnuts, cotton) | | | | | | | | | |
| Tanzania | | | | | | | | | |
| Barter terms of trade | 96.9 | 95.3 | 88.5 | 76.0 | 63.5 | 90.7 | 110.0 | 79.5 | 67.4 |
| Income terms of trade | 101.8 | 102.8 | 96.3 | 78.8 | 68.8 | 84.5 | 102.5 | 73.7 | 62.7 |
| (coffee, tobacco, cashews, cotton) | | | | | | | | | |
| Togo | | | | | | | | | |
| Barter terms of trade | 98.5 | 92.8 | 88.5 | 80.0 | 79.2 | 76.2 | 68.4 | 80.6 | 90.1 |
| Income terms of trade | 110.5 | 92.8 | 64.1 | 57.2 | 57.0 | 62.0 | 49.4 | 48.8 | 57.8 |
| (cocoa, coffee, cotton) | | | | | | | | | |
| Upper Volta | | | | | | | | | |
| Barter terms of trade | 99.0 | 101.7 | 102.8 | 108.0 | 91.9 | 101.7 | 105.5 | 101.7 | 92.6 |
| Income terms of trade | 106.9 | 130.7 | 110.0 | 140.2 | 181.6 | 214.0 | 156.0 | 229.5 | 245.8 |
| (cotton, sesame) | | | | | | | | | |
| Zambia (1971 = 100) | | | | | | | | | |
| Barter terms of trade | 100.0 | 82.1 | 113.6 | 104.8 | 91.8 | 84.7 | 104.6 | 98.1 | 127.2 |
| Income terms of trade | 100.0 | 142.6 | 97.9 | 126.1 | 125.6 | 169.6 | 133.1 | 92.9 | 90.4 |
| (maize, groundnuts, tobacco) | | | | | | | | | |

*Source:* *Accelerated Development in Sub-Saharan Africa – An Agenda for Action* (The World Bank, Washington DC, 1981).

primary or secondary education (Amin, 1978, Böhning, 1981, and Gaude, 1982). This pattern of migration deprives the rural areas of young educated persons and results in a preponderance in the rural population of children, women and old persons. Since it is traditionally the men who play the main role in land clearance and maintenance of soil fertility, their absence in large numbers can be expected to have adverse effects on agricultural output in addition to the imposition of a greater work burden on women and the old people – in itself a contributory factor to lower productivity (Bukh, 1979). It can also be expected to have a negative impact on absorption of innovations and overall managerial efficiency since extension services are typically directed at men who retain responsibility for overall management of the farm. As with the deterioration of the quality of land, the adverse impact of the prolonged absence of male adults on agricultural production and yields is gradual and cumulative.

*Disincentives to agriculture*

As in many other developing countries, the real returns to farmers from investment of labour, capital and enterprise in agriculture have been reduced by a variety of factors. The effect has been to reinforce the impact of deteriorating natural resources in stimulating the flight from the land. Different techniques have been used in different countries to extract resources from the agricultural sector. Unfortunately there are few studies which have attempted to derive comprehensive estimates of net resource transfers from agriculture, but some partial evidence is available. Table 2 shows the domestic terms of trade for some export crops in selected countries. These terms are naturally affected by the world prices for these crops but they are also influenced by domestic policies in such areas as exchange rate, trade protection, taxation and so on. The table shows a fairly sharp decline in domestic barter terms of trade for selected export crops for most years for countries such as Cameroon, Ghana, Kenya, Mali, Tanzania and Togo. On the other hand, the terms generally held up well for Malawi, Ivory Coast, Senegal, Nigeria and Zambia. Even in some of these countries, however, the export crops were taxed quite heavily. Coffee and cocoa growers, as, for instance, in Ivory Coast, received only 68 and 56 per cent of export proceeds in 1971–75; these declined further to 36 and 38 respectively in 1976–80. Likewise in Malawi, the smallholders received 42 and 28 per cent of export proceeds for tobacco in 1971–75 and 1976–80 respectively. The receipts for cotton were 68 and 75 per cent over the two periods (World Bank, 1981).

These indices of taxation of export crops do not measure the further effective taxation 'levied' by overvalued exchange rates and inefficient marketing systems. There is little doubt that the situation in both these respects has deteriorated quite considerably in most African countries in the 1970s. These two factors also affect the returns from domestically marketed products. Although less information is available on 'effective taxation' of domestically marketed food crops, until recent years many African countries tended to fix producer prices at relatively low levels in order to keep food prices low for urban consumers. However, relative food prices have risen quite sharply in recent years in a number of countries including Ghana and Nigeria.

With the deterioration of the overall economic situation and the intensification of foreign exchange shortages experienced by most African countries since the late 1970s, there is an increasing scarcity of basic consumer goods in the rural areas. In a situation like this, the terms of trade faced by farmers become irrelevant. In a growing number of African countries, the sheer unavailability of consumer goods in rural areas is exercising a strong disincentive effect on agricultural production.

The general economic difficulties have also affected the range and quality of support services for agriculture. In many countries there has been a deterioration in recent years in the quality and output of agricultural research stations and extension services. The supply of inputs like seeds, fertilizers and pesticides by public agencies has become increasingly less reliable. Above all, there is inadequate research effort to find solutions to the problems the African agricultural systems are confronted with and to generate a flow of appropriate innovations to enhance yields and labour productivity (Johnston, 1981). While the term 'collapse' is perhaps too strong a word, there can be little doubt of a serious rundown of agricultural support services and infrastructure in several African countries in recent years.

*Some exogenous factors*

Sub-Sahara Africa has suffered in the late 1960s and 1970s, perhaps more than other developing regions, from political instability, wars, and droughts. Just to mention some major upheavals and wars witnessed during this period,: the civil war in Nigeria; the prolonged struggle for independence in Mozambique and Angola which ultimately resulted in the mass exodus of the settler community and drastic reorganization of their economies; the Ethiopian revolution, civil war and war with Somalia; the prolonged war for independence in Zimbabwe; war between Uganda and Tanzania; civil war in Chad; continuing war in Western Sahara; not to mention the repeated acts of sabotage waged by South Africa on Angola, Mozambique and Zimbabwe and coups in several countries. There can be little doubt of the strong negative effect exerted by these events on overall and agricultural development. Apart from the diversion of scarce resources for purchase of military supplies and maintenance of armies, there is massive disruption of production and dislocation of the population. A partial but tragic indicator of this turbulence is provided by the 5 million officially-estimated refugees in Africa in 1980.

Agricultural production has been further adversely affected by a series of droughts. The best known of these is the prolonged drought in the early 1970s which had such a devastating impact on the Sahelian countries (Van Apeldoorn, Konczacki, and Sen, 1981). In terms of numbers of people affected, the droughts in the late 1970s and early 1980s affecting a number of countries in Eastern and Central Africa have perhaps been even more serious.

*Concluding remarks*

Although presented separately, many of the factors noted above are interrelated and often mutually reinforcing; for instance, the decline in soil fertility by reducing yields and income may further stimulate migration, while the selective nature of migration intensifies land deterioration. The squeezing of agriculture both intensifies migration and reduces resources available to the farmer to restore soil fertility. Even the occurrence of droughts has been linked to a deteriorating environment.

Even if there were agreement that the factors listed above are primarily responsible for agricultural stagnation in Africa, it is not possible to assign weights to these different factors. The relative importance of different factors is likely to vary from one country to another and often over time within the same country. From the point of view of policy, it is obviously important to have more precise ideas on the contribution to agricultural stagnation made by different factors. In principle, it is easier and quicker to adjust policies to remove or lessen the disincentive to agricultural production than, for instance, to find lasting solutions to the problems engendered by a transition from shifting to settled agriculture. Very little has been said here on the impact of the world economy on agricultural development in Africa. While there continues to be disagreement about the role played by the movements in world commodity prices in explaining agricultural stagnation, few would dispute that the immense rise in the price of fuel, the combination of inflation and recession in the industrialized countries resulting in reduced demand and low prices for some important export crops have had strong negative effects on African agricultural development both directly and indirectly through reduced development expenditure attributable to foreign exchange scarcities.

## PATTERNS AND PROCESSES OF DIFFERENTIATION

It is not possible to give precise estimates of the structure of and changes in rural income distribution over the period covered. There are few countries in sub-Sahara Africa which have reliable national household income or expenditure surveys at a given period, let alone comparable time series data. Nevertheless, it seems justified on the basis of the available quantitative and qualitative information to draw three broad conclusions regarding rural income distribution: there are considerable inequalities in rural income distribution, these inequalities have tended to widen over time, and in the 1970s, especially, large sections of the rural population have suffered declines in their incomes.

The quantitative evidence on overall and rural income distribution in a number of African countries has been assembled and analyzed elsewhere (Jain, 1975; Ghai, Lee and Radwan, 1979; and Ghai and Radwan, 1982). The Gini ratios for rural income distribution vary between 0.32 to 0.39 for Tanzania, Lesotho, Sierra Leone, Zambia and Sudan. This would make them comparable to the concentration in rural incomes in most Asian countries. The rural inequalities in Kenya and Botswana with Gini ratios of 0.50 and 0.49 appear high by international standards. While no comparable figures are available for other countries, there is some evidence to indicate that in countries where commercial agriculture has penetrated more deeply such as Ghana, Ivory Coast, Nigeria and Senegal, the indices of inequality would be higher than in the first group of countries mentioned above (Ghai and Radwan, 1982; Dumont et al, 1981).

Some indirect evidence on rural income inequalities is contained in Table 3 which provides estimates of Gini coefficients for land distribution in a number of African countries. Bearing in mind the usual qualifications that apply to data of this nature and the fact that in some countries the coverage is confined to traditional or smallholdings alone, the inequalities in land distribution in African countries appear substantially greater than might be deduced from the popular notions of land abundance, customary land tenure system and family based subsistence cultivation. They lend support to the estimates of income inequalities presented earlier. On the whole the estimates of land concentration appear well below those for Latin America but not too dissimilar to those in Asia. The majority of the African countries have land concentration ratios between 0.37 and 0.48 which makes them comparable to Sri Lanka, South Korea and Thailand. The higher figures for Kenya, Botswana and Ghana are nearer to those found in Philippines, Pakistan, Bangladesh and India (Ghai, Lee, Radwan, 1978).

These inequalities have resulted from policies initiated during the colonial period and from rural development strategies pursued in the post-independence period. The mechanisms and processes generating inequalities and impoverishment during the colonial rule have been studied extensively. It is, therefore, necessary only to recall the main features of these processes. Development during the colonial period followed two broad patterns. In the settler dominated colonies in East, Central and Southern Africa, the basis of differentiation and impoverishment was laid by policies comprising land alienation for white farms and plantations, consequent overcrowding of African peasants and herdsmen in 'reserves', and creation of a wage-earning class through partial or complete dispossession of land. These policies were buttressed by a discriminatory pattern of public expenditure concentrating infrastructural development in areas of white settlement. The result of these policies was the creation of an affluent immigrant community surrounded by a mass of impoverished peasantry and agricultural workers, and sharp regional differentials in levels of development.

The other pattern of development, exemplified by West African colonies, consisted of peasant cultivation of export crops. The ecological factors dictated the choice of wet coastal forest zones for the production of these crops. The social and economic infrastructure was concentrated in these areas, thus laying the basis for sharp regional differentiation. The rapid expansion of cash crops in countries such as Ghana and Nigeria resulted in the creation of a relatively prosperous class of commercial farmers. It also led to a modification of the traditional land tenure system creating a market in land and *de facto* individual ownership of land. The process of commercialization of peasant agriculture through cultivation of export crops spread through to other countries and was continued after independence. Cocoa and palm oil in Ghana; cocoa, palm oil and groundnuts in Nigeria; cocoa and coffee in Ivory Coast and groundnuts in Senegal and Gambia became the main cash crops. Even in the 'settler colonies', the policies were changed before independence to encourage peasant cash crop cultivation through settlement schemes and development projects. These policies were continued after independence and led to a sharp upsurge in smallholder production.

The cultivation of export crops was generally the first step in the differentiation process. Those who were fortunate enough to have land in the 'right' areas and were selected by the authorities as 'progressive' farmers experienced significant increases in incomes. This in turn provided the savings for further investment in land and expansion or diversification of production (Polly Hill, 1970). In many cases, trading or other non-farming activities provided the surplus for land acquisition (Clough, 1981). Earnings from jobs in the urban areas have been in some cases important sources of finance for purchase of land and livestock (Collier and Lal, 1980).

The state policies have greatly accelerated this process. Extension services, supply of credit, seeds, fertilizers, tools and other inputs have generally concentrated on the relatively more developed areas and the better-off farmers. In most countries the political, bureaucratic and business élites have used their positions in the state machinery to acquire farms or participate in subsidized agricultural development schemes.

These are some of the mechanisms which have led to the emergence of a class of relatively prosperous farmers variously called progressive, commercial or emergent. Some of the largest of them are urban-based absentee farmers. At the other end of the scale, a rapidly increasing number of households are confronted with pressures forcing down their meagre living standards. Land scarcity has been a problem in a number of countries or areas – Kenya, Malawi, Rwanda, Burundi, Zimbabwe, Lesotho, Swaziland, Mauritania and Niger, Southeastern Nigeria, Western Highlands of Cameroon, the Mossi plateau of Upper Volta and Senegal's northern Groundnut Basin. Pressure of population combined often with significant inequalities in land distribution is leading to the emergence of landlessness in some areas. More frequent is the existence of excessively small holdings forcing some members of the household to earn income through casual employment. The scarcity of land is also contributing to reduced yields and hence lower incomes through soil deterioration. It has also led to out-migration to the more arid zones as in Kenya where incomes are lower and more uncertain. For households already on the margin of subsistence with small cash incomes, a family misfortune or a drought can lead to irreversible loss of land or livestock. (Van Apeldoorn, 1981 and Sen, 1981). The rapid inflation combined with stagnant cash incomes and inflexible expenditure items have driven many into debt, sale of assets and penury. As already noted, the majority of peasant households, particularly in less advantaged areas, have been largely bypassed by government programmes for agricultural development while not escaping taxation and the impact of inflation.

The processes described above have tended over time to widen rural inequalities in most countries. It is, however, difficult to determine the net impact on income distribution of the pattern of agricultural development in the 1970s. Within the context of a marked slowdown in agricultural growth, export crops have fared worse than food and in some countries, like Ghana and Nigeria, the barter terms of trade have moved strongly in favour of food producers. What is less disputable is that a great majority of the rural population in a large number of African countries must have suffered a decline in their real incomes in the 1970s. This conclusion follows from declines in agricultural production per rural inhabitant in at least 25 countries and from the impact on farmers' incomes of a variety of government policies reviewed in the last section.

In conclusion it should be stated that during the period under review, a number of countries including Guinea, Tanzania, Mozambique, Angola, and Ethiopia have attempted to achieve rural development through different institutional systems with the objective, *inter alia,* of controlling polarisation of incomes and wealth. With the exception of Tanzania, either the experience has been too recent or too little is known about the outcome for a useful assessment to be made in terms of growth and distribution. The Tanzanian experience has been analyzed quite extensively. It would seem that certain features of rural institutional framework in Tanzania have operated to check differentiation but the growth in agricultural output has been disappointing.

This paper has attempted to survey and analyze growth and distribution in African agriculture. Owing to lack of availability of data on trends in rural income distribution in the 1960s and 1970s, it has not been possible to relate changes in income distribution in a systematic way to patterns and rates of agricultural growth. Further analysis must await the availability of better data and should be conducted at the country level.

## NOTES

[1] The work on this paper was done during my stay at the Institute of Social Studies, The Hague. I am grateful to the Institute and its staff for the facilities offered. For comments on an earlier draft I am indebted to Ms Muntemba and Messrs Ghose, Johnston, Majeres, Nook, Radwan, Smith, Szal and Van der Hoeven.

## REFERENCES

Amin, S. (ed.), *Modern Migrations in Western Africa,* Oxford University Press, London, 1974.

Böhning, W. R. (ed.), *Black Migration to South Africa,* ILO, Geneva, 1981.

Bukh, J., *Village Women in Ghana,* Scandinavian Institute of African Studies, Uppsala, 1979.

Clough, Paul, 'Farmers and Traders in Hausaland', *Development and Change,* London, Volume 12, No. 2, April 1981.
Collier, Paul and Lal, Deepak, *Poverty and Growth in Kenya,* World Bank, Staff Working Paper No. 389, Washington, 1980.
Dumont, René, *Paysans Ecrasés, Terres massacrées,* Laffont, Paris, 1978.
Dumont, René and Mottin, M. F., *L'Afrique Etranglée,* editions Du Seuil, Paris, 1980.
Dumont, René *et al, Pauvreté et Inégalités Rurales en Afrique de l'Ouest francophone,* ILO, Geneva, 1981.
FAO, *Production Yearbook,* FAO, Rome, 1980.
Gaude, Jaques (ed.), *Phenomène Migratoire et Politiques Associées dans le Contexte Africain,* ILO, Geneva, 1982.
Ghai, Dharam, Lee, Eddy and Radwan, Samir, *Rural Poverty in the Third World,* ILO, World Employment Programme, Working Paper, Geneva, 1979.
Ghai, Dharam and Radwan Samir (eds.), *Agrarian Policies and Rural Poverty in Africa,* ILO, Geneva, 1982.
Hill, Polly, *Studies in Rural Capitalism in West Africa,* Cambridge University Press, Cambridge, 1970.
Johnston, Bruce, 'Agricultural Production Potentials and Small Farmer Strategies in Sub-Saharan Africa' in *Two Studies of Development in Sub-Saharan Africa,* World Bank Staff Working Paper No. 300, Washington, 1978.
Johnston, Bruce, *Farm Equipment Innovations and Rural Industrialisation in Eastern Africa: An Overview,* ILO World Employment Programme Working Paper, Geneva, 1981.
Konczacki, Z. A., *The Economics of Pastoralism : A Case Study of Sub-Saharan Africa,* Frank Cass, London, 1978.
Sen, Amartya, *Poverty and Famines,* Clarendon Press, Oxford, 1981.
van Apeldoorn, G. Jan, *Perspectives on Drought and Famine in Nigeria,* Allen and Unwin, London, 1981.
World Bank, *Accelerated Development in Sub-Saharan Africa,* World Bank, Washington, 1981.

## DISCUSSION OPENING – RUFUS O. ADEGBOYE

This paper has described some of the problems of inequality in African agriculture but it has made no suggestions for improvement of or solutions to the problems raised.

It is not very impressive to talk of 5 million refugees in Africa. If these people are Africans could they be called refugees in Africa?

It is agreed that in an attempt to promote certain state development measures there is likely to be some damage done to agricultural development. For example, the concentration of industries in large cities and the importation of food stuffs which are produced locally but not well distributed could easily cause the farmer to move to the city or produce only for his family.

Solutions may be found in the need to develop communication partnerships between city people and farmers, banks and farmers, government and farmers. Extension workers, politicians, loan officers, co-operative officers, development planners and so on need to know the farmers' problems very well before attempting to help them. Similarly such international organizations as the ILO, FAO, the World Bank, and others must encourage the carrying out of basic village-level research projects in order to help developing countries to build up a reliable data bank.

## GENERAL DISCUSSION – RAPPORTEUR: E. A. SAXON

Considerable discussion centred around the role of multinational and national agribusiness in the context of growth and equity. Some speakers claimed that some of these tend to monopolize the supply of farm inputs and charge farmers prices much above world levels, while others may monopolize agricultural processing, extracting unreasonable profits. These activities raise problems of equity in developing countries that should be more fully explored in the context of the theme of this Conference.

A related issue is the plantation sector in which multinationals may also be involved, in some cases exerting undue influence on national governments. This may mean that investment policies are determined externally rather than by the country itself.

In reply, the speakers (Ranis and Ghai) said that this was an emotional subject and that there were both positive and negative aspects in the role of large corporations, for instance in East Asia they have contributed positively to growth and equity. In some countries large plantations have been nationalized and split up into small farms. Malawi is one of the few countries which invites investment in the plantation sector, leading to increases in employment and investment. While it is true that most of the profits have gone to better-off groups, expansion of the sector has yielded benefits overall.

A further query related to the conditions under which export promotion and import substitution become both feasible and effective. Professor Ranis said that most former colonial countries passed through an export orientation stage on the way to economic growth, but each case was different. Some East Asian countries concentrated on food, others on cash crops, with differing implications for development. Each country faced a difficult political decision as to when to shift from traditional to non-traditional exports. There is, for example, a large potential for South-South trade in manufactured goods, especially if some modifications are made in the goods produced.

One speaker commented that in all countries there were important differences in behaviour between small and large farms. Small farms are intent on maximizing food production and income in the short term and hence may fail to conserve resources, while large farms are better able to conserve resources. The source of growth can thus be undermined by the small farmer who cannot take the long-term view.

A specific query on Dr Ghai's paper was whether the Gini coefficients relating to income included non-agricultural income and how the Gini coefficients for land were estimated, seeing that there is a lot of fallowing in African agriculture. In reply Dr Ghai said that income data was from ILO and World Bank sources, and generally referred to income from agriculture alone. Land data related to holdings by the family at any one time, and did not include communal land. It was not clear what definition was used as regards cultivated and fallow land.

Participants in the discussion included Martin Upton, Sung-hoo Kim,

Frank Baffoe, M. G. Chandrakanth, H. Dequin, B.N. Verma and H.M.G. Herath.

C. L. J. VAN DER MEER

# *Growth and Equity – Experience in Developed Countries with a Market Economic System*

## INTRODUCTION

This paper focuses on the long term experience of growth and equity in the agricultural development of eight countries: three big ones: France, Germany and the United Kingdom; three small ones: Denmark, The Netherlands and Sweden; and two countries of recent European settlement: Australia and the United States. We have used data series on the total and agricultural labour force, and total Gross Domestic Product (GDP) and GDP from agriculture, both in current and constant prices. For most countries sufficient data are available from the mid-nineteenth century onwards: the United States 1840, France, Germany and the United Kingdom 1850, Australia 1860, Denmark and Sweden 1870, and The Netherlands 1920. The series allow us to compare long-term trends in relative income and production per worker in agriculture and other sectors and to estimate the terms of trade of agriculture versus the rest of the economy. Within the limited scope of this paper we cannot deal with the extensive information on equity from historical and farm income studies and we restrict ourselves to long-term development.

In the next section a broad sketch is given of agricultural development in the past two centuries. The third section contains an analysis of the data series. Successively the following subjects are treated: theoretical possibilities of patterns of growth and equity in agricultural development; the relation between production and demand; the expectations of the classical economists; the geographical spread of agricultural growth; the decline of the agricultural workforce; growth of GDP per worker; income per worker; and changes in the terms of trade. The final section contains concluding remarks about growth, equity and social change.

## POPULATION, ECONOMIC GROWTH AND AGRICULTURAL DEVELOPMENT

Most European countries experienced continuous population growth in the eighteenth and nineteenth centuries (Appendix A). The first half of the eighteenth century had been a period of agricultural depression with low real prices. )Abel, 1980; Slicher van Bath, 1963; Boserup, 1981; Grigg, 1980). After 1750, however, real agricultural prices increased steadily as a result of growing demand. Around the year 1800 and again during the years 1810–12 real prices rocketed, especially in the United Kingdom, which had become dependent on grain imports (Abel, Slicher van Bath). As in previous epochs of population growth agricultural production expanded in two ways. First, agricultural land was cropped more intensively. Less land was left in fallow, rough grazing was replaced by forage crops, natural fertilizers were used extensively, the share of root crops (turnips and potatoes) increased and multi-course systems, which had been in use in the Low Countries since the fourteenth century (Slicher van Bath, 1963) and still earlier in Northern Italy (Zangheri, 1969), spread around Western Europe. Second, more land was brought under cultivation and land reclamation was speeded up. Farmers' and peasants' incomes, and, stronger even, rents, rose considerably. Around 1800 in Southern England real wages had declined to about half the level of the first three-quarters of the fifteenth century (Brown and Hopkins, 1956) and on the continent the situation of wage earners was also bad (Slicher van Bath, 1963). In 1789 against the background of five decades of rapid population growth and increasing real food prices Malthus wrote his pessimistic population theory, which would have so much influence on economic thought.

However, soon this theory was refuted. The high price levels seem to have induced new technologies which were more productive and after the Napoleonic wars real grain prices declined rapidly, which Von Thünen and others attributed to over-production (Abel, pp. 239–40). The crisis lasted till around 1830. Population continued to grow, agricultural over-production disappeared, and grain prices started again an upward swing till the 1870s. Despite the low food prices of the 1820s real wages did not rise. Only after about 1830 did real wages start a slow but long upward movement, despite rising food prices, as intensification of agriculture and industrialization led to scarcity of labour (Collins, 1974). Boserup and several other economic historians have shown that in the past population growth was in general rather autonomous, that is not restricted by the production capacity as Malthus thought, but that the production capacity increased and declined in response to changes in population.

In the 1850s grain prices in the United States were still on the same level as in Europe and exports were limited. After the Civil War the great expansion to the plains started. Canals, railways and more efficient transatlantic traffic reduced freight rates drastically (Cochrane, North). Similar developments occurred in Russia. By the end of the 1870s European markets were glutted with cheap American grain and, to a lesser extent, Russian grain. The agricultural depression of the 1880s and 1890s came to an end because the frontier in the United States closed around the year 1900 (Cochrane). Increasing real prices stimulated Australia, Argentina, New Zealand and Canada to expand their infrastructure and to step up production of grain and animal production for export. World War I prolonged high prices, but afterwards prices fell, first in the 1920s and more severely in the 1930s, because of expansion of agricultural production and decreased demand caused by declining incomes in several countries. World War II and its aftermath pushed prices up, but after 1954 world market prices fell back to low levels.

At the end of the eighteenth century many countries had liberated trade in agricultural products. In the depression of the early nineteenth century Great Britain (to a lesser extent France and The Netherlands as well) protected its grain producers to a considerable degree. With the repeal of the Corn Laws trade in agricultural products was liberated again. However, during the agricultural depression at the end of the century several European countries introduced protection for their producers. The liberation of trade after the depression did not last long. During World War I all advanced countries interfered in agricultural markets and during the crisis of the 1930s they all introduced income support to their farmers. During World War II security of food supplies was the dominant policy aim but after the War policies reverted to price stabilization and support to protect farmers against a disastrous fall in income. In Western Europe, especially the EEC countries, relatively high prices induced a strong increase in land productivity and in the 1970s the EEC turned from a net importer into an exporter for most agricultural products.

The 1970s brought structural changes in the world economy. Oil crises, devaluation of the US dollar, failure to produce enough food in several developing and centrally planned countries, heavy price fluctuations in international markets, growth of GDP in the developed countries, and the slowing down of growth of productivity in US agriculture have changed the outlook. In other countries whose currency depreciated with the US dollar the terms of trade of agriculture tended to improve also (if governments permitted it). Most measures developed in the United States since the 1930s to curtail production and to support farmers were abolished in the 1970s (Hathaway). In ten years the volume of US grain exports more than doubled, the downward trend of price levels in international markets disappeared, and farm incomes in the United States are better than ever before.

## AGRICULTURAL GROWTH AND EQUITY

*Possible patterns of growth and equity*

What was the pattern of agricultural growth and how can it be explained? In combination non-agricultural growth, population growth and low income elasticity of demand for agricultural products could have three possible major effects. First, if supply of agricultural products were limited by soil fertility, as the classical economists expected, the terms of trade of agriculture would improve, and ultimately check economic growth. Second, because of low income elasticity of demand for agricultural products, productivity per man in agriculture could only follow the trend outside agriculture if the agricultural work force declined relatively and, later, even in total numbers. Third, income in agriculture could only follow the general trend if (for the sake of simplicity presuming constant income shares for land, labour and capital) the index of labour productivity times the net product price increased proportionate to wage levels outside agriculture.

*Production and demand*

The nature of growth in agriculture differs from growth in industry and services. During the past centuries the latter two have introduced large numbers of new products and many existing products have been improved. In agriculture only few new products were introduced and the quality of most agricultural products is still the same, or only modestly improved. Demand for agricultural products *per caput* increased less than real income *per caput,* because elasticity of demand falls to low levels when real income rises. The increase reflects improved diets with higher proportions of meat, fruits and vegetables. As a result total agricultural output in the Western world has increased only 50 per cent *per caput* since 1934–38 (estimated from data in FAO: State of Food and Agriculture, 1955–1981), which is much less than the increase in non-agricultural output *per caput.*

Since output growth has been accompanied by a growing share of non-agricultural inputs, real agricultural value added (GDP) *per caput* has increased less than output *per caput.* We observe great differences in GDP from agriculture *per caput* between countries over the past century (Appendices and Graphs). Over the whole period in the United States it has declined, particularly after the end of the nineteenth century; it ended in the United Kingdom at the same level as it was in 1850 and probably also in Germany (which is uncertain because of major changes in boundaries), but it almost doubled in other countries. The steady decline in the UK until 1940 and the steady increase afterwards is remarkable. In France, Germany and The Netherlands is increased rapidly after stagnation in the interwar period. In Australia, a low cost exporter with elastic supply, agricultural output fluctuates with international demand. In Denmark growth of agricultural GDP *per caput* stagnated after World War II, in Sweden it declined.

*The classical economists refuted*

The figures in this paper show that the classical economists were, in retrospect, wrong with respect to possibilities to expand agricultural productivity. Fertility of land turned out to be not just a constant factor, but to a large extent man-made, and, instead of food crises and real increases of rents and agricultural prices, the Western world experienced oversupply crises and 'declining importance of agricultural land' (Schultz).

*Agricultural growth in Europe and overseas*

Productivity can increase by a (relative) decline of input and by a (relative) increase of output. A considerable part of labour and other inputs on farms are fixed inputs and can often be considered as 'trapped' resources (Johnson) of which the allocation is governed by low 'salvage' prices, not by high 'acquisition' prices. This implies that for individual farms increase in productivity depends on increase in output rather than on decrease in inputs. This may be strengthened by economies of farm size (Tweeten). In the long run on the aggregate level, however, the decline of the labour force is the dominant variable. Given the low man/land ratio and low land productivity in countries of recent European settlement one would expect total production and certainly production per caput in these countries to increase faster there than in Europe, which it has not. Increase in productivity has taken place in different patterns during the nineteenth century. In countries of recent European settlement where labour was scarce and land abundant during the nineteenth century, and in some cases till far in the twentieth century, labour saving innovations, such as mechanization were induced, whereas in Japan and Europe with scarcity of land, and for most periods higher product prices, land saving innovations were pursued (Abel, p. 276; Hayami and Ruttan). In both patterns of technical progress the effect was a rapid expansion of production. In the twentieth century land saving innovations also became gradually widespread in countries of recent European settlement, but increases in land productivity have been relatively small.

*The decline of the agricultural workforce*

At the start of the epoch of modern economic growth the European countries had a vast agricultural workforce which constituted 60–65 per cent of the total workforce (except Great Britain and the Low Countries) (Appendices B and C). The countries of recent European settlement were still largely underpopulated with some concentration of settlers along coasts and rivers. As Dovring observed the agricultural populations remained fairly stable till 1950. There are several explanations for this. The introduction of new techniques in the nineteenth century was in general still low and population growth, especially in the new countries, was high. The non-agricultural sectors were relatively small and not yet able to absorb large rural masses. In the twentieth century the decline of the agricultural labour force was retarded by high product prices during the two world wars and unemployment and slow economic growth in the interwar period. In the 1930s there was even a tendency for unemployed town people to go back to the countryside (Bellerby). After World War II when in most countries the share of the agricultural labour force was near to 20 per cent a rapid decline of 25–70 per cent took place, slowest with 1 per cent per year in Australia and most rapid in Germany with 4 per cent per year.

*Growth of GDP per worker*

Acceleration of economic growth per worker (increase in labour productivity) started in most countries between the end of the eighteenth and the middle of the nineteenth century. Over the period 1870–1979 GDP per worker in agriculture multiplied by about ten times (Appendix G). For Sweden it was even 14 (see note on Germany in Appendices). Including the early decades of the period of modern economic growth the total multiplication factor can be estimated at about 12–15. It is remarkable that the differences between countries are small. In all countries the growth of GDP per worker in the non-agricultural sectors industry plus services (equals total minus agriculture) was slower than in agriculture but the growth pattern differed considerably between countries (Appendix F). Countries that had a high level of total GDP per worker in 1870 (not shown in the Appendix), the United States, Australia and the United Kingdom, experienced slower non-agricultural growth than Denmark, France and Germany.

For the period 1870–1913 and for countries for which data for previous decades are available, growth of labour productivity in agriculture was slower than outside this sector, except in Australia and Sweden; whereas in the period 1913–50 growth of GDP per worker in non-agricultural sectors lagged behind (the exception of Germany may be caused by changes in boundaries, see note in Appendices). In the period 1950–79 labour productivity in agriculture rose about twice as fast as in other sectors in all countries, except in Australia and Denmark where it rose only slightly faster.

Except in Sweden and the United States the slowdown of economic growth since 1973 in the developed countries is not accompanied by a declining growth of labour productivity in agriculture. In Sweden the main cause is declining agricultural production, in the United States agricultural production stagnates and the decline of the agricultural labour force has slowed down as well.

Over the whole period for which data are available on agricultural and non-agricultural growth per worker, all countries except France show a better performance of agriculture. The ratio of the indices of agricultural and non-agricultural labour productivity was 4.1 in Australia over the period 1860–1979, 3.1 in Sweden over the period since 1870 and 2.8 in the United Kingdom since 1860. The ratio for The Netherlands since 1913 is 2.5. For the United States where data are available on the period since 1840 the ratio is 1.5 in favour of agriculture, for Germany it is 1.2 since 1850 (see footnote Appendices) and for Denmark 1.1 since 1860. For France the ratio is only 0.85 since 1850, which result is stronger than in other countries affected by relatively slow growth of labour productivity in agriculture before 1870.

*Income per worker*

Average income in agriculture, measured as GDP in current prices per worker, has most of the time lagged behind that in other sectors (see Appendix H, Graphs). Exceptions are Australia where agricultural income was relatively high for most of the time, the United Kingdom where it has been relatively high since World War II and the United States after 1970. Relative income in agriculture has been particularly low in Sweden, France, The Netherlands and the United States. Since 1870 relative income in agriculture has increased strongly in the United States where it rose from 45 to 106 per cent of non-agricultural income and in Sweden from 25 to 52 per cent. Modest but still significant was the relative improvement of agricultural income in Australia (from 69 to 104 per cent), the United Kingdom (63 to 92 per cent) and The Netherlands after 1900 (33 to 53 per cent). In France it remained at about 50 per cent of non-agricultural income whereas in Denmark and (most likely) Germany it lagged behind. There are some similarities between countries. With the exception of Australia relative income in agriculture decreased from 1870–1900 (no data for The Netherlands), it increased in all countries till 1913 (in fact till around 1920). The interwar period was marked by depressed agricultural incomes, which is only partly revealed by the data in Appendix H. There were marked differences between various countries and years because of different government policies and differences in general economic conditions. During the period 1940–54 relative income in agriculture was high in all countries as a result of lagging supply, but afterwards it declined in the United Kingdom, The Netherlands, Australia, Denmark and Germany. In France it changed little, in Sweden it increased modestly and in the United States it rose from below 60 per cent in 1965 to around 100 per cent at the end of the 1970s.

*Terms of trade*

The terms of trade have been derived by dividing the (implicit) GDP deflators for agriculture and non-agriculture. With the exception of Australia and the United Kingdom the terms of trade for agriculture increased over the period till 1913. The general upward trend was interrupted at the end of the century. In fact the terms of trade reached a peak at the end of World War I and deteriorated rapidly afterwards. The depressed price levels of the 1930s were followed by the postwar and Korea boom, during which the terms of trade reached again a peak, in several countries a higher one than in 1913. After the Korea boom the terms of trade for agriculture decreased rapidly. In The Netherland, Germany and the United Kingdom the decline was about 60 per cent since 1950, in France, Denmark and Australia it was about 45 per cent and in Sweden one-third. In the United States the decline in the terms of trade was limited to only about 10 per cent.

## CONCLUDING REMARKS

We can now attribute the relative change in income in agriculture to the relative increase of production per worker in agriculture and non-agriculture and changes in the terms of trade. In most countries in the period 1870–1913 productivity in agriculture lagged behind but this was partly offset by improving terms of trade. In Australia the opposite occurred. In the period after World War I relative incomes in agriculture deteriorated because of worsening terms of trade and despite a growth of labour productivity in agriculture, which exceeded that in the rest of the economy. When the terms of trade turned in favour of agriculture after World War II the result was a strong relative increase in income. After 1950 labour productivity in agriculture rose in most countries almost twice as fast as in other sectors but its effect on relative income was in most cases more than offset by the halving of the terms of trade.

Of great importance for understanding who benefits from economic growth is W.A. Lewis's 'unlimited supplies of labour' model. It is clear that production per worker in agriculture can hardly grow without outside demand. As long as there is a large and elastic supply of labour in the countryside, whether it be as a result of continuous population growth, unequal distribution of land, or another reason, labour productivity and employment for the mass of the rural population will be low and remain low until a sufficient amount of labour is siphoned off to more productive employment elsewhere. For this reason one should expect that agricultural income in the early phases of development would lag behind.

Relative income in agriculture in the western world in the past depended on the relative strength of supply factors in agriculture (factors employed in agriculture, technical progress, imports and prices) and the demand factors for agricultural product (population growth, export demand and, to a lesser extent, the level of income). In the periods 1818–30, 1880–1900, 1920–40 and 1954–73 supply moved faster than demand. Most crises lasted long, not only because supply of factors of production in agriculture is inelastic and urban demand for rural labour grew slowly, but primarily because technical progress was the most important factor and was not very dependent on prices. Periods with lagging supply 1850–70, 1900–20, 1940–53, and the 1970s particularly in the United States, seem to have been caused by slowing down of technological progress, disruption of trade and rapid growth of demand.

Since the start of the epoch of modern economic growth, average product per worker in agriculture increased 10–15 fold which is a little better than growth of GDP per worker. Who benefited from growth in agriculture? The main beneficiaries were those farmers who formed the vanguard for new innovations and all consumers because they benefited from larger and cheaper supplies, but for the large majority of the farmers and rural labourers rapid growth has been a nightmare. Slowly but steadily they or their children moved to non-agricultural jobs. As Kuznets has pointed out rapid growth requires rapid structural change because of changing consumer demand and unequal growth between sectors. On the one hand there are the benefits for the consumers and the successful innovating producers and on the other hand there is the pain of structural change.

The development of agriculture implied a thorough change in society. However, family farms still are the dominant mode of production. Contrary to the expectation of Marx and many others, large capitalist farms employing large numbers of rural labourers did not develop. The expectation was based on the mistaken belief that economies of size and scale in agriculture, similar to industry, would make large capitalist enterprises economically superior (Mitrani, Ghayanov, Dovring). Increasing economies of size do exist but in most cases large family farms are big enough to realize resulting productivity gains and self-employed family labour appears more productive than a rural prolerariat.

*Acknowledgement* I am indebted to Professor R. van Hees, Mr T.J. Kastelein, Professor A. Maddison and Mr D. Strijker for their helpful comments, and to Mr B. van Ark, Mrs G. Jolink, Mrs M. Bernadina-Lukkien, Mrs A. Stanneveld and Mr P. van Veen for their assistance. Errors, however, are my sole responsibility.

## APPENDICES

| | France | West Germany | UK | Denmark | Nether-lands | Sweden | Australia | USA |
|---|---|---|---|---|---|---|---|---|
| A. Population in millions | | | | | | | | |
| 1760 | 25.2 | 18.3 | 11.1 | 0.8 | 2.0 | 1.9 | 0 | 1.6 |
| 1830 | 32.7 | 28.0 | 23.8 | 1.2 | 2.6 | 2.9 | 0.1 | 12.9 |
| 1870 | 38.4 | 39.2 | 31.3 | 1.8 | 3.6 | 4.2 | 1.6 | 39.9 |
| 1913 | 39.8 | 67.0 | 45.6 | 2.8 | 6.2 | 5.6 | 4.8 | 97.2 |
| 1950 | 41.8 | 50.0 | 50.4 | 4.3 | 10.1 | 7.0 | 8.2 | 152.3 |
| 1979 | 53.5 | 61.4 | 56.0 | 5.1 | 14.0 | 8.3 | 14.4 | 220.6 |
| B. Agricultural workforce in millions | | | | | | | | |
| 1850 | 7.20 | 8.30 | 2.02 | 0.65 | 0.55 | – | – | 4.55 |
| 1870 | 7.56 | 8.54 | 3.12 | 0.49 | (0.48) | 1.05 | 0.19 | 6.82 |
| 1910 | 8.69 | 10.54 | 2.40 | 0.54 | 0.64 | 0.98 | 0.44 | 11.84 |
| 1929 | 7.94 | 9.41 | 1.50 | 0.64 | 0.66 | 0.91 | 0.55 | 10.45 |
| 1938 | 7.28 | 9.01 | 1.27 | 0.59 | – | 0.86 | 0.61 | 9.69 |
| 1950 | 5.44 | 4.97 | 1.19 | 0.49 | 0.58 | 0.63 | 0.52 | 7.64 |
| 1979 | 1.87 | 1.54 | 0.63 | 0.21 | 0.28 | 0.24 | 0.40 | 3.30 |
| C. Agricultural workforce in per cent of total workforce | | | | | | | | |
| 1850 | 52 | 56 | 22 | 49 | 44 | – | – | 61 |
| 1870 | 50 | 49 | 22 | 52 | 35 | 54 | 31 | 53 |
| 1910 | 50 | 36 | 12 | 40 | 28 | 37 | 24 | 32 |
| 1950 | 28 | 24 | 5 | 23 | 15 | 18 | 16 | 13 |
| 1979 | 9 | 6 | 3 | 8 | 6 | 6 | 7 | 3 |
| D. GDP per caput (1913 = 100) | | | | | | | | |
| 1850 | 38 | 39 | 45 | – | 64 | – | – | 33 |
| 1870 | 51 | 50 | 68 | 44 | 76 | 38 | 74 | 50 |
| 1950 | 167 | 111 | 137 | 150 | 138 | 253 | 126 | 190 |
| 1979 | 495 | 355 | 257 | 345 | 336 | 536 | 246 | 364 |

| | France | West Germany | UK | Denmark | Nether-lands | Sweden | Australia | USA |
|---|---|---|---|---|---|---|---|---|
| **E. GDP from agriculture per caput (constant prices, 1913 = 100)** | | | | | | | | |
| 1850 | 73 | 77 | – | – | – | – | – | 95 |
| 1870 | 79 | 87 | 156 | 89 | – | 66 | 81 | 97 |
| 1950 | 89 | 54 | 98 | 135 | 96 | 122 | 137 | 86 |
| 1979 | 141 | 76 | 170 | 135 | 160 | 107 | 147 | 83 |
| **F. Non-agricultural GDP per non-agricultural worker (constant prices, 1913 = 100)** | | | | | | | | |
| 1850 | 33 | 42 | – | – | – | – | – | 40 |
| 1870 | 51 | 52 | 70 | 32 | – | 62 | 90 | 63 |
| 1929 | 159 | 108 | 97 | 107 | 138 | 115 | 95 | 120 |
| 1938 | 155 | 127 | 100 | 114 | – | 119 | 100 | 96 |
| 1950 | 144 | 125 | 124 | 122 | 135 | 172 | 104 | 156 |
| 1979 | 426 | 347 | 241 | 288 | 336 | 276 | 226 | 255 |
| **G. GDP from agriculture per agricultural worker (constant prices, 1913 = 100)** | | | | | | | | |
| 1850 | 89 | 50 | – | – | – | – | – | 58 |
| 1870 | 99 | 63 | 79 | 63 | – | 45 | 57 | 67 |
| 1929 | 118 | 85 | 135 | 132 | 130 | 94 | 106 | 129 |
| 1938 | 129 | 108 | 160 | 156 | – | 113 | 127 | 146 |
| 1950 | 168 | 86 | 215 | 228 | 173 | 237 | 212 | 201 |
| 1979 | 989 | 482 | 782 | 639 | 838 | 635 | 537 | 654 |
| **H. Ratio GDP per worker agriculture/non-agriculture (current prices)** | | | | | | | | |
| 1850 | 41 | 43 | – | – | – | – | – | 38 |
| 1870 | 46 | 65 | 63 | 88 | – | 25 | 69 | 45 |
| 1900 | 33 | 51 | 52 | 53 | 33 | 35 | 78 | 37 |
| 1913 | 37 | 57 | 52 | 62 | 37 | 43 | 89 | 45 |
| 1922 | 24 | 44 | 61 | 49 | 23 | 39 | 96 | 58 |
| 1933 | – | 44 | 69 | 47 | – | 31 | 106 | 62 |
| 1950 | 47 | 43 | 121 | 84 | 70 | 46 | 161 | 58 |
| 1970 | 40 | 37 | 86 | 60 | 68 | 44 | 91 | 72 |
| 1979 | 50 | 36 | 92 | 66 | 53 | 52 | 104 | 106 |
| **I. Terms of trade agriculture/non-agriculture (1913 = 100)** | | | | | | | | |
| 1850 | 41 | 55 | – | – | – | – | – | 57 |
| 1870 | 65 | 86 | 107 | 71 | – | 76 | 116 | 92 |
| 1900 | 81 | 75 | 100 | 76 | – | 81 | 103 | 66 |
| 1922 | 74 | 09 | 100 | 89 | 100 | 82 | 92 | 72 |
| 1933 | 119 | 77 | 81 | 49 | 63 | – | 75 | 49 |
| 1950 | 104 | 109 | 141 | 74 | 125 | 100 | 89 | 97 |
| 1970 | 64 | 59 | 72 | 43 | 80 | 67 | 67 | 63 |
| 1979 | 56 | 45 | 60 | 40 | 49 | 66 | 53 | 89 |

*Notes:* Preliminary statistical estimates, definitions between countries and over time differ. Where possible discontinuities over time were eliminated by linking series. In some cases additional estimates were obtained by interpolation. Underlining indicates discontinuity in the series because of changes in boundaries. For West Germany direct comparison of data before and after 1950 is not possible. As agriculture in the central and eastern part of the country was more important and probably more productive than that of the part which became the Federal Republic – to which data from 1950 onwards do refer – postwar GDP figures may be too low for agriculture and too high for other sectors. The limited space in this paper does not permit a detailed reference of sources, for detailed references the reader may refer to Kuznets (1971) and Maddison (1982). Completed series with notes, sources and definitions will be published elsewhere.

*Sources:* A. Population: data from A. Maddison (1982); B. Workforce: *Australia,* 1860–1900: N.G. Butlin (1964), 1900–63: M.W. Butlin (1977), and Dowie (1970); *Denmark,* 1870–1952: Bjerke (1955): *France,* 1830–1950: Clark (1957), Toutain (1963); *Germany,* 1850–1959: Hoffmann (1965); *The Netherlands,* 1850–99 Bos: (1959), 1899-1964: CBS (1979); *Sweden,* 1870–1950: Johansson (1967); *UK,* 1830–50: Mitchell (1962), 1855–1965: Feinstein (1972); US, 1830–1930: Lebergott (1966) and Clark (1957); data on recent years were obtained from ILO, OECD and national sources; C. Gross domestic product (Total and agriculture): *Australia,* 1860–1900: N.G. Butlin (1962), 1900–65: M.W. Butlin (1977); Denmark, 1870–1950: Bjerke (1955); *France,* 1825–1938: Markovitch (1966); *Germany,* 1850–1959: Hoffmann (1965); *The Netherlands,* 1850–99: Bos (1959), Theil (1971), CBS (1979); *Sweden,* 1861–1955: Johansson (1967); *UK,* 1950–1965: Mitchell (1975). Feinstein (1972); *US,* 1839–99: Gallman (1960) and Kuznets (1952), 1899–1929: Kendrick (1961), and Hist. Stat. of the US 1789–1945, after 1929: *US Dept. of Com.* (1981) and Hist. Stat. of the US Col. Times to 1957; data on recent years were obtained from UN, OECD and national sources.

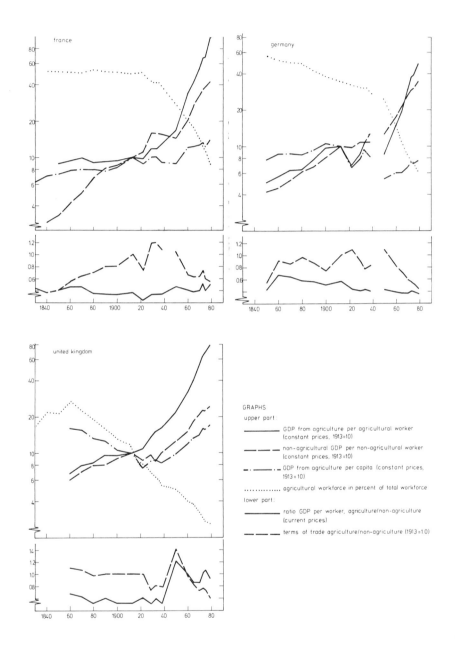

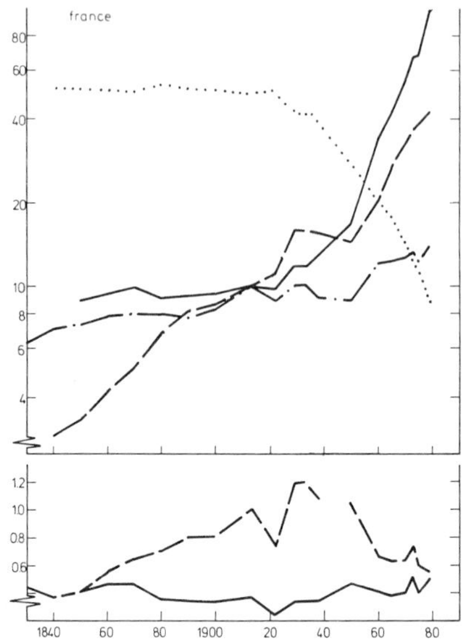


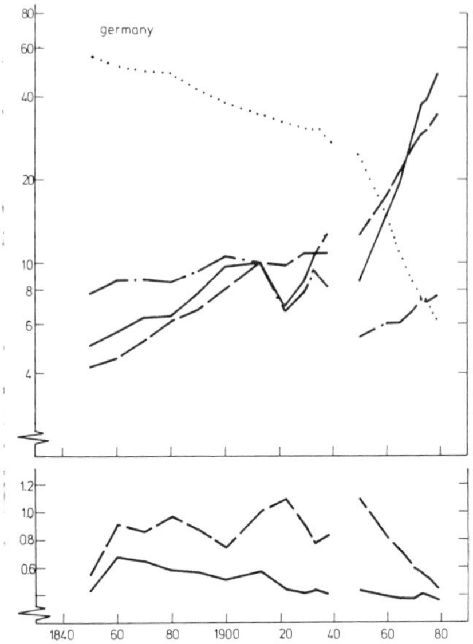


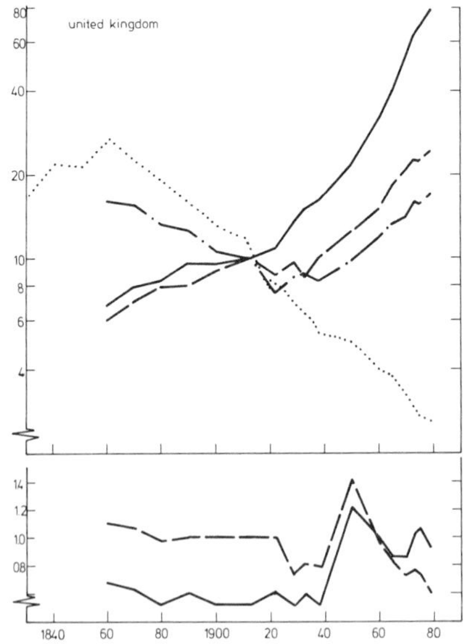


GRAPHS

upper part:

- GDP from agriculture per agricultural worker (constant prices, 1913=10)
- non-agricultural GDP per non-agricultural worker (constant prices, 1913=10)
- GDP from agriculture per capita (constant prices, 1913=10)
- agricultural workforce in percent of total workforce

lower part:

- ratio GDP per worker, agriculture/non-agriculture (current prices)
- terms of trade agriculture/non-agriculture (1913=1.0)

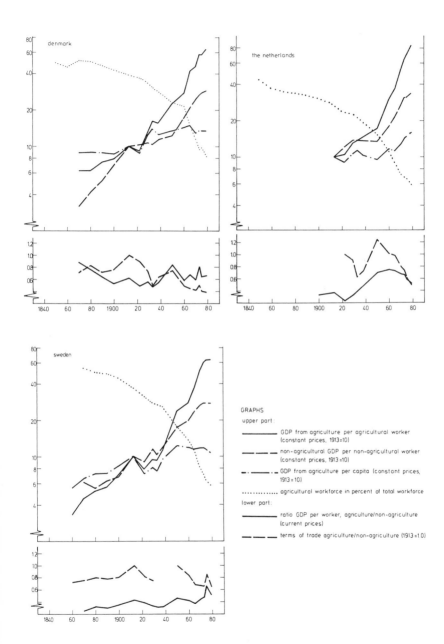

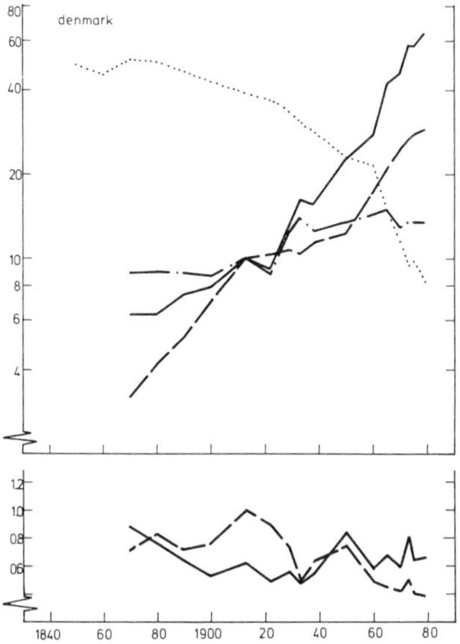


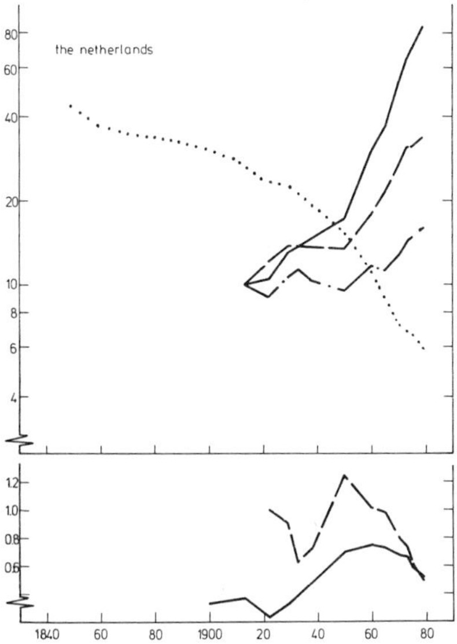


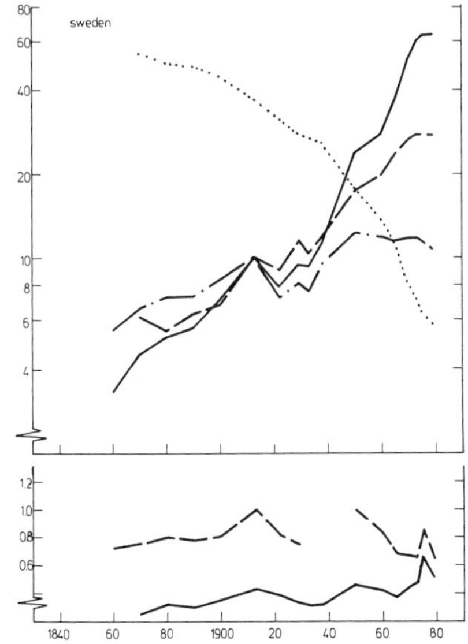


GRAPHS

upper part:

GDP from agriculture per agricultural worker (constant prices, 1913=10)

non-agricultural GDP per non-agricultural worker (constant prices, 1913=10)

GDP from agriculture per capita (constant prices, 1913=10)

agricultural workforce in percent of total workforce

lower part:

ratio GDP per worker, agriculture/non-agriculture (current prices)

terms of trade agriculture/non-agriculture (1913=1.0)

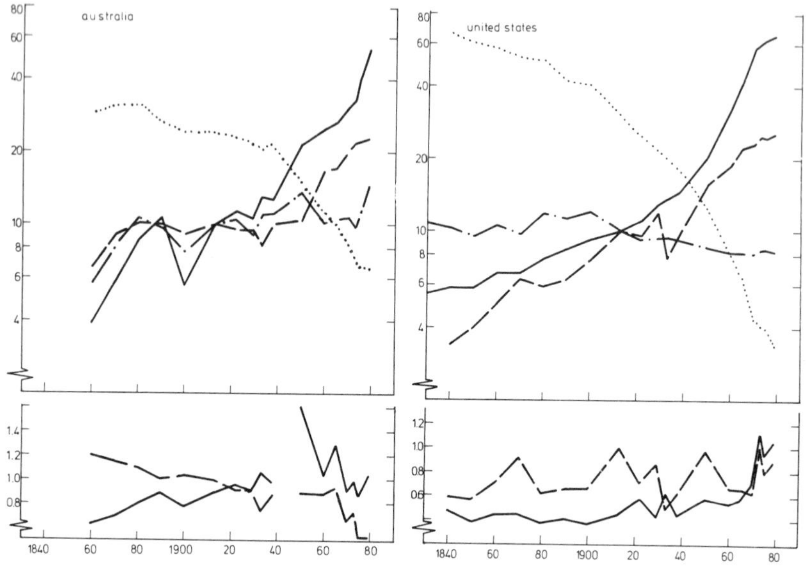


GRAPHS

upper part:

———— GDP from agriculture per agricultural worker (constant prices, 1913=10)

— — — non-agricultural GDP per non-agricultural worker (constant prices, 1913=10)

-·—·- GDP from agriculture per capita (constant prices, 1913=10)

............ agricultural workforce in percent of total workforce

lower part:

———— ratio GDP per worker, agriculture/non-agriculture (current prices)

— — — terms of trade agriculture/non-agriculture (1913=1.0)

## REFERENCES

Abel, W., *Agricultural Fluctuations in Europe From the Thirteenth to the Twentieth Centuries,* Methuen, London, 1980.

Bellerby, J.R., *Agriculture and Industry Relative Income,* Macmillan, London, 1956.

Boserup, E., *Population and Technology,* Blackwell, London, 1981.

Brown, E.H.P.H. and Hopkins, S.H.V., 'Seven centuries of prices and consumables, compared with builders' wage rates', *Economica,* 23 (1956).

Chayanov, A.V., *The Theory of the Peasant Economy,* ed. and introduced by Daniel Thorner, Basile Kerblay and R.F. Smith, Irwin, Illinois, 1966.

Clark, C., *The Conditions of Economic Progress,* 3rd edition, Macmillan, London, 1957.

Cochrane, W.W., *The Development of American Agriculture,* University of Minnesota Press, Minneapolis, 1979.

Collins, E.J.T., 'Labour supply and demand in European agriculture, 1800–1880', in Jones and Woolf (1974).

Dovring, F., *Land and Labor in Europe in the Twentieth Century,* Martinus Nijhoff, The Hague, 1965.

'The Share of Agriculture in a Growing Population', *FAO Monthly Bulletin of* AES, Vol III (1959), No. 8/9.

Grigg, D.B., *Population Growth and Agrarian Change,* Cambridge University Press, 1980.

Hayami, Y., and Ruttan, V.W., *Agricultural Development : An International Perspective,* Johns Hopkins Press, Baltimore, 1971.

Hathaway, D.E., 'Government and Agriculture Revisited, A Review of Two Decades of Change', in *Amer. JAE,* Vol. 63, No. 5, 1981, Proc. Issue.

Johnson, G.L., and Quance, C.L., *The Overproduction Trap in US Agriculture,* Johns Hopkins Press, Baltimore, 1972.

Jones, E.L. and Woolf, S.J., (eds.) *Agrarian Change and Economic Development,* Methuen, London, 1969.

Kuznets, S., *Economic Growth of Nations,* The Belknap Press of Harvard University Press, Cambridge, Mass., 1971.

Lewis, W.A., 'Economic Development with Unlimited Supplies of Labour', *Manchester School,* 1954.

*Growth and Fluctuations 1870–1913,* Allen and Unwin, London, 1978.

Maddison, A., *Phases of Capitalist Development,* Oxford University Press, 1982.

Mitrani, D., *Marx Against the Peasant,* Weidenfeld and Nicolson, London, 1950.

Schultz, Th.W., *The Economic Organization of Agriculture,* McGraw-Hill, New York, 1953.

Slicher van Bath, B.H., *The Agrarian History of Western Europe,* 500–1850, Arnold, London, 1963.

Tweeten, L., *Foundations of Farm Policy,* 2nd ed., Nebraska, 1979.

Zangheri, R., 'The historical relationship between agriculture and economic development in Italy', in Jones and Woolf (eds.) (1969), *op. cit.*

## DISCUSSION OPENING – W. J. ANDERSON

Professor van der Meer's paper has posed the question: what has been the impact of long term (1850–1979) economic growth on the productivity and income of the traditional agricultural sectors in eight western countries whose economic systems for pricing, allocating resources and income distribution were market oriented? The measurements used are comparative changes in the productivity, income and terms of trade between agricultural and non-agricultural sectors of those countries during that period. Canada would have fitted well with this group so I wonder why Canada was not included. I suspect that the general directions of trends would have been similar to those of the eight.

Secular trends and relationships common to all countries which stand out in the data are (a) the population growth rate was high in the early part of the period and tapered off; (b) the agricultural workforce declined as a proportion of the total workforce; (c) the rate of increase in productivity per worker in agriculture exceeded that of the non-agricultural sector by a considerable amount in most countries and the rate was much higher after 1913; (d) the chronic income discrepancy resulting from the interaction of growth and demand factors forced structural changes by putting downward pressure on agricultural labour returns; (e) for much of the period agricultural/non-agricultural terms of trade were less than 1.0, which is consistent with the unfavourable income ratios.

While these secular trends are discernible the number of departures from the trends is striking. From the data the impact of the see-saw between supply and demand and the shocks to the macro-economy which overrode the trends and generated alternate periods of prosperity and depression is apparent. These distortions provided an environment of uncertainty and instability which characterized the period of the study. The classical Malthusian-Ricardian model of population pressure on fixed resources resulting in subsistence income turned out to be a special case valid only up to about 1800 after which productive capacity and demand oscillated as to which was the dominant influence. The classical model had not taken into account the ingenuity of people to substitute technology for scarce factors, to develop and exploit new resources and to modify population growth through family planning. The release of the bounds on output and productivity, however, coupled with macro shocks from depression and war, led to instability as supply overreacted to demand changes. Instability has been a disturbing element but infinitely preferable to the problem of a secular trend towards subsistence.

Professor van der Meer calls attention to the impact of instability on income distribution (equity). He concludes that agricultural/non-agricultural income ratios in these countries depended on the shifting relative strength of supply factors, technical progress, imports and prices, and demand from population growth, exports and levels of income. He notes the periods in which supply moved faster than demand, which squeezed net returns and created adjustment crises, alternated with periods of lagging supply. Throughout the period the farm sector did not share equitably in the growing real income per caput and the variations between countries were considerable. Likewise among farmers, those who were in the vanguard to use high pay-off technology and invested at the right times profited handsomely. Those who came in late on the technological change and/or who made investments prior to a downturn fared very badly. Consumers were less affected by these cycles of demand and supply and generally benefited from agricultural growth and productivity.

The results are consistent with those expected from the combined forces of applied labour-saving technology, low price and income elasticities of demand, and slowing down in the rate of population growth. However agricultural adjustment problems and agricultural/non agricultural income discrepancies, made more prominent by instability, have not been acceptable socially and politically. Moreover the Malthusian spectre and Physiocratic perceptions have always been in the background politically, not to mention concerns for food security in the event of war. These socio-political reasons produced underlying agricultural fundamentalism among voters which favoured measures to offset instability and to correct what were judged to be market imperfections.

The uncertainties, the income pressures, the declining agricultural labour force and fear that the family farm was endangered, all associated with growth, resulted in agricultural policies with prominent elements of protection. This preoccupation with protection has spawned an array of ingenious national schemes involving supply management, price and income stabilization and implicit and explicit subsidies. Internally these measures have had all sorts of distorting effects on resource use and equity as certain commodities are favoured over others. Internationally these schemes distort trade by putting comparative advantage in the background. Van der Meer notes for example how the EEC has turned from a net importer to a net exporter of most agricultural products. The most serious effects of these measures are not internal because the countries can afford to subsidize and to sacrifice some comparative advantage. But the distortions of trade and resource use are more serious for poorer countries which need all the benefits from comparative advantage in world trade that their resources should permit.

The depression phases which agriculture has experienced in any country have come mainly from two sources. One has been new and cheaper competing supplies when other countries exploited technology and new resources. Agricultural expansion in one country created depression and adjustment problems in others. The other has been the major shocks to the macro-economy from war and depression. A third source of instability has been the business cycle. It has been observed that agriculture has been somewhat independent of the business cycle because (a) food consumption was only moderately affected by short-run fluctuations in the national income and employment and, (b) the old-style capitalist small-scale organization of farms, which combined management, labour and equity capital in the same person, precluded unemployment and modified short-run production adjustments, (c) the considerable degree of internal self-sufficiency in input supply characteristic of farm enterprises in the past provided a measure of independence from the general economy.

The last of those reasons is certainly invalid now. Farms which produce the bulk of the output are highly integrated with the business community and dependent on short-term loans to finance a large proportion of the inputs. This integration makes those producers vulnerable not only to inflation in input prices but to changing interest rates, the main instrument of monetary policy. Farmers now go bankrupt because the cash flow has turned out to be inadequate to cover rising input prices and interest rates on short-term loans. Inflation and exposure to financial markets has had a marked impact on land values since the mid-1970s, a period when inflation dominated the macro-economy. In addition to the discounted net income stream as the source of land value, land as a hedge against inflation became a dominant feature of the land market. The upward spiral in land prices has been aided by real interest rates, which have been 'zero or less after tax', and favourable tax treatment of capital gains, especially on land transferred as a family farm from one generation to the next. Recently, the high interest rate policy has deflated capital values including land. For established farmers with large equities these are paper profits and losses which do not destroy the business unit. For those producers who invested at high land values the result can be disastrous if they are squeezed between high interest rates on loans, inflation in input costs and less than buoyant commodity markets. It seems that uncertainty, always a major factor in growth and equity, has assumed even greater dimensions.

The road to progress has been a rough one indeed with alternating favourable and unfavourable cost-price relationships and always with inexorable pressures for structural change. The fact that productivity per agricultural worker has shown such a large increase is quite remarkable given the changing pressures from population growth, from additions to supply as new technological potentials were exploited and virgin land was brought into production, and from the shocks of economic boom and depression and two major wars. The secular growth in productivity, which the author notes as having been particularly rapid after 1913, is a tribute to research and development which has been supported mostly by governments, and to the effectiveness of production and resource management in the hands of small-scale capitalist managers. Resource adjustments required in the process of growth have produced returns to some people which are not equitable by socio-political standards. Instability and uncertainty have exacerbated this problem and together with considerations of equity have led to the adoption of protective measures by the rich countries. Stagflation and its remedies have enlarged the scope of instability. This added uncertainty, together with signs that the rate of increase in physical input/output ratios has slowed down, suggests that agriculture in these countries may be going through a period of slower growth in productivity. The combination certainly favours continued public intervention to protect agriculture.

VICTOR NAZARENKO

# *Economic Development and Social Justice: Experience of Developed Countries within the Socialist System*

This presentation sets itself as an object the analysis of some essential features of the experience of some European countries, that is the Soviet Union and socialist countries of Eastern Europe. With all their diversity of historic, natural and economic conditions they are characterized by a number of general regularities of socialist development in agriculture, its role under conditions of developed socialism and the state of economic development and social justice.

The presentation is dealing with a most important subject: how to solve the problem of stimulation of agricultural production development under conditions of the developed socialist society within the framework of the general economic development, and to make this development correspond to general social objectives of the socialist countries and achievements of the aims of the society.

First of all it should be mentioned that stimulation of the agricultural production development, in particular of food products, belongs to the most important tasks of the developed socialist countries. The recently adopted Food Programme of the Soviet Union proves it most expressively. It is the central economic objective of the 1980s.

It should be emphasized that total and per caput increase of agricultural production are major factors not only of economic but also of social policy in the development of socialist countries, as they are concerned with the problems of the living standards of the population, the rural population included.

The rise of farm production is achieved first through substantially increased capital investments into this branch of economy, through a shift to industrial production methods in agriculture. At the beginning the industrialization of agriculture was a source of capital investment in industry, now with the improved general economic potential it is used in general to supply capital investments in agricultural production.

TABLE I *Capital investments in agriculture*

(millions of national currency)

| Countries | 1960 | 1970 | 1975 | 1980 |
|---|---|---|---|---|
| Bulgaria | 405 | 559 | 783 | 385 |
| Hungary | 6271 | 21970 | 26187 | 30997 |
| G D R | 1898 | 4281 | 4906 | 4883 |
| Rumania | 5431 | 13102 | 18540 | 28008 |
| Czechoslovakia | 9753 | 9757 | 16558 | 16355 |
| U S S R | 5473 | 14401 | 23432 | 27020 |

*Note:* Table I is compiled on the basis of a uniform approach to agriculture and the data reflect only production capital investments.

These capital investments make up about 27 per cent of total capital investments in the economy of such a country as the USSR. One cannot help recognizing that it is a high level of investment, judging by the historical and current levels in many other countries. This development of capital investment apart from the development of agricultural production has created conditions for the partial release of working power, replacing labour by capital. In that way introduction of additional capital into this branch took place against a background of the movement of population from rural areas and in particular when the amount of people employed in agricultural production decreased.

The decreased number of people engaged in agriculture and the increased total agricultural production have made it possible to raise substantially labour payments in agriculture, the differences being observed in different countries. The additional sources of income for rural population, utilization of production from private plots and so on, are not taken into consideration in estimations.

It should be mentioned that the growth of the rural income has resulted not only from the objective rise of labour productivity, but also due to purposeful policy aimed at bringing closer the living standards of urban and rural populations; it is reflected, for example, in the system of purchasing prices, subsidies, cheaper credits, different budget assignments.

One of the methods to increase and maintain the level of labour payments in agriculture was the introduction of guaranteed minimum labour payments. This system was first introduced in the 1950s in the GDR and then it was spread in other socialist countries. For these purposes some countries are practising either the establishment of public funds or allocation of State credits to low profit farms for keeping up the level of labour payments. As a result the level of money payments in agriculture in some countries has approached that in industry, and in some cases it is even higher.

TABLE 2 *Average monthly level of labour payments in agriculture and in industry*

*(in units of national currency)*

| Countries | 1960 | 1970 | 1975 | 1980 |
|---|---|---|---|---|
| Bulgaria | 74 | 107 | 138 | 167 |
| | 80 | 124 | 150 | 197 |
| Hungary | 1416 | 2122 | 2717 | 3822 |
| | 1604 | 2089 | 2816 | 3883 |
| G D R | 370 | 529 | 700 | 727 |
| | 467 | 588 | 748 | 783 |
| Rumania | 703 | 1205 | 1531 | 2160 |
| | 829 | 1288 | 1602 | 2307 |
| U S S R | 55.2 | 101 | 127 | 149 |
| | 91.6 | 133 | 162 | 185 |
| Czechoslovakia | 1113 | 1806 | 2221 | 2488 |
| | 1442 | 1967 | 2338 | 2653 |

*Note:*
numerator – agriculture,
denominator – industry.

A number of countries manifest the tendency to more rapid rates of wage growth in agriculture as compared to industry. If we assume that the level of 1970 is 100, then, consequently in the Soviet agriculture, money payments have increased during the decade by 49 per cent and in industry by 39 per cent, in Czechoslovakia by 42 per cent and 36 per cent correspondingly, in G D R by 37 per cent and 32 per cent and so on. So, as a whole, the levels of labour payments in agriculture and in industry are approaching each other, although the corresponding differentiation in the complicacy character of operations and so on should be taken into consideration. In agriculture itself the level of payments in the public sector is approaching that of the co-operative sector. For example, in Czechoslovakia these levels became equal in 1972, in some countries in co-operatives the same level of payments is practised for agricultural operations on co-operatives and on state farms.

However the rise of money payments, important as it is, is not sufficient to fulfil the task of bringing closer the living standards of the urban and rural populations.

In this connection the progress of pensionary and social insurance systems are of great significance in agriculture. Initially this system was implemented on a wide-scale on state farms and then it was also introduced in co-operative enterprises. For instance since 1965 this system has been functioning in the Soviet Union on the basis of centralized funds for social insurance originating from the state budget and farm allocations. It should be emphasized that two-thirds of these expenses are covered by the state budget. Actually the process of unification of social insurance systems is proceeding in the urban and rural areas.

A similar process takes place in other countries as well. By the present time the terms of social insurance of the co-operative peasantry have been practically levelled with those of workers engaged in the government sector of the national economy. The centralized pensionary insurance of the co-operative peasantry has been under progress in Bulgaria since 1957, in Hungary since 1959, in Rumania since 1967 and in Czechoslovakia since 1964. Until recently there were differences in the age and rate entitlement for pension granting and this fact has brought about the difference at pensionary levels between co-operative peasants on the one hand and workers and employees on the other; the level of the former being much lower than that of the latter.

In accordance with new legislative acts, adopted in the COMECON countries in the 1970s, a uniform system of granting pensions and allowances for co-operative peasants has been introduced. This system offers equal opportunities for the utilization of social funds, allotted for the social needs of the population. In this way since 1975 pensions for co-operative peasants in Bulgaria have been calculated according to the same scale as for workers and employees. In Czechoslovakia since 1976, on the basis of the new pension law, the differences observed until recently in the field of social insurance between state and co-operative enterprises have been eliminated. In general the process of bringing the systems of social insurance for peasantry up to the level of the urban population is under way.

The solution of social problems of the rural population is now becoming an important factor in the state policy of stimulation of agricultural production. Technical progress is closely connected with the ever increasing importance of the human factor because of the ever growing role of highly skilled labour. At the same time the objective of the general social plan for bringing closer the living standards in the town and in the village should be implemented. It is being reached to a great extent due to the improved levels of incomes of enterprises and of individuals. However, in those zones and farms where it is impossible to solve the problems of production and social infrastructure by their own means, the state performs budget financing of these measures. This practice applies in all socialist countries. The most recent measures in this respect in the USSR are related to the Food Programme.

The Food Programme allocates 160 billion roubles for social development in rural areas in the 1980s, including special capital investments in areas showing unfavourable economic conditions.

An important aspect of state stimulation of agricultural production within the framework of the social policy is the integrated growth of the public and private sectors in agriculture.

There is a common feature – the constant tendency to an increased share of gross agricultural production coming from the state and co-operative sectors. This occurs due to the introduction of modern industrial production methods. In this connection the importance of private subsidiary farms has considerably declined within the total income of peasants.

In the past years this share was about 30 per cent in the USSR, 25 per cent in Bulgaria, 35 per cent in Hungary and over 50 per cent in Rumania. In the GDR in the overwhelming majority of co-operatives and in Czechoslovakia private subsidiary farms of the co-operative members do not play a significant part in the income of peasants, their commercial capacity being low in comparison with most COMECON countries. In those countries where private subsidiary farms play an important role in production, a policy of their production encouragement is practised. In this case private and social farms are not opposed and the process of integration takes place, specifically by means of agreements between co-operatives and peasants. Great experience in this respect has been accumulated in Hungary. In the USSR during recent years important measures have been adopted for the stimulation of the development of private subsidiary farms as an essential source of income for the rural population and food supply. But the main source of commercial produce is and will be large socialist agricultural enterprises – state and collective farms.

From the point of view of economic development concepts the problem of maximum stimulation of production is to be solved within the framework of implementation of the general social tasks of the society, involving the rural population. Some trends can be formulated which serve to fulfil the state regulation in developed socialist countries for the implementation of the objectives. First of all this is a system of planning, which with a certain difference among the countries, makes up the fundamentals of the mechanism.

The most important problem is the implementation of the entire process of planning as well as the economic activity on the basis of the applied economic instruments. They involve first of all the system of prices and price formation, establishment of conditions for profitable activity of the enterprises, having different specificities and located in different zones. So, the economic instruments of the state have to fulfil the functions for stimulation of production as well as for providing social justice.

The most important function among these economic instruments is the system of prices and the mechanism of price formation. In this case the most important task is stimulation of agricultural production and providing a definite level of profitability for different branches and areas. It is clear that this task is a complicated one and its solution depends on concrete economic conditions of some countries. Two main trends are to be observed: one of them is characterized by a high flexibility of the price organism, instability of purchasing and retail prices for agricultural raw materials and food. This system is mostly typical for a country such as Hungary. In some other countries, for example in the GDR and Czechoslovakia, a system of stable purchasing and retail prices is functioning and the state interferes in the price mechanism through periodical price correction and identification and a widely developed system of state grants and subsidies.

This system of price formation has also been set up in the USSR, where retail prices for food products do not change for long periods. Reconsideration of purchasing prices for agricultural produce, taking into account the changes in cost price for its production, periodically takes place. In practice it often means a periodical increase of purchasing prices for a number of farm products. The recent increase in prices was carried out in the USSR in May *this year* when the Food Programme was adopted. It is natural that conditions of stability of state retail prices for food products are connected with considerable budget subsidies intended to maintain price levels.

The price mechanism as a whole is orientated towards keeping low retail prices for food products and to a certain extent purchasing prices, reflecting cost price of agricultural production and an adequate profitability level. Of course it would be wrong to say that in such a complicated process as price formation all problems have been solved. In fact it is one of the most important trends of research in the USSR and in other developed socialist countries, since many economic problems of production, consumption and agrarian policy must be treated as a whole. One of the most important aims is the achievement of relatively equal economic conditions of production for various branches of agriculture.

This problem is treated in the regional plan. Differences in the location and in natural soil fertility create different conditions for profitable production and levels of incomes by the enterprises. Therefore different economic methods are used for levelling the conditions of farming. The system of zonal prices is functioning in the Soviet Union due to substantial climatic differences. This system reflects the conditions of production and the level of cost price of agricultural production in a certain zone. In some republics, for instance in Lithuania, differences in prices exist even inside the price zone. In other socialist countries uniform price systems for the entire country are used. However, in some countries, for example in Czechoslovakia, special grants are provided for farms located under the most unfavourable conditions – in mountains. Such levelling of conditions is promoted by land and income taxes, being one of the components of the funds for grant aiding farms under more unfavourable conditions. This practice is applied in the GDR and Czechoslovakia.

In the Soviet Union the system of income taxes was introduced into collective farms not long ago. In this case net income is taxable. Adequate income taxes were also introduced into state farms. These measures promote the allotment to the state of a part of differential land rent, which later on is used for other purposes in agriculture.

The analysis of a number of major trends in the economic and agrarian policy of developed socialist countries shows that they all put forward the objective of stimulating agricultural production. This stimulation proceeds first of all through intensification with wide utilization of capital investments and modern means of production. This development, however, is proceeding within the general social and economic framework of the society and simultaneously it is expressed by the achievement of social justice. Different as they are the means of state influence are directed just at this aim. However all this is an expressive creative process, which constantly puts forward new objectives for the government bodies and for economists. Therefore, the fulfilment of these tasks is a complicated process of scientific research.

## DISCUSSION OPENING – S.R. SEN

Yesterday afternoon, we had three papers on the experience of developing countries regarding growth and equity relationship in agriculture. There was evidence of a high degree of diversity. This morning we had first a paper from Dr Van der Meer regarding the experience of eight developed market economy countries. There was also diversity but it was somewhat less.

We have now a paper from Dr Nazarenko regarding the experience of six developed socialist countries. The diversity was relatively much smaller. I am thankful to Dr Nazarenko for providing us with some very interesting statistics about these six socialist countries. But all his figures are in current prices and different national currencies. This makes comparison over time and between countries very difficult. I wish Dr Nazarenko had used some common denominators in both these respects (for example 1960 prices and roubles) to facilitate comparison. However three facts stand out from his figures.

1 Agriculture is now getting a large inflow of capital from industry, which is a contrast with earlier years when capital used to flow from agriculture to industry. For example in the USSR agriculture now gets 27 per cent of total national capital investment, which is high by any standard.

2 The gap in per caput remuneration or income between industry and agriculture has narrowed down very considerably between 1960 and 1980, thanks, among other things, to this flow of investment to agriculture.

3 Fiscal measures are now playing a much greater role than physical controls in ensuring this greater equity, as compared to the practice in earlier decades.

The first set of questions that I have for Dr Nazarenko is: What difference has this made to the rate of growth of agricultural production? What is the rate now? Is it significantly higher than (a) what it was in earlier decades in these six socialist countries or (b) what it is now in non-socialist countries in comparable stages of development? If not, why?

Dr Nazarenko has mentioned that agricultural price policies are quite different in more industrialized socialist countries like the USSR and the GDR as compared to less industrialized socialist countries like Hungary and Rumania.

My second set of questions to Dr Nazarenko is: what is his evaluation of the relative merits of stable (or rigid) and flexible (or responsive) price policies? Yesterday Professor Ranis observed that flexibility is the name of development. Does Dr Nazarenko accept that as a proposition applicable only to underdeveloped market economy countries, or does he think that it is applicable also to underdeveloped socialist countries? Making the needed adjustment through subsidies, as in the USSR, instead of prices, may make for equity. But does it also make for economic efficiency?

As I was listening to the discussion yesterday afternoon and this morning, one thought occurred to me. Under certain circumstances, growth and equity moved in the same direction. Under other circumstances they moved in opposite directions. The stage of economic development, the trend of terms of trade, the readiness to adjust with changing circumstances, the nature of social control have all considerable relevance in this content.

My third set of questions is: what is the right combination and in what time horizon? *Prima facie,* it appears that possibly an undue stress on growth may result in greater inequity and an undue stress on equity may slow down growth. Each has its own short and long-term problems. Avoidance of extreme steps may have, therefore, some merit from this standpoint, whatever their other advantages may be.

## GENERAL DISCUSSION* – RAPPORTEUR: BRUCE L. GREENSHIELDS

In the general discussion it was suggested that one should not infer from Professor Van der Meer's paper that the growth experience of developed market economies is necessarily transferable to developing countries, because the latter group is getting a late start and is on a different track. Population and its rate of growth, concentration of market power, and capital needs are greater now. Also, the developing countries have no colonies to exploit, although the contribution of past exploitation to the agricultural development of developed countries was questioned.

Professor Van der Meer defended his use of a single-factor measurement of agricultural productivity because the contribution of land was relatively stable, as was the capital/labour ratio, but the latter assertion was questioned.

Nazarenko's data on capital investment were in current dollars; but they nevertheless depict real trends because prices were relatively stable over the period. The data on the changes in distribution of income show only intersectoral trends and they exclude off-farm income and income inputed from home production of food. If these sources were taken into account, it is possible that household income in the agricultural sector would exceed that of the non-agricultural sector. That would probably not be the case, however, on a per-hour basis.

Policies to raise the income of the agricultural sectors in socialist countries have favoured input subsidies rather than output price increases

*Papers by Van der Meer and Nazarenko.

that would raise retail prices. That agricultural productivity has increased in socialist countries in response to increased investment can be seen if the effects of weather and the time it takes for an increase in capital to bring about an increase in production are taken into account.

Participants in the discussion included Don Paarlberg, Frank Baffoe, George H. Peters, Ferenc Fekete and B.N. Verma.

# SECTION II

## *Concepts and Methodology – Analytical Aspects*

YUJIRO HAYAMI

# *Growth and Equity – Is There a Trade-Off?*

It has generally been agreed that a sustained increase in total factor productivity resulting from an organized effort to apply scientific knowledge to production processes underlay the rapid increase in national product in the economies which experienced the 'modern economic growth' *à la* Kuznets (1966). Agriculture is no exception to this rule. A large body of growth-accounting studies for developed economies shows almost unanimously that the part of agricultural output growth which can be explained by increases in conventional factors, such as land, labour and capital, is minor relative to an unexplained residual or 'technological change' broadly defined as a shift in a production function relating output to conventional inputs (Peterson and Hayami, 1977).

A traditional pattern of agricultural growth in developing countries was that the increase in agricultural output resulted mainly from opening new land for cultivation. However, due to the pressure of population explosion, unused land resources have been exhausted rapidly and, in many areas, cultivation frontiers have been pushed to a point where further land opening endangers ecological balance seriously. It is now a consensus that, in order to achieve agricultural output growth at a rate sufficient to meet the needs of developing countries, it is imperative to develop and diffuse modern agricultural technologies suited for their resource endowments and ecological conditions. Yet, it is common to assume a trade-off between growth and equity in the development of modern technology. It has been feared that gains from the technological advance accrue mainly to large farmers and landlords with a result of greater concentration of income and assets in the hands of a few. Such concern has been accentuated with the advent of the 'green revolution', the dramatic diffusion of modern varieties (MV) of rice and wheat in the tropics since the late 1960s.

Much of the discussion on this issue seems subject to confusion because (a) the effects of other factors, population pressure on land among others, are not properly separated from the effects of technology and (b) interactions between technological and institutional changes are not well understood. This paper aims to examine these conceptual issues in order to clarify the relation between growth and equity involved in the development of modern agricultural technology in developing countries.

## POPULATION PRESSURE AND TECHNOLOGICAL CHANGE

A popular belief of considering new technology a factor which promotes inequity in the rural sector is mainly based on a naive association between technological advance and growing inequality. Indeed, it is not difficult to find cases in which poverty and inequality multiplied side by side with the dramatic diffusion of MV. However, an inference based on the simple association tends to miss the real cause.

A major factor pressing change on income distribution in developing countries today is the strong population pressure on land. An explosive population growth in the Third World began in the second and the third decades of the twentieth century; it has further accelerated since World War II. The high population growth rates have resulted mainly from the decline in mortality rates due to the propagation of modern public health measures and extension of markets that prevented local crop failures from turning into famine. A similar increase in population was experienced by Western Europe and Japan in the beginning of modern economic growth; there industrial development provided sufficient employment opportunities in the urban sector to absorb more than the increments in total population. In most developing countries today, the population growth has not been accompanied by such structural transformation, because the population growth has been much faster and labour absorption by the industrial sector has been slower, due to the capital-using bias of modern industries, than in the early history of industrialization in developed countries. The ever-increasing rural population pressed hard on limited land resources. The man-land ratio has been increasing rapidly in developing countries, on the average, at a rate which would double the number of workers per hectare of cultivated land within a half century (Bairoch, 1975, pp. 5–8; Hayami and Kikuchi, 1981, pp. 39–40).

When the labour supply increases faster than the land supply, an increasing amount of labour will be applied per unit of land. If technology is constant, labour's marginal productivity and hence wage rates will decline along a fixed production function. If the labour application continues to increase, the diminishing return will intensify and the elasticity of substitution of labour for land will eventually become less than one so that labour's relative share of agricultural income decreases and land's share increases corresponding to any increment in labour input; this implies that the income position of tenants and agricultural labourers deteriorates relative to landlords and owner farmers. If the labour application per hectare increases further, a point will be reached beyond which the elasticity of substitution becomes so small that labour's income declines absolutely.

The negative effect of population pressure on income distribution through the labour market is coupled with the negative effect through the agricultural product market. The population growth implies a rightward shift in food demand. The increased food demand, when confronted with a fixed supply curve corresponding to a stagnant technology, raises food prices. The increase in food prices is a major gain to large farmers and landlords who sell a large portion of their food output in the market, while it is a major blow to agricultural labourers and marginal farmers who have to purchase foodstuff in order to supplement their own produce.

In the real world, both the labour demand and the product supply have not stayed constant. Substantial efforts have been made in developing countries to improve technology and land infrastructure, such as irrigation systems, so that both agricultural employment and food supply increased at rapid rates. However, those efforts have not been quite sufficient to overcome the strong population pressure on land; the upward shift in the production function has not been fast enough to counteract the decreasing return to rapidly increasing labour input per hectare. As a result it is common to observe that, side by side with the dramatic development of modern agricultural technology such as the MV diffusion, land rent rose at the expense of labour wage rates.

Thus, the situation in developing countries resembles the world of classical economists like Ricardo: as the growth of population presses hard on limited land resources under constant technology, cultivation frontiers are expanded to more marginal areas and greater amounts of labour are applied per unit of cultivated land; the cost of food production increases and food prices rise; in the long run, labourers' income will be lowered to a subsistence minimum barely sufficient to maintain stationary population and all the surpluses will be captured by landlords in the form of increased land rent. The way to escape from the Ricardian trap is to maximize efforts to develop agricultural technology so that the labour demand can increase faster than its supply and that the food supply can increase faster than its demand. Here is no trade-off between growth and equity. If growth is not enhanced, equity is impaired.

## DIFFERENT TYPES OF TECHNOLOGICAL CHANGE

If the basic cause of growing poverty and inequality is the population pressure on land, the technological change effective to serve for the dual goals of growth and equity should be land-saving and labour-using; in the Hicks definition it increases the marginal productivity of labour relative to that of land, thereby increasing labour's income share at the expense of land's share for a constant wage-rent ratio. If the technological change is biased in the opposite direction, it may add to the effects of population pressure in reducing wage rates and labour's income share.

Another important element in technological change is a possible bias for scale economies. The economies of scale usually stem from the lumpiness or indivisibility of production factors. If the adoption of a new technology requires a lumpy capital which cannot be utilized efficiently in a small operational unit, its adoption may be limited to large farmers. The high rate of return from the adoption of the new technology may work as a strong inducement for large farmers to accumulate more land through purchase of small farmers' holdings or tenant eviction.

The classification of agricultural technologies into mechanical technology and biological (or biological-chemical) technology has now been established. In general, the mechanical technology involves lumpy machinery capital which has a labour-saving effect. In contrast, the biological technology depends on divisible inputs such as seeds and fertilizer and is usually geared to increase output per unit of land area by applying a large amount of those current inputs together with greater crop care, more complex crop rotation and crop-livestock combinations. Thus, it is common to identify the development of mechanical technology as labour-saving and biased towards larger scale, and biological technology as land-saving and neutral with respect to scale or even biased towards smaller scale.

However, such associations do not necessarily hold. For example, irrigation pumps, though they belong to the mechanical technology, have a power to save land by increasing both the yield per hectare of crop area and the cropping intensity. On the other hand, some biological technologies developed in labour-scarce advanced economies are labour-saving by nature, such as the use of herbicides. In the United States the tomato varieties which have a sturdy skin and ripen at the same time were developed purposely to facilitate mechanical harvesting; this example shows that improved varieties which are neutral with respect to scale and factor use by themselves may enhance scale economics and labour-saving effects through their complementarity with mechanical technology. Moreover, the problem of capital lumpiness depends on institutional conditions. For example, the capital lumpiness of an irrigation pump is not a source of scale economies if its collective use by small farmers is organized efficiently. However, if small peasants have no access to credit, they might not be able to apply fertilizers and chemicals to an optimum level because of the bottleneck of a 'lumpy' cash requirement.

Thus, whether a certain technology or a combination of technologies serves for the dual goals of growth and equity depends on social and economic conditions. In organizing efforts to transfer technology to developing countries, a careful design is necessary to sort out and adapt various foreign-born technologies for local conditions and, at the same time, to modify social institutions and organization in recipient countries.

## TOWARDS GROWTH WITH EQUITY

Recent debate on growth and equity in agricultural development has centred on the 'green revolution'. The green revolution based on diffusion of improved seeds and increased application of fertilizers and chemicals is essentially an international technology transfer from developed countries in the temperature zone to developing countries in the tropics through adaptive research (Hayami and Ruttan, 1971). A natural worry is if the technology developed in different factor endowments and institutional conditions might be socially inefficient and inequitable in the socio-economic fabrics of developing countries. Popular arguments run as follows: green revolution technology tends to be monopolized by large farmers who have better access to new information and credit; efficient use of MV is difficult for subsistence peasants who have little capacity to purchase modern inputs such as fertilizers and chemicals; large profits resulting from the exclusive adoption of MV technology by large farmers stimulates them to enlarge their operational holdings by consolidating the farms of small non-adopters; it also induces mechanization, which reduces employment opportunities and wage rates for the landless population (Cleaver, 1972; Frankel, 1971; Griffin, 1974).

However, the empirical evidence accumulated in the past decade indicates that, in general, the MV technology diffused widely among farmers, irrespective of farm size and land tenure, in the areas where decent irrigation was available; its effect on employment was positive as evidenced by a significant increase in the real wage rates in the Punjab and other parts of North India where MV diffused widely at a time when real wage rates were constant or declining in other parts of India where MV diffusion was limited (Hayami, 1981; Hayami and Kikuchi, 1981, pp. 55–59; Ruttan, 1977). However, there is no denying that there were cases in which the small or poor farmers lagged significantly behind the large or wealthy farmers in the adoption of MV and related inputs; such cases tend to be found in the social environment characterized by extremely skewed distributions of wealth and power. Institutional reforms are desired to achieve a wider diffusion of technology so that the technology contributes to both growth and equity. Grabowski (1981) enumerates the necessary reforms:

> research activities must be directed at developing new seeds for the majority of farmers who lack irrigation. Research activities need to be oriented toward improving cultivation practices and irrigation techniques in order to increase cropping intensity. Credit must be made available to allow farmers with small farms to irrigate their land and thus increase their cropping intensities and allow them to make use of existing green revolution technology. Larger farmers' privileged access to machinery must be eliminated if the growth of employment is to be rapid. All of these require an increase in the power and influence of farmers with small farms, relative to those with large farms, on government decisions concerning rural research and credit priorities. This could possibly be accomplished through land reforms or, a less radical solution, the organization of small farmers into groups which could put pressure on government agencies to recognize and respond to the interest of small farmers.

No one will deny the desirability of such reforms. The problem is feasibility. It is a common observation that, in a society characterized by the monopoly of wealth and power by a few, institutional reforms are also twisted to serve the élites; a disproportional share of institutional credit and subsidized inputs intended to assist the poor, in fact, goes into the hands of the wealthy farmers because of their pull with government agencies; land reform regulations on land rent and tenure form often result in eviction of tenants and conversion of land use from labour-intensive crops such as rice to extensive crops such as coconuts. It is much more difficult to tailor institutions than to tailor technology so as to serve for the poor in a society characterized by extreme inequality. The relevant question to ask is whether, given the extreme inequality in wealth and power in developing countries, the development of the green revolution technology should be withheld for its possible adverse effect on income distribution. The answer is definitely 'no'. The MV technology has been diffusing in Asia wide enough to shift the labour demand and the product supply significantly without which the economies of developing countries would have moved several steps closer to the Ricardian trap of economic stagnation and greater inequality.

Equally important is the effect of technological change to induce institutional reforms. Technological change is a major factor to create disequilibrium in resource allocations under the existing institutions; institutional reforms are induced by the potential social gain resulting from the reforms to correct the disequilibria. In this perspective, if the existing institutions such as credit and land tenure represent a real constraint on the diffusion of technology, those institutions must be under strong pressure for reform. Whether such reform will be forthcoming depends on political will. However, it should be much easier to execute a reform to cut a pie more equally when the reform is expected to enlarge the pie than when it is fixed in size. Unless the development of new technology creates disequilibria which may be corrected by institutional reforms, it is unlikely that political will will be mobilized for the reforms. Neither growth nor equity can be achieved without the dialectic interactions between technological and institutional innovations.

The same dialectic process applies to the choice of research projects. For both growth and equity considerations it is desirable to allocate resources for developing technologies which can be adopted by a large number of poor farmers under unfavourable conditions in developing countries, such as organic fixation of nitrogen and better varieties suited for rainfed and flood water conditions. However, research on such technologies is much more difficult and takes much longer to achieve a major breakthrough, unlike the high-yielding, fertilizer-responsive MV for a well-irrigated condition. The backlog of technological potential accumulated in developed countries in the temperate zone that can be easily transferred to the topics through relatively simple adaptive research does not exist for the former as it did for the latter. If the modest research resources for international agricultural research systems in the 1960s were concentrated on such difficult research projects, no major breakthrough would have been made. Then, public attention and, hence, public funds, would not have been attracted to strengthening agricultural research systems in the tropics. The fact is that the 'green revolution' and 'miracle seeds', though the terms are very misleading, attracted public attention and contributed enormously to the expansion in the funding of both national and international agricultural research systems. As it has been recognized that the benefit of the 'miracle seeds' is limited to irrigated areas, increasingly more research efforts in the expanded research systems have been allocated for improvements in seeds and cropping systems geared to benefiting people in more unfavourable conditions. Likewise, the recognition that inadequate water supply is a major bottleneck to the diffusion of MV technology has induced both private and public investments in irrigation infrastructure.

Unless such dialectic interactions between technological and institutional innovations are maximized, we can hardly expect escape from the Ricardian trap. Thus, the first step in designing the effective agricultural development policy is to recognize that there is no trade-off between growth and equity in the long run.

However, the dialectic interactions between technological and institutional innovations do not always function effectively so that both growth and equity are enhanced. It is possible that in a society characterized by an extremely skewed distribution of wealth and power, technological and institutional innovations might be induced in a direction to benefit the élite, which does not coincide with a socially optimum direction. For example, in a rural society bifurcated into large estate owners and landless or near-landless population, the factor prices that are taken into consideration in the decision-making of the estate owners may be very different from the social opportunity costs. For the estate owners, unit labour costs may be substantially higher than market wage rates because a significant cost is involved in supervising a large number of hired labourers. However, the landed élite may have access to capital at a price cheaper than its social opportunity cost through such means as subsidized credits and overvalued exchange rates. In such a situation the research responsive to the demand of the landed élite may produce technologies biased towards a labour-saving and capital-using direction even if a socially optimum direction of technological change may be labour-using and land-cum-capital-saving. Those technologies, in turn, may strengthen the existing social system by making large-scale farm operations relatively more efficient.

Through such process, both social efficiency and equity are impaired. De Janvry (1973) identified this process as having resulted in stagnation and inequality in Argentine agriculture. In such societies, a vicious cycle of malinteractions between technological and institutional innovations might continue until eventual revolutions may stop it.

## REFERENCES

Bairoch, P., *The Economics of Development of the Third World Since 1900,* Methuen, London, 1975.

Cleaver, H.M., 'The Contradictions of the Green Revolution', *American Economic Review,* Vol. 62, No. 1, May 1972.

De Janvry, A., 'A Socioeconomic Model of Induced Innovation for Argentine Agriculture', *Quarterly Journal of Economics,* Vol. 87, August 1973.

Frankel, F.R., *India's Green Revolution,* Princeton University Press, 1971.

Grabowski, R., 'Induced Innovation, Green Revolution, and Income Distribution: Reply', *Economic Development and Cultural Change,* Vol. 30, No. 1, October 1981.
Griffin, K., *The Political Economy of Agrarian Change,* Harvard University Press, Cambridge, 1974.
Hayami, Y., 'Induced Innovation, Green Revolution, and Income Distribution: Comment', *Economic Development and Cultural Change,* Vol. 30, No. 1, October 1981.
Hayami, Y., and Kikuchi, M., *Asian Village Economy at the Crossroads,* University of Tokyo Press, 1981; and Johns Hopkins University Press, 1982.
Hayami, Y., and Ruttan, V.W., *Agricultural Development: An International Perspective,* Johns Hopkins University Press, 1971.
Kuznets, S., *Modern Economic Growth,* Yale University Press, 1966.
Peterson, W., and Hayami, Y., 'Technical Change in Agriculture', in Martin L.R. (ed.), *A Survey of Agricultural Economic Literature,* Vol. 1, University of Minnesota Press, 1977.
Ruttan, V.W., 'The Green Revolution: Seven Generalizations', *International Development Review,* Vol. 19, No. 4, August 1977.

## DISCUSSION OPENING – SECONDO TARDITI

Yujiro Hayami has examined in detail the relations between growth and equity in the application of modern agricultural technology in developing countries. He has clarified the effects of important factors, like population pressure on land and the interactions between technological and institutional changes. His excellent description of the problem is mainly based on positive economic analysis, and he concludes that 'there is no trade off between growth and equity in the long run'; but this statement is mitigated by the description of different situations where trade off does exist.

The general impression I gained was that proper agricultural policies could avoid situations of trade-off and foster a 'growth and equity' development. Unfortunately the normative side of the problem has not been developed in detail. Nevertheless I believe that it is of the utmost importance to examine carefully all agricultural policies with regards to their effects on growth and equity. I will try to focus on some aspects of the concept of 'trade off' between growth and equity and to classify different agricultural policies according to their positive or negative effects on growth, equity or both. I hope these concepts and methods will be useful for the discussion of our subject and complement those expressed in the paper.

*Concept of trade-off between growth and equity (Fig. 1)*
Since growth and equity are both components of social welfare we can think of a curve that expresses the highest possible rates of growth related to all different levels of resource distribution measured with one of the usual indexes.

This implies that different levels of resource distribution are related to maximum outputs of the optimally allocated resources. Through consequent social time preference rates, maximum possible rates of growth will be defined. All points on the curve will be economically efficient (production, exchange and output efficient) and this curve then may be seen as a particular expression of the well known 'welfare possibility curve', expressed through two measurable variables.

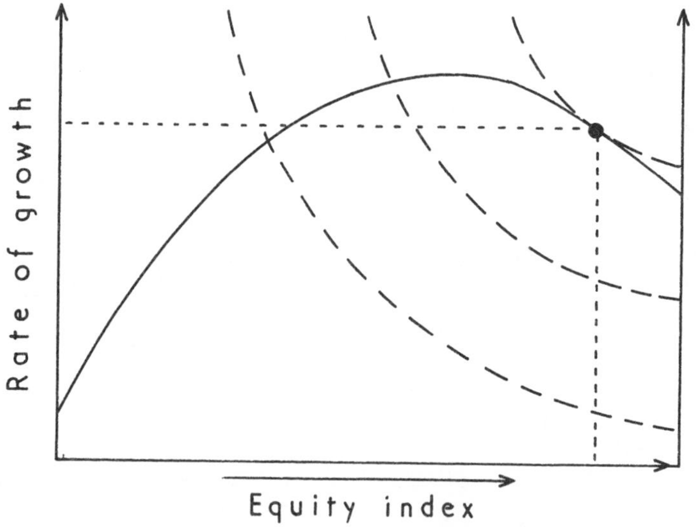


FIG. 1 Concept of trade-off between growth and equity

Let us put on the horizontal axis of a diagram an index of resource distribution varying from strong inequality to complete equality and on the vertical axis the rate of growth. The emerging curve that we may call 'social possibility curve' or 'social frontier' may have different shapes in different countries and in different periods of time according to the existing technology, factor endowment and social time preference. When the curve is positively sloped there is no trade-off between growth and equity, when it is negatively sloped there is trade-off. Moving from a strong inequitable distribution to a more equitable distribution, the curve should present a positive slope due to the fact that improving the resource endowment of the very poor will strongly increase their productivity and then the community's rate of growth. Then the curve should reach a peak and decrease, since lower savings and fixed labour supply should slow down the rate of growth. If we add on this diagram the well known social welfare function, we can find the optimal combination of growth and distribution which will always be located on a portion of the social frontier which is negatively sloped and presents then a trade-off between growth and equity equal to the marginal rate of substitution between growth and equity expressed by the community preferences. Like the social possibility curve, the social welfare function is different from one country to another as well as in various time periods, so that theoretical optimal combinations between growth and equity may differ considerably.

*Appraisal of technological change (Fig. 2)*
Starting from a feasible and efficient combination of growth and equity, the social frontier shifts upwards with a change in technology and the new

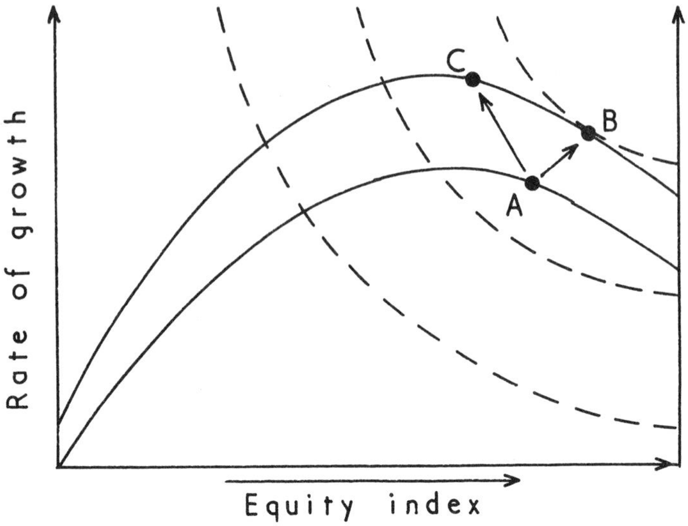


FIG. 2 Appraisal of technological change

feasible and efficient combination of growth and equity on the new social frontier may be located either north-east or north-west of the original situation.

In the first case the change in technology has generated a growth with equity improvement as dealing with 'labour using and land *cum* capital saving technological change' in the developing counties and no trade-off between growth and equity is involved. In the second case the new technology has generated more growth but less equity as when dealing with 'labour saving and capital using' technological changes in developing countries. In this case a trade-off between growth and equity is involved, as in the examples outlined in Hayami's paper.

*Classifications of agricultural policies (Fig. 3)*
Government intervention is usually examined in its real world context, that is in a 'second best' context, allowing for the non-complete realization of all conditions for Pareto efficient situations. The starting point of our analysis will then be a combination of growth and equity which is feasible but not efficient and is located inside the contour of the social frontier.

Agricultural policy measures may then move the existing locations north-west (growth with equity), north-east (growth with less equity), south-east (less growth and equity), or south-west (less growth with less equity). For example, a credit subsidy scheme for structural improvement of small holdings will be 'growth with equity' orientated (move north-east), while a traditional credit scheme requiring securities and being then out of reach of small farmers will imply a trade-off between growth and equity (move north-west).

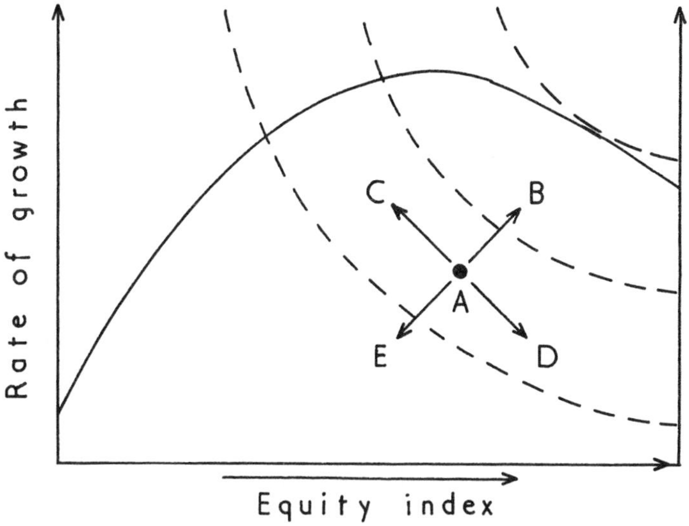


FIG. 3 Classifications of agricultural policies

On the other side a levy on agricultural products not justified on other welfare grounds may distort the price system and generate a global 'efficiency loss' together with a worsening income distribution since it is an income regressive burden for consumers and benefits mainly large farmers (move south-west).

A product subsidy policy will not be inequitable on the consumer side. and could be directed to particular groups of worse-off farmers. Together with some efficiency losses it will improve equity (move south-east), presenting again a trade-off case. When a trade-off between growth and equity is involved (move north-west or south-east) the slope of the welfare indifference curve in that point (the social marginal rate of substitution) will test the desirability of the trade-off generated by a policy measure which could increase or decrease the existing level of social welfare. Obviously, if alternative policies are discussed, the choice should be on the policy which allows the move on the highest possible indifference curve.

In the real world, problems are not clear-cut and each case must be studied in all its related effects before assessing total intensity of the trade-off between growth and equity. If the analysis is worked out on a partial equilibrium framework all relevant variables must be included.

A deeper knowledge of concepts and methodology needed to assess the effects of agricultural policies in this respect may surely allow a higher productivity of the agricultural economist's work towards increasing social welfare.

R. E. JUST, G. C. RAUSSER AND D. ZILBERMAN

# *Modelling Equity and Efficiency in Agricultural Production Systems*

## INTRODUCTION

Over the last decade, the attention of the development community has shifted from preoccupation with economic growth to emphasis on distribution. The development process is increasingly being assessed in terms of equity as well as growth. The traditional view held a distinct trade-off between efficiency and equity. Recent experience (particularly in Yugoslavia, China, and Korea), however, has cast doubt on this view. Similarly, the Kuznets hypothesis that inequality increases and then decreases, as income per caput grows, is no longer viewed as an iron-clad law. For example, on the basis of inequality measures in the Taiwan area (measured by the Gini coefficient G), Fei, Ranis, and Kuo have observed that:

> The Kuznets effect is a complex phenomenon that needs to be disaggregated. In its extreme form, it really is relevant only to the non-agricultural sector. In countries where agricultural activity is important – as it is in Taiwan and in most LDCs – growth does not necessarily conflict with equity, even before the turning point has been reached.

In the case of Taiwan, this study provides convincing evidence that the tendency of non-farm growth to increase G can be overpowered by the tendency to more egalitarian farm income growth; thus, the net effect can be to reduce inequality.

Thus, the distinct possibility exists that greater efficiency in resource use will assist in the achievement of a more equitable growth path as well as higher growth rates. The effective utilization and adoption of agricultural technology may, in fact, result in labour demand increasing faster than its supply, as well as food supply increasing faster than its demand. Recognizing the dialectic interactions between technological and institutional innovations, Hayami has even argued that the first step in designing an effective agricultural development policy is to recognize that, in the long run, there is no trade-off between growth and equity.

The vast majority of analytical frameworks that have been advanced for the evaluation of policies in LDCs, however, are primarily based on macro representations of the economy. Hence, few solutions have been offered that enhance both efficiency and equity. In evaluating equity issues, conventional macro or market-oriented analytical frameworks suffer serious limitations. For example, Krishna recently noted the fundamental inconsistency between recognizing the key characteristic of backwardness as pervasive fragmentation of labour and capital markets but yet using the ordinates of supply curves estimated from crude aggregate production or sales data as measures of the true opportunity costs of resources. Krishna further criticizes traditional analysis of aggregate gains and losses noting that the distribution of gains and losses between producers, as a group, and consumers, as a group, is of much less interest to policymakers than the distribution between rich producers and consumers and poor producers and consumers. Conventional welfare analysis, which is based on aggregate supply and demand relationships, sheds very little light on the distribution of gains between income brackets. When other objectives and structural features of poor economies are kept in mind, major arguments exist for second-best interventions which are neglected by conventional model formulations. Only by disaggregating conventional demand and supply analysis is it possible to correct some of the serious deficiencies of existing model formulations. This requires micro-based model formulations with explicit consideration of multiple objectives, in particular the equity and efficiency outcomes resulting from the implementation of various policies affecting the growth process.[1]

The purpose of this paper is to advance such a micro methodology for evaluating the efficiency and equity outcomes of various agricultural growth policies. The methodology is illustrated by way of a specific theoretical example. The example is necessarily simplified so that we may analytically derive the implications of the model by way of comparative statics. However, much more generality can be achieved in the context of actual empirical applications. A comparative static evaluation allows us to compare a host of different policies or governmental interventions. The model design is also readily amendable for the investigation of efficiency and equity consequences of integrated, comprehensive sets of policies. In an empirical context the model formulation admits the possibility that, for example, even though the distribution of income or landholdings might be quite stable under a single policy régime, egalitarian development strategies may be determined by integration of various policies. In fact, single policies, under certain economic environments, are shown to enhance efficiency as well as equity.

The major characteristics of the model formulation are presented in the next section. The mathematical representation of the model formulation is outlined in the third section, which emphasizes microeconomic behaviour as well as the aggregate or macro relationships for the agricultural production system. The fourth section presents some selected comparative static results for a number of governmental policies.[2] Finally, the last section presents some concluding remarks.

## THE GENERAL METHODOLOGY

The equity and efficiency impacts of selected governmental policies have been addressed by a number of different formulations, most of which are based on aggregate relationships. Generally, aggregate relationships are specified for an agricultural sector and a non-agricultural sector. The microeconomic foundations of these frameworks, however, are not generally specified. As a result, the thorny problems of aggregation are pushed aside.

The formulation in this paper, however, focuses on the agricultural sector alone in an effort to look at distributional issues within the sector. The sector is viewed as an aggregation of its parts; thus, the potential implications of various policies for both efficiency and equity are represented explicitly. The impact of governmental policies on agricultural production systems from the standpoint of both efficiency and equity is internally consistent at both the micro-level and the aggregate level. Within agricultural production systems, the general equilibrium effects of various policies are captured.

In the model formulation, land assumes a crucial role. As noted in numerous previous studies, the distribution of land has been found to be the dominant determinant of the distribution of income and access to non-land inputs (see, for example, Repetto and Shah, 1975 and several studies cited by Lappe and Collins, 1977). Given this focus, the model is structured to be able to evaluate land reform or the effects of redistributing land. The model formulation admits the possibility that redistribution of land is economically feasible without loss of output owing to the decline in the average productivity of land with an increase in farm size.

Along with the emphasis on the distribution of land, the model incorporates a number of important features including uncertainty, varying degrees of risk aversion, both fixed and variable costs of technology adoption, and credit constraints. It can thus be shown that the equity and efficiency effects of various policies depend critically upon the distribution of credit and risk preferences across various segments of the farm population. Although the example does not formally incorporate the distribution of human capital, it is a feature that can be easily accommodated with the methodology.

The driving force for growth in the model centres on new technology. Following the empirical results reported in Hayami, Ruttan, and Southworth, 1979, this feature of the model formulation simply recognizes that most output growth results from technology. Following this assumption, the model specification at the micro-level is essentially that which has emerged from the adoption literature. (For a recent survey, see Feder, Just, and Zilberman, 1982.) In this literature, the conventional wisdom is that constraints to rapid adoption involve factors such as the lack of credit, limited access to information, aversion to risk, inadequate farm size, insufficient human capital, absence of equipment to relieve labour shortages (thus preventing timely operations), and chaotic supply of complementary inputs (such as seeds, chemicals, and water).

Many development projects have sought increased growth through technological adoption by removing some of these constraints, for example, by introducing facilities to provide credit, information, orderly supply of necessary and complementary inputs, infrastructure investments, marketing networks, and the like. Some of these policies affect the fixed costs of adoption while others influence the variable costs. Thus, a general model specification must deal with both the discrete and continuous aspects of technological choice. This complicates the model specification but allows it to be used as a vehicle for evaluating a wide array of policies. In the model formulation presented below, the policies that are readily admitted include export subsidies or threshhold prices, credit funding enhancement, credit subsidies, fixed crop insurance, price stabilization, input subsidies, and extension programmes. This set of policies includes a number of instruments often pursued by governments of developing countries.

A complete analytical framework for investigating adoption processes at the farm level and its implications for both efficiency and equity must be based on a decision-making model for individual farmers determining both the extent and intensity of new technology utilization. Generally, decisions of a farm in such a model are assumed to be derived from the maximization of expected utility (or expected profit) subject to land availability, credit, and other constraints. Profit is a function of the farmer's choice of crops and technology. It, therefore, depends on his discrete selection of a technology from a mix of technologies and on a continuous choice of intensity with which to use the modern technology package.

To illustrate these points, the example below uses a stylized model involving two discrete technologies, traditional and modern. Given the discrete technology choice, income depends continuously on land allocation among crop varieties, the production function parameters of these crop varieties, the prices of inputs and outputs, and the annualized costs associated with the discrete technological choice. Given the land and variable input values, the perceived income may be regarded as a random variable embodying objective uncertainties with respect to yields and prices and subjective uncertainties associated with the farmer's incomplete information on the production function parameters.

The treatment of uncertainty and risk aversion must assume a central role in the model formulation if the risky perception of new technologies by individual farmers is to be captured. For this purpose there have been two major methods employed in both theoretical and empirical models. One approach employs *ad hoc* safety rules which are convenient and useful for planning purposes, especially using linear and nonlinear programming techniques (Roumasset, Boussard, and Singh, 1979). The other methodology, with a more sound axiomatic foundation, assumes expected utility maximization by farmers. The example below uses the latter approach. Utility of individual farmers is assumed to be negative exponential utility with normal yield distributions or quadratic utility. Under these assumptions, each farmer's objective function is linear in the means, variances, and covariances of revenues and is quadratic in the areas allocated to different crop varieties. The linear risk coefficient is assumed to vary with farm size thus preserving the tendency of absolute risk aversion to decline as farm size increases.

Most adoption studies also assume that the amount of land a farmer can operate each period is given; thus, he maximizes his expected utility subject to land availability. Imperfections in the credit and labour markets may also result in credit and labour availability constraints that affect the actual choice. The case of binding land and credit constraints is considered below, but labour constraints can be considered in a similar manner.

Once such a micro model of the decision-maker's problem is specified so as to be sensitive to the factor affecting individual farmers in developing agriculture, the methodology is applied as follows. First, response functions depicting the reactions (decisions, income, and welfare) of individual farmers to various policy, market, and informational factors is derived. Second, the distribution of information, human and capital resources, and preferences among farmers is estimated or specified. Third, the equity and efficiency performance measures of interest are determined by integrating the reaction functions of farmers with respect to the distribution of information, human and capital resources, and preferences among farmer. This integration can be done analytically in theoretical work and numerically in empirical work. Finally, the equity and efficiency effects of various policies can be analyzed accordingly.[3]

## AN EXAMPLE OF THE METHODOLOGY

To develop an explicit example of this approach that can illustrate the types of results that can be obtained, consider initially a single farm with fixed landholdings $L$ valued at price $p_L$ and a traditional technology involving a subjective distribution of net returns per hectare $\pi_0 = p_0 y_0$ with mean $E(\pi_0) = m_0$ and variance $V(\pi_0) = \sigma_0$ where $p_0$ and $y_0$ are the price and yield, respectively under the traditional technology. Suppose a new technology is introduced under which the farmer can allocate some of his land to the traditional crop (at traditional costs) and some of his land to a new crop (or a new method of producing the same crop).

The second crop (technique), the 'modern crop', may be a high-yielding variety or a cash crop utilizing a modern input such as fertilizers, insecticides, and improved seeds. On the other hand, it may be more vulnerable to weather variations so that there is a relatively greater degree of uncertainty regarding the returns per hectare. Additional (and subjective) uncertainty may also accompany the modern crop due to the fact that the farmer is less familiar with the new technology. Considering this factor, the modern crop may be viewed as more risky even if, in reality, it is not more susceptible to extreme weather situations than the traditional crop.

The production of the modern crop is presumed to require a cost of $w$ for the modern input per hectare to attain a subjective distribution of net returns per hectare $\pi_1$ with mean $E(\pi_1) = m_1$ and variance $V(\pi_1) = \sigma_1$. The (opportunity) cost of funds used to finance the modern input is given by $r$ so that $\pi_1 = p_1y_1 - w(1 + r)$ where $p_1$ and $y_1$ are the price and yield of the modern crop, respectively, and $p_1y_1$ is normally distributed. Also, suppose that net returns of the traditional and modern crops are correlated with $\text{corr}(\pi_0, \pi_1) = \rho$. Net returns for both technologies are assumed to be generated by a multivariate normal distribution with the relevant covariance matrix assumed to be positive definite. Also note that the variances and covariances include *subjective* uncertainty about yields and market access (prices) and may thus be influenced by both experience and extension efforts.

The farmer must either allocate all his land to the traditional technology or incur a fixed set-up cost, $k$, for the new technology in which case he can allocate his land in any proportion between the two technologies. Thus, the investment decision is a discrete choice whereas the land-allocation decision is a continuous choice.[4] In addition to the fixed set-up cost $k$ for which the annualized cost is $rk$, the farmer also incurs a variable cost, $w$ per hectare, for adoption. Both of these costs must be considered in the context of available credit $K$ in making the adoption decision. The credit constraint is

$$\text{I}(k + wL_1) \leq K$$

where $\text{I} = 0$ if the modern technology is not adopted, $\text{I} = 1$ if the modern technology is adopted, and $L_1$ is the amount of land allocated to the new technology.

Now assume that the farmer is risk averse with utility function $U(\cdot)$ defined on wealth, $U' >, U'' \leq 0$. Suppose that wealth, $W$, at the end of each season is represented by the sum of land value, $p_L L$, and the net return from production. Where $L_0$ is the amount of land allocated to the traditional technology, the decision problem is thus:

$$\max_{\substack{I = 0, 1 \\ L_0, L_1}} EU\,[p_L L + \pi_0 L_0 + I(\pi_1 L_1 - rk)] \qquad [1]$$

subject to

$$L_0 + IL_1 \leq L$$
$$I(k + wL_1) \leq K$$
$$L_0, L_1 \geq 0.$$

The results below assume that risk aversion is not so great or returns so poor as to prevent use of all available land. Thus, the land constraint can be replaced by a strict equality.

To solve this decision problem, first consider the choice of land allocation given the adoption decision. Assuming full utilization, the optimal decision with $I = 0$ is $L_0 = L$. Thus expected utility is

$$U_0(L) = EU[(p_L + \pi_0) L]. \quad [2]$$

Alternatively, given adoption, the objective of the decision problem in [1] becomes

$$\max_{L_0, L_1} EU[p_L L + \pi_0 L_0 + \pi_1 L_1 - rk] \quad [3]$$

subject to

$$L_0 + L_1 \leq L$$
$$k + wL_1 \leq K$$
$$L_0, L_1 \geq 0.$$

The solution to this problem is approximated by (see JRZ):

$$L_1 = \overline{L}_1 \equiv \begin{cases} 0 & \text{if } L_1^* < 0 \text{ or } k > K \\ L_1^* & \text{if } 0 \leq L_1^* \leq L \text{ and } (K-k)/w > 0 \\ (K-k)/w & \text{if } L > L_1^* > (K-k)/w > 0 \\ L & \text{if } (K-k)/w > L \text{ and } L_1^* > L \end{cases} \quad [4]$$

and $L_0 = \overline{L}_0 \equiv L - \overline{L}_1$

where

$$L_1^* = \frac{E(\Delta\pi)}{\phi V(\Delta\pi)} + LR \quad [5]$$

$$R = \frac{\sigma_0^2 - \rho\sigma_0\sigma_1}{\sigma_0^2 + \sigma_1^2 - 2\rho\sigma_0\sigma_1} \quad [6]$$

$$\Delta\pi = \pi_1 - \pi_0 \quad [7]$$

$$\phi = \frac{-U''(\overline{W})}{U'(\overline{W})} \quad [8]$$

$$W = p_L L + m_0 L + E(\Delta\pi) L_1 - rk. \quad [9]$$

Note that $\phi$ is the Arrow-Pratt coefficient of absolute risk aversion at expected wealth (see Arrow, 1971).

This result is intuitively clear from Figure 1 upon noting that (3) is a concave programming problem with linear constraints. Assuming full utilization of land, the optimal solution must lie on the line *ac*. Note that $L_1^*$ is the optimal solution for $L_1$ when negative choices for land quantities are possible (corresponding to the broken lines in Fig. 1). Thus, by concavity of the objective function, the optimum is at point c if $L_1^* < 0$. If credit is abundant (for example $K = K_1$ in Fig. 1), then the optimum is at point *a* if $L_1^* > L$. However, if credit is insufficient to allow complete adoption such as if $K = K_0$ in Figure 1, then the segment ab is infeasible because of credit limitations. Thus the optimum is at point *b* if $L_1^* > (K - k)/w$.

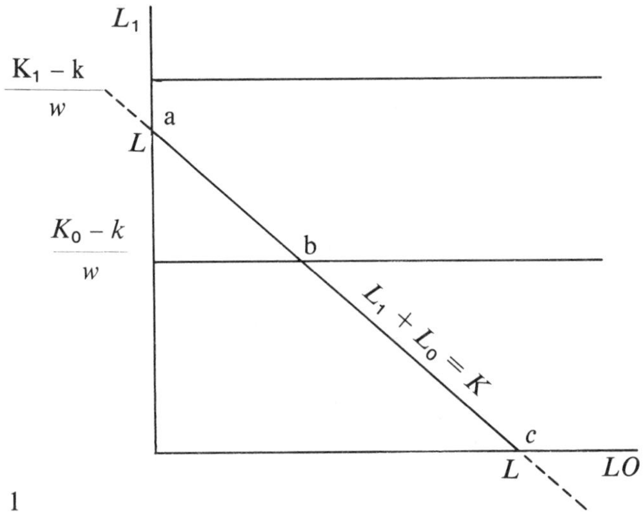


Fig. 1

To determine the technology choice, let

$$U_1 (L, \bar{L}_1) = EU[p_L L + \pi_0 (L - \bar{L}_1) + \pi_1 \bar{L}_1 - rk] \qquad [10]$$

Assuming either that the farmer is myopic (or considers future periods to be like the current one), the farmer selects the traditional technology if $U_0 > U_1$ and selects the new technology if $U_1 > U_0$.

Corresponding to (4), the expected 'welfare' of each farmer can be represented as follows:

$$\bar{U}(L) = \begin{cases} EU[(p + \pi_0) L], & \text{if } L_1^* < 0 \text{ or } k < K \\ EU[p_L L + \pi_0(L - L_1^*) + \pi_1 L_1^* - rk], & \text{if } 0 < L^* \leq L \text{ and } \frac{K-k}{w} > 0 \\ EU\left[p_L L + \pi_0\left(L - \frac{K-k}{w}\right) + \pi_1 \frac{K-k}{w} - rk\right], & \text{if } L > L_1^* > \frac{K-k}{w} > 0 \\ EU[(p_L + \pi_1) L - rk], & \text{if } \frac{K-k}{w} > L \text{ and } L_1^* > L. \end{cases} \qquad [11]$$

In this context, equity and efficiency issues can be investigated quantitatively once the distribution of microparameters among farmers is specified. The results here focus on the distribution of risk preferences, farm size, and credit availability with the farm(er)s assumed to be identical in other respects. This is done by first specifying a distribution of farm size and then specifying a relationship between farm size and risk preferences and credit.

Suppose the distribution of landholdings follows a Pareto distribution with density function

$$f(L) = (\gamma - 1)^{\gamma}\, \gamma^{1-\gamma}\, \overline{L}^{\gamma} L^{-\gamma-1} \quad \text{for } \frac{\gamma - 1}{\gamma}\overline{L} < L < \infty;\ \gamma > 1. \quad [12]$$

Note that the average farm size is $\overline{L}$ and that $\gamma$ is a measure of concentration of the farm size distribution. As $\gamma$ increases, the farm size distribution becomes more equitable with both small farms tending to become larger and large farms tending to become smaller.

Given this distribution of farm size, risk preferences as reflected by the coefficient of absolute risk aversion ($\phi$) are assumed to be related to initial wealth or farm size following the equation

$$\phi = \widetilde{B}\, W_0^{-\eta} = BL^{-\eta}, \quad 0 < \eta < 1, \qquad [13]$$

where initial wealth is $W_0 = p_L L$ and $\widetilde{B} = Bp_L^{-\eta}$. Absolute risk aversion is assumed to be constant for each individual farmer; however, $\eta > 0$ implies that larger farmers have less absolute risk aversion and $\eta < 1$ implies that larger farmers have more relative risk aversion following Arrow's arguments.[5] To simplify, the availability of credit is also assumed to be related to initial wealth or, equivalently, farm size, following $K = aL$.

For constant absolute risk aversion of individual farmers, the expressions in (11) can be represented as certainty equivalents. In particular, given (11), (12), and (13) and constant absolute risk aversion, the certainty equivalent is:[6]

$$C(L) = \begin{cases} U_0^* = (p_L + m_0)\,\overline{L} - \dfrac{B}{2}\sigma_0^2\, \overline{L}^{2-\eta}, \text{ if } 0 < L_1 \leq \hat{L}_1 \\[2ex] U_{11}^* = \left[p_L + m_0 + E(\Delta\pi)\dfrac{a}{w}\right]\overline{L} - \dfrac{B}{2}\dfrac{k^2}{w^2} V(\Delta\pi) L^{\eta} \\[2ex] \quad + B\dfrac{k}{w}\, v(\Delta\pi)\, \dfrac{a}{w} + R_v \overline{L}^{1-\eta} - \dfrac{B}{2} V \pi_0 + \dfrac{a}{w}\Delta\pi\, \overline{L}^{2-\eta} \\[2ex] \quad - E(\Delta\pi)\dfrac{k}{w} - rk, \text{ if } \hat{L}_1 < L_1^* \leq \hat{L}_2 \\[2ex] U_{12}^* = (p_L + m_1)\,\overline{L} - \dfrac{B}{2}\sigma_1^2\, \overline{L}^{2-\eta} - rk, \text{ if } \hat{L}_2 < L_1 \leq \hat{L}_3 \end{cases} \qquad [14]$$

$$U_{13}^{*} = [p_L + m_0 (1 - R) + m_1 R\,]\,\overline{L} + \frac{E^2(\Delta\pi)}{2\;BV(\Delta\pi)} L^{\eta}$$
$$- \frac{B\,\sigma_0^2\,\sigma_1^2(1 - p^2)}{2\;V(\Delta\pi)} \overline{L}^{\,2-\eta} - rk, \text{ if } L_1 > \hat{L}_3.$$

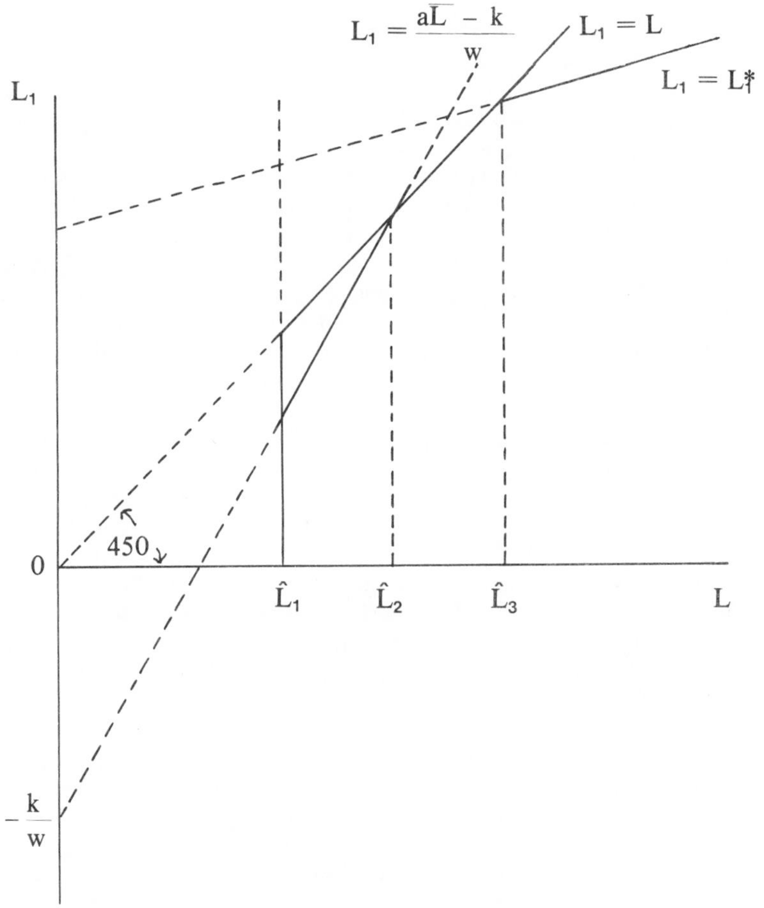


Fig. 2

The four expressions appearing in (14) thus provide a basis for evaluating the welfare effects (compensating or equivalent variation) of policy changes (Just, Hueth, and Schmitz, 1982). The four segments are graphically displayed in figure 2. In this figure, the intensity of adoption is measured by $L_1$ which is physically constrained to lie between the lines $L_1 = L$ and $L_1 = 0$. It is constrained to lie on or below the credit limitation boundary, $L_1 = (K$

$-k)/w = (aL - k)/w$. Subject to these limitations, the intensity of adoption follows the expression derived in (5) for $L_1^*$. Below $\hat{L}_1$, farm size is insufficient for fixed costs to be adequately spread to make adoption worthwhile. Between this boundary and $\hat{L}_2$, adoption becomes desirable but credit limitations prevent full adoption. On the interval defined by the bounds $\hat{L}_2$ and $\hat{L}_3$, full adoption occurs since credit becomes non-binding. At farm size $\hat{L}_3$ and above perceived risk becomes sufficiently large to induce diversification among the two technologies.

## EQUITY AND EFFICIENCY

On the basis of the above model, a number of analytical results have been derived in JRZ. These analytical results focus on the efficiency and equity effects of various governmental policies. The results clearly demonstrate that farm size within each of the decomposed class of farmers are unaffected by some policies and strongly influenced by others. For example, policies that enhance the perceived mean return of the modern technology (for example export subsidies and extension programmes) have no effect on the welfare of small non-adopting farmers, a unitary effect on full adopting farmers, and a less than unitary effect on partial adopters, in the case where the major barriers to adoption are risk aversion and set-up cost. In the case where the major barriers to adoption are credit instead of set-up cost, once again we have no effect on the small non-adopting farms, a greater than unitary effect on partial adopting farms, and a unitary effect on full adopting farms.

Turning to specific policies, first consider export subsidies or threshold pricing. For these policies, if the new technology pertains to a new crop, small non-adopters are unaffected while larger full adopters and partial adopters become better off thus widening the income distribution. Where risk aversion and set-up cost are the major barriers to adoption, the minimum scale required for adoption declines while the maximum size of full-adopting farms increases; thus, more adoption is induced. If the new technology pertains to an existing crop, then export subsidy or threshold pricing policies will cause an increase in aggregate farm income if the major barriers to adoption are credit and set-up cost. If the major barriers to adoption are risk aversion and set-up cost, the minimum scale required for adoption declines while the maximum size of full-adopting farms increases and the overall level of adoption is enhanced. However, if the major barriers to adoption are credit and set-up cost alone, adoption is unaffected and, thus, there are no efficiency effects. Hence, under export subsidies or threshold pricing policies, it is possible to achieve efficiency with less equity, no efficiency with less equity, and efficiency with improved equity.

In the case of a credit subsidy policy, small non-adopters are unaffected, while both larger partial adopters and full adopters are made better off. In the case where the major barriers to adoption are risk aversion and set-up costs, the minimum scale required for adoption declines while the maximum size of fully adopting farms increases and overall adoption is enhanced. If credit and set-up costs are the major barriers to adoption, then technological adoption is unaffected. Thus, this policy can result in efficiency with less equity or no efficiency with less equity.

The effect of a public credit programme that increases credit availability at the market rate of interest is to augment aggregate farm income if credit and set-up cost are the only major barriers to adoption. Under these barriers, small non-adopters and large full adopters are unaffected while the well-being of mid-size partial adopters is increased; the minimum scale required for both partial adoption and full adoption is decreased so that the overall adoption increases. Hence, for this policy instrument, growth with greater equity can be achieved depending on the distribution of available credit.

Crop insurance or price stabilization schemes have effects which depend upon whether the new technology pertains to a new crop or the existing crop. In the case of the new crop, these schemes improve aggregate farm income if the major barriers to adoption are risk aversion and set-up cost while farmer welfare is unaffected if the major barriers to adoption are only credit and set-up cost. For the case of the existing crop, the effect of actuarially fair crop insurance or mean-preserving price stabilization is to improve aggregate farm income according to the expected utility criterion if the major barriers to adoption are risk aversion and set-up cost, while farmer well-being is unaffected in the case where the major barriers to adoption are credit and set-up cost. Hence, this policy can result in growth with less inequity, no growth with no change in equity, and greater efficiency with increased equity in an expected income sense.

The effect of an input subsidy policy is to increase aggregate farm income. Small non-adopting farmers are unaffected, while the welfare of both fully adopting and partially adopting farmers is improved. In the case where risk aversion and set-up costs are the major barriers to adoption, the minimum scale required for adoption decreases while the maximum size of full-adopting farms is increased so the overall adoption increases. In the case where the major barriers to adoption are credit and set-up costs, the minimum scale required for adoption is unaffected while the minimum size of full adopting farms decreases so that overall adoption increases. Thus, it follows that this particular policy by itself results in greater efficiency with inequity.

Governmental intervention involving a subsidy on the fixed cost of adoption leaves small non-adopting farms unaffected while the welfare of larger fully and partially adopting farmers increases. The minimum scale required for adoption declines as the maximum size of fully adopting farms is unaffected in the case where the major barriers to adoption are risk aversion and set-up cost while the minimum scale associated with full adoption declines in the case where credit and set-up costs are the major barriers to adoption. Overall adoption increases in any case, and we are left with improved efficiency but greater inequity.

The effect of extension activities that improve farmers' subjective distributions of returns under the new technology or that reduce perceived search and learning costs connected with adoption is to increase average expected farmer welfare and the overall level of adoption. These increases are shared by larger farms with sufficient scale for adoption while farms below the minimum scale required for economic adoption are unaffected.

The effect of land-reform policies depends critically upon the nature of the barriers to adoption. For example, the effect of an increase in land endowment among adopting farmers with non-binding credit is to increase the intensity of adoption. The effect among adopting farmers with binding credit is to reduce the intensity of adoption since all land is allocated to the old technology.

The above thumb-nail sketch of the analytical results demonstrates quite clearly that single policies often prove unable to enhance both efficiency and equity. Export subsidy or threshold pricing policies prove effective in enhancing efficiency in some instances and ineffective in others. Without knowledge of the nature of the barriers to adoption, credit funding policies can be indeed precarious. We can only ensure the effectiveness of insurance or price stabilization schemes by combining such policies with credit-related policies to relieve potentially important barriers to adoption. The effectiveness of modern input subsidies also depends upon the nature of adoption barriers. Only by combining credit policies with modern input subsidies is it possible to ensure that small farmers benefit. Similarly, the influence of extension policies on equity outcomes depends upon its integration with other instruments. Only by combining extension programmes with other policies is it safe to infer that the minimum scale required for adoption will be decreased.

The above results reveal varying qualitative effects that can be achieved by different policies. They demonstrate the importance of different types of barriers to adoption and perhaps, more importantly, the need to operate with more than a single policy régime. It is particularly obvious that the pursuit of a single policy régime is most acute for small farms. The analytical results show how the pursuit of a single policy will generally result in a trade-off between efficiency and equity while a combination of policies may attain enhanced efficiency and equity simultaneously.

## CONCLUSION

The static representation advanced in this paper to investigate the efficiency and equity effects of various policies can be extended in a number of directions. The dynamic counterpart of the model presented in the third section involves an intertemporal optimization problem. At the beginning of each period, the type of technology the farmer will use is determined along with allocation of land among crops and the use of variable inputs. Moreover, equations of motion for the economic environment, human and capital accumulation, can be incorporated. In this formulation, at the end of each period, the actual yields, revenues, and profits are realized. This added information, as well as the experience accumulated during the period and the information on the outcomes obtained by other farmers, can be used to update the parameters that are used in the actual decision-making process for the subsequent period.

Other potential extensions include allowing not only the degree of risk aversion to vary across farmers but their *perceived* risk as well. In a dynamic context, the model can also be generalized to allow the criterion function (utility function) to vary over time as well as across farmers. To operationalize these and other potential extensions, however, requires a significant amount of empirical estimation. Even without such extensions, the model presented in the third section requires a considerable amount of empirical estimation.

Empirical analysis must begin by decomposing the farming population into relevant classes. This decomposition can be accomplished endogenously by the specification of a discrete/continuous behavioural model. The discrete choice relates to technology, while the continuous choice is the amount of land allocated across technologies. Available secondary data can be employed by a simultaneous discrete choice model of farmer behaviour (Hanemann). The explanatory variables appearing in this model include a vector of expected returns per hectare defined by capital technology, the variances and covariances of returns defined across crops and technologies, variable cost of modern inputs, the opportunity cost of financial funds, fixed set-up costs of various technologies, available credit, and the effect of various extension and learning activities on perceived return distribution.

Estimated relationships between the above explanatory variables and discrete technology choices and continuous land allocation choices is one component of the required empirical structure. A second component is an estimation of the distribution of landholdings. A third empirical component must relate farm size or other observable information to risk preferences. Estimation of this relationship will most likely require the use of primary data from representative samples. The final empirical component requires a set of linking equations between the policy instruments and the specified explanatory variables. For example, the empirical relationship between price supports and the vector of mean returns and the covariance matrix of returns across technologies must be determined.

Armed with the above four empirical components, a number of operational uses of the proposed framework are possible. First, one can simply evaluate numerically the effects of various policies through the four empirical components to determine the most effective integration of the various policies.

Secondly, the specification of a formal criterion function would allow the search for the optimal set of policies. Various trade-off relationships or alternative weightings in a scalar criterion function including two principal performance measures, efficiency and equity, could be specified, or a host of such criteria could be investigated through parametric analysis.

Another potential use of the four empirical components relates to the notion of political economic markets. In a positive analysis of government behaviour, the four components can represent a constraint structure which, along with a specified criterion function, can be used to infer *via* revealed preference methodology the weights across both efficiency and equity (Rausser, 1982). Such a positive analysis would allow economic researchers to effectively perform a role as social critics or as organizers of rural poor as suggested by Vyas, in this volume, and Krishna, 1982; that is, if past policies imply a value scheme which in some sense deviates from the public interest, then the implicit choice of trade-offs between efficiency and equity should at least be exposed. Along similar lines, various economic interest groups could also employ the four empirical components to determine which set of policies they are prepared to support or oppose.

In the final analysis, the proposed theoretical framework and its empirical counterpart will prove to be a valuable element in the tool kit of policy analysts if and only if sound data support systems are designed and maintained. The required data support system for the proposed framework is indeed demanding. Nevertheless, the expected benefits from designing and maintaining such a data support system may far outweigh its associated cost.

## NOTES

This work has been done as part of BARD project 1-10-79.

[1]There have been some multiple-objective programming approaches advanced in the development context (e.g., Loucks) but, as yet, there is a lack of sufficient micro detail.

[2]A more lengthy version of this paper which presents the formal propositions and proofs of the comparative static results is available upon request (Just, Rausser, and Zilberman, hereafter referred to as JRZ).

[3]With this background, one can view the methodology proposed here as an application of the general approach advanced by Johanson and Sato and applied elsewhere by Hochman, Zilberman, and Just.

[4]For simplicity, the variable input level per hectare associated with the new technology is assumed here to be predetermined. Some of the ramifications of assuming variable input per hectare to be a choice variable are investigated by Just and Zilberman.

[5]K.J. Arrow, 'The Theory of Risk Aversion', in K.J. Arrow (ed), *Essays in the Theory of Risk Bearing,* Markham, Chicago, 1971, Ch. 3.

[6]Note that the expression V is derived by approximating

$$\frac{dEU}{dL_1} = E[U'(\pi_1 - \pi_0)] \simeq 0,$$

by $E\ (\Delta\pi) - \phi\ [L_1\ V\ (\Delta\pi) + L\ (p\sigma_0\sigma_1 - \sigma_0^2)[\ = 0$ where $V$ donotes the variance operator and $\Delta\pi = \pi_1 - \pi_0$. Note also that the results appearing in (14) are formally derived in JRZ.

## REFERENCES

Arrow, K.J., 'The Theory of Risk Aversion', *Essays in the Theory of Risk Bearing,* Arrow K.J. (ed.), Markham, Chicago 1971.

Feder, Gershon, Just, Richard E. and Zilberman, David, 'Adoption of Agricultural Innovations: A Survey', Department of Agricultural and Resource Economics, Working Paper No. 225, University of California, Berkeley, 1982.

Fei, John C., Ranis, Gustav and Kuo, Shirley W. Y., *Growth With Equity: The Taiwan Case,* Oxford University Press 1979.

Hanemann, W. Michael, 'Discrete/Continuous Models of Consumer Demand', Department of Agricultural and Resource Economics, Working Paper No. 198, University of California, Berkeley, 1982.

Hayami, Yujiro, 'Growth and Equity: Is There a Trade-Off?' This volume p. 105.

Hayami, Y., Ruttan, V.W. and Southworth, H. M. (eds.), *Agricultural Growth in Taiwan, Korea and the Philippines,* University of Hawaii Press, 1979.

Hochman, E., Zilberman, D. and Just, R. E., 'Two Goal Regional Environmental Policy: The Case of the Santa Ana River Basin', *Journal of Environmental Economics and Management* 4 (1971): pp. 25-39.

Johanson, Leif, *Production Functions: An Integration of Micro and Macro Short Run and Long Run Aspects*, North Holland Publishing Company, Amsterdam, 1972.

Just, Richard E., Hueth, Darrell L., and Schmitz, Andrew, *Applied Welfare Economics and Public Policy,* Prentice-Hall, New York, 1982.

Just, Richard E., and Zilberman, David, 'Stochastic Structure, Farm Size, and Technological Adoption in Developing Countries', *Oxford Economic Papers,* (forthcoming).

Just, Richard E., Rausser, Gordon C., and Zilberman, David, 'Modeling Equity and Efficiency in Agricultural Production Systems', Department of Agricultural and Resource Economics, University of California, Berkeley, 1982.

Krishna, Raj., 'Some Aspects of Agricultural Growth, Price Policy and Equity in Developing Countries', Paper presented at the American Economic Association Annual Meeting, August, 1982.

Lappe, F.M., and Collins, J., *Food First – Beyond the Myth of Scarcity,* Ballantine Books, New York, 1977.

Loucks, D.P. 'Planning for Multiple Goals', in Blitzer, C.R., Clark, P.B., and Taylor, L., *Economy-Wide Models and Development Planning,* Oxford University Press, 1975.

Rausser, Gordon C., 'Political Economic Markets: PERTs and PESTs in Food and Agriculture', *American Journal of Agricultural Economics,* December, 1982, (forthcoming).

Repetto, R., and Shah, Vimal, 'Internal Policies for Income Redistribution: A Case Study in Rural India', Gujarat Institute of Area Planning, Ahmedabad, 1975.

Roumasset, J. A., Boussard, J.M., and Singh, I. (eds.), *Risk, Uncertainty, and Agricultural Development,* Agricultural Development Council, New York, 1979, Chapters 3 and 4.

Sato, Kazuo, *Production Functions and Aggregation,* North Holland Publishing Company, Amsterdam, 1975.

Vyas, V.S., 'Growth and Equity in Asian Agriculture: A Synoptic View'. This volume p. 52.

## DISCUSSION OPENING – L. GARRIDO EGIDO

I have found the model presented by Dr Just very interesting. This model, which integrates equity and efficiency, represents an important contribution and I wish to congratulate its authors.

It is, first of all, pertinent to make a preliminary comment on the concepts of efficiency and equity. Efficiency can be measured, both in physical and in monetary terms, by means of partial or global indices. Clearly, it is the latter that have to be used when measuring agricultural development, that is, this sector's technical progress. The indices used in the paper, however, are only concerned with economic factors. This is because the inclusion of social and political factors would present the problem of their quantification. Still, the concept of efficiency from both a collective and a long-term perspective, should include all aspects, like, for example, those relating to resource conservation and development, and to the attainment of an equilibrium state, of an effective social integration, and of the highest social welfare.

There is, therefore, need for a definition of these social and political objectives, upon which depend the efficiency level of agriculture, the development of which is assessed with respect to an equity level to be attained particularly via the distribution to both agricultural and non-agricultural groups of the benefits arising from such development. The question then is how to integrate these hard-to-measure elements into an agricultural development model which embodies an attempt to integrate efficiency and equity.

With respect to the distribution of the benefits from agricultural development, I wish to consider two questions.

Firstly, in most industrialized countries, modern techniques – high yield varieties, greater use of fertilizer and farm machinery and so on – have made higher yields and, as a consequence, overall agricultural productivity possible. Farmers' incomes will then be higher if agricultural prices will be kept at the same level by means of a governmental price policy. On the other hand, if agricultural prices are reduced, the benefits from agricultural development will be transferred to the consumers. Hence, the distribution of the benefits from agricultural development between farmers and non-farmers depends on Government policy, which is determined on the basis of a political option which takes the relation between farmers' and non-farmers' income levels into consideration. In the industrialized countries, however, the effort to improve the position of the agricultural sector through price manipulation has resulted in a relatively insignificant improvement. It has also resulted in production surpluses as a result of the abundant use of resources – especially labour – in agriculture. The combination of price and structural policies, as it has been implemented, has not been a solution. Could other actions be combined with these policies like, for example, direct income transfers in favour of certain agricultural groups? What should be the characteristics of these measures to ensure compatibility between efficiency and equity?

The second question concerns the different influence of technical progress in different areas. The use of new seed varieties has determined an appreciable increase in certain crops, though only in those areas for which such varieties proved appropriate. These regions have thus been able to improve their relative position *vis-à-vis* those which had to continue to use traditional varieties. Similar situations result from the use of other new techniques: mechanization, irrigation, more intensive fertilizer utilization and so forth.

From the above it follows that technical progress in the agricultural sector is either a cause of new regional disparities or it may exacerbate existing ones. This is so, even without taking into account all other consequences arising from an economy's general development which in their totality, and according to a study of the CEPE of the UN, exacerbate regional income disparities in less developed countries.

In the EEC, different policy measures are implemented to transfer income directly into mountain areas and into other less-favoured regions. In irrigated areas, some countries have adopted a measure which is related to farming enterprises. This is the case of Spain and Mexico, where the Governments have expropriated parts of large estates and financed some of the costs incurred. By so doing, while the goal of greater equity is pursued via the distribution of the benefits from irrigation, higher efficiency is obtained by the reduction in the size of large estates.

One may also wonder whether other measures would be available. An example would be the adoption of price differentials with the aim of reducing the price of those commodities produced in areas which are able to reap the greater benefits from the development of their agriculture. Another possibility might be the transfer of these benefits to the government *via* the levy of a land-tax. Could other measures be devised? Would problems be encountered in their administration? These are some questions which I think can be raised in connection with the paper of which Dr. Just has provided us with a fine exposition.

## GENERAL DISCUSSION* – RAPPORTEUR: ERIC MONKE

Contributors to discussion of the Hayami paper pointed out that the Ricardian approach to growth and distribution was not appropriate for all cases of agricultural development. The European case provides a counter example, where low population growth rates and extreme inequality prevailed in the presence of significant rates of economic growth. Other contributors identified sources of improved income distribution additional to the rightward shift in labour demand induced by new technologies. Human capital investment was suggested as a supply-side approach, which would raise labour wages *via* increases in worker productivity. Hayami's assertion that increased food prices favoured only large farmers was questioned. Increasing prices may lead to increased wage rates if labour supplies are limited since increased output prices will increase the value marginal product of labour, and thus shift the demand curve for labour rightward. Regarding the use of tractors, it was stated that they may be land-saving when they facilitate multiple cropping.

Discussion of the Just/Rausser/Zilderman paper questioned the viability of empirical estimation of the model. Difficulties in the process of preference identification were suggested as barriers to the estimation of an individual utility function. Additional problems were the requirement of the model that every individual utility function be estimated, and the derivations of a deterministic basis for the comparison of utilities across individuals, which is necessary to the valuation of equity effects. An advantage seen in

*Papers by Hayami and Just, Rausser and Zilderman.

the model was the incorporation of attitudinal variables, such as risk. Differences in attitudes towards risk may be a partial explanation of income distribution.

Participants in the discussion included H. von Witzte, M. G. Chandrakanth, Adolf Weber, H. M. G. Herath and H. L. Chawla.

SURJIT S. BHALLA AND MARK LEISERSON*

# *Issues in the Measurement and Analysis of Income Distribution in Developing Countries: Some Comparative Perspectives*

## INTRODUCTION

It would be foolhardy (not to say foolish) to attempt in a brief space a well-balanced review of the whole complex of issues surrounding the distribution of income in developing countries. This paper has a much more modest aim – to take a critical look at some of the analytic and empirical work over the past years in order to see what lessons, if any, may be derived for future research and, more particularly, for the incorporation of distributive and policy–alleviating objectives into development policy.

The emphasis on policy is important because explicit or implicit policy objectives and judgements are likely to have important consequences for ostensibly technical issues of measurement as well as for more theoretical questions of analytic design and specification. As has frequently been noted in other areas of economics, the work of even the most academic of economists tends to be sensitive to perceptions of major areas of policy interest. And the evolution of work on distributive aspects of development has both derived from, and contributed to, the changing perspectives within which specific policy problems are perceived as requiring greater or lesser attention.

The rest of the paper, therefore, tries to follow this evolution by characterizing successive stages of research on income distribution in terms of the types of problems addressed and their links to the framework of development policy concerns. Particular studies are singled out for illustrative purposes but we have made no attempt to be comprehensive.

*The views expressed should not be interpreted as necessarily reflecting those of the World Bank.

## STAGES OF RESEARCH

*Growth, inequality and decile shares*

In the policy environment of the 1950s and early 1960s, there was an emphasis on growth and the major policy focus was the improvement in per caput income. Distributional considerations took a secondary position to a concern with savings and capital accumulation. Indeed, one strand of thought in that period was that inequality might well be *necessary* for growth. The linkage came from acceptance of the current income theory of savings, according to which the rich were observed to save at a higher rate[1] Thus, higher savings out of a given pot required a higher inequality. This concern with savings and growth seems to have been a major influence on subsequent research[2] on the relationship between inequality and growth (that is, did higher inequality lead to higher growth) and between growth and inequality (that is, did higher growth lead to worsening inequality through differential savings rates, for example do the rich get richer?).

The growth-inequality relationship was given a specific sign by Kuznets, who postulated that:

> In the process of growth, the earlier periods are characterized by a balance of counteracting forces that may have widened the inequality in the size distribution of total income for a while, because of the rapid growth of the non-agricultural sector and wider inequality within it. It is even more plausible to argue that the recent narrowing of income inequality observed in the developed countries was due to a combination of the narrowing inter-sectoral inequalities in product per worker, the decline in the share of property income in total income of households, and the institutional changes that reflect decisions concerning social security and full employment. (1963, p. 67)

As mentioned by Bacha (1977) research 'tended to short-cut the inter-sectoral differentials stage' and instead of relating growth to inequality proceeded to relate inequality to the *level* of income. This testing was in search of what has now come to be known as the Kuznets inverted U-curve hypothesis, and it was mainly approached as an empirical issue.

Since historical data for individual countries was scarce, analysts were constrained to infer inter-temporal behaviour from cross-country evidence. The methodology employed was straightforward. Data on the size distribution of household income was converted into an inequality measure,[3] and this measure related to per caput income and/or growth. The literature generated by this triple thrust was enormous.[4] The basic results which emerged were:

(a) the empirical evidence, generally cross sectional, seemed to confirm the Kuznets hypothesis;[5]
(b) though some argued that the poor had become absolutely worse off (Adelman-Morris (1973)), the general finding was that this was not the case (Cline (1975)) but as implied by (a) above, the poor did seem to lose in relative terms.

The following two sections are devoted to a critical analysis of these and other results. The discussion is conducted at two levels: (a) the reliability of conclusions, and (b) their usefulness in terms of policy. The former is affected by the appropriateness of the methodology and the reliability of data. Two particular questions addressed are (i) availability of methodologically appropriate data and (ii) reliability of the available data.

*Availability of appropriate data*

What are appropriate data for the measurement of income inequality? Since concern is with welfare levels, a meaningful basis for comparison is with individual income rather than household income. This follows from the simple observation that individuals in a two-person household earning $4,000 cannot be presumed to be at the same welfare level as individuals in a four-person household earning $6,000. Adjustment of household income for family size has continuously been emphasized by Kuznets (1976): 'It makes little sense to talk about inequality in the distribution of income among families or households by income per family or household when the underlying units differ so much in size . . . . Before any analysis can be undertaken, size distribution of families . . . . must be coverted to distribution of persons (or consumer equivalents),' (p. 87). The issue is of more than theoretical importance since adjustments for family size can materially affect the estimates of inequality. Deaton (1981), for instance, finds that a re-ordering of households according to expenditure per caput in Sri Lanka decreases the Gini coefficient from 0.2535 to 0.2376. Lluch (1981) shows that in Brazil the per caput income distribution is substantially more equal than the household income distribution, that is the bottom 40 per cent has a share of 11.1 per cent (per caput) compared to a share of 8.7 per cent (household).

Apart from the unit of measurement, problems remain with the definition used to measure income and the 'proper' definition has received considerable attention in the literature. It has been convincingly pointed out that the distinction between measured current income and theoretically preferable estimates of permanent income is a non-trivial one. Lilliard (1977), using panel data for US households, finds that permanent income inequality is much less than current income inequality. Using a different methodology, and the assumption that work is a choice variable (that is a 'full income' model) Kuznic and DaVanzo (1979) arrive at full income estimates of inequality for Malaysia which are less unequal than the current income estimate (for example the bottom 40 per cent of individuals receive 9 per cent of actual income but 13.7 per cent of full income).

What these above considerations suggest is that conventional analysis of income distribution may be seriously misleading. Ahluwalia recognized this problem: 'There are a number of conceptual and definitional problems in measuring income inequality and available surveys do not display any uniform practice in handling these problems', (1976, p. 339). But the data are used, nevertheless, by Ahluwalia in obtaining the U-curve described earlier (see note[5]) and the effect of mixing per caput with household income distributions is ignored.

*Reliability of available data*

Notwithstanding the conceptual problems pointed to earlier, available income distribution data for most countries is notoriously deficient. In a comprehensive survey of income distribution data for Latin America, Altimir (1977) concludes on the basis of 49 different surveys and census results that 'the lack of nationwide coverage in a large number of the available surveys can rarely be compensated by using complementary sources', and 'to accept that a household survey or census accurately depicts "the" overall income distribution for the country in question would be extremely unwise as a starting point for analysis' (p. 91).

Uncritical use of data can be misleading even when the time-series data on inequality are available for a particular country. Korea, for instance, annually publishes results of urban and rural income surveys. On the basis of these data, Rao (1978) concluded that 'Korea is seen as a country which has been quite successful in combining rapid growth with improved equity' (p. 383). If true, this result would mean either that the Kuznets U-curve was not an appropriate representation of an average country behaviour,[6] or that policies followed by Korea have an 'abnormal' but desirable effect on income inequality.[7]

However, serious limitations of the Korean data were first pointed out by Choo in 1975, and 'adjusted' income distributions were constructed by Choo and Kim in 1978. Bhalla (1979) also adjusts the data for various 'omissions' in the surveys. (These omissions included all residents of townships (12.2 per cent in 1976), landless labourers, single households, and the very rich, among others.) These adjustments suggest that inequality in household incomes worsened during the time period 1970–76 (the share of the bottom 40 per cent of the households declined from 18 per cent of income in 1970 to 15.4 per cent in 1976) thus *reversing* the Rao conclusion mentioned earlier.

Like Korea, the Taiwan area's growth rate has also been impressive and it is of considerable interest to study the evolution of its inequality. But like Korea, Taiwan's income distribution data are questionable. Fei, Ranis and Kuo (1979) provide a detailed analysis of Taiwanese inequality, and themselves note that the data showing an increase in the income share of the bottom 40 per cent from 11.3 in 1953 to 20.3 per cent in 1964 are extremely questionable. Sample size is just one of the problems. In 1953, the sample size was 301 households; in 1964, 3,000. However, a major thrust of the analysis is in explaining the *decline* in inequality from a Gini level of 0.32 in 1964 to 0.29 in 1972. One of the stylized facts of the income distribution literature is the slow *change* in inequality that is observed in most countries in the absence of drastic redistributive policies. The change from 0.32 to 0.29 during an eight-year period is plausible. What is less plausible is that this change could have occurred in just two years. Closer inspection of data shows the following Gini levels: 1964:0.321; 1966:0.323; 1968:0.326; 1970:0.293; 1971:0.295; and 1972:0.290. Observations for 1964 to 1968 are undistinguishably close, as are the Ginis for 1970 to 1972. Such a break in the series suggests (but this is just speculation) that a significant change in comparability – either in survey design, administration or coverage – took place during the period 1968 to 1970. In the absence of detailed attention to this question (the authors only discuss the limitations of pre-1964 data) it is difficult to place much weight on the figures.[8]

Despite the nature and magnitude of problems alluded to above, it is far from our intention to dismiss the 'first' stage of research on income distribution in developing countries. Our purpose has been to document the various problems involved, and to caution against hasty or potentially misleading conclusions. The cross country analysis was forced on researchers, mostly due to lack of appropriate longitudinal country data. And, subject to appropriate caveats, much has been learned from this first stage research:

1 Policy makers, survey organizers and researchers are now much more sensitive and knowledgeable about appropriate data for the study of income distribution.
2 Reliable point estimates of income distribution for several countries are now available. This should be useful for any future studies on changes in income distribution.
3 The causation running from inequality to growth has been shown to be tenuous on both theoretical and empirical grounds.
4 As development proceeds, measures of relative inequality have been observed to remain fairly stable, or slightly worsen, providing weak confirmation for the Kuznets hypothesis.[9]

### *Absolute poverty – measurement and interpretation*

A second stage of research on income distribution (started even before the above mentioned first stage results had been reached) reveals, in a classical manner, the influence of policy on research. By the late 1960s and early 1970s, increasing concern was being expressed at the inadequacy of growth alone to 'deliver the goods'. 'Trickle down' was alleged not to work at all or to work too slowly, so that indirect alleviation of poverty via growth needed to be complemented by direct attacks on poverty. The shift in policy emphasis was strongly articulated by McNamara in his speech in Nairobi in 1973 on the problems of the absolute poor. Subsequent research, instead of emphasizing a trade-off between growth and equity, took as the policy goal the achievement of redistribution with growth.[10]

One feature of this research was to eschew relative inequality concepts like the bottom 40 per cent in favour of analytic focus on the problems and living conditions of the absolute poor. This shift had distinct advantages in terms of policy. The former approach was not particularly useful since target groups were not well defined. Discussions of Gini coefficients or the bottom 40 per cent did not identify the regional or occupational classification of the poor. It was increasingly recognized that from a policy point of view, it was easier (and more desirable) to *affect* changes in income levels for identifiable poverty groups rather than to attempt to affect changes in overall measures of relative inequality; several of the old problems carried over into the new emphasis – in particular, problems relating to proper identification and measurement.

Attempts at a definition of poverty and the drawing of a 'poverty line' have a long, and controversial, history (see Sen, 1978). An important characteristic of these definitions is that they differ across countries and time-periods. A level of income that reflected wealth in 1920 in the United States may reflect poverty in 1980. Analogously, a rich person in India may be poor according to American criteria. Thus, the poor in the two societies cannot be added or compared in any meaningful sense. This non-comparability, however, does not negate the relevance of the definition in either society. Rather it reflects an inherently relativistic aspect of poverty. Both the absolute and relative notions of poverty are concerned with welfare and income levels of the poorest. This fact can cause confusion, but it is important to note the fundamental differences between the two concepts.

A definition of absolute poverty must be relatively invariant with respect to time and geographical differences. Implicit in any definition of absolute poverty must be the notion that *at* the 'dividing line' people in different time periods or groups are in some sense at comparable levels of welfare. In other words, the concept of absolute poverty requires a cardinal measure of minimum economic welfare which is sufficiently invariant over time or between social or national groups to permit meaningful comparisons. In contrast, income levels associated with relative poverty (the lowest 20 or 40 per cent) can and do vary over time or between groups and societies.

The absolute definition requires a common methodology for assessing poverty while relative poverty does not. These differences imply that the two cannot be treated in an 'equivalent' manner. However, it *is* the case that an absolute poverty measure has a relative component to it. Choices about the dividing line are determined at least in part by 'relative' considerations. Nevertheless, an absolute poverty definition attempts to reduce the relative component to a point where valid comparisons can be made. It is only in this sense that the measure is 'absolute'.

Are there any objective criteria which can be used to define the absolute poor? One school of thought rejected attempts to establish elaborate objective standards for the poverty line and instead opted for a fairly arbitrary absolute poverty level (Ahluwalia et al., 1979). However, another whole line of research has sought a more objective and explicit specification of the poverty line via a nutritional norms approach to the measurement of poverty.

This approach emphasizes the consumption of one basic need – food. If it is assumed that a 'need' for food dominates all other needs (that is there is a low substitutability between food and other goods below the required level), then inadequate food intake can be used to represent absolute poverty.[11] Such a definition might then be meaningfully used for cross-country and inter-temporal comparisons. However, the specification of food inadequacy requires that a 'satisfaction' level be defined. This level can only have meaning in terms of nutrients like calories, proteins, vitamins and so on. In theory nutritional norms for each component of food can be used to test for adequacy. A 'short-cut' approach is to concentrate on calories under the assumption that calorie intake is closely correlated with the intake of other nutrients. Then, a level of expenditure at which the 'required' calories are purchased can be defined as the poverty line. This point is inferred from the joint distribution of average calorie intake and average income per caput.

This straightforward methodology was followed by Dandekar and Rath (1971) for India and Reutlinger and Selowsky (1976). However, this intuitively appealing approach has had its share of detractors. A major critic of this methodology was Sukhatme (1977). The fundamental problems he found in this approach were (a) an assumed perfect, but invalid, correlation between malnutrition and absolute poverty; (b) an assumption that average requirements are minimum requirements; and (c) an assumption that inter-individual variations in requirements are negligible or non-existent. As Sukhatme illustrates, if data on a healthy population are collected, and if 'requirements' are normally distributed, then the above methodology will indicate that half of the healthy population is malnourished (and therefore poor) and the other half is over-nourished, that is the entire healthy population is unhealthy (and poor?).

Some of these criticisms can be overcome if average requirements are adjusted for inter-individual variations. This is essentially the view taken by Reutlinger and Alderman (1980) and by Sen (1980), who defends the caloric approach by stating, 'The level of income at which an *average* person will be able to meet his nutritional requirements has a claim to being considered as an appropriate poverty line', and 'considerations of average nutritional requirements can be used for one perspective on poverty even when nutritional requirements vary from person to person', (pp. 4,5). However, as shown in Bhalla (1980), even this modification does not render the caloric approach generally useful for defining absolute poverty. The major inherent drawback is caused by the low elasticity of calorie consumption with respect to income. Thus, even small measurement errors in calorie requirements or consumption translate into large variations in the poverty line and in estimates of the population in poverty. For example, calculations based on the relationship between per caput consumption and income for urban Brazil in 1974, [12] show that if average requirements are varied from 2,321 calories to 2,030 calories per caput (a change representing the FAO and ENDEF requirements, respectively) the estimate of the poverty line changes from 15,400 cruzerios to 4,000 cruzerios, and the estimate of population in poverty changes from 99 to 50 per cent. A 13 per cent change in requirements changes the poverty line estimate by 385 per cent. Such a high elasticity of the poverty line estimate to a small error in measurement is not conducive to rigorous or objective specification.

That such small errors are inevitable with calorie intakes/requirements and so on is documented in detail in Bhalla (1980). First, it is more difficult to estimate the extent of calories consumed than to ask consumers about other variables, for example consumption expenditures. Second, recommendations of requirements vary according to FAO and other agencies, for example the US Food and Nutrition Board. Third, individual countries may have their own estimate of requirements. Finally, survey estimates of calorie consumption may vary from national food balance sheet estimates of consumption. Thus, without any consideration of conceptual problems relating to the use of average requirements, choice of 'data' alone would seem to determine whether 35 or 89 per cent of the population of Brazil is classified as malnourished/poor. Similarly, results published in Hanes (1974) would seem to indicate that 67 per cent of American males and 80 per cent of American females have a calorie intake below the FAO requirement levels.[13] If US recommendations are imposed, the corresponding 'malnutrition' figures are 46 per cent for men and 70 per cent for women. Since these results are based on individual intake data, these figures do not have any inherent biases. Comparison with other surveys (in particular the 1977–78 Nationwide Food Consumption survey) suggests that the Hanes data are fairly accurate. Thus, the inherent unreliability of the calorie approach would argue for extreme caution (if not rejection) in its use to establish an absolute poverty line.

An alternative to both the income and calorie approach to proverty measurement is the Basic Needs Approach. This method (Streeten and Burki (1978); ILO (1977); Grant (1978)) defines poverty in its most general form, that is a condition which reflects an inadequate purchase (or possession) of various commodities. Attempts at specificity have led to the following definition:

> There is not a single level of basic needs but a hierarchy. At the lowest level, basic needs are those that have to be met for *bare* survival. At the next level, basic needs may be defined as those that have to be met for *continued survival* and comprise a minimum of food and water, protection from *fatal* diseases and adequate shelter. At the third level, the satisfaction of basic needs covers continued *productive survival* and in addition protection from *debilitating* diseases, more food and some education. Finally, certain *non-material* needs may be added, like participation in making decisions affecting one's life and work, and the *relative* component of poverty (relative to the average income).
>
> (Streeten and Burki, 1978, p. 413, original italics).

Though the last attribute can be ignored, the definition of basic needs above is *roughly* comparable to a notion of absolute poverty. Even isolating the core basic needs – 'food (calories and proteins), clothing, safe drinking water and shelter' – there remain severe problems of estimation. Streeten and Burki estimate the number of people suffering from 'three core basic needs' to be approximately 800 million people in 1975, but it is doubtful that their measurement methodology can satisfy criteria pertaining to cross-country and inter-temporal comparisons.

Nevertheless, the concept of basic needs may serve a useful function in formulation and implementation of policy. The direct provision of some basic needs (running water, electricity, education, and so on) may be more effective than more general or more indirect measures of increasing welfare; moreover, specific targets are more easily defined. What is being contended here is that basic needs and absolute poverty are separate and distinct concepts, though obviously an overlap is present.

*Absolute poverty – interpretation of data*

Even if proper definitions are available, the problem of proper definition, and inference, remains. Given the political and policy importance of the subject, researchers should be cautious in inferring conclusions. For instance, a healthy debate in India ensued over whether absolute poverty (measured as the percentage of population below an 'arbitrarily' defined income line) had declined during the period 1960–61 to 1967–68. Bardhan (1974), Minhas (1974) and Vaidyanathan (1974) all found *different* estimates of poverty in 1967–68, though all concluded that poverty had not declined, and indeed shown some increase.

If persistent, an increase in poverty would be alarming. However, Ahluwalia's (1977) analysis outlines the importance of end-points in poverty analysis. In his study on poverty in rural India, Ahluwalia presents a profile of time-series of poverty in different states of India, 1957–58 to 1973–74. This 'time-series shows a pattern of *fluctuations*, with the incidence of poverty falling in periods of good agricultural performance and rising in periods of poor performance. Given the importance of weather induced variations in Indian agriculture, there can be little doubt about the important of such fluctuations and it is *crucial* to keep these in mind in assessing underlying trends' (1977, p. 319, our italics).

What the debate caused by choice of deflator and end-point underscores is the extremely complex nature of the subject. The fact that analysis of trends in absolute poverty suggests no immediate pulling of a policy lever, should not blind us to its importance. It is of grave policy concern to know about the welfare levels of the poor and their changes. This feedback can be related to growth performance, and the efficacy of various policies can be compared and assessed. Finally, it is a test of 'trickle-down': to what extent, and how fast, does per caput growth translate into the growth of incomes of the poor – a result that can only be achieved by time-series data rather than from cross-country regressions.

The final 'interpretation' issue relates to the inference of time-series behaviour from cross-country evidence. Unlike other variables (for example income elasticity of demand for food) cross-section estimates of poverty (or inequality) cannot be easily translated into time-series behaviour. This is because the control for initial conditions is crucial for analysis.

Analysis of data from Sri Lanka illustrates this point clearly. During the 15-year period 1963–1977, Sri Lanka was spending almost 10 per cent of its GDP on social programmes. It is of considerable interest, therefore, to measure the results of this unusually high expenditure. According to World Bank data, Sri Lanka does appear to be a 'positive' (or good) deviant with respect to *four* important social indicators – life expectancy, fertility, infant mortality and adult literacy. Cross-country regression data for 1975 confirms this tendency (Isenman, 1980, p. 239). An example of the possible deviation magnitudes involved has been measured by Sen using Isenman's life expectancy equation (data for 1975 or closest year):

$$\ln \textit{(life expectancy)} = 3.2 + 0.132 \ln \text{(per caput income)},\ R^2 = 0.7.$$

> From this, it is easily calculated that the income per caput corresponding to Sri Lanka's life expectancy of 69 years is $2,684 as opposed to its actual value of $130 in 1975 US dollars. Thus, the per caput income of Sri Lanka would have to be raised by a factor of 20.65 for it to have its *actual* life expectancy as its expected life expectancy based on income (Sen, 1980, p. 45).

The Sri Lankan record in enhancing social welfare is commendable and unambiguous. What *is* questionable is Sen's assertion that 'there is little doubt that the *social welfare programmes* of Sri Lanka place it at an advantaged position in terms of poverty removal and *longevity* increase given its income level' (1980, p. 44, our italics). In order to obtain a proper estimate of the effect of these programmes, *initial* conditions would have to be controlled for and one method of doing this would be to estimate the model in terms of first differences, that is 1975 level *minus* the 1963 level. This is not done either by Isenman or Sen. However, Table 1 of Isenman's paper suggests 'little' role for the social welfare programmes during 1963–1973. In this time period, life expectancy increased little (albeit from a high level) – 63 to 66 years, and infant mortality dropped from 56 to 46.[14] Thus, it is highly probable that Sri Lanka would appear deviant even with 1963 data for itself and 1975 data for other countries.

## CONCLUDING REMARKS

Despite the problems and pitfalls which researchers have faced (and which may have been given disproportionate attention in this paper) the past fifteen or twenty years have been an extraordinarily fruitful period of research on income distribution in developing countries. There has been a substantial accumulation of empirical data along with considerable progress in the clarification of conceptual issues arising in both theory and measurement. Moreover, this is one area where research efforts have been closely tied to questions of direct policy concern.

What conclusions may be drawn for future research directions? One that emerges clearly from the discussion in the previous sections is the importance of maintaining an historical perspective in any research on distributive issues. Perhaps the greatest current need on the empirical side is for time-series and longitudinal studies in order to decrease reliance on questionable inferences from cross-sectional survey. Closely related to this is the need for continuing analytic and empirical efforts to forge closer and better links between the economic and functional status of identifiable groups and the processes determining income generation, asset accumulation and access to economic oppotunities. This implies a shift away from analyses of size distribution *per se* towards investigation of the structure and operation of factor markets and the manner in which particular groups are affected by and respond to changes inherent in economic development.

Finally, and in many ways most important, the work on distributive aspects of development has been a major contributor to a broader view of development – one in which levels of economic welfare are seen as important determinants of the pace of economic growth. One of the potentially most rewarding frontiers for future research lies in the exploration of the relation between income levels and the contributions to growth arising from human resource development.

## NOTES

[1]Both the other theories of savings behaviour – the life-cycle and permanent income – do not postulate any dependence of the savings rate on the level of per caput income and therefore imply a zero effect of inequality on aggregate savings. This result is rejected by Bhalla's (1980) study of savings behaviour amongst rural households in India. However, Musgrove's (1980) cross-section study of 30 countries shows an insignificant effect of inequality on savings rates.

[2]Until, of course, the next major directional change – the concern with the absolute poor – see section on absolute poverty.

[3]A separate literature developed on the generation of inequality measures with desirable qualities. Popular measures included the Gini coefficient, the log. variance of incomes, the Theil index and the cumulative income shares of households ranked according to household income, for example the bottom 40 per cent.

[4]See Cline (1975) and Ahluwalia (1976) for a partial listing.

[5]In the most detailed study on the subject, Ahluwalia (1976), found the share of the bottom 40 per cent $= 70.6 - 44.4 \ln GNP^2 + 8.3 (\ln GNP)^2 + 12.0$ (socialist dummy), where GNP is in per caput terms. In this U-shaped curve, the turning point (that is the point beyond which income inequality would improve after deteriorating) was observed to occur at US $468 (1965-71$) –a level which included most LDCs.

[6]Time-series income distribution data for Taiwan also shows an increase of *equality* with growth. The data problems associated with Taiwan are discussed below.

[7]The former conclusion would follow because, as mentioned earlier, a cross-country regression is essentially used to derive implications about individual country behaviour over time. And the Korean data directly provides the latter result.

[8]We would like to thank Rakesh Mohan for discussions on this matter.

[9]Historical data for the US suggests no change in inequality in the period 1948–1970 (Chiswick and Mincer, 1972) and improvement in the period 1929–50 (Williamson and Lindert, 1980). Indian data suggests that there has been virtually no change in inequality since 1950 (Bardhan 1974). A theoretical formulation for the inevitability of the Kuznets curve has been provided by Robinson (1976).

[10]The policy shift in *research* was heralded by an important new book, Chenery et al., *Redistribution with Growth*, 1974.

[11]Empirical support for this intuitive view is provided by the fact that the poor often devote about 60–80 per cent of their budget to food purchase (Bhanoji Rao, 1981).

[12]These data are from the highly respected ENDEF Nutrition Survey. Further, the low calorie intake-income elasticity relationship is typical of most countries.

[13]This result is observed for the age-group 25–34 years. Similar results are observed for other age groups.

[14]During the preceding 10 years the changes were from 53 years to 63 years (life expectancy) and from 71 years to 56 years (infant mortality).

## REFERENCES

Adelman, I. and Morris, C.T., *Economic Growth and Social Equity in Developing Countries,* Stanford, 1973.

Ahluwalia, M.S., 'Inequality, Poverty, and Development', *Journal of Development Economics,* September 1976.

Ahluwalia, 'Rural Poverty and Agricultural Performance in India', *Journal of Development Studies,* 1977.

Ahluwalia, Carter, N.C., and Chenery, H.B., 'Growth and Poverty in Developing Countries', *Journal of Development Economics,* September 1979.

Altimir, Oscar, 'Income Distribution Estimates from Household Surveys and Population Censuses in Latin America: An Assessment of Reliability', mimeo, World Bank, 1977.

Bacha, Edmar L., 'The Kuznets Curve and Beyond: Growth and Changes in Inequalities', mimeo, World Bank, April 1977.

Bardhan, Pranab K., 'On the Incidence of Poverty in Rural India in the Sixties', in Bardhan and Srinivasan (1974).

Bardhan, and Srinivasan, T.N. (ed.), *Poverty and Income Distribution in India,* Statistical Publishing Society, Calcutta, 1974.

Bhalla, Surjit S., 'The Distribution of Income in Korea: A Critique and a Reassessment', mimeo, World Bank, 1979.

Bhalla, 'Measurement of Poverty: Issues and Methods', mimeo, World Bank, 1980.

Bhalla, 'Measurement of Permanent Income and its Application to Savings Behaviour', *Journal of Political Economy,* August 1980.

Bhanoji Rao, V.V., 'Measurement of Deprivation and Poverty Based on the Proportion Spent on Food: An Exploratory Exercise', *World Development,* Vol. 9, No. 4, 1981.

Chenery, H.B. et al., *Redistribution with Growth,* Oxford, 1974.

Chiswick, B. and Mincer, J., 'Time Series Changes in Personal Income Inequality in the US', *Journal of Political Economy,* Part 2, May/June 1972.

Choo, Hakchung, 'Some Sources of Relative Equity in Korean Income Distribution: A Historical Perspective', in Asian Manpower Studies, *Income Distribution, Employment and Economic Development in South East and East Asia,* Tokyo, JERC, 1975.

Choo, and Kim, Daemo, 'Probable Size Distribution of Income in Korea: Over Time and by Sector', Report submitted to Council for Asian Manpower Studies, Korea Development Institute, 1978.

Cline, William R., 'Distribution and Development: A Survey of Literature', *Journal of Development Economics,* December 1975.

Dandekar, V.M. and Rath, N., 'Poverty in India', *Economic and Political Weekly,* Nos. 1–2 (1971).

Datta, G. and Meerman, J., 'Household Income or Household Income Per Capita in Welfare Comparisons', World Bank Staff Working Paper No. 378, March 1980.

Deaton, A., 'Three Essays on a Sri Lanka Household Survey', Living Standards Measurement Study No. 11, World Bank, October 1981.

Fei, John C.H., Ranis, Gustav, and Kuo, Shirley W.Y., *Growth with Equity: The Taiwan Case,* Oxford University Press, 1979.

Grant, J.P., *Disparity Reduction Rates in Social Indicators,* Overseas Development Council, No. 11, September 1978.

Isenman, P., 'Basic Needs: The Case of Sri Lanka', *World Development,* Vol. 8, 1980.

International Labour Office, *Poverty and Landlessness in Rural Asia,* Geneva, 1977.

Kusnic, M. and DaVanzo, J., 'Income Inequality and the Definition of Income: The Case of Malaysia', The Rand Corporation, 1979.

Kuznets, 'Economic Growth and Income Inequality', *American Economic Review,* March 1955.

Kuznets, 'Quantitative Aspects of the Economic Growth of Nations: VIII Distribution of Income by Size', *EDCC,* January 1963.

Kuznets, 'Demographic Aspects of the Size Distribution of Income: An Exploratory Essay', *EDCC,* October 1976.

Lilliard, Lee A., 'Inequality: Earnings vs. Human Wealth', *American Economic Review,* March 1977.

Lluch, C., 'On Poverty and Inequality in Brazil', mimeo, World Bank, September 1981.

Minhas, B.S., 'Rural Poverty, Land Distribution and Development Strategy: Facts', in Bardhan and Srinivasan (eds.), *Poverty and Income Distribution in India,* 1974.

Musgrove, P., 'Income Distribution and the Aggregate Consumption Function', *Journal of Political Economy,* June 1980.
Rao, D.C., 'Economic Growth and Equity in the Republic of Korea', *World Development,* Vol. 6, 1978.
Rawls, John, *Theory of Justice,* Cambridge University Press, 1971.
Reutlinger, S. and Alderman, H., 'The Prevalence of Calorie Deficient Diets in Developing Countries', mimeo, World Bank, 1980.
Reutlinger, S. and Selowsky, M., *Malnutrition and Poverty,* World Bank Occasional Paper No. 23, 1976.
Robinson, S., 'A Note on the U Hypothesis Relating Income Inequality and Economic Development', *American Economic Review,* June 1976.
Sen, Amartya, 'Three Notes on the Concept of Poverty', ILO Working Paper No. 65, January 1978.
Sen, Amartya, 'Levels of Poverty: Policy and Change', World Bank Staff Working Paper No. 401, July 1980.
Srinivasan, T.N., 'Malnutrition: Some Measurement and Policy Issues', *Journal of Development Economics,* Vol. 8, 1981.
Sukhatme, P.V., 'Malnutrition and Poverty', Ninth Lal Bahadur Shastri Lecture, Indian Agricultural Research Institute, 1977.
Streeten, P. and Burki, S., 'Basic Needs: Some Issues', *World Development,* 6, 1978.
Vaidyanathan, A., 'Some Aspects of Inequalities in Living Standards in Rural India', in Bardhan and Srinivasan (eds.), *Poverty and Income Distribution in India,* 1974.
Williamson, J. and Lindert, P., *American Inequality: A Macroeconomic History,* Academic Press, 1980.

## DISCUSSION OPENING – SUSUMU HONDAI

The authors of this paper have focused their discussion on the analytical and empirical work over the past years in order to see what lessons may be derived for future research and for policy formulation to alleviate the poverty problem.

At the early stage of theoretical development, there was a great emphasis on growth, and distributional considerations took a secondary position. Indeed it was thought that inequality might well be necessary for growth. Since historical data for individual countries was scarce, most analyses done to infer intertemporal behaviour were from cross-country evidence.

However, these analyses utilized data which were not always appropriate or reliable. Most of the problems associated with the data mentioned in the paper are already well recognized. In relation to per caput and household income data, the authors have pointed out that meaningful basis for income distribution analysis is individual income rather than household income, since the welfare level of the individual depends on individual income. But the most important justification for looking at families rather than individuals is the fact of widespread income sharing within families. In a family, both economically active and dependent persons are included. The family is the unit that decides how to allocate the distribution of goods and services among its members. Another reason for choosing the family as a recipient unit is the difficulty in many situations of attributing incomes or earnings to a specific individual as in family-run farms or business. Still another is that property is jointly held, so that the income from the property is jointly received and not assignable to any one family member.

The next development of the research on income distribution mentioned in the paper was direct attacks on poverty. From the policy point of view, it is more meaningful to effect changes in income levels for identifiable poverty groups than to attempt to effect changes in overall measures of relative inequality for the contemporary developing countries. In this discussion, the authors identified the problems for defining poverty and made a detailed analysis associated with three definitions of poverty, arbitrary absolute poverty level, nutritional norms and the basic human needs approach. All the income adjustment and other fine points mentioned are useful and indeed indispensable in measuring the true extent of the poverty problems in LDCs.

With all the attention paid to theoretical complexities and definitional problems, I fear we may be moving quite far from where we want to be. The major goal in measuring absolute poverty is to quantify the extent of economic misery in a country or in the world so as to be able at a later time to assess progress toward its alleviation and more generally to learn how much the benefits of economic development are distributed. In other words, we ultimately want to assess changes in income distribution over time. In time-series comparisons, whatever biases and limitations there are in our definitions of poverty and in the data used to measure it at one time may reappear next time. If so, the indicated changes in the unadjusted data are likely to parallel the changes in the ideal distribution of income. What is important about the absolute line in a dynamic development context is that it be held constant in real terms. Thus, the usual types of figures on income, although not ideal in many respects, may serve as a useful guide to the economic position of the poor. Definitional issue and measurement complexities need to be addressed; but attention to them sometimes diverts attention from more pressing concerns: what produces poverty and is absolute poverty being alleviated with economic growth?

An important point in the aspect of absolute poverty is to gain a clear understanding of determinants of incomes at individual and household levels. Studies breaking down income inequality, for instance, those done by Fei, Ranis and Kuo, 1979, demonstrate that in the countries for which empirical studies are available, variations in labour income account for a larger fraction of total income inequality than do variations in all other income sources combined. This is partly because labour's functional share is higher than any other and partly because labour is the predominant income source. Hence an understanding of labour income inequality and its causes will be a central issue to the study of income distribution in developing countries. To attack this issue, we have to direct our research efforts more towards human capital analysis and earning function analysis. Analysis of the earning function examines the functional relationship between the income of a recipient unit and the factors thought to determine income. Future analyses in these areas will clarify functional income distribution which has been neglected for a long time and yield a high pay-off for intellectual effort.

MAHAR MANGAHAS

# *Measurement of Poverty and Equity: Some ASEAN Social Indicators Experience*

## THE SOCIAL INDICATORS MOVEMENT

Development work on 'social indicators' has been going on in ASEAN (Association of South East Asian Nations) countries for nearly a decade. In any given country, there are a variety of institutions involved. In addition to the central statistical agency, there are other government offices which are primary sources of important social data. Some institutions are in the academic sector. Some institutions are private. Resident offices of international bodies, such as the World Bank and the various UN agencies, make significant research contributions.

Thus the social indicators movement is not (nor should it be) coordinated in the sense of being centrally managed or uniformly conducted. Each institution has its own terms of reference, its set of resources, and its peculiar vulnerabilities, and must pursue its work within its own special frame. The social indicators movement should be seen as the aggregate outcome of all these agencies' separate accomplishments, rather than as the work of any single specialized agency in particular. It is necessary to look at the entire system because one agency can do what another cannot, and vice-versa, and there is nothing immoral about it.

The essential spirit of the social indicators movement is its thrust towards quantification of the conditions of previously neglected, but admittedly important, social concerns. The measurement activities have been meagre because the policy emphasis on poverty and equity is still fairly recent; yet, at the same time, the policy emphasis is hampered because the data are so scarce.

The conclusions of this paper are directed not towards any one institution in particular, but towards the system as a whole. The coexistence, at times complementary, at other times competitive, of several disparate institutions generating social statistics is a favourable condition for the system to respond to. On the other hand, a high degree of centralization of authority over statistical activities is, in my view, an unfavourable condition.

## POVERTY LINES AND GINI RATIOS

ASEAN data on poverty and inequality are still relatively scanty. Cross-sectional surveys of family income and/or expenditures are typically 4–5 years apart (Table 1). There has been little effort to keep the statistical designs of these surveys standard over time, and it is hazardous to draw time-trend conclusions. It is clear, nevertheless, that income inequality is relatively high, with the Gini ratio in the 0.40 to 0.50 region for almost all countries. Coupled with the relatively low levels of average income (except in Singapore), the inequalities imply that substantial numbers of the population are living in absolute poverty.

TABLE 1 *Gini concentration ratios of income inequality in ASEAN*

| Country | Year | Gini (%) | Remarks |
|---|---|---|---|
| Indonesia | 1976 | 52 | |
| | 1976 | 39 (Urban Java) | Refers to per caput |
| | | 30 (Rural Java) | consumption expenditures; |
| | | 34 (Urban outside Java) | |
| | | 32 (Rural outside Java) | |
| Thailand | 1962 | 41 | |
| | 1968 | 43 | |
| | 1972 | 50 | |
| Philippines | 1961 | 45 | |
| | 1965 | 50 | |
| | 1971 | 49 | 1975 procedure not comparable to |
| | 1975 | 55 | 1961–1971. |
| Malaysia | 1957 | 41 | |
| | 1967 | 44 | |
| | 1970 | 51 | |
| | 1973 | 48 | |
| Singapore | 1966 | 50[a], 46[b] | |
| | 1972 | 44[a] | [a]Pertains to individuals, not to |
| | 1973 | 46[a], 42[b] | households. |
| | 1974 | 43[a] | [b]Refers only to income from work. |
| | 1975 | 45[a] | |

*Sources:* M. Mangahas (1979), S. Ishak (1979).

TABLE 2 *Comparative poverty lines in five countries (Values per Caput per Year)*

| Country | Source | Year | | Poverty Line in local currency (a) | US$ exchange rate (b) | Poverty line in US$ of country purchasing power (c) = (a) ÷ (b) | Kravis adjustment factor (1970)[a] (d) | Poverty line in US$ of US purchasing power (e) = (c) x (d) |
|---|---|---|---|---|---|---|---|---|
| Indonesia | | | | | | | | |
| | | | | *Java:* | | | | |
| | Sajogye (1977) | 1976 | Rp. | 38,400 rural | 415 | 93 | 3.766 | 348 |
| | | | Rp. | 57,600 urban | 415 | 139 | 3.766 | 523 |
| | | | | *Outside Java:* | | | | |
| | | | Rp. | 40,000 rural | 415 | 96 | 3.766 | 363 |
| | | | Rp. | 60,000 urban | 415 | 145 | 3.766 | 544 |
| | World Bank (Oct. 1978) | 1976 | Rp. | 36,000 | 415 | 87 | 3.766 | 328 |
| Thailand | Meesook (1975) | 1968/69 | B | 1,000 | 20 | 50 | 2.822 | 141 |
| | World Bank (Sept. 1978) | 1975/76 | B | 1,800 rural | 20 | 90 | 2.822 | 254 |
| | | | B | 2,400 urban | 20 | 120 | 2.822 | 339 |
| Philippines | Mangahas (1977) | 1975 | p | 1,724 national | 7.3 | 236 | 2.061 | 486 |
| | Mangahas (1981e) | 1981 | p | 2,600[b] Manila | 7.9 | 329 | 2.061 | 678 |
| Korea | Suh (1979) | 1978 | W | 130,236 rural | 485 | 269 | 2.204 | 593 |
| | | 1978 | W | 155,160 urban | 485 | 320 | 2.204 | 705 |
| Malaysia | SERGPU (1978) | 1977 | M$ | 579 | 2.4 | 241 | 2.540 | 612 |

[a]Source of Kravis factors: M. Ahluwalia, N. Carter and H. Chenery 'Growth and Poverty in Developing Countries', World Bank Staff Working Paper No. 309, December 1978, Table 3.
[b]1,300 per month per family of 6; see Section 5 of this paper.

Table 2 summarizes absolute poverty lines selected from recent studies. Only the Malaysian line, it should be stressed, is an *official* one. For the sake of comparison, the poverty lines are first converted from local currency units to US dollars at the exchange rate applicable at the time, and then are given a rough adjustment for inter-country differences in the cost of living, using so-called 'Kravis factors' for which the base country of comparison is the US. Thus the final poverty lines in the rightmost column are in terms of purchasing power in the US in the base year 1970.[2]

It is remarkable that these poverty lines, after the Kravis adjustment, do not have an exceedingly wide range. At the head is Korea, with $600-700, followed by Malaysia with about $600, the Philippines with somewhat less than $500,[3] and then Indonesia in the neighbourhood of $400. The World Bank lines for Indonesia and Thailand should be carefully interpreted, judging that the Bank tends to be highly conservative. Its 'deep poverty' lines of nearly $300 for Thailand and about $325 for Indonesia do not seem to indicate a norm for the margin of poverty too different from that suggested for the Philippines. Meesook has stated that her Thai poverty line, which may seem quite different from the general pattern, is also an 'extreme poverty' line; in addition, its reference period is more than half a decade earlier than the other cases, and thus an additional correction for price inflation would be warranted.

It is also interesting to note that the ASEAN poverty lines reported here are not very different from some recently done for Latin America by Selowsky (1979). His poverty lines range from $215 to $237, in terms of local prices. If we likewise apply 1970 Kravis adjustment factors, then the corresponding poverty lines in US purchasing power range from $512 to $539.

## MALAYSIA: AN INDEX OF ETHNIC IMBALANCE

The concept of equity may be highly country-specific. This section describes an index recently introduced in Malaysia. It may be relevant to other societies which have similar problems of ethnic or tribal diversity.

One of the 'prongs' of the New Economic Policy in Malaysia is the restructuring of Malaysian society so that the identification of race with economic function and geographical location is reduced. Let $e_k$ be the proportion of persons engaged in some specific economic function, such as entrepreneurship, who are of ethnic group k, and $p_k$ be the proportion of group k in the population. If $e_k = p_k$ for all $k$, one could say that societal restructuring has been perfectly completed, and therefore ethnic imbalance is nil. On the other hand, one could specify entrepreneurship to be completely unstructured, when *all* the entrepreneurs come from only one ethnic group. Furthermore, the situation would be worse, the *smaller* the size of the ethnic group which monopolizes the entrepreneurship.

Now consider the expression $\Sigma\ (e_k - p_k)^2$ which obviously approaches zero as every $e_k$ approaches $p_k$, in the ideal situation. Suppose that an ethnic

FIGURE 1 *Malaysia: racial imbalance in occupational access, 1970 and 1975 target*

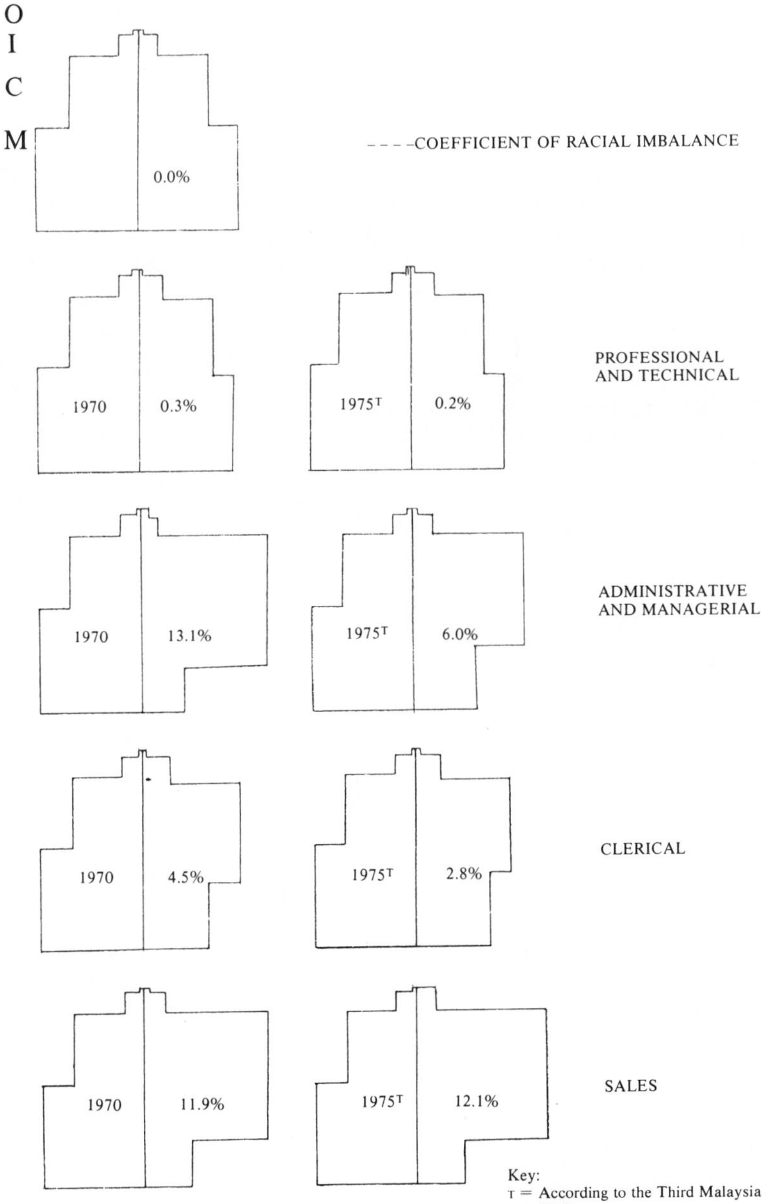


Key:
T = According to the Third Malaysia Plan;
M = Malays;
C = Chinese;
I = Indian;
O = Others;

group $j$ monopolizes a certain economic function. Then, for $k$ other than $j$, $e_k = 0$ and $\Sigma (e_k - p_k)^2 = \Sigma p_k^2$. It is supposed that $e_j = 1$. The worst possible monopoly happens when $p_j$ tends to zero, or when $(e_j - p_j)^2$ tends to one. Thus, the highest possible value which $\Sigma (e_k - p_k)^2$ can reach is $1 + \Sigma p_k^2$. This suggests an *Index of Imbalance,* ranging from zero to one:

$$c = \frac{\Sigma (e_k - p_k)^2}{1 + \Sigma p_k^2}$$

By using the squares of the discrepancies, (a) large discrepancies are emphasized much more than in proportion to their size, and (b) any given gain or loss in entrepreneurial share of one race is more serious the larger is the original discrepancy of the race which experiences the offsetting loss or gain. These would seem to be desirable properties for the index.

The diagram of the index is meant to suggest a physical structure, for example, the profile of an office building. The total *height* is 100 per cent or 100 'stories', but there are two wings, the left pertaining to population and the right, say, to entrepreneurs. Each wing is divided into sections according to height, the left wing according to the ethnic division of the population and the right wing according to the ethnic division of entrepreneurs. The structure itself consists of a stack of boxes corresponding to the ethnic sections; each wing has its own stack, and each box is square, as wide as the section is tall.

TABLE 3 *Coefficients of racial imbalance in Malaysia*[a]

| Economic Issue | (Per cent deviation from perfect balance) 1970 | 1974 | 1975 | 1978 |
|---|---|---|---|---|
| 1 Unemployment | 0.3 | 1.0 | 0.4 | |
| 2 Occupation | | | | |
| Professional and technical | 0.3 | 0.3 | 0.2 | |
| Administrative and managerial | 13.1 | 10.7 | 6.0 | |
| Clerical | 4.5 | 0.8 | 2.8 | |
| Sales | 11.9 | 10.3 | 12.1 | |
| Agriculture | 3.3 | 3.9 | 3.1 | |
| Production | 7.3 | 2.1 | 4.3 | |
| Service and other | 1.1 | 0.4 | 0.4 | |
| 3 Studies in colleges and universities | 0.7 | 1.1 | 1.4 | 1.4 |
| 4 Ownership of share capital | 42.0 | 31.2 | | 26.7 |

*Source:* Government of Malaysia (1979), Table 3 'Restructuring of Society, 1970–1978', pp. 112–119.

Note [a]Peninsular Malaysia only, except in the case of corporate sector ownership.

As a diagrammatic convention, the ethnic groups should be ordered according to population, with the biggest group at the base, and the smallest at the top. Observing the left wing in particular, the more fractionalized the population, the more the building will look like a narrow high-rise, vulnerable to strong winds, earthquakes, and so on; and the less fractionalized, the more it will look squat, big-based and formidable.

In the ideal situation, the right wing would be perfectly symmetical to the left wing (see the top of Figure 1). So when there is asymmetry, it is proper to say that the building needs to be 'restructured'. Since the sections of both wings must have the same ethnic order, the asymmetry can result in a bigger box stacked over a smaller one in the right wing.

Table 3 shows the application of the coefficient of racial imbalance to unemployment, occupation, access to local tertiary education, and ownership of share capital. In the first three cases, the population distribution by race which is used is that of the pertinent age/activity group. Figure 1 shows diagrammatically how occupational imbalance is to be reduced between 1970 and 1975, as per the Third Malaysia Plan. The greatest balance is clearly found among professional and technical workers (apparently this includes the civil service).

## THE PHILIPPINES: THE SOCIAL WEATHER STATION EXPERIMENT

One means of filling in data gaps is a special survey devoted to social welfare or well-being. Malaysia has now undertaken three nationwide rounds of such a survey (Government of Malaysia, 1979). At the Development Academy of the Philippines, the Research for Development Department is conducting a Social Weather Station (SWS) Project by means of quick-response well-being surveys. As the name implies, the objective of the project is to produce a quick reading of the 'social weather'. Two surveys were done in 1981 and another is planned for 1982.

This section summarizes some results pertaining to poverty and equity from the first SWS Survey of 500 household heads in March-May 1981 (Mangahas, 1981).

The SWS project emphasizes disaggregation of the data according to *socio-economic status* or SES. There are two SES concepts, one using the respondent's own subjective rating as to whether he is 'Poor' (mahirap), the second using the rough-and-ready techniques of consumer research to group households into purchasing power classes based on external appearances of consumer assets, mainly the dwelling.

Under the self-rating scheme, the 'Not Poor', the 'Border Line' (of poverty), and the 'Poor' in Metro Manila are found to be of roughly equal size. Under the class rating scheme, about 9 per cent are found to be ABs or 'upper class', 32 are Cs or 'middle class', 34 are Ds or 'Lower class' and 25 per cent are Es or 'very low class'. Both classification schemes have their separate merits; the correlation between the two is high but not exact.

The *poverty threshold income* is an indicator which incorporates both the cost of living and the people's own conception of their basic needs. The median poverty threshold is about ₱1,300–1,500 per family per month, and the average is ₱1,920. There is strong agreement between the 'Poor' and the 'Non-Poor' concerning the location of the threshold. Both among the 'Poor' and among the 'Non-Poor', those with a higher educational attainment claim a higher threshold level.

The incidence of poverty has very little relationship to age of the household head, except for being somewhat larger for the very oldest. Poverty is clearly inversely related to schooling. It drops markedly when one has at least attended some college: a college diploma makes a small additional difference. There is a residual of self-rated poverty (about 5 per cent) even for those with postgraduate attainment. The 'Poor' have a higher rate of open *unemployment* (about 9 per cent) compared to the 'Non-Poor' (6½ to 7 per cent); the overall open unemployment in the household heads survey is 7½ per cent[5].

The past year has been a difficult one in terms of material well-being. Those whose level of living deteriorated outnumber those whose level of living improved, 34% to 26%; for the others there was no change. The incidence of deterioration was higher among the 'Poor'.

Over the past three years, however, those whose lives improved outnumber those whose lives deteriorated, 42 per cent to 31 per cent. The incidence of improvement was much higher for the 'Non-Poor'; for the 'Poor', the ratio of gainers to losers over the past three years was only about 50:50. The class rating data suggest that it was in the middle class (Class C) in particular that the gainers had the biggest majority over the losers, over the past three years.

Over the next three years, those who expect their lives to improve highly outnumber those who expect a deterioration, 66 per cent to 13 per cent. This is out of those who could imagine the future, or only 80 per cent of the sample; non-responses were greatest among the 'Poor' (29%). In general, the degree of optimism about the future rises as material well-being already attained rises; but the peak of optimism seems to be reached, again, in the middle class.

The patterns of progress in well-being among households in Metro Manila are thus seen to be quite diverse. There are both ups (1978–1981) and downs (1980–1981). In some instances proportionately more benefits accrue to the poor, in some instances less, and in still other instances there is no pattern either pro- or anti-equity. Neither good news nor bad news dominates.

## CONCLUSIONS AND RECOMMENDATIONS

Since the ASEAN region has experienced tremendous economic growth, but with little improvement in distributive equity, the past structure of development policies and programmes needs to be modified (Mangahas,

1979). But though the general principles of redistribution are well-known, the problem is to discover the optimal mix and the new institutional forms which will work in each country context. There is a need for a responsive and vigorous social indicators movement, prompting some institutions in the statistical system to collect the relevant data so that all concerned can be guided by the objective facts.

*Monitoring of poverty*

There is a clear consensus that the problem of poverty takes precedence over the problem of relative inequality. The following actions are recommended:

1. Adoption of one or more official poverty lines.

   As a rule of thumb, there could be at least two lines set, say a poverty threshold and a subsistence threshold. We suggest the following as conservative, low-end guidelines:

   *Official poverty threshold:* US \$300[6] per caput per year

   *Official subsistence threshold:* US \$150[6] per caput per year

   Adjustment can be made for different family sizes and for differences in the cost of living in various locations. Annual adjustments can be made for inflation.
2. Identification of target poverty groups to whom the programmes are to be directed.
3. Adoption of quantitative long-term targets for poverty eradication, together with corresponding short-term and annual targets.
4. Annual reporting of the incidence of poverty with at least as much fanfare as the estimate of the GNP.
5. Experimentation with innovative techniques for monitoring poverty

*Monitoring of relative inequality*

The following new actions would be recommended:

1. Quantitative integration of planning for economic growth, poverty eradication and relative inequality reduction;
2. Clearer official conceptualization of inequity;
3. Monitoring of the variables needed for an adequate representation of inequity.

In general, the above recommendations are concerned with an *operationalization* of a much-needed distributive thrust in the data-collection systems in the ASEAN countries. The data gathered should be oriented towards answering the questions: *Who* benefits? *Who* bears the costs? When the data slide over these essential questions, as when they are limited only to aggregates or averages, or, worse, when the topic is not even on the statistical agenda, then a very important function of data, namely conscienticization, is lost. This is the important sense in which it is true that data are not really neutral, and is the main reason why the defenders of the socio-economic *status quo* are ever anxious to allege that there are 'insurmountable' technical, financial or even political problems with the development of data regarding distributive justice.

## NOTES

[1]The views expressed in this paper are the author's responsibility and do not necessarily reflect the official stands of DAP, UNICEF or any agency of the governments of Malaysia or Indonesia.

[2]To convert to base year *1980,* it would not seem to unrealistic to *double* these figures.

[3]Except for the 1981 Manila estimate.

[4]This index was designed during the UNICEF-assisted Malaysian Social Indicators Project of 1977/78, see Government of Malaysia (1979).

[5]Another DAP survey found a much larger unemployment rate among non-household heads.

[6]These are so-called 'Kravis dollars', of purchasing power in the US as base country; for the base year 1970, see Table 1 for the Kravis conversion coefficients.

## REFERENCES

Ahluwalia, Montek S., Carter, Nicholas G. and Chenery, Hollis B., 'Growth and Poverty in Developing Countries', World Bank Staff Working Paper No. 309, December 1978.

Government of Malaysia, *The Application of Socio-Economic Indicators in Planning and Evaluation of Development: Malaysia 1978,* Socio-Economic Research and General Planning Unit, Prime Minister's Department, April 1979.

Ishak, Shari, 'The Impact of Public Policies on Income Distribution in Peninsular Malaysia', *Economic Bulletin for Asia and the Pacific,* 30:2, December 1979, pp. 20–44.

Mangahas, Mahar, 'On the Construction of an Income Distribution Model: Baseline Data and Projections:' PREPF Equity Project Technical Paper, September 1977 (2).

Mangahas, Mahar, 'Indices of Ethnic Fractionalization and Imbalance', SERGPU/UNICEF Social Indicators Project Report No. 5, Kuala Lumpur, March 1978.

Mangahas, Mahar, 'Planning for Improved Equity in ASEAN, Hong Kong and the Republic of Korea', *Economic Bulletin for Asia and the Pacific,* 30:2, December 1979, pp. 1–19.

Mangahas, Mahar, 'What Happened to the Poor on the Way to the Next Development Plan?' paper presented at the Annual Conference of the Philippine Economics Society, 12 December 1981.

Meesook, Oey, 'Income Inequality in Thailand, 1962/63 and 1968/69' in CAMSJERC (1975)

Sajogyo, 'Garis Kemiskinan Kebutuhan Minimum' (The Poverty Line and Minimum Food Needs) *Kompas,* 4 November 1977.

Selowsky, Marcelo, 'Balancing Trickle-Down and Basic Needs Strategies', World Bank Staff Working Paper No. 335, Washington D.C., June 1979.

SERGPU, *Seminar Kebangsaan: Koordinasi Sistem Penilaian dan Penyelidikan Impek Pembangunan Sosio-Ekonomi,* Port Dickson, Malaysia, April 20–22, 1978.

Suh, Sang Mok, 'The Patterns of Poverty in Korea', Korea Development Institute, Working Paper 7903, 1979.

World Bank, *Thailand: Toward a Development Strategy of Full Participation,* Report No. 2059-TH, East Asia and Pacific Regional office, 1 Setember 1978.

World Bank, *Employment and Income Distribution and Indonesia,* Studies in Employment and Rural Development No. 51, Development Policy Staff, Washington, D.C., October 1978 (Draft).

## DISCUSSION OPENING – SUNG-HOOM KIM

Mahar Mangahas has made an excellent, extensive, in-depth survey of the ASEAN social indicators movement. In spite of the allegedly substantial proportion of people suffering from absolute poverty not only in ASEAN countries but also in other developing countries, the task of monitoring poverty and relative inequality has not been able to successfully attract respective attention in planning for national economic development programmes; also even the scholars in these countries have paid relatively little attention to this important issue, while concentrating on the techniques of measuring-such aggregates as national product and employment. In this respect, I think that Mahar Mangahas' recommendations concerning the monitoring task are legitimate and very timely. Most of my discussion will consist of adding some supplementary comments, rather than raising questions, to his paper.

My first comment is directed to the current debate between Sundrum (1976) and Sigit (1980-81) on the nature of the trend in income inequality, as introduced in Mr Mangahas' paper. It is interesting to note that Sigit in 1980 contended that 'it is not clear whether urban income inequality is definitely less than rural income inequality or even income inequality is growing or narrowing over time'.

In my opinion this contention should be viewed in the light of developmental stages in respective countries in order to arrive at a generally acceptable theory. When a country is at the stage where agriculture is dominant in the national economy, urban income inequality might appear to be less than its counterpart in rural sectors, simply because many poor or very poor people cannot find alternatives to remaining in the rural areas as simple farm-labourers and thus merely maintaining their subsistence livelihood there. But as industrialization *cum* urbanization proceeds as rapidly as seen in many developing countries, the poor and very poor including the destitute can more easily find alternative jobs in other than rural areas and they move to the urban industrial sectors. The rural-urban migration certainly transfers the rural poor to the urban sectors, but most of them still remain as naked-labourers. It is therefore natural to observe that the urban income inequality grows at a faster rate than that of rural sectors. At the same time, the overall relative inequality, too, is growing over time rather than narrowing, since government investments as well as other developmental programmes are more and more directed towards the urban/industrial sectors, causing relative poverty in rural sectors. Furthermore, rapid industrialization in developing countries is usually characterized by a handful of tycoon firms who take a lion's share of developmental profits. This fact implies that there are widening gaps not only between the urban and rural sectors but also between the 'haves' and the 'have-nots' in urban sectors. Within the rural areas themselves, there appears to be relatively narrowing inequality problems, as most of the rural poor find their way to rural-urban migration. These are the reasons why I believe the World Bank sees strong indications of increasing relative inequality but a narrowing one within rural areas in developing countries.

The second comment I want to make is that the social indicators movement should be able to identify factors underlining the very existence of the so-called vicious circle of poverty which has long been prevalent in developing countries. Age, education level, number of family members and location, all of which are introduced by Mr Mangahas on page 157, are, in my opinion, less meaningful or even superficial ex-post explanatory variables to determine the real chain of poverty. The current taxation policy, as found in most developing countries, is an example that helps explain how a majority of people (that is poor people) finance, if not sacrifice themselves for, a handful of rich people through the overwhelming indirect tax system. Without exploring the so-called structural problems and the built-in poverty-driven policies, the social indicators movement may remain only as a scholastic gesture.

In this context, I would like to emphasize the need for a preceding thorough survey (study) of the real reasons of a poverty-chain, before I join the author in declaring 'the past structure of development policies and programmes needs to be modified'. It is certainly high time to pursue plans and programmes concurrently to reduce income inequalities on the one hand and to enhance the general level of economic growth on the other. Lastly, I believe that those who stand in the frontier lines of the social indicators movement, should be able to clearly answer the question as to whether pursuing the equity-orientated policies and programmes, which aim to reduce social poverty and inequality, is less costly than pursuing the current efficiency-orientated developmental programmes in order to achieve the respective nation's ultimate goal of up-grading the quality of its people's life. In order to answer this conflicting question, the positive or negative relationships between current economic policies/programmes and consequent poverty/inequality events in the process of political, social and economic development need to be carefully examined. Without this, there remains a danger that the social indicators movement is simply a scholastic contender. At the same time, social indicators studies may be needed to delineate what should be the ultimate goal of national development and how this goal might be achieved in both the short-term and long-term.

With all these comments, I would like to join the participants in congratulating Mahar Mangahas on his pioneering work in measurement of poverty and inequality in ASEAN countries.

## GENERAL DISCUSSION*

The view was expressed that studies based on differences between groups missed the variability found within groups. This was important when comparing agricultural and industrial incomes as variability in the former was likely to be much greater.

It was felt that when considering 'social expenditure' it was important to distinquish between those social services that provide access to important 'public goods', such as education and health, and those measures which aim to redistribute current income flows, such as food subsidy programmes. The

*Papers by Bhalla and Leiseson and Mangahas.

former are likely to be more cost-effective.

Regarding income differences, it was stated that absolute as well as relative measures were important.

Participants in the discussion included Adolf Weber, S. Chiroapanda, Bruce Johnston, H. von Witzte and H.M.G. Herath.

FREDERIC O. SARGENT*

# An Economic Model of Rural-Agricultural Sectors

## INTRODUCTION

Models[1] to explain agricultural development and guide policy have proliferated in the last score of years. They have been developed by deductive reasoning from general theories, from empirical observations of a large number of cases, and from case studies of individual experiences. The list of models includes Rostov's five stages, Hirshman's unbalanced growth, Lewis's capital formation with underemployed labour, Frank's metropolis-satellite, Furtado's dependence theory, structuralism, import substitution, neoclassical model, and others. National economies whose experience has been extrapolated into development models include the United States, the Soviet Union, China, France, Sweden, Yugoslavia, Mexico, Brazil, Tanzania (Reynolds, 1975; Wilber, 1979). Special sectors such as industry, agriculture, or trade have been studied intensively with a view toward developing models. Each of these models provides useful concepts and examples and each one also has some limitation as a general theory. In spite of the many models which have been developed, there is general agreement among economists and administrators that there is still room for new models or revisions of those previously articulated (Britton, 1981). This paper presents a model developed by study of labour intensive agriculture in the United States.

The point of view and method of this paper is that of an institutional economist rather than a neoclassical, or neo-Marxist economist. The significant attributes of institutional economics that differentiate it from other theories are in (a) the function of theory, (b) the role of government, (c) the concept of man, (d) the ideal or model economy, and (e) addiction to a multidiscipline inductive methodology (Adams, 1980; Gruchy, 1947).

Neoclassical theory presents a rationale for the free market, competitive, capitalist economy. Neo-Marxist theory provides a critique of capitalism and advocates an equitable, classless society. Institutional economists

*The author appreciates the valuable suggestions of Reyes-Pacheco, Thomas Niles, Neil Pelsue Jr., and C. Lynn Fife.

emphasize a research method. Institutional economics has a pragmatic, inductive, multi-discipline methodology for solving socio-economic-political problems.

The preferred role of government in neoclassical theory is 'as little as possible'. In neo-Marxist theory the government evolves from central authority to 'as little as possible'. In countries led by adherents to both theories, governments play a dominant central role. The institutional economist recognizes this fact and accepts government as a fundamental institution.

Neoclassical economics assumes man is an individual, economic profit maximizer. Neo-Marxist assumes man is divided into conflicting classes. The institutionalist assumes man is an interdependent and social animal organized with others into social-political units capable of co-operative collective activity in the pursuit of multiple goals.

The ideal of society implied in neoclassical theory is a free market economy guided by the invisible hand. For the neo-Marxist it is a classless society following several preliminary stages. Institutionalists do not advocate an ideal model but their value premises and the literature indicate that they prefer central government planning in contrast to the neoclassical model and democratic, decentralized control in contrast to the Marxist model. A distinctive attribute of institutional economics is that it borrows concepts from several social science disciplines and treats values by investigation.

In this paper we assume that equity is a public value or goal coequal with productivity and efficiency (Schertz, 1981).

## DEFINITION OF THE RURAL-AGRICULTURAL (R-A) SECTOR

The unit of study in this paper requires a definition since it is not a conventional concept. The unit is a geographical and political region with special physical, social, political, and economic attributes. To define this concept it is necessary to differentiate it from the agricultural economists' concept of the 'agricultural sector' from the rural sociologists' concept of 'rural' and to contrast it with the urban-industrial sector.

### *The R-A sector vs the commercial agriculture (C-A) sector*

In US agricultural economic literature the term 'agriculture' refers to commercial agriculture. It refers to a summation of census data describing the larger, full-time, capital-intensive, more-profitable farms. It excludes small and part-time farms and does not refer to political units. The rural-agricultural sector concept of this paper refers to political units – that is towns, townships or counties which are rural and characterized by low-income and labour intensive, less-profitable agricultural enterprises. The conventional definition of agriculture is that of an industrial type sector. The rural-agricultural concept is a political, rural low-income region. The C-A concept refers to business units, the R-A concept to a socio-political unit (Colman, 1968; Brown, 1980).

In the United States these two concepts are spatially distinct. The commercial, capital-intensive large farm agricultural sector embraces midwest corn-hog farms, Wisconsin dairy farms, large western ranches, and feed lots, 100th meridian wheat farms, and California and Florida citrus groves and vegetable production.

The low-income rural-agricultural sectors are concentrated in the Appalachian region; the Ozark and Ouachita Mountain areas of Missouri, Arkansas, and Oklahoma; the northern counties of Minnesota, Wisconsin, and Michigan; northern New England (Vermont, New Hampshire, Maine); the Black Belt of the old South, along the US–Mexican border in Texas, New Mexico, Arizona, California; American Indian reservations in New Mexico and Arizona; the upper Great Plains; and upper New York (Colman, 1968). The total number of people in the R-A sector is difficult to determine as the census does not include this category. A recent USDA report states that there are nearly 10 million rural poor (Brown, Steward, and Ingalsbe, 1980). The total number of residents of R-A towns probably reaches 15 to 20 million.

Agriculture economists in the United States have focused their attention on the commercial, capital-intensive sector. They define the low-income sector as a social problem rather than an economic problem. Their prescription has been for low-income rural people to move out of agriculture and for rural poverty to be alleviated by welfare programmes not by market focused agricultural policies. This prescription has guided US policies for agriculture and rural areas for five decades (Bergland, 1981).

R-A sectors also differ physically from C-A sectors. R-A land is not prime agricultural land. It usually has poorer soils, more slope, and less water. Commercial agriculture is typically on the better soils, level land with adequate water. This spatial separation between the R-A and C-A sectors also occurs in many developing countries.

*The R-A sector vs 'Rural' sectors*

Sociologists contribute a great deal to the understanding of rural society but they do not define it in terms of political units. They study poverty, family, attitudes, organizations and so on, without specific regard to geographic areas and political units. While they do find that these characteristics vary between rural and urban areas they also declare that the rural-urban dichotomy is relatively unimportant (Dewey, 1960). Rural society, they hold, is similar to urban society but less developed. This paper makes an opposite assumption that rural society is significantly different from urban society in all critical attributes – government, goals, concept of land, values, mutual dependence, family organization, and way of life (Sargent, 1979).

Residents of rural towns practice direct democracy and self-government. Urban-Industrial regions, because of their size, must practise representative government. In New England, rural towns practise direct participatory democracy with annual town meetings where all interested citizens attend and vote. In rural communities, generally, local government organizations make many local decisions.

Public goals for land use in rural towns are more varied than those of urban governments. Urban goals feature growth in five categories – residential, commercial, industrial, parks, and utilities (Sargent, 1979). In rural areas, governments may pursue at least six goals that are not viable opportunities in urban areas: maintain a rural environment; protect natural areas; preserve wildlife habitats; foster extensive outdoor recreation; maintain natural aesthetic values; and protect wetlands, steep slopes, and higher elevations from development.

In the rural-agricultural sector attitudes of interdependence and co-operation take precedence over the attitude of competition (Sargent, 1979). In the US this attitude derives from the pioneer heritage where people had to work together to maintain security, raise a barn, harvest a crop, run a school, or celebrate a holiday. This attitude is still strong in many rural-agricultural towns in northern New England. An attitude of co-operation rather than competition is also dominant in agricultural sectors in many developing countries.

The concept of land ownership and use varies between rural and urban society. In urban areas, all land is considered developable space. Its value is determined by its distance from the city centre or transportation facilities and the cost of building. Swamps, or even open water, may be considered 'land' as they can be drained or filled and built upon; steep slopes can be levelled. In rural areas, land value is largely determined by its natural physical characteristics and productivity. Its wetness, permeability, fertility, slope, erodibility, elevation, microclimate, view, accessibility, or animal habitat are the natural characteristics that govern its value. Land ownership is valued as a basis for the rural way of life. It provides food, clothing, a store of value, a status indicator, a means of transferring wealth to the next generations, and a source of cash for emergencies or retirement (Sargent, 1979).

*The R-A sector vs the urban-industrial sector*

The R-A sector must be differentiated from the Urban-Industrial (U-I) sector in order to explain its growth and decline and justify special policies. The R-A sector is traditional rather than profit or market oriented. This fact has several ramifications. R-A areas have less quantity and quality of housing, education, municipal services, medical services, recreation, facilities, job opportunities, per caput personal income, and supply of capital (Colman, 1968).

The agricultural production process in R-A sectors differs from industrial production in a number of ways and each one leads to lower farm profits.

1 Many agricultural products are dependent upon biological and botanical growth cycles. The producer of these products cannot adjust production to market conditions in the short run to maximize returns. The industrial producers often can.

2 Agricultural production fluctuates with the vagaries of the weather. An agricultural producer cannot produce countercyclically to the

weather to benefit from weather-caused, price fluctuations. Industrial production is not weather-limited.

3 Traditional agricultural production is organized by sole proprietors who provide labour, management, ownership, and make savings by reducing necessary consumption. In industry the functions of ownership, management, labour, savings, and investment are provided by separate specialists. In neoclassical terms the small-scale family farmer is 'submarginal'. In Marxist's terms he would be considered 'precapitalistic'. In institutionalist terms he represents a basic institution – the family farm. Since agricultural production depends on family labour, the labour supply cannot be adjusted to seasonal or annual requirements. Hence, both underemployment and family labour exploitation are endemic. In industrial production, the labour input is adjusted to production requirements and all inputs are provided by specialists.

4 Demand for agricultural products is more inelastic than demand for manufactured products. The agricultural producer faces a horizontal demand curve; the industrial producer a sloping demand curve.

5 Agriculture is closer to pure competition than industrial production. Pure competition produces no economic rent or profit. Agricultural producers cannot increase their price by reducing their supply. Industrial producers generally enjoy an oligopolistic position in the market. They avoid price competition and employ price leadership, product differentiation, and advertising to obtain a monopolistic profit.

6 The equilibrium price of agricultural products tends toward the lowest amount that producers will accept – a return consisting of low wages, low returns to management, a required return to capital, but no economic profit. Industry requires the going rate of return to all factors plus an economic profit to assure continued operation.

7 Product differentiation is difficult for most agricultural products. Product differentiation with attendant higher prices is a general practice in the manufacturing sector.

8 Agricultural production requires close, personal management. This fact leads to increasing costs and diseconomies of scale. Industry, including the processing of agricultural products is favoured by decreasing costs and economies of scale. This leads to growth in firm size and eventual oligopolization. Firms become larger and develop the economic power to initiate vertical and horizontal integration and obtain monopolistic profits.

9 Agricultural production is generally located distant from central markets. Agricultural producers have high transportation costs that more distant agricultural producers must absorb. Industrial production is generally located in urban transportation centres.

10 The agricultural enterprises in the R-A sector are labour intensive, and hence, less productive and less profitable than industry which is capital-intensive.

In summary the R-A sector consists of separate, distinguishable, and significant political, social, and geographical units of low-income farmers and rural people whose characteristics distinguish them from the commercial-agricultural sector, the urban-industrial sector, and the sociologists' concept of 'rural' society.

## THREE PARTIAL THEORIES

A multidiscipline model of rural-agricultural sectors defined above may be constructed by combining three partial theories taken from five disciplines: (a) urbanization – the concept that central city growth is the central and dominant force in regional economic development (from regional economics); (b) natural resource determinism – the concept that the natural resource base is the major determinant of the location and rate of economic development (from resource economics and economic geography); and (c) government activism – the concept that the government role is to develop public goals, guide resource allocation, and influence income distribution (from institutional economics and political science). Let us review these three partial theories and then combine them to construct a multidiscipline model of R-A sectors.

### *Urbanization – the driving force of regional economic development*

Urbanization is a familiar concept in several social sciences – regional and resource economics, sociology, human ecology, economic geography, and history. The patron saint of this theory for economists is the German, Johann Heinrich von Thünen. In 1826, he published Der Isolierte Staat, which explained the location of economic activities by transportation costs and distance from the urban centre. Researchers in contributing disciplines have updated and augmented von Thünen's model to produce a complex economic development theory based on location and transportation costs.

The urbanization process may be compared to a wagon wheel. The city is a huge hub of industrial, commercial, and financial activity. The spokes are transportation arteries that extend to natural resources in the rural periphery. The spokes carry investment funds and entrepreneurs out to the rural area and bring back raw natural resources for processing, manufacture, and distribution. The hub city (or developed economy) has favourable terms of trade with all of the rural areas (or LDCs) from which it draws resources as its functions are more capital-intensive, mechanized, industrialized, productive, and profitable. The central city continuously accumulates capital and wealth and improved technology. As its area of dominance expands and as the urban centre expands, economic activity extends further into the rural hinterland but with diminishing levels of intensity. The direction, speed, and location of the urban-industrial growth into rural areas is governed by transportation facilities and costs and the suitability of the rural natural resources for economic exploitation. The dynamo that energizes the urban centre is found in the law of economic concentration which operates most effectively in urban centres. This urban-centred economic force is pervasive and strong. It dominates the growth process in the rural hinterlands.

Rural areas prosper when investment comes in but decline when the natural resource base is depleted or exhausted or more productive resource sources are found. They lack the urban centre's possibility of continuous cumulative growth, continuous capital accumulation, and profitable production.

*Natural resources – the spatial determinant of rural development*

The natural resource base of a rural area, plus the distance to the urban centre and the resource demands of the urban centre, determine the location and rate of rural development. Rural people are drawn into the process as labour when the urban entrepreneurs need manpower to develop and process the resources.

Rural natural resources include agricultural land, extensive recreational land, forests, mineral-bearing land, low-density residential areas, and ski slopes. The greater the quantity and quality of these resources, the greater their proximity to an urban centre; or the stronger the demand, the faster a rural area will develop. Rural areas with few or poor resources, or those too expensive to extract and exploit, or those a long distance from the urban centre, will be developed more slowly.

Erich W. Zimmermann, in his classic treatise, explained the central role of natural resources in economic development (Zimmermann, 1951). It was inherent in Zimmermann's theory that resources change with changes in technology and, therefore, so does their impact. This principle has been demonstrated in northern New England. With the replacement of water power by hydroelectric power and the settlement of more productive agriculture land in the West, the hill town communities in northern New England declined. Timber resources, plus a harbour, stimulated the development of many rural seashore communities in New England. They gradually declined after the timber resource was depleted, and wood was replaced by steel in boat building. The economic history of most small rural towns in northern New England can be explained in terms of several cycles of exploitation of the natural resource base.

In the very long run, rural areas tend toward an equilibrium between the carrying capacity of the resource base and the population. This equilibrium is achieved by inflow or outflow of people. The level of living at equilibrium is low when the resource base is poor and high when the resource base is varied and productive. This adjustment toward an equilibrium often requires several decades or even generations. Rural towns in Vermont have gone through a number of cycles of growth and decline based on resource discovery exploitation, depletion, and then decline. This has occurred on the basis of potash, lumber, grain, sheep, butter, cheese, milk, and tourism.

*Government management – allocating resources, developing public goals, distributing wealth*

Neoclassical economic theory minimizes and misrepresents the role of government. The value premise that market resource allocation is good and government interference is bad leads to a failure to see how government and market complement each other and a failure to adequately recognize the necessary functions of government. In capitalist, mixed, and socialist countries alike, the government has three necessary functions: (a) to establish public goals; (b) to participate with the market in varying combinations to allocate resources, and (c) to influence wealth distribution through taxing and spending policies. These three functions are carried out with varying degrees of efficacy at the local, regional, and national level. In northern New England, rural towns set their public goals which are invariably different from the public goals of cities. National and regional governments set national or regional goals and determine resource allocations to the public sector. The third function – influencing income distribution – is a major responsibility of national governments. National tax laws, credit subsidies, and spending programmes may favour various sectors in various degrees. A policy may favour the wealthy and rely on trickle-down to distribute income to others. It may feature a transfer of wealth from urban centres to the rural-agricultural hinterland. US agricultural policy has for several decades favoured large, capital intensive, commercial farms over small, labour-intensive, family farms. President Johnson's war on poverty programme provided an income transfer to low-income R-A regions. President Reagan's tax relief for high-income people constitutes a transfer from low-income to higher-income recipients.

The national government establishes the rules of the game concerning the distribution of wealth produced by natural resource exploitation. The extent to which the national government taxes this gain and the way it distributes it determines the income distribution pattern of the country.

## ECONOMICS OF THE R-A/U-I RELATIONSHIP

Utilizing these three partial theories we now have the building blocks for a model. Rural development or decline is the result of the interaction of these three major processes: (a) the urbanization process; (b) natural resource exploitation; and (c) the governmental action in developing public goals, allocating resources and distributing wealth. We can now develop an economic model based on these forces and the exchanges between the R-A sector and the U-I sector. The descriptive part of this model may be detailed in 10 propositions.

1 The urban-industrial centre and the rural-agricultural hinterland interact to constitute an economic system – one providing capital, manufactured products, and a market; the other, providing agricultural products and primary raw materials.

2 The energizer of this system is the urban-industrial centre. As this urban area grows in productivity, population, wealth, technology, and economic activity, demand for rural natural resources grows and investment capital is accumulated.

3 A circular urban-rural flow of money is established. Urban entre-

preneurs take savings from the urban centre of capital accumulation and invest it in the rural area to exploit the natural resources. Returns to capital, entrepreneurship and investors flow back to the urban centre. Wages for labour and small local expenditures remain in the rural area. This circle may have some modifications. Some capital is saved and invested by local people, but on the other hand capital intensive production spends very little in local wages or supplies.

4 A circular flow of people develops. Entrepreneurs and labourers go to the rural, resource producing areas when rural production is expanding. When the resources are depleted the rural economy declines and unemployed people move back to the urban centre. Those committed to the rural way of life remain.

5 A flow of resources occurs. Natural resources move from the rural sector to the urban area where they are processed or manufactured and distributed throughout the urban centre's trade area. Some are returned to the rural area as manufactured goods.

6 The urban-rural flows of capital, people, resources and goods continue until the rural natural resource is depleted. As rural resource production declines the rural level of living declines and a rural to urban flow of people commences.

7 These flows between urban and rural areas constitute an economic system that provides continuous growth at the urban centre and growth, decline, and stagnation cycles in the rural periphery.

8 The R-A sectors have inferior terms of trade *vis-à-vis* the U-I sector. This is because of the differential productivity between urban and rural areas. Rural-agricultural production is labour intensive, utilizing much hand labour, and is less profit-producing per caput. The U-I sector is capital-intensive, employing large inputs of machinery and technology and is more profitable.[2]

9 Governments set the rules for the relationship between urban and rural sectors. They may favour the urban capital accumulators and entrepreneurs, or they may tax U-I wealth and transfer it to the R-A sector in the interests of market stabilization or equity or they may do some of both. Government policy is critical.

10 Rural natural resources are exploited by the urban entrepreneur. Whether or not rural people are exploited depends upon their mobility, their alternatives, government policies, and resource ownership.

This urban-rural exchange constitutes a dynamic system. Urban centres expand continuously, drawing on an ever-widening circle of rural areas, until growth is restrained by government policies. Rural areas fluctuate according to the resource base. They may grow as long as the resources supply the fuel. If the resource base is depleted they can decline to a subsistence level economy. Rural areas in the United States have grown, declined, grown again, and declined again as the natural resource base was exploited and depleted; and then a new resource is discovered and, in turn, developed, exploited and depleted.

The direction and magnitude of these circular flows explains the relative poverty in the rural-agricultural sector. The most significant ratio is the amount of wealth produced and exported from the rural town to the city compared with the amount of wealth sent from the U-I sector to the R-A sector. Urban entrepreneurs and investors require a profitable return while rural workers will work for a minimum wage in order to pursue their preferred rural way of life or because they have limited alternatives. Urban areas have a near-monopoly on industrial technology, entrepreneurship and capital and so can charge a higher-than-competitive price for their products. Rural production is under conditions closer to pure competition and so wages are reduced to the lowest amount workers will accept. This means that the R-A sector has disadvantageous terms of trade *vis-a-vis* the U-I sector. The late E. F. Schumacker called this relationship 'internal colonialism' (Schumacker, 1977).

## GOVERNMENT POLICIES, AGENCIES, AND CONTROLS

The foregoing presents the spatial, physical, and economic framework of the U-I – R-A relationship and shows how economic forces operating under free market conditions lead to a low level of living for the R-A sector in comparison to the U-I and C-A sectors. To complete this model it is necessary to indicate the government policies that must be employed to mitigate and compensate this result. Governments may use a variety of policies, agencies and controls: supervised credit, co-operatives, taxation, subsidies, investments, and regulatory laws. The objective of these policies is to achieve a national goal of greater equity as well as greater productivity.

Direct government investment in social infrastructure and consumer subsidies is a proven method. Subsidies for housing, water supply systems, fish ponds, sewage disposal systems, schools, meals, playgrounds, community centres and health services will contribute the largest percentage assistance to the lowest income recipients (Johnson, 1980). This type of assistance found in antipoverty programmes of the L.B. Johnson administration in the United States was very effective in raising the floor of the level of living of people in R-A sectors generally.

The government planning process (local, regional, and national) may be co-ordinated as a tool to improve the R-A sector position. Potential centres of rural growth may be identified and supported through a national programme of decentralization of government facilities. These centres (in Latin America they are called *polos de desarrollo*) with national government assistance, can be encouraged to develop processing plants and small industries.

Taxation policies should be based on comparative productive efficiency. This would lead to heavier taxes on the more productive U-I and C-A sectors and lower taxes on the R-A sector.

Co-operatives, a supervised farm credit system, and a law to discourage corporate purchase of farmland are necessary institutions. Saskatchewan, Canada, provides one of the best examples of a cluster of policies that effectively promote the interests of the family farm dominated R-A sector rather than corporate farming and the commercial-agricultural sector. Co-operatives help the small producer or consumer to capture a larger proportion of the rural-urban flows of capital, wages, salaries, interest, and profits from the urban-manufacturing sectors. Co-operatives are also expressions of rural attitudes of mutual, local, self-dependence. Agricultural economists have long appreciated these aspects of co-operatives and have been in the forefront in advocating and supporting them as ameliorative rural institutions.

The issue of free trade versus managed trade has been debated in the literature for many decades. First British and then US economists advocated free trade while European and later LDC economists explain the necessity for managed trade and import substitution. This model helps clarify this controversy. Developing countries are predominantly rural-agricultural. Their terms of trade are generally disadvantageous *vis-à-vis* developed (urban centre) countries as they export more competitive and less profitable primary products and import manufactured goods. Free trade, based on comparative advantage, continues this unequal exchange. The economic returns to the LDC would not be sufficient to permit them to accumulate capital necessary for massive investments in more profitable, capital-intensive, industrial production. In order to escape the vicious circle of low productivity and poverty a LDC must change the structure of its trade. It must set goals of providing basic human needs to its own people and processing its own raw materials as well as exporting to earn foreign exchange. To accumulate capital to implement this programme it must take full advantage of trade which is the prime source of foreign hard currency. This can be accomplished only by managing trade to assure that all hard currency earned is invested in support of the national development plan rather than spent for luxuries or private consumption (Sargent, 1961).

## SUMMARY AND CONCLUSION

The polarization fostered by the conflicting theories of neoclassical and neo-Marxist economics inhibits development of an alternative model to explain and provide policies for rural-agricultural, low-income, labour-intensive sectors. The pragmatic and inductive method of the institutional economist can make a contribution. The basic concepts of urbanization, natural resource determinism, spatial analysis, and democratic government may be combined to produce a multidiscipline model. First we divide the economy into three sectors: urban-industrial, commercial agricultural, and rural agricultural. Next we analyze the relationship of these three sectors. Third we propose policies to achieve greater equity for the rural-agricultural sector.

## NOTES

[1]A model is 'a theoretical projection in detail of a possible system of human relationships (as in economics,...)'. Webster's *Third New International Dictionary,* unabridged, 1971.

[2]Mary H. Osgood states 'as distances from an urban center increase, so does the incidence of poverty. In the most distant and sparsely settled counties, the poverty rate is 2½ times that in metropolitan areas: nearly half (44%) of the nation's poor reside in nonmetropolitan areas', *Social Work,* Vol. 22, No. 1, January 1977, pp. 41–7.

## REFERENCES

Adams, John (ed.), *Institutional Economics,* Martinus Nijhoff Pub., 1980.

Bergland, Bob (ed.), *A Time to Choose: Summary Report on the Structure of Agriculture,* US Dept of Agriculture, Jan. 1981.

Bishop, C. E., (ed.), *The People Left Behind,* A Report of the President's National Advisory Commission on Rural Poverty, US Govt Printing Office, Sept. 1967.

Britton, Denis K. in Johnson, Glen, and Maunder, Allen (eds.), *Rural Change,* Gower for IAAE, 1981.

Brown, David L., Steward, Donald D. and Ingalsbe, Gene (eds.), *Rural Development Perspectives,* ESCS, US Dept Agriculture, 1980.

Colman, Wm. G. (ed.), *Urban and Rural America: Policies for Future Growth,* Advisory Commission on Intergovernmental Relations, US Govt Printing Office, Washington, D.C., 1968.

Dewey, Richard, 'The Rural-Urban Continuum: Real but Relatively Unimportant', *Am. J. of Sociology,* Vol. 66, No. 1, 1960.

Ferguson, Marilyn, *The Aquarian Conspiracy,* J. P. Tarcher, Houghton Mifflin, 1980.

Gruchy, Allan G. *Modern Economic Thought – The American Contribution,* Prentice-Hall, Inc., N.Y., 1947.

Johnson, H. Wayne, (ed.), *Rural Human Services,* F. E. Peacock, 1980.

Reynolds, Lloyd G. (ed.), *Agriculture in Development Theory,* Yale Univ. Press, 1975.

Sargent, Frederic O., 'A Suggested Trade Policy for Developing Agricultural Nations', *Canadian Journal of Agricultural Economics,* Vol. IX, No. 2, pp. 107–117, 1961.

Sargent, Frederic O., and Sargent, Blaine P., *Rural Water Planning,* Vervana Publishers, Ch. 15, 1979.

Schertz, Lyle P., 'The Quest for Equity', *The Rural Challenge,* IAAE. Occasional Paper, No. 2, p. 240, 1981.

Schumacker, E.F., *As If People Mattered,* 1977.

Wilber, Charles K. (ed.), *The Political Economy of Development and Underdevelopment,* Random House, N.Y., Second Ed., 1979.

Zimmermann, Erich W., *World Resources and Industries,* Harper, N.Y., 1951.

## DISCUSSION OPENING – FAISAL KASRYNO

The model presented by Professor Sargent is an institutional economics approach to rural development and is an appropriate model for explaining agricultural or rural development in developing countries.

Institutional economics basically contains two objectives: a) to explain the evolution of economics and b) to analyse the effects of institutions on resource allocation and income distribution. The usefulness of institutional economics in explaining economic phenomena rests on its ability to clarify some facts that appear at the outset to contradict classical and neoclassical economic predictions, such as the existence of tenancy together with wage labour and contracts indicate failure in the markets for some factor of productions. Rural institutions are dynamic and changing over time and vary across regions due to variations in prices, resource endowment as well as political aspects. For example *Bawon* is a rural institution that governs the harvesting labour share of the rice harvest and this varies between regions in Java and changes over time. In 1969/1970 *Bawon* or the harvesting labour share of rice was ⅙ of the yield in the northern plain of Java. In 1979/1980 the labour share declined to ⅛ or ⅒. If the share remained at ⅙, compulsory work was added by the inclusion of transplanting and weeding tasks in order to obtain the right to harvest and recieve ⅙ of the yield. These changes are the results of increasing population on a limited supply of land and nearly unchanged employment opportunities in the non-agricultural sectors.

A question that may need further discussion is whether rural institutions create inefficiency in resource allocation and income distribution or promote efficiency. If rural institutions, such as tenancy or land tenure, create inefficiency, should government abolish the institution, for example through agrarian and land reform or create or induce changes in other factor markets, for example by creating/inducing employment opportunities in the non-agricultural sector.

The economic model presented on pp. 169–170 is, perhaps, one that can be fitted into activity analysis such as I.O or L.P. models with multiple objective functions. If this is so, the question will be what is the relevance of the institutional economics approach in the model.

I think in explaining the existence and evolution of institutions or economic organization, such as contracts, conventional economic tools such as costs, benefits and equilibrium still can be applied. To explain resource allocation and income distribution and their changes over time and differences across regions, institutional economics can be used in conjunction with classical and neoclassical economics and not as an alternative. And this matter may need further discussion in this session.

Differences between the marginal productivities of factors of production and factor prices may perhaps be due to an inability to measure the level of inputs used, and the appropriate costs to be included, such as costs of information and supervision and political aspects. The solution by contracts or through institutions will approach the competitive market solution. Studies in Java have noted that imputed wage rates for the *Bawon* system and contract labour are nearly the same as market wage rates. Returns to factors of production (land and labour) in share tenancy arrangement were also nearly the same as the level of market land rent and wage rates, whenever appropriate costs were computed, such as supervision, information and search costs. To quote Roumasset, 1978:

> If property rights are well established, contracts are easily enforced, information costs are negligible, and numbers are sufficient to make attempts to monopolize unstable, then factor of production will be

allocated efficiently and receive their competitive factor payments, whether markets exist or not.

If search and information costs exist then the set of institutions which minimize excess burden or maximize the difference between benefits and costs will evolve. Problems of course will arise in measuring the excess burden. The role of government could be in providing information.

## GENERAL DISCUSSION – RAPPORTEUR: B. H. KINSEY

It was pointed out that the paper, while very interesting, may represent a minority viewpoint and raises two explicit questions: (a) What is the theoretical standing of the concept of a 'sector' defined in geographical terms? and (b) How is a 'resource' to be technically defined within this concept of a sector? It appeared possible, for example, for what was defined as a resource in the urban areas to be considered no longer a resource outside this area.

Experience in the UK indicated that, with a somewhat broader scope, it was not necessary to confine the definition of a sector to a geographical area. Boundaries have been defined for the 'less-favoured' areas in the UK but the definitional problem does not arise because additional categories – such as non-viable farms or an unfavourable age structure in agriculture – can be employed to identify the rural agricultural sector. There was also disagreement with the observation that the rural unemployed drift into the towns, as UK experience had shown the opposite – or at least that the unemployed 'back up' in the rural sector. The question was also raised as to what additional policy instruments were advocated by the author for improving the situation described.

It was also pointed out that value systems differ in rural and urban sectors, a fact which creates difficulties so far as achieving equity is concerned. What is the goal of the rural sector in relation to equity?

Concern was expressed as to whether the ecological considerations could be given due weight in the rural-agricultural sector model. Economics and ecological considerations may well dictate different patterns of land allocation to different activities. Is it possible to have a pattern of land use incorporating the concept of common property resource use?

Frederic Sargent responded that the importance of politics and political choice in relationship to resource ownership and use is recognised. The setting for the paper – the US state of Vermont – may impose restrictions on the general applicability of the model, but Vermont should be regarded in this sense as a laboratory, and other researchers will have to tailor the concepts in the rural-agricultural sector model to their own particular circumstances.

An improvement in social services is a common prescription for improving the situation of that part of the population living in the rural-agricultural sector, but the inefficiency of such services has to be both recognized and lived with – the latter because rural-agricultural dwellers do have different values. Surveys have been done to determine people's own definitions and concept of equity as well as their psychic value systems, and the differences are clearly revealed. It has also been established that ecological considerations rank as important in their value systems.

Participants in the discussion included Michel Petit, G. W. Furness, Takeo Misawa and M. G. Chandrakanth.

JOHN M. ANTLE

# *Infrastructure and Agricultural Productivity: Theory, Evidence and Implication for Growth and Equity in Agricultural Development*

## INTRODUCTION

The publication of T.W. Schultz's book *Transforming Traditional Agriculture* in 1964 marked a watershed in the economic development literature. As Schultz demonstrated in his analysis of the doctrine of surplus agricultural labour, much of the earlier development literature was based on the presumption – either implicit or explicit – that farm people do not make economically rational decisions and therefore do not allocate resources efficiently. Since the early 1960s an overwhelming body of economic research has shown that Schultz's hypothesis – that farm people are economically rational – is consistent with empirical fact. Other elements of the Schultzian model of agricultural development, closely related to the economic rationality of farm people, have also received much empirical support. Research has shown that farmers in traditional agricultures allocate resources efficiently, subject to the technical, economic and institutional constraints they face, and that sustained productivity growth depends on the successful adoption of new technology by farmers. Investments in agricultural research are necessary to create the new technology which is needed for productivity growth and investments in the human capital of farm people are necessary to provide farmers with the ability to learn of and use the new technologies.

The aim of this paper is to present theoretical analysis and empirical evidence in support of the hypothesis that another essential component of the agricultural development process – in terms of both growth and equity – is investment in the stock of physical infrastructure narrowly defined as transportation and communication infrastructure. The importance of infrastructure is demonstrated within the Schultzian model of agricultural development by observing that the economic rationality of farmers implies that their farm productivity depends on the perceived costs and benefits of the technological alternatives they face. It is argued that the effects of transportation and communications infrastructure on these costs and benefits are important determinants of the farmer's production technology choice and hence of farm productivity. These effects operate through the cost of new inputs from the non-agricultural sector (such as improved seed varieties and fertilizers) which accompany the new technology, the demand for the farmer's output, and the cost of economic and technical information associated with the new technologies. In addition to these microeconomic effects, it is argued that development of infrastructure increases aggregate agricultural productivity by increasing the efficiency of resource utilization on the aggregate level.

While the empirical evidence presented here supports the hypothesis that investment in infrastructure is important to agricultural productivity, it is also important to consider the implications of development of infrastructure for the equitable distribution of the benefits of technical change. The distribution issue is very important because it is often alleged that technical change may increase absolute income disparities across farm families, especially when land ownership is highly skewed, as well as across regions in a country. Analysis of the role infrastructure plays in the diffusion and adoption of new technology suggests that infrastructure projects promote productivity growth and may also lead to a more equitable distribution of the benefits of agricultural growth among farmers. The increased equity is due to the fact that the new technology is largely scale neutral but its productivity depends on the farmer's access to the technical information and inputs which complement it. Infrastructure investments produce benefits in the form of reduced costs for information and inputs which are complementary to the new technology, and these benefits are public goods which cannot be excluded from individuals. Therefore, development of infrastructure more equitably distributes the new technology, and hence its benefits, in the agricultural sector.

The paper begins with a brief discussion of theoretical foundations for the hypothesis that agricultural productivity is a function of transport and communications infrastructure. The second section surveys the empirical evidence on this hypothesis. The final section considers the implications of these empirical findings for both growth and equity in the agricultural development process.

## THEORETICAL FOUNDATIONS

Infrastructure may affect agricultural productivity at both the farm level and the aggregate or sectoral level. In this section each of these distinct dimensions of the productivity effect of infrastructure are considered.

To illustrate the farm-level effects of infrastructure let us consider a simple model of farmer behaviour under technical change. When new technologies are available to farmers they face the problem of choosing the best, or optimal, technology from the available technology set. For purposes of illustration, we assume farmers may choose a *production technology* $\tau$ from the set $T$ of available technologies; $\tau$ in turn defines the set of feasible input vectors $x$ associated with each technology. Together $x$ and $\tau$ characterize the farmer's production process. The set $T$ of available technologies is a function of agricultural research, $R$. In addition, the outcome of the production process depends on the farmer's ability to use the technology, so we define each technology as a function of the farmer's technical knowledge, $K$, and any other fixed factors of production, $Z$. Thus we let

$$\tau = \tau(K,Z),\ \tau \varepsilon T(R) \quad (1)$$

The farmer's production function is defined as

$$Q = \mathrm{f}(\mathrm{x},\tau) \quad (2)$$

and shows how output, $Q$, depends on the technology $\tau$ and the quantities of physical inputs $x$.

Infrastructure enters the model through price effects in product and input markets and information cost effects. The price effects are due to the well-known relationships between transportation costs and market prices of outputs and inputs (see, for example, Lele, 1971 and Rao and Subbarao, 1976); in addition, transport costs have a substantial effect on the non-monetary costs of gaining access to markets, especially in terms of the opportunity cost of time spent in transport. The information cost effects are due to the relationship between transportation and communications and the costs of acquiring the economic and technical information needed to use new technology. Defining $p_i$ as output and input prices and letting $TC$ represent costs of transportation and communication services, we may therefore write $p_i$ and $K$ as the following functions:

$$\begin{aligned} p_i &= p_i(TC, \text{ demand-supply factors}) \quad (3) \\ K &= K(TC, \text{ education, extension contact}). \end{aligned}$$

Prices thus depend on $TC$ as well as other demand-supply factors, and the farmer's accumulated technical knowledge depends on his formal education and the amount of extension contact he has as well as $TC$.

To complete the model we assume farmers make technology choices so as to maximize some criterion function $U(\cdot)$ which depends on profit and any other factors, such as risk aversion or home consumption, which may affect decision making. The farmer's decision problem is

$$\max_{x,\tau} U = U(\pi, \text{ other variables})$$

$$\text{subject to: } \pi = p_0 Q - \sum_{i=1}^{n} p_i x_i,\ (1), (2), (3). \quad (4)$$

Solution of this decision problem illustrates the channels through which infrastructure affects the farmer's choice of technology and hence his productivity. Through its price effects on the demand for the farmer's output and the supplies of inputs, the cost of transportation and communications may affect the economic incentives farmers perceive for use of the 'traditional' technology versus potentially more productive 'new' technologies. For example, the economic benefits associated with new technology should be less for farmers who face high transport costs because their villages are far from markets or connected to markets by poor roads. Compared to farmers with lower transport costs, farmers facing high transport costs receive less for the marketable surplus they produce and face higher cost for fertilizers and other inputs imported from the non-agricultural sector. The cost of acquiring technical knowledge, which is also essential to the successful adoption of new technology, is similarly affected by costs of transportation and communication services. A typical example is the farmer's access to extension programmes which depends on the cost to the farmer of travelling to extension centres and on the cost to extension workers of travelling to the farmer's village.

Another important dimension of infrastructure productivity concerns the interdependence of the benefits obtained from investment in infrastructure, research, extension, and education. As the above model illustrates, the adoption of new technology is a function of infrasructure. Therefore, the benefits of agricultural research, measured in terms of the aggregate productivity gains associated with the new technology (Schuh and Tollini, 1979) are a function of infrastructure, extension, and education. The same interdependencies hold true for investments in extension and education which are complementary to the new technology.

In addition to these farm-level productivity effects of infrastructure there may be additional aggregate productivity effects through a more efficient allocation of resources within the agricultural sector and between the agricultural and non-agricultural sectors of the economy. To illustrate these aggregate effects we may consider a two sector model, with the two sectors representing two agricultural regions or the agricultural and non-agricultural sectors. We can utilize the well-known theorem in international trade which states that factor price differentials between sectors cause the production possibilities frontier to be 'shrunken' inside the frontier attainable without factor price differentials (see Chacoliades, 1978, Ch. 20). Therefore, the *technical* efficiency of the aggregate production process is a function of the stock of transport and communications infrastructure which determines the size of factor price differentials across sectors of the economy. It should be noted that these differentials do not imply that the resource allocation is *economically* inefficient, given the prevailing transportion and communication costs; the reduction of aggregate productivity due to a less technically efficient resource allocation occurs even when all economic decision-makers behave rationally and all markets are competitive.

In conclusion, economic theory suggests transportation and communications infrastructure may have micro-level productivity effects due to the relationship between transport and communications costs, prices, information costs, and the productivity of farmers' technologies; and infrastructure may have macro-level productivity effects due to the relationship between factor price differentials and the aggregate production possibilities frontier.

TABLE 1 *Summary of production function studies on infrastructure and agricultural productivity*

| Study | Data | Infrastructure Variable | Elasticity of output with respect to infrastructure variable |
|---|---|---|---|
| Antle, 1980[1] | Farm-level, Indian rice, 1970–71, all-India | Transport cost proxy: distance from farmer's village to transport and communications facilities. | 0 to – 0.20, mean – 0.06 |
| Easter, Abel, and Norton, 1977[2] | District-level, Indian rice, 1959–61, 1966–68 | *Km* of hand surfaced roads per $Km^2$ of land area | 1959–61: 0.133<br>1967–68: 0.218 |
| Liang, 1981[3] | Regional per farm, Chinese wheat and rice, 1933 | Transport costs from farm to regional markets | Wheat: – 0.32<br>Rice: – 0.28 |
| Antle, 1982[4] | Aggregate US, 1910–78 | Value of transport and communication services | 0.17 |
| Antle, 1981[5] | Aggregate, 66 countries, 1965 | Value of transport and communications services per $Km^2$ of land area. | DC and<br>LDC data: 0.20<br>LDC data: 0.37 |

NOTES TO TABLE

[1]Farm-level Indian rice data for all-India; examined the effects of infrastructure, education, extension, irrigation, seed variety, rainfall, on the productivity of land, labour (hired and family), fertilizer and pesticide input, and capital. Increased transport costs were found to bias productivity of inputs.

[2]District level Indian rice data from Eastern rice areas; output was regressed on inputs (area, irrigation, fertilizer, tractors, labour, pumpsets) and technological factors (rainfall, soil type, infrastructure).

[3]Regional per-farm wheat and rice production, China; output was regressed on a transport cost variable only, without including other inputs. Input use was also found to be correlated with transport costs.

[4]Aggregate agricultural production, US; output explained as a function of inputs, stock of agricultural research, and infrastructure. Technical change found to be biased by agricultural research and development of infrastructure.

[5]Aggregate agricultural production for 66 countries (47 'developing' and 19 'developed'). Output explained as a function of land, labour, fertilizer, livestock, education, agricultural research, and infrastructure variables. Effect of infrastructure on productivity found to be larger than effects of education or agricultural research.

## EMPIRICAL EVIDENCE

This section summarizes recent empirical research on the relationship between infrastructure and agricultural productivity. Each of the studies reviewed employs a production function methodology, and some studies (Liang 1981, Antle 1982) also investigate the relationship between infrastructure and input use. Each of the production function models is a special case of the following general model: output $Q$ is a function of an input vector $X$, the technology index $\tau$, and a random disturbance $\varepsilon$. $\tau$ is a function of infrastructure, education, extension, agricultural research, and environmental variables. The production function is thus:

$$Q = f[X, \tau, \varepsilon].$$

The results pertaining to infrastructure and agricultural productivity are summarized in Table 1. As the table shows, the studies are based on data which differ widely in terms of their unit of observation, level of aggregation, time and place, and method of measuring infrastructure. Each of the studies found that a variable measuring either infrastructure service costs (such as transport costs), a capital stock, or service flows from a capital stock had a statistically significant effect on agricultural productivity. (It should be noted in interpreting the results presented in Table 1 that a negative elasticity should be obtained when the infrastructure variable is a measure of costs, and a positive elasticity should be obtained when the variable is a measure of a stock or service flow.) The aggregate studies tend to obtain a larger elasticity of output with respect to the infrastructure variable than the farm-level or regional studies, a finding that is consistent with the idea that the aggregate studies should measure the effect of infrastructure on both farm-level productivity and the aggregate efficiency of resource utilization. It is also notable that the effect of infrastructure on agricultural productivity is at least as large within and across less-developed countries as developed countries. This finding is consistent with the Schultzian model of agricultural development for it suggests that farmers in developing countries respond to changes in benefits and costs associated with infrastructure just as farmers do in developed countries.

We may conclude that all the evidence from these production studies supports the hypothesis that agricultural productivity is positively associated with development of transportation and communications infrastructure.[1]

## IMPLICATIONS FOR GROWTH AND EQUITY IN AGRICULTURAL DEVELOPMENT

The empirical research described in the previous section provides strong support for the hypothesis that transportation and communications infrastructure has a substantial effect on agricultural productivity, of an order of magnitude which may equal or exceed the effects of other important components of the agricultural development process such as research, education, and extension.[2] In interpreting these findings it should be emphasized that the production function studies measure the effect of infrastructure on production while *all other factors affecting production are held constant*. These estimates therefore can be said to measure an *external benefit* of investments in infrastructure in the form of increased agricultural productivity, benefits which are not ordinarily counted in cost-benefit analysis of infrastructure projects (see Adler, 1967).[3] Since the relative magnitude of these benefits appears to be substantial, it may reasonably be argued that consideration of these external benefits may significantly alter the optimal resource allocation in a country's development planning toward infrastructure projects, perhaps in place of other competing projects for agricultural research, extension, or education. In this regard it must be emphasized, as discussed in the first section, that the benefits of projects for investments in infrastructure, agricultural research, extension, and education, are generally mutually dependent. While in principle cost-benefit analysis could determine the priority of each alternative investment, in practice such analysis is very difficult to carry out. However, several facts suggest that investments in infrastructure should be given priority in agricultural development planning. First, when appropriate new technology has been developed, such as new seed varieties, experience suggests that most farmers can and do benefit from it if they have access to the seeds and complementary inputs. Second, the provision of other important services, such as education and extension, often depends on the existence of adequate transportation and communications infrastructure. Third, the aggregate effect of infrastructure, described above, is not dependent on the introduction of new technology, although this effect is likely to be much larger during the process of agricultural growth which requires resource mobility between sectors.

While the theoretical and empirical evidence presented thus far strongly suggests that investments in infrastructure play an important role in agricultural development, we need to consider the effects such investments have on the distribution of the benefits of agricultural productivity growth. For this purpose we note several pertinent facts about agricultural growth due to technical change. In the short run, producers who are early adopters of new technology benefit from reduced production costs relative to non-adopters. In the longer run, as more farmers adopt, the market price of output is bid down and the gains to early adopters are reduced or eliminated. The long run effects on welfare, measured in terms of changes in consumers' and producers' surplus, are known to be positive for consumers (both urban and rural) due to reduced food prices, but ambiguous for producers because the price of their output declines in the long run along with their costs.

With the above facts in mind, I will argue that the theoretical framework presented in the first section, in conjunction with other research on the characteristics of agricultural technology, suggests that investment in transportation and communication infrastructure which promotes productivity growth will lead to increased welfare for agricultural producers as a group and to a more equitable distribution of that welfare across producers. The increased welfare for producers as a group is due to the effect infrastructure has on demand for agricultural products. Not only will demand increase but generally the integration of farmers into larger markets will increase the elasticity of demand for agricultural products. It is easy to show that the higher the elasticity of demand, the more likely are the benefits of technical change to go to producers as increased producers' surplus. But how will the benefits of technical change be distributed across producers? Evidence suggests that most of the 'Green Revolution' technologies are quite scale neutral, and can and have been utilized on both very small and large farms when farmers have access to the information, inputs, and credit needed to utilize these technologies (for example see Sarma, 1982 for the case of India). Investment in transportation and communication infrastructure reduces the costs of obtaining information, inputs and credit for *all* farmers because these benefits are in the form of a public good. It is therefore difficult to prevent any individual from taking advantage of the benefits produced by investment in such infrastructure. It follows that development of infrastructure makes the new technologies available to more farmers and therefore results in a more equitable distribution of the benefits of technical change. Moreover, the equity effect of infrastructure should operate both in the short run as new technologies are introduced by making early adoption possible for more farmers, and in the longer run by making the technology available to a larger total number of farmers.

## CONCLUSIONS

In assessing the relationship between infrastructure and agricultural productivity we have found, first, that development of transport and communication infrastructure does appear to have a substantial effect on agricultural productivity at both micro and macro levels, and therefore does appear to be a necessary condition for agricultural growth, as suggested by the theoretical models presented in this paper. Therefore, we may conclude that project analysts can, and should, measure the productivity effects of infrastructure projects when evaluating alternative investments and formulating development plans. In addition to substantial effects on agricultural productivity growth, it has been argued that a more equitable distribution of the benefits of agricultural growth through technical change may be brought about by development of infrastructure. We may conclude that there appear to be strong justifications for investments in infrastructure in terms of effects on both agricultural productivity growth and the equitable distribution of the benefits of growth.

## NOTES

[1]These production function studies do not necessarily prove that the causality runs from infrastructure to productivity, and it can be argued that the causality may be reversed in some cases, for example, a certain region has a larger investment in infrastructure because it is more productive. Historical studies, however, do support the hypothesis made in this paper. See, for example, Cochrane, 1979, ch. 11, for an analysis of the importance of transport infrastructure to agricultural productivity in the US.

[2]Lockhead, et al., 1980, found in a survey of production studies that the average elasticity of output with respect to farmer education (years of schooling) is about 7 per cent for four years of elementary education. Somewhat less work has been devoted to measurement of the contribution of agricultural research. Evenson and Kislev, 1975, obtained an aggregate elasticity between 0.05 and 0.15, and Antle, 1981, obtained an aggregate elasticity of 0.10 to 0.17.

[3]Note that inputs and outputs also change as a result of, say, transport cost changes. The production function studies show that, in addition, there is an overall productivity gain which can be attributed to the use of more productive technology and a more efficient use of resources in the aggregate. This kind of benefit is referred to as a 'positive technological externality' in the project evaluation literature.

## REFERENCES

Adler, H. P., *Sector and Project Planning in Transportation,* World Bank Staff Occasional Papers No. 4, 1967.

Antle, J. M., 'Human Capital, Infrastructure, and Technology Choice in Agricultural Development', Unpublished Ph.D. dissertation, University of Chicago, 1980.

Antle, J. M., 'Infrastructure and Aggregate Agricultural Productivity: International Evidence', *Economic Development and Cultural Change* (forthcoming).

Antle, J. M., 'Research, Infrastructure, and Parametric Measurement of Biased Technical Change in US Agriculture, 1910–78', University of California, Davis, Dept of Agricultural Economics, Working Paper, 1982.

Chacoliades, M., *International Trade Theory and Policy*, McGraw-Hill, New York, 1978.

Cochrane, W. W., *The Development of American Agriculture, A Historical Analysis,* University of Minnesota Press, 1979.

Easter, W. K., Abel, M. E., and Norton, G., 'Regional Differences in Agricultural Productivity in Selected Areas of India', AJAE, Vol. 59, 1977.

Evenson, R. E. and Kislev Y., *Agricultural Research and Productivity,* Yale University Press, 1975.
Liang, E. P., 'Market Accessibility and Agricultural Development in Prewar China', *EDCC,* Vol. 30, October, 1981.
Lele, U. J., *Food Grain Marketing in India: Private Performance and Public Policy,* Cornell University Press, 1971.
Lockheed, M. E., Jamison, D. T., and Lau, L. J., 'Farmer Education and Farm Efficiency: A Survey', *Economic Development and Cultural Change,* Vol. 29, October, 1980: 37–76.
Rao, C. H. A. and Subbarao, K., 'Marketing of Rice in India: An Analysis of the Impact of Producers' Prices on Small Farmers', *IJAE,* Vol. 31, April–June 1976.
Sarma, J. S., *Growth and Equity: Policies and Implementation in Indian Agriculture,* IFPRI Research Report 28, November, 1981.
Schuh, G. E., and Tollini, H., *Costs and Benefits of Agricultural Research: The State of the Arts,* World Bank Staff Working Paper No. 360, October 1979.
Schultz, T. W., *Transforming Traditional Agriculture,* Yale University Press, 1964.

## DISCUSSION OPENING – TOSHIYUKI KAKO

I would like to begin by summarizing Dr Antle's presentation. Then, I will raise several questions which might be fruitful for further discussion.

Dr Antle's paper could be characterized as an attempt to expand the Schultzian model of agricultural development. As is well known, Theodore Schultz mentioned that the key factors of the growth of modern agriculture are new technology in agricultural production and improvement in the quality of human capital of farm people. He also pointed out that investments in agricultural research are necessary to create the new technology which is needed for productivity growth, and investments in the human capital of farm people are necessary to provide farmers with the ability to learn of and use the new technology.

The Schultzian model of agricultural development has been supported by many empirical studies. For example, Zvi Griliches, in his 1964 article, succeeded in explaining almost completely the growth of US agriculture by five conventional factor inputs and two non-conventional inputs. He estimated that non-conventional inputs, such as agricultural research and education, accounted for a substantial part of agricultural growth. Akino and Hayami, who carried out growth accounting research on Japanese agriculture, obtained similar results.

Dr Antle has added transportation and communication infrastructure as one of the components of non-conventional inputs. He has tried to prove theoretically and empirically that investment in infrastructure is efficient in terms of its effect on both agricultural productivity growth and the equitable distribution of the benefits of growth.

Investment in transportation infrastructure reduces the cost of transport. This, in turn, raises the prices received by farmers and reduces input prices. Farmers far from markets may respond with a significant added input of resources in production and significant increases in output.

Improvements in transportation infrastructure also increase the economic benefits associated with the new technology of the farmers who used to face high transport costs. Thus, it accelerates the rate of adoption of new technology by many farmers.

Next, investment in communication infrastructure reduces the cost of information and improves the diffusion of new technology to more farmers and to wider geographic areas, Thus it brings about a more equitable distribution of the benefits of technical change among farmers.

Dr Antle cited some empirical research in Table 1, and summarized the findings as follows: (a) 'The aggregate studies tend to obtain a larger elasticity of output with respect to the infrastructure variable than the farm-level or regional studies', and (b) 'The effect of infrastructure on agricultural productivity is at least as large within and across less developed countries as developed countries.'

He concludes that infrastructure has a substantial effect on agricultural productivity, of an order of magnitude which may equal or exceed the effect of agricultural research, education, and extension. Hence, he further concludes, investment in infrastructure should be given priority in agricultural development planning.

I would now like to raise four questions:

1 Dr Antle defined the infrastructure variable narrowly and included only transportation and communication. I think land infrastructure is important, too. Investment in land infrastructure includes the development of irrigation and drainage, which improve the quality of land, and contribute to increasing yields per ha as well as expanding the cropping area by facilitating multiple cropping (Hayami, 1981). Investment in land infrastructure is especially important in countries characterized by a growing population pressure on limited land resources. It has been observed that in India and Indonesia there was an under-investment of public funds for irrigation (Rao, 1975). According to some empirical studies, output elasticity with respect to land infrastructure took some positive values (K. W. Easter et al., 1977, India; Sidhu, 1974, Indian Punjab). Dr Antle states that he used irrigation as one of the explanatory variables of rice production in India. Would you give us some information on your findings? I also would like to know the reason why you defined infrastructure narrowly, including only transportation and communications and excluding land as well as social infrastructure.

2 Investments in transportation and communications are treated as one explanatory variable, but the effect of each may not necessarily be of the same order of magnitude, especially in countries where investments in human capital are not sufficient. On the one hand, transportation infrastructure can be utilized by all farmers, regardless of their education level or managerial ability. Communications infrastructure, on the other hand, can be better utilized by the more educated farmers. In countries with low rates of literacy, investment in education may be a prerequisite to the efficient use of communication infrastructure. So, in the analysis of LDCs, it seems more reasonable to treat transportation infrastructure and communication infrastructure as two separate variables and estimate output elasticity with respect to each.

3 Although development of infrastructure makes the new technology available to more farmers, this fact does not necessarily lead to a more equitable distribution of income. This is because all types of technical progress do not necessarily contribute to a greater equity in income distribution. The factor saving bias of the new technology, in a Hicksian sense, has an important effect on income distribution. Such technical changes as mechanization, which could be classified as labour saving, can reduce labour's income and deteriorate income distribution in labour abundant economies. Therefore Dr Antle's analytical method which examined the effect of infrastructure investment on income distribution, holding other things equal, is insufficient for me because, even if one can infer that investment in infrastructures has a positive effect on income distribution, the gains may be marginal compared with the effect of other factors on income distribution which are not treated explicitly in this analysis.

4 My last question concerns the interpretation of Table 1. In the aggregate studies the infrastructure variable consists of transportation and communication, but in the farm-level or regional studies only transportation is included. Is not this one of the causes of the difference in the estimates of output elasticity between the aggregate studies and the farm-level studies? I also would like to point out that reliability of the data may be quite different among countries. So we should be very careful how we interpret the results of the estimates in Table 1.

## GENERAL DISCUSSION – RAPPORTEUR: B. H. KINSEY

It was argued that the importance of the rural transport component of infrastructure was indisputable in terms of the growth dimension but more questionable in terms of equity. Analyses carried out in Bangladesh indicated that cost-reducing effects of rural roads accrued chiefly to those who already had a surplus to sell and who utilized purchased inputs. For this reason, improvements in rural transportation must be accompanied by other changes at the same time.

A warning was given that emphasis on irrigation could result in long-term irreversible deleterious effects on soil. In India, where 75 per cent of the cultivated areas is rainfed and not irrigated, equity considerations would suggest a greater focus on technology for dryland farming. Clarification was requested on the specification of the different components which had gone into the infrastructure variable and indicated that if investment on irrigation was not included, it was important and should be. There was disagreement with the opener's (Toshiyuki Kako) remark that there is under-investment in irrigation in Asian developing countries, arguing that in India what was lacking was investment on development to follow-up on the initial investment in irrigation.

Reference was made to an analysis which had been done on the investment in rural highways in Indiana. A negative coefficient was obtained for the relevant term in the aggregate production function used, and this was interpreted as showing that Indiana had become so interlaced with rural roads that it had actually reached the stage where the marginal returns to roads were negative. Results such as this suggest that it is possible to over-invest in infrastructure.

John M. Antle replied that he agreed fully that there was a need for a more dynamic approach to analysing the role of infrastructure but that a fairly long time series of data would be needed in order to do this. Because such series are rare in developing countries, his paper and previous work had relied heavily on aggregate data.

He agreed with the comments of the first speaker in the general discussion and pointed out, on the basis of Indian evidence, that where transport costs were previously very high, lowering them through improvements to infrastructure will benefit initially mainly the relatively wealthy. The evidence does suggest, however, that benefits will accrue to the poor later. The equity of distribution of the benefits arising from improved transport infrastructure had not been examined.

Participants in the discussion included M. D. Moazzem Hossain, M. G. Chandrakanth, K. S. Arun Kumar and R. L. Thompson.

# SECTION III

## *Structure and Pattern of Agricultural Growth*

NURUL ISLAM

# *World Agricultural Growth – Short and Long-term Aspects, Past and Future – An Overview*

## INTRODUCTION

World food and agricultural production has expanded in the past at an annual rate of 2.47 per cent from the mid-1960s to the end of the 1970s. There are, however, wide divergences among regions and countries. In the developed market economies where domestic demand for food and agricultural output is expanding rather slowly, production has outstripped demand growth. In the centrally planned developed economies there has been a slowing down in domestic production during the 1970s compared with the 1960s. An expanding demand, especially for livestock products, has resulted in growing cereal imports. The developing countries reveal widely different pictures in different regions or groups of countries. In general, demand growth (3.0 per cent annually) has outstripped domestic supply growth (2.84 per cent) in the developing countries as a whole, with a consequent rising import demand for cereals. In thirty-seven low-income countries during the 1970s, there has been a fall in cereal production per caput and in nineteen of them production also fell in absolute terms.

The basic fact is that food is in short supply in the majority of developing countries. Of 83 developing countries with populations over 1 million in 1980 (and excluding China), the food supply in 1978–80 was below nutritional requirements in 44 countries. They contained 1.24 billion people, more than half the total population of the 83 countries. In only 14 of the 44 countries (with just over 10 per cent of the population of the 44 countries) did average per caput calorie supplies increase during the 1970s – but not to the extent of meeting minimum national average nutritional requirements. These 44 countries constitute the core of the world food problem. Improved food distribution alone cannot solve even their present problems, quite apart from their growing food needs because of population expansion. They must depend on accelerating their own production and on the trade and assistance benefits of an improved world food system.

Over the years, the percentage of world cereal production which is internationally traded expanded consistently. The cereal imports of developing countries have expanded rapidly – more than doubled in the last decade. During this period the self-sufficiency ratio of many of the developing countries has declined. The developed market economy countries are predominant exporters of cereals in the world. This is especially true of North America: 67 per cent of the world cereal exports originated in North America in the late 1970s, with the United States providing 56 per cent of the world total, Canada 11 per cent, Australia 8 per cent, Western Europe about 7 per cent. Amongst the importers of cereals, the developing countries' share was 47 per cent, followed by Japan with 13 per cent, centrally planned developed countries with 20 per cent and Western Europe with 18 per cent. The imports of the developed countries, both market economy and centrally planned, consisted predominantly of coarse grains for feeding livestock.

The share of agricultural trade in world trade continues to decline but agricultural commodities remain a principal source of foreign exchange for developing countries. For the developing countries as a whole, earnings from agricultural exports constitute no more than 25 per cent or so; however, for low income developing countries, their share goes up to 50 per cent or more. Over the last decade and a half, the share of developing countries in world imports has increased, whereas that in world exports has declined. The agricultural exports of developing countries, other than cereals, fall into two categories: those which compete with developed country exports, consisting of temperate zone products, and those which are tropical non-competing products.

The competitive exports of developing countries which compete with developed country temperate zone products enjoyed a slower rate of growth in production than in domestic consumption. The competing exports appeared to have suffered a supply constraint arising from increasing domestic absorption of exportables in the developing countries. At the same time, in developed countries, the rate of domestic production increase exceeded that of demand growth, with an accelerated rate of increase in export surplus. The share of developing countries in world trade of competing products has declined over time. In respect of non-competing exports of the developing countries domestic consumption growth, at an annual rate of 2.48 per cent, exceeded demand supply at an annual rate of 1.83 per cent, thus restraining the growth of an export surplus. The trade in both these categories of non-cereal exports has been sluggish, contrasting sharply with buoyant trade in cereals and feedstuffs.

As is well known, a dominant characteristic of the world agricultural trade is the high degree of fluctuations in agricultural export earnings; both price and volume of trade in agricultural commodities fluctuate from year to year. The degree of fluctuations in export prices increased during the 1970s as compared with the 1960s; however, there was no evidence that instability of the volume of trade worsened from one decade to the next.

Interaction between domestic and external trade policies is nowhere more evident than in the field of food and agriculture. Domestic agricultural policies, including tax, subsidy and pricing policies, to raise, support or stabilize income or prices in the agricultural sector, have important implications for international trade in agricultural commodities. These policies are stimulated by multiple objectives, for example, to reduce income disparity between the agricultural and non-agricultural sectors; to reduce poverty in low productivity areas or income groups; to reduce dependence on external sources and to enhance the security of food supplies likely to be disrupted by political or stragic factors. Search for self-sufficiency in agriculture, either food or essential raw materials, has often led to levels of supplies which are beyond the limits of domestic demand, as well as of considerations of efficiency and costs.

The above, rather brief, overview of world food and agriculture reveals a mixed situation. The essential point, however, is that while global food and agricultural supplies meet demand growth, the developing countries face severe problems in food and agriculture. Hundreds of millions of people remain seriously undernourished. In per caput terms food production is regressing in an alarming number of countries and the international framework is failing to provide either a suitable policy climate to encourage a maximum contribution from agriculture to economic growth in poor countries or the material means to assist them to do so.

A substantial expansion of the rate of growth of food and agricultural production is indeed urgently required if the increase in demand of a growing world population with rising income per caput is to be met. The continuation of past trends would create an unbearable burden of food imports for developing countries and result in an increasing number of their undernourished population. Lack of progress in reducing hunger and undernutrition is not inevitable and there is no inherent reason why the sector should not contribute substantially to overall economic growth, including a more dynamic and sustainable agricultural trade. In particular, the growth of food output in developing countries could be accelerated substantially.

These are not simply wishful assertions. They are the findings of a careful assessment, country-by-country, of longer-term perspectives of ninety developing countries made in a very recent study by FAO, *Agriculture: Toward 2000*. One of the contributed papers[1] to this Congress goes into the detail of the study. But the essential findings are that it is feasible for agricultural output growth to be doubled by the end of the century, implying an increase of about one-third over the historical trend in developing countries. Food supplies in *each* of the 90 developing countries would be 100 per cent or more of minimum nutritional requirements by 2000 and even without improvement of the distribution of income, the numbers of seriously undernourished would be almost halved. The agricultural trade surplus of developing countries would be raised considerably in the Far East and Latin America. The deterioration in the food self-sufficiency of developing countries would be arrested even though their imports of cereal and livestock products would rise in absolute amounts. The developed countries would, of course, benefit from the expansion of agricultural trade. An acceleration in the rate of increase in production would require not only a large increase in investment in agriculture but also a significant shift in policies and institutions, both in developing as well as developed countries.

Three major and interrelated aspects of world agricultural growth, especially growth in the developing countries, are considered in the following sections. They are international assistance for accelerated growth in developing countries and its implications for international trade in agriculture and world food security.

## INTERNATIONAL ASSISTANCE FOR ACCELERATED PRODUCTION IN DEVELOPING COUNTRIES

Developed countries have a long-term interest in increasing food production in the poor countries. Cereal imports by developing countries which have already reached 100 million tons in 1981, would double – or more than double if the past trends in their per caput consumption and domestic production continue. This would throw an increasing burden on the developed, exporting countries with a pressure on prices at least in the short-run owing to inelasticity of output. In the long-run as well, if a growing and substantial proportion of world demand is to be met from North America, the likelihood of rising food prices in real terms cannot be ruled out, in the absence of significant technological breakthrough. Higher costs would depend on the timing and extent of increasing soil erosion, rising prices of water and energy-intensive inputs, diminishing returns from extension of cultivation to marginal less productive and fragile soils and from increasing application per acre of such inputs as fertilizer and pesticides. Consequent rising unit costs of food production could fuel inflation.

Growing food imports would also impose a heavy burden on international marketing and transportation facilities, including marketing and distribution networks in the developing countries. Moreover, financing of food imports on such a large and growing scale would require unrealistically high levels of either food aid or of rates of growth of non-food exports from developing countries. Widespread undernutrition and distress, following from food shortages caused by stagnation or slow growth in domestic production, would socially and politically destabilize poor societies with possible international consequences. Finally, a more vigorous expansion of food production in developing countries will stimulate their national growth; in turn, this will make them better customers for the manufactures, food grains and livestock products which the developed countries export.

Acceleration in domestic food and agricultural production would require shifts in domestic policies, higher priority and greater incentives as well as increased rate of national resource mobilization for the agricultural sector. Timely and adequate assistance, both technical and financial, from the international community is a *sine qua non*, because domestic efforts in developing countries, especially low-income countries, would be far from adequate.

The FAO Study, quoted above, indicates that a rate of growth in food and agriculture at a rate between 3.5-3.8 per cent in the next two decades would require an aggregate investment of between $1,700 billion and $1,400 billion (in 1975 prices) for the period 1980 to 2000. This includes investment not only in primary agriculture but also in storage and marketing, as well as in transport and processing. These four components amount to about $600 billion for the whole period. FAO estimates that the average annual investment requirements would rise to between $100 billion and $132 billion in the year 2000. In terms of the DAC/OECD narrow definition, which excludes transport and processing, annual gross investment requirements would rise to between $50 billion and $63 billion by 1990 and to between $74 billion and $100 billion by 2000 (all in 1975 prices). These requirements would imply a twofold increase in 1990 and a threefold increase in 2000 above the level of 1981. Annual gross investments would have to rise by three to four times the annual estimated flow in the late 1970s or in early 1980. Investment requirements, according to these estimates, would correspond to about 25 per cent of agricultural GDP of developing countries. The required level of annual aggregate investment for overall economic growth during 1980–2000 has been variously estimated at 25–30 per cent of GNP.

The FAO estimates that corresponding to such a large increase in investment, there would be large increases needed in external assistance to agriculture. Requirements, in terms of the DAC/OECD narrow definition, would rise to $12 billion a year in 1990 and $18 billion in 2000 (in 1975 prices). This implies a more than twofold increase in development assistance by 1990 and a three-and-a-half times increase by 2000. In 1980, the flow of external resources to agriculture amounted to $4.9 billion in 1975 prices, as against the estimated annual requirements of $8.3 billion for the period 1975–80. This would constitute 0.12 per cent of GDP of developed countries during the 1980s and 1990s as compared to 0.08 per cent in 1975. To realise this external resource flow would require either an increase in overall assistance or an increase in the share of agriculture in overall development assistance or a combination of both.

At present about 17 – 18 per cent of the total official development assistance goes to the agricultural sector. The percentage is much lower (10 – 12 per cent) for the average bilateral donor, whereas the multilateral financial institutions devote between 30–40 per cent of their total assistance to the agricultural sector. The current tendency to reduce the relative role of multilateral institutions would particularly adversely affect the agricultural sector. This, combined with a relative stagnation in total official development assistance, implies that achievement of the required flows of external assistance for the agricultural sector would necessitate a substantial reallocation of external resources to the agricultural sector; this is also the sector which plays the dominant role in low-income countries, to which priority in development assistance was, until recently, accepted by the donor community. The increasing emphasis on political, strategic and security objectives in the inter-country allocation of development assistance is bound to hurt the agricultural sector. In addition, a growing tendency to tie aid by sources and commodities, in an attempt to boost exports via external assistance, as a means of stimulating the domestic economy of the donor countries, has adversely affected the flow of programme assistance and local cost financing. This would have an unfavourable impact on the agricultural sector, since programme loans for agricultural inputs and local cost financing are not only essential for many agricultural and rural development projects, but also for promoting poverty-orientated programmes. The FAO Study indicates the need for a considerable increase – at an annual rate of 7 per cent compared with the rate of growth of gross output at 3.5–3.8 per cent in the use of current inputs (modern inputs like fertilizers, improved seeds and pesticides and so on) for the modernization of developing country agriculture. Non-agricultural inputs as a proportion of the gross value of farm output would need to rise from 20 to 30 per cent by 2000.

Thus, in the aggregate, gross investment would need to rise to 20 per cent of gross agricultural output. Gross investment in primary agriculture (excluding storage, marketing, transport and processing) during the period 1980–2000, on average, would be about 10 per cent of total investment for the economy, as estimated in some comparable studies. This compares with the share of agricultural GDP in the total GDP of about 13–14 per cent during the same period. It will be necessary to overcome the prevailing impression that agricultural development is relatively cheap or not capital demanding, even apart from the investment in rural physical infrastructure and so on, which is not included in the above estimates (rural roads or rural electrification are excluded). Labour productivity and agricultural output cannot be raised substantially without investment, however appropriately labour intensive is the strategy of development in labour abundant countries.

In the immediate future, overall growth prospects and resource availability both domestic and foreign, are unfavourable. It is important to ensure that the higher priority now being attached to agriculture does not suffer. Indeed, the more stringent the restrictions on resource availability, the greater is the need for allocations to high priority sectors to be preserved at the expense of less essential sectors, keeping in view the minimum and necessary degree of inter-relationship between sectors. In many areas of the developing world, prospects of obtaining substantial increases in agricultural output by increasing investment are high. They must be exploited. The agricultural sector provides the livelihood and employment for the majority of the world's poor. With the slowing down in overall growth rate, the poor would suffer most, and the agricultural sector needs greater attention in the interests of the poor as well.

## INTERNATIONAL TRADE ASPECTS

The principal policy questions in world agricultural trade are how to expand and stabilize it, both in response to growing demand and production and as an instrument for securing an efficient and growing agricultural economy.

*Protectionism*

How far is trade expansion hampered by trade barriers?

Protectionism in agriculture has persisted for a long time, and is pervasive. Non-tariff barriers, often in support of domestic support measures, are of much greater importance than tariff barriers in agricultural trade. Protectionism, an FAO analysis indicates[2] has increased in recent years, as trends in various measures of protectionism (that is differentials between domestic and world prices, as well as measures of producer subsidies in agriculture) indicate.

A recent study indicates that a 50 per cent reduction in agricultural protectionism in OECD countries would lead to increases in world trade to the amount of $8.5 billion in 1977 prices, of which increases of about $3 billion at the minimum would occur in the agricultural export earnings of the 57 most populous developing countries. The exports of OECD countries would expand by $1.7 billion as a result of liberalization. There would be reallocation of production and trade amongst the developed countries, with the United States, Canada and Australia enjoying a significant expansion of exports, as against losses sustained by France and Italy.

The increase in exports would amount to an increase of 15 per cent of the total exports of 79 commodities included in the analysis. For the developing countries it would lead to an increase of export revenue to the extent of 10 per cent of current value of exports in 1977 prices. The additional resource transfer to the developing countries, resulting from an increase in exports, would amount to $1 billion, the domestic resource cost of producing the export commodities being about $2 billion.

In spite of a broad international consensus, as evidenced in resolutions at various international fora, including FAO, UN and UNCTAD, on the need for a greater measure of liberalization in agricultural trade, progress to date is limited. There is an increased pressure towards protectionism. The Multilateral Trade Negotiations, first in the Kennedy Round and then in the Tokyo Round, were directed more towards trade in manufactured goods and towards tariff barriers. Moreover, trade liberalization under MTN was, to a large extent, concerned with developed countries rather than removing obstacles to exports of primary interest to developing countries. However, adoption of generalized preferential systems in favour of the developing countries was a step in the right direction; but a limited step, hedged in with many qualifications.

Agricultural protectionism can be reduced only if it is accompanied by significant adjustment in the structure and pattern of domestic agricultural production, which is buttressed by an array of domestic support measures. In a period of recession and unemployment, structural adjustment is most difficult: resources can be reallocated and output can be redirected more easily in a period of growth rather than of stagnation. Among the developed market economy countries, especially the United States, EEC and Japan, protectionism in agriculture has become the most intractable component in the overall trade negotiations. This is particularly so when agricultural surpluses of commodities such as sugar, cereals, dairy and meat products, accumulated through domestic support policies, seek competitive export outlets, often with subsidies (as in the EEC). The frequency of complaints in the GATT in respect of violation of its rules, confirms the intense protectionist pressure in several countries. At the same time it is paradoxical that in a period of inflationary pressures at home, cheap imports, which could exercise a deflationary impact, are kept out. The policy of controlling inflation *via* restrictionist monetary policies is aggravating recession and hence protectionist pressure from various interest groups.

Supply side measures to stimulate growth through greater investment and high incentives need to be combined with policies towards structural adjustment. Otherwise, to superimpose growth stimulating effects on the old structure would create further rigidities in the future.

As one looks towards the future, if developing countries are to significantly accelerate growth in their food and agricultural production, as a *sine qua non* for their overall growth they need to find expanding markets for their agricultural exports. At the same time, under the impact of rising domestic demand, resulting from rising incomes and population, their imports of basic foodstuffs and cereals will go up. In spite of the fact that they would produce more food, they will eat more as well; in the middle-income and high-income developing countries there will be a rapid increase in indirect consumption of cereals, that is *via* livestock products. This emphasizes the point made earlier that in an environment of overall growth there will be need and scope for adjustment in production and trade, but not for absolute contraction overall or even sectoral. For example, in a scenario of accelerated growth there would be no occasion for the developed countries undertaking an absolute reduction in output, even in respect of commodities competing with the exports of developing countries. As noted earlier, the FAO Study, *Agriculture: Toward 2000,* indicates that the developed countries will be able to expand significantly their output and exports of cereals to developing countries. Depending upon alternative scenarios of growth, developed countries would be able to expand their net export surplus by 80–150 per cent above the current level. Total cereal production in developed countries could then go up by 25–30 per cent. The developing countries, on the other hand, would generate larger exportable surpluses in tropical products ranging from beverages to rubber, bananas, tobacco, cotton and fruits and vegetables. In some of these products, the rate of domestic production growth in developed countries needs to slow down. In no case is there a need for absolute decline below the current level.

As the growth in demand would be mainly located in developing countries, those with substantial production possibilities could take advantage of growing export demand in cereals as well as in tropical products. In respect of commodities in which developing countries face competition with developed countries, that is rice, cotton, vegetable oils, sugar and so on, the increased intra-developing country trade will depend upon how far international trade is liberalized, and how far developing countries are able to increase productivity and build up transportation, markets, distribution and information networks for the promotion of trade amongst themselves.

World agriculture needs a long-term target or perspective for trade liberalization. The individual countries should in the first instance agree to slow down the pursuit of increased self-suficiency or expensive non-competitive surpluses through restrictive trade and domestic support measures. They should fix targets, if necessary commodity by commodity, as to the upper levels of the share of total domestic consumption which would be met from imports. A target of self-sufficiency ratios for protected commodities would over time help to prevent unplanned or unpredictable rises in domestic self-sufficiency and allow appropriate measures to be planned in advance by both importing and exporting countries.

## INSTABILITY IN PRICES AND EXPORT EARNINGS

Prices of agricultural products not only fluctuate but also many of them have shown a long-term downward trend in the last decade or so. Eleven commodities – tea, jute, rubber, bananas, wheat, maize, beef, soyabeans, palm oil, rice, and cotton – have shown downward trends in real prices during the period 1960–1980[3]. UNCTAD's Integrated Programme of Commodities was designed to stabilize and maintain prices of agricultural commodities in world trade; in addition, this was intended to strengthen the long-term earnings of developing countries from agricultural exports through expansion of research and development efforts and through their improved and more efficient marketing, distribution and processing, along with a greater participation of developing countries in incomes and earnings from these operations. High expectations were raised about the prospects of commodity agreements for twelve agricultural commodities which were included in the UNCTAD Commodity Agreement. An international agreement on the Common Fund generated confidence that both the developed and the developing – the producing and consuming – countries were eager and willing to accept the instrument of commodity agreements as a principal means of international price stabilization.

Actual experience of commodity negotiations in the last six or seven years has not fulfilled these expectations. Only one new international agreement, on rubber, has so far been negotiated; two existing agreements on sugar and cocoa have been renegotiated, but without universal participation. The EEC, with a growing export surplus of sugar, stays outside the Sugar Agreement, and the largest producer of cocoa, Ivory Coast, and the largest consumer, the United States, stay out of the Cocoa Agreement. The Coffee Agreement was extended in 1981 for another two years. The effectiveness of these price stabilizing provisions has been severely constrained, with the ruling market prices often lying substantially outside the 'price bands' included in the agreements. A careful and objective analysis of the long or medium term forces operating on the demand and supply prospects of a commodity is crucial to the success of selection of (a) a realistic and defensible 'price band' and (b) a relatively cost-effective size of buffer stocks.

The Common Fund agreement provided eventually for resources of only $750 million, of which $400 million is for buffer stock financing, rather than about $6 billion as was originally proposed. Principal reliance for resources was to be placed on borrowings from the capital market, which is plagued by abnormally high interest rates, and contributions from individual commodity agreements, which tend to jealously guard their resources. Individual commodity agreements were expected to receive substantial assistance from the Common Fund rather than the other way round; moreover, the expectation that each commodity agreement would face almost equal probability of lending to and borrowing from the Fund is not shared by the managers of existing commodity agreements. The success of the Common Fund is inextricably linked with the number and viability of commodity agreements. The limited success in reaching commodity agreements inhibits the prospects of the former.

The required number of countries have yet to ratify the Common Fund Agreement, thus delaying its operation at least by another year. In some developed countries there is an exaggerated ideological shift towards reliance on the 'magic of the market place', and an international commodity agreement is looked upon as interference with the market place.

Greater interest seems to be evidenced in the Second Window of the Common Fund (with a meagre sum of $350 million) designed to help research, development in the face of competition from synthetics and slow growth in demand, and improved productivity of export commodities included in an international commodity agreement, with or without buffer stock operations. Often the weakest commodities, in terms of long-term growth prospects, such as tea, sisal, jute, and so on, are the principal export earners of the poorest countries.

The producers of agricultural exports in developing countries do not receive more than a small fraction of the final consumer prices. If all processing stages for five major export commodities (rubber, cotton, jute, cocoa, coffee) were undertaken exclusively within developing countries, the current value of their export earnings would be increased by 25 per cent with a total gross income from processing of about $12 billion in 1980 prices.

An FAO analysis indicates that if potentials for agricultural growth are realized in the developing countries in the next decades, the annual requirements of investment in 1975 prices in storage and marketing alone would amount to about $4.5–$5.2 billion in 1990 and $5.8–$7.2 billion by 2000; corresponding annual requirements for investment in transportation and first-stage processing of agricultural commodities would be much higher – $18.6–$21.2 billion in 1990 and $25.4–$31.3 billion in 2000.

## WORLD FOOD SECURITY

International trade issues are closely linked with food security issues. Access to and assurance of supplies and access to markets are two sides of the same coin. Food security at the international level requires that access to supplies adequate to meet average nutritional requirements for all countries at all times is assured, especially at times of world food shortages and rising prices. This assurance is intended to meet the impact of fluctuations in output and prices on the availability of food supplies, especially in low-income food-deficit countries. The impact of shortages in food supplies falls most severely on the poor countries and on poor peoples.

The fluctuations in world supplies – traded in the world market – are the combined effect of fluctuations in a production and trade policy. To the extent that fluctuations in domestic production are not allowed to be reflected fully in fluctuations in consumption, either through changes in imports or exports, amounts traded in the world market would fluctuate to a greater extent than the domestic production would.

Moreover, since trade in cereals/food constitutes a small percentage of production, a given percentage fluctuation in production would be accompanied by a much higher percentage change in traded supplies.

In the course of the last two decades the degree of fluctuations in yield and production of cereals has increased. The average variation from trend in yield and production of cereals increased from 2.26 per cent in 1960–69 to 3.36 per cent in 1978–79 in respect of yield and from 2.57 to 3.32 per cent in respect of production for the same period. The largest degree of fluctuation occurs in the USSR. In the United States the degree of fluctuation increased from 3.19 per cent in 1960–69 to 10–38 per cent in 1970–75 in respect of yield; the average variation for developed countries is higher than that for developing countries and has increased over time.

According to some observers, uncertainty of cereal supplies in North America is likely to be aggravated in the future due to a variety of reasons. First, the likely frequency of climatic hazards is thought by a number of climatologists to be greater than recent historical experience might suggest. There appears to be a consensus that northern hemisphere weather in recent decades has shown less variability than evidence from a longer historical period would suggest, with the implication that levels of future production are at a greater risk from climatic factors. Second, concentration of cereal production on a limited and small number of varieties, as in the case of wheat, increases the genetic vulnerability of crops to epidemics (pests and diseases) under present farming systems. Third, risks of man-made hazards are also greater, due, for example, to risks of radiation from nuclear reactors.[4]

Aggregate world cereal production fluctuates less than production at the regional country level. A liberal international trading system partly mitigates the impact of fluctuations in a region or a country with food supplies moving from the surplus region to the deficit region or country.

That restrictive trade and domestic policies have aggravated fluctuations in world cereal prices is widely recognized. The fluctuating exchange rates and volatile interest rates in recent years have also contributed to the fluctuations in food and other commodity prices. Stock-holding costs are vitally affected by interest rates, and hence stocks vary in response to varying interest rates, resulting in variations in commodity prices.

International action to achieve a greater stability in prices of basic foodstuffs or cereals would contribute towards world food security. That the 1973–74 rise in food prices was disproportionately high in relation to the shortfall in production, was due, amongst other reasons, to the low level of stocks as well as to the speculative or panic purchases in all countries, both exporting and importing. A major influence was also the unexpected change in the grain import policy of the USSR which in order to maintain domestic livestock production compensated the shortfalls in the domestic availability of feedgrains by large-scale purchases in the world market.

The FAO International Undertaking on World Food Security, confirmed by the decisions at the 1974 World Food Conference, emphasized not only the role of adequate world food reserves for promoting market stability and food security, roughly estimated in the early 1970s as between 60 million tons (both coarse grains and wheat) and 30 million tons (wheat), but also the need for international co-ordination of national reserves. The management of national food reserves, including the criteria for and the manner of release and acquisition of reserve stocks in relation to quantifiable indicators of variations in world supplies or prices, was to be governed by an international agreement. FAO has estimated the minimum safe level of food reserves for food security at about 17–18 per cent of annual total consumption, that is 11–12 per cent of annual world consumption as pipeline stocks and 5–6 per cent as stocks to meet the probability of shortfall from the trend level of average world production.

Six years of negotiations on the conclusion of an international grains arrangement, with legally binding provision for international co-ordination of national reserve stocks on the basis of a set of 'trigger prices', ended in a stalemate in 1979. Subsequent negotiations for a more flexible agreement also failed to evoke acceptance. No viable and effective agreement seems to be in sight. FAO's Five Point Plan of Action, launched in the wake of failure of international grains negotiations on World Food Security, is the only available international framework for voluntary action with a view to adopting concerted measures for promoting world food security; the individual countries are requested to determine specific stock policies and targets as well as spell out criteria for the management of stocks so that once known, their consistency, adequacy and relevance for ensuring world food security can be assessed and monitored. Many countries, including developed exporting countries, are still unwilling to meet these requests.

Measures for meeting the rising and fluctuating import requirements for low income, food deficit countries are also important elements of FAO's Five Point Plan of Action. They include the early achievement of (a) the food aid target, set by the World Food Conference, of a minimum of 10 million tons and (b) the International Emergency Food Research target of 500,000 tons (as determined by the UN General Assembly Resolution in 1975) to meet emergencies. In response to the call by the FAO Plan of Action supported by the World Food Council and the UN General Assembly, a special Food Financing Facility has recently been established by the IMF as a modification of the Compensatory Financing Facility for export shortfalls to meet the exceptional import bills caused by either a fall in domestic production or a rise in import prices.

The current Food Aid Convention assures a food aid flow of 7.6 million tons of cereals but falls short of the minimum target fixed in 1974 of 10 million tons; however, the target itself is in need of upward revision in view of rising import requirements of the developing, especially low-income food-deficit, countries. The proportion of their imports met by food aid has been falling over the years, while their balance of payments gap caused by rising oil import bills and debt service payments continues to rise.

The International Emergency Food Reserve, placed at the disposal of the FAO/UN World Food Programme, reached its target of 500,000 tons for the first time in 1981; but being voluntary, partly bilateral and partly multilateral (partially earmarked for specific emergency use of country situation, even when multilateral), it is neither a stable nor an assured source of emergency assistance. It is not freely available to meet at short notice any emergency anywhere in the world.

Recently, the FAO Council and Conference have agreed upon an Agenda for Consultative and Possible Action in the event of an acute and large-scale food shortage. This agenda systematizes and extends the various criteria and indicators, quantifiable or otherwise, relating to production stocks, prices, exports and imports, which are needed to characterize or identify the emergence or occurrence of a large-scale and acute food shortage; it delineates the various measures which should be adopted by the international community, at national and international level, for conserving limited supplies and for managing stocks at times of shortages with a view to making supplies available through aid or commercial sales to vulnerable countries, including logistic and distribution arrangements. It further specifies the various alternative or concomittant institutional procedures and arrangements within the UN system or outside which need to be mobilized for meeting a food crisis.

Food aid, however, continues to be a subject of criticism. Food aid has multiple objectives; it can be and is provided in different forms and ways. Apart from being an instrument for relieving emergency food shortages, it can be a developmental tool, so long as it is neither a mere outlet for surplus disposal of food exporting countries, nor an alibi for domestic failures in production in recipient countries.

Project food aid related to socio-economic development projects through food for work projects or target group-orientated nutrition projects, including feeding programmes for vulnerable groups such as women and children, contribute to both growth and equity.

In a low-income country, an acceleration in income growth has an immediate and significant impact on food demand, especially when labour intensive technology and projects are the main thrusts of the development strategy. Rising food demand confronted with a low elasticity of domestic food supply causes an upward pressure on food prices. In this context, food aid can moderate a rise in domestic food prices and hence cost-push generated overall inflationary pressure.

Increased domestic food supply through food aid can discourage domestic production if food prices fall below the domestic opportunity cost of food production. Recent experience has demonstrated ways in which use of food aid to keep consumer prices low can be combined with measures to maintain incentive prices for domestic production. Dual prices could be introduced by driving a wedge between high incentive prices for farmers and the low concessional prices for 'target groups' of consumers. The differences between the two sets of prices can be subsidised by the sales proceeds of the food aid. Moreover, food aid can be used to build up buffer and food security stocks, without adding to current market supplies for consumption and not depressing prices.

An important international measure for promoting food security is the assurance of access to supplies for commercial purchases, so long as total import requirements are unlikely to be met from food aid at times of tight supplies and high prices in the world market. This is particularly so for low-income food-deficit countries, when they are likely to be 'crowded' out of the market, as in 1973–74, in the face of competition from high income importing countries. If the food deficit countries have national food security reserves they can draw upon them in times of domestic food shortages, as well as at times of tight world supplies and high prices, and avoid, at least partially, the resort to purchases on the world market.

In the absence of any international agreement, however, to maintain a minimum safe level of stocks which are available at times of shortages, each country is left to its own devices to build up stocks. The major exporting countries would build up stocks on the basis of their own assessment of likely fluctuations in domestic and export demand.

The objection has been raised that it is cheaper for individual developing countries to rely on imports rather than domestically held stocks to meet fluctuation in domestic production. Reliance on imports is liable to disruption because of changes in export policies including trade embargoes in the exporting countries due to either political reasons or domestic shortages, or through dislocations in transportation and distribution systems caused by wars, strikes or other logistic bottlenecks. The risks, both economic and political, in not having secure and independent access to and control over minimum food security stocks, are judged too great by many developing countries. Depending upon particular circumstances, each country should strive to achieve an appropriate combination of imports and domestic food security stocks.

The ability of developing countries to build up national food security stocks is inhibited by the lack of physical infrastructure, that is storage capacity, transportation, marketing and distribution facilities as well as by limited capacity to obtain food for stocks either from domestic production or from imports. Storage costs, especially in tropical conditions, can also be heavy. Most developing countries require financial and technical assistance to build up and operate food security reserve stocks.

FAO's Food Security Assistance Scheme provides such assistance but its resources, however, fall short of requirements. Since variation in production is likely to be less for a region or a sub-region than for an individual country, regional or sub-regional food security schemes like the Asian Food Security Reserve or a co-ordination of national stocks on a regional basis are an economical way of meeting the impact of fluctuations of supplies and prices. FAO estimates that developing countries (excluding China) need to invest $1 billion a year to build up the storage capacity for cereals alone in the next few years.

To avoid the extra cost of imports because of high prices at the time of worldwide shortages, developing countries could buy up from the world market stocks at times of low world prices and draw upon them at times of high prices. This would have a stabilizing effect on the world market, depending upon the amount of aggregate purchases by developing countries. The extent to which they would be able to do so would depend upon their access to financing facilities for not only the purchase of cereals but also for building storage capacity apart from meeting operating costs. An international agreement to help developing countries to make additional imports at times of low world prices should be supported by the provision of additional external financing, preferably through a modification of the existing buffer stock financing facility of IMF. The developing countries need to have discretion to use such stocks within the context of their own domestic needs and requirements related to their food security and price stabilization policies.

Stocks built up in developing countries are unlikely to be adequate to obviate the need for imports at times of tight world supplies. Long-term sales and purchase agreements could be reached between low-income developing countries (singly or in combination), on the one hand, and exporting countries, on the other, for ensuring secure access to adequate supplies for the former. To the extent that exporters are food aid donors, supplies under long-term agreements could be provided under varying degrees of concessional sales combined with purchases at commercial prices, the degree of concessionality increasing at times of high prices and decreasing at times of low prices.

## CONCLUSION

To sum up: world agricultural growth is conceived basically in this paper in terms of accelerating the rate of growth of production in developing countries. This is in the mutual interests of both the developed and developing countries. It would help correct the growing imbalances in world trade caused by rising food imports of developing countries. Furthermore, world agricultural growth would contribute to overall world economic growth.

Acceleration of agricultural growth in developing countries has implications for the developed countries both in the short and long-term. The primary responsibility for agricultural growth lies with the developing countries themselves. However, timely and adequate assistance is required from the international community. International action would be required not only in the form of greatly expanded financial and technical assistance; it would also be necessary for the developed countries to undertake over time an adjustment in the structure of their production and trade. In the near term future until the food deficit countries are able to increase substantially their domestic production, the developed, exporting countries are expected to harness their considerable production potential to generate a large export surplus, especially of cereals, in response to growing import demands of both the developing and the centrally planned countries.

In the short run, instability in production, in trade and in the prices of agricultural commodities, including in particular cereals, generates problems of food insecurity on the one hand, and of unstable and uncertain agricultural export earnings, on the other. The developed countries have not only an excess capacity for food production to respond to a fluctuating export demand, but also a greater ability, financial and otherwise, to hold stocks. The search for international measures or agreements for access to markets and assurance of supplies with a view to ensuring stability and security in the field of world food and agriculture should be high on the agenda of the international community.

## NOTES

[1]J. P. O'Hagan, et al., 'Agriculture towards 2000: long term perspectives in world food and agriculture', in *Rural Development for Growth and Equity,* IAAE Occasional Paper No. 3, Gower.

[2]*FAO Commodity Review and Outlook,* 1980–81.

[3]FAO Commodity Review and Outlook 1981–82. The real prices are current prices deflated by a composite index reflecting the overall structure of imports of the main exporters of each commodity concerned.

[4]H. Wagstaff, *Food Policy,* February 1982, Vol. 7, No. 1, P. 6567.

## DISCUSSION OPENING – JOHN CLEAVE

I am honoured firstly to be opening the discussion on a paper by such an eminent and influential person as Dr Nural Islam and secondly because the paper covers such an important topic, a subject which should be of concern to all of us. Indeed, I must congratulate Dr Islam on the wide range of his discourse which certainly has something for everyone here, whatever his area of specialization.

The paper makes some provocative assertions and raises some extremely important questions. In the limited time available, it is impossible to explore all of these. I would, therefore, like to focus on just a few propositions so as to stimulate the discussion which this paper deserves.

First, I want to suggest that the emphasis in the paper on the role of international assistance to improve the world food position is rather one sided: that the effectiveness of such investment will be reduced or negated unless rates of population growth can be lowered, and unless domestic policies are supportive. I would have liked to have seen both of these topics treated explicitly.

Population in the developing countries as a whole has been growing at more than twice the rate of the developed countries. As a result, while in the developed countries food production per caput increased by about 50 per cent, the gains in per caput production in the developing countries were modest. And, as Dr Islam points out, even among the developing countries the picture varies. In South East Asia overall agricultural output and food production have been rising steadily – to give, in the last decade, a per caput increase averaging 1.4 per cent a year. At the other end of the scale quite similar rates of production growth in Africa have been swamped by the population increase, resulting in a decade of declining production per caput. Population growth in Africa, in the very countries in which the 'food problem' particularly prevails, is, at 2.7 per cent a year, the highest in the world.

It is in particular – although not exclusively – to Africa that we must look when we say that 'food is in short supply in the majority of developing countries': to Africa, a continent with land still available and which, although periodically hit by adverse weather, was probably showing gains in production per caput averaging 1–1.5 to 2 per cent a year through the first 50 years of this century.

A recent World Bank Study attempted to isolate the sources of the recent slow agricultural growth on the continent. While it found that disruptions have certainly been caused by wars and civil strife, and drought and poor rainfall patterns in the 1970s have taken their toll, it has been the adverse policy environment which has been the prime cause. For example:

– there has been excessive emphasis on large scale government operated schemes, ignoring the enormous potential and responsiveness of the smallholder sector. State farms have been beset with problems of management, over-employment of staff, and under-utilization of machinery;

– price incentives for agricultural producers have been insufficient. Export crop producers have been heavily taxed while prices of food crops have been systematically set at below market levels. The average tax burden on export crops in the last decade has been in the 40 to 45 per cent range. This taxation has not only been direct, through export taxes or levies but, also indirect, through excessive marketing costs incurred by inefficient State-run boards and by overvalued exchange rates;

– in most African countries governments control producer and consumer prices for basic foodstuffs, seeking to provide incentives to producers but at the same time to protect consumers. In practice, consumers' interests dominate. Moreover, imported cereals have often become cheaper than domestic staples because of the over-valuation of many currencies;

– procurement and distribution of inputs is also monopolized by governments or para-Statal agencies in more than 60 per cent of African countries. These agencies have failed to deliver inputs at the right time at the right place and in the right amounts because of difficulties in adapting bureaucratic procedures to commercial operations.

– extension services have lacked recurrent resources and logistic support, and with a poor research base on which to build and faced with an adverse economic environment, have tended to be ineffective.

Unless the domestic policy environment is conducive to agricultural growth, international assistance simply will not be effective. It is significant that the decline in African food production occurred in a period when external sources of finance focused strongly on food production: between 1973 and 1980 about 5 billion dollars in aid flowed into agriculture, nearly half of this from the World Bank.

The second area I would like to touch on is that of trade and measures to improve world food security. Dr Islam's paper makes a lucid plea for international action to provide developing countries with access to adequate food supplies and to reduce price fluctuations, in particular by developing reserves and buffer stocks at appropriate levels.

Concern about world food security has in particular stemmed from the 1972 'world food crisis' when, at the time that the United States was reducing its stockholdings, both the USSR and India came on the market for substantial grain purchases. The run-down in stocks caused prices to soar, aggravated by panic buying. Demand and supply adjustments were rapid and the situation soon settled, but other factors have given developing countries concern about their dependence on external food supplies. Prices have been more volatile than formerly and at the same time food aid has declined. Major developed country blocs have increasingly insulated their consumers in times of production instability, making up their deficits by additional global trade. A further concern is the perception of unreliability of supplies from a few major supplying countries.

While these concerns are legitimate, the question I would like to raise is: do the risks justify enormous and expensive buffer stock operations? I would suggest not.

Prospects for global food security are certainly no worse than in the past. World food and agriculture production has been expanding over the past two decades at around 2.5 per cent per annum. Moreover, global food production has increased consistently at a rate faster than population growth for over 50 years. There is scope to continue this trend: new land is available in many parts of the world and high-yielding variety wheat and rice technology is currently used on less than 24 per cent of the land for which it is suited.

Moreover, the volume of food trade has increased four-fold in the last thirty years and the proportion of total grain production entering trade has tripled to 18 per cent, about half, by value, being feed grains. The efficiency of handling and shipping has significantly improved in recent years and the wider use of future contracts has removed some of the risks associated with market operations, although this is an area which many developing countries have still not exploited to the full.

Despite concerns to the contrary, there seems little risk that any country would not be able to obtain adequate supplies of food from the world market. The 600 million tons of grain fed to livestock provides a buffer stock at very low cost; we certainly should expect grain to be diverted from livestock production to direct human consumption if supplies become tight and prices rise. This is what happened in 1972–73 with reassuring efficiency and speed.

Against this, public sector buffer stocks are extremely expensive – especially in the tropics. Bank projects show costs ranging from about $80 per ton per year in parts of South Asia to over $150 per ton per year in land-locked African countries. In addition, turnover of stocks can be disruptive of local markets. If it costs anything up to $500 to use a ton of grain originating from a buffer stock, imports are clearly less expensive even under the most extreme market conditions.

In summary, then, I would suggest that in discussing Dr Islam's stimulating paper we should firstly address ourselves very seriously to population planning and improvements in the policy environment, both as alternatives and complements to investments to assist food production. (At a time when the international community is having difficulty maintaining in real terms the current level of development assistance it seems unrealistic to expect increases of up to 3½ times in the next few years. Conditions may improve, but whether they do or not we should seek to identify the optimum package of interventions to encourage growth.) Secondly we should explore ways of enhancing food security other than massive investment in and costly handling of stocks. The ultimate food security is an enhanced and more reliable local production of staples: and we should remember that, in many of the poorest areas of the world, such staples are often not internationally traded cereals.

JOHN W. MELLOR

# *Agricultural Growth – Structures and Patterns*

## INTRODUCTION

It is now nearly a quarter of a century since Bruce Johnston and I published our paper, 'The Role of Agriculture in Economic Development' (Johnston and Mellor, 1961). In that paper we recognized explicitly that the means by which agriculture is to be developed is closely related to the functions it is to perform. Hence we delineated an appropriate role for agriculture and in that context proceeded to expose the means by which agriculture could be developed to play that role efficiently. Both Johnston and I have further developed those basic ideas in several subsequent books and papers, (for example Mellor, 1966, Mellor et al., 1968, Johnston and Kilby, 1975, Mellor, 1976).

In our early paper we stated five classes of contribution by agriculture: (a) meet a rapidly growing demand for agricultural products associated with economic development (essentially a wage goods argument); (b) increase foreign exchange earnings by expanding agricultural exports; (c) supply labour to the non-agricultural sector; (d) supply capital, particularly for its own growth, for overheads and for secondary industry; and (e) serve as a market for industrial output. The agricultural development strategy follows from these objectives; the initial dominance of agriculture in the economy; the inevitable relative decline of agriculture with economic development; and the restraint imposed by diminishing returns given the relatively fixed land area on which most agricultures operate.

The basic prescription for agricultural development under the circumstances was 'expansion of agricultural production based on labour-intensive, capital-saving techniques relying heavily on technological innovations'. We also recognized a substantial period for 'establishing the preconditions for such growth' and a much later period, emphasizing 'expansion of agricultural production based on capital-intensive, labor-saving techniques'. Because the key intervening period 'requires an environment in which the possibility of change is recognized and accepted, and in which individual farmers see the possibility of personal gain, from technological improvement', it followed that in the preconditions phase 'improvements in land tenure are likely to be the most essential requirement'. In agricultural development, emphasis was given to 'nonconventional inputs' to complement the existing land, labour and capital resources. Explicitly noted are the large numbers of trained people needed by institutions for agricultural research, extension, supply of purchased inputs, particularly seed and fertilizer, and other institutional facilities. In the latter context, the principles for allocating this scarce personnel resource are discussed and major emphasis is placed on large expenditure for education.

These may now appear as rather widely accepted and even practical views. The agricultural development of Japan subsequent to the Mejie restoration (Ohkawa, 1964); of Taiwan (China) (and to a perhaps somewhat lesser extent Korea) (T.H. Lee, 1971); of the Punjab in India (Mellor et al., 1968); and, more broadly, much of contemporary Asia has followed this pattern at least in broad outline. In view of this we must ask why this has not been the pattern in much of Africa and why it has not been pushed more vigorously in significant parts of Asia. Further, after a quarter century of espousal of these views, what further lacunae can we find in the knowledge as then put forth.

Reticence in pursuit of this agricultural based strategy can be explained by three sets of factors. First, there has been explicit rejection of the basic premises with respect to the role of agriculture and a consequent very different set of alternative approaches to agriculture, with important structural implications. Second, a number of diversions have occurred arising from equity and ecological concerns which have been based substantially on ignorance of the context, the process and the results of technology based development – a point of view which although based on incorrect analysis served to reinforce the conclusions of those starting from very different premises. Third, Johnston and I drew insufficient attention to the requirements for conventional infrastructure and hence to the size of investment required in agriculture and the implications to the structure of both agriculture and industry. The latter represents an important lacuna in knowledge. Concurrently the alternative development strategy has suffered from an underestimate of food requirements, with a consequent and unexpected constraint on growth. It is important to sort out these forces because the next few decades are likely to be a period when food demand shifts more rapidly than supply and in which broad participation in growth will be essential to the political stability which is itself important to growth and development.

## DEVELOPMENT STRATEGY AND THE STRUCTURE AND PATTERN OF AGRICULTURAL GROWTH

All economic development strategies are intended to achieve transformation of the economy from one that is dominantly agricultural to one that is dominantly non-agricultural. This may be justified on the non-intellectual grounds of a sense of modernity arising from non-agricultural activities that cannot be ascribed to agricultural activities; to a geopolitical view that largely agricultural societies are militarily weak; or, on the economic grounds argued by Johnston and myself – that is, as incomes rise, people demand a consumption basket weighted increasingly towards non-agricultural goods and services while labour productivity is efficiently increased so as to produce the demanded quantity of agricultural commodities with a rapidly declining proportion of the labour force.

The difference between the strategy espoused by Johnston and myself and that of others is thus not in the objective, but rather it is in the role of agriculture in that process and the structure of agriculture and of industry as that objective is achieved.

*The Johnston-Mellor structure*

The Johnston-Mellor strategy is sharply different to the alternatives in the following three respects. Firstly, it emphasized consumer goods, both in the agricultural and non-agricultural sectors. Second, it emphasized increased employment both with respect to labour supply and to labour demand. Third, it emphasized international trade and comparative advantage and hence is not concerned with growth balanced to meet the domestic structure of demand as distinct from balance among complementary production processes. Each of the three features has important implications to agriculture's structure and development pattern. Each is complementary to the others. And, each represents a sharp contradiction to the alternative strategy.

Emphasis on consumer goods is of course central to an agricultural strategy, since agriculture is basically a consumer goods providing industry. But two other features should be noted. Low income labourers spend some 60 to 80 per cent of increments to income on food. Hence a high employment strategy must be a strategy of high rates of mobilization of food marketing. This point is spelled out explicitly in a recent paper (Lele and Mellor, 1981) which analyses the interacting food and labour markets and shows the importance of influences such as factor bias in technological change on the rate of labour mobilization. Because of the low elasticity of agricultural employment with respect to output, and the inelastic demand for food except among the labouring classes, growth in non-agricultural employment is important to creating adequate increases in income and markets for food.

Conversely, Johnston and I point out equally clearly that incentives to produce in agriculture require availability of non-agricultural consumer goods to provide an incentive to farm producers – while of course concurrently that farm market provides the incentive to the non-agricultural consumer goods industries.

As is clear from the above, an agricultural production orientation is an employment orientation (Lele and Mellor, 1972). This follows from the key role of wage goods in employment. W. Arthur Lewis made an important contribution in underlining this role, but was misleading in giving the impression that underemployed labour could be readily mobilized for non-agricultural employment, with its food supply automatically following (Lewis, 1954). In practice, increased employment requires increased food supplies, whatever the initial amount of underemployment (Lele and Mellor, 1981).

The interaction of agriculture, employment and trade is an important aspect of the agriculture based development model. It is the supply of wage goods (agricultural) which allows mobilization of labour and hence specialization in labour intensive goods and services for export (Mellor and Lele, 1975). Similarly, agricultural exports may themselves pay for import of capital intensive goods necessary as complements to otherwise labour intensive production.

The emphasis on consumer goods, on employment and on trade represent major points of departure of the Johnston-Mellor strategy from the alternative strategy. I will return to the implications of these departures to the structure of agricultural growth after a brief exposition of the alternative strategy.

*The Fel'dman-Mahalanobis structure*

It is most convenient to typify the alternative, non-agriculture based strategy by reference to Fel'dman, the Russian economist and intellectual father of the Soviet Union's development strategy, and P.C. Mahalanobis' strategy for the Indian Second Five Year Plan (for a full exposition see Mellor 1974). But the Harrod-Domar family of growth models is based on the same precepts and leads to the same conclusions. The Maoist strategy in China followed single-mindedly prior to, during, and subsequent to the Great Leap Forward and the Cultural Revolution is in the same genre (Tang and Stone, 1980).

For the purposes of this discussion three points need to be made about this class of development models (Mellor 1974).

First, these models focus single-mindedly on capital goods production. The rate of growth is a function of capital formation. Use of resources in consumer goods production is simply a diversion from growth which may give higher welfare in the short run, but at the expense of long-run growth and hence of long-run welfare. Since agriculture is a consumer goods industry, this strategy has no role for agriculture except as a provider of present welfare at the expense of future growth.

Secondly in these models it is capital that is limiting to employment not marketable surplus of wage (agricultural) goods and hence diversion of resources to agricultural production detracts from employment growth by reducing the rate of growth of the capital stock which is the key complement to labour. It is the assumption that capital-labour ratios are fixed that enforces this element. Since in practice in these models, the average capital intensity of production is high, these are in effect slow employment growth models, which, even granting a wage goods argument, which they do not, places only a small burden on agriculture.

Third, these are basically closed economy models. This reduces scope for decreasing capital-labour ratios through trade and hence increasing demand for food as a wage good. Similarly, the role of agricultural exports is largely ignored, a theoretical argument buttressed by arguing highly inelastic demand for agricultural exports.

Thus we see none of the roles for agriculture delineated by Johnston and myself playing a major role in this approach. Because employment grows slowly due to high capital labour ratios, demand for food grows slowly (and in any case it is assumed that food consumption can be regulated by fiat). Trade is downplayed and hence agricultural exports are downplayed. Employment grows slowly so there is little need to emphasize agriculture as a source of labour. Capital is not created in a consumer goods sector. And, demand for industrial consumer goods arising from a prospering agriculture serves to divert resources from capital goods production and therefore slows rather than accelerates growth.

*Implications for the structure of agriculture*

The Johnston-Mellor approach leads in practice to a vigorous, privately-operated smallholder agriculture which is technologically dynamic, commercializing rapidly, and, because of variation in control of resources and in enterprise, experiencing widening income disparities within the peasant farming sector.

Economies of scale in management of agricultural labour are such that it is unlikely that such an agriculture will be economically organized in large scale units, whether it be co-operative, collective, state farm or plantation. If public services are available, a small-scale sector will be highly competitive. If those supporting institutions are lacking, then a large-scale agricultural sector will not only result in an even more inequitous development pattern, but it will fail in at least two of the roles delineated for agriculture. It will be relatively more capital intensive, because of the diseconomies of scale in labour management, and hence its net contribution of capital to other sectors will be less. Similarly because of greater concentration of wealth, the demand stimulus from expenditure will tend to leak out of the country much more than will be the case for smaller farmers (Mellor and Lele, 1973). There is of course little role for a feudal agriculture in this strategy; it suffers from the same disabilities as a large-scale agriculture, plus lacking the incentive systems for rapid application of efficiency increasing technological change.

The alternative development strategy conversely calls for an entirely different approach to agriculture. That approach may take one of two quite divergent tracks. It cannot provide a rigorous, efficiency increasing peasant small-holder agriculture because it does not structure its industry to provide the consumer goods essential to farm producer incentives; nor can it generate export surpluses to import either consumer goods for incentive nor the agricultural producer goods needed for a high productivity agriculture.

On the one hand, the approach may attempt to maintain a peasant agriculture on as much of a self-sufficient basis as possible, with little growth in modern inputs, in consumer incomes or in consumption of urban goods. Production and consumption of locally produced consumer goods through labour intensive cottage industries is of course consistent with this approach – as long as there is no drain on the urban sector. Agriculture and the rural sector generally are seen as a holding area for labour, with little positive contribution to development, but with an important role of preventing labour from streaming into urban areas to create social discontent that would interfere with urban capital formation. This approach requires minimal training of people or building of expensive institutional and physical infrastructure.

On the other hand, the capital orientated approach may emphasize extracting a food surplus from agriculture – either for export as in the Soviet Union in the 1920s and 1930s, or for domestic urban consumption as in The People's Republic of China in the 1950s and 1960s. In this context large farms or conglomerations of farms may be attractive.

In this approach the strategy runs a grave risk of not mobilizing adequate food marketings even for the low level of urban consumption expenditure planned. Given that the strategy tends in practice to consistently underestimate food consumption, this is a serious shortcoming. It tends to result in large diversion of foreign exchange to food imports, for example, India in the early 1960s and the People's Republic of China in the 1970s. This is the basic rationale of the collective and state farm. They lend themselves to extracting a surplus for the urban areas.

*Inconsistent variants of the two models*

The Johnston-Mellor and the Fel'dman-Mahalanobis approaches are both rigorous, internally consistent models of growth. They work in practice and in theory. Each however has variants which are not internally consistent and which may lead to considerable grief.

In the case of Johnston-Mellor, which is after all an agriculture based model, the incorrect variant ignores the role of industry not only as an objective in itself, but as a necessary condition to agricultural growth. Thus inadequate investment is made in rural infrastructure which facilitates the transfer of capital either through taxes, prices, or direct investment from agriculture to industry and in foreign exchange allocations for rural based consumer goods.

In the case of the capital-based strategy the errors nascent in its variants are even more serious. The model is of course basically a closed economy model and hence difficulty is likely to arise in application to any small country.

A serious problem arises if the growth of the urban sector is in effect highly labour intensive, for example through rapid growth of a government bureaucracy as is now frequent in Africa. This swells the demand for consumer goods, particularly from agriculture, at the same time agriculture is not receiving the resources needed to respond; nor is the capital base being laid for rapid industrial growth. The result is bound to be the rapid growth in food imports we observe in Africa. That phenomenon is reinforced by the diversions to be discussed in the next section. Africa is the particular victim of the inconsistent versions of the non-agriculture based strategy and the currently fashionable diversions. The result has been large increases in externally financed food imports and slow growth.

*Equity implications of the two models*

Equity is a separate topic at the next plenary session, so I will only briefly sketch the equity implications of the alternative strategies.

The Mahalanobis-Fel'dman model makes no pretence of the production process contributing to the short-run reduction of poverty. The poverty reductions are strictly seen as long-term/short-term trade-offs. The more poverty alleviation now, the less later and vice versa. That is because poverty alleviation requires more consumption, and therefore diverts resources from the build up of capital. In the short run, poverty can only be reduced by redistribution.

The Johnston-Mellor model has powerful poverty alleviation forces. It is a high employment and a high food production model – both features essential to poverty alleviation. It is of course relaxation of the food supply/wage goods constraint on the one hand and the demand stimulation to high employment production processes which explain this poverty alleviation effect in a growth rather than a redistributional process. Of course within the peasant agriculture income disparities may increase. But, these will not be in favour of large-scale land owners nor against the landless.

Thus, there is a consistent economic logic to a development strategy that fails to invest in agricultural development. It should also be apparent that the industrial capital oriented strategy lends itself to a high level of government intervention since the points of development will be relatively few and concentrated. Conversely, the agriculture oriented strategy emphasizes sectors in both agriculture and non-agriculture with economics of scale that reach their maximum at a low output, calling for large numbers of firms and hence inevitably a major call on market forces for enforcing efficiency. Public sector intervention except for support services and broad influence on 'the rules of the game' will be uneconomic. Hence we find a close interaction between choice of development strategy and choice of political strategy.

## DIVERSIONS FROM AN AGRICULTURE BASED STRATEGY

Having made the intellectual case for sharply divergent strategies, with respect to the structure and pattern of agricultural development, it is important to point out diversions from the agricultural oriented strategy which are based on quite incorrect and logically inconsistent arguments. The three sources of this diversion relate to an agriculture based on new biological technology and high input levels. There is a concern for (a) the equity implications of commercialization of agriculture; (b) the energy consumption in a high input agriculture; and (c) the ecological effects of high input agricultures.

In addition, a hotch potch of other concerns reinforce these major sources of diversion: fears that commercialization of agriculture results in lower nutritional status, due to the increased relative attractiveness of non-food consumer goods; life style preference for small self-sufficient communities; and desire to reduce foreign assistance and hence preference for less capital oriented and less commercial rural development.

In the anti-commercialization approach to agriculture, five factors have been ignored. First, we seem to have little prospect of rapidly raising yields per unit area of land without crop varieties which require high input levels. Second, population growth alone requires expansion in production that no longer can be achieved primarily by increased land area under cultivation. Third, for decades into the future availability of energy for agriculture and most clearly nitrogen fertilizer from natural gas, does not face a major natural resource constraint as distinguished from capital and foreign exchange (export) constraints. Fourth, pollution levels from agricultural inputs are still low in developing countries and the need for more food very high. Fifth, the success of institutional approaches to equalizing access to inputs has been understated (for example the Taiwan area of China, Punjab of India and so on).

All of these diversions focus on opposition to biologically based high input agriculture. Such an agriculture is of course the core of any agriculture based strategy of development (Mellor and Herdt, 1964).

*Equity and agricultural modernization*

The equity and poverty alleviation of an agriculture based strategy has been stated above in terms of the employment and food consumption implications. The equity oriented opposition is based largely on the argument that the new agricultural technology is not scale neutral – that is, it works better on the larger farms than the smaller farms and thus tends to further skew income distribution away from the poor. The latter increased concentration of income would then result in a purchasing of land by the more well-to-do and further concentration of asset ownership. The unfortunate distribution effects were seen as particularly associated with high input levels and unequal access to those inputs. The empirical evidence to support this view is weak and depends heavily on (a) situations with poor input supplies, in which case political power allocates the scarce resources rather than economics; (b) observations documented by the misery making influence of population growth; and of course, (c) already exploitive land distribution systems. The alternatives for dealing with those situations are two: turn to the non-agriculture oriented strategy or emphasize equal access to inputs and other objectives which require even more trained personnel. Unfortunately, this diversion tends to be associated with a form of populism that shuns training of people for national level institutional development on the basis that such development is élitist, so the key to more egalitarian development is abjured. It is perhaps this element of anti-élitism which destroys the basis of agricultural development as clearly recognized in the early Johnston-Mellor paper and demonstrated so successfully in Japan, Taiwan (China) and the Punjab of India.

*Energy and ecology*

The energy and ecology arguments against an agriculture based strategy are more easily disposed of. The energy shocks of the mid and late 1970s raised concern about increasing agricultural production based on energy intensive use of fertilizers, water and pesticides. Similarly, the rising levels of pollution in developed countries brought a reaction against high input levels in developing countries.

It is sensible to spend on research to increase production efficiency including the productivity of inputs, as part of an agricultural based strategy. And, significant success has been achieved on the pest control side. However, it is crucial to understand that agriculture's key role arises from a process of commercialization and exchange which requires transport, low cost power and complex institutions. The alternatives are development without agriculture or no development at all.

## FUTURE MODELS FOR AN AGRICULTURAL STRATEGY

If one opts for an agriculture-based strategy of development, what oversights and errors might one note from the early writing of Johnston and myself. I note two major lacunae. We understated the capital requirements essential to moving agriculture and we understated the role of agriculture as a market for non-agricultural capital goods and services and the key mechanisms for it to play that role.

Our understating of capital requirements probably derived from observation of Japan and the Taiwan area where much of that infrastructure was in place before major yield increasing technologies occurred. Where the infrastructure of irrigation, transport, and power are lacking, very large investment is called for. We did not err in the view that this capital would have to come largely from agriculture. However, the burden cannot be carried by agricultural production alone. Rural consumer expenditure and rural based industries need to share in carrying these overheads. Thus one needs information on the size of these overheads, the optimal pattern of their provision, and the policies needed for their full and effective use. In this context, the timing and placement of rural services requires explicit attention. Since the investment requirements are large, a decision is forced as to the extent to which the development plan is to be based on agriculture or not. If the strategy is to be agriculture based, a commitment is required in financial allocations and in policy. Our early emphasis on low cost development of agriculture left room for equivocation on commitment to this strategy.

Closely related to this, Johnston and I emphasized agriculture's capital contribution coming in the form of taxes or low relative agricultural prices. Although we noted agriculture's role as a market, we saw this more as in conflict with the capital contribution and hence with a careful balance to be struck. This also resulted in a too restrictive attitude on agricultural prices. By emphasizing the market side more and recognizing the possibility of cost reducing technological change in industry, one can then depict agriculture as a sector providing a growing demand at constant prices for industrial goods produced at decreasing cost and hence with rising profits. It is the highly elastic and upward shifting demand arising from rising rural incomes that can provide the basis for a high rate of capital formation in the non-agricultural sector. These processes, the interaction with price policy, investment and rural policy generally need to be elaborated more fully.

Johnston and I specifically noted that in an agriculture based strategy, recognition would have to be given to the variability in agricultural resources and concentration on those regions most responsive to new technology. There is however a serious interregional problem, which I noted more fully later (Mellor, 1966). This is perhaps the most intractable structural problem we face in an agriculture based strategy of growth.

## REFERENCES

Bachman, Kenneth L. and Paulino, Leonardo A., *Rapid Food Production Growth in Selected Developing Countries: A Comparative Analysis of Underlying Trends, 1961–76*, International Food Policy Research Institute, Research Report No. 11, Washington, DC, October 1979.

Herdt, Robert W. and Mellor, John W., 'The Contrasting Response of Rice to Nitrogen: India and the United States', *Journal of Farm Economics,* Vol. XLVI, No. 1, Feb. 1964.

Johnston, Bruce F. and Mellor, John W., 'The Role of Agriculture in Economic Development', *American Economic Review,* Vol. 51, No. 4, Sept. 1961.

Johnston, Bruce F. and Kilby, Peter, *Agriculture and Structure Transformation Economic Strategies in Late-Developing Countries,* Oxford University Press, New York, 1975.

Lee, Teng-hui, *Intersectoral Capital Flows in the Economic Development of Taiwan,* Cornell University Press, Ithaca, 1971.

Lele, Uma, *The Design of Rural Development – Lessons from Africa,* Johns Hopkins University Press, Baltimore and London, 1975.

Lele, and Mellor, John W., 'Technological Change, Distributive Bias and Labour Transfer in a Two Sector Economy', *Oxford Economic Papers,* Vol. 33, No. 3, Nov., 1981.

Lele, and Mellor, John W., 'Jobs, Poverty and the "Green Revolution"', *International Affairs,* Vol. 48, No. 1, Jan. 1972.

Lewis, W. Arthur, 'Economic Development with Unlimited Supplies of Labour', *Manchester School,* May 1954.

Mellor, John W., *The New Economics of Growth – A Strategy for India and the Developing World,* A Twentieth Century Fund Study, Cornell University Press, 1976.

Mellor, *The Economics of Agricultural Development,* Cornell University Press, 1966.

Mellor, 'Food Price Policy and Income Distribution in Low Income Countries', *Economic Development and Cultural Change,* Vol. 27, No. 1, Oct., 1978.

Mellor, 'Models of Economic Growth and Land – Augmenting Technological Change in Foodgrain Production', in Islam, Nurul (ed.), *Agricultural Policy in Developing Countries,* Macmillan Press, London, 1974.

Mellor, 'Accelerated Growth in Agricultural Production and the Intersectoral Transfer of Resources', *Economic Development and Cultural Change,* Vol. 22, No. 1, Oct., 1973.

Mellor, 'The Functions of Agricultural Prices in Economic Development', *Indian Journal of Agricultural Economics,* Vol. XXIII, No. 1, Jan. – Mar. 1968.

Mellor, 'Towards a Theory of Agricultural Development' in Southworth, Herman M. and Johnston, Bruce F., *Agricultural Development and Economic Growth,* Cornell University Press, 1967.

Mellor, and Lele, Uma, 'The Interaction of Growth Strategy, Agriculture and Foreign Trade:

The Case of India', in Tolley, George S. and Zadrozny, Peter A. (eds), *Trade Agriculture and Development,* Ballinger Publishing Company, Cambridge, 1975.
Mellor, and Lele, Uma, 'Growth Linkages of the New Foodgrain Technologies', *Indian Journal of Agricultural Economics,* Vol. XXVIII, No. 1, Jan. – Mar. 1973.
Mellor, Weaver, Thomas F., Lele, Uma J., and Simon, Sheldon, R., *Developing Rural India: Plan and Practice,* Cornell University Press, 1968.
Ohkawa, K., and Rosovsky, H., 'The Role of Agriculture in Modern Japanese Economic Development', in Eicher, C., and Witt, L. (eds.), *Agriculture in Economic Development,* McGraw-Hill, New York, 1964.
Tang, Anthony M. and Stone, Bruce, *Food Production in the People's Republic of China,* International Food Policy Research Institute, Research Report No. 15, Washington, DC, May, 1980.

## DISCUSSION OPENING – H. S. KEHAL

Professor Mellor's very distinguished paper raises many important issues. It is interesting to note how he now looks back to interpret the substance of the Johnston-Mellor model (1961). In particular, he draws attention to agriculture's contribution to economic development under the following five categories: wage goods, foreign exchange, agricultural manpower for non-agricultural sector, capital flow and market contribution. He also elaborates his further contributions towards the theory of agricultural development in the post-1961 period. Then he makes a comparative study of the Johnston-Mellor strategy with an alternative strategy for development propounded by G. A. Fel'dman in the 1920s (which became the basis of Soviet planned development) and the strategy for India's development evolved by P. C. Mahalanobis in the early 1950s.

As is well known, Professor Mahalanobis was the architect of the development strategy of India's Second Five Year Plan. The strategy involved: (a) developing heavy industries as the key to long-run economic development; and (b) continuing production of consumer goods in small and labour-intensive industries to generate employment opportunities. The Mahalanobis model did not neglect agriculture but relied on increasing agricultural output by means of institutional measures such as land reforms, fixing of ceilings on holdings and distribution of land among the landless. Professor Mahalanobis maintained that these institutional changes would stimulate agricultural production, provide a large market for industrial output and serve equity objectives by transferring a part of national income away from those who largely spend on luxuries.

Professor Mahalanobis was convinced that industrial development would not be possible without 'an increasing supply of cheap food and raw materials'. Similarly, he expected that the long-run progress in agriculture would depend on large-scale industrial development catering to agricultural inputs like fertilizer, irrigation equipment and other capital goods. But in the short run, the approach to increases in agricultural production must be through institutional changes. Professor Mahalanobis suggested labour-intensive cultivation supported by community projects, village co-operatives, consolidation of holdings and other land reforms.

The discussion of the paper could logically centre around various inferences drawn by Professor Mellor and the policy implications of the Johnston-Mellor and the Fel'dman-Mahalanobis models. All this involves careful comparison of growth models with agriculture and industry orientations.

The actual growth experience of the past two-three decades, especially after the mid-1960s in Asia and Africa, offers the hindsight to look at the relative merits of the two alternative development strategies, viz the Johnston-Mellor and the Fel'dman-Mahalanobis models.

The underlying conceptual framework of the future growth strategy should meet the growth and equity objectives. Professor Mellor rightly refers to the need for poverty alleviation in the developing countries. And although the equity aspect of agricultural growth will be discussed in the next Plenary Session, the structure and patterns of agricultural growth have a bearing on the equity objectives.

Another problem which attracts attention is intersectoral balances and linkages. With the closing of the cultivation frontier, the future growth in agricultural output in developing countries will largely depend on more intensive use of inputs of industrial origin. This indicates the increase in sectoral interdependence and linkage effects of growth in the agricultural sector. This Session may discuss intersectoral relations especially in regard to prices, wages, incomes and technology in different sectors. The Session may also discuss various ways to realise the prospects of integration within and between sectors to achieve an effective use of resource endowments in various sectors.

The rapid growth of agriculture needs basic inputs like high-yielding seeds, fertilizers and water. However, their effective use requires suitable physical and institutional infrastructures. Professor Mellor has specifically mentioned the important role played by infrastructure in the agricultural development of the Punjab in his paper. Infrastructure development and external economies are closely related. Marshall (*Principles of Economics*) maintained that in the long-term development process, the external economies played a key role. External economies accrued to farm-firms in the Punjab with the expansion of infrastructural facilities like irrigation structures, regulated markets, co-operative credit, agricultural research and extension, consolidation of holdings and a network of village and market roads. By the mid-1960s, the Punjab had an infrastructure, both physical and institutional, which could support the introduction of the Green Revolution technology. A salient feature of agricultural growth in the Punjab in the post 1966 years has been the large-scale additions to and strengthening of existing infrastructural facilities as well as the creation of new types of infrastructure, thus generating further external economies.

Keeping in view that agricultural growth strategies have not been successful in some developing countries in Asia and large parts of Africa, as pointed out by Professor Mellor, this session may discuss the factors causing inadequate investments in rural infrastructure and ways and means of accelerating such investment to reap the external economies.

Among three E's, that is equity, energy and ecology, discussed by Professor Mellor in his paper, the line of discussion on the equity aspect of growth has been mentioned above. The introduction of 'new' technologies disrupt the existing ecological balance. It is suggested that fertilizers and pesticides contribute to environmental pollution. Increased use of non-conventional inputs has implications for the energy sector. Similarly, the success of the Green Revolution in certain regions of countries like India has disrupted the interregional balance. Professor Mellor refers to the interregional problems as the 'most intractable structural problem we face'. This Session may also deliberate on these success-related problems while discussing various aspects of structure and patterns of growth.

In conclusion, I may state that the paper presented by Professor Mellor is a fine exposition of the development of the theory and experience of agricultural growth since the 1950s. Professor Mellor is eminently suitable for enlightening this Plenary Session on structure and patterns of agricultural growth because of his long and outstanding contributions towards the theory of agricultural development, evolution of strategy for agricultural and economic development for the developing world, his high professional standing and the recent involvement in directing research from his position as director of the International Food Policy Research Institute. I deem it an honour that I have been asked to comment on a paper by such a distinguished man and I am highly grateful to Professor Kazushi Ohkawa for inviting me to open the discussion.

A. R. KHAN

# *Institutional and Organizational Framework for Egalitarian Agricultural Growth*

## INTRODUCTION: THE PROBLEM

In Asia, as in much of the developing world elsewhere, few countries have evolved an appropriate institutional framework for equitable growth of the agricultural sector of the economy. Much of the South Asian experience in recent decades can be characterized as relative stagnation with inequality while the typical South-East Asian experience is perhaps not too inaccurately characterized as growth with inequality.[1] Certain East Asian experiences have been claimed as solitary examples of growth with equality. The Taiwan area and South Korea are often cited as examples of non-socialist institutional reform leading to egalitarian growth of agriculture. Closer analysis, however, has made it increasingly clear that these are very much in the nature of special cases not likely to be easily replicated elsewhere. For quite some time it was believed that China held out an alternative, socialist example of reasonably rapid growth with a very high degree of equality. While the achievement of China must still be regarded as remarkable, recent official indictments raise serious questions about the effectiveness of the institutional-organizational framework of the commune system in generating an acceptably high rate of growth.

Institutional constraints on growth and equality in the agrarian societies have been a major concern of development theories. Such theories have frequently argued that existing institutions prevent both the attainment of higher output and its better distribution. To give an example, one of the widely held views among development economists is that the existing inequality in the distribution of land and the consequent prevalence of widespread labour-hiring in the countries of Asia not only perpetuate inequality but also limit output below the potential level by restricting the use of labour below the level that would obtain under egalitarian peasant farming based on family labour (because the market wage that dictates the quantity of labour hired for use is higher than the 'cost' of family labour). The implication is that an institutional change such as land reform, ushering in peasant farming based on family labour to replace currently widespread labour-hiring by larger farms, would promote both higher outputs and its better distribution.

This paper will argue that the above position represents an overly optimistic view. It neglects the important aspect of the cost of institutional change. Such cost arises out of a number of factors. Firstly, there is the cost of transition which is often critical for those poor Asian countries which cannot absorb such cost, in the form of lower output during the transition phase, without going through large-scale starvation. Secondly, every institution has its own systems of infrastructure and incentives which break down when the institution is overthrown. The new institution has to be provided with its alternative infrastructure and incentive systems. This entails cost in terms of the necessary time for adjustment and resources. The lack of these considerations makes the attraction of institutional change as the supposed sufficient vehicle for spearheading the process of egalitarian growth deceptively appealing. In reality the above costs almost always force a trade-off between growth and equality thereby robbing such institutional reforms of the attraction of appearing to promote both these objectives. The purpose of the paper is not to preach that one should abandon the path of promoting egalitarian growth through institutional change but to argue that the policymakers must be adequately aware of the costs involved and try to limit them as far as possible by avoiding over-optimism.

## INSTITUTIONAL CHANGE THROUGH EGALITARIAN LAND REFORM

An institutional change that is often recommended for those agrarian societies which are unprepared for or unwilling to make a basic change in their social systems is an egalitarian land reform of the Japanese-South Korean-Taiwanese type. It is argued that equality will be promoted by the egalitarian distribution of ownership of land to which, due to its scarcity, accrues a very high proportion of net output and that production will increase due to the much greater application of labour and effort as a result of the replacement of hired labour by family labour. The highly plausible theoretical argument is reinforced by the practical experiences of South Korea, the Taiwan area and Japan.

The fact that the experience has not been replicated elsewhere has generally been attributed by analysts to the lack of political will on the part of the political leadership and the power of those who own much of the land. It is frequently argued that in the above cases the problem of political will was solved by the presence of an occupation army and the power of the landowning classes had been eroded by the fact that they were (or were the collaborators of) the militarily defeated parties. The problems presented by the lack of political will on the part of the government and the political power of the landowning classes are real obstacles to land reform. However, to attribute the success in these East Asian cases entirely to the solution of these problems appears misleading.

In these East Asian cases, even in the pre land reform days, the operational landholdings were by and large small family farms, without much inequality in their size distribution, although the ownership units were distributed unequally. This is in rather sharp contrast to the phenomenon obtaining in contemporary developing Asia (particularly, South Asia) where the distribution of operational holdings is very unequal. In most cases the degree of inequality is greater in ownership distribution than in the distribution of operational holdings but the absolute inequality in the latter is very high.

The causes of this very different pattern of tenancy between East Asia and the contemporary developing Asia are not clear and is a priority area for interdisciplinary research. However, it is quite clear that the task of carrying out a highly egalitarian land reform was rendered a great deal easier in East Asia by the special characteristics of tenancy prevalent before land reform. The redistribution of ownership units could not have created much disorganization in so far as the operators of landholdings – the actual farmers – did not have to be disturbed significantly. Nor was it necessary for the new owner-operators to acquire entrepreneurial and technical knowledge which they, as tenant-operators, already possessed.

In much of the contemporary developing Asia the circumstances are vastly different in so far as the size of the operational landholdings – the farms – are highly unequally distributed. An egalitarian land reform of the East Asian type must bring about extensive redistribution among operational landholdings. Thus, some kind of a social upheaval is inevitable in carrying out land reform in these countries. This means that in order to face up to the task a much greater political will and organizational power will be required under these circumstances than was necessary in the East Asian cases.

Secondly, even in the unlikely event of finding the political will and organizational power, a good deal of time and resources would be required to replace entrepreneurship, knowledge and the overall infrastructural network. Those becoming farmers as a result of redistribution will need time to acquire entrepreneurial ability and technological and marketing know-how. More importantly, new channels of credit and investible resources will have to be established. All these will require time and resources. Although some of it will probably be offset by the greater labour use promoted by the institution of peasant farming based on family labour it is highly likely that aggregate output will fall in the short run. The extent of such fall and the length of the time period over which it takes place may be limited if the political will of the reforming government is adequately backed by a strong organization and sensible policies to improve skills, entrepreneurial abilities and command over resources of the new peasant owners. It is, however, unrealistic to think that such a major social change can be brought about at no cost to society.

On balance, the problem of adequate political will would appear to be the decisive factor. It should, however, be recognised that the need for greater political will derives from the greater obstacle arising out of the more highly unequal distribution of operational landholdings in these countries as compared to the successful East Asian cases.

## COLLECTIVE AGRICULTURE

The presence of political will, so rare a phenomenon in the contemporary non-socialist countries of Asia, is a frequent characteristic of revolutionary socialism. This has often led to thoroughgoing land reforms under its banner. However, revolutionary socialism looks upon egalitarian land reform as nothing more than a brief interregnum marking the transition towards the collective organisation of agriculture. An outstanding example is the case of the Peoples Republic of China which completed a land reform by 1952. According to all available evidence it resulted in a very egalitarian redistribution of rural income and the generation of a high rate of surplus for national investment.[2] And yet within 5 years – by the end of 1957 – private farming and land ownership as the partial basis of income distribution were virtually abolished. By then 96 per cent of the peasant families had been organized into advanced co-operatives under which land and other means of production ceased to be privately owned and the collective product came to be distributed entirely on the basis of work performed.

The arguments in favour of such rapid transition towards collectivization can be divided into two broad categories: those based on considerations of efficiency and those claiming that it would facilitate greater egalitarianism and quicker transition to socialism and, ultimately, communism. The first set of arguments emphasize the economies of scale, the greater ease in generating high rates of investable and marketable surplus to facilitate industrialization and the mobilization of labour to undertake capital construction. In the Soviet case these considerations – indeed the narrower ones pragmatically contributing to the needs of rapid industrialization – were decisive. Even in the Chinese case much of the arguments were based on considerations of efficiency and technical transformation of agriculture. Thus Mao Zedong, in his famous report 'On the Question of Agricultural Co-operation' in July 1955, argued that socialist industrialization was incompatible with peasant agriculture which would neither generate the required surplus nor create sufficient demand for the output of industry. But Mao also argued the case for collectivization on grounds of equity:

> As is clear to everyone, the spontaneous forces of capitalism have been steadily growing in the countryside in recent years, with new rich peasants springing up everywhere and many well-to-do middle peasants striving to become rich peasants. On the other hand, many poor peasants are still living in poverty for lack of sufficient means of production, with some in debt and others selling or renting out their land. If this tendency goes unchecked, the polarization in the countryside will inevitably be aggravated day by day. Those peasants who lose their land and those who remain in poverty will complain that we are doing nothing to save them from ruin or to help them overcome their difficulties. Nor will the well-to-do middle peasants who are heading in the capitalist direction be pleased with us, for we shall never be able to satisfy their demands unless we intend to take the capitalist road (Mao Zedong, 1971).

The argument that egalitarian peasant farming after land reform is an obstacle to the distributional goals of revolutionary socialism needs to be understood more clearly. At first, it would appear puzzling. A sufficiently egalitarian peasant farming could do away with wage labour so as to eliminate exploitation in the Marxist sense of the appropriation of surplus value. By continued enforcement of a land ceiling it should be possible to ensure this particular objective.

However, the two kinds of bourgeois rights that Marx talked about in the *Critique of the Gotha Programme* are preserved under this kind of peasant farming as sources of inequality. The first of these rights refers to the inequality in the distribution of rental income among peasant households due to unequal land and resource endowment. In a vast country like China anything remotely resembling strict equality in the distribution of land and assets would be impossible to ensure however thorough the land reforms may be. To curtail this right one must begin by collectivizing land and other assets and then gradually transfer their ownership from lower levels of collectives (for example teams) to higher levels (for example brigades and communes) until the level of ownership by all the people is reached.

The second type of bourgeois right arises out of the principle of relating earning to ability in so far as the latter is not proportionate to need. On this Marx was quite explicit in the *Critique of the Gotha Programme:*

> one man is superior to another physically or mentally and so supplies more labour in the same time, or can labour for a longer time... Further, one worker is married, another not; one has more children than another, and so on and so forth. Thus with an equal performance of labour, and hence an equal share in the social consumption fund, one will in fact receive more than another, one will be richer than another, and so on. To avoid all these defects, right instead of being equal would have to be unequal (Karl Marx, 1972).

Let us now examine these efficiency and equity arguments against the continuation of the post land reform egalitarian peasant agriculture in the context of achieving the goals of revolutionary socialism. The economies of scale argument is exaggerated in the context of a typical Asian agriculture characterized by a low degree of mechanization. Indeed, it is doubtful if there is any significant economy of scale in farming activities (excluding capital construction). In the mobilization of labour for capital construction there are significant economies of scale that can be taken advantage of under collective institutions. However, such advantage is at best a practical one: in principle, it should be possible to organize such activities by promoting co-operation among equal peasants. In terms of the mobilization of investable and marketable surpluses, again, there are clear practical advantages of collective institutions. It is far easier to collect marketable surplus from a few collective enterprises than from a vast number of peasants. A collective organization, like that of the Chinese communes, provides a framework for a simple system of concealed tax on lower collective units (for example teams) through the drafting of labour (who are given work points by their teams) for work at the higher collective units (for example communes).

While the substitution of peasant farming by collective farming provides some of the advantages of a practical nature noted above from the standpoint of efficiency, it has to face up to a very basic problem of efficiency in the organization of production, namely, the setting up of an incentive system. The nature of agricultural work is such that, as one moves out of the organizational framework of a peasant family into that of a collective, the evaluation of performance, the institution of a system of payments, the organization of management decisions and related matters become exceedingly difficult. If the basic accounting unit is small, as in the case of the *teams* of the Chinese communes, the problem of organizing an efficient system of incentives can still be approached. As the size of the basic accounting unit increases, supervision and evaluation of work become very difficult and the cleavage between payments and performance becomes large. The organization of incentives on a conventional basis becomes impossible.

From the standpoint of equity collective agriculture has little advantage over egalitarian peasant farming. The two kinds of bourgeois rights that are the sources of inequality under private peasant farming are also preserved under collective agriculture. The bourgeois right arising out of unequal access to land and productive assets need not be any greater under private farming than under a system of collectives in which the basic accounting unit is relatively small (for example an average team in the Chinese communes consisting of about thirty households). For such a small community in a homogeneous location it should always be possible to make land reform so egalitarian as to provide each household with roughly equal amounts of land and assets per person. The second type of bourgeois right is preserved under collective agriculture in so far as payments are based on the work performed (that is the socialist principle of 'to each according to his work').

Indeed, both in the Chinese communes and in the Soviet Kolkhozy evidence has been found that the income from personal plot is more equitably distributed than the collective income.[3] The present writer has tried to explain this phenomenon as follows:

> The distribution of income in the socialized sector, *in principle,* is proportional to the individual members' capacity to work. Individuals differ in terms of such capacity. In the socialized sector such differences in capacity result in larger income differentials because individuals work with relatively large amounts of capital and other resources. Thus the resulting distribution can be as unequal as individuals are in terms of ability. In the non-socialized sector there are such severe limitations on the volume of means of production per person that the differences among individuals' capacity to work cannot be fully translated into differential results of work. As a consequence, the distribution of income can be less unequal than that of the ability to work (Khan and Ghai, 1979).

For a sufficiently egalitarian peasant farming, under the usual kind of land and capital constraint observed in a typical Asian country, the same result would obtain in comparing the outcome of egalitarian peasant farming with the alternative of collective agriculture. The present writer has argued that in China the main gain in terms of improved rural income distribution was achieved by land reform and that since then further gain during successive phases of collectivization has been minimal (Khan, 1977).

Bourgeois rights can be restricted under the system of collective agriculture by raising the level of the basic accounting unit and by the gradual replacement of work done by need as the principle of payment. These, indeed, were tried in some advanced communes in China. It is, however, clear that these practices directly conflict with the conventional principles of organizing an efficient system of incentives. Both these restrictions on bourgeois rights result in the deviation of compensation from effort to such a degree that the material basis for efficient production breaks down unless the human agents of production cease to respond to the usual assumptions of being actuated by self interest (including the interest of the family and, perhaps, the immediate clan). Marx himself was so keenly aware of this problem as to realize that 'right can never be higher than the economic structure of society and its cultural development conditioned thereby'.[4] The precondition of successfully curbing the bourgeois rights is to bring about such a basic change in the attitudes and responses of the members of the labour force as to make them cease to behave in accordance with the standard assumption of orthodox economics that individuals, households and groups work for higher material consumption. In spite of the brief periods of experimentation in China this is by and large an uncharted path. No human society has yet succeeded in organizing itself on this basis for a substantial length of time and/or on a sufficiently wide scale.

For collective agriculture to provide significantly greater equality than a highly egalitarian, post land reform, peasant agriculture, bourgeois rights will have to be curtailed to such an extent as to make it impossible to set up an efficient system of incentives (in the absence of sufficient preparatory work in effecting basic change in human behaviour of proportions not experienced by any human society to date). This will render the collective system a far less efficient organization for productive efficiency in comparison with peasant agriculture. Attempts at hastening the path towards higher levels of collectivization, prompted either by considerations of expediency or by doctrinaire belief in the urgency or feasibility of curbing bourgeois rights, could easily create such great problems of productive efficiency as to require a backward step in the direction of restoring much of the elements of egalitarian peasant farming as the only available method of ensuring efficiency. Recent experiments in China with the so-called responsibility system indicate evidence of this. The lesson seems to be that revolutionary socialism should look upon egalitarian peasant farming, ushered in by post-revolution land reform, as a less temporary stage of agricultural organization and begin transition towards collective agriculture only after the subjective conditions have been fulfilled. As already indicated, a sufficiently egalitarian peasant farming is non-exploitative in the Marxist sense of eliminating the appropriation of surplus value. The bourgeois rights preserved under it can be modified significantly by using the instrument of fiscal policy. In any case, the existing forms of collectives are not able to curb these rights much more significantly.

## SOME CONCLUSIONS

1 Stagnation and growth with inequality in the rural economies of the contemporary developing Asia can be attributed, in substantial degree, to the prevalence of inappropriate institutions that are characterized by a high degree of inequality in the distribution of land and assets.

2 The change in these institutions – in particular, in the unequal distribution of land and assests – is highly desirable from the standpoint of the promotion of equality.

3 The hope that an appropriate institutional reorganization would *automatically promote egalitarian growth* is unrealistic.

4 Much of the hope of a non-revolutionary solution of the institutional problem of agriculture is based on the experience of East Asia. This hope is unlikely to be realized in contemporary developing Asia. Historical difference between East Asia and the contemporary developing Asia makes the cost of such reform in the latter a great deal higher in terms of the necessary political will, organizational ability and resources for an alternative infrastructure.

5 At least from the standpoint of the necessary political will revolutionary socialism appears to be a superior medium of instituting successful land reform. Such movements have, however, seen land reform as a short-lived transitional phase on the way to collective agriculture. The rapid transition to collectivization has by and large been promoted by the expediency and pragmatic need to generate high enough rates of investible and marketable surplus. The arguments of greater equity and efficiency have rarely been valid. The generation of greater equity without a loss of efficiency would require fundamental changes on the 'subjective' side by way of changing the responses of the human agents. Little preparatory work has ever gone into this. The problem is on the very frontier of human experience. But without some idea as to whether and how it can be resolved the transition to collective agriculture would appear to be premature.

## NOTES

[1] These are broad generalizations to which exceptions can be found. Growth of agricultural production in India during the 1960s and 1970s was about 2¼ per cent per year or just a shade higher than that in population. This was typical of South Asian growth rate. Agricultural growth

in Pakistan and Sri Lanka was a little higher while that in Bangladesh and Nepal was a little lower. In South-East Asia agriculture in the Philippines and Thailand grew at annual rates of over 4½ and 5½ per cent respectively. Indonesian growth rate was about 3¼ per cent over the two decades but higher during the 1970s. In both the South and South-East Asian countries inequality continued to be very high. This has been widely documented. For example see ILO (1977) and Griffin and Ghose (1979).

[2] See Charles R. Roll Jr. (1974) and Khan (1977).

[3] See Khan and Ghai (1979) for similar evidence in the Soviet Central Asian Republics and Griffin and Saith (1981) for that in the Chinese communes.

[4] The quotation is from Karl Marx (1972). Many Marxists suggest that a higher level of material well-being will automatically make it possible to de-emphasize material incentives. According to this view it will become easy to organize the distribution on the basis of the principle of 'to each according to need' once the economy attains a high level of material production. This, to the present writer, sounds like naive optimism which de-emphasizes the need to organize changes on the subjective front.

## REFERENCES

Charles R. Roll Jr., *The Distribution of Rural Incomes in China: A Comparison of the 1930s and the 1950s,* Harvard Ph.D. Dissertation, 1974.

Griffin, Keith, and Ghose, Ajit, 'Growth and Impoverishment in the Rural Areas of Asia', *World Development,* Vol. 7, 1979.

Griffin, Keith and Saith, Ashwani, *Growth and Equality in Rural China,* ARTEP, Bangkok, 1981.

ILO, *Poverty and Landlessness in Rural Asia,* Geneva, 1977.

Karl Marx, *Critique of the Gotha Programme,* Beijing, Foreign Languages Press, 1972.

Khan, A.R., 'The Distribution of Income in Rural China'.

Khan, A.R., and Ghai, D.P., *Collective Agriculture and Rural Development in Soviet Central Asia,* Macmillan, 1979.

Mao Zedong, 'On the Question of Agricultural Co-operation', in *Selected Readings from the Works of Mao Zedong,* Beijing, Foreign Languages Press, 1971.

## DISCUSSION OPENING – MICHEL PETIT

Dr Khan's paper tackles an important issue which no society, in Asia or elsewhere, can avoid: namely how to evolve an institutional framework capable of promoting agricultural growth and of reducing the inequalities in its distribution. The author is successful in avoiding the main risk in such a venture, that of being superficial while tackling such a broad issue in only a few pages. His purpose 'is not to preach but to argue that the policy makers must be adequately aware of the costs involved' (in promoting egalitarian growth). One can only applaud such a purpose.

This being said, my main task is not so much to praise the paper but to point out its limitations. Does the author fulfil his purpose? How well founded are his arguments? After an introductory section posing the problem which I have just reported, the second section, entitled 'Institutional change through egalitarian land reform', is very brief. It argues that the examples of land reform in East Asia cannot be easily replicated elsewhere because the costs of transition would be much higher in South and South-East Asia, due to a greater inequality of operational holdings before the reform. This can probably be accepted but does it justify the contradiction between the sentence asserting that it would be misleading 'to attribute the success in the East Asian cases entirely to the solution of the problems' linked to the lack of political will on the part of the government and the political power of the landowning classes as obstacles to land reform and the sentence stating: 'On balance, the problem of adequate political will would appear to be the decisive factor'? Personally, I could accept that these two sentences are not necessarily contradictory but making this clear would require to spell out better the interrelationships between economic and political factors. I shall come back to this later.

The following section deals with 'Collective Agriculture'. It implies that Khan would be happy if one could convince the socialists (the only ones capable of having the political will) to promote egalitarian peasant farming. To support his point of view, he criticizes the arguments usually presented both on grounds of efficiency and equity and taken here from Mao's writings on China. These arguments justify the rapid collectivization of agriculture after an initial period of egalitarian land reform following the socialist revolution. I must admit that the author's arguments on economies to scale and on the problems of setting up an adequate incentive system appear rather convincing to me. This is probably because I share what I believe to be his ideological leaning towards reformism. But are these arguments sufficiently well founded analytically to convince a Marxist? Frankly I doubt it.

In his analysis Khan quotes Marx's *Critique of the Gotha Programme:* 'right can never be higher than the economic structure of society and its cultural development conditioned thereby' in order to support the statement that 'Marx himself was keenly aware of this problem' (that is 'deviation of compensation for effort to such a degree that the material basis for efficient production breaks down unless the human agents of production cease to respond to the usual assumptions of being actuated by self interest'). The question here is that of the interrelationship among economic, institutional and human changes. For Marx and his followers, these relationships are of a dialectical nature. Thus, if one puts the above quotation by Khan in its broader context one can read:

> All these problems (referring to the inegalitarian nature of any right) are unavoidable in the first phase of the communist society, when it just emerges from the capitalist society, after a long and painful birth. Right can never be higher than the economic structure of society and its cultural development conditioned thereby.

In a superior phase of communist society, when the enslaving subordination of individuals to the division of labour and so on, will have disappeared, we will be able to escape once and for all from the narrow horizon of bourgeois right and society will be able to write on its banners: 'From each according to his capacities, to each according to his needs.'

Here Marx asserts very clearly the dialectical nature of the relationship through historical time between economic structure and right; (we can say) between economic and institutional changes. And it is the process produced by these interrelationships which brings about changes in the human agent. In my view the very mechanism of this process remains obscure and this obscurity regarding the relationship among economic, institutional and human changes is the main source of our analytical problems today. I would tend to criticize Khan for not emphasizing this point enough. Actually when he advocates 'begin transition towards collective agriculture only after the subjective conditions have been fulfilled', he ignores the main force behind collectivization, namely to establish socialist production relationships which are supposed to promote the emergence of a new man. Without necessarily accepting this Marxist view, I feel that Khan regresses compared to Marx because he seems to ignore the dialectical nature of the relationships among various types of changes and this brings me back to the point I raised above on the relationship between economic and political factors.

In conclusion I would like to repeat that A. R. Khan must be complimented for addressing himself to an extremely important and topical issue which is right at the core of the theme of our Conference on growth and equity. Whether or not he delivers as much as he promises can be disputed but undoubtedly the main limitations of his paper stem from very fundamental theoretical problems, regarding relationships between several scientific fields, which our profession has failed to solve so far. If I may be permitted to extend the argument, I would like to repeat a suggestion made earlier that a (fruitful) approach to these difficulties would be to develop what I have called an analytical political economy.

## GENERAL DISCUSSION* – RAPPORTEUR: J. P. HRABOUSZKY

The complementary nature of the three papers presented was also clearly reflected in the discussion. Mellor's paper set up a framework for strategies, Islam's paper explained some of the main international issues involved in the implementation of agricultural development strategies, while Khan's paper brought into focus many of the major difficulties of implementing the main steps towards more egalitarian structures in agriculture.

The many interesting comments dealt with the need to recognize the strong influence of demographic growth on agriculture, its impact in driving technological change and affecting many inter-sectoral relations, and also its crucial role on equity. The treatment of inter-sectoral links in relation to labour, capital, consumer goods, foreign exchange and incomes was recognized as the central element in the alternative models for agricultural development. Furthermore, the large variability in diverse situations in the real world needed to be matched by flexible interpretations of alternative models.

It was similarly emphasized that the transferability of experience from

*Papers by Islam, Mellor and Khan

land reforms towards more egalitarian structures is limited, especially with regard to the problems of the landless, and that in some cases second generation problems of otherwise successful reforms need attention. The importance of appropriate incentive structure as part of equality orientated organizational forms, together with development of physical and human infrastructure, were seen as necessary for external economies of scale to be realisable.

The discussion made it clear that the likely driving force for higher agricultural output in developing countries would remain domestic demand, but that exports were needed both in their role as providers of flexibility as well as enabling the exploitation of comparative advantages. Improvements in access to international markets, including intra-developing country trade, were necessary for its success.

The discussion also covered issues of international aid and food security. It was suggested that raising the level of international aid would be difficult under prevailing economic conditions and would be conditioned by the optimal use for growth and equity objectives and by improved domestic economic policies. On food security, comments emphasized the need for a careful balance between reliance on world markets, bilateral contracts and increased local and regional storage operations.

Participants in the discussion included Kirit S. Parikh, H. J. Padilla, George Peters, Ryohei Kada, Ferenc Fekete, H. F. Breimyer, G. Gaitani d'Aragona, H. L. Chawla and Yang Boo Choe.

FERNANDO HOMEM DE MELO

# *Technological Change and Income Distribution: The Case of a Semi-Open Less-Developed Economy*

Beginning in the 1950s the economics literature has given emphasis to the importance of technological change for economic growth in general, and for the increase in factor productivity in agriculture in particular (Solow, 1957; Griliches, 1963; 1964). In addition, several studies have been performed with the objective of estimating the rate of return of public investments in agricultural research, mainly for specific crops (Griliches, 1957, 1958; Akino and Hayami, 1975; Ayer and Schuh, 1972). Also, Evenson (1968) estimated a marginal rate of return of 48 per cent in the case of public investment in agricultural research in the United States.

More recently, on the other hand, attention has been given to the distributive effects of technological change. Bieri, de Janvry and Schmitz (1972) had already called attention to the lack of theoretical and empirical efforts in this area, at the same time as the public sector was investing large sums in agricultural research. Afterwards we had, among other contributions, the ones by Akino and Hayami (1975) for the aspects of rice research in the economic development of Japan; by Scobie and Posada (1978), investigating the impact of technological change in the rice sector of Colombia in terms of income distribution for families of consumers and producers; finally, by Hayami and Herdt (1977), about the effects of such a change in subsistence agriculture.

The present paper is one addition to this more recent line of emphasis, that is, the distributive implications of technological innovations and concentrates itself on effects for low income food consumers in less developed countries. In the words of Singer and Ansari (1978, p. 47), 'even the ultimate objective of development is a great deal more than a mere increase in per capita income; questions relating to the use and distribution of this income are as important dimensions of development policies as its increase'. Our main reference focus will be an economy characterized as 'semi-open', in the context of Myint (1975, p. 332), that is, in which 'a large part of the domestic economy must remain insulated from the impact of foreign trade and comparative costs...'. In such a case, very likely to be a common one in less developed countries, we intend to show that a pattern of technological change concentrated on exportables can impair the growth of domestic crops, alter relative prices of domestic-exportables and bring negative effects (real income) for low income consumers. Specific reference will be made to the large quick expansion of soybeans in Brazil, resulting from a process of technological change and the income distribution effects during 1967/79.

## TECHNOLOGICAL CHANGE, RESOURCE USE AND PRICE EFFECTS

The central idea in this part of the paper is to show how important technological innovations can affect resource use among the subsectors of Myint's 'semi-open' economy. An important innovation is here supposed to have a great deal of significance with respect to individual crops and regions benefited and with occurrence during a relatively short time interval. This innovation would have the necessary conditions for altering the composition of output as the result of changes in the expected returns to farmers of the available options. A possible outcome is the one in which resources are transferred from other activities to the one being favoured by technological change during the period of diffusion of the new knowledge. If the total cultivated acreage could increase, incorporating new lands, this expansion could be predominantly orientated towards the crops favoured by the innovations.

It is possible, however, that such a result could not be generalized. Relevant factors are the type of technological innovation, market conditions and the possibility of substitution among factors. Here we want to discuss the effects of land saving innovations[3], the so-called bio-chemicals (Evenson, 1974; Hayami and Ruttan, 1971). These innovations usually come from the work of selection and varietal improvement, including a greater response to fertilizer application. Also, they result in larger yields, practically cause no change in the final product and reduce production costs (Kuznets, 1972).

With respect to market conditions, reference is here made to the product demand, through the parameters, price and income elasticities, as particularly important for a greater generality of the results, that is, technological innovations affecting crop mix in favour of the benefited products. The higher the value of the price elasticity of demand, the more likely is the occurrence of such a result. This conclusion can be obtained from Castro (1974) who worked, for analysing distributive questions, with a two-stage production function with four factors: land and land-saving capital (bio-chemicals) on one hand, and labour and labour-saving capital (machinery) on the other, with a high degree of substitution in each stage but with low substitution among the two stages. Working with constant prices for all four factors, Castro has shown that the demand for land would increase if $S_T\eta + S_L P > P_T$, where S corresponds to factor shares of the aggregate factors (land plus bio-chemicals; labour plus machinery), $\eta$ to the price-elasticity of demand, P to the elasticity of substitution among the two subfunctions and $P_T$ to the same parameter in the land subfunction (land and bio-chemicals)[4].

Now, if we introduce the case of a 'semi-open' economy, Myint's type, the picture described would become clearer. The literature is beginning to register such circumstances with more frequence. For instance, Abbott (1979) mentions the case in which selfsufficiency is a national policy and the government allows consumption to increase or to decline with the level of domestic production. In addition, Castro and Schuh (1977) indicate that the choice of products is important for the determination of beneficiaries from agricultural research, because of the different demand price-elasticities. In the following, we assume the agricultural sector with two subsectors: exportables and domestic products. The distinction is based in each market's functioning, that is, if it is open or closed to international transactions.

In an open economy, domestic prices are determined by the functions of supply and demand of exports, while in a closed economy the relevant functions are the internal ones. This last case is, usually, a consequence of the adopted commercial policy, through instruments like tariffs, import licensing and, in the extreme, import prohibitions. Also, if we assume a 'small country' case in international trade, the domestic price of an exported crop is determined by the international price, the exchange rate and the marketing costs. In such a special case, there is an influence from prices of exported crops to prices of domestic crops, but not the reverse.

With such a situation in mind, we can analyse the likely distributive implications for families of consumers, with a process of technological change biased, in a certain time period, towards one or more of the exportable crops. If we consider the case of land-saving bio-chemicals the individual marginal cost curves and the market supply curve would shift to the right. With a perfectly elastic export demand, the cultivated acreage with the crop in question would increase[5], with all these effects occurring with a constant product price. This is the particular case where all the direct benefits from technological change are appropriated by domestic producers[6], including increases in land prices, mainly considering the location-specific nature of research results (Perrin and Winkelman, 1976).

When total acreage is fixed, the change in the expected rate of return for the exportable crop benefited by innovations would cause the attraction of resources previously employed in the domestic subsector (possibly, also, from other exportables) and, consequently, the real prices of domestic crops would increase. This would continue until a new equilibrium relative price is attained, always assuming no change in the commercial policy which brought the domestic subsector into existence. In other words, the composition of output would be affected in favour of exportables. A second possibility is when total cultivated acreage can increase. In such a case, the process would tend to be directed towards the favoured crops, in addition to the previous effect in regions already under cultivation. In the case the innovations are specific to a certain agricultural region of the country, the unfavoured ones could show an increase in the production of domestic crops – by assumption, crops not benefited by technological innovations – partly compensating the production fall in the former region.

Furthermore, if the so-called domestic crops are formed by important foods, in terms of budget shares of low income families, the price increase following the change in the crop mix would be like a tax with regressive incidence. As a result, the unbalanced nature of the process of technological change among crops with different market characteristics, could bring a worsening of income distribution (from the expenditure side). For that, it is necessary that we maintain the assumption of no changes in commercial policy or, alternatively, that the international market, at least for certain commodities, is not a supplier able to complement domestic production.

## EVIDENCE IN THE BRAZILIAN CASE

For quite some time Brazilian agriculture has been characterized by the existence of two subsectors, exportables and domestic crops, the first one being open and the second closed to international transactions[7]. Within the first group we have soybeans, oranges, sugar, tobacco, cocoa, coffee, peanuts and cotton, while the second one is formed by rice, edible beans, manioc, corn, potatoes and onions, most of them being important foods for low income families. In this part of the paper we intend to show that one of the main reasons for the tremendous growth in the production of soybeans from the early 1960s, was the development of technological innovations in Southern Brazil. In addition, such a growth was the causal factor for significant changes in the composition of output against domestic-food crops. Finally, we will attempt to show the effects of such changes on the index of food prices for families at different income levels.

However, it is important to point out at the beginning that technological innovation in soybeans was one of three factors favouring exportables in Brazil. The other two were (Homem de Melo, 1982): (a) The introduction, in 1968, of the system of exchange mini-devaluations, and (b) a favourable period of international prices, mainly during the first half of the 1970s. Consequently, the evidence of price effects to be later presented must be understood as the result of the above three forces, and not only from technological change in soybean production. We hope to show, however, that this last factor was of great importance for explaining the change in crop mix beginning in the second part of the 1960s.

Soybeans, in Brazil, represent the most recent example of a large expansion in area during a short time interval and with a limited geographic extension. In 1960 total soybean area was 177 thousand hectares, with 159 thousand in the state of Rio Grande do Sul. In 1980, on the other hand, the figures were 8,965 thousand and 3,988 thousand, respectively[8]. The increase in international prices started in 1971–72 and reached maximum levels in 1973 and 1974. In 1972 the total area was already at 2,292 thousand hectares. Certainly, the favourable period of international prices during the early 1970s made a positive contribution for that growth in area. However, that was not the factor at the origin of soybean expansion in Brazil, since during the 1960s those prices were practically constant in nominal terms. In addition, it seems relevant to indicate that several commodities had price increases during parts of the 1970s, but none of them had an expansion in area comparable (or, even, near) to that of soybeans.

TABLE 1 *Time of introduction and adoption of new soybean varieties in Brazil and effects on yields*

| Period | Average yield, Brazil (Kg/Ha) | New varieties |
|---|---|---|
| 1960– | | Amarela Comum, Abura, Pelicano, Mogiana. |
| 1960–68 | 1,060 | Hill, Hood, Majos, Bienville, Hampton. |
| 1969–74 | 1,394 | Bragg, Davis, Hardee, Santa Rosa, Delta, Campos Gerais, IAC–2, Viçosa, Mineira. |
| 1975–80 | 1,541 | IAS–4, IAS–5, Planalto, Prata, Perola, BR-1, Paraná, Bossier, Santana, São Luiz, IAC–4, UFV–1. |
| 1980– | 1,740 | BR-2, BR-3, BR-4, Ivaî, Vila Rica, Unîão, Cobb, Lancer, CO-136, IAC-5, IAC-6, IAC-7, UFV-2, UFV-3, Cristalina, Dokko. |

*Source:* Kaster and Bonato (1980), p. 421.

In Table 1 we show a summary of agronomic research in Brazil, in terms of new varieties, the time of introduction and the impact in actual yields. Two of those varieties – Santa Rosa and Hardee – were very important for the expansion of soybeans during the late 1960s and early seventies. The first one had its origin at Campinas Agronomic Institute, São Paulo, beginning with the introduction of American varieties and, later on, the development of lineage L–326 in 1958. In the mid–1960s it became commercially available in Rio Grande do Sul with the name of Santa Rosa. The variety Hardee, also of American origin, was studied and adapted at Campinas after 1965. Such facts also reveal the importance of international knowledge transfer for the process of technological change in Brazilian soybeans, mainly by making unnecessary a series of previous research work and leading, as in Guttman (1978), to a decline in research costs. Another related evidence of such importance is that from the 48 varieties recommended for planting in 1980, 26 had their origin in national programmes and 22 came from the United States, half of them in the form of lineages (Kaster and Bonato, 1980).

Several other agronomic aspects of the crop were emphasized over the years by the research centres: selection of Rhizobium's lineages, direct planting, control of weeds, diseases and pests, density and planting time. The indications are that in the late 1970s, soybean research was one of the most developed in the country. For instance, according to Kaster and Bonato (1980), in recent years this research has been involved in developing production systems for other regions besides Southern Brazil, like East and Centre-West regions. In addition, 'the research is aiming at developing a technology specific for soybeans production in regions with latitudes below 15° S. The perspectives for obtaining varieties specifically adapted to lower latitudes, as well as for knowledge about crop management are excellent, and new in the world' (Kaster and Bonato, 1980, p. 432).

TABLE 2 *Annual percentage rates of growth of domestic production in Brazil, 1960–69, 1967–76 and 1970–79*

| | Commodities | 1960–69 | 1967–76 | 1970–79 |
|---|---|---|---|---|
| 1. | *Domestic* | | | |
| | Rice | 3.20 | 2.47 | 1.46[a] |
| | Edible beans | 5.37 | –1.93 | –1.90 |
| | Manioc | 6.05 | –1.86 | –2.09[a] |
| | Corn | 4.74 | 3.55[a] | 1.75 |
| | Potatoes | 4.34 | 1.34 | 3.73 |
| | Onions | 3.87 | 4.77 | 9.27 |
| 2. | *Exportables* | | | |
| | Soybeans | 16.31 | 35.03 | 22.47 |
| | Oranges | 6.01 | 12.73 | 12.57 |
| | Sugarcane | 3.63 | 5.10 | 6.30 |
| | Tobacco | 5.30 | – | 6.16 |
| | Cocoa | 2.55 | – | 3.73 |
| | Coffee | –7.10 | –6.34[a] | –1.54[a] |
| | Peanuts | 5.89 | –6.80[a] | –12.06 |
| | Cotton | 1.51[a] | –1.99 | –4.41 |

*Source:* Production data from FIBGE – Fundação Instituto Brasileiro de Geografia e Estatîstica.

[a]This letter indicates the coefficient is not significantly different from zero at the 5 per cent level.

In Table 2 we show the rates of growth of domestic production during 1960–69, 1967–76 and 1970–79 for fourteen crops, among exportables and domestic. When examining such data, we note that from the 1960s to the 1970s Brazilian agriculture experienced important changes: after a relatively uniform performance among crops during the 1960s, in the 1970s the country had a substantial deterioration in the performance of domestic crops and a great expansion of certain exported ones, a process led by soybeans. The worst cases were manioc and edible beans, with large declines, while rice and corn had their production levels stagnated during the 1970s, at the same time population was growing at an annual rate of 2.47 per cent. When the first five domestic-food commodities of Table 2 were aggregated in terms of per caput caloric/proteic availability [9], the conclusion was an annual rate of decline, during 1967–79, of – 1.84 and – 2.09 per cent respectively (Homem de Melo, 1982a). Rice, corn and edible beans had their availabilities only slightly increased by imports over that period. These five domestic-food crops, in addition to cotton and pasture land, were the agricultural activities most affected by the substantial expansion of soybeans in Southern Brazil (Zockum, 1980).

Even when we consider other food products, like sugar, wheat, meat (beef, pork and poultry), eggs and milk, total per caput caloric/proteic availability declined during 1967–75 (annual rates of – 0.75 and – 0.76 per cent, respectively), with a small recovery during 1976–79. We also had a greater importance over time of wheat and sugar, the first one a traditional imported food which had a policy of price subsidies for consumers beginning in 1972 (Carvalho, 1981). During 1970–79, the growth rate of wheat availability was greater than that for domestic production, which indicates a more important role of imports. Without the policy of consumption subsidies and larger imports, the fall in caloric/proteic availability would have been even larger than that observed.

As a consequence of this unbalanced performance, in terms of domestic production and availability of food products, it seems relevant to investigate how different classes of family income were affected. To this end, we used the information from the family budget survey (ENDEF-FIBGE)[10] done in 1974–75 for the states of São Paulo, Rio de Janeiro, as well as South and Northeast regions (Homem de Melo, 1982a). Such data show important differences in consumption among expenditure classes[11] and regions. For instance, the share of rice and edible beans in total food expenditure varies between 21.1 and 27.9 per cent in the lowest income (expenditure class) and between 3.3 and 7.2 per cent in the highest one for the four regions[12]. Similar behaviour was observed for the shares of corn and its products, wheat and products (except in the Northeast), tubercle and roots (manioc, potatoes) and sugar. The contrary, however, occurs for meat and eggs/milk/cheese, that is, increasing shares as income rises. Also, a few important differences were observed in the Northeast: manioc is much more important in lower income classes, while wheat is more important for higher income classes.

These strong differences in consumption structures over income (expenditure) classes, as well as the distinct behaviour of physical availabilities, are good reasons for also expecting an uneven impact in terms of prices and real incomes for Brazilian families. This would occur through changes in market prices and consequent income effects, via each product's share in total food expenditure. After examining the behaviour of thirteen food items in São

Paulo during 1967–79, it was noticed that those with the largest increases were manioc, edible beans, beef, pork and corn (Homem de Melo, 1982a), three of them being domestic food[13], originating in the crop sector, and with greater relevance for lower income families.

As an attempt to verify the distributive effects of this situation, we estimated the increase of the food price index by income classes (based on ENDEF-FIBGE, 1974–75) for São Paulo, Rio de Janeiro, as well as South and Northeast regions. These indices were computed taking the shares (weights) of each product in total food expenditures for the two states and two regions of Brazil and the observed prices in São Paulo (Cost of Living Index). Excepting São Paulo, we are only approximating the situation faced by families over different income classes. It is expected, however, that the several prices vary mostly by reason of spatial distribution of production and consumption, without significantly affecting the rates of growth over time.

In Table 3 we show the estimated food price index only for the Northeast region. However, the direction of the change was the same in the two states and the other region analysed, that is, larger increases for the lower income families. In other words, these were the families mostly affected by the transformations which occurred in the composition of agricultural output, in response to technological innovations in soybeans and to changes in external variables (prices and exchange). The case of the Northeast region, however, was the most serious one and for that reason it is explicitly shown in Table 3. For instance, when we compare the lowest and highest income classes in terms of annual rates of growth of nominal food prices, we note that during 1967–79 they were 28.6 and 26.2 per cent respectively. Alternatively, a cumulated increase of 32.9 per cent more for the lowest income class. For São Paulo, Rio de Janeiro and South region the greater cumulated increase was 10.0, 12.7 and 8.7 per cent, respectively. For these different results among states and regions, we could mention two main reasons: (a) The greater importance of manioc and edible beans for lower income families in the Northeast as compared to other regions (26.7 against 2.4 per cent among the income extremes in that region, versus 14.2 against 1.4 per cent in the South). These two commodities were the ones with greater increases in prices during 1967–79. (b) The relatively small importance of wheat in the consumption habits of lower income families in the Northeast (4.2 against 10.0 per cent among the extremes in the Northeast, and 8.9 against 7.1 per cent in the South). We recall that, beginning in 1972, the Brazilian government subsidized wheat prices to all consumers, which in the Northeast had a regressive incidence. Results such as described, particularly those for the Northeast, can aggravate those obtained for nominal income distribution in Brazil with the census data of 1970 and 1980, in the sense of greater concentration of the real income distribution.

TABLE 3 *Indices of nominal food prices, expenditure classes, Northeast region, 1967/79 (1976 = 100)*

| YEARS | <1.0 | 1.0–1.5 | 1.5–2.0 | <2.0 | 2.0–2.5 | 2.5–3.0 | 3.0–3.5 | 2.0–3.5 | 3.5–5.0 | 5.0–7.0 | >1.0 |
|---|---|---|---|---|---|---|---|---|---|---|---|
| 1967 | 100 | 100 | 100 | 100 | 100 | 100 | 100 | 100 | 100 | 100 | 100 |
| 1968 | 126 | 124 | 123 | 124 | 123 | 122 | 122 | 122 | 122 | 121 | 120 |
| 1969 | 160 | 155 | 152 | 155 | 151 | 150 | 150 | 150 | 148 | 148 | 147 |
| 1970 | 198 | 191 | 188 | 191 | 186 | 185 | 184 | 185 | 183 | 181 | 181 |
| 1971 | 153 | 143 | 237 | 242 | 233 | 231 | 230 | 231 | 228 | 225 | 223 |
| 1972 | 319 | 302 | 291 | 300 | 284 | 280 | 278 | 280 | 275 | 270 | 268 |
| 1973 | 430 | 407 | 389 | 402 | 380 | 373 | 370 | 374 | 365 | 359 | 356 |
| 1974 | 557 | 533 | 514 | 528 | 504 | 497 | 495 | 498 | 490 | 483 | 479 |
| 1975 | 766 | 721 | 688 | 712 | 669 | 659 | 649 | 658 | 640 | 624 | 606 |
| 1976 | 1,133 | 1,033 | 970 | 1,012 | 932 | 914 | 897 | 912 | 876 | 848 | 817 |
| 1977 | 1,546 | 1,401 | 1,317 | 1,383 | 1,270 | 1,242 | 1,222 | 1,242 | 1,195 | 1,156 | 1,124 |
| 1978 | 2,087 | 1,947 | 1,856 | 1,925 | 1,799 | 1,770 | 1,743 | 1,768 | 1,720 | 1,671 | 1,631 |
| 1979 | 3,311 | 3,081 | 2,917 | 3,038 | 2,820 | 2,775 | 2,729 | 2,770 | 2,686 | 2,609 | 2,542 |
| Annual Rate | 22.6 | 28.0 | 27.5 | 27.8 | 27.2 | 27.1 | 26.9 | 27.0 | 26.7 | 26.5 | 26.2 |

*Source:* Primary data from ENDEF-FIBGE (weights) and FIPE – Fundação Instituto de Pesquisas Econômicas (Prices in São Paulo).

## CONCLUDING COMMENTS

This paper had the objective of investigating possible distributive implications of a pattern of technological innovations in a semi-open economy, that is, as composed by two subsectors in agriculture, exportables and the domestic one. The case we had most interest in was the one where the innovations were concentrated in crops of the exportables subsector during a certain time period. In such circumstances our conclusion was that the composition of output might change in favour of exportables. Without changes in commercial policy, prices of domestic crops would go up and if they are important foods for lower income families, real income distribution would be affected.

Attention was also given to the Brazilian case where a semi-open agricultural economy has long existed. In the domestic subsector important foods can be found, mainly in terms of budget shares for lower income families. We also gave particular attention to the technological innovations in soybeans, to its extraordinary expansion and to the transformations in the composition of output. Our final conclusion was that lower income families suffered the most from the behaviour of food prices during 1967–79. However, we also presented an important reservation: with the increase of certain international prices and modifications in the exchange rate policy, the results should not entirely be imputed to the unbalanced pattern of technological innovations, but to all factors together.

## NOTES

[1]Before the work of Bieri, de Janvry and Schmitz (1972) in the distributive area, we emphasize the contributions of Johnston and Cownie (1969), Falcon (1970) and Schmitz and Seckler (1970), where the focus was in the factor markets.

[2]An extension of the case presented by Hayami and Herdt (1977) is given by Nguyen (1977), that is, an open economy where the market price is subject to a ceiling, via imports.

[3]In the case of neutral technological change, two factors and the usual hypotheses, the demand for land with the favoured crop would increase if the price-elasticity of the product's demand is greater than one (absolute value). See Pastore and Mendonça de Barros (1976) and Ivenson (1975) for the case of demand for labour.

[4]See, also, de Janvry (1977) for a similar production function in two stages and four inputs. De Janvry indicates that bio-chemicals are highly output increasing even with an inelastic land supply and a constant level of labour-saving capital, as long as the elasticity of labour supply is high.

[5]In Myints (1975) words: 'In peasant economies, not excepting densely populated countries like India, peasant producers have been generally observed to respond to relative price changes by flexibly reallocating resources between subsistence production and cash crops, including export crops'.

[6]Schuh (1976) mentions this point for analysing the conflict of interests among producers and consumers with respect to financing agricultural research.

[7]See Homem de Melo (1982 b) for details of this segmentation and for evidence about prices–domestic and international – in both segments. We have shown that, for domestic crops, internal prices have been above the international ones.

[8]In 1980, soybean exports were US$ 2.5 billions, about 12 per cent of total Brazilian exports. During the 1960s, the rate of growth of cultivated soybean area in Brazil was 16.3 per

cent annually and went up to 20.7 per cent in the 1970s.

[9]That is, domestic production minus exports plus imports. We did not consider use as seeds, losses and change in stocks, because of lack of data.

[10]National Survey of Family Expenses, Fundação Instituto Brasileiro de Geografia e Estatistica.

[11]They correspond to consumption expenditures plus taxes as well as labour and retirement/ health contributions.

[12]The lowest and highest expenditure classes are not always coincident among regions.

[13]Even beef and pork meat are closer to the subsector of domestic products than of exportables. Some exports/imports were made during the 1970s, but in relatively small amounts when compared to domestic production.

[14]See Williamson (1977) for an analysis about wage goods and distributive inequality in the United States.

## REFERENCES

Abbott, P.C., 'Modelling International Grain Trade with Government-Controlled Markets', *AJAE* 61(1): 22–31, 1979.

Akino, M. and Hayami, Y, 'Efficiency and Equity in Public Research: Rice Breeding in Japan's Economic Development', *AJAE* 57(1): 1–10, 1975.

Ayer, H.W. and Schuh, G.E., 'Social Rate of Return and Other Aspects of Agricultural Research: The Case of Cotton Research in São Paulo, Brazil', *AJAE* 54(4): 557–69, 1971.

Bieri, J., de Janvry, A. and Schmitz, A., 'Agricultural Technology and the Distribution of Welfare Gains', *AJAE* 54(5): 801–8, 1972.

Carvalho, L.E., 'O Caráter Social da Politica de Subsidio ao Trigo', *Alimentos e Nutrição,* March 1981, pp. 32–42.

Castro, J.P.R., *An Economic Model for Establishing Priorities for Agricultural Research and a Test for the Brazilian Economy,* Ph.D Thesis, Purdue University, 1974.

Castro, J.P.R. and Schuch, G.E., 'An Empirical Test of an Economic Model for Establishing Research Priorities: A Brazil Case Study' in Arndt, T.M. et al. (eds), *Resource Allocation and Productivity,* University of Minnesota Press, 1977, pp. 498–525.

De Janvry, A., 'Inducement of Technological and Institutional Innovations: An Interpretative Framework', in Arndt, T.M. et al. (eds), *Resource Allocation and Productivity.* pp. 551–66.

Evenson, R.E., *The Contribution of Agricultural Research and Extension to Agricultural Production,* Ph.D Thesis, University of Chicago, 1968.

Evenson, R.E., 'International Diffusion of Agrarian Technology', *The Journal of Economic History* 34(1): 51–73, 1974.

Evenson, R.E., 'A Note on Distributional Effects of Technological Change in Agriculture', São Paulo, FIPE, Conference 'The Economics of Agricultural Research', Sept. 1975.

Falcon, W.C., 'The Green Revolution: Second and Third Generation Problems', *AJAE* 52(5): 698–710, 1970.

Griliches, Z., 'Hybrid Corn: An Exploration in the Economics of Technological Change', *Econometrica,* 25(4): 501–22, 1957.

Griliches, Z., 'Research Costs and Social Returns: Hybrid Corn and Related Innovations', *JPE,* 66: 419–31, 1958.

Griliches, Z., 'The Sources of Measured Productivity Growth: United States Agriculture, 1940–60', *JPE,* 71: 331–46, 1963.

Griliches, Z., 'Research Expenditures, Education and the Aggregate Agricultural Production Function'. *AER* 54: 961–74, 1964.

Guttman, J.M., 'Interest Groups and the Demand for Agricultural Research', *JPE* 86: 467–84, 1978.

Hayami, Y. and Herdt, R.W., 'Market Price Effects of Technological Change on Income Distribution in Semisubsistence Agriculture', *AJAE* 59(2): 245–56, 1977.

Hayami, Y. and Ruttan, V.W., *Agricultural Development: an International Perspective,* Johns Hopkins Press, 1977.

Homem de Melo, F., 'Disponibilidade de Alimentos no Brasil e Impactos Distributivos', *Trabalho para Discussao n.º 44,* Instituto de Pesquisas Economicas, Universidade de São Paulo, Feb. 1982.
Homem de Melo, F., 'Commercial Policy, Technology and Food Prices in Brazil', *Quartely Review of Economics and Business,* 1982, forthcoming.
Johnston, B.F. and Cownie, J., 'The Seed-Fertilizer Revolution and Labor Force Absorption', *AER* 59: 569-82, 1969.
Kaster, M. and Bonato, E.R., 'Contribuiçaò das Ciencias Agrarias para o Desenvolvimento: A Pesquisa em Soja', *Revista de Economia Rural* 84(3): 405-34, 1980.
Kuznets, S., 'Innovations and Adjustments in Economic Growth', *The Swedish Journal of Economics* 74: 431-51, 1972.
Myint, H., 'Agriculture and Economic Development in the Open Economy', in: Reynolds, L.G. (ed.), *Agriculture in Development Theory,* Yale University Press, 1975, pp. 327–54.
Nguyen, D. 'Intersector Distributional Implications of Agricultural Technical Progress in an Open Economy: An Extension', *AJAE* 59(2): 370–74, 1977.
Pastore, A.C. and Mendonça de Barros, J.R., 'Absorçao de Mao-de-Obra e os Efeitos Distributivos do Progresso Tecnologico na Agricultura', *Revista Brasileira de Economia* 30 (3): 263–93, 1976.
Perrin, R. and Winkelman, 'Impediments to Technical Progress on Small vs. Large Farms' *AJAE* 58(5): 888–94, 1976.
Schmitz, A. and Seckler, D., 'Mechanized Agriculture and Social Welfare; The Case of the Tomato Harvester', *AJAE* 52 (1970): 569–77.
Schuh, G.E., 'The New Macroeconomics of Agriculture', *AJAE* 58(5): 795–801, 1976.
Scobie, G.M. and Posada, R., 'The Impact of Technical Change on Income Distribution: The Case of Rice in Colombia' *AJAE* 60(1): 85–92, 1978.
Singer, H. and Ansari, J., *Rich and Poor Countries,* Allen and Unwin, London, 1978.
Solow, R.M., 'Technical Change and The Aggregate Production Function', *Review of Economics and Statistics* 39: 312–20, 1957.
Williamson, J.G., 'Strategic Wage Goods, Prices, and Inequality', *AER* 67(2): 29–41, 1977.
Zockun, M.H.G., *A Expansão da Soja no Brasil: Alguns Aspectos da Produçao,* Ensaios Economicos Nº 04, Instituto de Pesquisas Economicas – Universidade de São Paulo, 1980.

## DISCUSSION OPENING – J. VON AH

Professor Homem de Melo's paper deals with the problem 'Growth and Equity' as viewed from his Brazilian experience.

The agricultural subsector for export crops showed a spectacular increase in the total soybean acreage in the late 1970s. Improved new varieties met favourable price and demand conditions in the export markets. The agricultural subsector for domestic crops, however, was stagnating, even declining. While population still increased, food availability of traditional beans and manioc declined by 2 per cent per annum for low income groups. The situation was partly alleviated by Government subsidies on sugar, wheat and meats. Geographically, the north east of the country was especially badly affected and low-income families were hardest hit.

These findings seem to confirm Ruttan's general conclusions on effects of the so-called 'Green Revolution':[1]

- in areas of relative equality, its effect is strong in terms of productivity and equity.

- in areas with inequality (skewed distribution of land, prime land, wealth, power and so on) its effect is weak and increased the existing conditions of inequality.

In the case of this paper, *negative effects* are demonstrated on the nutritional status of people.

My comments will cover three areas of questions which appear to me important for judging possible effects of new technology on human nutrition. After all, equity of food distribution is an essential objective of *all* discussions on equity.

The first area covers questions of the data base and specifications, aggregations and disaggregations, namely:

- How meaningful is a national (or regional) average about nutrition in a large country like Brazil?
- Were the figures presented rural, farm, non-farm, family, local, male/female data?
- What is the share of subsistence food production without market exchange?
- Did the results present a trend or a cross-section of a fluctuation of good years/bad years? (A question I ask after reading yesterday's paper by Bhalla and Leiserson on 'Issues in the Measurement and Analysis of Income Distribution in Developing Countries: Some Comparative Perspectives'.[2])

A surprising quite recent publication was an article by Thomas T. Poleman, 'A reappraisal of the extent of World Hunger', in *Food Policy* of November 1981.[3] Poleman questions the basis of major surveys by FAO and the World Bank and USDA. He suggests that the real problem groups are mothers and small children.

How far did the Brazilian team worry about the above questions?

A second group of questions concerns theory and modelling. I have no arguments about the applicability of partial equilibrium analysis and Marshallian type approaches to the distribution of monetary costs and benefits of new technology between producers and consumers. My only question is whether the time and effort needed is available to formulate in urgent cases the relevant theoretical situation (I remind you of yesterday's papers by Hayami[4] and Just *et al.*[5]) for explaining what is happening and what policies should be initiated to solve problems of nutritional status.

Assuming the findings of de Melo on a deterioration of nutrition are correct, I have certain difficulties in blaming the soybeans for everything:

- What are the effects of overall price and trade policies of the Government?
- How about the Brazilian exchange rate policy which taxes in effect the agricultural sector?
- How about the growing of energy crops?
- Does the shared distribution of land have something to do with the problem at hand?

The paper presents more clear and straightforward conclusions on the relative position of areal productivity of soybeans versus other crops (for domestic *and* export use). In my opinion without improving the relative position of the traditional foods with soybeans in terms of better varieties and better prices, the process of product substitution will most likely persist.

There is a large task left for agricultural research of the biological type, and the designing of proper price policies.

Let me end with a third group of remarks. There is an enormous body of literature on the 'Green Revolution' which emphasizes strongly the negative effects, not the least, in forms of deteriorating equity. Our University of Friborg[6] has classified over 800 titles. My agronomist friends ask (with some resignation) 'Shouldn't it have taken place at all? What do you social scientists do with our good, successful work?'.

Without elaboration, it seems to me that scientists and biologists are expected to accomplish things that they simply cannot be expected to achieve. As a consequence I wish to put in a strong plea for a more intensive dialogue between agricultural economists and physical-biological scientists. With Schuh[7] I regret 'that there are social scientists who would have us throw the baby out with the bath water by abandoning technical change altogether, *rather than devise alternative policies to deal more directly with deleterious income-distribution consequences'*. – I add, naturally, that they have to be properly established first and identified as to their cause and nature.

I thank Professor de Melo for his stimulating paper. It would go beyond my competence to supplement the paper with suggestions for policy instruments; this task I leave, together with the author, to all of you.

## REFERENCES


[1]Ruttan, Vernon W., 'The Green Revolution: Seven Generalizations', *International Development Review*, 1977, 19, 4, pp. 16–23

[2]Bhalla, S.S. and Leiserson, M., 'Issues in the Measurement and Analysis of Income Distribution in Developing Countries', this volume pp. 139–52.

[3]Poleman, Th.T., 'A Reappraisal of the Extent of World Hunger', *Food Policy*, November 1981, pp. 236–252.

[4]Hayami, Y., 'Growth and Equity, Is there a Trade-off', this volume pp. 109–19.

[5]Just, et al., 'Modelling Equity and Efficiency in Agricultural Production Systems', this volume pp. 120–37.

[6]Fleck, F., Bortis, H., and von Ah, J., *The positive and negative effects of the Green Revolution* – A Documentation, Fribourg, 1982.

[7]Schuh, G.E., 'Approaches to Basic Needs and to Equity that Distort Incentives in Agriculture', in Schultz, Th. W. (ed.), *Distortions of Agr. Incentives*, Indiana University Press, 1978.

DANIEL W. BROMLEY AND B. N. VERMA

# *Natural Resource Problems in Agricultural Development*

## INTRODUCTION

The problems of natural resources in agriculture can be understood by a careful study of the institutional arrangements that indicate who controls natural resources, who uses those resources, who reaps the benefits of that use, and who must bear the costs. Markets and exchange (or resource allocation decisions in the planned economies) occur within a particular institutional structure that defines benefits and costs to different participants at the local level, and at the national level. While there are many possible approaches that we might take, an important yet often ignored perspective is that of the problems of resource use at the local (village) level. Because of the importance of these problems for local agricultural development our discussion will concentrate on local resource problems rather than on international markets for wood, minerals, and petroleum.

The rise of the open economy over the past two hundred years has meant that previous production systems are no longer local-demand constrained. That is, the local or village economic system was one in which production existed for local consumption. Such consumption was largely a function of local needs, and productive activities responded to those needs. Primitive economies exist in a few places even today where production is driven by domestic consumption needs. But the essence of 'modernization' has been to produce for export markets–that is, to engage in exchange in response to the prospect for gain arising from differential comparative advantage among regions. This comparative advantage has not always been as innocent as our textbooks would indicate. Indeed, it has been, for the most part, an artifact of colonial administration or colonial antecedents. In these settings, relative prices for labour and natural resources were not in any way reflective of the marginal social values at the local level but rather reflected the political and economic power of the colonial administration *vis-à-vis* the local (or national) structure. Even today, natural resource prices are often incongruous with relative values at the local level.

Open economic systems under an imposed constellation of relative prices for natural resources not only distort relative values to be placed on physical scarcity, but they break the practice of production being driven by local consumption needs. Scarcity is, after all, not a physical concept as much as it is a combination of control over natural resources through property arrangements, and an effort to create demand for certain resource properties or attributes. Property rights create the power to withhold commodities from the market and so to influence scarcity (Tawney, 1978).

In a small open economy local use-value and local exchange-value become supplanted by exchange value outside the economy. When buyers and sellers differ greatly in terms of political and economic power then efficiency in exchange must surrender the bulk of its normative appeal to the economist (Dobb, 1969; Mishan, 1971, 1974). Efficiency has no meaning without some reference to the distribution of income and power; the pauper can strike an efficient bargain with the millionaire.

The central issue in agricultural development activities as they relate to natural resources at the local level would seem to be one of understanding that: (a) relative prices for natural resources – and the institutional arrangements that produce those prices – often are an artifact of colonial rule; and (b) the export of natural resources – whether in the form of meat on exported livestock or of charcoal – means that local economic decisions often are dominated by reliance on external markets.

To gain a better understanding of how natural resource activities relate to the development process, we turn to a discussion of the major participants. We can then turn our attention to the process of development and the implications of this process for future agricultural development programmes sensitive to the special needs of natural resources.

## THE PARTICIPANTS

### *The local level*

All economic agents, whether individuals, households, or firms, operate within a set of institutional arrangements that both constrain and permit certain actions; this structure of institutions consists of individual and group *choice sets.* That is, each economic agent is constrained by the institutional structure of the culture in which that agent lives. A caste Hindu operates in an institutional structure that is both similar to, and different from, the institutional structure within which a Muslim lives. In the same village there are institutional arrangements that operate equally on both, but there are also some institutional arrangements that are not shared.

Some of the common elements of that structure would be those conventions and rules that define civilized behaviour; that is, community sanctions against murder, theft, arson, and so on. Yet another set of institutional arrangements would encompass economic exchange in the marketplace, landlord-tenant affairs, and the like. While terms of exchange (prices) might vary slightly depending upon one's religion or familial ties, the basic structure of economic exchange is set.

We refer to this set of institutional arrangements as *operating rules.* That is, the institutional structure at this level defines the environment within which individuals struggle to 'make a living' These rules define both individual and collective choice sets. Individual economic agents attempt to enhance their economic and social condition within the confines of choice sets. For the most part, the individuals have little influence over the nature of those choice sets. They must do as well as they can in an environment that has been defined for them. Indeed the essence of socializing the young is the process of teaching acceptance of those institutional arrangements.

Of couse within any particular socio-economic system a subset of individuals will possess the ability to impose a new structure of binding relationships on others. This is what Samuels would call voluntary freedom, and what Commons would call power. Accepting this set of operating rules at the local level is the prerequisite for accepting the notion that socio-economic life in the village is very highly defined and structured. We must also recognize that this structure gives rise to a unique concept of 'problematic situations' and thus to the preferred solutions to those problems. Very little that is new to the village can exist without confronting some of these institutional realities.

We would now like to draw a distinction between technology and technique. Technique is that set of tools and knowledge that comprises the production possibilities of the individual and the collective. By way of contrast, technology is a combination of technique and of institutional arrangements. When we talk of 'rice technology' in Asia we are speaking not only of a set of machines, seeds, tools, and knowledge about how to combine labour, land and water with these physical objects, we are also implying a particular set of institutional arrangements that defines land use patterns, water control practices, marketing opportunities, labour opportunities and obligations, and diet of the people. This is technology (Bromley, Taylor and Parker, 1980).

Much of what is done in the name of development is a process of introducing new techniques – seeds, machinery, ditches – but not new technology; the hardware but not the software (Cordell, 1978). We know that new techniques are readily adopted if they fit into the existing institutional structure, and if the losses of important participants in the village are not severe. But it is the possibility of loss that creates a certain resistance at the local level to any change. That is, there is tension at the local level in terms of the advantages and disadvantages that flow from the prevailing structure of choice sets. The prospects of a new configuration of advantages creates tension within the local setting.

There are, however, not only tensions at the village level, there are concordances as well. Most people prefer a better life for themselves and their family, all merchants want more business, farmers all want higher yields and prices, and all want a certain harmony and stability. Everyone is interested in what we call 'Pareto-safe' changes – those in which everyone is made better off. This belief in 'Pareto-safety' may help to explain the attraction of external assistance, whether that assistance comes from a regional or national capital, or from a foreign country. Somehow the perception exists that external assistance will be 'Pareto safe' – all will gain, and there will be no losers. The history of development assistance belies that perception.

*The national level*

Let us now turn to the national level. Here we find a structure of institutional arrangements that defines choice sets, but this level is also the locus of a constant search for a structure of operating rules that will induce individual economic agents – those individuals, firms and households in the economy – to operate in such a manner that certain collective goals are attained. After all there are people who must be fed, goods that must be produced, armies that must be maintained, imports that must be financed with exports, and so on. Those in government must abide by certain institutional strictures but they are also in a position to influence the choice sets of a large number of economic agents at the village level; here too, 'power' shows up as the legal and political ability to change the choice sets of economic agents. For example, if cotton becomes an important source of foreign exchange with which to acquire necessary (or desired) imports, then there is interest in enhancing the production of cotton. This might take several forms. The price of cotton might be influenced to make its production more attractive *vis-à-vis* other crops. Certain subsidies might be offered to cotton – related inputs or marketing requirements, cotton seeds might be sold at bargain prices, cotton gins might be constructed at government expense, or rail lines might be constructed to transport the crop. Entire irrigation projects might be created.

But there is another side to this. If at the national level cotton suddenly becomes a desired commodity, then it is possible that some other crop will become less desired economically; those who had been producing that particular crop might be hurt by the policy change. It is this prospect that epitomizes the second important tension in economic policy; the tension that results from a divergence between what is necessary or desired from the perspective of the national government and what is necessary or desired from the perspective of the individual economic agent.

*The international level*

Let us now introduce the third component of our system – the external development community. Activity here is also constrained by a set of institutional arrangements; which countries are to be helped, how much money is to be spent, the terms of that spending (loans, grants), the purposes for which it can be spent, and even the manner in which it can be spent. These institutional arrangements define in a very specific way what shall constitute 'development' as seen in the eyes of the external development assistance community. To be sure military and political considerations usually are important here.

This institutionalized definition of what constitutes development imposes important constraints on the national governments and on those at the village level. We have seen that at the local level there is a concept of 'Pareto safety' in which all are presumably made better off. The same concept often holds at the national level where external assistance is seen as a mechanism for achieving certain national goals without having to sacrifice others. Just as the local level is greatly influenced by the objectives of the national level, so is the national level greatly influenced by the objectives of the external participants in the development process. This influence is, for the most part, unidirectional. After all, the party with the funds will usually have an important voice in defining the nature of the enterprise.

The availability of money and the control over project design and evaluation means that the external level can essentially define the nature of the problem for both the national and the local levels. By having a major role to play in problem definition, it follows that the formulation of 'solutions' would also be strongly influenced.

This should not be taken to mean that there are not areas of concordance between the external component, the national component and the local component. Each participant shares the goal of improving life at the village level, and of solving important problems there. But, as with the national-local link, there can be disagreements over the specifics of what will be done. These disagreements imply that the external level imposes choice sets on the national level and in turn choice sets are imposed on the local level.

Consider the problems of the pastoralists in Africa. A variety of institutional constraints imposed as a result of colonial administration have eliminated a number of traditional responses to climatic variation. Hence, adaptations formerly made are no longer possible. The development community is often prone to define resource depletion as the fault of inappropriate technique and thus fences, tubewells and irrigation are perceived as the proper solution. These are the things that the external level is able and willing to finance and it is this aspect that permits both the external level and the national level to fail to comprehend the important interplay between institutions and technique that created the problem.

In summary, we view the development of agriculture as operating in a setting where tensions exist both within each of three levels and among three levels. Because the external level interacts with the local level through the intermediation of the national level, we can generally talk of a linear influence in which the external level imposes choice sets on the national level, which in turn imposes choice sets on the local level. It is not an overstatement to argue here that this structure defines what the development 'problems' are and also what the appropriate solutions are. For this reason, development assistance usually functions on projects – for projects embody precise responses to perceived problems, and projects allow one to obligate funds. These two aspects – projects and money – symbolize the essence of development as now practised.

Let us now concern ourselves with the nature of resource problems in agricultural development. We will retain the local-national distinction from above, but the external level will be discussed only briefly.

## THE DEVELOPMENT PROCESS

Because institutional arrangements define choice sets for individual and collective economic agents, natural resources have meaning to individuals (and to collectives) only with respect to a particular technical endowment and institutional structure. It is this structure that defines relative values. It is this structure that determines scarcity (and hence prices); and it is this structure that indicates which costs of resource use will be considered by those in a position to make decisions about use rates of natural resources. For instance, if the institutional arrangements over the discharge of toxic chemicals into a river are favourable to those wishing to discharge such wastes, then important costs are visited on others that can go unrecognized by the party responsible for those discharges. To say that they can go unrecognized is to say that they can be ignored. On the other hand, if the institutional arrangements are favourable to the potential victims, then the costs to those individuals (damages that would be incurred) cannot be ignored by those who would wish to avoid the costs of disposing of the wastes (Bromley, 1979, 1982; Mishan, 1971, 1974).

At the local level where resource-use decisions are made on a daily basis, the institutional structure is seldom the focus of analytical attention. Yet it is this structure that creates the incentives and sanctions for a particular pattern and time path of resource use. And, of equal importance, this structure influences the *appearance* of feasibility of external investments in the local natural resources. We stress the appearance of feasibility since new income streams are defined by this institutional structure, and those income streams predicted in project evaluation documents may sometimes bear scant resemblance to the actual situation once an investment becomes operational.

The distinction between rates of resource use and investments in existing (or new) resources is worth elaboration. Indeed, this distinction will serve to remind us that most of our attention in development programmes is focused on the investment aspect and little has been devoted to the management problem. How might we characterize the two types of activities?

By the *management problem* we refer to adjusting use rates of natural resources. Adjustments will not occur as a result of pleas directed at those who are currently using the resources; nor is it sufficient to plead for restraint on the part of would-be users. Rather, the management problem is really a task of institutional design – of creating a set of sanctions and incentives that will produce a pattern of resource use consistent with some social objective. At the local level one use pattern may be sought; at the national level quite another pattern. Usually, rules are promulgated at the national level in an effort to influence resource use at the local level. Unfortunately, the history of such rules shows that they arise only after serious resource depletion has occurred and that they are developed with little consideration given to pressures created at the local level, where people must somehow survive under a new institutional structure that appears to be quite arbitrary. This is usually compounded by the absence of any substitutes for the suddenly banned resource and by the administration of the new institutional arrangements 'from the top down'.

Examples are found in areas where deforestation is severe, and then suddenly all cutting of timber is outlawed. Such rules are usually accompanied by an indifferent – if not corrupt – enforcement effort that is characterized by what Myrdal refers to as the 'soft state'. This problem has been discussed in the context of African deforestation by Thomson.

On the other hand, the *investment problem* is one in which the physical capital stock of the local economy is augmented by the infusion of new financial and technical resources. We can relate the management problem to the investment problem by making reference to a renewable resource such as livestock forage. The management problem is one of adjusting current grazing patterns such that the forage resource is enhanced over time. When that adjustment fails to take place, serious depletion occurs (Swift, 1977). In a technical sense we invest in renewable natural resources, such as livestock forage, by reducing current use rates; foregone grazing now is an investment in the future resource. We can even think of the sacrificed income from such reduced grazing – the opportunity cost of more benign use – as the 'capital' cost of the investment.

The traditional investment problem in agricultural development has tended to focus on planting trees, or building irrigation structures, or planting range forage. But there has been a minimal concern with the institutional arrangements that control use rates of the various resources being augmented; not surprisingly, the record of success is not one to which we can point with pride.

This discussion of the distinction between investment and management was intended to highlight the extent to which we have been greatly concerned with the former and largely ignorant of the latter. This particular result is not an accident; rather, it grows out of the nature of development assistance as discussed in the previous section. Here we refer to the important role played by the external level on influencing problem definition and solutions at the national level. Of course this then dictates to a large extent the particular definition of problems at the local level as recognized by national governments and when problems are defined in a certain way, their solution is essentially co-determined.

The external participants in agricultural development also have other reasons for preferring to perceive of natural resource problems as investment problems. Investments can be formulated in terms of projects – a concept dear to the heart of most development administrators. Investment projects also can be defined in terms of financial commitments. Finally, the external country can appeal to its need to remain 'neutral' by not interfering with indigenous institutional arrangements. Investment projects are considered safe for the external participants for precisely the reasons that investment projects fail to deal with the very institutional failures that created a natural resource problem in the first instance.

We would not wish to leave the impression that the host country is innocent in this preference for investments in natural resources over programmes to improve natural resource management. Host governments and those interests represented by powerful élites like to think in terms of projects just as do the international development agencies. Secondly, host governments seem to have an affinity for the large grants and concessional loans that accompany investments. Finally, a host government would be subject to extreme political backlash if foreigners were found to be tampering with traditional institutional arrangements over natural resources. Put most simply, investments are politically safe for both the donor (external) and host (national) level, while management programmes are not. Investments have the aura of 'Pareto safety'; management programmes imply a redistribution of advantage within a fixed resource base. To wait for the payoff from an adjustment in current use rates is often considered too costly. How much more appealing to install physical infrastructure – ditches, trees, range grasses – and ignore the institutional arrangements that will ensure their long-run viability.

Recognizing the foregoing as the structure within which development activity will continue to operate is not to deny the chance for some improvements in how the process works so as to achieve the goals of all three of the participants. But an improvement will require a basic reformulation of the role of natural resources in the process of agricultural development.

Those of us who work in development must be ever mindful of the reality facing those living close to the margin of survival. That reality influences not only how they will define problems, but also their preferred solution to those problems. It will also influence their interest in the solutions that are imposed by both national and external actors in the development process.

Consequently, the development process as it relates to natural resource use should be designed in such a manner that the resource problems as defined by those at the village level carry significant influence *vis-à-vis* the problems as defined by national or foreign participants. The process must be such that the needs of the local participants are met and it must be consonant with the larger part of the existing technical and institutional structure at the local level.

These conditions are obvious to anyone who has spent time in the development business, but their relevance to the task at hand justifies their emphasis. Their immediate pertinence for a discussion of the role of natural resources in development compounds that justification.

## IMPLICATIONS FOR NATURAL RESOURCES AND DEVELOPMENT

Natural resources have socio-economic significance only with respect to a particular technical and institutional structure. The institutional structure defines who may control those resources, and that structure determines relative prices. To insist that relative prices are determined in markets is to beg the logically prior question of who controls the institutional arrangements that define any particular exchange process. This means that the benefits and costs of any particular action taken with respect to those natural resources are also determined by that institutional structure.

Forests and rangelands are depleted, water is rendered unfit for human consumption, farm labourers and their families are poisoned by powerful pesticides, soil is washed away. These situations persist because of a dissonance between technique and institutions. In central India the poorest families cannot afford cows or buffalo and so graze sheep and goats for a livelihood. The institutional arrangements that may have worked for cows and buffalo (a choice of technique) will most surely not work for sheep and goats (a different technique).

The failure of governments to create needed institutional change means that as population increases, more and more people will be forced to use land (and other natural resources) of decided inferior quality. In Latin America we see large ranches in the valley bottoms, while the *campesinos* are confined to the steep hillsides. Survival requires intensive cropping of these hillsides even though erosion is a serious problem. When the government finally decides to act it is more likely to deal with the symptoms of the problem by forcing the hillside cultivators to move. The larger institutional structure that allows ranchers to tie up large areas of fertile land – often to raise beef that will be exported – is rarely questioned by those with political power.

In summary, it is our view that economic development activities concerned with natural resources are misguided in two general respects. First, we tend to deal with technical innovation – new technique – to solve institutional problems. Second, when institutional change is employed, it is often for the wrong reasons, directed towards the wrong problem and carried out at the wrong level. To a certain extent this is the result of an incorrect definition of the problem (Runge, 1981; Runge and Bromley, 1979). But it also results from an unwillingness to confront those who possess political power.

Technical change has the advantage of being apparently 'Pareto safe', while institutional change holds certain threats for those currently advantaged by the *status quo.* Economists feel comfortable dealing with technical change and quite uncomfortable with institutional change, largely because of our training where we learn that market exchange will produce economic efficiency. But it also can be traced to the belief that the structure that defines the market – here termed institutional arrangements – is not an area of legitimate scientific enquiry (Tribe, 1972). With this view of the role of the 'objective' scientist, we are circumscribed from bringing analytical skills to bear on the very structure that determines natural resource use patterns in the developing countries. Until we begin to analyse this structure, our contribution to a science of natural resources and economic development is destined to be irrelevant.

## REFERENCES

Bromley, Daniel W., 'Land and Water Problems: An Institutional Perspective', *American Journal of Agricultural Economics,* Vol. 64, December 1982.

Bromley, Daniel W., *Economic Issues in Forestry as a Development Program in Asia,* Center for Resource Policy Studies and Programs, School of Natural Resources, University of Wisconsin, Working Paper No. 16, April 1982.

Bromley, Daniel W., Taylor, Donald C. and Parker, Donald E., 'Water Reform and Economic Development: Institutional Aspects of Water Management in the Developing Countries, *Economic Development and Cultural Change,* Vol. 28, January 1980.

Bromley, Daniel W., *The Development of Natural Resource Economics: Concepts and Their Relevance to the Developing Countries,* Center for Resource Policy Studies and Programs, School of Natural Resources, University of Wisconsin, Working Paper No. 14, June 1979.

Commons, John R., *Legal Foundations of Capitalism,* University of Wisconsin Press, 1968.

Cordell, John, 'Swamp Dwellers of Bahia', *Natural History,* June/July 1978.

Dobb, Maurice, *Welfare Economics and the Economics of Socialism,* Cambridge University Press, 1969.

Mishan, E. J., 'The Postwar Literature on Externalities: An Interpretative Essay', *Journal of Economic Literature,* Vol. 9, March 1971.

Mishan, E. J., 'The Economics of Disamenity', *Natural Resources Journal,* Vol. 14, January 1974.

Myrdal, Gunnar, *Asian Drama,* Vintage Books, New York, 1972.

Runge, Carlisle F., 'Common Property Externalities: Isolation, Assurance, and Resource Depletion in a Traditional Grazing Context', *American Journal of Agricultural Economics,* Vol. 63, November 1981.

Runge, Carlisle F. and Bromley, Daniel W., *Property Rights and the First Economic Revolution: The Origins of Agriculture Reconsidered,* Center for Resource Policy Studies and Programs, University of Wisconsin, Working Paper No. 13, January 1979.

Samuels, Warren J., 'Welfare Economics, Power, and Property', in Warren Samuels and A. Allan Schmid (eds.), *Law and Economics,* Martinus Nijhoff Publ., Boston, 1981, Ch. 1.

Swift, Jeremy, 'Pastoral Development in Somalia: Herding Cooperatives as a Strategy Against Desertification and Famine', in Michael Glantz (ed.), *Desertification: Environmental Degradation in and Around Arid Lands,* Westview Press, Boulder, Colorado, 1977, Ch. 11.

Tawney, R.H., 'Property and Creative Work', in: C.B. Macpherson (ed.) *Mainstream and Critical Positions,* University of Toronto Press, 1978, pp. 135–151.

Thomson, James T., 'Ecological Deterioration: Local-Level Rule Making and Enforcement Problems in Niger', in Michael Glantz (ed.), *Desertification: Environmental Degradation in and Around Arid Lands,* Westview Press, Boulder, Colorado, 1977, Ch. 4.

Tribe, Laurence H., 'Policy Science: Analysis or Ideology', *Philosophy and Public Affairs,* Vol. 2, Fall 1972.

## DISCUSSION OPENING – SOHEI MARUTA

It is a great pleasure for me to put the main issues and questions to a paper with such deep philosophical thought that includes a substantial analysis to the theme but not merely a functional one. It seems to me that the fundamental characteristic of this paper is to inquire into the essential meaning of natural resource problems and economics in agricultural development, through careful study from the view point of institutional arrangements and structure where that means the control and uses of natural resources, reaping the benefits and bearing the costs. The authors mention that the central issue in development activities as they relate to natural resources is one of understanding that: (a) relative prices for natural resources and the institutional arrangements that produce these prices are an artifact of colonial rule; and (b) the export of natural resources means that local economic decisions are dominated by reliance on external markets.

In the second section they analyse the participants or actors in the development process, classified into three categories – the local level, the national level and the international level, that is, social subjects. This is the reason why it is the participants who define the way in which agricultural development programmes are formulated, designed, evaluated and implemented. Then the development *process* is dealt with, since natural resources are usually handled in the context of an investment problem instead of in the context of a management problem. Lastly, implications for natural resources and development are mentioned.

The paper has an important significance, so let me designate some questions:

The authors mention that natural resources have meaning to individuals and to collectives only with respect to a particular institutional structure. It is this structure that defines relative values, that determines scarcity and hence nominal prices, and that indicates which costs of resource use will be considered concerning use rates of natural resources. That is true. Standard economics, however, refers to such an institutional structure through monopoly-oligopoly analysis, while econometrics does it by quantifying to give parameters into structural equations, such quantities are means that define the quality, that is the institutional structure, as Hegel said. Accordingly, it seems to me that the authors' thinking and the standard economic or econometric approach supplement each other.

Second, they also mention that it is this structure that creates the incentives and sanctions for a particular pattern and time path of resource use, so that I feel resource economics is resource economic law or jurisprudence, while economics exclusively deals with the *effects* of economic behaviour.

Third, this approach is useful in the diagnosis of development policy, but what shall we do to development programming?

In any case, it is not easy to completely hold the concept of institutional arrangements or structure that is a key-concept, so that it is difficult for me to put any critical comments. Nevertheless, I would like to mention something about the first part of the central issues mentioned by the authors.

'The institutional arrangements produce relative prices for natural resources, and the former are an artifact of colonial rule', say the authors. I agree with most of what they say about initial conditions, because human beings cannot live in a vacuum but only in an historical reality. But logical explanation is often reversed against a generating process. We can often look at the reversal between the former and the latter. It seems to me that eminent general principles prevail through different social phenomena with various initial conditions. Accordingly, I feel that the authors as well as Knut Wicksell need to establish more historical facts. In such a case, many devices will be required to make suitable social indicators measure complex phenomena.

Nevertheless, at present when the raison d'être of economics is doubted, this paper is invaluable, especially since it stresses the appearance of feasibility, and it deals with the particular institutional structure in less-developed countries.

## GENERAL DISCUSSION* – RAPPORTEUR: REINOLDO I. ADAMS

The Brazilian situation was considered a special case. It was felt that Brazil had undergone recent reorganization in the research system and there was a need for more in depth benefit/cost analysis of its results. Credit and price policies may have been as important as research in recent years to explain the expansion of soybean production. Also not necessarily higher food prices resulting from technical changes benefiting export crops would reduce real income for small farmers. If these farmers were food crop producers they could have benefited.

There was a general agreement on Bromley's approach to Natural Resource Economics specially on the need for more institutional change. A suggestion was made for more interaction with other approaches, like the French 'agrarian system'. Policy developments are also of special importance. A conclusion was drawn that property rights and the distribution of ownership of resources together affect fundamentally the prices of products and resources. Thus there is a connection between ownership and resource allocation. A major concern was placed on who is going to benefit from technical change and to what extent, as, for example, should the 'Green Revolution' ever have been undertaken or not? Finally, there was an emphasis on the natural resource problem related to the institutional changes. It fails because the markets for institutional change fail. It implies that government must create institutional changes. But is government not part of the problem? Might it not be better to get government to withdraw from modification of property rights? The question relies on who is the government. The government acts in the interests of the groups who support it. Thus government is not always interested in institutional change.

Participants in the discussion included Michel Petit, Richard Meyer, G. J. Tyler, D. H. Penny and Ian Wills.

*Papers by de Melo and Bromley and Verma.

DIOYO PRABOWO

# *Demand for and Supply of Basic Food Products in the ASEAN Countries*

## INTRODUCTION

The Association of South East Asian Nations or ASEAN is faced with a rapid increase in the demand for food. In the majority of ASEAN member countries, neither has food production kept pace with the increase in demand stemming from population and income growth, resulting in dependence on imports of varying magnitudes, nor has there been stability in food production as large parts of ASEAN are still dependent on the intensity of the monsoon.

Food self-sufficiency is one of the principal aims of the national development plans of the ASEAN member countries. At the same time, there is a reasonable degree of economic complementarity among the ASEAN countries since while some member are food deficit, others are surplus. There are, therefore, opportunities for intra-regional co-operation.

Article B.1 of the Declaration of ASEAN Concord, signed in Bali in February 1976, states that the member countries should all assist each other by giving priority of acquisition in respect of food (rice). The Declaration also enjoins the member countries to intensify their co-operation in the production of basic commodities, particularly food. The Economic Ministers' Meeting in Kuala Lumpur in March 1976 asked the ASEAN senior officials to study the basic commodities that might be included in the co-operation scheme. The ASEAN Meeting of Experts on Agricultural Planning held in Indonesia in August 1976 specifically stressed the need for a study of supply and demand for food and other strategic agricultural products. The study would enable ASEAN to assess the demand for food and other strategic agricultural commodities over the horizon 1975–90 and the production potentialities in meeting it. The study would also help to estimate the input requirements for achieving the production potential so that ASEAN member countries could take co-operative action in meeting the requirements.

The immediate objectives of the study are to estimate, for the period 1975–90:

(a) the domestic and regional demand for ASEAN for rice and corn (maize), and
(b) the production potential in the region.

## REGIONAL DEMAND FOR RICE AND CORN.

Demand is defined here as the sum of demand for food for human consumption and demand for non-food uses. Population and income are the most significant determinants of the demand for food. Consequently one needs to measure the income elasticity in order to estimate the future demand.

The various types of non-food uses were estimated independently for seed, waste, feed and industrial uses. Seed requirements depended to a large extent on the area sown. Waste was estimated as a proportion of domestic supply. For livestock feeds, the requirements were estimated on the basis of projected animal production. With regard to other industrial uses a continuation of past trends was assumed in most cases.

The probable demand for food was projected by individual country and the estimates were subsequently aggregated for the whole ASEAN region. Three alternative projections were made. Alternative I was formulated by taking the normal population growth rates and the most likely income growth rates in the ASEAN countries. Alternative II projections were based on a more optimistic expectation of population and income growth rates. Correspondingly more pessimistic assumptions of population and income growth rates relative to the most probable levels were made to generate Alternative III projections.

### *Rice*

The main importance of rice in the ASEAN region is its being a primary source of carbohydrate. Almost two-thirds of the daily intake come from rice. An important component of the index of food prices as well as the cost of living, rice is also important from the employment aspect. In all ASEAN countries, except Singapore, more than 50 per cent of the labour is employed in agriculture, a large part of which is in rice production. In the ASEAN region therefore, food literally means rice and the two terms are used interchangeably. The food balance sheets indicate that throughout ASEAN only in the Philippines did annual rice consumption remain stable at around 90 kilograms per caput. Thailand recorded the highest per caput consumption of 154 kilograms and Singapore the lowest.

Indonesia, a rice deficit country, recorded the highest income (expenditure) elasticity of 0.56. A 10 per cent rise in the per caput income, other things being constant, would raise rice consumption in Indonesia by 5.6 per cent. In Singapore the income elasticity of demand for rice was negative (−0.01). For Thailand, a major rice exporting country, the estimate was a low income elasticity of 0.046. The estimates were 0.14 and 0.22 for Malaysia and the Philippines respectively.

The total demand for rice, food and non-food is shown in Table 1. It can be seen from Table 1 that the rice consumption of Indonesia alone is more than the equivalent of the amount consumed in the other four countries in ASEAN altogether. The importance of Indonesia to the rice demand is reflected by its share in the total rice consumption of the ASEAN. Under Alternative I the rice consumption (food and non-food) of Indonesia in 1981 was 1.3 times the consumption of the rest of ASEAN. It is projected that the ratio would be 1.4 times in 1985 and 1.5 times in 1990. It is projected that the annual rate of growth of the demand for rice in the ASEAN region would be 4.05 per cent during 1981–85 and 3.92 per cent during 1985–90 using Alternative I. Under Alternative II the annual rate of growth would be 4.12 and 4.05 per cent for the period 1981–85 and 1985–90 respectively. Under Alternative III the annual rate of growth would be 4.00 and 4.11 per cent for each period.

TABLE 1 *Rice: Total demand (food and non-food uses) in ASEAN, 1981–85, 1990.*

(million metric tons)

| Country | | 1981 | 1982 | 1983 | 1984 | 1985 | 1990 |
|---|---|---|---|---|---|---|---|
| | | | | *Alternative I* | | | |
| Indonesia | | 20.38 | 21.34 | 22.34 | 23.39 | 24.47 | 30.20 |
| Malaysia | | 1.78 | 1.83 | 1.90 | 1.97 | 2.03 | 2.39 |
| Philippines | | 4.91 | 5.05 | 5.21 | 5.37 | 5.53 | 6.42 |
| Singapore | | 0.18 | 0.18 | 0.19 | 0.19 | 0.20 | 0.20 |
| Thailand | | 8.82 | 9.03 | 9.25 | 9.47 | 9.69 | 10.93 |
| | ASEAN | 36.07 | 37.44 | 38.89 | 40.39 | 41.92 | 50.14 |
| | | | | *Alternative* II | | | |
| Indonesia | | 20.53 | 21.52 | 22.56 | 23.64 | 24.78 | 30.92 |
| Malaysia | | 1.73 | 1.78 | 1.84 | 1.90 | 1.97 | 2.38 |
| Philippines | | 4.91 | 5.05 | 5.22 | 5.38 | 5.54 | 6.43 |
| Singapore | | 0.18 | 0.18 | 0.18 | 0.19 | 0.19 | 0.20 |
| Thailand | | 8.77 | 8.97 | 9.17 | 9.38 | 9.59 | 10.67 |
| | ASEAN | 36.12 | 37.50 | 39.17 | 40.49 | 42.07 | 50.60 |
| | | | | *Alternative* III | | | |
| Indonesia | | 20.09 | 20.98 | 22.00 | 22.89 | 23.90 | 29.66 |
| Malaysia | | 1.73 | 1.79 | 1.85 | 1.91 | 1.98 | 2.40 |
| Philippines | | 5.02 | 5.18 | 5.36 | 5.54 | 5.73 | 6.77 |
| Singapore | | 0.18 | 0.18 | 0.19 | 0.19 | 0.19 | 0.20 |
| Thailand | | 8.96 | 9.20 | 9.45 | 9.63 | 9.95 | 11.30 |
| | ASEAN | 35.98 | 37.33 | 38.85 | 40.16 | 41.75 | 50.33 |

*Corn*

In countries like Indonesia and the Philippines corn is second only to rice as a staple food. The per caput corn consumption in 1975 was highest in the Philippines and lowest in Singapore. In the Philippines, corn is primarily consumed as a staple food in Visayas region. In Indonesia corn is consumed by people in areas like East Java and Madura. The average consumption per caput in ASEAN was 16.74 kilograms per annum in 1975. With a total population of 185.65 million (excluding Thailand) the demand for corn in 1975 for the whole region would be 3.11 million metric tons. The income elasticity coefficients for Indonesia, Malaysia and the Philippines showed a negative sign indicating that corn is considered an inferior food in the ASEAN region.

TABLE 2 *Corn: total demand (food and non-food use) in ASEAN, 1981–85, 1990*

(thousand metric tons)

| Country | 1981 | 1982 | 1983 | 1984 | 1985 | 1990 |
|---|---|---|---|---|---|---|
| | | | *Alternative* I | | | |
| Indonesia | 2,242.00 | 2,284.00 | 2,326.00 | 2,372.00 | 2,396.00 | 2,607.94 |
| Malaysia | 322.49 | 334.38 | 357.26 | 382.15 | 394.03 | 647.58 |
| Philippines | 3,094.92 | 3,200.56 | 3,311.76 | 3,425.54 | 3,553.89 | 4,225.76 |
| Singapore | 278.46 | 241.50 | 255.50 | 269.58 | 285.82 | 379.85 |
| Thailand | 384.00 | 398.00 | 412.00 | 427.00 | 436.00 | 516.00 |
| ASEAN | 6,321.87 | 6,458.44 | 6,662.52 | 6,876.27 | 7,065.74 | 8,377.13 |
| | | | *Alternative* II | | | |
| Indonesia | 2,212.16 | 2,246.12 | 2,285.16 | 2,318.28 | 2,344.47 | 2,533.76 |
| Malaysia | 311.80 | 333.58 | 356.35 | 381.13 | 392.91 | 547.10 |
| Philippines | 3,082.00 | 3,185.21 | 3,293.89 | 3,405.05 | 3,530.69 | 4,187.58 |
| Singapore | 278.44 | 241.48 | 255.51 | 269.55 | 285.59 | 379.79 |
| Thailand | 384.00 | 398.00 | 412.00 | 427.00 | 436.00 | 516.00 |
| ASEAN | 6,268.40 | 6,504.39 | 6,602.91 | 6,801.01 | 6,989.66 | 8,164.23 |
| | | | *Alternative* III | | | |
| Indonesia | 2,262.08 | 2,304.87 | 2,347.89 | 2,395.14 | 2,435.63 | 2,697.11 |
| Malaysia | 313.20 | 335.20 | 358.20 | 383.20 | 395.20 | 553.20 |
| Philippines | 3,143.11 | 3,258.04 | 3,378.91 | 3,502.76 | 3,661.61 | 4,372.66 |
| Singapore | 278.46 | 241.50 | 255.54 | 269.58 | 285.63 | 379.85 |
| Thailand | 384.00 | 398.00 | 412.00 | 427.00 | 436.00 | 516.00 |
| ASEAN | 6,380.85 | 6,537.61 | 6,752.54 | 6,977.68 | 7,214.07 | 8,518.82 |

Corn demand for industrial uses account for 4 per cent in Indonesia and 2 per cent in the Philippines of the total corn demand. The estimates of future corn consumption for animal feeds were based on the projected number of dairy cows, hogs and chickens. It was assumed that the share of corn in the animal feed would remain constant.

Table 2 shows that under Alternative I the Philippines would have the highest demand at 3.6 million metric tons in 1985 and 4.2 million metric tons in 1990. Following the Philippines is Indonesia with 2.4 million metric tons in 1985 and 2.6 million metric tons in 1990. The changes in the population and income growth rates under Alternative II and III would not change substantially the estimates under Alternative I.

## REGIONAL SUPPLY OF RICE AND CORN

The probable output of food was projected by individual country and the estimates were subsequently aggregated for the whole ASEAN region. The projection methodology consisted of several steps. First, the historical performance of agricultural production was analysed and summarized statistically. The primary objective was to establish objectively the historical basis for projecting future production by measuring the nature of the response of crop production to the various inputs and other influences and by estimating how the production technology has changed regularly over time.

There are several alternatives which are potentially applicable to specify the econometric relationships between agricultural production and the explanatory variables. Which formulation is appropriate was not always intuitively obvious at the start of the analysis. Most alternatives had to be tried and the final choice had to be based on and supported by comparative empirical results. Therefore, the second step was the evaluation and the selection of alternative parameters from the statistical results. The statistics included the coefficients of production elasticity which are a measure of responsiveness of output to changes in production factors such as land, fertilizer or prices; the trend factor which was used to estimate the contribution of natural advances in production technology; and the rates of growth of the major inputs of production which were employed as a historical basis for projecting future input levels. Third, the selected estimates of parameters, together with an updated set of base period quantities for each country, were applied to project the growth in input utilization and subsequently the changes in agricultural production.

The major shortcoming inherent in the trend projections emanated from the assumption that the forces which generated the observed pattern of production would remain in the future. To the extent that the assumption is realized, the trend projections could be regarded to closely approximate the forecast of probable production. Where the assumption is not a tenable proposition, it was considered more logical and correct to take into consideration the factors which would impinge on the historical trends.

TABLE 3 *Trend projections of domestic output of food in the countries of ASEAN, 1981–85 and 1990*
(thousand metric tons)

| Commodity/Country | | 1981 | 1982 | 1983 | 1984 | 1985 | 1990 |
|---|---|---|---|---|---|---|---|
| Milled Rice | | | | | | | |
| Indonesia | | 19,696 | 20,355 | 21,014 | 21,672 | 22,331 | 25,624 |
| Malaysia | | 1,179 | 1,191 | 1,204 | 1,216 | 1,228 | 1,290 |
| Philippines | | 5,052 | 5,197 | 5,342 | 5,487 | 5,633 | 6,359 |
| Thailand | | 12,410 | 12,704 | 12,997 | 13,290 | 13,583 | 15,050 |
| | ASEAN | 38,337 | 39,447 | 40,557 | 41,665 | 42,775 | 48,323 |
| Corn | | | | | | | |
| Indonesia | | 2,863 | 2,766 | 2,669 | 2,573 | 2,477 | 1,995 |
| Malaysia | | 42 | 44 | 45 | 47 | 49 | 57 |
| Philippines | | 3,306 | 3,423 | 3,539 | 3,656 | 3,773 | 4,358 |
| Thailand | | 3,248 | 3,400 | 3,553 | 3,705 | 3,858 | 4,620 |
| | ASEAN | 9,459 | 9,633 | 9,806 | 9,981 | 10,157 | 11,330 |

Government plans, programmes and targets do exist and they definitely influence the historical pace of development and the changes in the various sectors of the economy. This realization brought an inevitable adjustment in the trend projections. This was the fourth stage in the projection methodology.

TABLE 4 *Projections of most likely or probable domestic output of food in ASEAN member countries, 1981–85 and 1990*
(thousand metric tons)

| Commodity/Country | | 1981 | 1982 | 1983 | 1984 | 1985 | 1990 |
|---|---|---|---|---|---|---|---|
| Milled Rice | | | | | | | |
| Indonesia | | 21,070 | 21,911 | 22,752 | 23,593 | 24,434 | 29,038 |
| Malaysia | | 1,433 | 1,491 | 1,549 | 1,607 | 1,665 | 1,959 |
| Philippines | | 4,815 | 4,971 | 5,128 | 5,284 | 5,440 | 6,223 |
| Thailand | | 12,069 | 12,348 | 12,634 | 12,925 | 13,224 | 14,825 |
| | ASEAN | 39,387 | 40,721 | 42,063 | 43,409 | 44,763 | 52,045 |
| Corn | | | | | | | |
| Indonesia | | 3,305 | 3,320 | 3,333 | 3,347 | 3,362 | 3,433 |
| Malaysia | | 42 | 44 | 45 | 47 | 49 | 57 |
| Philippines | | 3,390 | 3,589 | 3,715 | 3,889 | 4,071 | 4,625 |
| Thailand | | 3,224 | 3,369 | 3,513 | 3,658 | 3,802 | 4,526 |
| | ASEAN | 9,961 | 10,322 | 10,606 | 10,941 | 11,284 | 12,641 |

The trend projections of rice and corn are summarized in Table 3 while the revised projections are presented in Table 4. The revision was based on a review of plans and targets for 1981 to 1985 and the resource constraints faced by various countries. The adjusted projections incorporated the perceivable binding effects of land availability and the impact expected from government initiatives in food and agriculture.

## DEMAND AND SUPPLY IMPLICATIONS

This section integrates the probable supply and demand situations and provides some implications for agricultural production and foreign trade. Table 5 presents a picture of domestic production compared with the most likely level of internal absorption for the ASEAN region in 1985 and 1990. The prospects show a favourable potential balance for the ASEAN region with respect to rice and corn.

## RICE

The production orientated programmes in the rice sectors in ASEAN countries have been found instrumental in sustaining the advances in output. On the other hand, population and income changes have steadily and surely raised rice consumption over the years. Nevertheless, the ASEAN region as a whole could look forward to a favourable situation with respect to foodgrains. The production sufficiency ration (PSR) for rice has values over unity which indicate that there would be a potential exportable rice surplus from the ASEAN region through 1990. Total domestic ouput would exceed the regional requirements by about 2.84 million metric tons in 1985 and 1.5 million metric tons in 1990.

Looking at individual cases reveals country differences with respect to the nature of production constraints, potentials and strategy for increasing the domestic ouput of rice in individual countries. The production patterns among countries and the projected exportable rice surplus for the ASEAN countries as a group indicate strongly some opportunity for intra ASEAN trade in rice.

Thailand continues to occupy its position as the main rice exporter with a potential exportable surplus rising from 3.53 to 3.89 million metric tons in 1985 and 1990. Singapore produces no rice crop and would have to meet its domestic needs wholly through imports. Malaysia could become the largest rice importer among ASEAN countries since domestic production would potentially supply only about 82 per cent of internal consumption both in 1985 and 1990. Maintaining relative self sufficiency, the Philippines would continue to produce rice primarily for internal consumption only, since foreign trade in rice is not a major orientation.

Together with Thailand, Indonesia remains in the centre of the rice situation. Its large population and recent advances in rice production

TABLE 5 *Probable domestic output and internal absorption of rice and corn in individual ASEAN countries, 1985 and 1990*

(million metric tons)

| | 1985 | | | | 1990 | | | |
|---|---|---|---|---|---|---|---|---|
| | Supply | Demand | Potential Balance[1] | PSR[2] | Supply | Demand | Potential Balance[1] | PSR[2] |
| 1. Milled Rice | | | | | | | | |
| Indonesia | 24.43 | 24.47 | −0.04 | 0.99 | 29.04 | 30.20 | −1.16 | 0.95 |
| Malaysia | 1.67 | 2.03 | −0.36 | 0.82 | 1.96 | 2.39 | −0.43 | 0.82 |
| Philippines | 5.44 | 5.53 | −0.09 | 0.98 | 6.22 | 6.42 | −0.20 | 0.97 |
| Singapore | – | 0.20 | −0.20 | 0.00 | – | 0.20 | −0.20 | 0.00 |
| Thailand | 13.22 | 9.69 | +3.53 | 1.36 | 14.82 | 10.93 | +3.89 | 1.35 |
| ASEAN | 44.76 | 41.92 | +2.84 | 1.07 | 52.04 | 50.14 | +1.90 | 1.03 |
| 2. Corn | | | | | | | | |
| Indonesia | 3.36 | 2.40 | +0.96 | 1.40 | 3.43 | 2.60 | +0.83 | 1.32 |
| Malaysia | 0.05 | 0.39 | −0.34 | 0.13 | 0.06 | 0.65 | −0.59 | 0.09 |
| Philippines | 4.07 | 3.55 | +0.52 | 1.15 | 4.62 | 4.23 | +0.39 | 1.09 |
| Singapore | – | 0.28 | −0.28 | 0.00 | – | 0.38 | −0.38 | 0.00 |
| Thailand | 3.80 | 0.44 | +3.36 | 8.64 | 4.53 | 0.52 | +4.01 | 8.71 |
| ASEAN | 11.28 | 7.06 | +4.22 | 1.60 | 12.64 | 8.38 | +4.26 | 1.51 |

*Source:*

[1] + and – signs indicate surplus and deficit respectively

[2] Production sufficiency ratio

ensures that Indonesia would influence heavily the potential rice balance in the ASEAN region. A traditional (and in fact the world's largest) importer, Indonesia hopes to soon meet all its rice intake from domestic sources, particularly around 1985. A fast growth in production was recorded starting in the latter part of the 1970s as a result of the Special Intensification Programme (Insus). However, there is a distinct possibility that the rice situation in Indonesia could slide back in 1990 when the growing intakes due to population and income growth would overtake domestic rice output by 1.16 million metric tons. It is indeed feasible to cover up the potential rice shortfalls in 1990 through further production intensification and land developments for rice cultivation outside Java.

A close examination of historical evidence and the growth rate of harvested rice area implied by the 1985 targets in ASEAN countries would support the conclusion that a further acceleration of rice production would have to come from technical changes. The harvested rice area could not be expanded as fast as during the earlier decade.

In terms of global outlook, the ASEAN rice output as forecast would increase faster in 1985 and 1990 relative to the change in world production. Averaging 13.4 per cent of world rice output in 1974–76, the ASEAN rice production would increase to about 15.09 per cent in 1985 and 15.43 per cent in 1990. The share of Thailand in the export markets amounted to 15.66 per cent of the total in 1976–78. The exportable surplus of Thailand would constitute about 26.67 per cent in 1985 and rise to 27.78 per cent of the projected world exports in 1990. Therefore, Thailand is going to be an increasingly important supplier in the world rice market. For the ASEAN region as a whole the share of its exportable rice surplus in the world trade would be slightly lower.

*Corn*

The ASEAN region is projected to have excess supplies of corn in 1985 and 1990. The favourable balance was based on the upgrading of corn yields in major producing countries. The assumption was that the development and diffusion of high yielding corn hybrids would improve average farm yields in the Philippines, Indonesia and Thailand. If so, domestic supplies would exceed demand well into the 1990s in these countries. Considering that existing productivity is rather low compared to potential corn yield levels, there exists a substantial leeway for corn production to increase in the ASEAN region.

The Philippines would continue as the largest corn producer in ASEAN whereas Thailand would have the biggest exportable surplus due to a comparatively small domestic absorption. In the Philippines, as in Indonesia, corn is normally utilized both as human food and as animal feed. Taking only feed corn, the comparative intakes in Thailand and the Philippines *vis-à-vis* their respective meat outputs would suggest that the former consumes a lower proportion and that corollarily there is a greater utilization of other feedstuffs in meat production.

The apparent differences in feeding technology may have important implications for other countries. For instance, although the overall corn balance in the Philippines indicated a surplus, only the supply of food (white) corn is more than adequate and the internal requirements of feed (yellow) corn continue to exceed the domestic output. A similar situation exists in Indonesia. Preferred by feedmillers, yellow corn is imported for feed while government procured corn could not be disposed of easily in the market.

Corn consumption is dependent on prices. As an inferior food, corn can compete if its price is relatively low compared to the rice price. In Indonesia the price support for corn is linked with the rice price rather than with the world price of corn. The relatively high price support induces production but at the same time dampens the demand of the feedmilling industry for indigenous corn and makes corn a relatively expensive substitute as food.

The constraints to corn production and utilization rest with the technology, production cost structure, quality and variety of corn available. Without a better technology, favourable corn production potential in ASEAN would not be effectively and competitively utilized. In the immediate future it would be practical as well as economical to find out what other feedstuffs and agricultural by-products (and to what extent) can replace yellow corn in the ration. The substitution of other feed ingredients for yellow corn would alleviate the excess demand and relax some of the constraints on accelerating meat production. In the long run there would be substantial gains from improving corn production technology by developing and diffusing adaptable varieties of corn.

At the present time ASEAN corn output represents an insignificant proportion of the world's output of course grains. As forecast, the ASEAN output would constitute only about 1.30 per cent of the projected world production of coarse grains in 1985 and 1990. In terms of global exports the share of Thailand is estimated to improve marginally from 2.86 per cent in 1974–76 to 3.41 per cent in 1985 and 3.80 per cent in 1990.

## DISCUSSION OPENING – MASAHIKO SHIRAISHI

I am particularly interested in this paper by Dibyo Prabowo because I am working with an Indonesian Team from Gadjah Mada University and Pajajaran University on a socio-economic study of rice farming and marketing in Indonesia. We have already published a report on a case study of Gadingsar village in Central Java in April 1982. So I should like to comment mainly on the agricultural situation in Indonesia.

I have three points. Firstly, cassava is a very important food, as well as corn, in Indonesia. I would like to know how one should estimate the demand and supply of cassava. Secondly, according to IRRI statistics, I notice that only 38.8 per cent of the rice area is technically irrigated in Indonesia, while 40 per cent is rainfed, 16.5 per cent upland and 4.7 per cent deep-water. I think rice production and introduction of modern varieties of rice depend on this basic structure in future as adoption of HYV rice depends on the land-use pattern for rice in Indonesia, that is, irrigated, rainfed, upland, deep-water.

Thirdly, Indonesia produces about 50 per cent of ASEAN rice. From my survey in Indonesia, about 75 per cent of the rice produced by farmers is used for home consumption and the amount marketed is thus only 25 per cent of the total.

I would like to know the near future position concerning marketing structures, agricultural co-operatives and the traditional harvesting and other institutions.

M. AVILA, L. A. NAVARRO AND J. LAGEMANN[1]

# *Improving Small Farm Production Systems in Central America*

The purpose of this paper is to provide selected results of an applied research process being implemented by the Tropical Agricultural Research and Training Centre (CATIE)[2] to develop and test improved crop and animal production systems for low income farmers in specific areas representing the typical ecological zones of Central America.

## THE CENTRAL AMERICAN SETTING

Central America includes Guatemala, Honduras, El Salvador, Nicaragua, Costa Rica and Panama. In 1979 these countries had a population of 22 million of which 52 per cent was rural. In the same year, the estimates of yearly income per caput were $872 for all sectors and $401 for the agricultural sector. Crops, pastures, forestry-woodland, and other areas including non-utilized, occupied 12.5, 22.3, 47 and 18.2 per cent, respectively, of the total land area of 486,570 square km (FAO, BID).

The region can be divided into three ecological environments (Table 1). Population density and the intensity of agriculture are relatively greater in WDT areas, lower in LHT areas. However, all three ecological zones are of considerable importance in terms of these characteristics.

TABLE 1 *Distribution of land, human population and farms in Central America according to ecological zones.*

| Ecology | Land | Population | | Farms | |
|---|---|---|---|---|---|
| | % | % | per km² | % | per km² |
| Semi-Arid Tropics (SAT) | 23 | 28 | 44 | 27 | 3.5 |
| Wet-Dry Tropics (WDT) | 37 | 50 | 47 | 53 | 6.6 |
| Lowland Humid Tropics (LHT) | 40 | 22 | 19 | 20 | 1.9 |

*Source:* CATIE[a]

Farming systems in SAT areas reflect the availability of soil water which is the most limiting factor. Rain-fed systems, by far the most common, favour the production of drought resistant varieties of maize and sorghum and other crops and the management of small stocks of animals which are fed partially from crop residues, particularly during the dry season. Rainfall patterns severely limit cropping alternatives and intensify agricultural activities during certain periods of the year, thereby exacerbating labour shortages.

The WDT zone provides the most favourable environment for both human settlement and agricultural production. Most large cities are located here, implying a high food demand, pressure on land, and need for appropriate technologies. Farming systems in this zone are highly diversified to include annual (maize, beans, cassava and vegetables) and perennial crops (coffee, sugar cane and banana) as well as livestock (cattle, swine and chickens).

Farming systems in the LHT are the least intensive and tend to favour perennial crops (banana, cacao and African oil palm) and beef cattle. Year-round abundant rainfall, temperature and radiation permit immense biomass production but there is also a very fragile ecological and soil environment. Thus research priorities in technology development include proper soil management, weed control and increased labour productivity.

Identified as a major sector in all the ecological zones described, the small farm sector, grossly defined as farms less than 35 hectares, controls approximately 25 per cent of the total farm land and accounts for less than 20 per cent of the total farm input expenditures, while income per caput is less than $100 per year (CATIE, 1981a). These farmers provide two-thirds of the active rural labour force and produce 80 per cent of the total food, excluding rice, for the region. Their participation in rice, perennial crops, and livestock production, which the region exports, amounts to 36,29 and 21 per cent of the total production value. Given the present forecasts for population growth, economic expansion and energy costs for the region during the next twenty years, small farmers will continue to be one of the most important social and economic sectors in Central America.

Therefore, if the economic development of the region is to progress further, particularly in terms of income generation and equitable distribution, there is a need to mobilize the resources of this sector. In this respect, this paper is well attuned to the theme of this Conference.

## THE OVERALL RESEARCH STRATEGY

Three main features distinguish the strategy of CATIE. The focus is on small farmers in an effort to raise food production and income levels in the agricultural sector. The interdisciplinary approach is used to develop technology for improved farming systems. There is a strong determination to support national institutions by working together with their staff on country-related problems and by providing graduate and short-term training programmes (CATIE, 1978).

CATIE, together with local institutions, conducts research to develop *in situ* production technologies suitable to the various target areas with the active participation of farmers in all phases of the methodology. A production system must be studied and understood before it can be modified or improved. Thus the process of applied research follows logical steps: area selection and description, analysis of predominant production systems, development of innovations, testing under farmer conditions, and diffusion of improved systems (CATIE, 1978; Navarro, 1979; Lagemann, 1982).

The role of the social scientist in the research process is to collaborate in assessing farmers' resources and productivity, designing appropriate technology or systems, evaluating the probable impacts of these alternatives and training national professionals in applied socio-economics (Avila and Navarro, 1979).

## SELECTED RESULTS IN TYPICAL AREAS

Although CATIE has been carrying out farm-level research in crop and animal production in all countries of the region, reference to only four areas in different countries will be used to illustrate research methodology and progress[3].

### *Technology development in food crops in the semi-arid area of Tejutla, El Salvador*

Tejutla, located 64 kilometres north of San Salvador, is a small community with 11,500 hectares and 10,155 inhabitants. The rainy season is short, extending from May to December. Both the onset and end of rains are erratic and furthermore there is a severe 'canicular' period, a dry spell lasting as long as 30 days, during the June–July weeks. The lack of soil water is complicated by the mountainous configuration of the terrain and the edafic conditions of the shallow Lithosols and Grumosols that predominate in the area (CENTA). Under these ecological conditions and the low development of the public infrastructure and markets, the farming systems tend to be very traditional. In a survey of 56 farms, 1 to 18 hectares in size, 63 per cent maintained small herds of cattle of less than 10 head, and 75 per cent had some supplementary small animal enterprises, 1 to 10 chickens and 1 to 2 pigs. Perennial crops and forestry activities include a few fruit trees and other drought resistant species, some for fuel.

Food grain production is the only farm activity for all farms under 2.1 hectares and the principal farming activity for 95 per cent of all farms. Gross incomes ranging from $600 to $1,200 per year were reported by farmers with 2.1 to 4.9 hectares, the larges subgroup according to the survey (CATIE, 1979)[4].

The cropping systems within the area show their adjustment to the two over-lapping and short-cropping seasons which are determined by the bimodal rainfall pattern. Since most farm activities are labour intensive, the concentration of agricultural activities during certain periods of the year produces labour problems during the cropping season and high rural unemployment during the off-season which may last up to half the year.

The most common cropping pattern, practised by 95 per cent of farmers in Tejutla, includes maize seeded at the beginning of the rainy season and sorghum added as a relay-intercrop a month later (maize/sorghum). This pattern demonstrates the risk-spreading strategy of the farmer since it allows a good harvest of maize in September and sorghum in December during favourable rainy seasons, or at least a good harvest of sorghum during drier years. Both the common H-3 hybrid maize and the local sorghum cultivar included in the pattern are well adapted. During grain maturity in October, and even after harvest which is often delayed to December due to labour shortage, the local cultivar of sorghum maintains a good proportion of green foliage. This adds an advantage to the maize/sorghum cropping pattern within the farming system because the field residues are used for direct animal feeding during the dry season.

The maize/sorghum based cropping system was selected for research in Tejutla because it is also widely used elsewhere in the semi-arid tropics of Central America.

Tested technical recommendations are selected to improve crop yields and returns to labour and capital investment per hectare and also to maintain the traditional advantages of the system. Most evaluation trials are carried out on farms with the participation of farmers to ensure that the resulting technology requirement is maintained within the resource endowment and the interest of target farmers (CENTA). As shown in Table 2, the farmers' system was studied and quantified and moderate adjustments were designed to be tested; these included vegetation management before seeding, use of fertilizer, and soil insect control. The results were favourable except in the case of net returns to working capital. The farmers use very low levels, if any, and thus obtain high returns. Subsequently, additional tests in 10 sites involving the substitution of the H-11 hybrid maize for the common H-3 resulted in average maize yields of 2149 kilogrammes per hectare.

TABLE 2 *Yield, costs and economic efficiency indicators of farmers' and improved maize/sorghum cropping system,* per hectare

| | Farmers' System | Improved System Increase % | Criteria | Farmers' System | Improved System Increase % |
|---|---|---|---|---|---|
| Maize, kg | 1,750 | 31.9 | Net Income (NI), $ | 254 | 46.6 |
| Sorghum, kg | 1,100 | 74.8 | Net Family Income, $ | 590 | 36.5 |
| Operational costs (OP),$ | 336 | 16.4 | NI/MD, $ | 6.16 | 19.5 |
| Man-days (MD) | 84 | 43.2 | NI/OC, $ | 2.41 | –15.9 |

*Source:* CATIE, 1979

There are other cultivars of sorghum with higher grain yields, but they lack the additional characteristics required by the farmers.

The resulting recommendations for developing the maize/sorghum cropping system are ready for evaluation under the exclusive management of a large number of farmers in Tejutla and other areas previous to its final diffusion. These evaluations, called validation within the methodology, will be implemented in 1982.

*Farming systems in the wet-dry area of Jinotega, Nicaragua: the importance of cash crops for small farm development*

The Jinotega region in Nicaragua has a high concentration of small farms in comparison to other parts of the country. Of all surveyed farms 75 per cent own less than 10 hectares and the average farm size is 6.4 hectares[5]. Farmers cultivate their crops on hilly lands as 60 per cent of all fields are situated on slopes of between 10 and 50 per cent. The prevalence of stones in parts of the region prevents the introduction of mechanized cultivation methods. Average family size is 8 with 1.5 man-equivalents available for farm work.

Land use consisists of annual crops (2 hectares; added effective hectarage of two cropping cycles), perennial crops (0.8 hectares) and pasture or fallow (3.7 hectares). Of all smallholders 88 per cent rear a few chickens and 72 per cent of the farms own on average 2 pigs which are produced mainly for family consumption. Cattle production is found on only 32 per cent of farms, which own an average 7 head.

Crop production is labour intensive due to the fact that, apart from ploughing with oxen, all activities are carried out by manual labour (Table 3). Labour for crop production represents 72 per cent of total farm demand, whereas livestock production is labour extensive. General farm activities constitute 54 man-days, and off-farm work about 70 man-days per year. Labour intensity per enterprise varies considerably with onion cultivation having the highest demand on a per hectare basis. The labour distribution shows three peaks within a year: at the beginning of each cropping cycle, in May and August, and (in the coffee producing areas) during harvest period from November to January. Most of the hired labour, which amounts to 100 man-days per farm, is used during these peak labour periods. Increase of crop production area with present cultivation methods seems unlikely due to labour bottlenecks.

Maize and bean production are relatively low due to risky rainfall conditions in the region, and in comparison, maize and beans in association proved to be more stable and with higher yields. Vegetable production, compared to grains, is very intensive and carefully managed. The value of cabbage and lettuce production amounts to C$17,000 per hectare, and for onions to C$44,400 per hectare. Vegetables were introduced to the region about 15 years ago and are actually, in addition to coffee, an important cash crop in the area. Average coffee production with 580 kilogrammes of dried coffee per hectare is very low compared to similar areas in Central America or to experimental results in Jinotega. Livestock production is managed extensively with an average production of C$6,300 per farm. Poor husbandry practice is the principal

TABLE 3 *Labour use, production and productivity of small farmers in Jinotega, Nicaragua,* March 1981–February 1982: N= 63 farms

| Labour use, man-days[a] Per farm | $\bar{X}$ | C.V. % | Per enterprise | $\bar{X}$ | C.V. % |
|---|---|---|---|---|---|
| Crop production | 236 | 102 | Maize | 68 | 92 |
| Animal production | 40 | 128 | Beans | 75 | 87 |
| General farm activities | 54 | 97 | Maize/beans | 90 | 48 |
| Total farm | 330 | 88 | Cabbage + lettuce | 150 | 75 |
| Off-farm activities | 70 | 132 | Onions | 260 | 80 |
| | | | Coffee + fruit trees | 92 | 57 |

| Production and productivity Per farm[b] | $\bar{X}$ | C.V. % | Per enterprise | Tons/ha | GM/ha | GM /MD |
|---|---|---|---|---|---|---|
| Value of total product. | 33000 | 110 | Maize | 0.9 | 12 40 | 18 |
| Thereof: | | | Beans | 0.5 | 3100 | 41 |
| Basic grains | 7200 | 150 | Maize + beans | 0.9+0.4 | 4000 | 44 |
| Vegetables | 8100 | 100 | Cabbage + lettuce[c] | 17000 | 14400 | 96 |
| Coffee + fruit trees | 11400 | 247 | Onions | 12.0 | 41100 | 158 |
| Livestock | 6300 | 187 | Coffee + fruit trees | 0.58[d] | 12100 | 131 |
| Net farm income (NFI) | 23900 | 105 | | | | |
| Off-farm income | 2800 | 144 | | | | |
| Total family income | 26700 | 95 | | | | |
| Gross margin (GM)/ha crops | 7000 | 197 | | | | |
| NFI/man-equivalent | 15900 | 140 | | | | |

[a]8 hours of work of a male adult equivalent.[b] Córdoba (C$) = US$0.033 in the unofficial market.[c] Value of production.[d] Yield for dried coffee only.
*Source:* Tienhoven, N., Icaza, J. and Lagemann, J., 1982 (forthcoming).

cause of low productivity of the livestock enterprise.

Gross margins per hectare and man-day vary greatly between different farm enterprises. They were extremely high for onions, followed by coffee, cabbage and lettuce, and finally, by beans, maize and beans in association; maize only had the lowest returns.

The value of whole farm production averaged C$33,000. The coefficient of variation is high (110%), minimum values are in the order of 3,000, maximum values close to 220,000. The great variation in performance results principally from differences in husbandry practices and management capacities of the farmers. The amount of cultivated land and labour use explains only a relatively small part of the total variation observed.

Value of production was highest from coffee and fruit trees, followed by vegetables, basic grains, and livestock. These results demonstrate clearly the importance of cash crops within the whole farming systems studies. The average values on productivity are rather low compared to other areas in

Central America, but the results from the better farmers indicate that significant improvements are possible.

Usually 'testing of technology' follows the diagnostic and experimental stage. However, a 'pretest' was conducted simultaneously with the diagnostic stage on the assumption that there are some innovations available from the same area or from similar areas. The technical package was identified in collaboration with national institutions and meetings with local farmers. A maize/bean intercropping package with improved varieties, increased plant densities, and fertilizer application raised maize production by 300 per cent and bean production by 50 per cent. Production costs were higher compared to normal farmers' practices, but net income per hectare increased by 90 per cent and production risks were lower. Although the package was evaluated by researchers and farmers as successful, its adoption might be limited due to a higher Marginal Benefit-Cost Ratio for onion production which is the predominant cash crop in one of the testing zones.

From the evidence presented, it can be concluded that farming systems in the highlands of Jinotega are highly diversified. Yields of grains are low, and they are principally produced for subsistence. Significant yield improvements are possible. However, given present price relations, they offer few incentives compared to other crops. Coffee and vegetables are the crops which provide the largest share of total farm revenue. These cash crops have attracted considerable attention during the last years and should be regarded as the key crops for the future development of Jinotega.

*Designing and testing an improved cattle production model in the Wet-Dry area of La Nueva Concepción of Guatemala*

La Nueva Concepción, located 150 kilometres southwest of Guatemala City, is a community formed by an agrarian reform programme in 1954. There are 1,415 family farms, each of 20 hectares.

The rainy season averages 130 days (May-October) and the annual rainfall varies from 1,619 to 2,500 mm. The dry season is very severe; irrigation is possible only by digging deep wells, although a few farms are near streams.

The soils are of alluvial origin and are relatively fertile. Soil drainage conditions are favourable; the land is flat and there are no obvious soil deficiencies. Of the total population 95 per cent are employed in agricultural activities such as cattle, maize, plantains, sesame, rice, and other minor enterprises. Since approximately 95 per cent of all farms have cattle and there is economic and biological potential for increased production, it was identified as a key component to improving farm-level productivity. Thus an applied research programme was initiated in 1979 (ICTA-CATIE, 1982; CATIE, 1981b).

From a survey of 66 farms, 97 per cent had cattle in combination with annual or perennial crops, and 97 per cent of the farms with cattle manage it as a dual purpose operation, that is, milking the cows once a day with restricted suckling of the calves; the remaining 3 per cent are specialized beef units. On pasture management, 75 per cent of the land area is in improved grass species and 45 per cent has rotational grazing. As supplements, common salt is used on 86 per cent of the farms, minerals on 10, commercial concentrates on 18, molasses on 37, and crop residues on 92 per cent of the farms. Vaccination and control for parasites are done routinely on 87 per cent of the farms.

Estimates of biological and productive indices of the system were made: stocking rate 2.2 animal units/hectare, annual calving rate 44 per cent, milk production 505 lt/cow/year, and gross income $362/hectare on a yearly basis.

The research team identified three key limiting factors to improving productivity and net income: a) poor feeding systems, particularly during the dry season when protein content of available feedstuffs is extremely low, b) inadequate health programmes, and c) lack of information on the management and performance of the dual purpose system (ICTA-CATIE).

To tackle these problem areas, component and system research was begun. In this paper only the results for system management will be reported. On the assumption that the existing levels of productivity could be substantially increased in the short-run by introducing currently available technologies, a model simulating the basic features of the farmers' system was modified to include key improvements related to the restrictions described above. The physical model implemented in early 1980 under experimental conditions served to analyse and understand its performance and to demonstrate work progress to farmers. After one year of operation, the results were favourable, and thus, a similar model was established on one farmer's plot, but a few changes were made to suit his particular needs.

The improved model was tested under the management of the research staff (IMR) and of the farmer with limited assistance of the research staff (IMF). These results are compared to the typical above average farmer of the area (TAF). All three systems were monitored using farm records kept by research field assistants.

The principal difference in the management is that in the IMR molasses and urea were used as supplements throughout the year, and feed preparation for the dry season was necessary because of the high stocking rate, whereas in the IMF he preferred not to use molasses and urea. The TAF, however, normally depends on whatever feedstuffs are available during the dry season such as crop residues, low quality pastures, and molasses.

Considerable improvements were achieved with the improved models compared to the TAF, in terms of birth rate, calf mortality, and calving interval (Table 4). The IMF, though, did not perform as well as the IMR in all these aspects. In the dual purpose system the milk-beef production ratio is subject to modification within certain limits. For example, the IMF farmer was relatively more interested in selling milk than in feeding the calves well, and thereby he effectively reduced weight gains. In the case of TAF the same option is possible, but his productivity levels in both milk and beef are lower.

In terms of economic profitability, the IMF did not perform as well as the

IMR, but it almost doubled the levels of net returns to labour and to total investment obtained by the TAF. In the case of the TAF, the total net income is unfavourable and certainly he cannot operate in the long-run with such technology at current input-product price relationships.

TABLE 4 *Results of testing the improved cattle production model in La Nueva Concepción of Guatemala: January-December, 1981*

| Variable | Improved model managed by: research staff | farmer | Typical above-average farmer |
|---|---|---|---|
| Cows, head | 23 | 18 | 30 |
| Labour use, man-days/ha | 70.5 | 67.7 | 64.6 |
| Total costs/cow/year, $ | 335.4 | 373.8 | 366.0 |
| Stocking rate, AU/ha | 5.7 | 4.0 | 3.0 |
| Birth rate, % | 88.0 | 77.7 | 71.4 |
| Calf mortality rate, % | 0 | 5.9 | 10.0 |
| Calving interval, mo. | 13.5 ± 2.0 | 13.5 ± 1.8 | 15.6 ± 2.4 |
| Milk prod./ha/year, lt | 3739.0 | 2223.9 | 1449.6 |
| Milk prod./cow/year, lt | 849.4 | 1111.9 | 623.3 |
| Weight gain/calf/day, gr | 374 | 279 | 255 |
| Gross margin/ha/year, $ | 806.3 | 386.3 | 357.4 |
| Total net income/year, $ | 779.5 | –151.9 | –1000.6 |
| Net return to labour, $/man-day | 5.13 | 2.27 | 1.23 |
| Net return to total investment, % | 9.63 | 5.26 | 3.26 |

*Source:* ICTA-CATIE

In conclusion, it is possible, using available technologies, to improve the present productivity level of the farmers' system in this area. However, it is necessary to explore additional technological alternatives while simultaneously testing integrated models for a longer period and on more farms. Of course an increase in product prices to the farmers would certainly stimulate interest in better technologies and thus increase productivity, otherwise the cattle system may disappear.

*Transferring dairy production technology in the lowland humid area of Rio Frio in Costa Rica*

Specialized dairy production under tropical conditions is a challenge for professionals since the transfer of such technology, developed in temperate zones, encounters ecological, biological, and management barriers.

For many years CATIE has been experimenting with this system and has designed and tested a small-scale prototype. It has an area of 3.7 hectares of African star-grass *(Cynodon nlemfuemsis)*. The 20 cows and 8 young stock represent the product of a crossbreeding programme involving Criollo, Jersey and Ayrshire breeds.[6] Their milk production potential is comparable to that of the specialized European breeds with the added advantage that they are highly resistant to tropical diseases and parasites (Avila et al., 1980).

The basic feeding source is grazed forage. Pasture management consists of 2 days of grazing and 21 days of rest for each of the 24 paddocks and the application of 250 kg of nitrogen/ha. A high stocking rate is maintained and a minimal supplementation of 3 kg of molasses with 3 per cent urea is fed daily to each cow. Calves receive some concentrates and 200 lt of milk during their first two months.

Investment in infrastructure is minimal: a milking parlour, elastic fences on the periphery and lanes, a faeces depot and electric fences for rotational grazing. The system is designed as a one-man operation. High productivity levels result from well-kept records and a simple health programme.

Some efficiency indices estimated during the 1979 year were as follows: stocking rate 6 AU/ha, birth rate 89 per cent, calf mortality 5 per cent, total costs/ha ₵23,750, variable costs/ha ₵8,702, milk production/cow 2,918 lt, milk production/ha 16,673 lt, net income/ha ₵9,454 and net family income/man-day ₵124. These indices have been fairly stable over 5 years.

Based on this experience, CATIE was asked to transfer this model to agrarian reform colonists in Rio Frio as a means of providing a viable production alternative to farmers and satisfying the local demand for milk.

TABLE 5 *Land use and socio-economic characteristics of the colonists in Rio Frio in November, 1977*

| | | | |
|---|---|---|---|
| Land area, ha | 10 | Level of formal education: | % |
| Under cultivation: | | 1-3 yrs. of schooling | 54.2 |
| Pastures, % | 40 | Completed primary | 35.9 |
| Crops, % | 13 | Started secondary | 8.8 |
| Colonists with bank loans, % | 52 | Completed secondary | 1.1 |
| Average loan, ₵* | 9000 | Previous occupation: | % |
| Age of the colonist, yrs. | 36 | Landless labourer | 80.0 |
| No. of children | 3 | Non-agricultural labourer | 14.6 |
| Average age of the children, yrs. | 3.5 | Other | 5.4 |

*Source:* CATIE, 1982
*In 1979 US$ = ₵8.54

Rio Frio is located in the northeast part of the country, covering an area of 27,000 hectares at an altitude of 130 metres above sea level. The soils have a clay texture and low fertility severely limits cropping activities. However, the high temperature and rainfall levels throughout the year favour forage production. A diagnosis of farmers, background, resources and production alternatives was made (Table 5). Production enterprises (maize, beans, rice, milk and swine) generated a yearly gross income of ₵2,451, which the government subsidized with ₵8,789 per family.

To solve the key problems a comprehensive strategy was adopted. First, a careful selection of candidates was made to choose farmers with the most experience or interest in dairy production. Second, the project staff had to be directly involved in all aspects: planning, approval and supervision of credit, purchasing animals from similar ecological areas, model implementation, and marketing. Third, a simple training methodology was based on the demonstration of management practices and working hand-in-hand with the farmer.

The results after 4 years of operation are impressive (Table 6). At present the total milk production of the 22 farms on which the Project staff has records is some 650,430 lt a year, of which 70 per cent is transported to other areas of the country. The government has discontinued the subsidies.

TABLE 6 *Comparison of the milk production system before and after Project implementation in Rio Frio: average figures for 22 units*

| | 1977 | 1981 | | 1977 | 1981 |
|---|---|---|---|---|---|
| Area in pastures, ha | 4.0 | 9.5 | Total credit ¢* | 9000 | 135000 |
| Grazing paddocks, no. | 2.3 | 24.8 | Milk production, lt/day | 6.6 | 81 |
| Cattle, head | 4.1 | 32.5 | Gross family income | ¢8789 | 84700 |
| Producing cows | 1.0 | 15.0 | Farm production, % | 27.9 | 100 |
| Dry cows | 0.3 | 5.0 | Government subsidy, % | 72.1 | 0 |
| Heifers | 1.8 | 5.3 | Net income, ¢ | – | 23547 |
| Calves | 1.0 | 7.2 | | | |

*Source:* CATIE, 1982

*In 1981 US$ = ₡30 on the unofficial market

In general, the achievements demonstrate that the combined efforts of both institutions were successful in forming a team to train and help the colonists apply appropriate technology for dairy production. The project is presently operated and managed by the national institution.

## POLICY IMPLICATIONS

Research organization and progress in crop and animal production for small farmers in Central America have improved substantially in the last few years. The experience gained thus far indicates that there are technologies that can increase productivity levels and that small farmers do respond to technological opportunities, though the sector is not favoured by price policies.

There are, however, a few factors worth mentioning that will determine prospects for research to benefit the target group. First, the question of political stability has caused activities directly involving peasants to appear conspicuous. Second, support for the stability and development of personnel skilled in research and extension should be given priority by national policy makers. Third, to some international aid agencies the cause of the income problem lies with poor extension capabilities, and therefore they do not value research. Finally, national research and extension programmes on crop and animal production are not integrated to focus adequately on the farmers' systems.

## NOTES

[1]The authors are grateful to O. W. Deaton, R. A. Moreno and G. Páez for their apt comments.

[2]The Centro Agronómico Tropical de Investigación y Enseñanza (CATIE) is a non-profit institution with headquarters at Turrialba, Costa Rica.

[3]The results presented in this paper are the joint product of CATIE and the following institutions: Centro Nacional de Tecnologia Agraria (CENTA) of El Salvador; Dirección General de Técnicas Agropecuarias (DGTA) of Nicaragua; Instituto de Ciencia y Tecnologia Agricolas (ICTA) of Guatemala; and Instituto de Tierras y Colonización (ITCO) of Costa Rica. Financial and/or technical support for the work in El Salvador was provided by USAID-ROCAP, IDRC and EEC; in Nicaragua by GTZ; in Guatemala by IDB and USAID-ROCAP; and in Costa Rica by ITCO.

[4]In this report the local currency is used only for Nicaragua and Costa Rica due to unstable exchange rates with the US dollar.

[5]A few farms over 50 hectares were excluded from the survey.

[6]The 'criollo' is a breed brought to America by the Spaniards in the sixteenth century.

## REFERENCES

Avila, M., Deaton, O.W., Ruiz, A. y Romero, F., 'Análisis de Sistemas de Producción Animal del Pequeño Productor', documento presentado en el Curso de Proyectos de Desarrollo rural del Banco Mundial, Turrialba, Costa Rica, 1980.

Avila, M. y Navarro, L.A., 'The Contribution of Farm Management Economics to CATIE's Research Effort', presentado en el Seminario Iowa State/IICA/CATIE, Turrialba, Costa Rica, 1979.

Banco Interamericano de Desarrollo, *Progreso Económico y Social en América Latina: Informe Anual 1979,* Washington DC, 1980.

CATIE, *A Farming Systems Research Approach for Small Farmers of Central America,* Turrialba, Costa Rica, 1978.

CATIE, *Descripción de una Alternativa para el Sistema de Producción Maiz Asociado con Sorgo,* Turrialba, 1979.

CATIE, *Formento de la Producción de Leche en Las Colonias del ITCO: Informe Final del Proyecto ITCO/CATIE,* Turrialba, Costa Rica, 1982.

CATIE, *Research and Training for Developing Crop Production Technology for Small Farms in CATIE's Mandate Region,* Turrialba, Costa Rica, CATIE, 1981a.

CATIE, *Sistemas de Producción para Pequenas Fincas: Segundo Informe Anual del Proyecto CATIE/ROCAP,* Turrialba, Costa Rica, 1981b.

Centro Nacional de Tecnologia Agropecuaria (CENTA), *Informe Anual 1980: Programa MAG/CATIE,* San Salvador, 1981.

Food and Agricultural Organization, *1980 Production Yearbook,* Rome, 1981.

ICTA-CATIE, *Programa de Producción Animal: Informe Anual 1981,* Guatemala, 1982.

Lagemann, J., 'Farming Systems Research as a Tool for Identifying and Conducting Research and Development Projects', *Agricultural Administration* (accepted for publication on February 1982).

Navarro, L. A, 'Generación, Evaluación, Validación y Difusión de Tecnologias Mejoradas y Apropiadas para Pequeños Agricultores', presentado en Chile en el Seminario de la Investigación Agricola en los Paises en Desarrollo, Turriálba, Costa Rica, 1979.

Tienhoven, N., Icaza, J. and Lagemann, J., *Farming Systems in Jinotega, Nicaragua,* Turrialba, Costa Rica, CATIE, 1982 (forthcoming).

## DISCUSSION OPENING – HSI-HUANG CHEN

The well-written paper by Avila, Navarro, and Lagemann is very informative. It discusses the research process and technological development necessary for improving small-scale farming systems in three typical ecological zones of Central America. The main purpose of the research strategy is to develop new technology for food production and for income generation.

The paper describes how a production system was analysed and tested to determine whether current technologies and cropping patterns were suited to the sample target areas; how the new technology and farming system was developed for small farmers; and how the present farming technology was improved in order to increase productivity. It seems that most research and development efforts focused on the improvement of biological potential for increasing production which, in turn, was identified as a key point in the improvement of farm-level productivity. I agree that technological innovation is a necessary condition for small farm development. I also agree that it is necessary to explore additional technological alternatives while simultaneously testing integrated models for a longer period and on more farms. The paper illustrates the major progress in farm-level crop and animal production research. However, the authors do not clearly show how the farming system has been improved, what kind of new technology has been adopted to achieve the research purpose, and by what process this technology was selected.

My comment on this paper is that the small-scale of farming in Central America limits farm diversification and hinders economic planning for small farms. In this paper, none of the research methods are designed to specifically address themselves to these small-farm problems. Assuming that there is a knowledge gap these problems of small-scale farming could be researched at CATIE and the resulting techniques transmitted to each target area for piloting, demonstration and dissemination. This would facilitate attempts to increase both food production and farm incomes. It is likely that a more comprehensive micro-economic analysis would yield data of more use to the agricultural experts responsible for exploring technological alternatives and to the policy-makers confronted with determining the role of the small-farm production system in the national agricultural production policy.

I suggest that the CATIE research would form an appropriate economic base for this research programme. From the economic point of view, there are three priority areas which could be adopted for small-farm farming research: these are (a) the economics of subsistence-type farms and the economics of the farm household; (b) the economics of farm labour and; (c) farm practices and management. I think such economic analysis is useful in evaluating the performance of the small-scale farming system, in identifying its problems and constraints, and in guiding its adjustment to facilitate future expansion.

With respect to the dissemination of new technology, there are two problems which demand more attention. Firstly, one of the most important factors influencing farmer participation is the degree of risk implied by the new technology. Many farmers may be deterred from participating if they perceive the risks associated with the new technology are too high. Thus, government policy support is required to provide incentives which encourage the adoption of new technological innovations. Secondly, if the new production technology is developed in a relatively short period of time, corresponding modification of the institutional structure to support the extension of the new technology to a large number of farmers may not be undertaken. The development of new technology also requires the creation of a new institutional system to respond to these new conditions. Moreover, all new technological development should be in harmony with national agricultural development targets. Failing this, all research efforts are in vain.

Finally, I would like to say a word concerning small-farm development. The small-scale farmers used to be the rural poor. Any innovations for use by small farmers should aim to achieve the dual purpose of increasing food production and improving the farmers' standards of living. Technological innovations alone are not a sufficient condition for improving small-farm production. The premise of improving the small-farm production system is to identify needs, devise and initiate research programmes to meet them, and to bring these resulting schemes to completion.

## GENERAL DISCUSSION* – RAPPORTEUR: MOHIUDDIN Z. AMIN

On the paper by Prabowo the following points were raised: (a) a larger demand projection for rice was forecast in Repelita III than that projected in the paper, (b) income distribution aspects of demand were not shown in the paper, and (c) demand for substitute foods was not estimated.

The author replied to these questions by stating that there were indeed some future demand projections of rice and other cereals in a few Indonesian programmes, like Repelita III, which were more comprehensive. Regarding the second point he stated that there had not been many studies of the income distribution aspects of production in Indonesian agriculture, hence no definite reference could be made to this aspect. Finally price information on cereal substitutes was not available and hence this could not be incorporated in the analysis for the paper.

On the paper by Avila, Navarro and Lagemann there were four participants who raised a few questions. The important queries were as follows: farming system research is often too narrow in leaving out problems of marketing and infrastructure, thereby restricting its effectiveness. How were the differences between experimental yields under controlled conditions and farm yields under practical management estimated? Finally, were innovative technologies identified and adopted?

The first author of the paper replied to these questions by stating that the farming system research is a 'bottom-up' concept of development, it is

*Papers by Prabowo, and Avila, Navarro and Lagemann

complemented by policy-setting research at regional and national levels to the extent that such support is essential for improvements at farm level. Estimation of different yields at the experimental level and the practical farming level is essential for policy recommendations for farmers and hence on-farm research on this aspect should minimize the difference. Finally, he explained that for dissemination of innovative technologies previous research results were extrapolated from other areas and experience of research and extension scientists were heavily drawn upon to design appropriate technologies for dissemination in the project areas.

M. HAWKINS, S. LEAVITT AND R. NORBY*

# Operation of Market Mechanisms in Accelerating Agricultural Growth

Accelerated growth of the agricultural economy is not possible without the existence of an adequate market mechanism. In an enlightened economy, the concepts of equity and self-initiative should also be linked with the market mechanism. Most nations work hard at developing market mechanisms which fit their environment and economic order. The functions of marketing are dutifully examined and action is taken to upgrade storage, processing, transportation, information flows, and so on. Planners expect incredible results and, indeed, sometimes, especially in the early stages of agricultural development, productivity increases can be dramatic. Thus, in the early stages of development, functional analysis and market reorganization can be effective in fostering growth in the agricultural sector.

History, however, illustrates that as food production more nearly meets consumer needs, initiative, innovation and efficiency tend to fall. Market concentration, aided and abetted by private or government marketing organizations, seems to dictate rigorously defined market channels, with a minimum of interest in price exchange mechanisms and in daily or weekly price haggling sessions. The discipline of the marketplace is directed towards operational needs of the system, including the needs of the retailer, wholesaler, processor and consumer. The exchange functions of marketing give way to cost-plus accounting as the system evolves from many relatively small partners in the system to fewer but larger successors. The latter firms tend to downplay activity directed towards pricing activities and export markets and devote their energies to a demanding standardized domestic consumer market. The mature marketing scene is therefore depicted by a concentrated domestic marketing effort, with total consideration being given to the elements of operational efficiency.

## THE MATURE MARKET

There is evidence of informal structural arrangements (Hawkins and Norby,

* The authors would sincerely like to thank Ms Evelyn Shapka and Ms Judy Warren for editing and typing the many drafts of this manuscript.

1977) which negate the exchange system's effectiveness in reflecting supply and demand. Daily and weekly price haggling appears to have become only a point of historical interest.

Equity and growth within the mature market concern only the taxing authorities and national planners. Marketing events for firms in the mature market are developed around (a) weekly standing orders; (b) formula pricing tactics; (c) private label practices; (d) public relations; (e) image differentiation; (f) products with long shelf-life; (g) one-stop shopping centres with exclusive retail space; (h) excessive retail selling space; and (i) vertical integration (Hawkins, 1979) – providing peace and serenity for all in a regularized domestic market. Governments and marketing agencies pursue the common goals of redistributing wealth outside of the marketplace, limiting growth principally to the domestic scene, and avoiding at all costs price competition and the rigour of a noisy marketplace where occasional pain is a way of life.

The problem with this 'commercial pastoral' life is that food prices rise at a faster pace than consumers relish due to restriction of output. Internal equity issues between labour and management begin to dominate events and growth stagnates. It is now a matter of history that when an economic system decides that small agricultural producers and processors are redundant to the industrialization of food production, then eventually the resultant costs of marketing and producing food will be paid for through shortages and/or higher prices.

## THE PROBLEMS

The questions therefore become: (1) 'Can we develop a marketing mechanism which promotes equity and accelerated growth in the agricultural sector without promoting excesses of market structure concentration and oligopolistic conduct within the food marketing system?' and (2) 'Can we foster the innovativeness and drive of the small producer and processor while exploiting the economies of scale of the larger operator?' The task is to direct government attention away from the 'big picture' towards providing an atmosphere where the relatively smaller agricultural producers can co-ordinate their activities in production and marketing in such a manner as to maintain equity and growth within the food system.

This paper will present an example of this producer co-ordination which is presently occurring in the Province of Alberta in Canada. The paper will briefly outline the history of the Alberta Pork Producers Marketing Board (APPMB) and will attempt to develop conclusions from its experience. The authors regret the narrowness of the analysis. However, we trust that our intimate knowledge of this situation will be more useful to the IAAE membership than would an overzealous attempt to extrapolate and generalize our personal experiences to areas beyond our environment.

## BACKGROUND

The groundwork for the establishment of Canadian marketing boards took place in the State of Queensland, Australia, in the early 1900s. News of the legislation passed there for the formation of marketing boards by agricultural producers soon found its way to the Province of British Columbia in Canada. From there the news spread through Canada, arriving in Alberta in 1956. Over a thirty to forty year period, Canadians evolved the original Australian precept into a system built around a supervisory/regulatory body called a marketing council, or 'super board.' The Marketing of Agricultural Products Act of Alberta is administered by the Alberta Agricultural Products Marketing Council, an appointed body that reports to the province's Minister of Agriculture. It is a political body which serves at the discretion of the Minister; thus, it acts as the arm of government directing marketing initiatives to approximately ten Alberta commodity boards.

Briefly put, the government places the powers of regulating quantities and commodity prices within the Council. It is interesting to note that although the Council has the legislated authority to regulate retail behaviour, it has to date confined its actions to the farm level. At this level, the Council delegates to producer-elected marketing boards such powers as the producers approve in referendums or through unanimous consent. Therefore, after a series of producer plebiscites, the APPMB was established in 1968 to undertake research, promotion, political lobbying, and to conduct a public teletype auction of pigs.

## INTERIM COMMENTS

At this point in the paper several observations should be noted. The Alberta Agricultural Products Marketing Act is generous to agricultural producers. That is to say, the objective of the government is to foster producer participation in the marketing of their products. One could comment that within the overall guidelines of government policy, the producers are trusted to run their own affairs. This situation is made possible through control and feedback mechanisms which make certain that boards carry out their individual mandates. These mechanisms include: (a) supervized secret voting by ballots for elections and major changes in regulations; (b) approval of yearly operating statements, budgets and marketing fee checkoffs by all producers; (c) verbatim minutes of board and director meetings sent to each Council member; (d) occasional Council attendance at board meetings; and (e) the holding of regular meetings between the Council, its member boards and the Minister. Through the Council, the boards have been granted fairly specific regulations. Within these regulations, the boards have substantial freedom to act. If producers as a group have shown tangible support to a proposition, amendments to the regulations are made fairly readily.

## THE TASK

Since the inception of the APPMB, the goal of hog producers has been to develop a market system which accelerates agricultural growth while maintaining market discipline, producer involvement and equity considerations. How well has the APPMB fulfilled these obligations? Has the Board met the additional criterion of market efficiency?

In 1979, researchers in the Department of Rural Economy undertook a comprehensive study and evaluation of APPMB operations. The research attempted to link changes in institutional policies with economic criteria. Several publications are pending and the M.Sc. thesis of Mr S. Leavitt, currently with Cargill Grain Ltd., forms the basis of the context and much of the analytic work behind this paper. Our thoughts reflect 30 years of personal study in this areas and an intensive, objective evaluation of a working marketing system by a gifted student. Our total task, therefore, is to blend and expand the theoretical basis for market analysis of a marketing system with a case study situation to see if a link can be made between theoretical relationship and actual market activity.

## INSTITUTIONAL FACTORS

During the 1960s, hog producers in Alberta became concerned about the structure of the hog industry. Manning (1965) indicated that 'less than 5 percent of the total number of hogs marketed were sold at public auction in Calgary and Edmonton, and this small number established the base prices for most of the other hogs sold'. There may have been advantages in this system for the larger producers as the 'packers introduced various means of awarding producers, such as premium payments, quick payment, quick kill, assembly and transportation cost subsidies, and other prearranged formulas' (Andersen, 1971).

If a perfectly competitive market exists, neither the buyers nor the sellers can exert more market power than the other. However, market power is strengthened for either buyers or sellers as one side becomes highly concentrated. Reschenthaler (1980) implies that a number of costs affecting market power show up under the heading of poor performance. Examples are inefficiencies in allocation, technology and dynamics. Additionally, as competitive forces are reduced, 'firms in an oligopoly might not try as hard to keep their costs down or artifically depress prices of resource inputs'.

The hog producers in Alberta acted collectively when they became aware of the market power existing among the packing plants. Galbraith (1952) implies this reaction when he states: 'Power on one side of the market creates both the need for, and the prospect of reward to, the exercise of countervailing power from the other side. The first begets the second'.

Hog producers and producer organizations related to the industry began submitting marketing plans to the Alberta Department of Agriculture for approval in the early 1960s. In the fall of 1965, the newly appointed Agricultural Products Marketing Council urged the organizations which had submitted plans to co-operate on a consolidated proposal acceptable to all sectors of the industry. The organizations sponsoring the three basic plans were the Western Hog Growers' Association, the Alberta Livestock Co-operative, and the joint organization of the Alberta Federation of Agriculture and the Farmers' Union of Alberta[1]. No agreement on consolidation was made. The Marketing Council then advised all swine and farm organizations that the Minister of Agriculture had approved a proposal to conduct an opinion poll of hog producers concerning the type of marketing plan they favoured.

In the fall of 1968, the results of the opinion poll indicated that the producers favoured the joint FUA/AFA proposal which called for the establishment of a hog marketing board under which all slaughter hogs were to be sold through a single selling agency. The provincial government began action to make the Alberta Hog Producers' Marketing Board a reality, and on 31 October 1969, the Board officially opened its telebid system of selling hogs.

Since the Board's implementation, it has undergone various developments and policy changes. Some of these alterations include Board involvement in domestic and foreign pork marketing contracts, insurance programmes, price pooling, bid/acceptance selling system, promotional activities and court action against the packing plants. Appendix A summarizes the development of the Board and events which have affected it. Using quantitative techniques, the following section will review the analysis which attempted to link the institutional changes outlined in the Appendix with empirical data obtained from the marketplace.

## SUMMARY OF ANALYSIS

Space and time do not allow complete documentation of the research results. Briefly summarized, the research findings were as follows:

### *Concerning conduct among the pork packing plants in Alberta*

1 Despite wide fluctuations in hog marketings, the four major packing plants exhibited constant market shares during the periods studied.
2 Short-run price fixing was suggested.
3 Price leadership was exhibited.
4 Cost-plus pricing of hogs was evident.

### *Concerning market information*

1 The Board has instituted regular summaries of wholesale and retail pork prices.
2 Hourly, daily and weekly market information has become available by phone and is published in numerous publications.

3 Actual price and quantity figures are supplied to government and business, at no cost to the user.
4 Delegates to the Board are also instrumental in circulating information to producers.

*Concerning operational efficiency*

1 The costs of insurance coverage on transit pigs were cut approximately in half.
2 The number of assembly yards were cut from several hundred to six; thus, the actual costs of assembly were almost cut in half.
3 Pigs were directed to the nearest slaughter facility, thereby limiting shrink costs.
4 The Board received substantial income from the 'check float' mechanism. Interest from this source paid a considerable part of the Board's operation.[2]
5 Data processing has reduced paper costs and payment times and the information flow generated also benefits the total industry.
6 The Board assumed the cost of supervizing carcass identification from the federal government, thus saving the taxpayer a sum of money.

*Concerning pricing efficiency*

1 The Board established a trading company in order to (a) expedite export of live hogs and (b) find places to slaughter hogs during labour strikes, thus improving market arbitrage.
2 Domestic contracts with local processors, as well as export contracts, on a cost-plus basis, with Japanese buyers, have been undertaken.
3 The Board has purchased a packing plant operation in order to modify the structure of the marketplace.
4 Prices for Alberta pigs appear to more closely approximate other Canadian markets since the Board started.
5 Price differences with major US markets appear to have narrowed considerably.
6 There would appear to be some evidence that the level of real hog prices was higher after the Board came into effect. However, variability of real prices increased substantially. The latter situation led the Board to pool daily prices for all producers.

## ADDITIONAL REFLECTIONS

The two year study into the APPMB clarified and reinforced previous observations. The producer-controlled body had improved market efficiency. Not quite as clearly did it present the case for increased growth and equity in the marketplace.

Previous to the Board's operation, large commercial operations received substantially higher prices for their pigs than small producers. In addition, many bonuses were available to large volume producers such as fast kill, fast payment, free trucking, delayed kill premiums, and guaranteed dollar premiums. The large number of producers who accounted for a relatively small percentage of total pigs slaughtered became noticeably upset. Political pressure grew. Therefore, the Board's implementation of one price for all producers found considerable political favour. It would appear that the new system was able to eliminate discrimination between producers while improving or maintaining operational efficiency. Thus, equity between producers in regard to access to the market and terms of trade became reality.

The Board has also had to come to grips with alleged collusive conduct on the part of the processing industry. Evidence of alleged staged auction sales, rigid market shares, a lack of market arbitrage and active tampering by meat processors and assemblers with telecommunication sales network led the Board towards active intervention in the marketplace.[3] Reinforcing the drive for producer activism was the abdication of the market regulator role by the Council and various other government regulatory organizations.

The newly formulated political and economic activity instituted by the Board was financed by an additional producer checkoff on the sale of each pig. In point of fact, this fee is now several times higher than the amount of the producer-collected funds going towards the handling and selling of each pig. In addition, the APPMB has engaged a small, talented, high-priced group of experts to help it plot its course. The Board has become a democratically elected political force with economic power and has made considerable progress in handling operational, equity and growth factors in its production and marketing environment. The Board's impositions on the system have been limited in abuse of power by the two-way flow of pigs and pork products across North America, the Marketing Council's supervisory role, and by the competition of meat alternatives in the consumer food basket. In addition, election procedures, which involve limited terms for officers and financial accountability to member producers, have generated turnover in the players and have created new imaginative thrusts in management. The individual producer can produce whatever pigs he desires, responding to market ebbs and flows. In addition he is financially supported by a joint government-producer income averaging plan and he has the final confidence that his elected proxies are directing the attack for equity, growth and market efficiency.

Thus, the system has retained the discipline required of a competitive marketplace, while allowing individual producers to demonstrate self-initiative and innovative desires in their production units. It has recognized the necessity of economies of scale in a narrow consumer market and now works actively in maintaining the volumes of hogs necessary for the survival of the existing meat processors.

# APPENDIX A

*Flow chart of significant events affecting the Board*

31 October 1969 – AHPMB officially started selling hogs.

May 1973 – The Board negotiated first of a series of contracts with Japan for hog exports.

July 1973 – Formation of the Producers' Hog Indemnity Fund.

1974 – Board given authority to negotiate directly with processors or buyers.

1975 – Board terminals established to influence hog flow to packing plants.

November 1977 – Hu Harries completes report on the hog price relationship.

March 1978 – Board implements daily producer price averaging.

March 1978 – Board starts marketing hogs under advanced buyer bidding.

June 1978 – Producer toll free code-a-phone market information service.

1978 – Incorporation of the Alberta Hog Trading Company.

April 1979 – Sale of frozen pork to Korea.

May 1979 – Name change from 'Hog' to 'Pork'.

November 1979 – Appeal of the Board's bid/acceptance system and domestic contracting launched by two major processing firms.

February 1980 – Three processor firms' partial boycott starts.

February 1980 – Minister Schmidt announces his intention to establish a Hog Marketing Review Committee.

February 1980 – Board discontinues use of teletype: receives offers by telephone, telex, letter or teletype circuit.

March 1980 – Board and individual plaintiffs file $73 million statement of claim against packers for restraint of trade.

March 1980 – Marketing Council passes motion to take over Board operations through A.R. 99/80.

April 1980 – A.R. 99/80 is repealed by Council.

May 1980 – Temporary Stop-Loss Program announced by Minister Schmidt.

December 1980 – The Board purchases Fletchers' Fine Foods Limited packing plants in Red Deer and Vancouver.

## CONCLUDING COMMENTS

The task of this paper has been to present a situation wherein the marketing mechanism has been utilized to accelerate growth in the agricultural sector while retaining marketing efficiency, equity and the role of self-initiative. The marketing system examined utilized co-operative action by producers, computerized mechanisms, and imaginative government legislation to jar the mature market structure towards the aforementioned goals.

It is important to note that the described system has only one weapon to use in the face of market collusion or government restriction. Awareness and unbiased technical knowledge of the marketplace are the principal means of directing political pressure towards legislative or producer-directed changes.

Accelerated growth in agricultural development would appear to be possible with an elected producer-backed market mechanism. It is also apparent that operational efficiency gains are similar to those available in concentrated mature market systems which owe their existence to economies of scale, market power or government decree.

## NOTES

[1] For a detailed description of the three marketing plans proposed and the development of the Board, see M. H. Hawkins, S. S. Leavitt and L. Leiren, *Development and Operation of the Alberta Pork Producers Marketing Board,* Revised Rural Economy Bulletin 12, Edmonton: University of Alberta, Dept of Rural Economy, 1981.

[2] 'Check float' is the amount of money tied up in uncashed producer payment checks. The total amount involved is remarkably constant. Interest on this money is paid by the banks to the Board. Previously these payments had gone to the packers.

[3] Legal actions by the APPMB and the Canada Department of Justice are pending.

## REFERENCES

M. H. Hawkins and R. Norby, *The Implications of Vertical Integration by Food Retailers on the Canadian Pork Marketing System,* Occasional Paper No. 2, Edmonton: Rural Economy, University of Alberta, November 1977.

M. Hawkins, 'The Competitive Environment in the Canadian Food System' (Paper presented to Organization and Direction of the Food System in the 1980s seminar, at Edmonton, Alberta, 11 – 12 June 1979).

Travis W. Manning, *Performance of the Hog Marketing System in Alberta,* Agricultural Economics Research Bulletin No. 4, Edmonton: University of Alberta, July 1967, p.9.

Richard S. Andersen, 'An Economic Analysis of Daily Hog Price Fluctuations and Supply Response', unpublished M.Sc. Thesis, University of Alberta, Edmonton, 1971, p. 14.

G. B. Reschenthaler, 'An Analysis of the Competitiveness of the Pork Industry in Alberta', paper presented to the Hog Marketing Review Committee, Edmonton, 24 June 1980, p. 9. Mimeographed.

J. K. Galbraith, *American Capitalism: The Concept of Countervailing Power,* Houghton Mifflin, Boston, Mass.: 1952, pp. 111 and 113.

## DISCUSSION OPENING – MICHAEL HAINES

In recent years it has become fashionable to stress the role of marketing in encouraging agricultural development. Some writers, particularly those from the straight marketing and business disciplines, have even gone so far as to assert that marketing improvement is *the* key factor in development, both in the developed and the developing world. This view has led to the great emphasis on the role of agri-business. In the same period, the acceptance by many people of the fact that input supply, agricultural production, processing, retailing and ultimate consumption are simply part of an integrated food production and marketing system (characterized in French by the term *agro-alimentaire*) has stimulated renewed interest in the developed world in a problem which has been ever present in the developing world: namely, whether *growth* is more important than *equity* or vice-versa; that is the theme for this conference. That both these concepts are important has always been recognized; the *problem* has always been to design a system such that it achieves a satisfactory trade-off between them – satisfactory normally being conceived from the farmer's point of view.

The fact that most agricultural products require processing, and that most processing activities exhibit considerable economies of scale, has led to the growth of very large firms which, it has been widely believed, exercise considerable power over the farming sector and may cause a loss of consumer sovereignty. This view of the situation has been widely accepted by agricultural economists, and considerable efforts have been devoted to devising institutional arrangements which would allow the exploitation of economics of scale without permitting exploitation of the farmer. This paper offers a case study of one recent attempt to prevent the exploitation of small farmers by an oligopoly of four hog processors in Alberta. The solution discussed is the establishment of a marketing board to countervail the power of the oligopoly, and thereby ensure that all producers receive the same price and are offered the same terms of trade (where before the establishment of the Board larger producers obtained better terms than small producers). There is therefore *equality* of treatment, but this may not represent *equitable* treatment. Indeed, what may have been created is a producer monopoly which may well countervail the power of a processor oligopoly, but may not have increased the revenue and consumer satisfaction of the total system, simply redistributing it among the participants. It may have ensured better treatment of small farmers, but at the expense of efficient, planned, large-scale, low cost production which would be beneficial to the largest group in developed countries – that is, consumers. I am not arguing that what the Board has achieved in improving operational efficiency has not been beneficial; it clearly has – costs of collection and so on have been reduced by 50 per cent, which is a major achievement. Similarly, illegalities have been detected and prosecutions put in hand, which is also important. What I am more concerned about is that the Board was established and is controlled, albeit democractically, by one sector of the marketing system to protect, as I understand it, the interests of small producers against large producers and against other sectors of the agri-food system.

The authors say that hog purchasers were offering special terms of trade and inducements to larger producers, and that the farmers were right to object and call for government intervention to prevent this. At the present time there is a similar campaign by small retailers in the United Kingdom and we have seen such action in France. The Robinson-Patman Act was a legislative response in the United States to a similar complaint by retailers. Marketing Boards and co-operatives have been established by government and farmers throughout the world based on similar reasoning. In many cases these activities have failed to achieve all that their sponsors sought because in effect they are trying to put the clock back, and more importantly they are damaging other sectors of society. In the case of the retailers, they are preventing consumers from obtaining food at lower prices, and the same is often true of attempts to protect small farmers. I must say that I am not persuaded of the case that 'when an economic system decides that small agricultural producers and processors are redundant to the industrialization of food production, then eventually the resultant costs of marketing and producing food will be paid for through shortages and/or higher prices'. Certainly where state ownership is concerned this may be true, but in Europe and, I suspect, North America, many consumers would argue that high prices (or high taxes) are the *result* of attempts to keep small farmers, processors, and indeed retailers in business, and not that the demise of these smaller businesses is the cause of high food prices. Clearly it depends on whether there are further economics of scale to be exploited by larger units, and this may in turn depend upon research and technology which is often funded by the State but benefits larger and more industrialized producers, who are often better able to produce growth in output.

This paper then raises again the main issue to which this conference is devoted, namely growth and equity, that is *a question of objectives.* If we want equity (or as it seems to me in this case, equality of treatment) then we may have to live with low levels of growth since growth in output nearly always results from the use of more resources, both financial and technical, which smaller farmers do not have. Efforts to protect small farmers may therefore be counter-productive both to other producers and certainly to the marketing system as a whole, whereas it is the planning by the food industry and large retailers which I would argue has led to increases in consumer satisfaction (which is the aim of all marketing activities).

The second question raised by the case study is one of *means*. If it is decided by the state that on political grounds it is necessary to protect a particular group, what is the best method of so doing? The authors of the paper show that the Alberta Hog Marketing Board has achieved many of the objectives which were sought. This is a common experience in many developed countries where marketing boards exist although not in LDCs. They allow the producer to exercise a high degree of freedom in his production decisions while at the same time imposing, after his initial consent, a certain minimum level of discipline, and it is this statutory discipline which overcomes the problems of the voluntary co-operative. This Marketing Board seems to be totally producer-run, although some others have a number of independent members, while others may contain representatives of the processing and retail trades and consumer groups. It seems to me that this last structure, which is more representative of the system as a whole, is more in line with modern marketing thinking, and this seems to me to be one topic worthy of discussion today.

There is, finally, another general point which is of considerable importance in a number of countries, and has received a great deal of attention in Canada, the United Kingdom and so on. Many countries now face a situation in which the market for agricultural commodities is no longer growing and conditions of surplus exist. What is required, therefore, is a means of equitably preventing the growth and later even reducing output, so that producers' incomes can be maintained without imposing unacceptable costs on consumer and taxpayers. I, for one, would welcome the views of the authors of this paper on the idea that a broadly-based Marketing Board involving all participants of the marketing system plus the government might be the most acceptable means of achieving this end.

A. S. WATSON

# *Marketing Policy in Relation to Agricultural Development**

## INTRODUCTION

Agricultural marketing has a problem of its identity as a subject for academic inquiry and agricultural economists have vastly differing perceptions of its appropriate subject matter. In broad outline, these perceptions range from the firm-orientation of the 'marketing concept' favoured by most business schools to a view of agricultural marketing as a branch of applied economics, most often neo-classicial in inspiration, directed towards the study of marketing functions and institutions. Since commentators on agricultural marketing appear to be unsure on questions of theory and methodology, it seems necessary to spend some time discussing these differences in outlook before attempting to address the difficult question of the importance of marketing policy to agricultural development. A useful starting point is to sketch out the introductory discussion on agricultural marketing contained in two (English language) review articles published during the 1970s (Breimyer, 1973; Bateman, 1976) and to comment on a change of emphasis between successive editions of a standard textbook on the subject (Kohls and Downey, 1972; Kohls and Uhl, 1980).

Breimyer categorized three different approaches to agricultural marketing: the 'what happens' school, the co-ordinating role of marketing, and market development. The 'what happens' view is essentially descriptive and is suggestive of the existence of a one-way flow of products along a marketing chain from producer to consumer. The second approach, the co-ordination role, potentially has more analytical content as it emphasizes that economic processes are at work in the distribution and transformation of agricultural products and it leads directly to the realization that marketing margins are the prices of marketing services, or collections of services, and not merely differences in prices between different points of the marketing chain. Marketing margins, and the performance of marketing functions, are therefore to be explained in terms of economic theories relevant to the

*The advice and encouragement of my colleagues J. W. Cary, L. R. Malcolm and N. H. Sturgess is gratefully acknowledged.

behaviour of marketing firms and institutions. A refinement of the co-ordination concept of marketing was made by Phillips (1968) who stressed that economic research in agricultural marketing should be concentrated on the provision of information to market participants rather than the study of middleman functions, which Phillips regarded as problems in production and consumption of the various services performed in the marketing chain that do not require special methods of economic analysis. Phillips was critical of traditional definitions of marketing because they were too general to be useful and because they diverted attention from an important aspect of economic activity, that of obtaining information. The third approach, the 'market development' school, recognized by Breimyer, represents the attempt to apply merchandizing and promotion-based techniques of product differentiation, developed for the industrial sector, to problems of agricultural marketing. As discussed in the next section, it is prescriptive rather than descriptive or analytical.

Bateman, in his review of agricultural marketing, went a long way further towards accepting the marketing concept espoused by the industrial marketeers. Whilst Bateman gives a detailed treatment of traditional supply/demand analysis as it has been applied to agricultural marketing, his attitudes are far closer to the business marketing philosophy than would be the sympathies of most agricultural economists, or at least would have been until the 1970s, when a (minor) paradigm-shift seems to have occurred in the agricultural marketing literature. Changes like this are subtle and inherently hard to document. Business marketing is probably more influential inside large agricultural marketing organizations than would be suggested, say, by its formal representation in the professional activities of agricultural economists or their published literature. This influence seems to be growing and the reasons for it ought to be considered. It is interesting to note that the United States textbook by Kohls (co-authored with Downey and Uhl respectively, in its 1972 and 1980 editions) has always followed a standard approach in its introductory chapters, emphasizing functional and institutional approaches to marketing. The 1980 edition changes tack perceptibly. In fact, Kohls and Uhl describe the marketing concept glowingly as 'the third successive business philosophy of the Industrial Revolution' (p.42) following the production-engineer orientation and sales orientation of earlier periods. Such an extravagant claim is some justification for an attempt to explore the reasons for this changing emphasis in discussion of agricultural marketing.

## A CRITIQUE OF BUSINESS MARKETING

A central tenet of the philosophy of business marketing is the so-called marketing concept – 'the idea that the customer is not merely the person who happens to be at the end of the line but that his needs and wants should dominate the whole pattern of activity within the firm; firms should be market-oriented and not product-oriented' (Bateman p.172). In some ways, this is an example of a statement of principle without any content because it is not really a testable proposition that might provide a guide for action or an agenda for research, except in terms of market research to describe the characteristics of consumers. Most obviously, it is not clear how consumer wants could be determined or how conflicts of interest between consumers, or between consumers and producers, would be resolved. Arndt (1981) has pointed out that this prevailing ideology of marketing is based on a postulate of a lack of conflict of interest between consumers and producers and an instrumental view of the consumer.

The marketing concept has its particular focus on specific management problems of individual economic units engaged in marketing – be they farmers, commercial firms, co-operatives, State-sponsored marketing boards or governments. By its very nature it is not concerned with questions related to marketing policies for industries which involve wider issues relating to economic efficiency and equity. Consequently, the theory that is relevant to business marketing is most likely to be obtained from other areas of social science, in particular, various branches of psychology, rather than economics. It is only to be expected that the behavioural sciences will be more important if the emphasis is on consumer behaviour.

The most pervasive idea from economics that seems to be involved in much of the literature on business marketing is the concept of price discrimination. The real subtlety of marketing specialists is found in the sophisticated ways that markets can be segmented. It is obvious, however, that price discrimination can be a double-edged sword from the viewpoint of consumers, taken as a group, even if price discrimination is successful in raising aggregate revenue and/or reducing costs of distribution for producers. The claimed 'consumer' orientation of business marketing may be, in practice, more about getting more money out of them. The alleged consumer orientation of the marketing concept should not be confused with the sorts of impulses embodied in the doctrine of consumerism, which is more of a reaction to the cruder ideas of business marketing than an endorsement of its objectives and methods. Arndt (p. 298) has noted that: 'By natural instinct, marketing tends to be tempted to colonize further non-traditional marketing spheres under the flag of convenience of "Societal Marketing" or "Broadened Marketing"'.

In principle, there is nothing undesirable, or unusual, in a situation where different sub-disciplines exist to explain and elaborate phenomena at the firm and industry level. An analogous dichotomy between farm management and production economics was discussed by Longworth and Menz (1980). It is probably not sufficiently emphasized that both the theories of the firm and of the household were developed to explain how firms and households are linked to (and by) markets, and how output is distributed, rather than to derive insights into the individual behaviour of firms and households. There are few 'economic men', outside the ranks of economists, for traditional economics is not concerned with the behaviour of people but with the behaviour of commodities (Boulding, 1956).

The firm-orientation of business marketing is highlighted by the fact that its teachers and practitioners rely on case-studies to elaborate its methods. This is a sure sign that there are no general principles of marketing strategy that are based on a theoretical framework that is capable of consistent application. The lack of rigour in business marketing is further indicated by the following two quotations from a standard marketing text (Kotler, 1967):

> Creativity is a valuable ingredient in every facet of business but plays its most conspicuous role in the marketing area. The firm is pitted against other firms in a never ending struggle to win the attention and patronage of highly elusive customers. Conventional marketing is likely to lead only to conventional sales results. To achieve exceptional results, companies must develop creative ideas which, in the realm of products, advertising, merchandising, and sales presentation, distinguish their offerings from those of competitors (p.246).

> But certainly all the rules in the world cannot substitute for creative inspiration. And some of the best advertisements arise from breaking the rules (p.247).

Taken on their own, these statements are harmless enough but we are left in the dark, as ought to be expected, as to what 'creativity' actually is or what it means to make the jump from the 'conventional' to the 'exceptional'? What then is the attraction of business marketing to its adherents? In the first instance, the modern industrial economy has extreme specialization of economic functions and fine division of labour – even the most eclectic or superficial ideas about marketing may be preferable to no ideas at all. The sub-discipline of business marketing is oriented towards practical activities; it is in some ways ideal for a bureaucratic institution interested in the improved performance of well-defined functions but not wanting much basic questioning of its fundamental objectives. For example, marketing boards in many countries turn a blind eye to the fact that they have been established by governments in the 'public interest' when they advertise agricultural products: this may be in the interests of the producers of the particular product but it will be generally to the detriment of other producers, and consumers, unless the promotional activity results in lower costs of distribution. Although business marketing is easy to criticize, even to caricature, for its generality, one should not deny that it can be useful to intelligent practitioners. The saving grace of business marketing may be that its all-embracing view of economic behaviour, and its willingness to borrow methods freely from many sources, may be useful in particular problem-solving applications. The problem, however, as with all 'multi-disciplinary' or 'systems approach' attitudes to research or problem-solving, is to put empirical substance for the rhetorical shadow of 'marketing' and to restrain those who see it as some sort of panacea for farmers' problems, which may have altogether different causes and remedies. In its worst versions, business marketing is the obverse of the fundamentalist notions that middlemen are parasites and that the source of all value derives from the producer.

## CONVENTIONAL APPROACHES TO AGRICULTURAL MARKETING

In most countries agricultural marketing institutions and the serious study of agricultural marketing are both responses to measures that have been taken by governments given the problems of farmers caused by low agricultural prices. The most common reaction of farmers to economic difficulties is to blame the marketing system (Watson and Parish, 1982). Thus, there is considerable overlap between the subject-matter of courses in agricultural prices and agricultural marketing. A useful point of separation would be that price policy concerns the determination of absolute price levels; whereas marketing policy concerns the determination of price differentials, around the absolute price, that reflect location, time, quality and form characteristics of commodities.

Under competitive conditions, the theory of agricultural marketing would not be difficult, or very interesting, because the 'law of one price' is such a powerful idea in an exchange economy. This would still be the case if competition were restricted at some stages of production or distribution, because the various margins around administered prices may still be determined competitively by whatever means, and at whatever level, the flat, or absolute, price is established. The law of one price asserts that prices within a competitive market will be uniform after the costs of adding (or substracting) place, time and form utility are taken into consideration. Moreover, the process of competition is justified in orthodox theory because competition not only allows the use of known information on costs to establish prices, it is also asserted to be an efficient method of generating the economic information necessary to guide business decisions in a situation where, perforce, the economic 'facts' helpful to make those decisions are transient in nature (Hayek, 1978). The process of competition has to be considered both vertically, between marketing channels, and horizontally, between firms operating at the same stage.

Even if the theory of marketing were straightforward under competitive conditions, there is enough to interest the analyst of agricultural markets as they adjust continuously to new information concerning costs and demands for the various services that are provided. One consequence of this concept of 'one price' is that even though considerable caution will need to be exercised in applying theories of market economies to less-developed countries, there is considerable common ground in studying price relationships for the (external) trade of such countries.

The critical factor determining the development of agricultural marketing institutions in a mixed economy will be whether fiscal (subsidy/tax) or regulatory devices are used to achieve agricultural price and income objectives. This will be independent of the actual levels of protection (nominal or effective) that are achieved by intervention in price and marketing systems, but will be essentially determined by various features of the agricultural, political, financial and taxation institutions of individual countries. Thus, of the export-orientated agricultural economies, New

Zealand has extremely wide-ranging controls applied to the marketing system (Veeman, 1980), whereas the United States relies more on the price mechanism to co-ordinate marketing activities for its export trade. Australia and Canada are in a hazy, intermediate, position – in the former case, more because of the constraints on 'orderly marketing', brought about by the division of powers under the Australian Constitution, than a deepseated commitment to the economics of *laissez-faire.* Amongst the protected agricultural economies of western Europe, the United Kingdom is characterized more by marketing boards than its new-found partners in the European Economic Community where fiscal methods have long held sway as instruments for price and income support. This is largely because the taxation and social security systems of some European countries were unable to deliver the desired transfers to farmers in an agricultural system where the rates of adjustment of farm size and population were insufficient to achieve satisfactory urban-rural income relationships.

Conventional micro-economics is a powerful antidote to some of the more persistent fallacies that surround discussion of agricultural marketing. Mindless measurement of irrelevant indicators of marketing efficiency such as the 'farmer's share of the consumer's dollar', the dubious benefits of product promotion for farmers taken as a group and the massive waste of intellectual effort through econometric forecasting of prices are three obvious cases in point.

## MARKETING AND AGRICULTURAL DEVELOPMENT

There are substantial differences between the agricultural marketing systems of developed and developing countries. Although these differences are so marked as not to require detailed description, it is salutary to note that all marketing systems perform essentially the same physical and economic functions. A much more interesting question to consider is whether differences in marketing systems are an important cause of differences in rates of economic growth or whether they are mainly a symptom of economic prosperity. The former view is implicit in the more extreme versions of the philosophy of business marketing discussed previously in this paper, whilst the latter sentiment is consistent with the observation that almost invariably the demand for marketing services increases as incomes rise. The relationship between income and the demand for marketing services will, of course, be working in the other direction in a period of declining incomes.

An important link between marketing policy and the process of agricultural development is that the emergence of specialized marketing activities involves more division of labour as farmers substitute greater concentration on production activities for direct participation in marketing. The (theoretical) benefits of this division of labour are twofold: lower costs of production obtained through specialization and lower costs of providing the marketing services *per se.* Discussion of the advantages and disadvantages of the division of labour is as old as economics itself. Adam Smith claimed in the opening sentence of the *Wealth of Nations,* that 'The greatest improvement in the productive powers, and the greater part of the skill, dexterity and judgement with which it is anywhere directed, or applied, seem to have been the effect of the division of labour'. Smith stressed the importance of the division of labour for three main reasons: increased dexterity of labour, saving of time, and the invention of machines to assist labour (Groenewegen, 1977). These economic processes involve both learning and financial development that will allow production (and marketing) to proceed whilst labour is employed until output is forthcoming.

The distinction drawn by Adam Smith 'between productive and unproductive labour is probably the most maligned concept in the history of economic doctrines' (Blaug, 1970, p.56), but it is important to note that it had nothing to do with the traditional distrust of middlemen based on the view that the service industries are somehow less important than economic activities directed towards the production of tangible outputs. What was at issue was the difference between economic activity that results in capital accumulation and activity that services the immediate needs of households. The analysis of the process of economic growth envisaged by Smith has been formalized by Hicks (1965) in the following relationship:

$$g = k.p/w - 1$$

where $g$ is the rate of growth of output, $k$ is the proportion of productive labour (the savings ratio), $p$ is the productivity of labour and $w$ is the wage rate. In this simple model, productive labour is equivalent to what nowadays would be called gross investment whereas unproductive labour corresponds to the consumption sector. Productive labour is therefore labour that produces a surplus over and above the wages paid to it, and thus contributes to capital accumulation, and does not mean labour in particular occupations. In this 'growth' model, which is more a description of the growth process than a linked sequence of growth through time, the growth of the 'economy' depends critically on the productivity of labour, $p$, which Smith believed would be enhanced by the division of labour.

There is an important sense in which the development of specialized marketing institutions represents the mirror image of the development of a sophisticated financial system that will also aid the process of saving and capital accumulation that is necessary for agriculture to become more productive – this is consistent with the useful working definition that agricultural marketing is the study of the economic processes at work as agricultural products flow from the producer to the consumer and money moves in the opposite direction. Again, it is interesting to address a further 'chicken and egg' question as to which of these two phenomena needs to be acted upon first to encourage development, at least in the context of capitalist economic development. There would seem to be intuitive reasons for arguing that if the financial system can be 'got right' then the marketing arrangements will follow. McKinnon (1973) has argued a convincing case for the development of a financial system that encourages the holding of financial assets rather than a situation where:

> a significant proportion of the physical capital of the economy will be embodied in inventories of finished or semi-finished goods that are not used directly for production or consumption. A small farmer may keep unduly large rice inventories as the embodiment of his savings – a portion of which the rats eat every year (p.63).

The essence of McKinnon's theory is that real money balances and physical capital are complementary rather than competing assets because money can be thought of as a conduit through which accumulation takes place. Increasing the value of the real stock of money and increased real interest rates will encourage farmers, and other small savers, to shift from inefficient and inflexible self-financing to external financing as their savings become aggregated in an evolving financial system. This breaks down the fragmentation of the economic system with its extreme divergence in rates of return and calls forth new net saving and diverts investment from inferior uses.

## CONCLUDING COMMENTS

In an agricultural context, the most fruitful approach to marketing would seem to be to emphasize the co-ordination role of marketing, since this highlights the important role of prices in the organization of production and consumption. By its very nature, agriculture will remain a disaggregated sector in most conceivable economies. Appropriate marketing adjustments can be expected to follow, rather than to lead, the process of agricultural development, which will depend more on increases in output based on education, and investment in infrastructure and at the farm level.

Although the business marketing approach may contribute to the operational problems of private or public marketing organizations, it does not have much useful information to offer concerning those more fundamental economic issues affecting trade, development and the prices and incomes received by agricultural producers.

## REFERENCES

Arndt, J., 'Marketing and the Quality of Life', *Journal of Economic Psychology,* Vol. 1, No.4, December 1981.

Bateman, D.I., 'Agricultural Marketing: A Review of the Literature of Marketing Theory and of Selected Applications', *J.A.E.,* Vol. 27, No. 2, May 1976.

Blaug, M., *Economic Theory in Retrospect,* Heinemann, London, 1970.

Boulding, K.E., *The Image,* University of Michigan Press, 1956.

Breimyer, H.F., 'The Economics of Agricultural Marketing: A Survey', *R.M.A.E.,* Vol. 41, No. 4, December 1973.

Groenewegen, P.D., 'Adam Smith and the Division of Labour: A Bicentenary Estimate', *Australian Economic Papers,* Vol. 16, No. 29, December 1977.

Hayek, F.A., 'Competition as a Discovery Procedure', Chapter 12 in F.A. Hayek, *New Studies in Philosophy, Politics, Economics and the History of Ideas,* Routledge and Kegan Paul, London, 1978.

Hicks, J., *Capital and Growth,* Oxford, 1965.

Kohls, R.L. and Downey, W.D., *Marketing of Agricultural Products* (4th ed) Macmillan, New York, 1972.

Kohls, R.L., and Uhl, J.N., *Marketing of Agricultural Products* (5th ed) Collier Macmillan, 1980.

Kotler, P., *Marketing Management,* Prentice-Hall, Englewood Cliffs, New Jersey, 1967.

Longworth, J.W. and Menz, K.M., 'Activity Analysis: Bridging the Gap Between Production Economic Theory and Practical Farm Management Procedures', *R.M.A.E.,* Vol. 48, No. 1, 1980.

McKinnon, R.I., *Money and Capital in Economic Development,* The Brookings Institution, Washington, 1973.

Phillips, J., 'A Revised Approach to Marketing', *R.M.A.E.,* Vol. 36, No. 1, March 1968.

Veeman, M.D., 'New Zealand Marketing Boards' in Hoos, S., *Agricultural Marketing Boards – An International Perspective,* Ballinger, Cambridge, Mass., 1979.

Watson, A.S. and Parish, R.M., 'Marketing Agricultural Products' in D.B. Williams, *Agriculture in the Australian Economy* (2nd edition) Sydney University Press, 1982.

## DISCUSSION OPENING – J.C. ABBOTT

In his introduction Professor Watson brought up some of the more provocative elements of his paper. I am going to leave it to his audience to respond to them.

Our theme is marketing policy and agricultural development. I would like to complement Professor Watson's paper by directing our thoughts more specifically to the kind of marketing needed to promote agricultural development at an earlier stage, and the influences that have had an effect on policy-making for this in the developing countries. The goal, there, has been to build a marketing infrastructure suited to the needs of small farmers and, by offering them easier access to favourable markets and to fertilizer and other inputs, to bring into the commercial economy the large number of family producers who continue to farm along semi-subsistence lines. The development instruments are better roads, market facilities and storage, provision of market information and implementation of guaranteed minimum prices for major agricultural products through marketing board and co-operative purchasing systems. Now some of these approaches are being questioned. The co-operative system was dismantled in socialist Tanzania as too costly. Last year the state agricultural marketing board of Senegal was summarily abolished. Considerable development effort may have been wasted. I should like to put forward two propositions:

1 The university teaching of developed countries, the visibility of their institutions and the attitudes of their aid agencies have been a significant distraction. Developing countries have been led into projects which they have not the resources to implement and maintain.

2 This distraction has been the more potent because of the social and informational gap between those who are actually engaged in agricultural

marketing in many developing countries and those who take official policy decisions.

Let us look at what can happen in practice. Aid and development agencies find a natural satisfaction in building roads in developing countries up to the standards of their own countries – but if afterwards they will not be maintained much of the original investment is wasted. There is one country where major roads have been built and rebuilt two or three times at ten to fifteen year intervals under successive aid programmes. Similarly, helping a country maintain a steady supply of spare parts and effective repair facilities may give much better returns than furnishing successive fleets of new transport vehicles to specialized institutions and projects. Fostering growth of a locally operated general carrier system with agencies established to organize return loads is a useful strategy for effective transport utilization. Construction of storage by public bodies with aid and development money has always been risky. Because their decisions tend to be taken centrally and in response to allocations of blocks of funds that must be spent, public organization investments in stores and other fixed facilities are often wastful. Fertilizer stores constructed for the extension service in Iran cost three times per ton capacity those put up by private distributors. A decade or two ago we were campaigning against the building of big silos where small scale multi-use hangars were much more appropriate. Even these can go wrong when built to meet standardized precepts under a big loan programme. Of those recently built for farmers bringing stocks to rural assembly markets in Northern India hardly any are being used by farmers in practice. The credit and handling procedures for this are just too cumbersome.

To fill gaps in existing marketing channels or to supply new inputs and product outlet needs governments have tended to set up new co-operative and state marketing systems with external assistance. In FAO we have maintained a specialized bibliography of material on marketing in the developing countries. Fifteen years ago the literature tended to present co-operatives and state enterprises as the panacea for all ills. The bibliography supplements of recent years are full of reports on the problems of such enterprises and how they can be resolved.

Commonly quoted as a justification for the focus on public and co-operative enterprise was the reluctance of private enterprise to accept the risks of innovation. Perhaps this should be restated as reluctance of the government and aid donors to give private enterprises the resources and incentive to take the risks and to let them begin on a small scale.

Until very recently, the role of the rural assembly market as an instrument for change and progress has been neglected. Affording access to large numbers of rural people the market can be an economical natural integrator of a range of development activities. Yet many development programmes would have nothing to do with these markets. In Brazil and India surveys have shown that increasing the density of organized rural markets attended regularly by wholesalers has stimulated a significant expansion of farm output within two or three years. This response, moreover, came almost entirely from the smaller farmers because they were the ones handicapped by distance from outlets for their produce where pricing and services would be competitive. Once we thought that setting up an official market news service where none existed was the first and minimum step in a programme to improve marketing infrastructure for producers and consumers. It was assumed to give high returns for a low cost. A disconcerting number of such services set up under aid projects have stopped rather soon after external assistance ceased – with only muted regrets. Again, I suspect, the need has been seen in developed country terms: coverage and presentation have not been adapted to local requirements. Provision of practical advice on marketing to the farmer is another essential service. In practice it is done best under production contracts for marketing and processing, with the contracting enterprise supplying the field staff and advice that is specific. The advice given to farmers under general extension programmes tends itself to be general, with the agent a post box for government policy rather than someone who can work out the best marketing strategy for individual farmers in their particular situation. Stabilization of prices to reduce producers' market risk is generally an effective generator of expanding ouput. Production economists still see the market risk as the greatest deterrent for the small farmer in India. The relative decline in production of pulses and oilseeds there as against rice and wheat is attributed very largely to this. Certainly the announcement before the planting season and effective implementation of guaranteed minimum prices to farmers for the two major crops has been strategic in building up production to match population growth.

Operation of a price stabilization system requires a very cool head. General awareness that the government is fixing the base price can attract great political pressure. Only too easily costs can be forced up to an uneconomic level or the intake specifications eroded to the point that heavy physical and quality losses are incurred on stocks in storage. This does not mean, however, that I have in any way lost my optimism that we can continue to make progress with marketing infrastructure as an instrument of agricultural development. My current project is to put together a set of case studies on marketing successes in the developing world – private, co-operative and public institutions.

## GENERAL DISCUSSION* – RAPPORTEUR: K.S. ARUN KUMAR

In the discussion on the paper by Murray Hawkins et al. the following questions were put:

1 Were there any limitations on the Board's activities?

2 What circumstances led to its success and is any empirical evidence available?

3 Was there any government subsidy and who pays for the cost of the operations?

*Papers by Hawkins, Leavitt and Norby, and Watson.

4 Are the needs of retailers met?
5 Is there any interference with exports or imports?

In reply Dr Hawkins said that the Marketing Council was generally ineffective in supervising the Board's activities which might adversely affect the interests of consumers. The circumstances which led to its success (and empirical evidence is available for use by the University of Alberta) include a concerted interest by producers to correct processor abuses in the marketing system, genuine improvements in operational efficiency, an improved market information system, and a sound financial position. Operating costs were paid by producers and there is no subsidy. Retailers co-operate actively with producers through the Board which has no powers concerning exports or imports.

He concluded that while marketing boards in Canada have met the objectives of producers, there is considerable discussion as to whether or not they have harmed the interests of consumers.

Regarding the paper by A.S. Watson, the comment was made that more thought should be directed towards the kind of marketing needed to promote agricultural development at an earlier stage. It was suggested that the rural assembly markets had been neglected and these were an essential instrument for change and progress. By affording access to large numbers of rural people, the market can be an economical natural integrator of a range of development activities.

Dr Watson, in reply, stated that he shared some of the scepticism expressed regarding the transfer of marketing institutions and felt that the FAO ought to consider documenting failure as well as success.

Participants in the discussion included M. G. Chandrakanth, R. R. Piggott and Robert Bohall.

# SECTION IV

## *Equity for Rural People*

NILS WESTERMARCK

# *Postwar Trends in Income Distribution and Dispersion in Profitability among Different Farm Groups*

Problems involved in income distribution among farmers can be examined from various aspects. Without any doubt we are faced by a wide spectrum of intricate and politically sensitive governmental actions but simultaneously the problems are intimately connected to natural conditions, progress in research, advisory services, human ability, educational level of the farmers and so on, and of course also to the implementation of land reforms. In order to make it possible to deal with the topic in a tolerable way I consciously confine my paper to developed countries only. My reasons for doing so are first the lack of empirical figures from developing countries for a long enough period and, secondly, the disturbing impact of more or less successfully implemented land reforms in the Third World which does not enable time period comparisons to be made. In short it exceeds my capacity to reproduce a global picture.

My main interest focuses around the problem whether, and if so to what extent, a trend towards a widening income gap between better-off and less well off groups of farmers has arisen within the decades since World War II. There exist in this respect at least two conflicting forces or phenomena, namely on one hand the research and technological development which logically has favoured farmers with better education, farmers provided with higher mental ability and larger amounts of economic resources, farmers operating farms situated in more fortunate natural regions, and so forth, versus farmers belonging to opposite categories. On the other hand, governments in many welfare countries have, particularly in the 1960s and 1970s, taken measures to level out the social and economic differences between the two categories.

An established element in the welfare policy of many developed countries is to support the low income groups of citizens with social and economic measures in order to bridge the gap between the poor and the well-to-do as well as to level regional disparities. Such a policy is in my opinion quite in conformity with endeavours towards equity and to warrant all citizens a satisfactory standard of living. Such a policy cannot, however, imply parity or equality such as to attain a similar income and welfare level for all people. Such a state of affairs is an utopian one and would certainly completely spoil the enterprising spirit of human beings, especially that of the entrepreneurs.

The aim with regional policy matters as to agriculture is at least in principle to bring forth an internal levelling of incomes between small and large farms and a geographical one between climatic zones, lowland and highland settlement, and so on. Since a considerable proportion of the activities in less-developed regions in welfare nations is related to agriculture and forestry, the population in those regions usually has a level of income falling below the national average income per caput.

The role of regional policy in general economic and social policy naturally varies from one country to another but the bases of regional development policy are similar: to promote a distribution of economic resources that is conducive to full employment and growth and which enables people living in different parts of the country to share in the general progress of the nation. The economic and social policy measures to remedy drawbacks may for instance imply subsidies for interest payments on loans for financing investment, transportation subsidies, higher prices for some products, state subsidized prices for purchased means of production, and so forth. It is a generally known phenomenon that research and development since the war have made tremendous achievements. Technological progress is always intimately related to the level of human knowledge and skill and to the degree of enthusiasm and belief in the future that inspires individuals but also to their physical capacity. The chief objective is that 'agricultural policy should be shaped so as to contribute to the realization of the general aims of the regional policy'. This means that agriculture must deliberately be guided in such a way as to alleviate the task of maintaining settlement especially in the least favoured areas; that is areas suffering from stagnation, depopulation, diminishing employment and with a low income level. The governments in many European high income countries have also taken action in order to stabilize the number of people involved in farming, including forestry, in the least favourable areas by stimulating investment increases first and foremost there. Referring to Leagans (1979, p. 50) of Cornell University, his compilation of data indicates that smallholders remain low income producers more because they lack the requisite means of production than because they are unwilling to make technical innovations when they first become available or profitable.

During the last three decades I have carried out three long series of research, partly in Finland and partly in Sweden, with the purpose of finding out the influence of the farmer's mental ability, his vocational theoretical education and his age on the economic results, as well as the effect of intensified advisory services and individual farm planning (Westermarck, 1974). The results from my Swedish study were, briefly, that in all size groups the net farm income, as well as the total net income, for the subgroup of farmers with at least agricultural vocational secondary school was higher than that of farmers with only formal primary school education.

Later on, two research projects of mine were carried out in Finland with the aim of elucidating the influence of intensified individual advisory services and farm planning on management and economic success on Finnish family farms. The research lasted fifteen years. For reasons of comparison, control farm groups located in the same region and belonging to similar size groups but without the same services had to be chosen. An examination of economic progress, whether on a basis of the total net income, the net farm income or the so-called coefficient of profitability, revealed that a marked successive improvement of profitability had taken place in the study farm groups but no corresponding development was seen in the control farm groups.

In a Norwegian investigation (1969) it was found out that farmers with agricultural school education carry on their farming operations more profitably than farmers without the corresponding education. It was, however, pointed out that other factors also exercise an influence on the results obtained.

The researches here mentioned are of course not the only ones carried out as regards the influence of education and mental ability on technological progress and income level. They have to be taken only as examples. My conclusion from the findings with relevance to this paper is, nevertheless, that intensified advisory services directed towards particular target groups as well as differences in the educational level and mental ability between groups contribute *ceteris paribus* to widen the income gap. We may also recall that in areas characterized as economically weak there is often a relatively low level of general and vocational training, especially among the older farm people.

Although the area of arable land is an incomplete expression of the size of a farm business unit it is nevertheless commonly used in official statistics. In proceeding further I also shall use this magnitude. In doing so the following question arises: to what extent do there exist differences as to the vocational educational level of farmers, mental ability, and economic resources between different size groups and particularly is it possible to establish that any trend has taken place during the postwar period either in one direction or another? Unfortunately the statistics on Finland are a very imperfect means of indicating a possible trend. We are therefore committed to one year only, namely 1976. The statistical figures comprising 320,000 farmers and farmers' wives show the following picture:

| Size Group | Farmers and farmers' wives with vocational theoretical education in per cent of total |
|---|---|
| < 10 hectares | 5.5 |
| 10-30 hectares | 16.0 |
| > 30 hectares | 33.2 |
| Total | 10.9 |

The figures clearly indicate that farm couples operating larger family farms possess a higher vocational theoretical level than farm couples on medium sized or small farms. Without any doubt we may state that this has also been the case previously. The wives have been included because they play a very significant role as partners in farming in Finland. Several investigations and surveys carried out in different countries indicate that a positive correlation exists between the use of advisory services and the farm size in hectares (Vainio-Mattila and Tauriainen, 1969; Hoiberg and Swope, 1979; Westermarck, H. 1973). As well as in vocational education so also in involvement in farm advisory services it is therefore obvious that the small farmers have been in an inferior situation. Disequilibrium as regards educational level and involvement in advisory services must, however, not *a priori* express differences in inherited mental ability. A chance to obtain education may very well depend simply on, for example, the existence of some private fortune or be insisted on by parents or other close associates.

Unfortunately I have, in spite of determined attempts, failed to receive any empirical material to elucidate the most interesting question as to the inherited mental ability of farmers operating farms of various size. Nevertheless, however, we may be able to accept the hypothesis that both theoretical vocational education practice outside the home farm and involvement in advisory services enrich the farmers' knowledge and capacities, provide new impulses, widen their views, and therefore provide a stimulus from an early stage to create higher potential capacities in the farmer as an entrepreneur and his willingness to accept benefits in research and new technology.

A very pessimistic opinion upon the situation prevailing among low-income farmers (individual gross sales under $10,000) as to their attitudes to extension's responsibility is expressed in the US report of the Extension Committee on Organization and Policy (1967). Some quotations from the report are elucidative: 'Low farm income stems from many causes. Without sufficient resources, and management skills to take advantage of modern agricultural technology, these farm families slip further and further into debt and despair. But in contrast to larger farm operators many understand neither the causes nor the possible solution to their farming problems. Moreover, they are generally not inclined to seek help from educational and government agencies. They also fail to understand that their net incomes will decline if they cease to improve their farming operations.'

The Nobel Prize winner Schultz (1978, p. 47) is very resolute in proclaiming his opinion as to the role of governmental policy measures and the influence of mental ability upon economic disequilibrium:

> The value of the ability to deal with disequilibria is high in a dynamic economy. In my opinion, two important inferences can be derived from the economic dynamics of agricultural modernization. First, economic disequilibria are inevitable. They cannot be prevented by law, by public policy, and surely not by rhetoric. Second, the function of farm entrepreneurs in perceiving, interpreting and responding to new and better opportunities cannot be performed efficiently by governments.

Taking into account what I have already here mentioned and bearing in mind the remarkable technological postwar development, it is logical to assume that technological development has favoured the already better-off and widened the economic disequilibrium. However, on the other hand we have to consider the contradictionary aspects, namely the governmental policy measures executed to level the disparities. How successful have these actions been and what is the final outcome of the phenomena? In tackling this complicated question I requested and also received empirical data and information from some developed countries which have taken measures to level the disparities. I wish to start with Finland.

In *Finland,* like in many other European countries, farm records are kept based on book-keeping. However, we have to recall that figures obtained from book-keeping farms do not constitute a statistically random sample of the great mass of farms because farm account activity is carried out by voluntary efforts. Consequently the participants must be considered on average somewhat more alert and prosperous than the great mass of farmers. This is of course a weakness which we, however, cannot keep away from in a free society. I am not speaking of accounts compulsorily kept for taxation purposes which are not applicable for representing the truly existing situation.

In order to illustrate the postwar development I have selected a rather homogenous and typical Finnish region, namely Central Finland, where almost all the farms regardless of size are family farms and the principal agricultural income is produced from livestock, mainly milk cattle husbandry.

| *Size group $<$ 10 ha* | 1959–61 | 1969–71 | 1977–79 |
|---|---|---|---|
| Number of farms | 120 | 55 | 22 |
| Net farm income, mk per ha | 552 | 656 | 2804 |
| Ditto per lu[1] | 2306 | 3087 | 14023 |
| Coefficient of profitability | 0.72 | 0.43 | 0.48 |
| *Size group $>$ 30 ha* | | | |
| Number of farms | 24 | 19 | 37 |
| Net farm income, mk per ha | 274 | 495 | 1618 |
| Ditto per lu[1] | 2158 | 6886 | 28253 |
| Coefficient of profitability | 0.88 | 1.14 | 0.93 |

[1] lu = one labour unit corresponding to 2000 work hours in agriculture per year

In comparing the figures for the two size groups the number of small farms during the last period unfortunately has considerably declined, due to several reasons, but mainly because of a shift over the part-time farming with lesser interest in agriculture proper or they have enlarged the acreage to exceed 10 ha. This diminishes to some extent the significance of a comparison in time. Nevertheless the tendency for a widened gap between the two groups in favour of the group with larger farms is clear. The coefficient of profitability is calculated by dividing the net farm income by an amount made up of an interest claim of five per cent for invested capital plus the value of the labour input of the farm entrepreneur and his family calculated at the normal wage rate for hired labour.

What measures then has the Finnish government executed to level the income gap? First, we may say that price policy has during the postwar period favoured livestock producers, who are predominantly small and medium-sized farmers. If we thus commence from a weighted index figure of 100 for all livestock producers during the first three-year-period of 1959-1961, the corresponding figure for the second period rises to 174 and for the last period to 449, and for milk separately to as high as 824. The corresponding rise in the nominal price index for food grains has simultaneously been as low as from 100 to 194. In spite of these facts we, therefore, have to conclude that the price policy measures have not been able to narrow the gap. We must, however, take into consideration the fact that the comparison includes only agriculture proper and not income from forestry or other sources. On the whole my paper deals with agriculture only because to take into account other sources of earnings also and to penetrate the influence of technological development in agriculture on incomes from forestry and so forth within the frame of empirical figures appears to me to be too complicated a topic. We may, therefore, say only that observations from many countries indicate that during the postwar decades small farmers are likely to earn more extras in addition to income from agriculture proper.

Secondly, a pervading phenomenon in Finland during the three last decades has been that several public measures to support agriculture, especially on the geographically less favoured small farms and farming in remote regions, have been strengthened. National budget calculations show that all support measures in total represented 2 per cent of the national gross agricultural income in 1969–61, the corresponding share in 1969–71 was 4 per cent, and in 1977–79 11 per cent. The main part of the support has been directed to the small farms in the remote regions. In order to get a clear picture of the magnitude of all special state support directed to individual farms, three different model farms have been constructed with the same production line, namely, mainly production of milk. The figures below illustrate the trend during the last three decades.

The figures clearly indicate, firstly, that the rate of subsidies has risen and, secondly, that the subsidy measures have particularly been directed to small farms in remote areas, as for instance northern Finland. As a corollary it has to be mentioned that in northern Finland practically no large farms exist. It must in this connection be stated that necessary as the measures to support the less developed areas and the small farms have been, they have brought about a surplus of live-stock products, especially milk, exceeding the domestic consumption. It is, however, not possible here to penetrate the complexity of all intricate matters involved in agricultural policy with subsidies and so on to get rid of the surplus. Each medal has at least two sides.

| | The share, in percent, of state subsidies in the gross return from agriculture | | | |
|---|---|---|---|---|
| | 1950 | 1960 | 1970 | 1980 |
| A small farm of 8 ha in northern Finland | 16 | 19 | 17 | 32 |
| A small farm of 8 ha in southern Finland | 1 | 1 | 5 | 18 |
| A large farm of 30 ha in southern Finland | 0 | 0 | 0 | 9 |

I now introduce to you findings from *Belgium* where Bublot (1974) and his colleagues have carried out several analyses dealing with the income dispersion on farms keeping accounts. During the period 1966–1970 the average income per labour unit increased yearly at the rate of 10.9 per cent. On a regional basis the annual growth rate varied from 12.5 to 7.4 per cent. The most interesting finding was that within the same region the situation was marked by a growing differentiation among its farmers. The regional distribution curve on income per labour unit was, however, characterized by a flattening trend. This phenomenon was interpreted in such a way that price policy in Belgium has had a marked effect in reducing income dispersion, whilst the changes in the technical conditions of production have had an opposite effect. Another Belgian, Thonon (1977, p. 137), reports as follows: 'Farm incomes fluctuate considerably from year to year, partly because of variations in the prices of inputs and outputs and partly due to changes in their volume. Although 66 per cent of the increase in the volume of production can be attributed to technological advance, it has had only a minor impact on the level of farm income due to the depressing effect of increased output on production prices'.

Sneesens (1979), also from Belgium, has analysed the dynamics of income dispersion between farms from 1962 to 1975 in the Belgian Loamy area. Among the determining factors are mentioned the development of the technical conditions of production and the price policies adopted. The results show that price policy had had a very marked effect in reducing income dispersion, whilst the changes in the technical conditions of production had had an opposite effect. Family income dispersion had overall been reduced by 5.1 per cent, which verifies the equalizing role price policy can play in agriculture. Sneesens emphasizes that the effect of price policy upon internal income distribution between farmers has often been under great criticism and much misgivings have been expressed. He states that public authorities had succeeded in favouring small farms by influencing price relationships. But he continues by mentioning that the use of relative prices to reduce inequalities is limited by the more or less rigid restrictions imposed by the need to maintain market equilibrium. The German von

Witzhe has severely criticized Sneesens' research for methodological reasons but it is not meaningful here to discuss the dispute between the two economists. (See the *European Review of Agricultural Economics,* Vol. 7, no. 1, 1980.)

In information obtained from *Austria* by correspondence it is pointed out that the income gap between the large and the small farms has widened in postwar years. This development is due to the fact that the large-scale farmers are more alert and have better possibilities to take advantage of modern technology. In other words, Austrian governmental measures to even the disparity have not been effective enough. A German investigation reported by Rintelen (1968) indicates that the income disparity in *West Germany* has become more acute, and provided all farms were run at maximum efficiency the disparity would be even greater. The reasons for the rapidly widening disparity are mainly that progress in agricultural engineering, in arable farming and crop cultivation as well as in the food processing industries, favours some particular districts and sizes of farm more than others.

*Switzerland* is, in Europe, traditionally considered the founder of introducing and pursuing farm accounting among farmers. The activity was commenced already in 1901 and has been ever since continued on a broad and systematically well developed basis. Simultaneously Switzerland is one of the most developed countries which has long traditions regarding the levelling off of regional income disparities in farming and rural areas, with substantial financial and social state support also in order to maintain settlement in remote mountain areas. The Secretariat of the Swiss Farmers Union has, at my request, put together for my disposal numerous valuable empirical figures from Swiss book-keeping farms for the period of 1946–79. It is neither possible nor relevant to give a comprehensive account of the report forwarded to me but it is of great value to give a summary. It indicates the interesting phenomenon that between farms of various sizes during the early postwar years the differences strongly grew but later on a tendency in a smoothing direction has come about. Two main causes for the latter phenomenon are stated, namely:

- a more intensive line of production on the small farms, with an increase in the number of livestock and cultivation of fruit, vegetables, and vineyards.
- the disappearance of numerous low income and less profitable small farms resulting in the survival of only the most progressive and profitable ones.

To what extent, however, is this phenomenon also due to governmental policy actions? In order to bridge the income gap between regions, or at least reduce it, the Federal Swiss Government supports agriculture at a high level. That the subsidies spent on the benefit of farming are very significant is clear when mentioning that in an investigation from 1976 around 25 per cent of the net farm income of the book-keeping farms located in the valley districts consisted of subsidies in one form or another, the corresponding figure for the book-keeping farms in the mountain districts was around 38 per cent. A policy along those lines must notwithstanding produce an effect; but how many countries can afford and are willing to sacrifice so much for agriculture and rural development?

The development in *Norwegian* agriculture is characterized by a somewhat similar trend as that in Switzerland with the exception of the northernmost and most unfavourable region of Norway where the gap throughout has widened. Thus in the more favourable districts the farm income per farm was on average for the group below 10 hectares 60 per cent of the corresponding income for the farm groups with 20-30 hectares in 1958-60, in 1968-70 it was 46 per cent, and in the period 1978–80, 55 per cent. Norwegian agricultural policy has during a long period of years endeavoured to prevent too strong a disparity and as far as possible to create equality and has thus partly succeeded. This was particularly the case in the 1970s.

From a very recent *Japanese* report ('The State of Japan's Agriculture', 1980) I cite the following statement:

> The number of small-scale farmers leasing their land to others has increased, strengthening their image as lenders of agricultural land. On the other hand large-scale farmers are renting more land, expanding their scale by this means. These trends can be attributed to the aging of the labor force, the widening of the gap in profitability by scale of the operation, and the gap between small-scale farms and large-scale ones has widened. This is a reflection of an increase in profitability of the greater mechanization and integration of rice cultivation under way in larger farms.

What conclusions may we then draw from the material collected and the statements received from the seven developed countries discussed here? Has the income gap between the better-off and the worse-off groups of farmers increased within the decades since World War II or not? Within the frame of findings from the countries referred to, the reports from four countries denote that technological development has been conducive to widening the gap. Public measures have not managed to mitigate this cleft. Only in Switzerland and partly in Norway and perhaps also in Belgium have governmental actions to support small farmers and farmers in remote regions, in order to smooth the gap, borne fruit. Such an achievement has, however, been possible only because government has during a long period of time with considerable and single-minded action supported the worse-off groups of farmers.

## REFERENCES

Extension Committee on Organization and Policy, Report of the Project III Committee, Washington DC, 1967.

Norges Landbruksökonomiske Institutt, Yrkesutdanning og lönnsomhet i jordbruket, Saermelding No. 12, 1969.

Schweizerisches Bauernsekretariat, Die Einkommensdisparität in der Schweizerischen Landwirtschaft, Probleme und Lösungsmöglichkeiten, (Mim.) Brugg, 1979.
Einkommenunterschiede in der Landwirtschaft (Mim.) Brugg, 1981.
The Ministry of Agriculture, Forestry and Fisheries. 'The State of Japan's Agriculture 1980', A Summary Report (Mim.), Tokyo, 1981.
Bublot, G., *Economie de la Production Agricole,* Louvain, 1974
Hoiberg, E. and Swope, C., *Iowa Farm Families Use of Extension,* Co-operative Extension Service, Iowa State University Pm-876 February 1979.
Leagans, P., *Adoption of Modern Agricultural Technology by Small Farm Operators: An Interdisciplinary Model for Researchers and Strategy Builders,* Cornell International Agricultural Mim., New York, 1979.
Rintelen, P., 'Die Einkommendisparität in der deutschen landwirtschaft und ihre ursachen', *Agrarwirtschaft,* Vol. 17, No. 8, 1968.
Schultz, T.W., *Politics versus Economics in Food and Agriculture,* Princeton University Press, 1978.
Sneesens, J-F., 'Dynamics of Farm Income Dispersion in the Belgian Loamy Region', *Eur. R. Agr. Eco.,* Vol. 6, No. 2., 1974.
Thonon, A., 'Technological Progress and Price Variations, and Their Effect on Farm Incomes in Belgium, 1954 to 1972', *Eur. R. agr. Eco.,* Vol. 4, No. 2, 1977.
Vainio-Mattila, I. and Tauriainen, J., *Maataloudellisen neuvonnan tarkoituksenmukaisuutta ja alueellista organisaatiota koskeva tutkimus* (Mim.) Helsinki, 1969.
Westermarck, N., 'Peer Farmers' Role in the Adoption of Recommended Practices', *Acta Agraria Fennica* 129, 1973.
Westermarck, N., 'The Influence of Certain Entrepreneurial Variables on Economic Success in Farming', *Eur. R. Agr. Eco.,* Vol. 1, No. 4, 1974.
Von Witzhe, H., 'Dynamics of Farm Income Dispersion: A Comment', *Eur. R. Agr. Eco.,* Vol. 7, No. 1, 1980.

## DISCUSSION OPENING – G. BUBLOT

I shall open the discussion with seven comments which I will try to present very briefly.

1 It is difficult to *establish* in a rigorous way the dispersion of farm income and its trend over time. The economist has access to accounting data from a very limited number of farms constituting a sample which is hardly ever drawn up according to the requirements of statistical analysis.

The studies cited by Professor N. Westermarck show a remarkable number of similarities. In the European countries to which the cited works refer, as well as in Japan, it is observed that there is a clear trend towards a wider dispersion of farm incomes over time.

2 The latter, difficult to establish, is yet more difficult to *interpret,* because it is the result of many causes, among which are the region, the main production activities of the farms and their size, the level of farm education and management. Moreover, they operate together, that is in an indissociable and simultaneous way, which makes it difficult to identify their individual effects and, as a consequence, to know exactly where the cause of the observed phenomenon lies.

3 The formulation of the problem implies that at any time, *farm incomes are subject to some dispersion.* This is a manifestation of the

persisting extreme diversity in the conditions of agricultural production and comes from the fact that the greatest share of this – soil, fertility, situation, size, aptitude, and so on – accrues to the farmer.

4 Professor Westermarck strongly emphasizes the *importance of the human factor* as an explanatory element of the differences between farm incomes. It is often observed in the countries of Western Europe that the oldest farmers have the smallest farms, the worst education and the lowest incomes. But the opportunity cost of their labour is similarly the lowest and the differences between incomes would be much less if these were expressed, not in absolute terms, but in comparison with the real opportunity cost of the farmer's labour.

The same may be said so far as the regions are concerned: the farmers' incomes are often lowest in the regions which are less developed in economic terms. The regional differences between incomes would be less if the latter were expressed in terms of the opportunity cost of labour in the regions being compared.

5 In most of the studies cited, *mechanical progress* is considered to be an important cause of the increasing dispersion of farmers' incomes. The most efficient techniques are adopted at a greater rate than that at which the outdated ones are removed. The adoption of a high yielding machine is not accompanied by the immediate disappearance of machines with lower perfomances. As a result a growing dispersion in the capacity of the machines being used is observed and, as a consequence, an increasing dispersion of working times required by the different production activities and, ultimately, of output and income per man. Now, other things being equal, especially the region and the production activity, the material costs per hectare are no greater in the large farms than in the small ones. The former thus benefit, at no greater cost, from the enormous possibilities of mechanization, which would then explain to a great extent the increase in income dispersion.

6 From a broader point of view, this is only one facet of the *increasing differentiation between farms,* a process by which they become more and more different, not only as regards materials used and revenues received, but also regarding the choice of types of production. The investments are becoming so heavy and so specific, that farms can no longer equip themselves for a wide range of production activities; they therefore reduce their range of activities, specialize, and, as a result, see the level of their income and its evolution over time conditioned by factors specific to each activity.

7 The increasing dispersion of incomes is full of implications for *agricultural policy.* Some measures tend to reduce it, such as assistance to small farmers and to less favoured regions; also the growth of progressive taxation, in countries where it is observed. But the impact of price policy is more controversial. It is a matter of fact that the fundamental option of agricultural policy is a choice of the best compromise between attaining income parity and the efficient allocation of resources. But whatever form they take, agricultural policy measures

should be based upon a clear definition of the objectives to be achieved which probably requires a clearer notion of equity. I express here a personal opinion that the present conference has not adequately defined this concept. Doubtless economists hesitate to define and to clarify a concept presenting many facets which are not purely of an *economic* nature, like social ethics, distributive justice, welfare and so forth.

In conclusion, the dispersion of incomes irresistibly bring to mind the image of athletes engaged in an unending competition which increasingly accentuates the differences between the positions of each of them, notwithstanding the continuous elimination of those at the rear.

The attention paid to income dispersion in the developed countries has its roots in the fast and irreversible transformation of peasant agriculture into farm businesses and the pre-eminence of income considerations which this involves. It seems also that income dispersion is increasing in the developing countries; but farmers there are less sensitive to income, and conditions are less conducive to perceiying and measuring it.

As with many works, the excellent essay of synthesis of Professor Westermarck's asks more questions than it answers. By this fact it must enrich discussion and open the way to further research.

SABURO YAMADA

# *Intersectoral Inequalities between Agriculture and Non-agriculture: Implications of the Japanese Experience*

## INTRODUCTION

Intersectoral inequalities or income disparities between the agricultural and non-agricultural sectors have been much discussed by agricultural economists since the subject was first raised by Petty (1690) nearly 300 years ago. Drawing from the scanty empirical evidence available up to that time Petty concluded that 'there is much more to be gained by manufacture than husbandry, and by merchandise than manufacture'. Later, Clark called this 'Petty's Law'. He devoted himself to collecting empirical evidence for many countries relating to the law, and found general patterns of structural changes in connection with intersectoral inequalities as well as with the process of economic development (Clark, 1951). There has been much discussion on income disparities between farmers, or rural people, and non-agricultural workers, or urban people, in relation to out-migration from the agricultural sector to the non-agricultural sector, or referring to rural poverty and income distribution problems (Schultz, 1953; Bellerby, 1956; Lewis, 1958; Fei and Ranis, 1964; and Schuh, 1982).

Intensive empirical studies on changes in the intersectoral inequality of output per worker as well as in the structural transformation in the course of Modern Economic Growth (MEG) were made by Kuznets (1963 and 1971). From those studies, which covered mainly the Western developed countries, he derived an important hypothesis that income inequality tended to widen in the early phase of MEG, then narrowed in the later phase. This the well known 'Kuznets' U-shape curve'. If this law can be applied to contemporary developing countries, the inequality which is one of the important problems of their economic and social development must necessarily occur there. How about the actual performance? Empirical studies covering developing countries were undertaken by Chenery and Syrquin (1975) and Ahluwalia (1976). Although the curve was confirmed using cross-section data, historical evidence using time series data is still not clear-cut.

To obtain a better perspective on the trends of changes in inequality and various related aspects for contemporary developing countries, Japan's long-term experience, for which quantitative data have been estimated and analysed by Ohkawa and his associates (Ohkawa and Shinohara, 1979), may present a good 'bridge' between the developing and developed countries, because it is a record of a latecomer with surplus labour in an earlier period of MEG under unfavourable resource endowments (man/land ratio), which characterize a majority of contemporary developing nations particularly in Asia.

The purpose of this paper is to provide internationally transferrable knowledge on the secular trends in intersectoral inequalities and related factors in the course of MEG, which may be derived from the Japanese historical experience.

## ANALYTICAL FRAMEWORK

### *Concepts of intersectoral inequalities*

Three kinds of intersectoral inequalities are to be focused on in this paper: (a) inequalities in output (GDP) per worker; (b) inequalities in personal factor income per worker; and (c) inequalities in per caput income between farm and non-farm households. Wage differentials are not discussed explicitly. These concepts will be discussed, using both real and nominal prices respectively. Indicators of inequalities are measured as the ratios of various economic variables between the two groups. The agricultural sector or farm households will be used as the bases or denominators of these ratios.

Differences in output per worker are the most conventional indicators of inequality based upon aggregate macro statistics. *Output per worker in real terms* can be considered as a simple rough indicator of partial average labour productivity without making any adjustments for changes or differences in labour days or hours, quality, and composition. It may indicate the level of technology by sector in a crude sense. *Output per worker in nominal terms* reflects changes in terms of trade as well as real productivity among the sectors. In general, a higher rate of productivity increase in a sector leads to lower prices relative to the other sectors if the markets work competitively. Thus, the inequality in this concept tends to change more slowly than the real productivity gaps between the sectors. A price support for a less productive sector brings about the same effect. The sectors to be compared are the agricultural sector and the non-agricultural sector, but this will be defined more precisely later on.

*Personal income per worker* means labour income per worker for the non-agricultural sector and the sum of labour income and land rent per worker for the agricultural sector. In Japan agricultural land belongs to the farmers themselves or landlords-cum-cultivators in general, except for a particular period to be referred to later. Thus, farmers' income is a mixed income of imputed wage and rent. To get these factor incomes, sectoral output was multiplied by their respective factor shares.

*Per caput household income* is income per caput, including income from the major occupation and side-jobs by all the family members as well as from asset ownership. The households being compared are farm households on the one hand and non-farm households on the other. Households are basic units, particularly in rural areas, both for production and consumption. In general, consumer prices differ between rural and urban areas. Such price differentials as well as price changes are adjusted in the case of *per caput household income in real terms,* so that this indicator must be more appropriate than the nominal term figures to compare income disparities between the two types of household in a real sense.

*Dualistic growth and sector classification*

In explaining the Japanese experience of intersectoral inequalities, the concept of 'dualistic growth', that is the co-existence of 'modern' and 'traditional' sectors (Ohkawa, 1972), is applied here. 'In the Japanese economy, modern sectors are those which use techniques and forms of organization imported from the West. Traditional sectors employ techniques and organization indigenous to Japan' (Ohkawa and Rosovsky, 1968). The classification of sectors of the economy in this paper follows Ohkawa as well as Kuznets (1971). Agriculture, forestry, and fisheries are treated as typical traditional sectors and are called the 'A sector'. Manufacturing, mining, construction, transportation, communications and public utilities are considered as typical modern sectors and are called the 'M sector'. The remaining part of the sector is called the 'S sector' which has mixed characteristics. The non-agricultural sector which consists of M and S sectors is termed the 'NA sector'.

The traditional versus modern dichotomy in the literature has mainly referred to differences in production techniques. In addition, however, I would like to stress the co-existence of 'different ways or preferences of living' between rural and urban people, which can be considered as an additional aspect of the traditional-modern thesis. The traditional ways of living would prefer relatively indigenous living standards, a self-sufficient subsistent life, and a mutually helping large family size depending on inherited asset bases. In contrast, the modern way of living would prefer Western standards, a purchasing-base life, and independent small family size depending on recently acquired asset bases. Such contrasting characteristics of two types of life styles would be common in the earlier period of economic development. In this regard, farm households could be expected to typify traditional ways of living while urban worker households those of modern ways of living. Farmers' traditional behaviour, referring not only to production aspects but also to life style preferences, will be used to explain the existence of wide intersectoral inequalities later on.

*Phasing of the dualistic growth*

A phasing approach, namely, demarcating the entire period of modern economic growth into identifiable and relatively unified phases of growth, is useful not only in examining the modern Japanese experience but also in making Japan's historical experience internationally transferrable. In considering the changes in relative growth rate and share of the A sector in the economy, labour market conditions in the A sector, and structural transformation, three phases of economic growth are defined based upon Ohkawa's various studies, as well as Minami's (1973) and Yamada's (1980).

## JAPANESE HISTORICAL EXPERIENCE

*Phases of Japan's dualistic growth*

*Phase I:* 1885/89 to 1915/19. Modern economic growth emerged in this phase as indicated by a sustained high growth rate of the M sector as seen in Table 1 (Ohkawa and Rosovsky, 1965). However, the shares of the A sector in the total number of workers and in GDP were still high, the growth rate of the A sector was relatively high compared to later periods and accelerated through technological development in agriculture (Hayami, et

TABLE 1 *Salient characteristics of the Japanese economy by phases*

(in per cent)

| | Phase I | | Phase II | | Phase III |
|---|---|---|---|---|---|
| | Ia<br>1885/89<br>to<br>1905/09 | Ib<br>1905/09<br>to<br>1915/19 | IIa<br>1915/19<br>to<br>1935/39 | IIb<br>1955/59<br>to<br>1960/64 | 1960/64<br>to<br>1975/79 |
| Growth rate of GDP | | | | | |
| Total | 3.4 | 3.9 | 3.3 | 10.1 | 7.9 |
| A Sector[1] | 1.5 | 2.3 | 0.7 | 1.8 | 1.4 |
| M Sector[1] | 6.1 | 6.5 | 6.2 | 17.1 | 9.6 |
| Growth rate of workers | | | | | |
| A Sector | 0.1 | −0.7 | −0.4 | −2.9 | −4.9 |
| M Sector | 1.5 | 3.2 | 1.8 | 4.6 | 2.1 |
| Growth rate of prices | | | | | |
| A Sector | 5.1 | 6.2 | 1.3 | 4.6 | 7.8 |
| M Sector | 3.5 | 6.3 | −0.0 | 0.7 | 4.3 |
| Share of A sector[2] | | | | | |
| in Total Workers | 73–67 | 67–58 | 58–45 | 37–30 | 30–12 |
| in GDP | 43–36 | 36–31 | 31–18 | 15–10 | 10–5 |

*Sources:* Ohkawa and Shinohara, 1979; *Labour Force Survey,* 1980; and *Annual Report on National Accounts,* 1981.

*Notes:* [1] See the text for definitions of the A and M sectors.

[2] Two figures mean changes from the first at the beginning period to the last at the end period.

al., 1975). Phase I may be characterized as a phase of dualistic growth in which the development of the modern sector was heavily dependent on the positive performance of the traditional sector. This phase is divided into two sub-phases, *Phase Ia* (1885/89 to 1905/09) and *Phase Ib* (1905/09 to 1915–19). The major difference between them is growth in number of workers in the A sector: number of workers was increasing in Phase Ia but decreased in Phase Ib. Such change was important as 'the first turning point of the labour market conditions' in the traditional sector. However, the essential characteristic of the entire Phase I was still that of 'labour suplus' or 'unlimited supplies of labour'.

*Phase II:* 1915/19 to 1960/64. the M sector maintained sustained growth during this phase, though interrupted by World War II. But the A sector stagnated significantly in the prewar sub-phase, Phase IIa (1915/19 to 1935/39). As industries rapidly developed, opportunities for non-farm investments increased, and the shift from 'innovation landlords' to 'parasitic landlords' progressed in this period (Hayami, et al., 1975). Under this situation, the rate of technological progress in agriculture slowed, being discouraged in particular by the increasing inflow of cheap rice from colonies and by the unfavourable terms of trade for agriculture during the Great Depression. In Phase IIb (1955/59 to 1960/64), the postwar economic spurt occurred. The growth rate of the M sector was extremely high at 17 per cent per annum, while that of the A sector remained less than 2 per cent. Labour inflow to the NA sector from the A sector began to increase and by the end of this phase, surplus labour in the A sector disappeared. There is a consensus that the period around 1960/64 was 'the second turning point of the labour market', from the phase of unlimited supplies of labour to the phase of limited supplies of labour (Minami, 1973). Phase II is characterized as a phase of dualistic growth where the modern sector achieved an accelerated sustained growth leaving the traditional sector behind, which resulted in significant structural transformation during the period (Table 1).

*Phase III:* 1960/64 to 1975/79 (onward). The growth rate of the M sector in this phase was not as high as in the previous phase but still remained at a high level of about 10 per cent in spite of the oil crises and the world economic depression. But growth in the A sector was low. Consequently, the outflow of labour from the A sector increased and the number of workers in the A sector decreased by about 5 per cent per annum under the condition of limited supply of labour. Thus, the agrarian structure as well as agricultural technology have been fundamentally altered by development in the A sector. Phase III can be characterized as a phase of dualistic growth where the traditional sector is forced to transform by the modern sector's development under conditions of limited supply of labour.

### *Inequalities in output per worker between agriculture and non-agriculture*

The ratio of output per worker between the M and A sectors in real terms (the real M/A ratio), which is a rough indicator of productivity differences between the M and A sectors, shows an increasing trend in both the pre and post-war periods (Table 2, Panel A). This implies that the productivity gaps between the modern and traditional sectors have widened as a whole. This trend was significant in Phases Ia and II. In Phase Ia the number of agricultural workers increased and the rise in agricultural productivity remained relatively small. In Phase IIa agricultural growth slowed and in

TABLE II *Selected indicators of intersectoral inequalities, Japan*

(in per cent)

| | Phase I | | | Phase II | | | Phase III |
|---|---|---|---|---|---|---|---|
| | Ia | | Ib | IIa | | IIb | |
| | 1885/89 | 1905/09 | 1915/19 | 1935/39 | 1955/59 | 1960/64 | 1975/79 |
| A Ratios of output per worker | | | | | | | |
| M/A, real | 1.5 | 2.8 | 2.8 | 5.1 | 2.0 | 2.7 | 3.0 |
| M/A, nominal | 2.4 | 3.3 | 3.4 | 4.8 | 3.6 | 4.1 | 2.8 |
| NA/A, real | 3.7 | 4.2 | 3.6 | 4.1 | 2.8 | 3.2 | 2.8 |
| NA/A, nominal | 3.5 | 3.6 | 3.0 | 3.7 | 3.2 | 3.8 | 2.7 |
| B Ratios of factor income per worker | | | | | | | |
| NA'/A', nominal | 2.7 | 2.6 | 2.2 | 2.5 | 2.6 | 3.0 | 2.3 |
| C Ratios of household income per caput | | | | | | | |
| NF/F, nominal | 1.9 | 2.2 | 2.1 | 3.0 | 1.4 | 1.4 | 0.9 |
| NF/F, real | 1.3 | 1.5 | 1.4 | 2.1 | 1.2 | 1.3 | 0.8 |

*Sources:* The same sources as Table 1; Otsuki and Takamatsu, 1978; Minami, 1981; Yamada, 1980; *Farm Household Economic Surveys,* various issues; and *Family Income and Expenditure Survey 1963-1980,* 1981.
*Note:* See the text for explanation of each ratio and the meaning of M, A, NA, NF and F. Real terms data were obtained by deflating nominal data by respective price deflations for which base years were 1934/36 for data before World War II and 1975 for data after the war.

Phase IIb the industrial spurt was so big that agricultural improvement could not catch up. In contrast agricultural improvement slowed down in Phases Ib and III. In Phase Ib agricultural development was significant and in Phase III agricultural mechanization, which led to productivity increases for agriculture, was induced by the substantial labour outflow from the A sector to the M sector.

Since the terms of trade have changed favourably for the A sector against the M sector during the entire period, the rise in the nominal M/A ratio was much smaller than the real M/A ratio in Phases I and II. Significantly, the nominal M/A ratio declined distinctly in Phase III, which was brought about mainly by the high price support policy for agricultural commodities in this period.

The ratios of output per worker between the NA (= M + S) and A sectors (the NA/A ratios) both in nominal and real terms have different trends than the M/A ratios. Changes in these ratios were much smaller than for the M/A ratios and show no particular secular trends for the entire period.

The S/A ratios had declining trends (not presented in Table 2) and the NA/A ratios are the weighted average of the trends of the M/A and S/A ratios. This may imply that the mixed characteristics of the S sector have stabilized the expanding inequality between the M sector, a typical modern sector, and the A sector, a typical traditional sector. It should be noted, however, that the intersectoral inequalities in output per worker between the A and NA sectors narrowed not only in Phase III but also even in Phase Ib.

The most important finding is the fact that sharp declines appeared in the nominal M/A and NA/A ratios during Phase III. Thus, the 'Kuznets' U-shape curve', has occurred for the Japanese economy at least in nominal terms recently.

*Relatively stable intersectoral gaps in personal income per worker*

Output per worker is not the same as labour return per worker because output contains interest on capital and land rent as well as returns to labour. Thus, factor shares should be taken into consideration in comparing the levels of personal earnings per worker by different sectors. The labour share of the NA sector had a distinct declining trend in the prewar period, then levelled off after the war (Minami, 1981), while the labour share was rather stable for agriculture for the entire period (Yamada, 1980). Farmers or landlords-cum-cultivators received not only their labour return but also land rent as well. Thus, land rent is also added to their personal income. But the rent received by absentee-landlords must be omitted from the income of the A sector. It is impossible to estimate such rents precisely for all periods. I made a tentative estimate only for Phase IIa when absentee landlords were significant, as stated earlier. The figures NA'/A' in Panel B in Table 2 are the adjusted ratios of NA/A in Panel A to compare such personal income between the NA and A sectors. Note that the adjusted ratios become small and stable except for 1960/64. Income gaps per worker between the NA and A sectors are smaller and more stable than indicated from the conventional ratios of output per worker.

*Per caput income disparities: an explanation by traditional behaviour of farmers*

As observed in the above section, there have been sizable productivity gaps between the A and NA sectors in all the phases of dualistic growth in Japan. Even though the adjusted ratios of factor income per worker are much smaller than the productivity ratios, these ratios show that NA ratios are more than twice those for the A sector for the entire period. Why and how did such significant intersectoral inequalities continue to exist for such a long time? One explanation is the 'traditional behaviour' of farmers and their families. To compensate for low productivity or low earning per worker in the A sector, it has been common for wives, older family members, and even children to work on the farm, particularly in the prewar period. In this period, the average number of farm workers per farm household was 2.5 persons. They worked not only on the farm but also in off-farm jobs, if such employment opportunities existed. In the prewar period, however, there were not many such job opportunities in rural areas. Many rural youngsters left home to work in urban areas and sent remittances to their parents. But the job opportunities in urban areas were not enough to absorb all excess rural labourers so that many people remained in rural areas as 'surplus labour' in Phases I and II. The share of the income from off-farm jobs in the total farm household income is estimated as about one-fourth in the 1930s. In the post-war period it has increased continuously reaching three-quarters of the total income in 1980. This has been brought about by the significant expansion of off-farm job opportunities even in rural areas along with the post-war economic growth. At present 'part-time family farming' is one of the significant characteristics of Japanese agriculture (Kada, 1980). By working more total hours than non-farm people, farm household income was raised to some extent in the prewar period and to a greater extent in the post-war period. However, since the family size of the farm households has always been larger than the non-farm households, income per caput has been lower in the farm households than in the non-farm households.

How have the disparities in income per caput between the farm and non-farm households changed in the past? A problem is that there are few reliable data to examine this question for the prewar period. For the post-war period we have randomly sampled household economic surveys, by which we measure the income gaps. For the prewar period, however, there were no such data available and we have to resort to data estimated using simplifying assumptions. In this paper I have utilized the estimates by Otsuki and Takamatsu (1978). These are not adjusted for differences in family size and in price levels between the farm and non-farm households, for which I have made the adjustments. The series of the ratios of income per caput between the farm and non-farm households thus adjusted are presented in Panel C in Table 2 as the nominal and real NF/F ratios.

The real NF/F ratios, which adjust both the family size and the rural-urban price differentials, reveal that the gaps are not as large as indicated in Panels A and B, and are rather stable around 1.3 to 1.5 during Phases I and II, except for 1935/39. These levels and patterns are very close to those of personal consumption per caput estimated by Ohkawa (1973). In 1975/79. the ratios became less than 1.0, which means that per caput income of farm households has exceeded the incomes of non-farm households in Phase III. This might be reflected by an increase in urban to rural migration of people who recently came back from urban areas to their native rural areas. The appearance of such reverse indication of income per caput between the farm and non-farm households must correspond to the observed u-shape curve phenomena in output per worker. Except for the 1975/79 case, there have always been differences in income per caput between farm and non-farm households. How can sustained gaps be explained? The existence of 'traditional behaviour' of farmers can explain them to a considerable extent.

For the majority of farmers, who are used to living in rural areas according to their traditional ways, there must be a preference for living in rural areas rather than to move from there to urban areas, even if there exist monetary income differences between the two areas. It is difficult to estimate such preferences empirically. Of course, some of the younger generation would have no such preference so that they might be eager to find jobs in urban areas. But as the mode of the majority of rural people in the prewar period in particular, such preference should exist under associated various social and institional circumstances (Bellerby, 1956). We may assume that the rather stable levels of 1.3 to 1.5 in the real NF/F ratios we have seen in the prewar period might be reflecting the fact that there would be a kind of socially genuine equilibrium situation existing between rural and urban people which acted as a social stabilizer in the prewar period, except for Phase IIa in which the ratio increased substantially.

## CONCLUSIONS: IMPLICATIONS OF THE JAPANESE EXPERIENCE

After World War II many countries became independent. At that time their economies and societies were essentially 'traditional', but soon after 'modern' sectors were established and developed along with the international transfer of technology and capital. Thus, 'dualistic growth' started there some time after their independence. The patterns of the growth are not necessarily the same for each country because their initial conditions and development strategies were not the same. However, there are some common economic characteristics, particularly in Asia and Africa: these are the large agricultural share in the economy, unfavourable man/land ratios, high population pressure, and the existence of large technological backlog transferable from abroad.

What changes have appeared in the intersectoral inequalities there under these conditions in the past? There is evidence to indicate that the productivity gaps between the A and M sectors, or the traditional and modern sectors, have widened in most Asian countries during the past two decades (Yamada, 1981). Such expanding gaps were smaller in nominal terms because the terms of trade have changed in favour of the A sector in many cases during the same period. These changes are consistent with the Japanese experience we have observed above. During the period income disparities per caput between the F and NF households had no particular trend in the case of Taiwan, China (Kuznets, 1980) and the disparities fluctuated along with the changes in policies in the case of Korea, according to official statistics. These two economies are relatively developed, but have not yet entered Phase III, though their own development phases do not necessarily correspond to the Japanese experience.

Some implications can be drawn from the Japanese experience to obtain a better perspective on the trends in the intersectoral inequalities in the contemporary developing countries. These are as follows (using the terminologies in Table 2):

1 The real M/A ratios will continue to widen, while the nominal M/A ratios will widen more slowly than the real ratios because of favourable changes in the terms of trade for the A sector. However, the rates of change will differ according to their different phases. The key factors are the trends in changes in agricultural workers and agricultural development relative to industrial growth.

2 The NA/A ratios will show more moderate changes than the M/A ratios because of the mixed effects of the changes in S/A ratios which will differ by countries.

3 The NA'/A' ratios will show more moderate changes than the NA/A or M/A ratios. These ratios will be rather stable in many countries.

4 The real NF/F ratios will be stable in most countries; but in some countries, such as NICs, these may fluctuate according to the rapidity of structural transformation and development policies, particularly price policies. However, if some countries fail in appropriate agricultural development corresponding to population growth and general economic development, the ratios will increase.

5 The traditional behaviour of farmers and rural people and their off-farm jobs should not be disregarded in social stabilization in order to offset the possible income inequalities generated from economic growth. In relation to this issue, the healthy development of farm households or family farming units in rural areas, not only in production aspects but also in living or consumption aspects, is imperative.

## REFERENCES

Ahluwalia, M., 'Inequality, Poverty and Development', *Journal of Development Economics,* Vol. 3, No. 3, December 1976.

Bellerby, J. R., *Agriculture and Industry Relative Income,* Macmillan, London, 1956.

Chenery, H. and Syrquin, M., 3Patterns of Development, 1950–1970, Oxford University Press, 1975.

Clark, C., *The Conditions of Economic Progress,* Macmillan, London (2nd ed), 1951.

Fei, John C. H. and Ranis, Gustav, *Development of the Labor Surplus Economy: Theory and Policy,* Illinois, Richard D. Irwin, 1964.

Hayami, Y., in association with Akino, M., Shintani, M., and Yamada, S., *A Century of Agricultural Growth in Japan: Its Relevance to Asian Development,* University of Tokyo Press, 1975.

Kada, R., *Part-time Family Farming: Off-farm Employment and Farm Adjustments in the United States and Japan,* Centre of Academic Publications Japan, Tokyo, 1980.

Kuznets, S., 'Quantitative Aspects of the Economic Growth of Nations: VIII Distribution of Income by Size', *Economic Development and Cultural Change,* Vol. XI, No. 2, January 1963.

Kuznets, S., *Economic Growth of Nations: Total Output and Production Structure,* Harvard University Press, 1971.

Kuznets, S., 'Notes on Income Distribution in Taiwan', in Klein, L. R., Nerlove, M., and Tsiang, S. C. (eds), *Quantitative Economics and Development: Essays in Memory of Ta-Chung Liu,* Academic Press, New York, 1980.

Lewis, W. Arthur, 'Unlimited Labour: Further Notes', *Manchester School of Economics and Social Studies,* January 1958.
Minami, R., *The Turning Point in Economic Development: Japan's Experience,* Kinokuniya, Tokyo, 1973.
Minami, R., *Nihon no Keizaihatten (Economic Development of Japan),* Toyokeizai Shimposha, Tokyo, 1981.
Ohkawa, K., *Seikatsu Suijun no Sokutei (Measurement of Living Standard),* Iwanami. Tokyo, 1953.
Ohkawa, K., and Rosovsky, H., 'A Century of Japanese Economic Growth', in W. Lockwood (ed.) *The State and Economic Enterprise in Japan,* Princeton University Press, 1965.
Ohkawa, K., 'Postwar Japanese Growth in Historical Perspective: A Second Look', in L. Klein and K. Ohkawa (eds), *Economic Growth: The Japanese Experience Since the Meiji Era,* Richard D. Irwin, Homewood, 1968.
Ohkawa, K., *Differential Structure and Agriculture: Essays on Dualistic Growth,* Kinokuniya, Tokyo, 1972.
Ohkawa, K., 'Personal Consumption in Dualistic Growth', in K. Ohkawa and Y. Hayami (eds), *Economic Growth: The Japanese Experience since the Meiji Era,* The Japan Economic Research Centre, Tokyo, February 1973.
Ohkawa, K., and Shinohara, M. (eds), *Patterns of Japanese Economic Development: A Quantitative Appraisal,* Yale University Press, 1979.
Otsuki, T., and Takamatsu, N., *An Aspect of the Size Distribution of Income in Prewar Japan,* International Development Centre of Japan, June 1978.
Petty, W., *Political Arithmetik,* R. Clavel and H. Mrtlock, London, 1690.
Schuh, G.E., 'Out-migration, Rural Productivity, and the Distribution of Income', in R. H. Sabot (ed), *Migration and the Labor Market in Developing Countries,* Westview Press, Boulder, Colorado, 1982.
Schultz, T.W., *The Economic Organization of Agriculture,* McGraw-Hill, New York, 1953.
Yamada, S., 'The Secular Trends in Input-Output Relations of Agricultural Production in Japan, 1878–1978', paper presented at the Conference on Agricultural Development in China, Japan and Korea, Taipei, December 1980.
Yamada, S., 'Generality and Regional Speciality in Economic Development: A Comparative Study of Economic Development in Asian Countries, 1960–1978' (in Japanese), *The Memoirs of the Institute of Oriental Culture,* No. 87, The University of Tokyo, November 1981.

## DISCUSSION OPENING – PHILIPPE LACOMBE

The paper given by our colleague Mr Yamada seems to me to be an excellent example of quantitative history, allowing both the relative importance and the performance of the agricultural sector to be viewed in perspective. In respect of various sectors of the Japanese economy and of different phases of the nation's economic history, Mr Yamada has examined a synthesis of the economic indicators for productivity and for the returns per worker or per family. Through this long-term study, we are able to follow the way in which disparities developed, whether of productivity or of return, and to examine the factors which gave rise to them, on the basis of the relationship between agriculture and the economy as a whole.

This study can therefore be seen as belonging to that category concerned with inter-sector relations. Mr Yamada himslef relies upon it in seeking particularly to prove the hypothesis that disparities were somewhat accentuated at the beginning of the process of economic development, followed by a subsequent reduction. The whole of the research was carried out with the aim of being able to transfer the knowledge gained to other situations.

Based as it is on quantitative data, this study calls in the first instance for some observations on the statistics used in it. We would do well to look on the one hand at the alleged disparities and, on the other, at the explanation put forward for their persistence. Finally, we need to ask ourselves some questions about the possible general applicability of these results.

### *1 The statistical questions*

My comments can be summarized under three headings, as follows:
(a) Only mean averages are examined. Perhaps because of the impossibility of doing so, Mr Yamada does not at any point consider those factors which indicate dispersion: these would have been extremely useful, in the first place for showing the significance of the averages and, secondly, in looking at the reproduction of the disparities revealed in terms of those averages.
(b) To clarify reality, Mr Yamada makes adjustments to his statistical series. These adjustments, justifiable in intention, are in fact difficult to achieve. If we look only at the case of returns on land: part of this is derived from non-farming owners, whilst another fraction is incorporated with the return on the labour of working farmers. Mr Yamada goes on to estimate this return and the way in which it is divided up. The analysis is thus concerned with returns which, in part, are calculated or estimated and which do not represent a true, actual return. There is a probability that the returns alleged to accrue to working farmers are not in fact achieved.
(c) The extension of the two-job pattern to Japan is such that it cannot but complicate population censuses: the attachment of those with two jobs to a particular category of employment is difficult precisely because they belong to more than one category. This state of affairs can import bias when working out the statistical denominators.

### *2 The identification of disparities*

On average, disparities decrease if agricultural productivity increases either through improved performance or through a reduction in manpower, or if prices increase. They increase when the situation is reversed. They are therefore subject to the influence of technological development, of patterns of behaviour among farmers, of non-agricultural employment and of prices: Japanese economic history provides us with extremely interesting evidence on these macroeconomic relations. They may be more or less classical, but they are decisive if we are to understand the development of agriculture. The hypothesis put forward at the start of the paper, however, postulating a reduction in disparities, is not fully verified. It is not verified by the totality of factors. So far as productivity is concerned, it is validated only in terms of nominal value, during the present period of time, and it is strongly influenced by recent fluctuations in agricultural prices occasioned by price support programmes.

These results appear to me to demonstrate that there is no automatic, general, spontaneous tendency towards a reduction of inequalities. Rather than seeking desperately to indicate a trend, the interest lies in showing the interplay of the mechanisms which can accentuate or reduce the disparities. For that very reason, however, there is a need to study the behaviour patterns of those who manage the mechanisms, that is, farmers, suppliers, customers, the State, consumers.

Parity and disparity constitute the result of social groups confronting interests contradictory to their own and placed in differing situations which bring with them behaviour patterns some of which are imposed on others. Examination of these patterns of behaviour leads us to a third series of comments on the persistence of disparities.

### 3 *The persistence of disparities*

This is in effect explained by Mr Yamada as being the traditional behaviour pattern of farmers, often bringing together several activities (part-time farming) which results from a preference for an existing situation, even where that works against their own interests.

I agree wholly with the stress laid on the extent of part-time farming in Japan, but it does not seem to me to be a measure of the reduction of disparities. Rather, it is an indication that parity of agricultural with non-agricultural incomes cannot be achieved by farmers from agricultural production alone. Even if, by reason of part-time farming, the congruence of farm and non-farm incomes is close to unity, part-time farming still shows the disparities. Mr Yamada explains that the persistence of the income disparities, of which the farmers are the victims, is due to their preference for carrying on activity in a rural environment, conserving a style of life as well. Far from being based on any socio-psychological preference, no matter what disparity, this pattern of behaviour really results from the absence of accessible alternatives. Given their circumstance, many farmers do not have any alternative; their only logical possibility is to carry on their agricultural production, possibly combined with an activity outside the farm.

It is of course this lack of alternatives which results in these disparities being perpetuated, with society profiting from it. If farmers were able to become masters of their own situation and to control their own production, as certain states or commercial operators are able (or attempt) to do, the disparities would be less. Their perpetuation is not something given by nature but is produced by social organization.

That is the reason why I do not share his optimistic approval of an acceptable, justified disparity of between 1.3 and 1.7 to the disadvantage of farmers. I would invite him to consider this relationship from the point of view of stimulating inter-sectoral exchange or of social balance. There is nothing which allows us to assert that such a relationship is normal or natural. It results from the workings of the social system and from unequal relations between social groups.

If Mr Yamada bases his argument on this socio-psychological preference, he doubtless does so to widen our often over-simplified economic explanations. This concern I share; but such an enlargement of view should not lead us to imprecise, uncertain concepts. In my view, an enlargement of view needs to result from examining circumstances, the behavioural patterns resulting from those circumstances and the contradictions which may also flow from them.

I am surprised that the behaviour of the other consuming parties involved are not examined. Who benefits from the growth of agricultural production? Does the modern sector benefit from it? What is the State's role? Just staying in the area of quantitative techniques in which Mr Yamada excels, analysis of the distribution of the productivity gains will enable us to clarify these questions.

*4 The general application of the results*

To sum up, Mr Yamada shows a readily understandable concern to come up with knowledge transferable to other countries, particularly developing countries. It seem to me that the circumstances of Japan are manifestly too different for us to be able to follow him in that argument, unless in terms of considerations which are so generalized as to be banal.

I should like to suggest an alternative reading of his work. He has thought of it as allowing general trends to be spotted before their existence is shown to be proved. To me it is more a description of the case of Japan, with all its specific circumstances; and this is essential if one is to go on to make comparisons. Rather than as a framework for identification, I see it as a framework for comparison. Looking from the point at which we are in this work, there is more to be got from an analysis of one example and from its comparison with others than from seeking, on the basis of a single example, to identify general trends.

These remarks, which I have been charged with putting forward, should not be allowed to detract from a most positive impression of this meticulous work, truly worthy of a professional researcher and which, quite apart from its own inherent quality, suggests a number of complementary studies. I should therefore like to thank Mr Yamada most cordially for his outstanding achievement.

## GENERAL DISCUSSION* – RAPPORTEUR: J. P. G. WEBSTER

These two papers created a good deal of interest and there were many who commented on the contents.

One participant noted Professor Westermarck's definition of equity which concerned a 'satisfactory' income. If this was accepted we should be concerned with how many people were *below* this level rather than with the spread of incomes. He also raised the question of the sensitivity of the income measures to the valuation of family labour. Should this be on the basis of opportunity costs rather than some sort of substitution cost as is often done? Also we should be concerned with total household income

*Papers by Westermarck and Yamada.

rather than simply that part of household income which is agricultural in its origin.

Another participant warned that an increase in dispersion of agricultural incomes may also imply a reducation in the dispersion of across-sector incomes. If larger farmers get richer, agricultural incomes may thus get closer to industrial incomes. He also asked Dr Westermarck to spell out the relationship between managerial ability and farm size.

A participant from the United States indicated that his country's experience mirrored that of the six countries studied by Westermarck. An USDA study had shown that larger farmers benefit more than smaller farmers in the areas of price policy, credit, taxation, and extension and research services. Proposals to modify the situation had recently been shelved. He also said that small farmers derived a large part of their incomes from non-agricultural services. Other participants enquired of Dr Yamada as to the reasons for changes in relative incomes. As compared with Western Europe, income per worker seemed low. Why? However labour productivity in European agriculture seems to have grown faster. What were the reasons behind this? Is growth in Japanese agriculture limited by technical bottlenecks or by adverse effects of high growth in the non-agricultural sector.

Other points raised included questions about the apparent non-neutrality of technology with respect to small and large farmers. One extension worker noted that many small farmers, when defining their objectives, included such non-economic variables as 'independence' and 'rural way of life'. Perhaps we should attempt to measure utility rather than income.

Dr Westermarck in reply, thanked participants for their comments and questions. He agreed with the opener with respect to the use of opportunity cost as a means of valuing family labour. But how to measure it? He accepted the need to include off-farm income, but said that it could not be included if the aim of the study was to look at differences in technical efficiency between groups of farms, for example large versus small. He also indicated that some of the questions raised could be answered only by a national income approach and not by his more micro-orientated methods.

Dr Yamada, also in reply, accepted that there were statistical problems in the derivation of the ratios in his paper. Examples included the imputation of rents and income from part-time farming. These were difficult problems when considering a study dealing with a hundred years. He also emphasized the distinction between the 'traditional' and the 'modern' way of life – with its different sets of values. Whilst he accepted that Japan was unique, there were perhaps lessons which countries with similar population growth rates and stages of agricultural development might find useful. Both technical bottlenecks and the availability of off-farm jobs could partially explain some of the relationships seen. But also important were the institutional aspects of land ownership and the maintenance of high rice prices leading to high land prices. Farmers often would not sell their land even if the agricultural portion of their income has fallen to a very low level.

Dr Yamada had then to stop because time had run out. He apologized to those questioners who had not been adequately answered.

Participants in the discussion included D. K. Britton, M. Upton, D. Rossetti, M. Viallon, M. Ruf, Y. Suzzi, R. J. Dancey, D. Paarlberg, C. H. Van der Meer, M. G. Chandrakanth and Yang Boo Choe.

YOSHIHIKO SUGAI AND A. R. TEXEIRA*

# *Income Disparities among Groups of Farmers: With Special Reference to Brazil*

## INTRODUCTION

Equity standards have not been given much attention by Brazilian agricultural policy-makers. Recently, when the economy reached a growth pattern that characterized the 'Brazilian Miracle', equity issues were given attention, mainly by the academic community. With the rapid growth of the Brazilian economy the academic community came together to agree with the fact that the growth of the national economy is resulting in further concentration of wealth (Langoni, 1973).

The Brazilian Government showed sensitivity to this fact and sponsored various studies which showed some interesting causes of the increase in the country's income disparities that had not been taken into consideration in reorientating the country's general economic and agricultural policies. Little attention has, however, been given to equity problems even after it was recognized that economic growth worsens income disparity. This brings up the problem of the economic development process that is fundamentally related to the interaction between the agricultural sector and the industrial sector. Many early development plans placed primary emphasis upon industry, largely ignoring agriculture, and accepting the preconception that 'redundant labour' in the agricultural sector could be drawn upon both for the industrial work force and for producing the food to maintain it. However, too often the needed food supplies were not implemented in agriculture (Fei and Ranis, 1964).

The basic problem is that low productivity in agriculture can limit economic growth. Industrialization and agricultural development plans must be made together. Agriculture is the source of manpower for industrial expansion, it is the source of essential supplies for maintaining a growing industrial population and of exports to be traded for industrial goods, and it is the chief potential source of savings for non-agricultural investment (Heady, 1969).

The present paper is addressed to the equity patterns among farmers in

*The authors are indebted to Levon Yeganiantz for review and comments.

Brazil. Rather than going deeply into specific problems, the paper attempts to characterize some general features, trying to find some bearings on the policy tools commonly used by the Brazilian authorities.

## BRIEF OVERVIEW OF THE AGRICULTURAL SECTOR PERFORMANCE OF BRAZIL

The historical evaluation of the Brazilian economy, and indeed of the society as a whole, has frequently been described in terms of a series of commodity cycles, each emanating from a specific export product boom. With the exception of a gold and diamond boom during the eighteenth century, these cycles have been associated with agricultural exports.

These cyclical export booms have been responsible for the major changes in the Brazilian economy, influencing such basic socio-economic characteristics as the size and degree of decentralization of administration, the location of industrial activities, land tenure, income disparities, the distribution of wealth, the racial composition of the population, and attitudes toward savings and consumption. Within the rural sector itself each of the cycles inevitably had an impact on the composition of output and distribution of wealth and income.

Since the end of World War II, Brazil's gross domestic product has grown rapidly. The average rate of growth was around 7 per cent per annum in real terms. The agricultural sector in this period has expanded at an average annual rate of about 4.5 per cent and its share of gross domestic product was reduced from around 27 per cent to 12 per cent. Agricultural exports, including processed farm products, have been significant, accounting for two-thirds to three-quarters of total exports during the last three decades.

Aggregate agricultural performance in this period has been good and the sector has played its development role by contributing foodstuffs, savings, raw materials, labour and foreign exchange to the secondary and tertiary sectors. However, there have been large variations through time in the relative performance of the major agricultural product groups and among the several major regions of the country.

## MAIN AGRICULTURAL POLICIES

This section examines the following policy tools: agricultural credit, the special subsidy programme for wheat, the coffee programme, the beef programme, some input subsidies, the agricultural land and settlement programme, taxation, and research and extension.

### *Agricultural credit*

Subsidized credit has been a primary tool of Brazilian agricultural policy in order to compensate the sector for the discriminatory impact of other policies (for example, control of food prices, surcharge on agricultural products, industrialization based on import substitution sometimes resulting in increased agricultural input costs,) and to stimulate agricultural investment and ouput. The total amount of this credit has reached a level of around 70 to 100 per cent of the value of agricultural production. The interest rate on agricultural credit in relation to the inflation rate is relatively low. This means that the agricultural sector is subsidized by this credit. Ordinary agricultural production and investment credits were charged nominal interest rates of 13 to 21 per cent with lower rates available through many of the special programmes. These rates compared with a general price inflation of around 40 per cent per annum in 1976–78, 77 per cent in 1979, and nearly 100 per cent in 1980 and 1981. The distribution of credit is very much skewed by crop groups. According to the 1975 to 1977 estimates of the Central Bank and Bank of Brazil, about one-fifth of the value of all crop-specific production loans went to soybean producers. About 80 per cent of the total production credit went for six crops: soybeans, wheat, rice, corn, coffee, and sugarcane. These six crops account for about 60 per cent of the gross value of total crop production. The domestic consumption crops, black beans and cassava, account for about 17 per cent of the value of crop production and received only 4 per cent of crop-specific production credit. The major export crops, soybeans, coffee, sugarcane, cotton and cocoa, received around 50 per cent of total agricultural production credit. These divergencies can be explained by the smaller size and more remote locations of bean and cassava growers as compared to the grain and export crops producers. It also reflects the general impact on incentives to use modern inputs. The distribution of credit among regions is also skewed. Thus, in 1977, the Northeast received only 12 per cent of crop credits. At the same time, the Southern States received 46 per cent of total crop credit, reflecting the heavy concentration of wheat and soybeans. Lower income groups have a higher number of loan contracts but less in quantity of the credit. On the other hand, the larger income group received more than half the total agricultural credit from a small number of loan contracts. Giving a large amount of subsidized credit to a small group of Brazilian farmers has had a significant impact on income distribution in the agricultural sector. Where credit is used to improve productivity and lower production costs, market forces pass some or all the gains on to the consumer in lower prices, the recipient of credit clearly benefits to the detriment of non-recipients who suffer the same decrease in price but without equal access to cost-reducing inputs and advanced technology. The more price-inelastic the demand for the product, the greater the fall in the product price. This provokes the greater pressure of low prices on that group of farmers who did not receive credit. Further, these farmers who produce the basic foodstuffs, such as beans and cassava, will suffer more since they face a more inelastic demand than do export crop producers.

If access to credit is unevenly distributed or demand elasticities markedly different, recipients are enabled to bid inputs away from non-recipients, thus changing the pattern of agriculture input utilization. The more price-elastic the demand for the product, the less will be the impact of expanded output on product price and, hence, the greater the incentive of the farmer to bid up the price of needed factor inputs away from crops with inelastic demand. In general, export crops and those commodities best protected by the government programme enjoy a higher demand elasticity and are thus most likely to bid up factor prices. Consequently, the small farmers who produce the less price-elastic products will suffer from high input prices. Recently an added effort was made to extend credit to the many small farmers in the more remote areas of the country who had previously not enjoyed effective access to institutional credit. The credit policy has been able to help agriculture execute its function of supporting economic growth but in spite of its beneficial effects it has caused great disparity among the groups of farmers in the agricultural sector.

*The special case wheat subsidy*

Wheat is not ideally suited to the edafo-climatic conditions in Brazil, and the technology of production is rather demanding. Consequently, signficant producer subsidies have been required in times of low world wheat prices. On the consumer side a substantial consumer subsidy on wheat consumption in recent years has led to significantly increased demand, which, combined with several years of poor harvest, has resulted in expanded wheat imports. Thus, in spite of an increased acreage planted to wheat, imports still provide more than one-half of consumption needs.

A major obstacle to self-sufficiency in wheat production is the increasing use of wheat products stimulated by low retail wheat prices. As a consequence, imports still supplied, on average, 60 per cent of domestic consumption during the second half of the 1970s. The distortion in the cost of wheat and wheat products to consumers in turn affects competitive product demand. Low wheat prices resulted in a 55 per cent growth in wheat consumption per caput during the 1970s. This included some diversion to livestock feed. Consequently, traditional food (and feed) sources, such as corn and cassava, became more expensive flour sources than wheat. Corn and cassava are traditionally small-farmer crops. Thus, to the extent that substitution by wheat has led to reduced demand and lower prices for these crops, small-farmer incomes have been adversely effected by the consumer subsidy.

*The coffee programme*

Coffee growers would have favoured a larger share of the world market, but not at the expense of a decline in the domestic price. For them, the best policy would have been a high domestic price, unlimited purchases of coffee by the government at high prices and aggressive sales abroad, even if this entailed a lower external price. This course of action would have ended in a further expansion of coffee production in Brazil, an even larger accumulation of stock and a large cost to the government in supporting the domestic price. The world market share of Brazilian coffee exports fell from 44 per cent in the 1950s down to 33 per cent in 1966. In order to keep the domestic price high, a subsidy programme to eradicate approximately 500 million trees during 1966–1970 was executed. The areas where coffee was eradicated were encouraged to produce an export grain crop. Diversity resulted in labour problems since coffee is a highly labour intensive crop. In fact this programme caused unemployment in the coffee production areas. Labourers unemployed due to the coffee eradication programme put pressure on the small farmer group that needed off farm or farm employment, resulting in rural migration to cities in search of new jobs and creating a large number of migrating farm labourers who left their small farm activities.

*Beef cattle programme*

Price control is set on beef at the retail level. In addition, a high export target was set for beef. Thus, the control of the foreign exchange rate has had very strong influences in this sector. On the producer side, this group received special credit for long-term loans with low interest rates and this credit represented a heavy subsidy for this group. The primary condition for access to this credit is ability to mortgage, usually, farm land. Thus, the credit has been strongly linked to large beef cattle farmers. At present this special programme of credit has become stagnant, although the land factor for the eligibility for credit has been eliminated.

*Some input subsidies*

The import-substitution industrialization policies have influenced the use and costs of modern inputs. The tariffs levied on imported chemicals, farm machinery and tractors are substantial and significantly increase input costs to farmers seeking to adopt modern production practices. This negative effect is offset, however, for those farmers who have access to subsidized credit. This is well illustrated by considering fertilizer and tractor credit. Fertilizers are heavily utilized in Brazilian agriculture, consumption reaching around 3.4 million metric tons of nutrients in 1979. The distribution of consumption is very variable between different crops. Thus almost 75 per cent of total fertilizer used during 1975–1977 went to six crops: soybeans, wheat, sugarcane, coffee, rice and corn. Demand for fertilizer thus comes primarily from the farmers who produce export crops, although a growing use by other producers is evident over the period.

With respect to machinery, especially tractors, the users are again mainly the large farmers. Tractors, as well as other agricultural machinery, are financed by long-term credit. With nominal interest rates lagging well behind the inflation rate, the implicit subsidy has grown in importance over time.

*Agricultural land and settlement programme*

Land policy has suffered great variation in Brazil. There are still large agricultural frontier areas which are not incorporated into agricultural production. In some regions there are 3 inhabitants per square kilometre and on average 14 inhabitants per square kilometre. At the other extreme there are regions where the land tenure system puts a heavy pressure on those farmers without land. In these regions there are constant claims for the need for agrarian reform. Through the historical consequences of the land tenure system, Brazilian society has not favoured the sector of small farmers. As already pointed out, the fact of land owning has been the prerequisite for participating in other benefits, such as credit, especially subsidized credit. The availability of subsidized credit pushes up the price of land regardless of its utility as a productive input, because the ownership of land is in most cases necessary to qualify for credit. Thus, when credit is as highly subsidized as it is in Brazil, some proportion of the credit can be expected to be applied, either directly or through the release of the borrower's own financial resources, to the purchase of land simply to establish eligibility for still more subsidized credit and to benefit from the speculative land price increases thus generated.

Recently, Government policy tried to correct this situation primarily by initiating the following four programmes: (a) a land settlement scheme for the frontier areas and helping landless small farmers to obtain titles to land, (b) elimination of land ownership as a condition for access to agricultural credit, (c) special land occupancy (squatter) rights – if a farmer occupies and cultivates public land for more than five years, he can get a title to the land, (d) land tax programmes aimed to force efficient utilization of land for agricultural production.

*Taxation*

The industrialized region, Southern and Central Southern States, has adopted a lower tax rate on moving agricultural commodities as compared to the North and North East States that are less industrialized and, lacking alternative sources of income, has taxed the movement of produce. Because of the sizeable revenues generated by its strong industrial base, the Southeast, particularly São Paulo State, is able to set a lower tax rate on farm goods than the economically weaker states of the North East where most small farmers are located. This tax affects the small farmers who produce domestic food-stuffs.

*Research and extension*

Policies intended to improve technology have had an important impact on Brazilian agriculture. Brazilian research and extension expenditures have increased over the last ten years. According to the National Research Council and National Agricultural Research Corporation (EMBRAPA) data for 1977–78, the main research expenditures are still for the export crops which absorb more than 60 per cent of total research expenditure, as compared to basic food-stuffs, such as cassava and beans, which share less than 8 per cent of the total, even though the government has made great efforts to increase the productivity of the latter products since the middle of the last decade. These basic foodstuffs have low yields, so there is a good chance to improve them. For example, the more intensive use of improved seeds in crops like corn and beans constitutes a potentially important source of growth. The low rate of use of improved seeds and the low levels of national yields in both crops suggest the existence of a wide margin for improvement. Research and extension to develop and disseminate improved seed should thus be given high priority. These basic food crops have not received heavy research investment traditionally. Consequently, the producers of these crops, especially small farmers, will benefit from this policy.

## FARM GROUPS AND INCOME DISPARITIES

A few Brazilian studies concerning equity questions related to agricultural sector classify farmers using the following criteria: (a) production organization and capital-labour relationships with emphasis on the situation of land ownership (Perez, 1975), (b) farm income classification based on the production factors (land, capital, labour) and technology (Grawunder, 1976).

Four groups of farmers are defined using a combination of the above criteria and also considering the products: (i) Small disadvantaged subsistence farmers, small tenant farmers, share croppers and squatters. A sizeable portion of this group is found in the Northeast. Farmers of this group are also found in some small parts of other poor areas of the country, Central-East and South; (ii) Small to medium size commercial farms located near urban centres. A high percentage of the farmers in this group are owner operators; (iii) Large scale livestock enterprises; (iv) Large commercial enterprises primarily orientated to export crops (coffee, cotton, sugarcane, cocoa and, more recently, soybeans).

Historically, the first group has been given little attention by the Government. A few ideas are commonly offered to better this group's situation: resettlement of these small farmers on new lands; creation of agribusiness to absorb surplus labour; development of new alternative crops that could generate more income; migration into the industrial sector.

Of these four alternatives, the last one is the most natural procedure historically. All alternatives have high costs. Migration to urban centres has produced the increase of the slums on the borders of the major cities, that force high pressure on the labour market with increased rates of unemployment and criminality in these areas.

Family labour in the second group would also reach the cities. Being closer to the city they have easier access to schools. Once they get education, they do not return to the farm. Being more exposed to changes in the market, the farmers in this group ought to respond to training programmes which would better their capability to adjust to the signals of the market. Further, closer to cities, the lower transport costs of the products should enhance their comparative advantage. Recently the Brazilian government created a programme for 'horticultural cities' to make use of the locational advantages of this farm population around the capital cities. Only a few of the state capitals, however, have this programme as yet.

The third group is a small one (in terms of farmer population), although the farmers included in it occupy about half of the country's pasture. Taking the cattle raising activity in isolation, the farmers in this group have recently been left to natural market forces without any special favourable policy measures. With an inflation rate of 100 per cent, however, beef cattle have experienced stable or even decreasing nominal prices. The belief that the situation could be improved by investment in the meat marketing system, has led the government to subsidize slaughter-houses, cold storage and so on. Such a policy has proved to have benefited the large meat marketing firms. These are also the owners of a significant part of the beef cattle herd in the country. The integration of the cattle raising operations with the slaughter-houses compensates for the low revenues of the producing phase of the proccess.

The distortions caused by the policies related to the beef marketing sector are numerous. They are beyond the scope of the present paper despite their very interesting equity effects. Cattle farmers are not among the low income groups in Brazil. This paper does not dwell on considerations about ways and policies to improve their incomes.

The farmers in the fourth group have the highest incomes. Their expenditures on modern inputs account for more than 60 per cent of their total costs. They depend heavily on agricultural credit. The emphasis of the government is towards export and this indicates that this group will tend to get the most benefit from the present agricultural policies.

## CONCLUDING COMMENTS

The agricultural sector has made a significant contribution to the overall economic growth and development of Brazil. However, the distribution of income and equity has not been significantly improved in relative terms, even though in absolute terms there may be some improvement.

Among the more common policy orientations used by Brazilian society over its history, it is fair to say that equity considerations were not among the most important ones. Even though agricultural policies did not take into consideration the equity dimension, they did affect strongly the equity standards of the rural society. The rural poor left without society's attention in the form of better education, health care, and social security, have historically tended to migrate to the urban area. In these new areas, they got more access to such amenities, even though they were not directed especially to the poor classes of the population. These migration patterns of rural poor in Brazil reflected their rationality and the way they exposed their problem to the whole society.

The dimension of the country and the diversity of conditions showed no natural ways out of the rural poverty problem which is free of creating other problems for the Brazilian agricultural sector. If the Brazilian society does not change its agricultural economic policies, this income disparity is likely to keep increasing.

## REFERENCES

Fei, John C. H. and Ranis, Gustav, *Development of the Labor Surplus Economy: Theory and Policy,* Yale University Economic Growth Centre, Irwin, 1964.

Grawunder, Atos F., *The Southern Brazil Agricultural Sector: The Income Problem,* University of Wisconsin, 1976 (Ph. D Thesis.)

Heady, Earl O., 'Developing Economically and Politically Consistent Policies: the Problem of Equity', in CARD, *Food Goals, Future Structural Changes, and Agricultural Policy: A National Basebook,* Iowa State University Press, 1969.

Langoni, Carlos Geraldo, *Income Distribution and Economic Development of Brazil (Distribuição da Renda e Desenvolvimento Econômico do Brasil),* Editora Expressão e Cultura, Rio de Janeiro, 1973.

Perez, Luiz Henrique, *Characterization of Brazilian Agricultural Areas by Production Patterns (Caracterizacão de Áreas Agrícolas Brasileiras segundo suas Formas de Produção),* Piracicaba, ESALQ, 1975, – Tese, MS.

## DISCUSSION OPENING – JEUNG HAN LEE

Sugai and Filho classify Brazilian farmers into four groups mainly in terms of the commodity produced. They also evaluate eight public policies or commodity programmes the Brazilian government presently pursues with respect to effects on income distribution among farm groups, and among regions which are not specifically well-defined. The authors strongly insist that each of these policies or programmes has contributed to increasing income disparities among farm groups. In conclusion, the authors insist that 'If the Brazilian society does not change its agricultural economic policies, this income disparity is likely to keep increasing.'

I have several comments in mind. First of all, despite the fact that the policies or programmes are noticed as the main causes of income disparities, there is no indication as to how much of farm income distribution is worsened against certain groups of farms due to implementation of these policies or programmes. It can happen that the effect of one policy, for example the subsidized credit, is offset by that of another, for example tariffs levied on imported inputs, indeed as the authors have recognized. Nonetheless, can we strongly insist that a set of policies has made the income disparity worsen, without supporting empirical evidence? Is this set of policies or programmes the most and only important factor affecting the equity or income distribution of Brazilian farmers?

Secondly, as we all know, a certain policy normally brings about several different effects, some of which may be undesirable. The authors discuss this undesirable effect only, without paying attention to desirable ones, which perhaps have contributed greatly to economic development in Brazil. For example, it is known that the programmes of price support and subsidized credit for wheat during the decade of the 1960s made possible substantial growth in agricultural output and transformation of the economy from extensive range livestock to intensive crop production. Hence total output, factor productivity, employment and farm incomes were greatly increased.

Thirdly, all the implication delivered by the paper seems to suggest that there exists income disparity between the small subsistence farm subsector and the rest of the farm sector, rather than among groups of farmers, and, perhaps, between the north-eastern region and the rest. Considering that the subsistence small farms are concentrated in the north-eastern region, the main determinant of the existing farm income disparity may well not be the kinds of policies or programmes the authors have discussed. It may be the small size of farm, landlessness, poor infrastructure, lack of off-farm employment opportunity, lack of human capital, and so on. Therefore the abolition of the present government policies may not in fact contribute to correcting the existing income disparity.

Lastly, it is also known that in the Brazilian economy the basic problem in the agricultural sector is not so much the distribution of income within the sector, but the absolute poverty of people in the agricultural sector relative to the non-farm sector. At any rate, what would be alternative policies in achieving Brazilian economic development goals, including equitable income distribution within the farm sector as well as between the farm and non-farm sectors, if the eight policies or programmes evaluated should be changed? Is it also desirable to change the programmes which are related to land settlement, land rights, land tax, and research and extension intended to help the small subsistence farmers the authors discussed in the text?

ENO J. USORO

# *Agricultural Resource Activation and the Problem of Rural Poverty in Nigeria*

In recent years, scientific knowledge gained through education and contact has contributed significantly to noticeable economic changes and improved standards of living principally in the Third World urban locations. The transmission of the benefit of such revolutionary development leverage or of their effect to rural areas cannot be adduced for their impact on transforming the socio-economic conditions within the rural area – that known cradle of rural poverty – in the Third World. The purpose of the present sketch is to summarize, from the Nigerian experience, those inhibiting obstacles to effective adaptation of introduced ideas and knowledge into the Nigerian rural setting on a scale that could activate and mobilize enough resources for the improvement of the standard of living of the rural poor.

Over the years, significant interest (expressed through rural agricultural policy resources, implementation procedures, administrative organization, and investment expenditure allocations) has been shown by various Nigerian governments in the attempt to raise rural living standards through increases in agricultural output. Enchanted by agricultural research results in biological and engineering sciences, the government has encouraged the gradual adoption of micro-orientated ideas drawn from general scientific knowledge (high-yielding crop varieties, selective fertilizers, irrigation construction and so on) in rural agriculture, but with minimal effects. Therefore, useful as the policy measures may be, the present emphasis on improved agricultural productivity as the single approach to combat the problem of rural poverty ignores the social environmental barriers – cultural, economic and political – which constitute obstacles to the transmission of productivity benefits to the rural poor.

## POLICY THRUST AND SOCIAL-ECONOMIC CUM POLITICAL CONSTRAINTS

The implication of the first legal land reform attempt in Nigeria (Land Use Decree No. 6 of 1978) may suffice to illustrate the incongruous divergence between the objective of increased productivity in agriculture and a corresponding reduction in rural poverty. Essentially the thrust of the decree was on evolving a uniform tenure system and encouraging the development of privately owned large-scale commercial agricultural enterprises, whose indirect demonstration effect on rural farmers and possible employment opportunities could improve the level of rural agricultural practices as well as the rural standard of living. The legal protection provided would-be agricultural entrepreneurs against possible local land conflict, plus government financial support through the Agricultural Credit Guarantee Scheme Fund Act (Act No. 20 of 1977)[1], ensured a smooth transition from traditional to modern agricultural practices and enhanced levels of rural well-being. Thus, implied in the policy and the measures adopted is the false hope that modern large-scale commercial agriculture will, by itself, circumvent the social and cultural problems of traditional agriculture and rural poverty.

Clearly articulated in the land reform decree is the 'battle cry' for upper and middle class capitalist farmers drawn from both the rural and urban population. These are entrepreneurs, who with superior social relations, access to decision-makers and commercial organizational ability, can maximally benefit from biological science research advice and economic inputs, from the adoption of appropriate cultivation techniques, the utilization of extension services and subsidies and the recruitment of local labour from the rural farming communities. These paragons of agricultural progress (our would-be commercial farmers) comprise the core of agricultural lieutenants who, guided by profit motives and encouraged by policy, no longer operate within traditional social and cultural constraints. But this approach leaves the majority of our rural farming population – the rural poor – in limbo, and creates social and political problems of a dimension that may defeat Nigeria's overall commitment to the eradication of rural poverty.

By emphasizing efficiency in rural agricultural resource allocation, organization and ouput flow under the management of the property-owning class, government policy erroneously ignores the size and magnitude of the participating rural farmers, their agricultural problems, past creative and productive capacities and their experience gained through years of traditional farming as irrelevant to rural agricultural development and improvement in the farmers' well-being. Thus rural farmers are alienated from participation in a scheme formulated for their benefit through the extent to which resources are devoted to affecting large-scale changes over small select areas, as against small-scale changes over large areas. Therefore, policymakers' insensitivity to the limited capacity of commercial agriculture to transform traditional institutions in organizing production, renders its agricultural bias anti-poverty programme operationally ineffective.

Equally important in alienating the possible beneficiaries of the programme – the rural poor – from active participation is the divergent interest between the politically powerful entrepreneurs and the politically defenceless rural farmers. For, while the former is conscious of the benefits of the programme which they view primarily in political and economic terms, the latter harbours a fear of the possible consequences of land displacement, loss of dignity, self-confidence, respect and the erosion of their known traditional way of life. These pessimistic attitudes (which derive from their feeble political strength, emanating from their low level of literacy, absence of organization with a leadership able to challenge the power elite) engenders mistrust of government bureaucratic programmes for rural development.

The rural farming communities' weak political bargaining power poses several rural organizational and implementation problems with adverse consequences for the improvement of the living standard of its poor members. Thus the communities' inability to participate or be consulted about traditional socio-cultural and economic issues relevant to evolving a rural anti-poverty oriented programme (which requires the co-operation and active involvement of its members), inhibits the formulation of a pragmatic plan with a rural focus. This weakness underlines the observed urban directed strategy for rural agricultural planning, the government's conservative financial expenditure on improvement in purely traditional agricultural activities, as well as the disproportionately heavy taxation burden on rural farmers during the heydays of the Marketing Boards (Bauer, 1954). It is therefore tempting to speculate that as long as the rural farmers' political weaknesses persist, rural poverty could remain a feature of the Nigerian countryside.

The capitalist ideological alignment of the Nigerian Power élite represents yet another societal constraint which prohibits enthusiastic support for rural anti-poverty programmes. The known capitalist inordinate desire for wealth accumulation through profit oriented private enterprises, reinforced by their perception of poverty as the consequences of individual failings (for which the extended family system and not the society should be held responsible), explains to a large extent, the power élite's callous attitude towards rural anti-poverty schemes. Thus, despite government intervention, the power élite's capitalist attributes discourages wholehearted involvement in the formulation and implementation of a poverty programme for which they perceive themselves as prospective losers.

Viewed from its urban-oriented goals, government policy concern over rural agriculture does not represent an attempt to alleviate rural poverty, but rather seeks to satisfy the present and future demands for agricultural output. For, if the policy was meant to play a dual role – inducing increases in agricultural output *and* improving the standard of living of the rural poor – measures could have been incorporated to ensure

(a) the creation of a structural framework designed to increase the effective activation of rural resources;
(b) the minimizing of the political and ideological constraints to policy implementation, and
(c) the creation of possible increases in the rural poor income through expenditure on incentive inducing measures.

## MEASURES FOR ALLEVIATING NIGERIAN RURAL POVERTY

Policy strategy for the development of rural agriculture and of improvement in the living standard of the rural poor is not pursued for the separate development of an isolated group, but as part of a national planning strategy that mobilizes farmers for the task of nation building. Since our planning objective incorporates the desire to eradicate rural poverty, the search for a corresponding strategy must recognize those problems that are peculiar to our rural conditions and seek solutions appropriate to the framework of our rural institutions. For unlike industrial planning, management and production in manufacturing enterprises, a borrowed technology and the lofty ideas of management cannot be successfully transplanted into traditional rural agricultural settings. The specific nature of the region's problems, the farmers' long process of trial and error in resolving them, their adaptation to the requirements of farming in particular locations, their knowledge about the availability and relative costs of local resources, and their organizational methods encouraging self-reliance and revitalizing communal traditions must all be taken into account. Thus, in the process of policy formulation, a strategy should develop that focuses on the farmers, their well-being and their future.

The process of evolving an effective structural measure relevant to the eradication of rural poverty through agricultural output increases in the present context depends on rectifying at least two policy defects in perception. First, acknowledging 'people' and their basic human needs as the primary concern, and concern with agricultural output increases as secondary. Secondly, willingness to understand the traditional intricacies of rural organization and operation. It cannot be denied that rural farmers command defined sets of practical information or stocks of knowledge about traditional agriculture that could assist in guiding the evolution of new techniques appropriate for rural agricultural transformation. Thus the policy-makers must 'understand the farmer, not patronise him: assume that he knows his business better than we do, unless there is evidence to the contrary' (Polly Hill, 1970).

The relevance of understanding rural communities can be realized by examining how policy changes can be brought about in one of the most important structural measures that adversely affect the rural poor in Nigeria – farm-size. In a country where a communal land use system and its consequential land fragmentation has deprived many rural families of a decent means of livelihood, prospects for acquiring large-scale farms require evolving an acceptable co-operative system that could adopt modified farm practices to advantage. Unavoidably, such a system touches upon land tenure. Land to the farmers is a source of livelihood to be preserved, if possible, for the future. Thus irrespective of the land decree, large-scale land-use treads on explosive political and emotional grounds. Therefore as a starting point, the formulation of a policy involving large-scale land-use requires knowledge of the history of social and political relations within and among rural communities. In addition it requires continuous dialogue with rural farmers that could elicit their understanding of the possible courses of action open to them. This way the rural farmers have a participatory role to play in ascertaining community response to any proposed changes. These would be changes which recognize the relationship between the earning capacity of individual families and farm size as a means of alleviating the problem of rural poverty.

Measures adopted to effect farm structural changes alone without also effecting administrative structural reorganization may be inadequate to counteract the inordinate interest of the political power élite in a rural anti-party programme. The physical remoteness of bureaucratic administrative authorities (the official local representatives and guardians of the farmers' interest) from rural areas ostracizes farmers from participatory administrative and political decision-making. This absence of an effective communication channel between both (government administrators and rural farmers) under the prevailing condition of the latter's lack of political cohesion, renders ineffective an attempt by farmers to challenge the interest and authority of the power élite. Therefore, the creation of more local government units sufficiently compact (in which elected rural farmer representatives are incorporated) provides a possible communication link with policymakers through official local government representatives and at the same time challenges the existing dominant influence of the urban power élite on decisions affecting rural communities.

Structural defects and organizational deficiencies have, in planning rural agricultural development, restricted government rural area investment commitments to purely select indirect schemes such as primary education and access roads that do not convey immediate benefit to the rural poor. While such indirect productivity measures may benefit enterprising rural farmers, they cannot deal with poverty associated with ill-health – a characteristic of the rural poor – in a country where free medical delivery services are limited; nor can it alleviate the heavy tax burden – a direct antithesis of rural anti-poverty measures – on the rural poor. Thus, increased government expenditure on rural public health and the adoption of such fiscal measures that make the tax burden less regressive (by relating it to the ability of individuals to pay) equally portrays policymakers' awareness of the nature of indirect benefits that recognize the low income earning capacity of the rural poor and of their physical well-being.

## CONCLUSION

Rural poverty in Nigeria is real and its problems intractably complex. In spite of government consciousness and concern, the economic interest and political influence of the power élite, manifested through the country's capitalist ideological bias, rescinds policy thrust to the disadvantage of the rural poor. Urban orientated policy measures, plus incorporated borrowed ideas which disregard traditional experience and ignore farmers consultation, weaken the implementation of a policy meant to activate rural resources for the benefit of the rural farmers and the rural poor.

Rural development policy may be perceived as a set of principles developed to guide the management of the rural sector's affairs. Its elements are the relevant ideas that go to make up the concept of the system. Thus if the ideas are external to the system, so are the goals, the assumptions made about the situation to be met, the selection of alternative courses of action, the determination of optimum ways of implementation, and finally the ultimate system itself that emerges. In our own case, the initial specification of our goals in social and economic terms requires policies directed to the development of the human potential of the group. This means evolving a modified yet identifiable system that retains the basic characteristics of rural agriculture, but comes to grips with the practical problems which face the rural poor, the rural farmers and the nation.

## NOTES

[1] The Federal Government and the Central Bank of Nigeria have so far contributed ₦51.3 million and ₦34.2 million respectively out of the ₦100 million provided for in the Act establishing the fund.

## REFERENCES

Federal Republic of Nigeria, Land Use Decree No. 6 of 1978, Lagos 28 March 1978.

Bauer, P. T. and Yamey, B. S., 'The Economics of Marketing Reform', *Journal of Political Economy,* Vol. LXII No. 3, June 1954.

Polly Hill, *Studies in Rural Capitalism in West Africa,* Cambridge University Press, 1970.

## DISCUSSION OPENING – D. H. PENNY

The issues raised in this paper are as old as the first plantation ever established in the New World. They are also as new as the 1978 'land reform' laws in Nigeria that were passed to facilitate the establishment of large commercial agricultural enterprises whose 'indirect demonstration effect on rural farmers and possible employment opportunities could improve the level of rural agricultural practices as well as the rural standard of living' (Usoro, p. 360). The act provides 'legal protection' to 'would-be agricultural entrepreneurs [capitalist farmers] against possible local land conflict' (p. 360).

Usoro's paper presents a well-argued case against the plantation system for Nigeria. It also has many useful lessons for other countries.

His paper can be briefly summed up as follows. Economic growth can beget rural poverty; the 'agricultural production approach' to rural poverty is probably too narrow; the people who own or manage large-scale commercial farms (or plantations) often have good connections in the upper echelons of government and can therefore get special treatment; the self-same people are substantially cut-off from the peasants and from the traditional social and cultural constraints (that apply in the rural areas); the government ignores or at least underestimates the knowledge of the peasants; the support given by government to the capitalist sector makes the peasants wary and sceptical of the value of programmes aimed directly at them; to be effective, anti-poverty programmes need the active involvement of the people affected; the new élite loves accumulation (of money) and appears to believe that poverty is due to the failings of individuals. In the final sections of the paper Usoro argues that human needs should be the first consideration and that nothing really effective can be done to alleviate poverty unless officials have a good understanding of rural organization. He also says that officials should be closer to the people, and that the main aim of development policy should be to build on indigenous institutions, including the wisdom of the rural people, and not to rely on alien imports like plantations.

I have only two small criticisms to make of the paper: first, the author tells us far too little about the actual circumstances of the village people in Nigeria and how their economic performance and potential differs from that which is likely from the new capitalist farms; second, his suggestion that 'officials should strive to become closer to the people' might not be politically feasible, given the realities of the market system. It would also have been interesting to hear something of how things have worked out in Nigeria since the law was passed in 1978.

There are a number of interesting parallels with what seems to be happening in Nigeria and with Indonesia's historical experience of plantations. In a 1963 paper, Zulkifli and I compared the productivity of peasants and plantations on the East Coast of North Sumatra, Indonesia, an area where estates and smallholdings have long co-existed, by no means always happily. The estates and the smallholdings described in the paper were neighbours; they were on the same sort of land, which meant that the land could have been used equally well for rubber or for rice, and they were equally close to the major market. The smallholdings were completely subsistence-oriented and no improved varieties of rice, fertilizer or pesticides were used. The productivity comparison was as follows:-

| | Estates | Smallholdings |
|---|---|---|
| Value added per hectare | Rp 7,500 | Rp 9,800 |
| Value added per man employed | Rp16,700 | Rp 8,900 |

The average labour force per hectare on the estates was 0.45 persons per hectare; it was 1.1 persons per hectare on the smallholdings.

The comparison would have looked rather different if we had compared rubber smallholdings with rubber estates, but even here it is likely that the household incomes of the peasant rubber growers would mostly have been higher than those obtained by the plantation labourers, even though value added per hectare, and more particularly per man employed would have been higher on the estates.

Most comparisons between estates and smallholdings involve production units where the same crops are grown. However when the comparisons are between the best uses of land by peasants and the best uses of land by plantations in the self-same district, the comparison is much less likely to favour the plantations, if at all.

The following Indonesian figures for 1981 illustrate what I mean. A plantation with an average rubber yield of 1000 Kg per hectare (drc) produces the gross equivalent of 1830 Kg of milled rice. If paid out costs are deducted, then value added per hectare is 1640 Kg (Barlow and Muharminto, 1982, p.125). A typical rice smallholding, with the capacity to produce two crops per year, will produce 3500 kilogrammes milled rice equivalent (mre) per year, or 3150 kilogrammes net (value added). The household income of the peasant will be 3150 kilogrammes, assuming that his farm is one hectare in size. (Many peasant farms are larger than this in the Outer Islands of Indonesia.) On the estate, the daily wage was just over 5 kilogrammes more a year. If his wife worked, too, she would expect to get about the same. The one hectare peasant farm shows a substantial advantage when it comes to value added per hectare and per man; it shows an even greater advantage over the plantation when it comes to labour use per hectare, for labour's share of the 1640 kilogrammes mre on the estate was just 450 kilogrammes (or 27 per cent), whereas the family would get almost all the value added, 3150 mre, from the rice farm.

I believe that these comparisons are in the spirit of Usoro's paper, and it will be interesting to see what happens in Nigeria. In the meantime, however, it should probably be pointed out that many national governments and international aid agencies continue to use incomplete and inadequate economic calculations to justify giving priority to investments in plantations. (Etherington's 1974 paper shows what happened in Indonesia's tea industry.)

If the goal is accumulation rather than the most economic use of the land then plantations are perhaps to be preferred, for it has long been known that it is easier to get profits – and taxes – from the docile labour forces on plantations (Mandle's 1972 article is good on this point) than it is to persuade peasants to share their earnings with the people who live in cities.

In conclusion, I hope that conference participants will be stirred by Usoro's paper to do further research on the economics of land use so that we can all get a better picture of estates versus small holdings and of the long-term social and political, as well as economic, consequences of preferring the one over the other.

## REFERENCES

Barlow, C. and Muharminto, 'The Rubber Smallholder Economy', *Bulletin of Indonesian Economic Studies,* Vol. 18, No. 2 1982.

Etherington, D. M., 'The Indonesian Tea Industry', *Bulletin of Indonesian Economic Studies,* Vol. X, No. 2, pp. 83–113 July 1974.

Mandle, J. R., 'The Plantation Economy: An Essay in Definition', *Science and Society*, Vol. 36, No. 1, pp. 49–62 1972.

Penny, D. H. and Zulkifli, M., 'Estates and Smallholdings: An Economic Comparison', *Journal of Farm Economics*, pp. 1017–21 Dec. 1963.

## GENERAL DISCUSSION* – RAPPORTEUR: J. A. EVANS

In general discussion of Dr Usoro's paper some scepticism was expressed about what had been achieved for farming people either by schemes for small farms or large plantations and the view was expressed that the value system had to be altered radically. It was also thought that the new attention given to peasant farmers by agricultural economists was an important sign of changing values generally. Others questioned whether the problem was as acute as the paper suggested or indeed whether it was peculiar to developing countries. Income support for farmers unable to help themselves was a possibility considered in some developed countries, though this was essentially a social rather than an agricultural measure. More information was sought about the aims and probable outcome of the 1978 Decree as to whether farms of the large size described were in fact expected, whether the ultimate aim was just to promote some increase in average farm size and whether landlessness would result.

In reply Dr Adegboye pointed out that the 1978 Decree had been introduced after long explanation and debate. Some progress was being made both in land acquisition and in increasing output. Land left unfarmed under the traditional tenure system was being brought into production but it was not the aim to produce landless people. He took the view that free education and medical services, though indirect in effect, were better than income support.

In general discussion of Dr Sugai's paper, information was sought about the experience of small farmers in the export sectors such as citrus. It was suggested that the unfavourable outcome for poor farmers of all kinds of policies might be explained by the way the political process was structured and operated. One view of the basic problem was that ways had not been found of developing commercial farming without further depressing the position of small farmers.

In reply Dr Sugai said that strategies were being sought to improve the lot of small farmers, for example mineral exploitation in the north of the country was being combined with development schemes for agriculture. Quantitative evidence certainly existed to support his analysis but the present paper aimed to indicate only the broad lines of the argument.

Dr Filho, who had collaborated in the paper, stressed that although there was a deliberate emphasis on policies which had a negative effect on small farmers the paper also showed that changes had been made where possible to modify these effects. Among exported crops citrus was an important new crop, though it was concentrated in one region. Promotion of soya beans for

*Papers by Sugai and Texeira and Usoro.

export would help farms of all sizes. It was true that small farmers had no say in policy, but he believed Brazil was looking for ways of reducing inequity and was conscious of the need to feed her own poor people adequately.

Participants in the discussion included R. I. Molla, R. W. Bohall, J. M. Slater, M. E. Andal, W. Zohlnhofer, P. von Blankenburg and T. Tuma.

RYOHEI KADA

# *Changing Rural Employment Patterns: Role of Off-farm Employment for Balanced Rural Development**

## INTRODUCTION

In the early decades of development, employment objectives were often treated as a by-product of economic growth, which emphasized industrialization as a leading element. Today employment and equity are considered to be the central issues of development goals. We now realize that without steady development of the agricultural sector and of rural areas, overall economic development will be hardly achieved. Considering the fact that the urban-industrial sector has often limited capacity to absorb the growing rural labour force, there are two alternatives for employment expansion. One is to enhance the labour absorptive capacity within agriculture, the other is to create rural off-farm employment. This paper focuses on the latter alternative.

The aim of this paper is threefold. First, we attempt to give an overview of the extent and nature of off-farm employment in both developed and developing countries. Second, we attempt a theoretical analysis to explain the rationale for off-farm employment or part-time farming. Finally, we examine the viability and policy implications of off-farm employment for sustained rural development.

Employment patterns in rural areas are alway changing[1]. One well-known fact is that the relative share of the agricultural labour force has been declining in the process of industrialization and urbanization. The other important change, which has been frequently neglected, is the shift toward more off-farm employment in rural areas of both the developed and the developing world. Statistical evidence shows that an increasing percentage of the rural labour force is engaged solely or in part with off-farm employment. Rural off-farm activities are becoming an important source of income in many developing countries. Though the nature and implications are essentially different, advanced countries have also shown a general trend of increased part-time farming, a combination of farm and off-farm employment by farm households[2].

* This paper also represents an outcome of the discussion in the Seminar on Mixed Households (Part-Time Farming) at Ljubljana, Yugoslavia, 22–24 June 1981.

TABLE 1 *Distribution of employed labour force between agricultural* and non-agricultural activities in rural areas: selected countries*[1]

| Category | Country | Year | Primary employment | | Cropped area per agricultural worker |
|---|---|---|---|---|---|
| | | | Agricultural | Non-agricultural | |
| | | | % | % | ha.[2] |
| Rural areas, excluding urbanized settlements | Kenya | 1969 | 72 | 28 | 0.48 |
| | Iran | 1972 | 67 | 33 | 4.63 |
| | Colombia | 1970 | 77 | 23 | 1.82 |
| | Indonesia | 1971 | 72 | 28 | 0.63 |
| | Thailand | 1972 | 82 | 18 | 0.84 |
| | Philippines | 1970 | 72 | 28 | 1.16 |
| | Korea, Rep. | 1970 | 81 | 19 | 0.38 |
| | Taiwan (China) | 1966 | 51 | 49 | 1.12 |
| | India | 1966/67 | 80 | 20 | 0.50 |
| Rural areas, including rural towns | Colombia | 1974 | 57 | 43 | |
| | Philippines | 1970 | 60 | 40 | |
| | Korea, Rep. | 1970 | 75 | 25 | |
| | Taiwan (China) | 1966 | 49 | 51 | |
| | India | 1966/67 | 76 | 24 | |

*Sources:* [1] Extracted from the statistics arranged by Anderson, D. and Leiserson, M. W., *Rural Enterprise and Nonfarm Employment*, A World Bank Paper, January 1978, Table 1., pp. 17–18; [2] Calculated from Food and Agriculture Organization, *Production Yearbook*, for the year 1970.

**Includes agriculture, forestry, fishing, and hunting.*

Until now, however, neither agricultural economists nor developmental scientists have to any extent studied part-time farming (or off-farm employment in more general terms) as a major field of professional emphasis. They have tended to consider this phenomenon as either a transitional pattern in the economic development process or simply a secondary, insignificant matter. The fact is that off-farm employment has been expanding and plays under some conditions an important role for sustained rural development.

## EXTENT AND CHARACTERISTICS OF OFF-FARM EMPLOYMENT

It is not easy to identify and measure statistically the extent of off-farm employment, due mainly to the lack of statistics on rural off-farm employment in many developing countries. Furthermore, there exists no formal definition for rural off-farm employment, nor is there any clear distinction between rural and urban areas.

A recent World Bank paper, however, has attempted to compare the levels of rural non-farm employment in some developing countries. It reports that for most of the 15 developing countries where recent statistics are available, the percentage of the rural labour force primarily engaged in non-farm work is, as a minimum estimate, between 20 and 30 per cent. The report also shows that when somewhat urbanized larger rural towns are included, the non-farm percentage of the rural labour force is raised substantially to roughly 30 to 40 per cent[3], as is shown in Table 1.

In Asian countries, where nearly two-thirds of the Third World's population live, work outside farms may have even greater potential importance because of the way agriculture is developing. Land fragmentation has produced a number of landless and nearly landless people. Larger more wealthy farmers are often adopting inappropriate and expensive farm machines, reducing the demand for hired farm labour. Hence, off-farm employment offers an important source of income for rural families, especially the poorer ones.

In already developed countries, too, off-farm employment and incomes are a significant component of farm households today. In Japan over 80 per cent of the total farm households have one or more members of the family working off-farm; in the United States over 50 per cent of the farm family income was obtained from off-farm sources in recent years. Table 2 shows to what extent major OECD countries have part-time farming units relative to the total number of farms in recent years. It should be noted here that the percentage of off-farm income to total family income has increased in the last decade or so in most of these countries.

Causes and motivations for combining off-farm employment with farming are numerous, depending upon the type of farming and resource endowments of individual farm households and the land and labour market situations of the area concerned. But basically they are classified into 'push' and 'pull' factors. Among important push factors are limited opportunities to expand farm incomes, due probably to small farm size or lack of capital and technological progress within agriculture which enables shorter hours of labour input. On the other hand, a most important pull factor is increased off-farm employment opportunities, due mainly to industrial growth and transportation development[4].

Differences among countries in terms of the extent of off-farm employment can be explained by both economic and non-economic factors. But two factors seem to be particularly important. One is the degree of agricultural opportunity, a typical example of this being the average farm size. It is generally observed that the smaller the farm size, the greater percentage of income tends to be gained from off-farm sources. The other factor is the degree of industrialization and the location of non-farm employment opportunities. The high figure for off-farm employment in Taiwan, for example, is due not only to an extremely small farm size but also to well-developed decentralized industries, together with short commuting distances, all of which are well constrasted with the experience of Thailand[5] where the man/land ratio is relatively small.

TABLE 2 *Extent of part-time farming in some OECD countries*

| Country | Year | Full-time | Part-time Class I[1] | Part-time Class II[1] | Average farm size |
|---|---|---|---|---|---|
| | | % | % | % | ha |
| Japan | 1965 | 21.5 | 36.7 | 41.8 | 1.0 |
| | 1975 | 12.5 | 25.4 | 62.1 | 1.1 |
| West Germany | 1965 | 40.9 | 25.7 | 33.4 | 8.9 |
| | 1975 | 45.2 | 15.3 | 39.5 | 13.8 |
| United States | 1959 | 55.1 | 15.0 | 29.9 | 121.2 |
| | 1969 | 45.7 | 14.3 | 40.0 | 155.6 |
| Norway | 1972 | 33.4 | 21.5 | 44.1 | 17.6 |
| Austria | 1973 | 45.8 | 10.5 | 43.7 | 19.4 |
| Switzerland | 1975 | 48.6 | 9.1 | 42.3 | 8.7 |
| Italy | 1970 | 62.4 | 5.0 | 32.6 | 6.9 |
| Netherland | 1975 | 74.1 | 6.3 | 18.4 | 11.6 |
| France | 1970 | 77.4 | 5.8 | 16.8 | 22.1 |
| Canada | 1970 | 69.4 | 10.7 | 19.9 | 187.5 |

[1]Full-time farming is roughly defined as where no income from off-farm work is obtained; part-time farms are divided into two categories: Class I (Class II) is the farm in which less than half (over half) of the household income comes from off-farm sources, or less than half (over half) of the operator's working time is devoted to off-farm employment.

*Sources:* *Part-Time Farming in OECD Countries: General Report* (Paris, OECD, 1978); *Production Yearbook* (Rome, FAO, 1975).

As the economy of a nation develops, the characteristics of off-farm employment change, usually from subsistence orientated to modern industrial activities. At the early development stage, traditional manufacturing such as weaving cloth and leather-making are dominant; cottage industry, simple food processing, or petty trading may also be prevalent. Later, off-farm employment tends to shift to become more capital intensive in nature and geographically it moves from rural to urban areas. At any stage of development, however, off-farm employment can provide the farming population with additional employment and incomes.

Another important aspect of off-farm employment is that such work plays an important part in evening out employment opportunities over the year in rural areas. Agricultural work by its nature has usually a large swing between near full employment in peak periods, such as planting and harvesting, and nearly total unemployment in the slack season. That is why off-farm work typically rises when farm work falls and falls when farm work rises. Off-farm work, if it is properly adopted, can decrease seasonal or disguised unemployment.

## ROLE OF OFF-FARM EMPLOYMENT IN THE DEVELOPMENT PROCESS

We may now be able to summarize the potential role of off-farm employment in rural development. The following are three basic functions that can be played by off-farm employment, assuming that off-farm work is appropriately distributed and is spread to the desired segment of the rural population. This has been deduced from the post-war experiences of Japan, the Taiwan area, and Korea[6].

### *Employment Expansion Effect*

Off-farm activities in rural areas directly expand employment opportunities for the rural population. This is partly because it can utilize a disadvantaged labour force, such as women and the elderly who otherwise would have little opportunities to work in the modern sector. Also, off-farm work can even out labour utilization over the year since agricultural works are highly seasonal. Another advantage of rural off-farm employment is that it can provide additional employment in a relatively inexpensive way. This comes from the fact that such off-farm work tends to adopt more labour-intensive technology than the modern industrial sector in urban areas and usually uses local resources for local needs.

### *Income Distribution Effect*

As pointed out earlier, off-farm employment is an important source of income for many rural families, especially those poorer families who possess little or no farmland. Various surveys indicate that the less land a farm family manages, the more off-farm work it does and the greater share of income is obtained from off-farm sources. This negative correlation between farm size and the level of off-farm income indicates that off-farm employment can contribute to a more equitable distribution of income in rural areas. This appears to have greater significance to Asian countries where farmland is relatively scarce and fragmented and population density is very high, including a number of landless people.

*Linkage Effect*

Off-farm employment may bring about a closer linkage between agricultural development and industrial development, a factor which has often been lacking in development efforts. When off-farm employment is created, the level of farm family income is increased, which in turn increases the demand for both non-food consumption goods and agricultural inputs produced in the industrial sector. Rural off-farm employment can also reinforce the economic ties between urban and rural areas without worsening unemployment in already urbanized areas. Hence, off-farm activities may be considered to be an intermediary for a closer linkage between the rural agricultural and urban industrial sectors.

## A THEORETICAL APPROACH FOR LABOUR ALLOCATION BETWEEN FARM AND OFF-FARM

The structural transformation of economies has been analysed by development economists using the macroeconomic analytical tools of dualistic growth models. But dualistic models usually work on an implicit assumption that the transfer of labour occurs discretely, that is labour is employed strictly in either one sector or the other. Not enough investigations have been undertaken to analyse theoretically the adjustment process at the micro-level. In particular the existence of part-time farming or off-farm employment taken up by farm households has seldom been taken into account in orthodox economic thories[7].

In this section, we present a simple theoretical model to explain why such farm households with off-farm employment exist and how they respond to the changing structure of labour and land market conditions which take place with overall economic development. This model is a conventional income/leisure utility maximization type[8].

We first assume that the farm household possesses the following utility function and tries to maximize its utility level, given its production function and exogenous parameters.

$$U = U(A, M) \tag{1}$$

where $A$ is the total labour hours provided by the members of the whole household in a year and $M$ stands for the amount of household income earned for the same period. This utility function is expressed as ordinary indifference curves which are upward sloping to the right in the income/labour diagram. Hence, it follows that:

$$U_A < 0; \; U_M > 0 \tag{2}$$

where $U_A = \delta U/\delta A$ and $U_M = \delta U/\delta M$.

The slope of the indifference curve, which is expressed as $-U_A/U_M (>0)$, measures the amount of $M$ which is required just to compensate for a marginal increase in the family labour. According to Nakajima's terminology, we call this the marginal valuation of family labour. Since we assume that the utility function is a continuous, twice differentiable, monotonically increasing function of income ($M$) and leisure ($\bar{H} - A$), it is reasonable to assume that:

$$\frac{\delta}{\delta A}\left(-\frac{U_A}{U_M}\right) > 0, \text{ and } \frac{\delta}{\delta \mathrm{M}}\left(-\frac{\mathrm{U_A}}{\mathrm{U_M}}\right) > 0' \qquad (3)$$

The farm production function is assumed, again for simplicity, as the function of the labour input to the farm operation ($A_1$) and of the fixed amount of owned farmland ($\bar{B}$). It is assumed that no rental market for land exists.

$$F = F\,(A_1; \bar{B}) \qquad (4)$$

The marginal product of labour of this production function is assumed to be non-negative and always decreasing, that is, $F_{A_1} \geqq 0$, and $F_{A_1 A_1} < 0$.

We also assume that the farm household has employment opportunities off the farm. Hence the farm household as a whole may obtain income not only from farming but from off-farm employment. Then the total household income is expressed as the following equation:

$$M = P.F\,(A_1; \bar{B}) + w.\,(A - A_1) \qquad (5)$$

where $P$ is the market price of farm product; $w$ is the fixed wage rate per hour; and $(A - A_1)$ is the amount of labour hours employed off-farm that is non-negative and has some limit, *i.e.*, $0 \geqq A - A_1 \geqq \bar{T}$.

By maximizing the utility function (1) subject to the income equation (5), we can get the following first-order conditions, solving $\delta U/\delta A = \delta U/\delta A_1 = 0$:

$$P.F_{A_1} = -\frac{U_A}{U_M} = w \qquad (6)$$

These conditions imply that in equilibrium the marginal product of labour on the farm must be equal to the wage rate, and that the marginal valuation of family labour should also be equal to the off-farm wage rate. From the equations (5) and (6), we obtain the optimum amount of labour input ($A_1^*$ and $A^*$) and the corresponding income level $M^*$.

An example of this equilibrium condition is depicted in Figure 1. This figure illustrates the case where the farm household takes up at least some off-farm employment (that is, $A^* - A_1^* > O$) and obtain off-farm income, $w.\,(A^* - A_1^*)$. The equilibrium points are at $Q$ and $R$, which determines the level of farm and off-farm labour input, respectively (or, $Q'$ and $R'$ in the

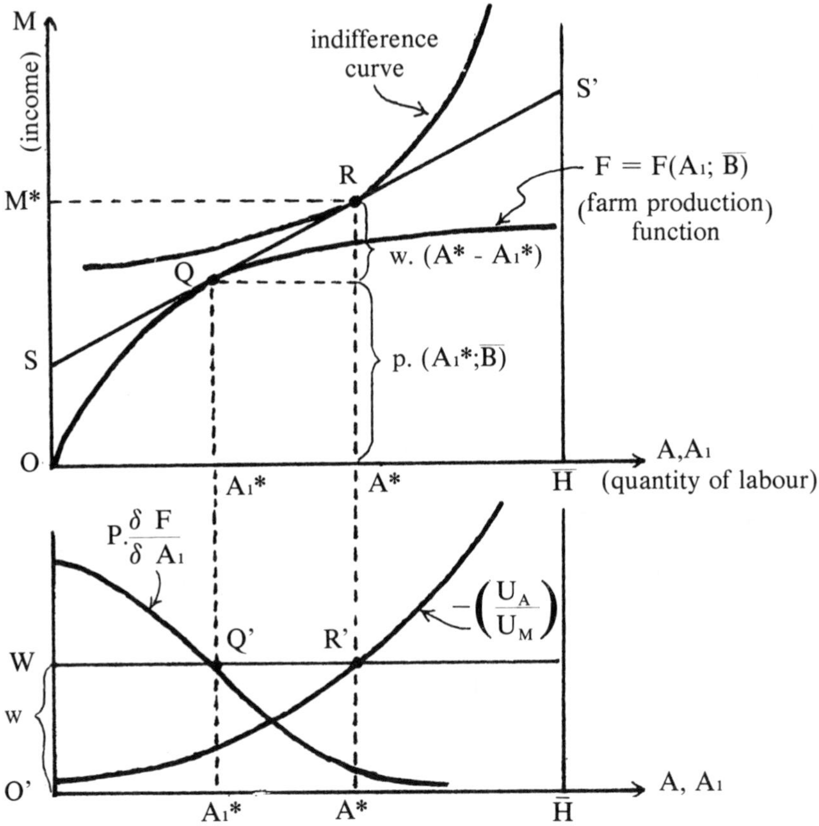


FIGURE 1 *Subjective equilibrium of the farm household faced with off-farm employment opportunities*

lower diagram showing the equilibrium of marginal values). It should be noted that there is no guarantee to obtain equilibrium at R that stands on the off-farm wage line *SS'*; in some other case where the farm production function takes a much higher position than the one shown in Figure 1, no off-farm work may be taken up. Alternatively, when the farm household takes up off-farm work up to the limit ($\overline{T}$), the equilibrium is represented by a corner solution, and the following equilibrium conditions hold:

$$P.F_{A_1} = -\frac{U_A}{U_M} < w;\ A - A_1 = \overline{T} \qquad (6')$$

## CONCLUDING REMARKS

*Off-farm employment as a vehicle for sustained rural development*

The above theoretical analysis indicates that taking up off-farm employment can be a rational behaviour of farmers in which they adjust themselves to changing conditions of the labour market. The model also implies that other factors, such as wage rate increases, labour saving technical progress within agriculture, and more and longer off-farm work opportunities, may shift the labour allocation pattern toward relatively greater off-farm employment. In concluding this paper we examine some implications and required conditions of off-farm employment for sustained rural development.

Considering that off-farm employment takes up a substantial share of the contemporary rural labour force in the developing world and that it is situated at the interface between the urban industrial sector and the rural agricultural sector, off-farm employment should be taken into account as an important vehicle for a balanced and sustained rural development strategy focusing on growth and equity, particularly in areas where the man/land ratio is high.

Although it may be admitted that off-farm employment plays such important roles as employment expansion, more equitable income distribution and rural urban linkage creation, there are many difficult and complicated issues to be solved. Among those crucial issues are: (a) whether off-farm employment has a reasonable labour absorptive capacity; (b) how to provide such work opportunities to the needed segment of the rural population; and (c) whether or not off-farm employment brings about any negative effects on agricultural production and resource use[9].

With respect to the labour absorption capacity, it should be noted that creating jobs in the urban industrial sector usually requires far more capital than the creation of jobs in the rural agricultural sector. In this context, off-farm employment tends to have technology with a lower capital/labour ratio than in the modern industrial sector which often uses a highly capital-intensive imported technology. A lower capital/labour ratio means that off-farm employment located in rural areas possesses a higher labour absorptive capacity per unit of capital investment. To be more successful, therefore, the choice of technology should be rather small-scale, locally adapted so that a less skilled labour force can have an access to it.

Finally, it must be noticed that off-farm employment alone cannot guarantee the sustained economic development of rural areas. Agricultural productivity has to be raised in order to have balanced development. Productivity increase in agriculture not only increases the demand for industrial inputs but also releases more labour hours to be utilized in off-farm activities. In sum, off-farm employment should be integrated with overall rural development efforts. Growth of off-farm activities in rural areas depends not only on government efforts to relocate non-farm industries but also on the steady growth of agricultural productivity.

## NOTES

[1] For a detailed review on this, see P. Gregory, 'An Assessment of Changes in Employment Conditions in Less Developed Countries', *Economic Development and Cultural Change,* 28–4, July 1980.

[2] See for a general discussion of part-time farming in developed countries, S. I. Krasovec, 'The Future of Part-Time Farming', in *Proceedings of the Twelth IAAE Meeting for 1964,* pp. 246–75, London, 1975; also see Kada, R. *Part-Time Family Farming,* Centre for Academic Publications Japan, Tokyo, 1980.

[3] See D. Anderson, M. W. Leiserson, *Rural Enterprise and Nonfarm Employment,* A World Bank Paper, January 1978.

[4] For a detailed description on this, see R. Kada, *Part-Time Family Farming.*

[5] For a recent experience of Thailand, see T. Onchan, and Y. Chalamwong, 'Rural Off-Farm Employment and Income of Rural Households in Thailand', paper presented at the International Seminar on Off-Farm Employment and Rural Industrialization, FFTC/ASPAC, Tokyo, October 1981.

[6] For the experience of Taiwan, see Ho, S.P.S., 'Decentralized Industrialization and Rural Development: Evidence from Taiwan', *Economic Development and Cultural Change* 28–1, Oct. 1979; see also for a comparative study of Korea and Japan, R. Kada, 'Employment Creation in Rural Areas: The Achievement of Saemaul Undong and Further Development'', in Lee, M.G. (ed.), *Toward A New Community,* Seoul National University, April, 1981.

[7] Exceptions in this area are: C. Nakajima, 'Subsistence and Commercial Family Farms: Some Theoretical Models of Subjective Equilibrium', in C.R. Wharton, Jr.*et al., Subsistence Agriculture and Economic Development,* Aldine, Chicago, 1969; J. E. Lee, Jr. 'Allocating Farm Resources between Farm and Nonfarm Uses', *Journal of Farm Economics* 47–1, 1965; and S. Hymer, and S. Resnick, 'A Model of an Agrarian Economy with Non-Agricultural Activities', *American Economic Review* Sept. 1969.

[8] This section is an application of the subjective equilibrium theory of family farms, see C. Nakajima, *Subsistence and Commercial Family Farms,* pp. 165–96.

[9] For a review and detailed discussion of labour absorption capacity of agriculture, see S. Ishikawa, et al., *Employment Expansion in Asian Agriculture,* ILO–ARTEP, Bangkok, March 1980; see also Hara, Y., 'Off-Farm Employment in Economic Development: Some Theoretical Considerations', paper presented at the International Seminar on Off-Farm Employment and Rural Industrialization, FFTC/ASPAC, Tokyo, October 1981.

INDERJIT SINGH

# *The Landless Poor in South Asia**

## INTRODUCTION**

The majority of the world's poor are among the 625 million people residing in the rural areas of South Asia[1]. Poverty is massive both in absolute numbers and as proportions of the rural populations. According to various studies, by 1980 an estimated 265 million people (48 per cent of the rural population) in India, 52 million in Bangladesh (78 per cent) and 38 million (58 per cent) in Pakistan were living below the country-specific 'poverty lines' in rural areas[2]. Although the data as well as the 'poverty lines' leave much to be desired, the absolute numbers in poverty are very large and increasing everywhere in South Asia.

The majority of the rural poor are (a) small and marginal farmers – owner cultivators, tenants and part tenants – with operational holdings less than two hectares and (b) agricultural labour households with little or no land who rely mainly on casual wage employment for their livelihood. Any measure to redress their poverty must concentrate on increasing productivity on small farms and employment opportunities for both groups. In particular the concern centres around the so-called 'landless'. It is widely believed that (a) they comprise a majority of the poor; (b) their numbers and proportions are increasing dramatically; (c) they are being by-passed by programmes designed mainly to benefit the landed; (d) the benefits of growth do not 'trickle down' to them; (e) few if any programmes have proved successful in increasing their incomes; and (f) apart from a radical programme of land redistribution little can be done to improve their prospects. Some go so far as to argue that growth has actually increased their poverty.

* The following paper is a very abbreviated version of that presented at the Conference. Space limitations prevented publication of the full paper but, as the author indicates below, its contents will probably appear as a publication of the World Bank. (Ed.)

** This paper draws heavily on the draft of my book *Small Farmers and the Landless in South Asia,* which is being submitted to the World Bank for publication. Numerous references to that work are referenced as Singh (1982), with appropriate chapters and pages indicated. The views expressed in this paper represent those of the author and not necessarily those of the World Bank.

More recently there has been an upsurge in the concern over the 'landless' as evidenced by a rash of recent publications on the subject[3], so much so that a certain cynicism has set in[4]. The major concern is that by identifying the rural poor with the 'small farmer', many policies and programmes currently being undertaken by both national governments and international agencies may be irrelevant or even counter-productive. Esman (1978) has succinctly summarized this concern:

> One of the principal fallacies in the discussion of rural poverty in the third world is to regard the rural poor as an undifferentiated mass of 'small farmers' ... with relatively small but secure holdings, which with the help of improved technologies and cropping practices, inputs, production incentives and marketing could provide a decent livelihood . . .
>
> In some countries there are many small farm households which more or less fit this image, and have a reasonable chance of providing decent family livelihoods under prevailing institutional conditions. They need and could benefit from the help of government and development agencies. But they are seldom the majority of rural households and they are certainly not the poorest. Below them in status, influence and material welfare are landless workers, tenants and sharecroppers and marginal farmers whose holdings are so small, often so fragmented, and of such poor quality that they cannot provide a livelihood from their holdings and must therefore deploy a large proportion of their family labour supply off the farm. While some marginal farmers could be helped by improved infrastructure, technologies, inputs and other measures identified with small farmer strategies, . . . in many cases and size and quality of their holdings make this unlikely, even when governments are prepared to undertake the greatly increased expenditures that these measures would require.
>
> Conceiving the rural poor casually as 'small farmers' contributes to the continued neglect of those in the lower strata who are much poorer and in many countries far more numerous. Since we believe that any effective strategy of rural development must take explicitly into account the poor majority, we focus on the landless and near landless – those groups who are below the category of the 'small farmer'.

In the course of this paper we will examine some of these contentions to see if they stand up to the evidence from South Asia. In particular we will try to clarify the concept of 'landlessness' and to outline what programmes, if any, have succeeded in alleviating their poverty.

## WHO ARE THE LANDLESS?

The problem of 'landlessness' is grossly exaggerated. Part of the problem is conceptual, and part of the problem is inadequate or poor data. Some of it is due to misleading and sloppy interpretation of the data and some may even be politically motivated through a desire to exaggerate the problems of poverty by showing that currently designed growth strategies are bypassing 'a large majority of the rural poor who are landless'. What are the facts?

*Conceptual Confusion*

At least three alternative definitions for the 'landless' in rural areas are tenable: (a) those who *own* no land; (b) those who *operate* no land; and (c) those whose *major* source of income is wage employment. Each definition includes different but not mutually exclusive subsets of the rural population (typically these subsets overlap) and has different implications both with regard to the control over rural and other assets and how incomes are derived from them. The three are often hopelessly confused. Data on 'landlessness' *per se* is meaningless without adequate means to differentiate between these categories. Perforce, data are not up to the task.

TABLE 1 *India: agrarian profile and landlessness in rural India (Household numbers in millions)*

| | | Owning land | Not owning land | Row total |
|---|---|---|---|---|
| Operating land | | | | |
| (a) NSS: | 1960–61 | 51.81 (71.5) | 1.62 (2.2) | 53.4 (73.7) |
| (b) NSS: | 1970–71 | 54.7 (69.8) | 2.2 (2.8) | 56.9 (72.6) |
| (c) (Est.) | 1980–81* | 64.38 (67.0) | 3.33 (3.47) | 67.7 (70.5) |
| | | (Group A) | (Group C) | (A + C) |
| Not operating land | | | | |
| (a) NSS: | 1960–61 | 12.2 (16.8) | 6.8 (9.4) | 19.0 (26.3) |
| (b) NSS: | 1970–71 | 16.1 (20.5) | 5.4 (6.9) | 21.5 (27.4) |
| (c) (Est.) | 1980–81* | 23.6 (24.56) | 4.78 (4.97) | 28.38 (29.5) |
| | | (Group B) | (Group D) | (B + D) |
| Total | | | | |
| (a) NSS: | 1960–61 | 64.0 (88.3) | 8.46 (11.7) | 72.46 (100.0) |
| (b) NSS: | 1970–71 | 70.8 (90.3) | 7.6 (9.7) | 78.4 (100.0) |
| (c) (Est.) | 1980–81* | 87.98 (91.6) | 8.11 (8.4) | 96.1 (100.0) |
| | | (A + B) | (C + D) | (A + B + C + D) |

*Note:* Figures in brackets give percentage of total in each year.
*Sources:* B. Minhas (1970); NSS, 16th Round, 1960–61; NSS, 25th Round, 1970–71; taken from Singh (1982), Chapter 2.

The best way to look at the data on 'landlessness' is to construct a four-way classification on the basis of both ownership and operational distributions: (a) those who own land and operate it or a class of *owner-operators* (group A); (b) those who own land but do not operate any – rentier class of *'landlords'* or 'absentee owners' who presumably rent out all their land

TABLE 2 *India: percentage of landless households not owning and not operating land, select states, 1954–55, 1961–62 and 1971–72*

| State | Percentage of households not owning land | | | Percentage of households not operating land | | | Percentage of households owning but not operating | | Percentage of households neither owning nor operating | | Percentage of landless households leasing in land |
|---|---|---|---|---|---|---|---|---|---|---|---|
| | Round | | | Round | | | Round[2] | | Round[2] | | Round |
| | 8th | 17th | 26th | 8th[1] | 17th | 26th | 17th | 26th | 17th | 26th | 26th |
| Punjab | 36.86 | 12.33 | 7.14 | 38.92 | 39.09 | 58.61 | 30.51 | 52.90 | 8.58 | 5.71 | 66.83[3] |
| Haryana | - | - | 11.89 | - | - | 48.00 | - | 41.05 | - | 6.94 | |
| Gujarat | - | 14.74 | 13.44 | - | 25.41 | 33.75 | 11.78 | 25.47 | 13.63 | 8.28 | 55.98 |
| Andhra Pradesh | 30.12 | 6.84 | 6.95 | 42.80 | 37.95 | 36.05 | 32.03 | 29.68 | 5.92 | 6.37 | 83.58 |
| Bihar | 16.56 | 8.83 | 4.34 | 23.84 | 21.71 | 20.65 | 15.28 | 17.52 | 6.43 | 3.13 | 83.56 |
| West Bengal | 20.54 | 12.56 | 9.78 | 24.30 | 33.88 | 30.94 | 24.21 | 23.09 | 9.67 | 7.85 | 86.65 |

*Notes* [1] Gives percent of non-agricultural holdings deemed comparable by Sanyal to 17th and 26th round; [2] 8th round estimates are not available; [3] Includes Haryana.
*Source:* NSS data reported by SK Sanyal (1977) in Sarvekshana; taken from Singh (1982).

(group B); (c) those who do not own any land but operate some by renting-in from others – a class of *pure tenants* (group C); and (d) finally a group that neither owns nor operates any land – *purely landless* (group D). The all-India NSS data on this four-way classification for 1960–61 and 1970–71 (and extrapolated to 1980–81 on the assumption that similar trends have continued) are presented in Table 1. Such a classification was first made by Minhas (1970) using the 1960–61 data and we have added the 1970–71 NSS data and extrapolated. Evidence from *Indian* data which are the most complete shows that (a) 'landlessness' in terms of 'those who own no land' is small (10 per cent), and has declined in both relative and absolute terms, (b) 'landlessness' in terms of 'those who operate no land' is larger (around 28 per cent) and has increased in both relative and absolute terms, while (c) 'landlessness' in terms of 'those who neither own nor operate any land' (intersection of the first two) is very small (around 7 per cent) and has declined in both relative and absolute terms. Further, a substantial portion of 'those who operate no land' – nearly three-quarters – are owners of land. It is actually only the last category that has no access to land either through ownership or tenancies.

The all-India data hide marked regional differences. Sanyal (1976) has analysed the NSS data for six Indian states. This is quite revealing and is given in Table 2. 'Landlessness' in terms 'of those not operating any land' has increased significantly in many agriculturally dynamic states (Punjab, Haryana, Gujerat); but this should not be a cause for alarm, as it is the result of a larger proportion of the rural population moving away from agricultural occupations towards a growing and dynamic non-farm sector. In some agriculturally stagnant states (W. Bengal and Bihar) this type of landlessness has actually declined. These types of data on 'landlessness' suggest the *ambiguity* of the concept as it fails to distinguish between the consequences of dynamic from stagnant processes that have the same outcome – fewer people owning or operating land!

Mead Cain (1981) in a recent paper suggests that much of the NSS data has an upward bias because it shows many households 'owning land' when most likely they own only non-arable land – probably homestead plots. Although even these plots are used to grow crops, in some cases an adjustment is justified and Table 3 gives his adjusted figure for India. The evidence clearly suggests that 'landlessness' in terms of 'those who own no land' has been *declining* in spite of the oft repeated claims to the contrary[5].

Much that has been written on 'landlessness' in *Bangladesh* is replete with confusion on definitions and data sources. No consistent set of data exists that allow us to say anything about *trends* in 'landlessness', although these have been inferred from a large set of disparate and non-comparable sources. What little is firmly known suggests that (a) 'landlessness' in terms of non-ownership of land is significant (29 per cent of all rural households), (b) the percentage of 'landless labour' to total rural households is large – around 30 per cent, and (c) this latter category has been growing in both relative and absolute terms and this trend may have accelerated in recent years[6]. As Cain (1981) points out 'we have some confidence that the

TABLE 3 *Total landlessness and near-landlessness among households in rural India according to national sample survey data, 1954/55 – 1971/72*

(Households in millions)

| Size of ownership holding (acres) | 8th Round[1] (1954–55) | | | | 17th Round[2] (1961–62) | | | | 26th Round[3] (1971–72) | | | |
|---|---|---|---|---|---|---|---|---|---|---|---|---|
| | % | Adj. | Cumulative % | Adj.[4] | % | Adj. | Cumulative % | Adj.[4] | % | Adj. | Cumulative % | Adj.[4] |
| 0.00 | 23.09 | (30.8) | 23.09 | (30.8) | 11.68 | (27.5) | 11.68 | (27.5) | 9.64 | (25.6) | 9.64 | (25.6) |
| 0.01 – 0.49 | 18.01 | (8.0) | 41.10 | (38.8) | 26.23 | (10.4) | 37.91 | (37.9) | 27.78 | (11.8) | 37.42 | (37.4) |
| 0.50 – 0.09 | 6.16 | (6.2) | 47.26 | (45.0) | 5.31 | (6.3) | 44.22 | (44.2) | 7.45 | (7.4) | 44.87 | (44.8) |

*Notes:* [1] For the 8th Round, ownership was defined as right of permanent and heritable possession; landholding was inclusive of all land, regardless of purpose to which put; [2] For the 17th Round, ownership was defined to include ownership-like possessions; [3] For the 26th Round, ownership and landholding were defined as for 17th round; [4] (Adj.) gives the adjusted figures after correcting for errors in NSS data by *excluding* homestead land and leaving the proportion of households with *arable* land in each ownership category.

*Sources:* 8th: NSS Report No. 36, Appendix 3, Table 15, p. 71 and Table 8, p. 64. 17th: NSS Report No. 144, Table 3(1), p. 7 and Appendix 1, Table 2, p. 13. 26th: NSS Report No. 215, Table 2, p. 67. Tables taken from M. Cain (1981) 'Landlessness in India and Bangladesh: A Critical Review of Data Sources', The Population Council, New York (Working Paper No. 71, May 1981).

percentage of rural landless households at 29 in 1978, but beyond that little can be said'.

Nothing can be inferred directly about 'landlessness' – magnitudes of trends – in *Pakistan* because data are practically nonexistent. This is a serious lacuna in the agrarian data base. Data can however be 'constructed' from a number of sources and they show that (a) the proportion of rural households 'not operating any land', as well as the proportion of landless agricultural labour households as a percentage of all rural households, nearly doubled in the 1960s – from around 9 per cent to around 20 per cent. But this reconstruction is very weak and involves many assumptions about the data[7].

What this evidence suggests is that apart from the shaky data the concept of 'landlessness' – whether in terms of 'not owning' or not 'operating land' – though of some value – should not be of primary interest. Nor do trends in 'landlessness' signify much in and of themselves. They need to be examined along with other evidence on the changing agrarian structure. Instead one should concentrate directly (a) on the conditions of cultivation for those who *operate* land – the size of holding, its productivity and tenurial status – and (b) on the conditions of *wage employment* for those who depend primarily upon wage labour in rural areas for their incomes[8]. For this a close look at the occupational distribution of rural labour households is more helpful. To this we turn next.

*Rural labour households*

Neither the magnitudes nor trends in 'landlessness' *per se* are of primary interest. Of greater interest are those rural labour households that depend *primarily* on wage employment in rural areas, or more specifically in agriculture (agricultural labour households). Both sets include not only the so-called 'landless' but also many marginal and small farmers who operate owned land, as well as small tenants who lease-in land and who have to supplement their farm incomes by wage employment. It is to this set of 'households' that the term 'landless' and 'near landless' is often loosely applied. The majority of the rural poor come from these groups.

*Labour force composition*

Data on rural labour are sparse, except for India, and they often conflict as they come from a variety of sources, but they all show that the *proportions* as well as the *absolute numbers* of rural households who have to depend primarily on wage employment are *increasing.* As a corrollary those dependent primarily on farming as a source of income are declining.

The available data on the composition of the rural labour force by 'usual activity status' in South Asia are given in Table 4. A third of the rural population in Pakistan and Bangladesh and over two-fifths in India participated in the rural labour force. A quarter of these in India, a third in Pakistan and nearly half in Bangladesh were working on their own farms – that is were operating land as farmers or tenants. In India nearly two-thirds of the rural labour force are casual or agricultural labourers; in Bangladesh

TABLE 4 *South Asia: composition of rural labour force by usual activity status, 1972–78*

(In millions)

| | Pakistan | | India | | Bangladesh | | South Asia |
|---|---|---|---|---|---|---|---|
| | 1974 | Est. 1978 | 1972-73 | Est. 1978 | 1974 | Est. 1978 | (Est. 1978) |
| Rural population | 50.0 | 56.0 | 455.0 | 493.0 | 65.0 | 78.0 | 627.0 |
| Rural labour force | 15.0 (30.0)[1] | 17.0 (30.3)[1] | 200.0 (44.0)[1] | 218.0 (44.2)[1] | 16.0 (24.6)[1] | 24.0 (30.8)[1] | 260.0 (41.5)[1] |
| Proportion of rural labour | (100) | | (100) | | (100) | | (100) |
| Working on own farm | 0.9 (6) | 6.4 | 50.6 (25) | 55.4 | 7.5 (48) | 11.6 | 73.0 (28) |
| Working as casual wage earners/agr. labour (Min) | 0.9 (6) | 1.0 | 78.0 (39) | 86.0 | 4.0 (25) | 6.0 | 93.0 (36) |
| Working as helpers | 4.6 (30) | 5.1 | 45.6 (23) | 49.7 | 4.3 (27) | 6.6 | 61.0 (24) |
| Working as non–agricultural sector and/or seeking work | 4.3 (28) | 4.8 | 25.1 (13) | 27.5 | [2] | [2] | 32.0 (12) |

*Notes to Table 4 – opposite:* In Bangladesh only the Agricultural Labour Force was considered. While those working on own farms include part owners generally, a pure share cropper is also included here. In India the available breakdown was for farm and non-farm work combined. It was assumed that 74 per cent of the labour was for agricultural activities. For Pakistan the 1972 Agricultural Census gives higher estimates for labour force than the Labour Force Survey used here. 1978 estimates assume there is no change in the labour force structure from that which is known.

[1] Percentage of total rural population. Figures in brackets give the percentage of the rural labour force in each category.

[2] Included in other categories.

*Sources:* Government of Bangladesh, 'Agrarian Structure and Change: Rural Development Experience and Policies in Bangladesh', Dacca, May 1978, p. 64; World Bank, 'Economic situation and Prospects of India', Report No. 2431, April 1979, Table 1.8; Government of India *'Draft Five Year Plans 1978–83, Vol. II',* Planning Commission, New Delhi, 1978, Table 1, pp. 100–3, 127. Government of Pakistan, Ministry of Finance, Planning and Gronomic Affairs, 'Labour Force Survey, 1974–75', pp. XIX, 67, 81.

---

25 per cent and in Pakistan only 6 per cent. These rely primarily on wage employment. But not all are dependent on agriculture. A quarter of the rural labour force in Pakistan and about 15 per cent in India work in non-agricultural occupations (data for Bangladesh are unavailable).

To what extent these large differences, in proportions of the population participating in the labour force, reflect poor data bases – for only the Indian data can be deemed anywhere near reliable – is uncertain; but the magnitudes involved are very large. In 1978 of 260 million in the rural labour force an estimated 93 million (36 per cent) were 'casual wage earners' or 'agricultural labourers', while another 61 million (24 per cent) were working as 'helpers' or were 'permanent labourers' on other farms. Only 73 million (28 per cent) worked on their own farms, while some 32 million (12 per cent) worked in the non-agricultural sector and/or were seeking work.

## *Magnitudes and Trends*

### (a) *India*

The trends in the rural labour force and its composition are harder to quantify due to lack of comparable data. The best comparable data are Indian and these are presented in Table 5 on a regional basis[9]. In the Indian data which is most comprehensive, rural labour households are defined as those households whose major source of income is 'wage paid manual labour', that is if 'wage employment for manual labour contributed more towards its income in the 356 days preceding the data of the survey than other two sources taken individually'. The emphasis is on 'manual' and on

TABLE 5: *India: changes in rural labour, 1964–65, 1974–75*

| | Rural house-holds | Rural labour households: As % of (1) | Rural labour households: All | Rural labour households: with land | Rural labour households: without land (millions) | | Agricultural labour households: As % of (1) | Agricultural labour households: All | Agricultural labour households: with land | Agricultural labour households: without land (millions) |
|---|---|---|---|---|---|---|---|---|---|---|
| **1964–65** | | | | | | | | | | |
| North | 16.5 | (15.2) | 2.5 | 1.1 | 1.4 | (8.5) | (13.4) | 2.2 | 1.0 | 1.2 |
| West | 17.5 | (22.3) | 3.9 | 1.4 | 2.5 | (14.3) | (18.9) | 3.3 | 1.3 | 2.0 |
| South | 18.3 | (33.3) | 6.1 | 2.4 | 3.7 | (20.2) | (30.0) | 5.3 | 2.0 | 3.3 |
| East | 18.2 | (29.7) | 5.4 | 2.8 | 2.5 | (13.7) | (24.2) | 4.4 | 2.4 | 2.0 |
| All India | 70.4 | (25.4) | 17.9 | 7.7 | 10.1 | (14.4) | (26.6) | 15.2 | 6.7 | 8.5 |
| **1974–75** | | | | | | | | | | |
| North | 19.6 | (18.9) | 3.7 | 1.7 | 2.0 | (10.2) | (14.8) | 2.9 | 1.4 | 1.5 |
| West | 19.7 | (25.4) | 5.0 | 2.3 | 2.7 | (13.7) | (21.3) | 4.2 | 2.0 | 2.2 |
| South | 21.1 | (40.8) | 8.6 | 3.9 | 4.7 | (22.3) | (34.6) | 7.3 | 3.3 | 4.0 |
| East | 21.7 | (35.0) | 7.6 | 4.2 | 3.4 | (15.7) | (29.5) | 6.4 | 3.6 | 2.8 |
| All India | 82.1 | (30.3) | 24.9 | 12.1 | 12.8 | (15.6) | (25.3) | 20.8 | 10.3 | 10.5 |
| **Decade % Change (Increases)** | | | | | | | | | | |
| North | 20.0 | | 48.0 | 55.0 | 43.0 | | | 32.0 | 40.0 | 25.0 |
| West | 13.0 | | 28.0 | 64.0 | 8.0 | | | 27.0 | 54.0 | 10.0 |
| South | 15.0 | | 41.0 | 63.0 | 27.0 | | | 38.0 | 65.0 | 21.0 |
| East | 19.0 | | 41.0 | 50.0 | 36.0 | | | 45.0 | 50.0 | 40.0 |
| All India | 17.0 | | 39.0 | 57.0 | 27.0 | | | 37.0 | 54.0 | 24.0 |

*Notes to Table 5 – opposite:* (Figures in parenthesis give rural labour and agricultural labour households as % of all rural households.)

*Note:* Agricultural labour (drawing over half of their incomes as wages for agricultural work) households are 85 per cent of rural labour (drawing wages for labour in rural areas) households and 22 per cent of all rural households.
*Source:* GOI, Ministry of Labour, 'Rural Labour Enquiry 1974–75'.

---

'wage payment' – in cash or kind – so that we are concentrating on precisely the subset of occupations those without skills or assets would be engaged in. *Agricultural labour households* are a subset of rural labour households in that they are engaged in mainly agricultural activities – 'farming, dairying, horticulture, livestock or any practice performed on a farm as incidental to or in conjunction with farm operations and depend on wage labour as a primary source of income in the previous year'. (See *Rural Labour Enquiry 1974–75,* Summary Report.) Several features of the 1974–75 data need to be noted:

(a) of nearly 82 million rural households in India *only a third* (some 30 million households) could be classified as rural labour households – that is those primarily dependent on wage labour[10];
(b) of these over four-fifths (84 per cent), over 25 million households but only a *quarter* of all rural households could be classified as agriculture labour households – that is dependent primarily on wage employment in agriculture and related activities;
(c) there is considerable regional diversity, with the proportion of rural households that are labour households far higher in the East (35 per cent) and South (41 per cent), than in the North (19 per cent) and West (25 per cent)[11];
(d) of all rural labour households, a little more than half (51 per cent) were 'without land' – that is cultivated neither owned or leased-in land and hence were totally dependent on manual wage labour, but these constitute only 15.6 per cent of all rural households. (Again these proportions are higher in the South (22 per cent) and lower in the North (12.2 per cent) and West (13.7 per cent;).) So while a *third* of all rural households are primarily dependent on wage employment, only a *ninth* are *totally* dependent on it. These are the rural landless labour households.
(e) rural labour households have increased at a rate faster than rural households – this growth has been in excess of 4 per cent per annum in all regions of India except the West; agricultural labour households have increased similarly but at a slower rate of around 3.5 per cent per annum;
(f) the number of rural labour households 'with land' has increased at the highest rate and their proportion also increased significantly;
(g) the average size of rural and agricultural labour households increased from 4.51 to 4.7 for the former and from 4.47 to 4.76 for the latter in the decade[12].

The dynamics of the rural labour force in India are clear. While the absolute and relative numbers of those dependent primarily on manual wage labour have increased, the proportions of those dependent *totally* on wage labour have gone down even though their absolute numbers have not. Thus of 30 per cent of the rural households primarily dependent on wage employment, about half are landless labourers, but the other half are small and marginal farmers. This means that the significant increases in the ranks of agricultural labour have occurred through a process where an increasing number of those with small or marginal holdings have been pushed increasingly to rely upon wage employment, until it has become a primary source of income for them. We have already documented the main processes that have contributed to this outcome: (a) the subdivision of holdings into smaller and smaller cultivating units *via* inheritance and in the face of increasing population pressure on land; (b) the repossession of land held by tenants; (c) some distress sales of land by poorer farmers and to these may be added; (d) a rapid rise in the cost of living which may have forced small farmers to supplement their incomes *via* wage employment, so that labour displaced cultivation as a principal source of their income[13].

*(b) Bangladesh*

Although the use of wage labour is fairly widespread in Bangladesh there is very little data on rural labour households. What little data are available have to be pieced together from a variety of sources, are recent and are summarized in Table 6. The estimates obtained are at best sketchy, but they indicate the broad dimension of the numbers. About 40 per cent of all rural households (between 4.5 – 5.0 million) can be classified as rural labour households – that is, those dependent primarily upon manual wage employment – in recent years. Of these about 75 per cent depend primarily upon manual wage labour in agriculture. Households not owning and not operating any land and which can be presumed to be wholly dependent upon manual wage employment constitute between a quarter to a third of all rural households. If we took the lowest figure for 1978, this last category would account for a population of over 13 million, while those dependent primarily upon manual wage labour in rural areas would be around 23 million[14].

Fewer rural labour households in Bangladesh operate land than in India. One recent study of over 2,300 rural labourers who participated in the Food for Work programme in 1976 showed that 57 per cent had no land, while another 29 per cent operated less than one acre and only 13 per cent operated more than one acre. But again significantly, not more than two-thirds of the rural labourers were *totally* dependent on wage labour, even in this case. Again as in India, although the proportion of households 'neither operating nor owning land' may have declined (the figures are suspect, because the surveys are not strictly comparable), the proportion dependent *primarily* on wage employment specially in agriculture have increased dramatically.

TABLE 6: *Bangladesh: rural labour households in Bangladesh*

| | | 1973–74 | 1977 | 1978 | % Change 1973–74 to 1978 |
|---|---|---|---|---|---|
| 1 | Rural population (mil.) | 67.6 | 69.0 | 76.0 | 12.4 |
| 2 | Rural households (mil.) | 11.1 | 11.8 | 13.3 | 19.8 |
| 3 | Households operating only leased-in land (mil.) | 0.4 | 0.6 | 0.7 | 75.0 |
| | (%) | (3.6) | (5.1) | (5.8) | |
| 4 | Households not owning (a) and not operating any land (mil.) | 3.7 | 3.3 | 2.8 | – 39.3 |
| | (%) | (33.3) | (27.9) | (23.3) | |
| 5 | Estimated rural labour households (mil.) | 4.4 | 4.7 | 4.8 | 9.1 |
| | (%) | (39.6) | (39.8) | (40.0) | |
| 6 | Estimated agricultural labour households | 2.8 | 3.4 | 3.5 | 25.0 |
| | (%) | (25.2) | (28.8) | (29.2) | |
| 7 | Average household size | – | 4.81 | 4.72 | – |

*Note:* (a) Those who owned no land other than homestead land.
(Figures in parentheses give percentage of all rural households in the category.)

*Sources:* 1. GOB and WB population estimates; 2 Januzzi and Peach (1977, 1978); 3. GOB Agr. Census (1960); 4 MSA (1967–68) cited in WCAARD and Robinson; 5. HES and BDs data cited in Jabbar (1978) and assumptions on labour force in WB Economic Report.

### *(c) Pakistan*

Data on rural labour households in Pakistan is the scantiest of all. It also has to be pieced together from a variety of strictly non-comparable sources. Further, all we have to go on are estimates that are *residually* derived from the Agricultural Census and some direct estimates of agricultural labour from the Population Census. These broad estimates are given in Table 7. The figures are sketchy and probably unrealistic as they have been 'assembled' as it were from a variety of sources. Data on rural population and agricultural labourers are from the Population Census. The estimates depend crucially on the average size of rural households used. Since various estimates on household size are given, the estimates on rural labour in the table could also differ significantly. But nonetheless they are instructive.

To begin with, although the rural population increased considerably, the growth in the population of agricultural labourers increased far more slowly. The absolute number of agricultural labourers increased by some 20 per cent, but their proportion in the rural population *fell* from around 18 per cent in 1961 to 15 per cent in 1972. The remainder of the increase in 'rural households not operating land' – some 151 per cent in the decade – must have gone into other non-agricultural or non-wage occupations. This is confirmed by the rapid growth in non-farm employment and auxiliary sectors in the rural areas of Pakistan[15].

TABLE 7: *Pakistan: rural labourers in Pakistan*

| | | 1961 | 1972 | % Change 1961–1972 |
|---|---|---|---|---|
| 1. | Rural population (mil.) | 42.9 | 65.3 | 52.2 |
| | Punjab | 25.6 | 37.8 | 47.7 |
| | Sind | 8.5 | 14.2 | 67.1 |
| 2. | Rural household size | 5.5 | 5.8 | |
| 3. | Rural households (mil.)[a] | 7.8 | 11.3 | 44.9 |
| 4. | Farm households (mil.) | 4.9 | 4.0 | –18.4 |
| 5. | Rural households not operating land (mil.)[b] | 2.9 (37.2) | 7.3 (64.6) | 150.7 |
| 6. | Agricultural labourers (mil.) | 7.6 (17.7) | 9.7 (14.8) | 27.6 |
| | Punjab | 4.8 | 5.8 | 20.8 |
| | Sind | 1.6 | 2.4 | 50.0 |
| 7. | Agricultural labour[c] households (mil.) | 1.4 | 1.7 | 19.5 |

*Notes:* [a] Derived by dividing population by household size; [b] Residually derived (3 – 4); [c] 6 ÷ 2.
(Figures in parentheses are percentages of total rural households.)
*Sources:* 1. Census of Pakistan, 1961,, vol. 3; 2. Pakistan Economic Survey, 1977–78; 3. Pakistan Housing Economic and Demographic Survey Vol. 2; 4. Part 1, 3 and 5; 5. All (I) – (IV) cited in M.H. Khan (1979) and GOP/FAO; 'WCARRD Country Paper for Pakistan' (p. 39 for household size); 6. M. Afzal (1974).

Agricultural labourers increased by 50 per cent in Sind compared to 21 per cent in the Punjab between 1961 and 1972; but the rural population increased by 67 per cent and 48 per cent respectively. So there must have been an increase in non-wage occupations in rural areas in both states – more so in the Punjab. But in what occupations? The 1972 Agricultural Census shows that out of a total of 5.5 million 'agricultural households', 4 million operated farms, but 1.5 million were classified as 'livestock holders'. We do not know how many livestock holders there were in 1961, but Naseem (1979) has argued that livestock provides an important supplementary source of income for the landless, so that a decline in farming households has been offset by an increase in livestock households. He cites the considerable increase in the acreage to fodder during a period in Pakistan when draft animals were being replaced for farm power to substantiate his arguments. He concludes that during this period a large number of small and marginal farmers were forced to sell or leave their land and eke out their existence with livestock (buffaloes for milk) and specially small stock (goats). Further he reports an increasing trend towards hiring of wage labour on farms and suggests that on a 'crude measure of landlessness' (landless = rural-farming households), that 'from a low of 10 per cent in 1960 landlessness increased to about 48 per cent in 1972[16] . . . it ranged from 45 per cent in NWFP to 54 per cent in the Punjab'. These statements are probably conjectural at best. More likely, out-migrants and employment in non-wage occupations absorbed much of the increase in the non-farming population. These changes are not dissimilar to those in East Punjab where non-farming households have also increased dramatically and a high proportion of them are engaged in non-wage employment.

A detailed study by Eckert (1972) from a survey he carried out in the Punjab in 1971 is the only one of its kind for Pakistan that has as its focus rural labour and rural employment. Using his sample from 40 villages he estimated the occupational distribution: 69 per cent of the households were land owners or cash and kind tenants. Of the remaining 31 per cent of the non-farming households, some 13 per cent were classified as labour households (6 per cent permanent and 7 per cent temporary). The remaining 18 per cent were classified as artisans or shopkeepers. This is a different picture from that presented by Naseem. For 1970–71 he estimated some 3.2 million labourers and over 5.2 million artisans and shopkeepers. The artisan and shopkeeper category is specially large and included a number of trades whose income levels 'were tied to the prosperity of the village and this for most villages was related to the productivity of agriculture'. He estimated that perhaps 60 per cent of the hired labourers were only temporarily employed, worked one-third as many days as permanent workers (11.3 days/month against 29 days) and faced a constant struggle to find work. Temporary workers (called *kamees*) are most often used in harvesting operations by almost all farms while permanent workers were employed mainly on large farms. He estimated that 'more than 2 million Punjabis in the landless labour class of rural residents lived at the level of half a rupee per day per person'.

Wages, generally, rose in the Punjab. A 52 per cent increase in nominal wages in five years 1965–66 to 1970–71 was reported by Eckert for peak time operations – rice transplanting in this case. Artisan incomes also rose in real terms. A comparison of income per caput showed permanent labourers not much worse than tenant farmers, while temporary workers had incomes at least 10 per cent below their levels[17].

Apart from the higher growth and productivity experienced in the West

Punjab, another factor affecting the composition of the rural labour force is migration. Rural-urban migration and, recently, migration for work abroad is a contemporary fact of some magnitude. Eckert's study found that 19 per cent of the households in his survey had an out-migrant and an equal amount had access to remittances as an important augmentation to their incomes and affected the investment pattern[18]. But the out-migrants are least likely to have been landless labourers or even tenant farmers as his study also found. So in spite of recent talk of 'rural labour shortages', as a result of out-migration to the Middle East it is unlikely that the main beneficiaries of this process have been the unskilled and assetless labourers, for the simple reason that they do not have either the means to migrate or the skills to market. Nonetheless rural-urban migration in the West Punjab has also been high, reducing the potential labour supply in rural areas. Eckert claimed that 'over one million labourers have left Punjabi home villages to take work elsewhere'[19].

Recent data on the overlap between marginal farmers and agricultural labour are unavailable, but data from the 1961 Census showed that in Pakistan, out of a total of 3.2 million agricultural labourers only half a million were purely landless, the rest rented or owned some land in addition to wage employment. Some landless labourers are also engaged in a variety of other occupations – blacksmiths, carpentry, cloth weaving, pottery – and perform services or supply goods throughout the year for payment at harvest time. As such they comprise the service sector at the village level. The payment is often in kind and as a share of the produce. As different trades have been affected differently, some of these 'landless' have done better than those with land. In particular those with skills – the artisan class, blacksmiths, carpenters, and leather workers – have benefited from the general regional prosperity and are deemed in short supply. It is the temporarily hired landless labourers, those without skill and employed for less than half a month on average who are akin to agricultural labour households elsewhere in the subcontinent. They accounted for around only 8 per cent of all rural households in the West Punjab.

At the national level there are no other data pertaining to the magnitude and conditions of rural labour – a gap that is serious if one is to understand what is happening in the rural areas. Even given these crude figures it would be safe to conclude that although rural labour households have been increasing in number, their relative weight in the agrarian structure may have declined in Pakistan. In their place are increasing numbers of non-farming households relying on livestock and other artisan, trade related activities with wage labour to supplement their incomes. The proportion of the population relying wholly on wage labour is likely to be small and declining. This is in sharp contrast to the rest of the subcontinent except the Northwest – East Punjab and Haryana – where similar conditions prevail.

In spite of the varying numbers there is one feature that needs to be clearly emphasized – that 'small farmers' and 'agricultural labourers' are eventually overlapping categories. Since farmers with small or marginal holdings depend heavily on wage labour the distinction made between small

TABLE 8: *India: distribution of agricultural labour households*[a] *by area of land cultivated, 1974 – 75*

| Size group of land operated (Acres) | North | West | South | East | All |
|---|---|---|---|---|---|
| Nil | 51.1 | 53.5 | 54.8 | 44.4 | 50.8 |
| 0.0–0.5 | 19.1 | 12.1 | 16.6 | 27.3 | 19.3 |
| 0.5–1.0 | 15.2 | 5.1 | 9.0 | 11.8 | 9.9 |
| 1.0–1.5 | 8.0 | 6.7 | 7.8 | 8.7 | 7.9 |
| 1.5–2.0 | 2.5 | 3.3 | 2.6 | 2.4 | 2.6 |
| 2.0–2.5 | 2.3 | 5.5 | 3.8 | 2.9 | 3.7 |
| 2.5–5.0 | 1.5 | 9.1 | 4.1 | 2.2 | 4.2 |
| Over 5.0 | 0.4 | 4.7 | 1.4 | 0.3 | 1.6 |
| All | 100.0 | 100.0 | 100.0 | 100.0 | 100.0 |
| Millions | 2.92 | 4.19 | 7.23 | 6.39 | 20.72 |

[a] Those households which have over 50 per cent of their incomes from agricultural wages.
*Source:* GOI, Ministry of Labour, 'Rural Labour Enquiry 1974–75'.

cultivating households and rural labour households is improper because they are not mutually exclusive sets. Table 8 with data from India illustrates this feature very clearly. It is wrong therefore as some writers have done to distinguish 'small owners', 'small tenants' and 'agricultural labourers' as separate categories and then to 'add up' the proportion of rural households in each. This is a form of double counting.

## SOME FINAL NUMBERS

Despite the extreme diversity in South Asia and the difficulty with data comparability, we have been able to classify all rural households who depend primarily on wage incomes into three mutually exclusive categories:

*(a) Landless rural labour households*
Those 'who do not operate any land' and who have to rely mainly on wage employment often as casual agricultural labourers for their livelihood but partly also in the rural non-farm sector from employment in marginal activities. Raising farm productivity can provide benefits to them only

indirectly via an increased demand for labour, where and when it is forthcoming. In 1980 there were some 20 million households in this category and they accounted for 17 per cent of all rural households and 13 per cent of the rural population.

*(b) Near landless households*
Those with less than one acre (0.4 hectares) of operated area. The present holdings of this group of farmers are too small to provide a subsistence standard of living, even allowing for productivity increases that are likely in the future. These households are akin to the landless in their dependence on rural wage incomes as a major source of livelihood. They can also supplement their wage incomes through a variety of on-farm ancillary activities such as dairying and poultry. In 1980 the near landless accounted for 13 per cent of all rural households and 12 per cent of the rural population in South Asia; they also accounted for 22 per cent of all cultivated holdings and 4 per cent of the cultivated area.

*(c) Marginal farmers*
Those with between 1 and 2.5 acres (0.4 – 1 hectares) of operated area, whose holdings at present levels of productivity are too small to provide an adequate standard of living but whose incomes per caput could be improved substantially by future productivity increases. Nonetheless they still depend primarily on wage incomes to supplement their incomes from farming which provides them only with below subsistence incomes. In 1980 marginal farmers accounted for 17 per cent of all rural households and 16 per cent of the rural population in South Asia; they also accounted for 25 per cent of the cultivated holdings and 8 per cent of the cultivated area.

The data are given in Table 9[20]. These three groups together accounted for 47 per cent of all rural households and 41 per cent of the rural population in South Asia in 1980[21]. These groups accounted for some 55 million rural households with a total population of 272 millions in 1980.

In addition there are some 19 million *small farmers* – those households with between 2.5 and 5 acres (1-2 hectares) of operated area whose holdings at present levels of productivity provide a standard living close to the margin of subsistence. Though they do not depend primarily on wage incomes they participate in wage employment to supplement their meagre farm earnings. Although future farm productivity increases could definitely provide them with an adequate standard of living they will continue to supplement these by seeking wage employment. In 1980 these households accounted for an additional 16 per cent of all rural households and 17 per cent of the rural population in South Asia; they also accounted for 21 per cent of the cultivated holdings and 14 per cent of the cultivated area.

## CONCLUSION

It is true that the landless and near landless numbers in South Asia will

TABLE 9: *South Asia: estimates of small farm and landless households and population in 1980 (based on 1970–80 population changes and 1970s proportions)*

| | Pakistan | | | India | | | Bangladesh | | | TOTAL SOUTH ASIA | |
|---|---|---|---|---|---|---|---|---|---|---|---|
| | H (mln) | FS | P (mln) | H (mln) | FS | P (mln) | H (mln) | FS | P (mln) | H (mln) | P (mln) |
| Landless rural labour (non cultivators with income from wages over half of total income) | 2.0 | 4.5 | 9.0 | 15.0 | 4.4 | 66.0 | 3.0 | 4.6 | 13.8 | 20.0 (17.0) | 88.8 (13.3) |
| Near landless (cultivators operating less than 0.4 ha) | 0.2 | 4.9 | 1.0 | 14.0 | 5.0 | 70.0 | 1.1 | 5.1 | 5.6 | 15.3 (13.0) | 76.6 (11.5) |
| Marginal farmers (cultivators operating 0.4 to 1.0 ha) | 0.5 | 5.0 | 2.6 | 16.9 | 5.3 | 89.6 | 2.3 | 6.2 | 14.3 | 19.7 (17.0) | 106.5 (16.0) |
| Small farmers (cultivators operating 1.0 to 2.0 ha) | 0.7 | 5.3 | 3.8 | 15.9 | 6.1 | 97.0 | 2.0 | 7.1 | 14.2 | 18.6 (15.8) | 115.0 (17.3) |
| Sub-totals | 3.4 | – | 16.4 | 61.8 | – | 322.6 | 8.4 | – | 47.9 | 73.6 (62.4) | 386.9 (58.1) |
| All rural households | 10.1 | 5.8 | 58.6 | 93.6 | 5.6 | 524.2 | 14.3 | 5.8 | 82.9 | 118.0 (100.0) | 665.7 (100.0) |

*Sources:* As described in *Annex* 3.I. in Singh (1982).
*Note:* H, FS and P refer to households, family size and estimated population respectively.

continue to grow and with them the numbers of the poor will also continue to increase. The incidence of poverty too may increase in areas where agricultural stagnation persists. This is due fundamentally to (a) the underlying demographic pressures and (b) the failure of these economies to transform themselves rapidly by providing adequate employment in the industrial sectors. The result has been that the agricultural sector has had to provide employment and opportunities in lieu of failed industrialization. In the long-run *only* reducing the rate of population growth and increasing opportunities in the non-agricultural sector of these economies can eradicate poverty. But in the meantime – in the next decade or two – there are many programmes that can be pursued that have proved to be beneficial to the landless and near landless. These include (a) irrigation, (b) 'green revolution' HYVs and land-intensification and the extension and research to make them possible, (c) dairying, and (d) employment guarantee schemes and rural work or food for work programmes. But most critically those programmes that will accelerate the rate of agricultural growth and reduce the rate of population growth will provide benefits *directly* as well as *indirectly* to the landless through increased employment. Growth has not in general been 'immizerizing' and the 'green revolution' though a mixed blessing in some respects has had considerable benefits for the landless poor.

Of course redistributive land reforms would go a long way in relieving the plight of the landless in some areas, but it is an unlikely panacea for the vast problems of rural poverty in South Asia. In the long-run, mass poverty will only be eradicated by the industrial transformation of South Asia. On this path the economies of the region are now embarked.

## NOTES

[1] *South Asia* throughout this paper is used to denote the three largest countries of the subcontinent – Bangladesh, India and Pakistan.

[2] For India see Ahluwalia (1977), for Pakistan see S.M. Naseem (1977) and for Bangladesh see A.R. Khan (1977). The proportions in poverty from the 1970s are extrapolated to get the 1980 populations.

[3] See for example ILO *Poverty and Landlessness in rural Asia,* Geneva, 1977 and M.J. Esman *Landlessness and Near-Landlessness in Developing Countries,* Cornell University, 1978.

[4] 'The very recent fad about and display of interest in the landless is less due to a charitable concern on part of the established officialdom and academia than due to a very real bout of enlightened self interest arising out of the threat of disintegration to the established order in the face of the growing trend of landlessness and agricultural stagnation', S. Adnan et al. (1978).

[5] Esman (1978) for example. He also gives figures for the 'landless and near landless' in India of 53 per cent and for Bangladesh at 75 per cent. In an earlier version of his study he gave figures of 79 per cent for India and 88 per cent for Bangladesh.

[6] See Januzzi and Peach (1980) on the 1978 results of the Land Occupancy Survey. Others who have given widely varying figures include Jabbar (1978), Abdullah et al. (1976), M. Hossain (1978) and A.R. Khan (1977). For details see Singh (1982) Chapter 2.

[7] For example we estimate some 0.6 million agricultural labour households in 1961 increased to 1.6 million by 1972. See Singh (1982) Chapter 2 for details.

[8] As Adnan et al. (1978) state: 'the liberal meaning of the term "landless" is far to imprecise and heterogeneous for any serious undertaking to identify the poorest target groups . . . . The moral from this would be that from the policy maker's point of view, identifying the landless and assetless "target groups," mere landholding stratification is not enough, given the significance of other forms of means of production in the non-agricultural sector'.

[9] The figures differ from Table 4 both because they are for different years and because Table 4 refers to the rural *population,* while Table 5 refers to rural *households.*

[10] This is lower than the proportion of the rural labour force, some 39 per cent, classified as 'casual or agricultural labourers' in 1972–73. The discrepancy can arise because individual members of households otherwise not classified as 'rural labour households' could still be seeking wage employment as casual or agricultural labour.

[11] Indian states are allocated to four broad regional groupings for analysis as follows: *North:* Jammu and Kashmir, Himachal Pradesh, Punjab, Haryana and Uttar Pradesh; *East:* Assam, Bihar, West Bengal, Nagaland, Mizoram, and Arunachal Pradesh; *West:* Rajasthan, Maharashtra, Gujarat and Madhya Pradesh; and *South:* Karnataka, Kerala, Andhra Pradesh and Tamil Nadu. These regions account for 22 per cent, 27 per cent, 24 per cent and 27 per cent of all rural households respectively and are not totally arbitrary sets. See Singh (1982).

[12] Data not shown in Table 5. See Singh (1982).

[13] Some of the households listed as rural labour in 1974–75 may have been tenants whom their landlords listed as labourers to conceal their tenancies. The extent of this bias is not known. See Singh (1982), Chapter 2, on the changing agrarian structure in South Asia.

[14] See Singh (1982) Ch. 2 for discussion of data sources.

[15] See Singh (1982), Ch. 8.

[16] Our table shows an increase from 38 per cent to 65 per cent, but Naseem is unclear about his definition.

[17] The annual incomes per caput cited are: large farmers (Rs 1102), small farmers (Rs 318), tenant farmers (Rs 200), permanent labour (Rs 192) and temporary workers (Rs 173, Eckert (1972) p. 57.

[18] The role of remittances as sources for investible capital is equally important in E. Punjab.

[19] Over what period of time is not mentioned.

[20] The 1980 projections are based on the agrarian structures prevalent in the 1970s and the population changes estimated between 1970–1980. See Singh (1982), Chapter III for details.

[21] Recall that family size is positively related to size of holding so that the proportion of households is larger than the proportion of population accounted for by poorer households. We are also aware that land size without reference to productivity means little. Still these are fairly meaningful groupings. See Singh (1982) for details.

## REFERENCES

Abdullah, Abu, Hossain, M. and Nations, R. 'Agrarian Structure and the IRDP – Preliminary Considerations', *The Bangladesh Development Studies,* Vol. IV, No. 2, April 1976.

Adnan, S., Khan M. et al., 'A Review of Landlessness in Rural Bangladesh 1877–1977', Rural Economics Program, Dept of Economics, University of Chittagong, Bangladesh, 21 August 1978 (mimeo).

Ahluwalia, M.S., 'Rural Poverty and Agricultural Performance in India', *Journal of Development Studies,* April 1978.

Cain, Mead 'Landlessness in India and Bangladesh: A Critical Review of Data Sources', paper No. 71, Population Council, New York, May 1981.

Eckert, J. B., Badar, M. A., Akbar, M., and Mausha M., *'Rural Labour in Punjab: A Survey Report',* Survey Unit, Planning and Development Department, Govt. of the Punjab, Lahore, July 1972.

Esman, M. J., *Landlessness and Near-Landlessness in Developing Countries,* Rural Development Committee, Cornell University, 1978.

Government of India, *Rural Labour Enquiry 1974–75: Summary Report,* Labour Bureau, Ministry of Labour, Govt of India, 1978.

Hossain, Mahabub, 'Agrarian Production Structure in Bangladesh', in *Agrarian Structure and Change: Rural Development Experience and Policies in Bangladesh,* Ministry of Agriculture and Forests, Government of Bangladesh, 1978.

ILO, *Poverty and Landlessness in Rural Asia,* Geneva, International Labour Organization, 1977.

Jabbar, M.A., 'The Land Tenure System in Bangladesh', in *Agrarian Structure and Change: Rural Development Experience and Policies in Bangladesh,* Ministry of Agriculture and Forests, G.O.B., 1978.

Jannuzi, F.T. and Peach, J.T., *The Agrarian Structure of Bangladesh: An Impediment to Development,* Boulder, Westview Press, 1980.

Khan, A.R., *The Economics of Bangladesh,* Macmillan, London, 1972.

Khan, A.R. et al., *Employment, Income And The Mobilisation of Local Resources – A Study Of Two Bangladesh Villages,* ILO, Asian Employment Programme, Bangkok, 1981.

Khan, M. H. *The Economics of the Green Revolution in Pakistan,* Special Studies in International Economics and Development, Praeger, New York 1975.

Minhas, B.S., 'Rural Poverty, Land Distribution and Development', *Indian Economic Review,* April 1970.

Naseem, S. M., *'Rural Poverty and Landlessness in Pakistan',* 1977.

NSS 'Tables On Landholdings: Twenty-sixth Round, July 1971–September 1972' (All India and Statewise Reports for Punjab, Kerala, Gujarat and Maharashtra), National Sample Survey organization, Department of Statistics, Ministry of Planning, Government of India, Feb. 1976.

NSS 'Tables with Notes On Some Aspects Of Landholdings In Rural India, 16th Round (July 1960–June 1961)', National Sample Survey Organization, Department of Statistics, Ministry of Planning, Government of India.

Sanyal, S. K., 'Trends in Some Characteristics of Land Holdings – An Analysis for a Few States', *Sarvekshna,* Part I: Vol. 1, No. 1, July 1977, pp. 1-13; Part II, Vol. 1, No. 2, Oct. 1977, pp. 65–76.

Singh, Inderjit, *Small Farmers And The Landless In South Asia,* World Bank, Draft monograph manuscript, June 1982.

## DISCUSSION OPENING – MUBYARTO

The topic concerning the poor, especially the landless poor, has by now become quite familar to all of us, not only for agricultural economists but for social scientists in general. Even the general public are quite aware that in the developing countries the landless in agriculture or the rural sector are always part of the society who are poor because they are the majority of the rural population who own no wealth or assets to earn a regular income. They only own their labour and its utilization depends more on the owners of capital who are much fewer in number. The result is that this labour has a very low price. Dr Singh starts his paper by saying that there is usually still confusion about who are the landless, because there are at least three groups:

(a) those who own no land;
(b) those who operate no land and
(c) those whose major source of income is wage employment in rural areas.

And then he asks what are the facts? The question is interesting because this indicates that he wants to present facts and nothing but facts. We should be interested to know whether he succeeds or not in obtaining and presenting facts. The problem we face is that the three groups of the rural poor mentioned above, especially the small farmers and agricultural labourers, are in fact overlapping which makes it difficult to estimate the exact number. Consequently it is also difficult to formulate precise policies to solve their problems.

Dr Singh recognizes and suggests that underemployment in the rural-agricultural sector is high. But on the other hand he warns us that available statistical data on this are highly unreliable. In other words he seems to suggest that our conventional concepts of unemployment, underemployment and disguised unemployment are not alway relevant and should be used with great care. This is of course not a new problem, we are only reminded of it again.

I am very interested in and I agree with Dr Singh's statement that although employment and income opportunities have increased for rural labourers, the conditions of employment have become more risky: material conditions may have improved but the sense of personal security has probably deteriorated.

Let me close my opening of the discussion by asking some general questions:

1. Dr Singh provides us with a lot of statistics on rural landlessness and rural poverty but the impression we get is that we still need more statistical data especially at the district level. Do we really still need yet more statistical data?

2. In the long run, mass poverty will only be eradicated by the industrial transformation.
What precisely is meant by 'industrial transformation'?

3. Some of us have been in the 'business' for 20–25 years. The poverty and the landless were there 25 years ago and are still here today. Research workers have been working hard during the period. Do we now have any well developed theory to help analyse the roots of the problem or do we really need any new theory at all? If we think we have enough theories already do we think that the problem is really not the theory but its implementation?
If there are policymakers in LDCs who say 'no more seminars, please, just act'. What should we say to them?

5. It has been said that all conventional concepts on unemployment and under or disguised unemployment are misleading. What is the substitute? What concepts do we need?

6. Can we easily compute growth rates at the district level in order to study the trickle down effect? Is it not asking too much?

7. The more you collect statistics the more the likelihood is that we know less and less about poverty and moreover we will have less faith in poverty statistics.
What should we suggest to our research workers?

## GENERAL DISCUSSION* – RAPPORTEUR: H.M.G. HERATH

Regarding the paper by Ryohei Kada, the analytical distinction between farm, off-farm and own-farm income was felt to be very useful for policy purposes. The existence of off-farm employment helps equalize incomes between groups, particularly for those groups with very little land. However, the question of what the farm household does with the income obtained through off-farm activities had been ignored in the paper and this further information was considered desirable. The point was also made that the root cause of why part-time farming develops in some countries and not in others had not been made clear. It was felt, in particular, that Dr Kada's suggested causes, namely the pattern of farm sizes, existence of transport facilities and location of industry, may in fact be dependent on the relative importance of part-time farming. It was also suggested that the income equalizing effects of part-time farming may be limited by interregional differences. A study done by the Department of Agricultural Economics of Reading University on Cyprus was cited as an example. The possibility of expanding off-farm employment for equity purposes was generally felt to be a prudent approach.

There was criticism that despite the critical analyses by Dr Singh, the definition of landlessness was still not clear, particularly with respect to the issue of renting in and renting out land. Many agreed with Dr Singh's conclusion that landlessness, poverty and rural unemployment were based on highly exaggerated estimates. The point was made that Dr Singh supported his conclusions by analysing data from the Punjab and Haryana, which was felt to be insufficient from which to generalize the findings for the whole of South East Asia. Also, the observation that the female component in labour has been rising, particularly after 1971, had not been explained. The need to consider rural public works as a strategy for raising rural wages was emphasized. In reply it was stated that the observations were made not only by analysing data for the Punjab and Haryana but also data from all states of India.

Participants in the discussion included M. Upton, H. E. Breimyer, F. Baffoe, K. Ahuja, Arun Kumar, Richard Meyer and Surjit Bhalla.

*Papers by Kada and Singh.

# SECTION V

*Strategies and Policies in Agricultural and Rural Development*

BRUCE F. JOHNSTON AND WILLIAM C. CLARK*

# *Rural Development Programmes: a Critical Review of Past Experience*

In our view the fundamental objective of rural development programmes is to reduce and eventually to eliminate acute poverty (although we certainly recognize that major attention must be given to the rate as well as the 'pattern' of agricultural development). Measured against this strategic long-term objective, national and international development efforts have failed in many countries, especially in the 35 low-income developing countries.[1]

It has been estimated very roughly that in 1980 some 750 million people in developing countries were living in 'absolute poverty'. The 1.3 billion people living in low-income countries account for a large percentage of the world's population living below a poverty line, however that poverty line might be defined. Some 70 per cent of the population and labour force in those countries still depend on agriculture for employment and income; the most widespread and intractable problems of poverty are to be found in the rural regions of the low-income developing countries.

A retrospective analysis by Vyas (1979) of changes in the number and size distribution of farm households in India epitomizes the problem. Between 1953–54 and 1971–72, the number of farm households in India increased from 49 to 81 million; the average size of farm holding declined from 6.3 to 3.8 acres. Even more significant as an indicator of the increase in rural poverty, the number of 'marginal' farm households with less than 1 acre more than doubled, rising from 15 to 36 million in less than 20 years. It is true that the marginal and landless households bore the brunt of the increasing pressure of population on the land. It is not true that 'the small were getting smaller because the big were getting bigger'. The number of 'big' and 'large' farmers declined, and there was a decline in the average size holding in every size category.

The proximate causes of the increased extent of rural poverty in India and in other low-income developing countries are obvious: the growth of population and the continued dominance of agriculture in their labour force

* This review briefly summarizes some of the principal themes in our recent book, *Redesigning Rural Development: A Strategic Perspective* (1982). A number of extracts from the book are included with the kind permission of Johns Hopkins University Press.

because of limited expansion of non-farm job opportunities. India's rate of population growth of some 2.2 per cent has been relatively slow as compared to other developing countries. Moreover, it has declined a little whereas for the other low-income developing countries population growth rose from an average rate of 2.4 per cent in the 1960s to 2.6 per cent in the 1970s. On the other hand, the share of agriculture in India's labour force only declined from 74 per cent in 1960 to 71 per cent in 1979, a small change even compared to other low-income countries (World Bank, 1981, pp. 166, 170). But identifying these proximate causes tells us little about the critical question: what has gone wrong? What kinds of policies and programmes are likely to be more effective during the next two or three decades? We interpret our assignment as a challenge to look back on the experience of the last twenty to thirty years and from that strategic perspective to offer some answers. Given the complexity of the issues of rural development, our perspective is necessarily partial, our answers necessarily tentative. For the sake of brevity, however, we offer them as assertions. We have examined the relevant evidence in considerable detail and discussed some of the qualifications and caveats in Johnston and Clark (1982). It is worth emphasizing, however, our conviction that policy analysis 'can be no more than a guide, an aid, to better policy design' (Johnston and Clark, 1982, p. 265). Moreover, only action in specific country situations can improve the lot of the rural poor. Theory, research, and analysis can provide only limited guidance in the design and implementation of the intervention programmes that are needed. Because mistakes and short-falls are inevitable, we stress the need for improved trial-and-error learning that better integrates theory and practice in a continuing process of policy redesign.

## SOME PITFALLS OF ANALYSIS

Some battles can be won by piecemeal action. To attain the basic, long-term goal of overcoming poverty, however, we must think and act *strategically*. Our actions must be guided by a recognition of the inter-connected determinants of rural well-being, of both complementary and competitive effects of individual programme actions on one another, and of the long-term consequences of policy choices.

An essential starting point for analysis of the complex, ill-structured problems of rural development is an understanding of the nature of a country's rural development problems. There is, of course, great diversity among developing countries in their physical environment, economic resources, historical circumstances, political régime, and many other dimensions. Nevertheless, the subset of low-income developing countries have in common a number of characteristics that tell us a great deal about what changes are most *desirable*. These countries also face similar constraints that are important in determining the kinds of change that are likely to be *feasible*.

*Feasibility and desirability*

A tendency to equate the feasible with the desirable is one of the most common pitfalls of the historical debate over development. One version of this pitfall is to assume that because a certain goal is desirable, it must be feasible as well. But especially in the lower income developing countries, resources are scarce, needs are enormous, and there is never enough money, time, or trained manpower for all of the important tasks that demand attention. The pursuit of the desirable may often be infeasible, wasting the scarce resources it consumes.

The converse pitfall assumes that because a certain goal is feasible, it must be desirable as well. But the use of resources for any task in the developing world is likely to entail substantial opportunity costs. Thus, a hard-nosed penchant for doing what works almost always means not doing something else. Opting for programmes simply because they appear to be feasible is likely to preclude the search for other options that could have greater impact in reducing rural poverty.

A conventional view of planning emphasizes procedures in which objectives are first established and then the means required to attain those objectives are determined. The attractive logic of this approach is misleading. Instead, good policy analysis emphasizes the need for *mutual adjustment of ends and means:* the definition of objectives must be shaped by the availability of resources – and vice versa to the extent that available resources can be enlarged or deployed more effectively. This stress on the need to mutually adjust ends and means has important implications for the design of strategies for rural development. In particular, it emphasizes the importance of making hard decisions about priorities. That is an especially difficult challenge. In our judgement the nature of the problems confronting the contemporary low-income countries emphasizes the importance of attaining multiple objectives: (a) accelerating the expansion of farm output; (b) generating productive employment opportunities (both within and outside agriculture) for a growing labour force; (c) reducing the particularly serious manifestations of poverty (especially malnutrition and excessive mortality and morbidity among vulnerable groups); and (d) creating an environment favourable for slowing the rate of growth of population. The design and implementation of strategies for rural development capable of achieving those four objectives is not easy. But there is persuasive evidence that it is a feasible goal, although there is no reason to be optimistic that in all or even most cases the obstacles to success will be overcome. On the other hand, because of the severity of the resource constraints that characterize the lower income developing countries, achieving a significant reduction of the poverty that is so widespread in these countries by relief and welfare programmes is, we believe, simply not feasible (Johnston and Clark, 1982, pp. 68–69).

*Ineffectiveness and lack of consensus*

Another pitfall that has compromised development efforts has been the ineffectiveness of development advisors in creating the consensus necessary for effective action. Instead of cumulative progress in advancing understanding, we have seen the typical behaviour of an immature field: a tendency to jump from controversy to controversy and to flit from fad to fad (Ravetz, 1971). An able practitioner has argued that good policy analysis requires a systematic effort 'to evaluate, or to order, and structure incomplete knowledge so as to allow decisions to be made with as complete an understanding as possible of the current state of knowledge, its limitations, and its implications' (Morgan, 1978). When applied to a problem as complex and ill-structured as development, a host of variables and changing interrelationships among those variables must be considered. Consequently, complete knowledge and understanding are impossible. Furthermore, judgements and decisions by policymakers will inevitably be influenced by opinions, subjective preferences, values, and vested interests. Therefore, good policy analysis should order and structure our incomplete and imperfect knowledge 'in ways that are open and explicit' and should avoid drawing 'hard conclusions unless they are warranted by unambiguous data or well-founded theoretical insights'.

Development specialists have not given enough attention to arriving at an agreed understanding of the fundamental conditions and constraints that characterize different types of development situations. Too often our objective has been to demolish an opponent's theory and to establish the superiority of some alternative version of the 'truth.' Such an emphasis on claims and counterclaims is singularly inefficient in identifying the really important issues on which there is inadequate understanding or faulty or insufficient evidence and thereby gradually broadening the areas of consensus. In the absence of a workable consensus on what needs doing and how it is to be done, it is difficult to overcome the inertia of a government bureaucracy and undertake new initiatives. At the same time, in the absence of patient and persistent efforts to advance understanding and to build consensus for well-considered programmes, there will be a tendency for governments to undertake hasty and sporadic action to respond quickly (and ineffectively) to the latest crisis.

### *Cogitation and interaction*

A third pitfall concerns the tendency to exaggerate the role of 'intellectual cogitation' as an approach to social problem-solving. The terms 'intellectual cogitation' and 'social interaction' have been introduced to describe two alternative approaches to social problem-solving (Wildavsky, 1979; see also Lindblom, 1977, chapters 19, 23). The approach of intellectual cogitation assumes that we are equal to the task of *thinking through* solutions to our problems. The social interaction approach takes a more sceptical view of our capacity for calculation and analysis and relies on *acting out* solutions through social processes of politics, markets, bargaining, and other interactive techniques. Comprehensive economic planning is a form of intellectual cogitation that is arguably desirable but wholly infeasible. The approach is infeasible not only because it exceeds man's cognitive capacities but in addition it presumes the existence of agreed upon criteria of goodness or value on which alternative solutions can be judged (Lindblom, 1977, p. 322). As Herbert Simon (1971, p. 47) has argued, 'the dream of thinking everything out before we act, of making certain we have all the facts and know all the consequences, is a sick Hamlet's dream'.

The interactive approach of acting out solutions also has its limitations. We have just noted that the feasible is not always desirable; and a predilection for 'getting on with it' may have a high opportunity cost and entail undesirable long-term consequences. Policies that promote a dualistic pattern of agricultural development based on the 'crash modernization' of a subsector of atypically large and capital-intensive farm enterprises tend to foreclose the option of achieving a broadly based, employment-orientated pattern of agricultural development involving the progressive modernization of a large and increasing fraction of a country's small-scale farm units. Furthermore, interaction learns only randomly from its own experience, and it is incapable of learning from the experience of others.

Policy analysis seeks an integration of cogitation or thinking-through approaches and interactive, acting-out approaches which recognizes explicitly the strengths and limitations of each. Clearly, there is a need for systematic reflection on the key problems and issues, the major constraints, and the feasible opportunities for advancing development. Such reflection on and analysis of past experience provide valuable guidance for the design of programme interventions. The challenge is to make the best choices knowledge can buy, but at the same time to be prepared to learn from our inevitable mistakes in a continuing, interactive process of policy design, implementation, and redesign.

## POLITICS, POWER, AND PERSUASION

Some will no doubt feel that the analytical pitfalls we have singled out are of small importance relative to the dominance in the existing political power structure of vested interests opposed to changes that benefit the rural poor. Such a 'politics first' perspective often leads to the view that a revolutionary change in the existing power structure is a 'prerequisite' for designing and implementing development strategies that will be effective in eliminating poverty (see, for example, Griffin, 1979; de Janvry, 1981).

We do not deny the importance of political factors. But it is too simplistic to attribute the failures of development efforts to a lack of 'political will' and the pernicious influence of vested interests. In one sense it is certainly true that failures of development programmes are 'essentially' political failures. The decisions of policymakers that shape a country's development strategy are bound to influence 'who gets what, when, and how'. But we believe that bewailing the unequal distribution of power is no more conducive to resolving the 'essentially political' problems of development than bewailing the unequal distribution of rainfall is to resolving 'essentially agricultural' problems.

Some development situations are doubtless so thoroughly dominated by power-holding interests totally opposed to economic and social progress that analysis simply has no role to play. But the proper role of policy analysis is precisely 'speaking truth to power' (Wildavsky, 1979) – and speaking it clearly and persuasively enough that the resulting development efforts actually do improve the lot of the poor. If only because politicians invariably have many concerns and only limited resources, the policy environment will never be 'optimal' as viewed from our perspective as policy analysts concerned with advancing the interests of the rural poor. As Hirschman (1971) has argued, the practical requirement is to 'think in terms of sequences in the course of which a forward step in one direction will induce others . . . ' (pp. 19–20). Leys (1971, p. 133) brings in the political dimension explicitly when he stresses the need to assess as realistically as possible 'what changes – social and political, as well as economic – are within the politicians' "means"' and what are not; and what patterns or sequences of change, among those that are practical, will carry the process of economic development farthest and fastest at the least cost in the politician's resources'. Thus we must learn to understand the constraints that define feasible programmes; and those constraints are related to the world of power as much as to those imposed by nature and by the scarcity of economic, budget, and manpower resources. But constraints, unlike a 'precondition', are something that can be modified and relaxed by well-chosen policies and actions. Development is the result of numerous short-term actions at the tactical level. If those actions are to have a cumulative impact, they must be related to a long-term, strategic perspective.

Because of our frustration and relative impotence as we confront self-interest and the venality of some powerful groups, the temptation is strong to conclude that incremental progress is impossible and revolution is a necessary precondition. Hence, there are many who would agree with de Janvry (1981), p. 268) when he says, in effect, that the need is not for policy analysis but rather to 'foment collective action and class consciousness' and to bring into existence 'mass-based democratic régimes'.

Before we reject the possibility of a reformist approach and conclude that incremental improvements are infeasible, let us be sure that our own house is in order. After all the poor have been known to suffer as much from ill-conceived programmes designed to help them as from well-conceived programmes designed to exploit them. Indeed, faulty analysis or self-delusion may be more serious problems than self-interest and venality. And those are failings that we, as policy analysts, should be able to do something about. The seriousness of opting for revolution is underscored by the historical fact that revolutions devastate the lives of many people – especially the poor. Even in the most favourable circumstances, a revolutionary change in a country's power structure is only a first step. Above all in low-income countries, the elimination of poverty depends primarily on generating a higher level of income by means that ensure that the expansion of opportunities for productive employment is more rapid than the growth of the economically active population. Consequently, as A. K. Sen has argued, a 'shift in focus to technological and institutional details is long overdue. . . . The most serious problems lie, not in the grand design, but in what has the superficial appearance of "details"' (as quoted in Hunter, 1978, p. 37). We believe that regardless of the ideological orientation of a country's political régime, the success of efforts to eliminate rural poverty will require interventions in three programme areas.

## A THREE-PRONGED STRATEGY FOR RURAL DEVELOPMENT

A general conclusion suggested by a policy analysis perspective is that we should focus on the more serious failings of rural development programmes and on the most feasible and desirable opportunities for mitigating those failures. Our analysis of the constraints and opportunities relevant to today's low-income countries leads us to conclude that three areas of historical failure merit priority attention:

1 The failure to design and implement effective strategies for fostering broad-based agricultural development.
2 The failure to reduce excessive mortality and morbidity among infants and small children and the interrelated failure to slow the rapid growth of population and labour force.
3 The failure to create effective problem-solving organizations at the local level and to improve the performance of development bureaucracies.

This diagnosis is the basis for our advocacy of a three-pronged strategy for rural development. The first 'prong' relates to the need for a broadly based, employment-orientated pattern of agricultural development. Expansion of opportunities for productive employment, both inside and outside agriculture, is of central importance. Fuller and more efficient utilization of the relatively abundant resource of human labour can facilitate the expansion of output while at the same time generating the incomes that enable the poor to raise their levels of consumption. This analysis and empirical evidence emphasize the importance of tightening the labour supply/demand situation if increases in returns to labour are to be achieved.

The second prong involves strengthening a very limited set of social services. This includes education, as is now generally recognized. Because of their importance and past neglect, we stress particularly the need for interventions directed at the interrelated problems of malnutrition and chronic ill-health among infants and small children. In addition to the high human and economic costs associated with impaired child development and the excessive mortality rates among these vulnerable groups, the risk that small children will not survive to maturity is also a major obstacle to the spread of family planning. Considerable attention has been given in the past few years to the decline in fertility in the developing world. A number of middle-income countries and two low-income countries – China and Sri Lanka – have indeed achieved remarkably rapid declines in fertility. It is hardly coincidental that virtually all of the countries that have realized significant declines in fertility since 1960 have also sharply reduced infant and child mortality rates (Johnston and Clark, 1982, pp. 145–47).

Our third prong concerns organization programmes designed to strengthen the institutional infrastructure and managerial skills needed for rural development. The neglect of these problems is in part a consequence of the tendency for economists to focus on what to do while neglecting the 'details' of how to do it. More than a decade and a half ago Hsieh and Lee (1966) asserted that 'the main secret of Taiwan's development' was 'her ability to meet the organization requirements' (pp. 103, 105). This lesson has, however, been largely ignored in spite of the accumulating evidence that organizational requirements are not easily fulfilled and require serious and sustained attention. Success in implementing the first and second prongs of an effective strategy for rural development is unlikely unless the organizational requirements are met.

Analysis of the interrelationships among activities in these three areas emphasizes that programme interventions can have significant complementary as well as competitive impacts on each other. We have suggested that the components of a rural development strategy can be designed (and redesigned) in ways that maximize their capacity for mutual support and minimize the risk that action in one programme area will compromise efforts in other areas. This is obviously a difficult challenge, especially since development specialists are far from being in agreement concerning the need for priority attention to simultaneous action in these three programme areas.

The greatest danger of the three-pronged perspective described here is that it will be interpreted as a recommendation to adopt any and all programmes which may be advocated in the production, consumption, or organization areas. No interpretation could be further from our actual intent. On the contrary, widespread and sustained progress towards improving rural well-being requires that only a very few of the highest priority, most mutually reinforcing programmes should be undertaken at all. Strategic choice means choosing *not* to do a vast number of tactically attractive things. Our emphasis on the necessity of an appropriate balance between production orientated and consumption orientated activities highlights this key requirement of strategic design.

The need to conserve scarce resources, to undertake only those tasks most central to the improvement of rural well-being, is equally acute when we consider the organizational components of a development strategy. A strategic perspective means using all available forms of social organization – including political, market, and traditional structures – for the tasks which they can be made to perform reasonably well, while preserving scarce administrative talent for focused intervention when and where it can do the most good. Effective production and consumption programmes can be expanded only with the growth of organizational capacity for their effective implementation. This focus on the need to develop organizational competence directs attention at another major theme of our strategic perspective – the importance of time and timing.

Improving rural well-being is an inherently time-consuming process.

Historical experience teaches that, at best, broadly-based and sustainable progress will be measured in decades, not years. In part, the pace of development is limited by fundamental structural demographic constraints: even under the most optimistic of assumptions, today's late-developing countries will remain predominantly rural societies into the twenty-first century. Perhaps even more significant for policy design, however, is that development is essentially a learning process: the growth of organizational competence and personal knowledge are as fundamental a requirement as the growth of capital in the conventional sense. Because most of the 'answers' to development questions are not known by anyone, because even those answers which are known by some must be laboriously passed on to others, because all answers must be adapted to specific places and times, the learning process of development necessarily entails a great deal of trial and error.

This much-needed persistence has too often been lacking in rural development strategies. The desire to bypass the errors, to teach answers instead of facilitating learning, is strong – and disastrous. Impatience for immediate results has often encouraged relief and welfare approaches to improving rural well-being. Such short-term activities, however, almost invariably lead to the neglect of more fundamental long-term tasks: building organizational and technical capabilities and strengthening the capacities of local people to meet their own needs. Failure to pursue rural development strategies that are focused on programmes to strengthen indigenous capacities to accelerate the growth of output, expand employment, improve health and nutrition, and slow population growth will mean that the number of people suffering the deprivations of rural poverty will continue to increase.

Those of us who have emphasized the relevance of the experience of Japan and the Taiwan area of China have been guilty of teaching answers instead of stressing the need for a learning process leading to a continually improving sequence of programme designs. In particular, we have been much too slow to take account of a major limitation of technology transfer based on their experience. Because of the relatively homogeneous character of agriculture in those two areas and the dominant importance of irrigated production, there was enormous scope for expanding farm productivity and output by relying mainly on improved seed-fertilizer combinations for rice and a few other major crops. In countries with different and more heterogenous conditions, including major reliance on rainfed production, it is necessary to confront the more difficult task of identifying a number of strategies adapted to a variety of agroclimatic conditions and crops. Experience at ICRISAT, for example, suggests that in areas where rainfall is variable and only marginally adequate, there is a need for improved methods of soil and water management in order to realize the yield potential of improved varieties and fertilizer. Little sustained and systematic attention has been given to the task of evolving equipment and tillage innovations for that purpose that meet the needs of smallholders with very limited cash income and purchasing power (Johnston, 1981).

The development 'failures' that we have noted are failures about which something can be done. It must not be forgotten that only a decade or two ago many of today's middle-income countries faced constraints and conditions comparable to those of today's low-income countries. A number of those countries have made substantial progress in improving the well-being of their people because they *did* pursue strategies for rural development emphasizing vigorous and sustained production, consumption, and organization programmes similar to the three prongs of the strategy that we have advocated.

We believe that the efforts of today's low-income countries to emulate such successes will be facilitated to the extent that the development debate within these countries and the international development community can be focused constructively on fundamental constraints and opportunities, on the longer term implications of strategic policy decisions, and on systematic efforts to learn from both successes and failures.

## NOTES

[1] To be sure, some progress has been made even in the low-income countries. Between 1960 and 1980 GNP per caput increased at an annual average rate of 1.7 per cent in real terms (but was still only $250 in 1981); life expectancy at birth increased by a little over 20 per cent (but was still only 51 years in 1979, mainly because infant and child mortality rates are still shockingly high); adult literacy was about 40 per cent higher in 1976 than in 1960 (but was still only 39 per cent). (China is excluded from these figures; see World Bank, 1981, pp. 6, 134, 170).

## REFERENCES

de Janvry, A., *The Agrarian Question and Reformism in Latin America,* Johns Hopkins University Press, 1981.

Griffin, K., *The Political Economy of Agrarian Change,* Macmillan, London, 1979.

Hirschman, A. O., *A Bias for Hope,* Yale University Press, 1971.

Hsieh, S. C. and Lee, T. H., *Agricultural Development and Its Contributions to Economic Growth in Taiwan,* Joint Commission on Rural Reconstruction, Taipei, 1966.

Hunter, G., 'Report on Administration and Institutions', in Asian Development Bank, *Rural Asia: Challenge and Opportunity,* Supplementary Papers, Vol. IV, *Administration and Institutions in Agricultural and Rural Development,* Asian Development Bank, Manila, 1978.

Johnston, B. F., 'Farm Equipment Innovations and Rural Industrialisation in Eastern Africa: An Overview', World Employment Programme Research Working Paper WEP 2-22/WP.80, International Labour Organisation, Geneva, 1981.

Johnston, B.F. and Clark, W.C., *Redesigning Rural Development: A Strategic Perspective,* Johns Hopkins University Press, 1982.

Leys, C., 'Political Perspectives', in Seers, D. and Joy, L., *Development in a Divided World,* Penguin, England, 1971.

Lindblom, C. E., *Politics and Markets,* Basic Books, New York, 1977.

Morgan, M.G., 'Bad Science and Good Policy Analysis', *Science,* Vol. 201, No. 4360, 15 Sept, 1978.

Ravetz, J. R., *Scientific Knowledge and Its Social Problems,* Clarendon Press, Oxford, 1971.

Simon, H. A., 'Designing Organizations for an Information-Rich World', in Greenberger, M., *Computers, Communications, and the Public Interest,* Johns Hopkins Press, 1971.
Vyas, V. S., 'Some Aspects of Structural Change in Indian Agriculture', *Indian J. Agri. Econ.,* Vol. XXXIV, No. 1, Jan.–Mar. 1979.
Wildavsky, A., *Speaking Truth to Power: The Art and Craft of Policy Analysis,* Little, Brown and Company, Boston and Toronto, 1979.
World Bank, *World Development Report, 1981,* Oxford University Press, 1981.

## DISCUSSION OPENING – WILHELM BRANDES

This excellent paper shows all too well the broad experiences the authors have gained in their theoretical and practical work with planning and execution of rural development programmes. My problem is that I completely share the views expressed by Professors Johnston and Clark. When now making a few additional remarks I am running the risk of touching points which may have been covered already by the authors' recent book which I could not get hold of in time.

Let me first say a few words about the optimal degree of complexity of rural development programmes or projects (Ruthenberg, 1981, p. 9). In order to attack the problems of certain portions of the rural population (in particular the very small farmers and the landless) in a more direct way than in the 1950s and 1960s, emphasis has shifted over the last decade from technology-dominated agricultural programmes to integrated rural development programmes. Such a shift inevitably has significant impacts on the complexity of the organizational task. My impression is that in many cases the decline in efficiency resulting from too much complexity has been underestimated. I feel that one has to live with the following trade-off: some programmes appear rather ideal, on paper; but they work poorly. Other programmes appear not so well-designed, in particular with regard to providing assistance to low-income groups; but due to their simple organizational structure, they function well and give, at least indirectly, some relief to poor people. I am in complete agreement with Uma Lele (1975, p. 188) when she states: 'The approach recommended . . . involves beginning with only the few simplest interventions to remove the most critical constraints and allows the programs to evolve in scope through time-phasing of activities.' A good example for a programme following this philosophy is, in my view, the well-known *Training-and-Visit-System* in agricultural extension (Benor and Harrison, 1977). To design programmes that are both feasible and desirable also means, as has been stressed by the authors, not doing some tactically attractive things which, within the environment we have to work, is easier stated than done. As we all know, the problem of optimal complexity is far from being solved, and a lot of learning-by-doing remains to be done to devise programmes that are not too far from optimal for the great variety of different situations.

Next I wish to speak about value judgements that have to be made when dealing with absolute versus relative poverty, however both might be defined. In developing countries many situations exist where some measures would alleviate absolute poverty while allowing relative poverty to grow. Other measures would lead to a more even distribution with only minor reductions in absolute poverty. In the real world zero-sum games are the exception rather than the rule. Let me clarify the nature of the value judgement required by giving an example I often use in class. I assume two population groups, *A* and *B*, with initial incomes of 90 and 200, respectively, where 100 might be defined as the absolute poverty level. Implementation of project 1 would lead to a distribution of 120 and 300. If, on the other hand, project 2 were realized, the income of group *A* would grow to 100 while group *B* would experience a decline from 200 to 150. When discussing this, I was intrigued that a substantial portion of my students did not bother about Pareto optimality but preferred project 2. In my view, nothing is wrong with such a choice. It is clearly a question of value judgement. What I would like to see happen whenever rural development programmes are planned and implemented is that the responsibles enter into a dialogue (a) to estimate possible trade-offs between the attacks on absolute and relative poverty and (b) if such trade-offs should exist, to agree on explicit value judgements concerning absolute and relative poverty.

Let me finally mention another set of value judgements: the social discount rate (time preference). Whenever resources are limited for a certain period of time, which I presume is the rule, those resources can, roughly speaking, be used for present consumption or for investments generating possibilities for future consumption. Quite often the existence of this trade-off is not clearly enough examined, and the opportunity costs of basic-needs approaches are not adequately considered. Again, a dialogue among the responsibles aiming at the estimation and evaluation of such trade-offs appears to be useful. While great emphasis on the basic-needs approach implies *ceteris paribus* a high social discount rate, advocates of revolutions have, at least implicitly, a low discount rate. They put a relatively low weight on the fate of the present population compared to the hope for better economic and social conditions of future generations; a hope that, as the authors show, can be futile.

## REFERENCES

Benor, D. and Harrison, J. Q., *Agricultural Extension: The Training and Visit System*, Washington, 1977.

Lele, U., *The Design of Rural Development: Lessons from Africa*, Baltimore and London, 1975.

Ruthenberg, H., 'Is Integrated Rural Development a Suitable Approach to Attack Rura Poverty?', *Quarterly Journ. Int. Agriculture*, 20, pp. 6–14, 1981.

A. T. BIROWO

# *Rural Development Planning and Implementation*

## INTRODUCTION

Rural development efforts have been designed during recent years using indicators (for example, income, food availability, literacy, calorie intake, health facilities and so on). It has been possible to construct dividing lines between segments of the population using such social indicators. A common concept has been the poverty line or, more elaborately, the relative poverty line and the absolute poverty line. Closely related to these concepts are attempts to define what, in a given society, are the basic necessities for a segment of the population in order not to fall below the poverty line. The concepts are interrelated and many attempts have been made to list those needs (basic needs, basic human needs etc.) which have to be satisfied if an individual or a group of individuals is to be above the poverty line.

The first attempts to define basic needs were made by ILO and IBRD. The strategy of the latter emphasizes growth and the direct alleviation of poverty. The distribution of the benefits of growth is supposed to be guaranteed by the governments concerned. Direct distribution programmes should provide everyone with a minimum of food, housing, health and so on. This will mean more assistance which is more orientated to target groups of poor in the poorest countries. Such programmes are calculated to reduce the worst misery at the least cost and with the greatest speed. The ILO approach also aims at satisfying non-material needs such as human rights, participation and autonomy. ILO stresses the redistribution of assets, income and power. This implies modification in income distribution and changes in the structure of production. At the World Employment Conference in 1976, this strategy was recommended to be adopted by each country.

To-day, there is a rather broad consensus that more emphasis should be given to rural development activities. However, when looking more thoroughly into this, it is apparent that different people will interpret rural development in their own way. This means that a whole range of activities are named as rural development but which may have a content of great variation. Programmes could be very comprehensive, attempting to cover a wide spectrum in the rural society. Similarly, there may be projects that are very sharply focused on only one aspect, for example, increased food production. Even though it may be true to state that most planners agree upon poverty eradication as the key objective of rural development, there are various opinions on the methods by which this will be achieved.

IBRD has made great efforts to elaborate a thinking and a policy on rural development. In 1971 it initiated investigations to gain its own experience of past and on-going projects in Africa (IBRD, 1975). The intention was to find ways of designing projects that would 'reach' large numbers of the rural population and require low financial resources and trained manpower per person reached by the project. The investigations indicated that very few rural development projects existed which simultaneously emphasized the three major aspects of rural development projects: improving living standards, mass participation and making the process self-sustaining. The IBRD views rural development as a strategy designed to improve the economic and social life of the poor.

Development is about human beings. It is about great numbers of poor people most of whom are living in rural areas. They are dependent upon agriculture, not for livelihood only but for survival in many instances. Their poverty ranges over a wide spectrum: malnutrition, hunger, disease and poor health, ignorance, laborious methods of agricultural production, isolation (through their living in remote areas without access to road, schools and alternative employment). It should be emphasized that increased food production is only one single factor for development. Admittedly the focus on production has been there for a long time. The argument has been the need for food of a world population which is growing very fast. Food and population have been at the top of the list of priorities.

As to production, it should be borne in mind that the world has proved that as a whole it can produce the amount of food that is needed for the global population. Secondly, it should be recognized that no hungry or poor people have money to buy these essentials that will meet their most urgent needs. Food is also produced by fishing. Frequently, production takes place in close association with forestry, altogether forming a complex rural life system based upon subsistence. In this system agriculture competes for scarce resources of labour, skill, time, cash, etc. To these people development will certainly mean different things (safe drinking water, better schooling facilities, money to buy food, improved health facilities, as well as specific wants by groups or individuals). This will introduce another dimension of poverty, namely lack of participation. Full participation of the poor is vital if the process of development is to be selfsustaining. Nowadays, participation is also included in most development projects. The problem is, however, that those who are supposed to participate are excluded from most of the decision-making since they have no control of or access to the existing power system. Instead, this system will obviously stifle any initiatives that poor people may have had or might have taken. This introduces still another dimension of poverty, namely the lack of power.

Rural development is a process of change in societies, whereby poverty will be reduced and the creativity and existing knowledge of the poor fully utilized. The poor should have access to the resources of society and the environment and be encouraged to achieve control of resources that are introduced – at reasonable costs – from outside their rural environment in order to make available resources more productive of amenities, services and goods required and wanted by the poor and their governments. There has been no common understanding of what rural development is or how it should be organized in order to attack the problem of poverty. This disappointing fact may stem from an unclear understanding of the problem area itself and of the analysis required. Rural development takes place in a political context and it means nothing but a social transformation in rural areas by which poverty will be eradicated through attacking the existing power structure. This has not been conspicuous in past development thinking which has assumed a social framework that will change without conflict. Transformation means that those without power must gradually gain it to achieve some basic needs at the expense of those who already possess considerably more than basic needs. The concept of rural development should only be used if it is defined in a clear and functional way and will attack the roots of the problem: why is there poverty? The problem area is complex and a variety of measures may be undertaken. These must be properly organized and integrated. In this paper, more attention will now be placed on the Indonesian experience in rural development efforts.

## POLICY ISSUES IN INDONESIAN AGRICULTURAL AND RURAL DEVELOPMENT

Agricultural policy issues for Indonesia in this and the next decade are centred around three problems. First, how to maintain the rate of rice production increase of the past two years while speeding up the rate of increase in non-rice food production. The policy issues involve decisions concerning subsidies for input prices and output prices as well as marketing policies in general. Appropriate policies for increasing corn production will be especially important to ensure an adequate supply of this crop for the growing livestock industry.

The second important problem is how to increase export earnings from cash crops to offset the prospect of the decline in oil export revenues. The current export earning of these crops was US $ 1.4 billion in 1978 and is expected to reach US $ 3 billion in 1983 and US $ 6.5 billion in 1988. The cash crop subsector was neglected until the 1970s but the Government is now involved in major replanting, rehabilitation and new planting projects so that these earnings can be attained. The most serious problems in the cash crop sector are related to the lack of qualified technical and managerial personnel and the extreme shortage of extension workers.

Finally, there are the problems of unemployment and underemployment. Although manufacturing industry has grown rapidly in recent years this sector is still too small to contribute significantly to general employment. The problems of unemployment and under-employment are closely related to poverty in Indonesia, especially in the rural areas. While the investment programme in the estate crops sector is expected to create jobs for some additional 130,000 staff and 2.2 million smallholders and to raise the income of some 4 million rural families, the challenge is still much bigger. With a population growth of 2.3 per cent per annum, the labour force increases by 3.2 per cent, or between 1.5 million to 2.0 million entrants every year.

## RURAL DEVELOPMENT PROGRAMMES

At present, several departments have special programmes to help the poor or economically weak groups. These include the Departments of Agriculture, Industry, Mining and Energy, Manpower and Transmigration, Trade and Co-operatives and Public Works, Public Health, Social Services and Finance.

Since almost half of the Departments have special programmes for the poor, and in reality the whole Cabinet must implement the general equity programmes since 1979, it is almost impossible to isolate these special programmes. The two important sectoral departments, Agriculture and Industry, have some overlapping in carrying out the programmes for the rural poor. If the incomes of the poor are derived mostly from agricultural activities, then the agriculture department may help by introducing some programmes in agricultural education and extension. However, in many instances their income may be derived more and more from non-agricultural activities, that is from trading, handicraft or small scale industries. This means that the Department of Industry and perhaps also the Department of Trade and Co-operatives, should have more means to help or to encourage their development.

In the beginning of the third five-year plan, when a special State Minister of Co-operatives was appointed, it was declared that co-operative organization would be used to achieve equity. This declaration marks the beginning of increased governmental assistance to the co-operative in the form of more subsidy, easier credit and preferential treatment in rice procurement and in fertilizer distribution. But this government action has raised serious doubts about the success of promoting the co-operative cause. There are four characteristics of co-operative organization which should be distinguished:

(a) the co-operative as an ideology;
(b) the co-operative as a tool of economic policy;
(c) the co-operative as part of community development; and
(d) the co-operative as a business enterprise.

In Indonesia the four characteristics tend not to be carefully separated with the result that each group promotes it own interest by using another for purposes of its missionary zeal. For example, the leaders of the co-operative movement are pushing co-operation as an ideology and accusing the government of not having sufficient political will to promote it. On the other hand, the government, even though it says that the co-operative must become a sound economic organization, nevertheless always uses it as a tool for implementing government economic policy. In 1973 it was used to implement the government rice procurement policy and now it is used to help achieve the equity objective. Indonesian economists in general usually adopt the view that a co-operative is nothing but a business enterprise. They argue that there are three types of economic organization: state enterprise, private enterprise, and the co-operative, and each has the right to exist. In their view the co-operative must be able to compete with the other two economic organizations. This is the so-called capitalistic view where, as in the United States or Scandinavian countries, the co-operative enterprise competes well with other businesses. Perhaps the most appropriate view is the last one which considers co-operation as part of community development. This is related to the basic spirit of community among people in rural areas. If this view is adopted, the only way to measure the success of the co-operative is by the degree to which it strengthens the spirit of co-operation.

There are two reasons why the rural co-operative has failed in the past: first, it has been unrealistically assumed that the farmer always prefers a co-operative rather than some other organization; second, that it is capable of serving all members of the village community. The second assumption is unrealistic if we remember that the co-operative as a business enterprise can best serve only the farmers who own 0.7 hectare of sawah or more, which is the minimum size for a farmer's level of subsistence. In most villages in Java this constitutes less than five per cent of the rural population.

The transmigration programme is always linked with land and agrarian reform. This means that transmigration is seen as a means of solving population pressure in Java-Bali and, at the same time, as a programme to move the landless farmer to the outer islands. In the Sukarno period (1945–65), there was a Ministry of Co-operative, Transmigration, and Community Development which indicates the very close relationship of the three. Recently the Ministry of Transmigration was changed to the Ministry of Transmigration and Manpower, implying that transmigration is now considered as a means to increase the mobility of manpower from one region to another and not necessarily involving only Javanese farmers. It is hoped that transmigration can become an important way to speed up regional development in the outer islands.

However, despite the government's vigorous attempt to achieve better results in the transmigration programme, it is difficult to avoid the impression that it has become a routine organization. Targets were set high but non-achievement is very common. Overall the achievement during the period 1969/70 – 1980/81 has been rather satisfactory (87 per cent), but the very high target of the third five-year plan of 500,000 families had only achieved about 20 per cent toward the middle of the plan period. Transmigration is recognized as one of the most difficult government programmes at the present time. There are three reasons for the apparent difficulties. First, it involves over half a dozen governmental agencies which are difficult to co-ordinate. Second, the outer islands have never become attractive places for the young people of Java. On the contrary, there is still a tendency for young people from the outer islands to be attracted to Java. Thirdly, there has been an apparent lack of imagination and dynamism in tackling the problem. For example, in order to draw skilled and energetic transmigrants to pioneer the opening up of new settlement areas, especially at the initial stage, there is a great need for an incentive system and the provision of special facilities. There is surely a need to create and increase the spirit of urgency in carrying out the transmigration programme.

The development of rural industries is now considered by many writers as a promising way to achieve equity. It is called rural non-farm employment, a topic which is being studied more carefully in many developing countries. In Indonesia the government has attempted to promote these small-scale rural industries, for example, by setting up BIPIK, a special agency to provide technical and managerial guidance (1974) and PPIK (Centre for the Development of Small-Scale Industries) in 1977. In 1979 the government started to build several 'mini industrial estates' to provide infrastructural facilities for small-scale industries. A special preferential credit system is provided through KIK (Small Investment Credit) and KMKP (Credit for Working Capital). But the problems are still numerous. The chronic complaint of small-scale industries had been and still is the lack of funds. A comprehensive survey in Central Java in 1974 found that the problem of credit, marketing, and the purchase of raw materials are all closely related. Credit is needed mostly to purchase raw materials which have to be purchased in the open market. The marketing of the products is not efficient because small-scale industries are in a very weak position and hence rely more on the middlemen or the merchants. Many of them also require consumption credit which is usually considered inseparable from production credit. For the cottage and small-scale industries, the household and the business is difficult to distinguish, so that it is very common that the Bank would provide credit for living costs. Further, the study found that without exception all businesses, big and small, considered capital shortage as the most serious constraint to growth. But it is interesting that there is a tendency for the constraint to increase with the growth of the industries. On the other hand, the difficulties of finding raw materials tend to be greater for the smaller industries than the bigger ones. This indicates the real need for co-operation among small-scale industries in order to obtain inputs and to market their output.

The government has for years attempted to develop co-operation among small businessmen. If there is a successful co-operative, with a strong and loyal membership, then it is easy for the government to aid the officers of the co-operative. But so far co-operation has not worked well. On the one hand, membership is low and loyalty is weak because the co-operative cannot provide good services. Most prospective members would join a co-operative if it was a means of obtaining credit. If these small businessmen do not work together in a co-operative organization and instead compete with each other in obtaining raw materials and in marketing their products, then they will become an easy target for the middlemen.

## THE CAUSES OF THE FAILURE AND SUCCESS OF RURAL DEVELOPMENT

There are both failures and successes in the implementation of rural development programmes. One of the difficulties in evaluating the programmes is that it is not easy to distinguish between agricultural and rural development. There is a tendency to confuse or to use the two terms interchangeably or at best to combine the two terms. By combining the terms agricultural and rural development we usually hope that both the production aspect and the distribution aspect are considered.

Many writers on rural development now define rural development as the effort to improve the living standard of the rural poor. For example Uma Lele (1975) defines it as: 'improving living standards of the mass of the low-income population residing in rural areas and making the process of their development self-sustaining'.

From this definition we can conclude that the emphasis is not just on how to increase agricultural or food production, but on how to increase the welfare of the rural poor and how to make the process self-sustaining. Of course, in reality, the effort to increase their living standards will involve their own efforts to increase agricultural and food production, including livestock and fishery. This is understandable if the process of this development is going to be self-sustaining. In other words, if the rural poor are to improve their living standards, their main livelihood, that is agriculture and agriculture related activities, must be sustained and strengthened. Even if in the beginning, some kinds of subsidy or external assistance are needed for the low-income population, this assistance should not be expected to continue forever. But in order for this to happen, the rural economy must be moving and must widen its scope beyond the usual limited borders. This means that there must be an expanding market for the commodities produced by the low-income population.

The achievement of these objectives certainly requires government policies that provide continuous incentives to rural production, an efficient administrative system and appropriate institutional arrangements. If the traditional institutional arrangement guarantee the effectiveness of certain production and marketing systems, then this must be maintained and even strengthened. From past experiences, the success of certain programmes depends upon:

(a) good co-ordination and good leadership;
(b) patience in the programme implementation and
(c) good co-operation between government and private organizations.

The presence of good leadership is very important in each project and with this leadership, co-ordination with other government agencies is made easier. Since strong leadership is crucial, it is absolutely necessary to identify the right and capable leaders for each project. The second element of success is patience in the implementation of programmes, and especially when this is orientated to the achievement of fixed targets; otherwise then there is a likelihood that whatever the success achieved, it is not going to be satisfactory. Finally, it is necessary to realize that government agencies have very limited capacity to undertake rural development programmes by themselves. They must rely on the support, co-operation and participation of private organizations. With active participation there will be a guarantee that the programmes will be sustained, even if the government agencies pull out from the rural areas. In fact it is perhaps a prerequisite for the programme to identify local private organizations as a counterpart to the government agencies, before the programme is started. These are the organizations which are expected to run the programme after it is considered to have reached the self-sustaining stage.

It is logical to conclude that without the above conditions for success, any programme of rural development will fail. If co-ordination and leadership are poor, if there is too much obsession to achieve certain physical or numerical targets, and if there is no hope of local private support for the programmes, then certainly any programme is doomed to fail.

Perhaps, however, we can be more specific on this and present some signs which may give rise to the possible failure of projects. Some of these signs or characteristics are as follows:

1 The project which is imposed from above and is not developed from below.
2 The project which has no possibility of surviving without continuous government subsidy.
3 The project which has no connection with the human development of the rural population.

It is clear that the above characteristics of 'bad' projects are self-evident and, it seems, can be easily avoided. However, experience has shown that more often than not, these 'bad' characteristics can be found again and again. The question is then, why? What are the reasons, for introducing such projects? One of the reasons is that government agencies everywhere have the tendency to formulate projects from behind the desk, because they must propose these projects every budget year. If they do not receive sufficient information from the field, then 'behind the desk projects' are easiest to formulate. These type of projects, however, will eventually fail.

## PERSPECTIVES

There are three options available to government to solve the poverty problems in rural areas. The first is growth-orientated policies to increase the productivity of labour in agriculture. Included in this policy are agricultural intensification, transmigration, rural public works and so on (Birowo, 1981). This policy, if efficiently implemented, means that it will automatically increase the productivity of land and capital which are limited in their supply. This growth-oriented policy has been implemented since the beginning of Repelita in 1969 through a variety of subsidy systems for credit, fertilizer and other agricultural inputs.

The second set of policies are the so-called equity-orientated policies designed to help stimulate economic activities in the rural areas. These include the village subsidy programme, the subsidy to Kabupaten and others which are better known as the INPRES programme. These programmes have succeeded in improving rural infrastructures such as roads, small irrigation dams and bridges; although admittedly these rural infrastructures do not specifically help the rural poor.

The third set of policies are equity-orientated policies which involve policies to distribute assets and incomes. These types of policies are indeed the most difficult to implement because they involve the need to change the existing power structure in the rural areas. Land and agrarian reforms have been attempted since the early 1960s but the result has been disappointing. In view of the growing number of landless and near-landless, which means an increasing percentage of under-employment, this equity-orientated policy should emphasize creating more rural employment and improving the incomes of the poor.

From the foregoing analysis it appears that the challenges to eradicate poverty in rural areas are very great indeed. Even if the overall economy grows at a respectable level and equity-orientated policies achieve significant results, we will still find a large number of people below the poverty line in the year 2000. In the year 2000 there will still be wide diversity of richness and poverty among regions and many resource poor regions will still be sparsely populated, while the people who remain will still be poor. It is impossible to depend solely on the government to alleviate poverty. There is a real need to be convinced that prosperity, happiness and peacefulness in rural areas cannot be 'granted' by the government. The people themselves must act. The criteria for success in human development are not the satisfactions of material requisites of wellbeing, even though those are very important, but on the ability of rural people to play their own role in determining their destiny.

## REFERENCES

Birowo, Achmad T. and Hansen, Gary E., 'Agricultural and rural development: an overview', in Hansen, Gary E. (ed.), *Agricultural and Rural Development in Indonesia,* Westview Press, Boulder, Colorado, 1981, pp. 1-30.

Bengtsson, Bo (ed.), *rural development research: the role of power relations,* SAREC, Stockholm, 1979.

Moebyarto, Sayogyo and Tjondronegoro, S., 'Poverty, equity and rural development', in Moebyarto (ed.), *Growth and Equity in Indonesian Agricultural Development,* Indonesia

Yayasan Agro-Ekonomika, Yogyakarta, 1982.
IBRD, *Rural Development Sector Policy Paper,* World Bank, Washington, 1975.
Uma Lele, *The Design of Rural Development: Lesson from Africa,* World Bank, Johns Hopkins University Press, 1975.

## DISCUSSION OPENING – LIEM HUY NGO

It is a great honour for me to be able to comment on the paper of Dr Birowo. First I would like to start with a general observation that some aspects, orally presented by Dr Birowo, were not covered by his paper. But I am grateful to him, because through his oral presentation some questions relating to his paper were clarified.

Dr Birowo's paper covered 3 main areas:

1. The objectives and different concepts of rural development to tackle rural poverty.
2. Based on the Indonesian experience, some policy issues in agricultural and rural development, such as, the Co-operatives Development Programme, the Transmigration Programme, the Rural Industrialization Programme and various factors determining the success and failure of these government programmes and projects.
3. The perspective of policies in solving rural poverty based on options which are growth-orientated and equity orientated.

These three areas were clearly described and analysed by Dr Birowo.

Since many fundamental aspects found in Dr Birowo's paper, for instance those relating to social indicators, poverty line, basic needs concept, Indonesian development programmes and their causes of success and failure, have already been discussed implicitly or explicitly in the last sessions of the Conference and/or in the discussion groups and since time is limited, I would like to focus my remarks on a few points which are, in my view, not explicitly elaborated in Dr Birowo's paper and oral presentation. These points are also very important in the planning and implementation of rural development programmes and especially in the achievement of the equity goal.

*Focusing on the rural poor target groups.*
I agreed with the author when he mentioned that 'it is apparent that different people will interpret rural development in their own way'. These different interpretations of rural development have somehow consequences in the design, planning, implementation and even evaluation of rural development programmes/projects. Rural development is not only to focus on the satisfaction of basic needs and eradication of rural poverty but its programmes should also focus on the target groups – on the rural poor. In the planning process, the rural poor has been seen usually as a homogenous group. This is not true. Technological and institutional change and growing population have enforced the heterogenity of the rural poor. Within the

group (small tenants, small fishermen, agricultural and non-agricultural landless farmers, near-landless farmers) may exist a certain competition for access to a fixed amount of farmland. Identification, planning and implementation of different projects for the rural poor require information and knowledge about the composition of the rural poor, that is their socio-economic situation, their perceptions, their needs and behaviour, their relation to a given system. This information will not be limited only to the rural poor as target groups but also to the other groups with which they interact (for example landlords, middlemen, dealers, public employees, professionals).

The author is right in mentioning that the poverty problem is complex. I believe that we have to understand more about the complexity of rural poverty. This includes the identification of different problems, constraints and their inter-relationships which hinder the target groups to access to physical, economic and socio-political resources. Here I think you have a gap between economic theory used at the macro level and the situation at the micro level. The realities and situation at the micro level can explain the behaviour, the rationality of the rural poor, why they do not participate in the development process, why they are resistant to government programmes and projects, why they are adverse to change and so on. Experiences in the past showed that their resistance to development efforts led them to adopt certain behaviour which is sometimes not understandable for planners 'behind the desk' (using the author's expression) and/or which cannot be included in certain econometric, simulation models. This means that in order to obtain growth and equity, target-group-orientated and employment-orientated rural development programmes should be adopted. It seems that the realization is more likely to be achieved if efforts are concentrated at the regional level – taking into account both the macro and micro level.

*Co-operation with non-governmental organizations.*
I will not concentrate any discussion on the factors affecting the successes and failures of rural development programmes and projects. These factors are well pointed out by the author in his paper. I agree with Dr Birowo about these factors.

The most interesting thing which was pointed out was the fact that the success of certain programmes depends on good co-operation between the government and the private non-governmental organizations. It is not usual – at least in rural development literature – to hear that good co-operation between government and NGOs is one of the major factors affecting the success and failure of rural development programmes and projects. But Dr Birowo did not describe clearly the role of these NGOs. In some instances, the rural poor lost confidence in the government because they did not benefit much from its development programmes. In this situation NGOs can serve as a bridge to get back the confidence of the poor.

The role of NGOs is supposed to be not only to run the government programme after it is considered to have reached the self-maintaining stage – as mentioned by the author – but NGOs can also mobilize the poor and attend to their needs.

The experiences of these NGOs with the grassroots, their flexibility in developmental works and their skills in some sectors covering basic needs such as health, nutrition, education, housing, certainly can be used in the identification, planning, implementation and evaluation of the development programmes/projects. However, in the process of co-operation, one has to consider the fact that the non-governmental organizations are not a homogenous group; they differ from each other by size, area of activities, linkages and – very important – they have different ideologies. Therefore it is difficult to identify areas of co-operation not only between government and NGOs but also among the NGOs themselves.

Since I understand that delegates from various NGOs involved in developmental works are also present at this Conference, it would be useful if Dr Birowo could elaborate more the experiences of co-operation between the government and private organizations and clarify – if possible – what the types of private organizations are, what is their role in rural development and what are the problems perceived, at least from the view point of the government, regarding this co-operation. This co-operation is not an easy task. It requires a sincere political will from the government side. The sincerity should not stay only at the national level; but it also has to go down to the local level where these private non-governmental organizations operate.

*Organizational structure and institutional arrangements*

Dr Birowo has stressed, in his oral presentation, the overall organizational structure and the planning and implementation mechanism based on the Indonesian Five Year Plan and some rural development programmes. However, he did not elaborate how this structure and these mechanisms affect the decision-making process, local level participation and the target groups.

The co-ordination problem between the different agencies – as pointed out by the author in his discussion of the transmigration programme in Indonesia – is only the consequence of the organizational set-up. Very often decentralization is proclaimed by the central government. But in analysing working relationships and the interactions of planning, as well as in studying the relationships between the administrative staff and the project staff, one could raise the question as to whether central government is really willing to distribute power to local government. The success and failure of efforts in rural development are not decided by a country's type of political régime and its ideological motivations. Rather the key to this most important problem is to be found in organizational structure and institutional arrangements.

Finally, I would like to congratulate Dr Birowo for his efforts in presenting to us the very practical and realistic issues of rural development planning and implementation in Indonesia.

G. H. PETERS AND A. H. MAUNDER

# *Efficiency, Equity and Agricultural Change with Special Reference to Land Tenure in Western Europe.*

## INTRODUCTION

This paper is parochial in dealing only with Western Europe. Despite the geographical limitation, which also implies restriction to developed areas, European conditions are sufficiently diverse to provide highly relevant examples of the complex effects which land tenure can have on efficiency and equity. It is also stressed that the European situation is continuously altering in response to economic change, and is frequently affected by general legislation, particularly taxation provision, as well as by law specific to land holding itself.

*Tenure and efficiency*

Theoretical work on tenure and efficiency normally stresses the distinction between *owning* and *operating* land. At one end of the spectrum both functions may be vested in one person or small family group, though the size of their operation can range from very small peasant proprietorships to large-scale owner-occupation. Economically one of the great problems of adaptation becomes that of adjusting man-land ratios as conditions change, since for many institutional reasons the land market may be imperfectly adapted to exchanges of land[1]. More generally the existence of a labour market can also be of considerable importance since it allows labour application to exceed that available to a family group should the marginal hiring cost be exceeded by the value of the marginal product. Both points relating to markets are equally relevant to conditions of tenancy and will reappear.

In the efficiency context, following Schickele (1941), there is a critical distinction between 'durable' and 'non-durable' inputs. The former comprise land and fixed capital; the latter include labour and all other intermediate inputs. Efficiency of allocation clearly demands that the marginal rates of substitution between durable and non-durable inputs should in all cases be the same, and that they should relate to the relative prices of inputs. Since in owner occupation there is unified control of both classes of input a rational operator should attempt to ensure that the efficiency conditions are met, provided, among other things, that he has unencumbered ownership, access to capital and is not inhibited by the uncertainties of biological production. It is also clear that land should be allocated to those best able to utilize its full capabilities; in short there needs to be an element of competitive pressure within the land market to secure any indicated land reallocation and to preserve freedom of entry for newcomers of superior efficiency.

Any form of tenancy involves divergence between ownership and operation, and a multiplication of problems. Tenancy may be based on a share or a cash rental, and there may be numerous stipulations relating to length of leases, compensation for unexhausted improvements at the termination of a tenancy, responsibility for repair and upkeep of durable inputs, control of cropping practices, provision for rent review during the course of a lease and arrangements for eviction and ending of a tenancy agreement. There are various standard criticisms of tenancy. For example share tenancy has long been regarded as potentially defective on the grounds that a tenant will not apply non-durable inputs to the point at which their marginal cost equates to the value of marginal product, for the tenant who bears the cost only obtains some share of the benefit[2]. Cash rent tenancy can also be inefficient if the split in control between durable inputs, now supplied by the landowner, and non-durable inputs, supplied by the tenant, results in breaches of the equi-marginal principle. Tenants, for example, may under-supply if they are insecure or do not receive compensation for improvements; landlords similarly may under-supply if they are unable to secure rent increases adequate to balance the cost of any new investment made. A significant advantage of tenancy, on the other hand, can be division of responsibility since the role of landownership involving care for layout and for buildings, as well as access to long-term capital, can complement the farming skills of tenants (Walston 1978). However Schickele regarded the problem of divergent control as overriding and this prompted him to declare that owner-occupation is probably more conducive to efficiency than cash rent tenancy. This argument, however, is by no means clear cut. Indeed following the recent work of Currie (1981) it appears that any broad statement relating to the merits of 'systems' is likely to be misleading since the potential variations in tenure form can be considerable. Currie himself ends his survey with a note in favour of 'tripartite' arrangements involving landowner, capitalist farmer and worker. The point stressed is that such a system, if it works in accord with rather stringent conditions, can allow markets to function for all factors to satisfy the marginal conditions. He notes, in particular, the importance of the man-land ratio and the need to adjust scales of operation to ensure efficiency across the operating structure.

### *Tenure and Equity*

Still by way of introduction it remains to consider the relation between efficiency and equity. Suppose in a tripartite system that the size distribution of operating units is well adjusted to fit the managerial abilities of farmers, tenure laws satisfy the needs of both parties and workers are protected against exploitation. Efficiency conditions can thus be satisfied. However inequity could be diagnosed if there is a marked discrepancy between the wealth, income and political power of landowners and that of other members of society. The replacement of private landowners by institutional or state ownership, on some agreed terms, might be recommended though this need not lead to any change in the operating structure. By contrast a latifundia system may be inequitable and also inefficient since it can prevent attainment of an optimum man-land ratio. At the other end of the scale, social and political systems can be found widespread throughout Europe which have quite different effects stemming from particular concern to secure equity between members of farming families in matters of inheritance. This was embodied, particularly, in the Napoleonic laws which codified the equality of joint heirs, the limitation of testamental power available to a current owner of land and prohibition of attempts to shape future inheritance. This is not universal in continental Europe – in Germany the law varies from area to area, while in Denmark division is prevented. However from the viewpoint of this paper the effect of law and custom has often been to create a pattern of small farms, many of which also suffer from gross fragmentation with associated inefficiency in operation[3].

## THE OPERATING AND OWNERSHIP STRUCTURE OF EUROPEAN AGRICULTURE

A necessarily brief résumé of European conditions, so far as the countries of the EEC are concerned, appears in Table 1. For the moment the important points to notice concern the average size of holdings (col. 4) where the United Kingdom has an easy lead (64.3 ha in 1975, almost three times the figure for Denmark and France). The United Kingdom also has the lowest percentage of part-time farmers, and a very low number of farms in the 1-5 hectare group, first place of both characteristics being taken by Italy. The country with the highest incidence of tenancy is Belgium, followed by France, Netherlands and the United Kingdom (col. 5).

### *Tenure in Britain*

In Britain[4] conventional wisdom has it that the landlord-tenant arrangements have operated with greatest efficiency. Though it must be emphasized that the small farm problem is not absent in Britain, an important historical legacy has been a size structure of operating units well adapted to basic farming conditions, and untrammelled by fragmentation. However it cannot be concluded from this that tenure controversy is absent in Britain. The issue has become of great topical concern with strong debate about the merits of the landlord-tenant system, the degree of tenant security to aim at, and the most appropriate way to ensure that adaptation to agricultural change can occur.

Landlordism evolved in Britain out of a manorial system in which land was held in fragmented portions by peasant farmers who were subject to the

TABLE 1 *The operating and ownership structure of European agriculture*

| | Holdings[d] (000's) 1979 | Per cent holdings 1979 | | Average size: ha 1975 | Per cent area tenanted 1975 | Per cent farm size increase 1960–75 | Per cent holders part-time 1975 |
|---|---|---|---|---|---|---|---|
| | | 1-5 ha | > 50 ha | | | | |
| Belgium | 97[a] | 29.1[a] | 3.8[a] | 13.9 | 73 | 70 | 25 |
| Denmark | 120 | 11.3 | 9.6 | 22.6 | 14 | 44 | 13 |
| France | 1103 | 19.4 | 13.5 | 24.3 | 47 | 43 | 19 |
| W. Germany | 807 | 32.1 | 3.7 | 13.8 | 29 | 48 | 18 |
| Ireland | 260[b] | 17.3[b] | 7.4[b] | 20.5 | 8 | 20 | 15 |
| Italy | 2145[b] | 68.2[b] | 1.8[b] | 7.5 | 17 | 10 | 40 |
| Luxembourg | 6 | 19.5 | 15.3 | 23.5 | 42 | 75 | 11 |
| Netherlands | 132 | 24.2 | 2.8 | 14.4 | 44 | 31[c] | 8 |
| United Kingdom | 260 | 14.5 | 31.3 | 64.3 | 43 | 28[c] | 7 |
| Average/Total | 5175[b] | 41.9[b] | 6.3[b] | 16.9 | 35 | 40 | 27 |

*Notes:* [a]For 1978; [b]For 1975; [c]Due to break in series figures show change between 1960 and about 1970; [d]Holdings of 1 hectare and over; [e]Part-time is defined as spending under 25 per cent of time on the holding.
*Sources: The Agricultural Situation in the Community and Yearbook of Agricultural Statistics,* Eurostat; *EEC Agricultural and Food Statistics,* June 1974, MAFF.

overriding control of a feudal lord. These arrangements operated for centuries until overtaken by 'enclosure movements' which were particularly powerful in the 'agricultural revolution' of the eighteenth century. Enclosure, it is said, resulted in the formation of estates divided into self-contained rented farms which were adequately equipped with fixed capital items at the expense of the landowner and subject to cash rent tenancy. In its orginal form it was underwritten only by common law and custom. Governmental intervention, except in passing Enclosure Acts sanctioning initial changes in layout, did not affect the relation of landlord and tenant. It was not until 1875, and the first Agricultural Holdings Act, that tenants became statutorily eligible to compensation for improvements and entitled to a minimum period of one year before a notice to quit could become operative.

Ownership was heavily concentrated. The 'New Domesday' Survey of 1875 showed that most of the land belonged to a few hundred families who enjoyed an opulence contrasting starkly with the conditions of agricultural workers who made up the base of the tripartite system. Landlordism has been in decline ever since as a result of complex causes stemming partly from periods of economic adversity and partly from the effects of legislation. Estate duty, payable on the death of the owner of property, is often pictured as the major destroyer of the landed estate. However, when introduced in 1894 duty was low, and when it became stiffer in 1924 agricultural land was protected by rebate to 45 per cent of the level incurred for other property. Political power had a part to play in this. Nevertheless it could be claimed that the landlord-tenant system, powerfully reinforced by the custom of primogeniture, represented a valuable form of ownership structure which it would be unwise to disrupt with dramatic suddenness.

It was during the inter-war years that economic depression began to have an effect. Rented land was 88 per cent of the total in England and Wales in 1910, 75 per cent in 1924 and 62 per cent by 1950. An interesting controversy in the inter-war years concerned land nationalization, *not* on grounds of equity or out of a desire to dispossess landlords without compensation. The argument was that the system worked effectively only when landowners had access to capital and were prepared to invest in improvement. However under capital scarcity a takeover was seen as a way of refurbishing the system by allowing in state funds and simultaneously maintaining the independence of tenant farmers. This argument (revived by Walston in 1978) contrasts with discussion of land nationalization earlier in the century among the radical wing of the British Liberal Party which was concerned more with distribution of ownership as an equity issue, rather than with farming efficiency. The British Labour Party is now again raising similar issues.

The next important development was the Agricultural Holdings Act of 1948 which codified wartime practices. The Act provided a technical position in which tenancies were deemed to be year to year, but ejection of a tenant was only possible in limited circumstances such as bankruptcy or bad husbandry. In effect it became extremely difficult for a landlord to obtain repossession, except on the death of a tenant. The 1948 Act, since it created very secure tenancies, also had to provide a mechanism for fixing rents. If negotiation between landlord and tenant proved unsuccessful either party could refer the dispute to arbitration. However the instructions to arbitrators were initially vague and unsatisfactory, although stiffened by more precise provisions in 1958. The results were that the movement of rents became sluggish and large disparities began to appear between those paid by secure sitting tenants and by new entrants fortunate enough to have an opportunity to bid for a farm available for letting. In the land market this was reflected in large 'vacant possession premiums'. Land sold subject to tenancy has generally been lower priced (£951 per hectare in 1976 for example) while land available with vacant possession has been much more sought after and highly valued (£1,814 in 1976). Security of tenure and the behaviour of rents persuaded many landowners to sell farms, whenever they became available, at the high vacant possession price, or indeed to sell to tenants at a compromise price. This process went on rapidly after 1950 (rented land 62 per cent of total) pulling down the rented proportion to 48 per cent by 1960.

A further blow to landowners came in 1974 with the conversion of estate duty into capital transfer tax. Hitherto all land enjoyed relief from the full rigours of taxation; now the concession was to apply only to owner-occupied farmland, rented land would not qualify, and would face a higher tax bill. The change also significantly tightened the tax legislation in the sense that avoidance became more difficult. It used to be said that estate duty was a 'voluntary' tax paid only by those incapable of organizing their affairs in a tax efficient way. That situation changed markedly in 1974 (Peters, 1980).

Even more powerful have been the effects of the Agriculture (Miscellaneous Provisions) Act of 1976, which was also passed by a Labour government. Though it should have been apparent that the CTT provisions would gradually reduce land offered in the rental market, the 1976 Act sought to protect *tenants* by allowing virtual *inheritance* of tenancy through two further generations. Various relatively minor conditions had to be fulfilled but in general it provided impregnable and possibly very long term security for a family and, by the same token, a long term obligation on the part of the landowner. The results are predictable. Whenever land 'falls in' to the control of a landlord (for example by the death of a tenant without heir) he is most unlikely to make a new letting which might tie land to three generations of family occupation. Results of a survey by agricultural valuers show that only 8.5 per cent of the area of land becoming available was let out afresh, while 24.7 per cent passed to a new tenant under the Act, either unopposed or after appeal to the Agricultural Land Tribunal. Of the remaining 66.8 per cent some 30.2 per cent was taken in hand by landlords who would farm themselves, 19.7 per cent was sold and 16.9 per cent was taken in hand to become the subject of a partnership with a farmer rather than a strict tenancy. This effectively means that the traditional landlord system (where the landowner was an 'individual') has come under severe attack and, apart from the rump of protected tenancies, could become increasingly difficult.

## EFFECTS OF TENURE

It might have been thought that there would be clear evidence to help in comparison of the landlord-tenant and owner-occupation systems. Clearly the switch away from the former cannot be taken as representative of some sort of economic 'natural selection' since the causes lie in taxation and legislation. Empirical work available in Britain comparing operating efficiency suggests that no clear-cut differences emerge. The 1973 NEDC report could not demonstrate any convincing relationship between tenure and productivity (NEDC 1973). More detailed investigations by B. Hill and D. K. Britton (1978) suggested some tendency for smaller tenanted farms to have superior efficiency ratios to similar owner occupied properties but statistically significant differences in performance could not be established over all size groups. There is, however, some other evidence pointing to the advantages of maintaining a market in rented property. The process of agricultural change normally involves a decline in the man-land ratio and an enlargement in the size of operating units. This is usually easier to accomplish if tenancy is a possibility.

European statistics are difficult to interpret because of definitional changes. Over the years some of the countries with large tenanted sectors (for example Belgium) have experienced the greatest increase in farm sizes (see Table 1). Very little change occurred in Ireland and Italy where owner occupation predominates. While these aggregative data are not unambiguous (note Denmark, West Germany and France) there is more convincing evidence in detailed studies of the actual process of farm enlargement. Indications are that this has been achieved more often by renting rather than buying extra land. The point was strongly emphasized in a study of structural change in the Central Midlands and Devon (England) by Hine and Houston (1973). Similarly in Sweden, despite an active policy for farm enlargement through purchase, Bolin (1974) estimated that two-thirds of the land used for increasing farm area came from renting. One author of this paper (Maunder) has also observed an association between size change and the proportion of land tenanted in detailed studies of Italy, where there is considerable internal variation in the importance of tenancy. Similar results seem to hold for the regions of France.

It will be appreciated that the tentative conclusions which are emerging lead to an obvious problem. Preservation of tenancy normally implies the preservation of private land-owning. As we have seen in Britain, capital taxation is widely accepted on equity grounds, hence there can be conflict with efficiency. However, it is probably fair to record the view that the current acute problems of the landlord-tenant system stem mainly from the 1976 provisions with their blocking of the market in tenancies. In the light of the earlier theoretical discussion it is clear that tenants do require security; but in Britain the pendulum has probably swung too far.

In Britain controversy centred on a combination of efficiency and equity arguments have not been restricted to the tenanted sector. There is an influential view, associated with Sutherland (1981), that the present legislative climate is damaging the efficiency of the owner-occupied sector, and producing its own set of inequities. His argument stems from the belief that there are no significant economies of scale in British agriculture beyond a farm size of 300 acres (121 ha). This is a rough judgement since conditions vary between farming sectors. However, whatever the detailed situation might be, it is a fact that the capital transfer tax concessions which can be obtained from the preferential treatment accorded to agriculture are raising land values generally. At the top of the farming ladder this provides a strong equity base, cushions mismanagement and confers large capital gains on a privileged set of owners. Sutherland therefore proposes abolition of concessions to farmers who own more than 300 acres. In this case, if economies of scale are absent, equity and efficiency considerations pull in the same direction. Indeed it could be contended that many forms of concession to agriculture (including generous support prices) inflate farm real estate values (Trail 1980) and act as a barrier to new entry. The way into farming has never been easy (the old tag has it that one can become a farmer only through parsimony, patrimony or matrimony), but in Britain because of influences in both the tenanted and the owner-occupied sectors it is becoming increasingly log-jammed.

Following the earlier discussion of European conditions it might be supposed that the most obvious problem is a defective operating structure associated with sub-optimal sizes, fragmentation of holdings, and problems of transfer between generations. All of these difficulties are present in various degrees, though it is important not to over-emphasize them or regard them as general. In Denmark and the Netherlands, for example, farms are comparatively small yet agriculture is widely regarded as being of noted efficiency. The countries do, however, contrast in the extent of tenancy (14 per cent in Denmark, 44 per cent in the Netherlands). Conditions in Belgium are even more puzzling. Tenancy is the rule, with occupiers having rents controlled by legislation, they enjoy virtually automatic renewal of leases which are normally for nine years, heirs have the right of succession and landowners cannot resume occupation unless they wish to farm their land themselves or have it farmed by successors. However despite these restrictions farm sizes have expanded, and though competition for land must be restricted Belgium consistently rates highly in agricultural productivity calculations. More acute problems are to be found in Western Germany, parts of France (notably Brittany) and in Italy. As a typical example, in Western Germany smallness is accompanied by awkward fragmentation; 25 per cent of farms are split into 6-10 parcels and 26 per cent have 11 or more. As in other mainland European countries an official land consolidation organization is attempting to improve the situation but progress is limited. In 1975–77 some 4,725 farmers exchanged 10,800 hectares but this slow rate, if anything, is declining. For various reasons there are attractions in traditional systems, as shown in a Belgian survey (Everret, 1974) which indicated that out of 459 farmers questioned only 43 per cent were clearly in favour of a consolidation programme and 39 per cent were opposed.

A frequent problem is that there is often a direct conflict between *equity within families* and the efficiency of the farm. Even when family settlements manage to preserve a farm intact (or at least in its previously fragmented form) the new operator, unless the previous generations were able to build up considerable external assets or the family is small, can be faced with financial obligation to relatives and a consequent shortage of working capital. In considering the building-up of small holdings to viable size there can be some advantages, as noted earlier, in having a strong element of tenancy within the ownership structure though this can be nullified if security of tenancy becomes extreme. In this connection in Western Germany leases are customarily for 9-12 years, but heirs again have the right to succession. In Italy tenancy for working farmers is of indefinite length, they have a right to pre-emption in cases of sale and heirs again have right to succession (Scully, 1977). It is inevitable, under such conditions, that progress towards consolidation and a more efficient operating structure must be inhibited.

It is clear then that so far as state intervention in the relationship between tenants and landowners is concerned, there are two important sets of provisions which limit the adaptability of farming systems. These are the provisions relating to security of tenure and those relating to rent determination. Regarding the former, while most European countries, as already described, give full, if not excessive, security to tenants, Italy at one extreme extends this protection even to very short-term and grazing tenancies, while at the other, Denmark with a high degree of owner-occupation has little tenancy legislation as such[5]. So far as rents are concerned, Britain is unusual in attempting to base rent determination on the free market. It is more common to find that rents are set by reference to some objective assessment of agricultural productivity, often in the fairly distant past. Owners and tenants indulge in various complex and ingenious devices to try and overcome the effect of these provisions. Where this proves impossible the result at the best is structural stagnation but at the worst it can lead to the actual abandonment of land from agriculture. The basic trouble, from the equity point of view, is that these tenure provisions were designed to protect poor tenant farmers from large and rapacious landlords and have little reference to new situations where in many areas of mainland Europe both parties are drawn from the same social and economic class.

## CONCLUSIONS

In the light of all its complexities the European scene is one in which any clear policy prescription becomes inadvisable if not impossible. Recalling earlier theoretical discussion, the route to efficient operation, when viewed in neo-classical terms, is to be found in the existence of markets which allow all factors of production to be transferred between use and user with minimum friction. In agriculture it is widely recognized, however, that tenancy can only operate efficiently if there are safeguards against arbitrary landowner action. Though in the light of discussion it would be foolish to generalize, continental Europe appears to suffer from an owner occupation system which inhibits structural adaptation and in many areas preserves a system of small fragmented farms which are ill adapted to modern needs. Concurrently with this, when tenancy is present as an important alternative it tends to be hemmed in by excessive and complex rules which go beyond necessary bounds and *also* inhibit adjustment. Over the years ahead we must hope to see national and EEC action being devoted to the creation of a more flexible land-owning and tenure situation designed to aid in the build up of larger holdings offering greater income earning opportunities. In Britain, which has a different legacy and traditionally a much more open system, it is regrettable that recent policies have been choice restricting. The damage likely to be done may not be severe, given Britain's far more effective operating structure. The more difficult, and more urgent, problem is that of creating efficiency when a start has to be made from the baseline of ultra-restrictive land policies represented by conditions in many areas of continental Europe.

## NOTES

[1] Generalization is dangerous when dealing with land ownership. The Irish 'conacre' system, as one example, does allow convenient short-term leasing in a predominantly owner occupation system.

[2] The brevity of the discussion reflects the rareness of share tenancy in Europe, except in Italy where it is still less than 10% of land area and is diminishing.

[3] Northern Spain provides some classic examples of fragmentation. According to Guedes (Guedes, 1981) a 2.2 hectare farm in Burgos was divided into 64 plots averaging 0.024 hectares per plot. In the case of particularly favoured seed beds division between inheritors can result in plots literally the size of a handkerchief.

[4] Britain will be treated in some detail since it is home ground. However it is also a comparatively easy spot to start what could, if space allowed, be an enormously elaborate survey. For further details and for other EEC countries see various EEC reports on *Factors influencing ownership, tenancy, mobility and use of farmland;* Bergmann (1981), Harrison (1981), Fløystrup-Jensen and Dyreborg-Carlsen (1981) have been published to date. [Further reports are now available for Belgium and Luxemburg, Italy, the Netherlands and W. Germany (ed.)]

[5] It is interesting to note that the tenanted portion of the total agricultural area of Denmark increased from 7 per cent in 1966 to over 15 per cent in 1980 (Landøkonomisk Oversight, 1981).

## REFERENCES


Bergmann, D., *Les facteurs qui influencent la propriété, l'affermage, la mobilité et l'utilisation des terres agricoles en France,* Commission des Communautes Europeennes, Informations sur l'agriculture No. 76, Luxembourg, 1981.

Bolin, O., *Lantbruksnämndernas mal, medel och ander i rationaliseringsprocessen,* Institutionen för ekonomi och statistik, Uppsala, 1974.

Currie, J. M., *The Economic Theory of Agricultural Land Tenure,* Cambridge University Press, Cambridge, 1981.

Everret, H., 'Farmers Attitudes to Land Consolidation: A Sociological Survey of the Sandy Areas of E. Flanders', *Cahiers de l'Institut Economique Agricole* No. 171, 1974.

Fløystrup-Jensen, J. and Dyreborg-Carlsen, B., *Factors Influencing Ownership, Tenancy, Mobility and Use of Farmland in Denmark,* Commission of the European Communities, Information on Agriculture No. 73, Luxembourg, 1981.

Guedes, M., 'Recent Agricultural Land Policy in Spain', *Oxford Agrarian Studies,* Vol. X, 1981.

Harrison, A., *Factors Influencing Ownership, Tenancy, Mobility and Use of Farmland in the United Kingdom,* Commission of the European Communities, Information on Agriculture No. 74, Luxembourg, 1981.

Hill, B. and Britton, D. K., 'Differences in Efficiency by Farm Size and Tenure', Paper to AES Conference, December 1978 (mimeograph).

Hine, R. C. and Houston, A. M., *Government and Structural Change in Agriculture* MAFF, HMSO, London 1973.

*Landøkonomisk Oversight, 1981,* De Danske Landbofeninger, København, 1981.

National Economic Development Office, *Farm Productivity: A Report on Factors Affecting Productivity at the Farm Level,* London, HMSO, 1973.

Peters, G. H., 'Some Thoughts on Capital Taxation', *Journal of Agricultural Economics* Vol. XXXI, No. 3, Sept. 1980.

Schickele, R., 'Effects of Tenure Systems on Agricultural Efficiency', *Journal of Farm Economics,* Vol. 23, No. 1, February 1941.

Scully, J. J., *Land Tenure in the European Community,* Newsletter on the Common Agricultural Policy No. 3, Commission of the European Communities, Brussels, 1977.

Sutherland, A., 'Capital Transfer Tax: and Obituary', *Fiscal Studies* November 1981, and 'Capital Transfer Tax and Farming', ibid., March 1980.

Trail, B., *Land Values and Rents: The Gains and Losses from Farm Price Support Programmes,* Bulletin 175, University of Manchester, Manchester 1980.

Walston, Lord, 'Land Ownership', *Journal of Agricultural Economics,* Vol. XXIX, No. 3, September 1978.

## DISCUSSION OPENING – ZULKIFLY HJ. MUSTAPHA

The authors have given us a brief but comprehensive account of land tenure systems, in particular in Britain, and within the space limitations provided, have also mentioned some issues pertinent to tenancy and the relationship of tenure and efficiency and equity in the scenario of structural change.

The land tenure system, despite standard criticisms of being defective, has to a certain extent provided efficiency of the farm and equity. This is normally observed only in a particular legislative and policy environment. Particularly in the case of the landlord-tenant system, efficiency of the farm may and usually does appear in the form of effective and efficient utilization of productive resources by tenants in those situations where they felt secure and that the use of land provided them with good incomes or a high share of the returns. Assured high returns from the land would in turn encourage a positive response from the landlord towards improvement in the landlord-tenant relationship and further improvement of the land; thus assisting towards greater efficiency. Equity can be seen more in terms of accessibility and availability of opportunities for tenants, who formerly were landless, to generate employment and income through the economic use of productive resources.

However, more often than not, the landlord-tenant system may be defective as regards efficiency and equity. Under this system either in the form of share tenancy or cash rent tenancy, there is often a tendency towards insecurity of tenure and a lower share of the returns for the tenants. This often results in inefficiency. In addition, inequity in tenure systems also exists. This is seen in terms of differences in wealth, ownership, income, and economic power between the tenants and the landed groups, as well as between members of farming families.

The paper has provided some indication of the relationships between tenure and efficiency and equity, but it does not adequately and appropriately discuss all the various issues in tenancy systems that may have affected efficiency and equity and which often have very significant implications to the issues at hand and to growth in general. To have included these issues in the discussion would have been stimulating as tenancy, particularly the landlord-tenant system, affects not only the developed countries but also, and to an important degree, the developing countries. This, I presume, was no fault of the authors but was due to space limitations..

I have, however, a few points in opening this paper for discussion: First, I suggest that the land area or the size of units of production and its implications to efficiency and equity in any tenancy system needs elaborations and further discussion. I view this issue as significant owing to the fact that size has often been argued as being one of the central issues relating to efficiency on the farm, in particular, and equity in general. It has been observed that land holdings in developing countries are generally smaller, to the extent of being uneconomic, when compared to the developed countries for both landlord-tenant and owner-occupation systems.

In the owner-occupation system, as a result of inheritance and the social system, in particular in Islamic countries, land holdings have been continually sub-divided and fragmented from generation to generation into smaller and smaller units. It is claimed that such small units of production, usually less than two hectares, limit the opportunity and potential for higher productivity and income, thus resulting in low reinvestment on the land. This has led to inefficiency on the farm. At the same time, with variations in the ownership pattern based upon the size of holdings, it gives rise to inequity among members of the farming population.

In the case of the landlord-tenant system, the production units among the landlords are also generally small. Also there often exist absentee landlords who normally involve themselves with economic activities in urban centres and, with the land being inherited, neglect their land but have high expectations of the returns from their tenants. Such practices, in most cases, have also led to the inefficient use of the land. Inequity, however, is already reflected in the ownership structure.

My second point concerns the issue of exploitation under the landlord-tenant system which I think would have a direct effect on efficiency, but was not discussed in the paper. I am certain that exploitation exists in the landlord-tenant system both in developed and developing countries. Often, both in share and cash rent tenancy, it is the tenants who are on the losing end. They not only have to pay high rents but also often receive a low share of the returns. This has discouraged improvements to the land which would have increased efficiency, and the continued exploitation leads to inefficiency on the farm and, to a certain extent, economic and social injustice and other related socio-economic problems.

Thirdly, legislation and policies pertaining to tenancy always try to achieve the ideal, that is to eliminate or at least minimize the complexities of problems in tenancy. However, one must be cautious of its successful implementation. As indicated in the paper, legislation and policies have not successfully eliminated tenancy, but instead preserved tenancy systems and the prevailing ownership structures. The preservation of tenancy may indicate a perpetuation not only of inefficiency and other evils of tenancy, but also may perpetuate inequity. Thus, defects remain in terms of both efficiency and equity.

In conclusion, I think we should be critical of any tenancy systems and the legislation and policies undertaken through State intervention. What should be done, maybe, is to work within prevailing tenancy systems to activate efficiency and equity so as to make them less defective.

## GENERAL DISCUSSION* – RAPPORTEUR: STEPHEN K. POLLARD

The general discussion on Johnston and Clark's paper centred on several key aspects of rural development: employment, poverty and equity. The question was raised as to whether Johnston and Clark's use of the terms relief and welfare in describing certain programmes, for example school-lunch programmes, that are essential for improved equity in LDCs, was correct. Further, there was doubt whether strategies appropriate for middle-income countries are applicable to present-day LDCs. Better co-ordination between population policy and economic policy is indicated, given the severity of the population problem. Examples of economic development policies which would reduce fertility are raising incomes of the poor and increasing education levels, particularly of women. It was questioned whether agricultural development strategies will generate employment in agriculture as this seems to be the case only when multiple cropping is undertaken. Therefore we must rely on infrastructural development in rural areas to increase rural employment. A more radical approach was called for to rural development and change; emphasizing that the Johnston and Clark strategy could not achieve desired goals. On a similar note it was claimed that there is nothing new in the Johnston and Clark strategy and one must be aware of the power groups and self interests at work when developing rural development strategies. In response, Professor Johnston agreed that there was nothing new in what he and Professor Clark proposed, but also that many economists were too concerned with macro models and production projects. Further, the basic needs component of their strategy is an important element in alleviating rural poverty. On the question of population, he agreed that it was too important an issue to leave to the demographers and that we, as agricultural economists, need to be aware of this.

Discussion on the paper by A. T. Birowo centred on the role of

*Paper by Johnston and Clark, Birowo, Peters and Maunder.

government co-operatives and non-governmental organizations in promoting rural development. It was suggested that government sponsored co-operatives would not be effective in meeting farmer members' interests. Birowo replied that this was not the case in Indonesia. Furthermore, rural co-operatives *and* non-governmental organizations provided ways and techniques to improve rural conditions in Indonesia.

Discussion on the paper by Peters and Maunder focused on the relationships between landlord and tenant and equity under different forms of agricultural tenure. It was stated that the growth in developing countries that facilitates agricultural equity is industrial growth. Hence, recent industrial recessions in the US and Europe will impair achievement of equity in agriculture tenure. The issue was raised that tenants can be more efficient than owner-operators. Further, tenants may be in a position to exploit the landlord if the tenants can conceal output from him. Mr Peters responded by stating that tenants may not always be more efficient than owner-operators. Tenure systems needed to be examined to better understand whether a complete ownership of the land by producers is both efficient and equitable.

SAÚL TREJO REYES

# *Regional Income Inequality in Mexican Agriculture and Government Policy*

Mexican agricultural development over the present century is widely considered a great success story. Agricultural output has in general kept pace with the food requirements of a population that grew from 15 million in 1910, on the eve of the Mexican Revolution, to 20 million in 1940 and 70 million in 1980. During the last 40 years output per caput grew more than fourfold. Agricultural product grew from 100 to 525, while national product increased from 100 to 1300. However, agricultural output per caput grew only 50 per cent, and as a result the country was forced to import foodstuffs during the last decade. During the period following 1940, the agricultural labour force has grown from 3.8 to somewhat less than 7 million, so that output per worker is now 3 times greater. However, the increase in rural income has by no means been equitably distributed among different regions and human groups. Rather, productivity differentials and income inequality have widened, not only between urban and rural dwellers, but also within the rural sector. That this has been so under a government grown out of revolution and committed to equality shows the great difficulty in distributing government resources to attain equity objectives. It also shows how the increasingly urban character of the Mexican economy and society has conditioned rural development policies along a road to inequality.

Until early in this century Mexican agriculture, and Mexican society as a whole, had developed predominantly in the central highland plateau. The coastal areas, as well as the North and Northwest, had been held back in their development both by climate and by distance from the central region where Mexico City is located. Thus in 1899 the central region accounted for 49 per cent of crop value. This share diminished steadily to 35 per cent in 1939 and 27 per cent in 1959 (Reynolds, 1970). Beginning in the 1930s, the Federal Government started an intensive policy of agricultural investment, directed toward increasing the land area under cultivation, primarily in regions hitherto underdeveloped. Cropped land area increased from 6.3 to 10.8 million hectares between 1940 and 1960 and a further increase to 16.4 million hectares took place between 1960 and 1978. Irrigated land area increased from 1.9 to 3.0 million hectares between 1940 and 1960 and to 4.8 million hectares in 1978. Thus the ratio of cropped land to labour increased from 1.57 hectares per worker in 1940 to 2.31 in 1979. Despite what would appear as a lessening of population pressure on arable land in this period, 1940 also marks the start of a still ongoing process of rural-urban migration that has completely transformed the character of the country from rural to urban. In 1940 the total labour force was 5.9 million, of which 3.8 million, or 64 per cent, was in agriculture. By 1960 the figures were 11.2 million, 6.1 million, and 54 per cent. In 1980 the total labour force was about 21 million, of which at most 7 million, or 33 per cent, were in agriculture and other rural activities.

It may be said that modern Mexican development portrays a race between the growth of the labour force, which definitely accelerated after 1940, and the creation of new employment opportunities. The fact that the agricultural labour force continued to increase during the period of rapid urbanization may be attributed to four factors: (a) opening of new land to cultivation; (b) government investment in rural infrastructure; (c) government expenditure on social welfare in the rural areas; and (d) private capital accumulation in agriculture. Given that these four elements have operated in a different manner both through time and in different regions of the country, they have contributed to an increase in regional income differentials over time.

As may be seen from the labour force figures, between 1960 and 1980 the agricultural labour force rose at most 15 per cent, while the urban labour force rose 170 per cent. This latter figure may be overstated but even so the difference is enormous. Practically the whole of the increase in rural population migrated to the cities after 1960. Data for the period previous to 1960 is scarce; however, the differential rate of development for five regions may be seen from the share of agricultural production that each of them accounted for in 1939 and 1959:

TABLE 1 *Share of Agricultural Production: Regions of Mexico*

| Region | 1939 | 1959 |
|---|---|---|
| North | 25 | 23 |
| Gulf | 19 | 17 |
| North Pacific | 11 | 18 |
| South Pacific | 10 | 15 |
| Centre | 35 | 27 |
| Total: | 100 | 100 |

*Source:* Reynolds (1970).

It should be pointed out that during the last five decades rather diverse policies have been followed with regard to government investment in agriculture. During most of the 1930s a policy of land distribution and support to small landholders was followed, and co-operative organizations were given various types of government assistance. During the 1940s this policy was substituted for one of support to commercial agriculture. Co-operative type associations fell out of favour, large-scale individual farming was favoured and agricultural investment emphasized increases in irrigated acreage, generally in new regions. The land was distributed in larger units and at the same time traditional agriculture was neglected. During the 1950s an intermediate course between support of modern and traditional agriculture was followed. During the 1960s investment in modern agriculture again became relatively more important. Beginning in 1952 the share of agriculture in government investment began to fall from 20 to about 12 per cent by 1970. By then it was evident that the relative neglect of agriculture in favour of urban activities, as well as the decreasing marginal productivity of new investments in irrigation, given that the best locations had already been developed, was resulting in a lessened dynamism of the sector. At the same time it became evident that rural poverty and the resulting migration to the cities were becoming problems of unmanageable dimensions. Thus, without neglecting commercial agriculture, rural development investment was again increased. By 1976 investment in agriculture and rural development had again reached 20 per cent of government investment.

Between 1960 and 1979 more specific indicators of the regional impact of government policies may be used. The first is the distribution of federal government investment expenditure in different states and in different types of activities. We shall analyse two periods. The first, 1959–70, encompasses two administrations; the second, 1971–78, includes the administration in power from 1971 to 1976 and the first two years of the following government period. Per caput federal investment in different states for the period from 1959 to 1970 ranged from US$120 (at 1970 prices) to US$985. There are seventeen states in the range from US$120 to $320. Sixteen of these form a compact region that includes Central Mexico and all but one of the Pacific coastal states in Central and Southern Mexico. The pattern is repeated in 1971–78 with relatively minor changes. Total investment does not always accurately reflect the effects on the population, since the benefits of industrial and petroleum public sector investment accrue to Mexico City in large part, regardless of location.

With regard to investment in agriculture and in social welfare activities, a degree of concentration similar to that for total investment occurs. In both periods agricultural investment has been concentrated in a few zones where irrigation could be developed. As a result these states, all outside the central region referred to above, have accounted for a very high proportion of the increase in agricultural output. Their role has been particularly important with regard to exports.

## AN EXPLANATION OF REGIONAL INCOME INEQUALITIES IN MEXICAN AGRICULTURE

Five elements may be considered in order to explain regional differentials in rural incomes. They are the following:

1 Relative capital-labour and land-labour ratios.
2 Factor productivity differences, stemming from use of different technologies and organizational models.
3 Labour mobility in response to income differentials.
4 Relative rural-urban prices.
5 Government income transfers.

The first two elements determine physical output-to-labour ratios in agricultural activities. The latter two relate to the individual worker's ability to obtain money income either through sale of his output or through working for pay outside his own plot. Included in the last one are prices of industrial goods, which also determine in a direct way welfare levels of rural inhabitants and their families. Also part of government transfers are social welfare expenditures, which represent a transfer of income in kind to the rural inhabitant.

As a result of the differential access of the population to the above named elements, income inequality is very high in Mexico. Although there are no regional or sectoral data on income distribution, it is useful to analyse the overall distribution of income, since the various groups are rather easily identified. Table 2 shows income distribution in 1950 and 1977. The Gini

TABLE 2 *Size distribution of income in Mexico by deciles*[1]

| Decile | 1950 | 1977 | 1977[2] | Annual Real Increase % |
|---|---|---|---|---|
| I | 2.43 | 1.08 | 2.31 | −0.2 |
| II | 3.17 | 2.21 | 4.41 | 1.5 |
| III | 3.18 | 3.23 | 6.88 | 2.9 |
| IV | 4.29 | 4.42 | 9.41 | 3.0 |
| V | 4.93 | 5.73 | 12.20 | 3.4 |
| VI | 5.96 | 7.15 | 15.23 | 3.5 |
| VII | 7.04 | 9.11 | 19.40 | 3.8 |
| VIII | 9.63 | 11.98 | 25.52 | 3.7 |
| IX | 13.89 | 17.09 | 36.40 | 3.6 |
| Xa.[3] | 10.38 | 12.54 | 26.71 | 3.6 |
| Xb. | 35.10 | 25.45 | 54.21 | 1.6 |
| Total | 100.0 | 100.0 | 213.0 | 2.8 |

*Sources:* 1950, *Population Census;* 1977, Secretaria de Programación y Presupuesto, *National Income and Expenditure Survey.*

[1] In 1950 each decile represented 450,000 families; in 1977, 1.1 million.

[2] This column shows each decile's real income in relation to its 1950 income. Thus, if national income in 1950 may be considered as 100, in 1977 it was 213. The per caput income of the lowest ten per cent of the population was 2.43 in 1950, and 2.31 in 1977.

[3] Each of these last two rows represents 5 per cent of the population.

TABLE 3 *Government investment, welfare and income levels by state*

| Region | Welfare rank 1970 | Current (US$) income 1965 | Rank | Govt Investment Rank 1959-70 | 1971-78 |
|---|---|---|---|---|---|
| Northwest | | | | | |
| Baja California | 3 | 756 | 3 | 9 | 12 |
| B. California Sur | 7 | 628 | 6 | 3 | 3 |
| Sonora | 5 | 728 | 4 | 12 | 10 |
| Sinaloa | 15 | 500 | 8 | 7 | 14 |
| Nayarit | 25 | 267 | 20 | 29 | 18 |
| North | | | | | |
| Chihuahua | 9 | 390 | 12 | 13 | 20 |
| Durango | 18 | 274 | 18 | 17 | 24 |
| Northeast | | | | | |
| Coahuila | 8 | 632 | 5 | 6 | 11 |
| Nuevo León | 2 | 916 | 2 | 16 | 17 |
| Tamaulipas | 6 | 542 | 7 | 5 | 7 |
| Centre-North | | | | | |
| Aguascalientes | 4 | 284 | 17 | 15 | 22 |
| San Luis Potosí | 24 | 207 | 23 | 25 | 29 |
| Zacatecas | 29 | 163 | 29 | 32 | 30 |
| Pacific-Centre | | | | | |
| Jalisco | 11 | 331 | 15 | 30 | 30 |
| Colima | 17 | 335 | 14 | 8 | 5 |
| Michoacán | 26 | 172 | 27 | 24 | 15 |
| Centre | | | | | |
| Querétaro | 19 | 228 | 21 | 14 | 16 |
| Guanajuato | 20 | 215 | 22 | 20 | 28 |
| Hidalgo | 27 | 157 | 30 | 23 | 13 |
| México | 16 | 430 | 9 | 27 | 26 |
| Tlaxcala | 22 | 110 | 32 | 31 | 27 |
| Puebla | 21 | 205 | 24 | 28 | 31 |
| Morelos | 10 | 268 | 19 | 22 | 23 |
| Gulf-Centre | | | | | |
| Veracruz | 12 | 426 | 10 | 11 | 8 |
| Pacific-South | | | | | |
| Guerrero | 30 | 171 | 28 | 18 | 19 |
| Chiapas | 32 | 192 | 25 | 21 | 9 |
| Oaxaca | 31 | 115 | 31 | 26 | 25 |
| Peninsula | | | | | |
| Tabasco | 28 | 343 | 13 | 2 | 4 |
| Campeche | 13 | 418 | 11 | 11 | 6 |
| Quintana Roo | 23 | 173 | 26 | 4 | 6 |
| Yucatán | 14 | 295 | 16 | 19 | 21 |
| Federal District | 1 | 1100 | 1 | 1 | 1 |
| National Average: | | 455 | 9 | | |

coefficient changed from 0.504 in 1950 to 0.496 in 1977. As may be seen from Table 2, the bottom 50 per cent of the population received 18 per cent of total income in 1950 and 16.7 per cent in 1977. However, the lowest decile's share fell from 2.43 per cent to 1.08 per cent. This group's real income remained approximately constant over the period, while deciles $\overline{\text{V}}$ to $\overline{\text{X}}$ obtained rather substantial increases in their incomes. The fact that the Gini coefficient remained practically constant results from the fact that some of the intermediate groups increased their income share at the expense of the top decile. Thus, while the relative lot of the poorest group worsened, in equity terms this was somewhat compensated by the income gains to middle groups, obtained to a great extent as a result of the urbanization process.

Table 3 shows an ordering of relative welfare at the state level. An index was computed using 1970 Census data for sixteen variables. It also shows an estimate of output per caput by state for 1965, with a maximum of US$110 and a mean of US$455. If the 31 states and the Federal District are ranked according to their income levels, it may be seen that 14 of the 16 states that received the highest per caput federal investment in 1959–70 occupy the first 14 positions in terms of income per caput at the state level. In 1971–78, 12 of those 14 still remained in the top places in terms of government investment per caput.

If these investment figures are broken down, the most interesting aspects for our purpose are those relating to investment in agriculture and in social welfare. With regard to agricultural investment, 10 of the fourteen states with the highest investment in 1959–1970 also are among the fourteen top states in terms of per caput incomes. Social welfare investment expenditures are also highly concentrated. In 1959–70, 10 of the 14 states with the highest per caput investment are also among the top 14 states in terms of income. In 1971–78, it is the same. The above shows the close relationship between income levels and the distribution of government investment expenditures. It also shows that, with the exception of the Mexico City area, government investment expenditures have been concentrated outside the region where traditional agriculture is a way of life. Thus it may be seen that in so far as the population of these areas has been able to increase its welfare level substantially, it has sought to do this through migration, either to the capital city, to the United States, or to other areas, primarily the northern border.

*Rural-urban migration.*

In order to determine the importance of different factors in explaining rural-urban migration, a model based on Todaro's work was tested for the Mexican case. Maximization of individual welfare would imply that the decision to migrate is a function of relative expected earnings and unemployment. Specifically, the following model was used:

$M_i = M_i\,(L_i, w_i, w_d, U_i, U_d, D)$ , where

$M_i$ = Migration between 1960 and 1970 from state i to the Federal District

$L_i$ = Labour force in state i in 1970

$w_i$ = Minimum wage in state i

$w_d$ = Minimum wage in the Federal District

$U_i$ = Underemployment rate in state i, defined as the share of the labour force with incomes below the state minimum wage in 1970

$U_d$ = Underemployment rate in the Federal District, defined in a similar manner

D = Distance from the capital of state i to the Federal District.

## REGRESSION RESULTS

| | Const. | L | D | $w_i/w_d$ | $U_i/U_d$ | V* | $R^2$ |
|---|---|---|---|---|---|---|---|
| M | 2.4939 | 1.0146 | −0.5482 | - | - | −1.1576 | 0.88446 |
| (t) | (3.9523) | (10.3227) | (5.5041) | - | - | (3.3586) | |
| M | - | 1.0021 | −0.5418 | −0.9586 | 1.0464 | - | 0.88656 |
| (t) | - | (10.2138) | (5.5901) | (2.9147) | (4.0700) | - | |
| M/L | 4.5339 | - | −0.5526 | - | - | −1.1537 | 0.7071 |
| (t) | (8.1078) | - | (5.9210) | - | - | (3.4174) | |
| M/L | - | - | −0.52040 | −0.6200 | 1.6727 | - | 0.6985 |
| (t) | - | - | (5.5632) | (1.9192) | (6.8523) | - | |

* $V = (w_i/w_d)(1 - U_i + U_d)$

Results obtained show very clearly the importance of these variables, all with the expected signs, as may be seen in the above chart. Given the policy that had been followed until a few years ago with regard to minimum wages, these reflected rather well the relative level of development of different states. Thus it may be seen that income differentials affect rural-urban migration directly. The same may be said of relative underemployment levels.

In dealing with the question of how well migratory flows have contributed to an equalization of income levels throughout the country, it is necessary to rely on indirect evidence, since reliable income figures by state at different time intervals are not available. Personal income distribution figures, as shown in Table 2, indicate that an increase in the degree of inequality for the poorest ten per cent of the population has been accompanied by an apparent stability in this group's real income over time. At the same time, from the fifth decile upwards, income gains have taken place at a rate substantially higher than the average, at the expense of the share of the top five per cent of the population. The poorest ten per cent of the population represents, almost completely, rural inhabitants. This group is about a fourth to a third of rural population, and it is made up predominantly of landless labourers and owners of very small plots of land. These groups have been the target of government policies over the last decade.

Government expenditures to improve the welfare of the poorest groups in rural areas have been directed primarily at the following areas:

1 Health, through setting up rural clinics in the poorest areas in order to provide basic medical care to poor peasants. Also, a programme to provide medical services to some groups of rural labourers.
2 Education, through an increase in expenditures to serve the needs of the most isolated groups of rural inhabitants.
3 Nutrition, by means of a programme of rural stores to lower the prices of basic processed foodstuffs to the rural population, which traditionally has paid the highest prices for all products.
4 Productivity. Beginning in 1980, a programme of increased support prices for production of staple food, primarily corn, was put into effect. It was coupled with subsidies to lower the prices of seeds, fertilizer and credit, primarily to subsistence farmers, in order to increase agricultural production and the productivity of land.

The latest indirect evidence would seem to indicate that the high rate of growth achieved by the Mexican economy in 1978–81, an average of 8.5 per cent anually, has meant a high rate of employment creation and therefore increased job and income opportunities for the rural labour force. However, this has been a short-run change. The more important question in this regard is the extent to which a rapid increase in aggregate demand resulting from the oil boom has meant lasting changes in the welfare levels of the rural population. Recent aggregate economic changes have affected at least three of the five elements that explain regional differentials in rural incomes; labour mobility as a result of increased opportunities for non-agricultural employment, relative rural-urban prices, and government income transfers to the rural population. As a result of the changes initiated, and of good weather conditions, agricultural output increased by 18 per cent in 1981 and cropped area increased almost proportionately.

Despite the above, it is evident that agriculture cannot absorb any more workers; on the contrary, the impossibility of earning the levels of income which better communications and urban influences have led rural inhabitants to aspire to, has meant a continuing exodus from rural areas to the largest cities in Mexico. Since, as was mentioned above, a large part of the rural population has not improved its welfare level at all during the last thirty years, it appears that agricultural price policies and an excess supply of labour have kept rural wages, and incomes for the poorest groups, near the subsistence level. These workers lack any marketable skills. The fact that their number has increased at the same rate as the total population means that government policy in general has not been effective in reaching marginal populations, although rapid growth in the last few years has given many of them a way out of rural poverty. For these people, progress has meant increasing inequality. It is significant that temporary migrants to the United States do not in general come from the poorest states, but rather from the Central and Northern regions, which have a long history of such migration. These states have traditionally enjoyed higher average incomes, and have also had a higher rate of migration to the large Mexican cities.

Given the adverse influence of government policy on regional equality and/or rural-urban income differentials, it may be asked what types of alternative policies might have been followed to promote equality. It would seem that Mexican policies in this respect have varied widely over time, and yet the basic problems have remained. The unemployment and under-employment problems that Mexico has traditionally faced receded into the background in the last few years as a result of the oil boom. Despite this fact, the poverty level prevalent in a large part of the agricultural sector has meant that private saving capacity in traditional agriculture is very low. Therefore, given the insufficient rate of creation of urban employment as well as the exploding labour force, rural income increases have depended on government investment or income transfers. In some cases these have been a way of calling forth the savings potential implicit in underutilized rural labour. However, in general this aspect has not been emphasized. Thus the rate of increase of rural incomes has been limited by the amount of government resources effectively transferred and by the prevailing organizational patterns. Of course, in some areas with favourable resource endowments, the effect of government transfers on productivity and capital formation has been rather high.

Given that government investment funds for agriculture have been clearly insufficient for the sector as a whole, emigration has been a way to avoid a drastic fall in rural incomes, as well as a means by which rural families have received transfers from their urban members. This process seems to have worked most clearly in the central region of the country where subsistence and traditional agriculture prevails. Migrants, as Table 4 shows, have gone, in large part, to Mexico City.

Despite the fact that in many regions rural welfare levels seem to have increased as a result of government investment expenditures, rural-urban income differentials, as well as productivity differences between agriculture and other activities, have widened. Thus, relative incentives to migrate out of agriculture remain high. Given the size of the agricultural labour force and the prevailing levels of rural incomes, it is evident that, even if the past rate of migration to the cities continues over this decade and the next, rural population at the end of the century will still be about twenty million, compared to approximately twenty-four at present. Thus, the demand for productive agricultural investment will remain unabated.

That the region surrounding Mexico City has been traditionally the area of poorest agriculture is accounted for in terms of land and capital per

TABLE 4 *Net migration by state and region*

| Region | ('000s) Up to 1960 | 1960–70 | Total | Total/1970 Pop. (per cent) |
|---|---|---|---|---|
| Northwest | 279 | 183 | 462 | 11.0 |
| Baja California Norte | 256 | 139 | 395 | 39.0 |
| Baja California Sur | −16 | 10 | −6 | −4.4 |
| Sonora | 76 | 21 | 97 | 8.4 |
| Sinaloa | −46 | 18 | −28 | −2.1 |
| Nayarit | 9 | −5 | 4 | 0.7 |
| North | −26 | −87 | −113 | −4.3 |
| Chihuahua | 115 | 1 | 116 | 6.9 |
| Durango | −141 | −88 | −229 | −23.6 |
| Northeast | 278 | 131 | 409 | 9.1 |
| Coahuila | −39 | −55 | −94 | −8.1 |
| Nuevo León | 124 | 154 | 278 | 15.7 |
| Tamaulipas | 193 | 32 | 225 | 14.7 |
| North Central | −412 | −309 | −721 | −26.8 |
| Aguascalientes | −42 | −12 | −54 | −15.2 |
| San Luis Potosi | −152 | −126 | −278 | −20.8 |
| Zacatecas | −218 | −171 | −389 | −38.9 |
| Central Pacific | −557 | −271 | −828 | −13.5 |
| Jalisco | −254 | −8 | −262 | −7.6 |
| Colima | 11 | 15 | 26 | 10.2 |
| Michoacán | −314 | −278 | −592 | −24.3 |
| Central | −959 | 223 | −736 | −6.2 |
| Queretaro | −97 | −24 | −121 | −23.9 |
| Guanajuato | −331 | −166 | −497 | −20.9 |
| Hidalgo | −189 | −121 | −310 | −24.8 |
| Mexico | −189 | 660 | 471 | 11.7 |
| Tlaxcala | −61 | −36 | −97 | −22.0 |
| Puebla | −151 | −136 | −287 | −10.9 |
| Morelos | 59 | 46 | 105 | 16.3 |
| Gulf Central | 39 | −15 | 24 | 0.6 |
| Veracruz | 39 | −15 | 24 | 0.6 |
| South Pacific | −277 | −309 | −586 | −10.8 |
| Guerrero | −74 | −114 | −188 | −11.2 |
| Chiapas | −42 | −38 | −80 | −4.9 |
| Oaxaca | −161 | −157 | −318 | −15.0 |
| Peninsula | −87 | −18 | −105 | −5.4 |
| Tabasco | −34 | −6 | −40 | −5.0 |
| Champeche | −9 | 11 | 2 | 0.8 |

| | | | | |
|---|---|---|---|---|
| Quintana Roo | 10 | 24 | 34 | 37.4 |
| Yucatán | −54 | −47 | −101 | −12.7 |
| Mexico City | 1,722 | 473 | 2,195 | 30.4 |

*Sources: Population Census,* 1960, 1970.

worker, as well as by the persistence of traditional cultural traits. That government policy has been unable to alter the status of the poorest inhabitants significantly despite the large sums invested over almost fifty years shows that the problem is not exclusively of an economic nature. Lacking any coherent blueprint about the objectives of government policy with regard to rural inhabitants or the ways in which such objectives would come about as a result of different actions, successive administrations have simply emphasized different programmes, either to transfer income or to increase productivity. However, at any one time expenditures have been thinly spread and the organizational models of rural society have not always been aimed at achieving widespread participation in efforts and decisions. Corruption has also been an important factor in maintaining the productivity of government's rural expenditures rather low.

In other regions of the country, where due to irrigation and larger plot sizes initial factor endowments have been more favourable, rural productivity and incomes have grown continuously. In such areas, the real wages effectively paid to rural workers have also apparently increased over time, as the index of rural wages shows. It is clear that only in those regions with favourable factor endowments have modern agriculture and organizational patterns developed. In areas where this has been the case the labour force in agriculture has been sharply divided into landowners and workers. However, the latter have at least been able to earn the minimum wage, which is far above the level of income that poor peasants obtain in the regions where traditional agriculture is prevalent.

## REFERENCE

[1] C.W. Reynolds, *The Mexican Economy, Twentieth Century Structure and Growth,* Yale University Press, 1970.

## DISCUSSION OPENING I – CHAMHURI SIWAR

This paper deals with a typical trend that is happening in most LDCs, that is, the growth that leads to further inequality. The author initially describes the success story of Mexican agriculture in terms of the growth in agricultural output, rural incomes and productivity, but not without the consequence of the growth of productivity differentials and increased income inequality which results from uneven agricultural investment, rural-urban migration and differences in factor endowments.

With regard to government policies, the author chooses government investment in the agricultural sector as an index of the government's support for the agricultural sector. He uses the size of the government investment as the indicator. This approach contains one inherent weakness in that it does not tell us about how the investments were spent, that is, whether or not it has been in support of the commercial and modern agricultural sector with the consequent neglect of the traditional sector. Also the profitability of each investment was not reported, nor were the distribution of gains and losses from the investments. Specifically it would be interesting to know how the gains and losses from such investments were distributed among the landless, small, medium and large-sized farmers. The failure of government policy, as pointed out by the author, lies with the ineffectiveness of government programmes in reaching the marginal population. The author asked what alternative policy might be followed. It seems that the history of government investment in agriculture has traditionally favoured commercial and modern agriculture, concentrated in a few zones where irrigation could be developed, with an apparent neglect of the traditional sector. It is not surprising that the result is increased income inequality between the rural-urban sector and also within the rural sector itself. To improve income inequality within the rural sector, a natural course to follow would be to emphasize investment and development programmes in the traditional sector. By specifying the rural target groups, investment and programmes may then be directed to them to alleviate poverty.

Another factor that contributed to the increase in regional income differences was said to be rural-urban migration. The extent to which this migration occurs was summed up in that after 1960 practically the whole of the increase in the rural labour force migrated to the cities. The author uses a model, similar to that of Todaro's, to determine the importance of different factors in determining rural-urban migration. It seems to me that it is not enough to look into the decision to migrate based on relative expected earnings and unemployment. Other factors, such as the levels of education, the costs related to migration, the availability of kin in urban centres, would strongly influence the decision to migrate.

The other side of rural urban migration, that is, the impact on the agricultural sector, specifically on agricultural and labour productivity and incomes, has not been analysed. In a situation of agricultural labour surplus one would expect that rural-urban migration would increase agricultural and labour productivity and ultimately labour's income, through increased farm size and farm opportunities.

A declining trend in the agricultural labour force is a prerequisite for improved agricultural incomes as experienced by most developing countries. As such, rural-urban migration should be encouraged to a point where agricultural land could be worked optimally and rural labour force meets its demand. This would help to raise rural wage rates and reduce rural-urban wage differentials and would by itself reduce rural-urban migration. On the urban side, the influx of labour to the urban centres, along with the inability of the urban sector to provide adequate employment opportunities, would ultimately reduce urban wage rates. This would act as a deterrent to a further influx and further growth would hopefully reduce regional income inequality.

## DISCUSSION OPENING II – DAVID COLMAN

The paper touches (in a rather disjointed way) upon two different dimensions of income inequality; (a) regional income inequality; and (b) inter-personal income inequality; and it also touches (econometrically) upon rural-urban labour migration which is part of the system's mechanism for equating incomes and opportunities.

The issues are not principally addressed at the agricultural sector level, but at the aggregate level. That is to say that Table 2 presents the income distribution for the Mexican population as a whole (not for rural or agricultural families) while Table 3 presents rankings of states in terms of average income per caput for the population as a whole.

The data in Table 3 are used to illustrate the direct relationship between income levels in states and government expenditure in states, suggesting that government policy favours the better-off states. Since regional agricultural expenditure by the government has also correlated well with overall government expenditure it, too, has tended to go to the better areas and thus does not appear to have been primarily aimed at equity objectives.

One (possibly interesting) observation arises with respect to the data in Table 2 on the changing income distribution over time. It is an observation which relates to comparable statistics in other papers and is the relationship between the population in the bottom decile in 1950 and that in 1977. Naïvely one might assume that there is some family relationship (despite the growth in the number of families in the decile from 4.5 million to 11 million). However the possibility is that there may be a large income mobility related to the family income cycle. Thus those in the lowest decile may be largely older and single parent (smaller) families in both periods, such that a high proportion of those in the bottom group in 1977 were, when younger, in a higher group in 1950. In other words, figures like this gloss over a number of interesting questions.

The rural-urban migration analysis is based on a simple pooled cross-section/time-series model. The results accord well with expectations and are robust (in that deflating M by L does not greatly affect the parameters on the explanatory variables other than L). The only other thing which it would have been useful to have explained is the rationale for variable V when the intercept term is supressed.

The inclusion of this brief section on rural-urban migration provides a peg on which to hang a whole discussion of market mechanisms for reducing income inequality, for the results indicate market forces working strongly to relocate labour. There are other equilibrating mechanisms which might operate, such as, lower prices for wage goods in poorer areas; a tendency for some movement of labour intensive industries to poorer areas; and migration of individual family members on a temporary basis. The cumulative effect of these will clearly not bring about regional and interpersonal income equality. But the question we might ask is how large are the effects of government policies to reduce income inequality likely to be relative to the effects of 'normal market' equilibrating mechanisms.

MEDHI KRONGKAEW

# *The Rural Public Works Programme and Income Distribution in Rural Thailand*

## INTRODUCTION

One major difference between the present Thai Government under General Prem Tinsulanonda and previous governments is that Prem's Government has made a very conscious and concrete effort to promote rural development through reduction in rural poverty and improvement in rural income distribution. The larger amounts of central government's budget in Thai history have so far been spent on public works programmes primarily to help the rural population; a special rural poverty plan has been set up and appended to the Fifth National Economic and Social Development Plan; and several areas throughout the country have been designated poverty areas so that the government can concentrate their efforts in helping them. One of the reasons that prompted the present Government to take these measures could be the growing realization that the outcome of past development efforts in the last two decades, though satisfactory in terms of overall rate of growth, has not been equally distributed among various sectors of the population, with the farm sector which is the largest sector probably enjoying the least benefits. Certainly it could be accepted that the number of poor families has declined even in absolute terms in the last decade or so, but it is still doubtful to say that the extent or magnitude of income disparities within the rural areas or between rural and urban areas has also declined.[1] Whatever the case may be, there is still much to be done in the rural areas of Thailand regarding the issues of poverty eradication and improvement in income inequality.

It is the intention of this short paper, therefore, to focus on one specific measure which the present Government has initiated to combat rural poverty and income disparities: the Rural Job Creation Project (RJCP).[2] First, the paper will discuss the current state of poverty and income inequality in rural Thailand. Then it will proceed to describe the nature and operation of the RJCP. And finally, the impact of the RJCP on rural poverty and income distribution will be assessed and policy recommendations offered.

## POVERTY AND INCOME DISTRIBUTION IN RURAL THAILAND

The main purpose of this section is to paint a broad picture of the poverty and income distribution situations in the rural areas of Thailand, without engaging in a detailed discussion of the causes and characteristics of such situations, in order that the readers will be able to see a rationale behind the launching of the national public works programme of the present government.

As for the poverty situations in rural Thailand various studies have been conducted to find out who the poor are and whether they have changed their positions through time.[3] Various techniques were used to determine the poverty lines or poverty band, but it seems that the technique used by Oey Astra Meesook (1979) for the World Bank has gained the most acceptance among researchers in this field. This is the technique where the poverty or cut-off income is derived, first, from the amount of money needed to satisfy minimum food requirements of an average person, then other non-food expenses are computed and added into it. Based on this poverty income, the incidence of poverty in rural Thailand, that is the percentage of the total population which is under the poverty line, can be estimated. This is shown in Table 1 for 1962/63, 1968/69, 1975/76 for all regions, and 1979/80 for the Northeastern region only.

It can be seen from Table 1 that, according to the estimates by Meesook, the incidence of poverty in rural Thailand secularly declined from 1962/63

TABLE 1 *Incidence of poverty in Rural Thailand; 1962/63, 1968/69 and 1975/76.*

| | (% of total population) | | | |
|---|---|---|---|---|
| Region | 1962/63 | 1968/69[a] | 1975/76 | 1979/80 |
| North | 66 | 37 | 36 | - |
| Northeast | 77 | 67 | 48 | 67[b] |
| Centre | 40 | 16 | 15 | - |
| South | 46 | 40 | 35 | - |
| Whole Kingdom | 61 | 43 | 37 | - |

*Source:* For 1962/63, 1968/69 and 1975/76, the data were adapted from Oey Astra Meesook (1979, p. 52). For 1979/80, the figure was obtained from the preliminary result of the Socio-economic Survey of the Northeastern Region, 1978/80 conducted by the National Statistical Office.

*Notes:* [a]The rural areas for this year include both the villages and sanitary districts, whereas in 1962/63 and 1975/76 only villages were included. The percentages shown in 1968/69, therefore, slightly understate the true poverty situation in rural areas for that year.

[b]The same cut-off or poverty income as in Meesook was used here, that is 1981 baht per person per year, adjusted by the price index of 138.1 for 1979/80 (1975/76 = 100.0).

to 1975/76 in all regions of the country. Some researchers may argue against the use of price indices in adjusting the poverty income upward which understate the true price situation in rural areas, making the incidence of poverty in later years lower than it should be. But there should be little doubt that the poverty situation has substantially improved between 1962/63 and 1975/76. However, the most recent estimate by the National Statistical Office, for the Northeastern region for 1979/80 only, shows the incidence of poverty at 67 per cent, an increase more or less to the level of 1968/69. Although this latest estimate only shows the poverty proportion in one region, and the situation could be different elsewhere, it has served to dampen the enthusiasm that one could draw from the decline in the rural poverty trend as shown from 1962/69 to 1975/76.

TABLE 2 *Gini co-efficients of rural income distribution in Thailand*

| Region | 1962/63 | 1968/69 | 1971/73 | 1975/76 | 1979/80 |
|---|---|---|---|---|---|
| Money Income | | | | | |
| North | 0.2566 | 0.4008 | 0.4945 | 0.2020 | |
| Northeast | 0.3370 | 0.5249 | 0.4747 | 0.3184 | |
| Centre | 0.3360 | 0.4380 | 0.5334 | 0.1859 | |
| South | 0.2921 | 0.3654 | 0.5293 | 0.2293 | |
| Total Income[a] | | | | | |
| North | 0.3080 | 0.3450 | 0.5590 | 0.2780 | - |
| Northeast | 0.2640 | 0.3473 | 0.3780 | 0.2500 | 0.3863[b] |
| Centre | 0.3750 | 0.3917 | 0.4130 | 0.2610 | - |
| South | 0.3700 | 0.3249 | 0.4140 | 0.2970 | - |

*Sources:* Adapted from Krongkaew (1980); Meesook (1975b) and Wattanavitukul (1978). All these estimates were based on the results of the Household Expenditure Survey of 1962/63 and the Socio-economic Surveys of 1968/69, 1971/73, 1975/76 and 1979/80 (for the Northeast only).
*Notes:* [a]Total income includes money income, in kind or non-money income and imputed rent.
[a]Already adjusted for imputed rent.

Whereas absolute poverty may have declined between 1962/63 and 1975/76, the relative poverty or inequality in income distribution in rural areas has not performed equally well. In fact, the inequality has worsened. As can be seen from Table 2, the extent of income inequality, as shown by Gini coefficients, increased steadily between 1962/63 and 1971/73 both for money income and total income of rural households. But this worsening trend in rural income distribution seemed to have been arrested in 1975/76 when the Gini coefficients for that year showed a remarkable reduction in income disparities. The improvement in income equality for 1975/76 was so large and so sudden as to create a sense of doubt regarding the survey data and/or the addition of income components. Another unusual point is that normally the distribution of total income would show greater equality than the distribution of money income, because those households in the lower (poorer) end of the income distribution would derive most of their incomes from non-money sources thus improving income equality. But the estimates for 1975/76 show *lower* Gini coefficients for money income than total income for households in all regions except in the Northeast. This sense of doubt for 1975/76 was reinforced by the latest estimate for the Northeast which shows a Gini coefficient of 0.3863 which is much higher than in 1975/76. Indeed, this coefficient of income inequality is highest of all the estimates from 1962/63.

All in all, it could be concluded that the poverty and income distribution in rural Thailand is still unsatisfactory and a matter of much concern. The average income of rural households may increase steadily throughout the latter part of the 1960s and the 1970s so that the number of households falling under the poverty line also steadily declined. But this trend may have already stopped, slowed down, or even reversed. And throughout these periods income inequality within the rural areas themselves may have increased all the time. This, apparently, must be the rural scenario which was taken by the present government and that which prompted them to launch the first rural Job Creation Programme in 1980.

## THE 1980 RURAL JOB CREATION PROGRAMME

This national public works programme was established on 1 May, 1980, soon after Prem became Prime Minister in early March of the same year and was to go on for 4 months until the end of August. The 1980 RJCP was not the first major public works programme in modern Thai economic history. Indeed the first large-scale public works programme covering the whole country was instituted 5 years earlier under M.R. Kukrit Pramote's Government (known as the Tambon Development Programme I) where 2.5 billion baht was spent for the entire project by all Tambons in the Kingdom. The programme had proven to be very politically popular, so it was repeated in the following year under a new government and a larger budget (3.5 billion baht and known as the Tambon Development Programme II). Yet another rural public works programme costing 1.6 billion baht was created in 1978 under another new government (the Rural Economic Rehabilitation Programme). The 1980 RJCP was the first rural public works programme under the present government, to be followed by two more RJCPs in 1981 and 1982. The budgets for these three programmes for 1980, 1981 and 1982 were, respectively, 3.5 billion baht, 3.5 billion baht and 1.8 billion baht.[4]

The purposes of the 1980 RJCP can be stated as follows:

(a) to help augment the incomes of farmers in the rural areas across the

country who suffered from drought in the previous year, by creating jobs during the slack season in which those farmers could come to work;
(b) to stop or slow down the migration of the rural population to cities or urban centres;
(c) to enable the rural population to increase their infrastructural assets, such as irrigation ditches, water reservoirs, roads and so on, for their farm production and livelihood;
(d) to promote development planning at the lowest level of public administration and stimulate greater local grass-root participation in self-government.

It is quite evident that the primary intention of the government was the income augmentation of the rural population; the other objectives were subsidiary or by-products of this aim, and rural jobs or employment were the means to achieve these ends. The hardship experienced by farmers in most provinces as a result of general drought conditions in 1979 tied in very well with the general ill-being of the rural households, as pointed out in the earlier section, to give an added weight to the appropriateness and timeliness of this rural public works programme.

All 71 provinces except Bangkok Metropolitan Areas were covered by this programme. There were 2 types of projects to be supported under this RJCP: (a) Project Type I was the construction and/or improvement of water resources for farm or household uses which included digging ponds, water wells, water canals, drainage ditches; construction of irrigation dams and spillways; repair of embankments; and the like. (b) Project Type II was the construction and/or repair of other public works, mainly roads and bridges. Because water resources were more important, the central government has specified that no less than 70 per cent of all projects must be of Type I. And because the primary emphasis of this programme was rural employment, one important condition governing all types of projects was that the cost of labour must constitute at least 70 per cent of the total cost.

The money was allocated to each province according to the following formula:

$$M_i = \frac{P_i / H_i}{\Sigma_i (P_i H_i)} \times K$$

and $H_i = 0.25\,(R_i / \overline{R}_i) + 0.75\,(Y_i / Y_{wk})$

where $M_i$ = money allocated to province $i$
$K$ = total RJCP budget
$P_i$ = rural population of province $i$
$H_i$ = index of hardship in province $i$
$R_i$ = amount of rainfall in province $i$ in 1979
$\overline{R}_i$ = mean rainfall for province $i$
$Y_i$ = income per caput of province $i$
$Y_{wk}$ = income per caput of the country

Once the province had received its allocated money, it would then further allocate the money to the districts and villages under its jurisdiction under the general guideline recommended by the central government. The provincial authorities also screened and selected projects submitted by the Tambon or Village councils within the allotted budget.

TABLE 3 *Physical results of the 1980 RJCP and the numbers of rural labour employed.*

| | North | Northeast | Centre | South | Total |
|---|---|---|---|---|---|
| Project Type I | | | | | |
| – Number of projects classified into: | 10,986 | 18,653 | 12,043 | 4,948 | 46,630 |
| (a) Water wells (units) | 4,993 | 3,824 | 1,796 | 1,617 | 12,230 |
| (b) Ponds (units) | 2,144 | 11,932 | 2,738 | 509 | 17,323 |
| (c) Water reservoirs, dams, embankments (units) | 1,379 | 3,627 | 391 | 439 | 5,836 |
| (d) ditches, canals (km.) | 10,791 | 2,096 | 7,993 | 5,040 | 25,918 |
| (e) other[a] (units) | 125 | 138 | 125 | 153 | 540 |
| Project Type II | | | | | |
| – Number of projects classified into: | 1,666 | 5,066 | 913 | 1,048 | 8,693 |
| (a) bridges (units) | 183 | 135 | 75 | 78 | 471 |
| (b) roads (km.) | 2,361 | 5,610 | 824 | 1,416 | 10,212 |
| (c) other[b] (units) | 169 | 271 | 131 | 74 | 645 |
| Number of Workers Employed | | | | | |
| Type I Projects | 786,305 | 1,535,975 | 588,159 | 202,351 | 3,112,790 |
| Type II Projects | 126,933 | 412,787 | 55,264 | 46,465 | 641,449 |
| Total | 917,233 | 1,948,762 | 643,423 | 248,816 | 3,754,239 |
| Actual Expenditures (million baht) | 665.3 | 1,284.3 | 488.9 | 323.8 | 2,762.3 |

*Source:* Krongkaew et al., 1981.
Notes: [a]water tanks, drainage pipes, etc.
[b]school buildings, youth centres, community halls, etc.

Table 3 summarizes the overall results of the RJCP at end of the programme. The overwhelming majority of projects involved earthworks, so the method of wage payment in most regions was by piece rate, that is the amount of earth or soil removed (in cubic metres), except in the North where the more prevalent method of payment was a daily wage rate. The hiring practices by the Tambon councils were usually 'come all, hire all'. Altogether, more than 3.7 million workers were employed in the Programme throughout the country between 1 May and 31 August, 1980.

## IMPACT OF THE 1980 RJCP

In order to find out about the impact of this RJCP on income, employment and other socioeconomic variables, an evaluation subcommittee was set up to take a sample survey of the workers, non-workers and various administrators in the programme. The evaluation subcommittee randomly selected 6,793 workers to be interviewed from 276 villages in 70 districts in 21 provinces throughout the country. Another 562 non-workers were also selected randomly to be interviewed, as well as all the village headmen, district officers and governors of the sampled areas.

The results of the survey showed that the actual number of people who worked in the RJCP was less than that reported by the government. This was because many workers had worked in more than one project. Taking this into consideration, the number of workers in the RJCP for the whole country was estimated at 2.875 million divided into 0.913, 1.949, 0.643 and 0.249 million for the North, Northeast, Centre and South, respectively. As the rural labour force in 1980 was estimated at around 14.3 million, those who found work in the RJCP amounted to more than 20 per cent of the rural labour force during May to August that year. As the average number of days worked was about 13 days, the total number of man/days created by the RJCP was about 37.4 million.[5]

On the question as to whether the RJCP had really helped provide jobs for the rural unemployed during the slack season, the survey results showed that it had. When asked to give reasons for working in the RJCP, the majority of workers answered that they did not have work to do at that period. (35.6, 26.0, 53.6 and 24.0 per cent of all the reasons for North, Northeast, Centre and South, respectively.) Not only that, it was also found that about 44,000 workers who worked in the RJCP had worked in Bangkok and other urban centres just before they joined the RJCP. This could be interpreted as the reverse migration effect of the RJCP.

On the income effects of the RJCP, the survey results showed that the average cash income received by workers in the Programme was about 877 baht for the whole country, or 706 baht for the North, 775 baht for the Northeast, 1125 baht for the Centre and 1170 baht for the South. This cash income represented about 10 per cent of the normal average earnings of an average farmer for the whole year. Although this amount of cash income should reasonably augment the total income of poor households who worked with the RJCP, it seemed, from looking at the distribution of average earnings by size class of gross income, that the richer workers tended to have received more income from work in the RJCP. A simple regression of average earnings on size class of family's gross income confirmed the above suspicion as the following estimates show (figures in parentheses are t-values):

$$1.\ CY_N = \underset{(4.236)}{452.4} + \underset{(4.089)}{0.0118}\ GY_N \qquad R^2 = 0.4419,\ N = 24$$

$$2.\ CY_{NE} = \underset{(15.387)}{789.5} - \underset{(-0.268)}{0.0008}\ GY_{NE} \qquad R^2 = 0.0181,\ N = 24$$

$$3.\ CY_C = \underset{(12.455)}{1019.7} + \underset{(1.125)}{0.0021}\ GY_C \qquad R^2 = 0.0426,\ N = 24$$

$$4.\ CY_S = \underset{(9.478)}{1014.3} + \underset{+(1.349)}{0.0038}\ GY_S \qquad R^2 = 0.0762,\ N = 24$$

$$5.\ CY_{WK} = \underset{(20.400)}{751.1} + \underset{(5.486)}{0.0052}\ GY_{WK} \qquad R^2 = 0.5631,\ N = 24$$

where CY = cash income received from RJCP ; GY = gross income of worker in question; and subscripts N, NE, C, S, and WK represent North, Northeast, Centre, South and Whole Kingdom, respectively.

It can be seen that for the majority of cases the coefficients of gross income variable all have plus signs except in the Northeast. But then, in the Northeast, the magnitude of the gross income parameter was very small and insignificant. The $R^2$ for the Northeast was also the smallest. So it is probably safe to argue that, for any individual worker, the RJCP tended to benefit the richer worker more than the poorer worker. To test this belief again the evaluation team used the amount of land holding as the independent variable to explain the size of earning in the Programme, and the results of the estimation (shown below) were reasonably significant, thus confirming the first estimates:

$$1.\ CY^*_N = \underset{(2.944)}{600.9} + \underset{(4.763)}{8.8541}\ L_N \qquad R^2 = 0.4142,\ N = 14$$

$$2.\ CY^*_{NE} = \underset{(11.357)}{698.5} + \underset{(1.333)}{1.9589}\ L_{NE} \qquad R^2 = 0.1290,\ N = 14$$

$$3.\ CY^*_C = \underset{(9.095)}{1005.1} + \underset{(1.670)}{4.4131}\ L_C \qquad R^2 = 0.1885,\ N = 14$$

$$4.\ CY^*_S = \underset{(6.741)}{1036.5} = \underset{(0.653)}{3.3030}\ L_S \qquad R^2 = 0.0343,\ N = 14$$

$$5.\ CY^*_{WK} = \underset{(13.723)}{750.4} + \underset{(3.293)}{4.2953}\ L_{WK} \qquad R^2 = 0.4747,\ N = 14$$

where CY* = cash income received by workers who had different sizes of land holding; L = size of land holding (in rais); subscripts N, NE, C, S and WK represent North, Northeast, Centre, South, and Whole Kingdom, respectively. The results show that the coefficients of the independent variable all have positive signs and are statistically significant at least at the

10 per cent level, except only for the South. The $R^2$ may be small on the regional estimates, but for the overall national estimate, it was not too unsatisfactory.[6]

One important question which may be asked in a similar context is : considering the Programme as a whole, has it improved the rural income distribution? By adding the cash income into each worker's total gross income and comparing the 'before' and 'after' distributions, one can perhaps draw some conclusion about the income redistributional effect of the 1980 RJCP. The results of this are shown in Table 4.

It is quite clear from Table 4 that, as a result of the RJCP, the income distribution of households in the rural areas in most regions of Thailand improved, as indicated by smaller Gini coefficients. It was only in the North where the distribution of income after the RJCP had become more unequal than before the RJCP. This perhaps could be explained by the fact that the prevalent payment practice in the North was to pay daily wages to workers in the programme instead of paying piece rates. Therefore, poorer workers who would like to work harder to earn more wages were not able to do so. Moreover, the daily wage system was more conducive to abuse by well-to-do or influential persons who would get their names listed in the work force but did not do much work.

## CONCLUSION

It could be concluded, therefore, that although the 1980 RJCP tended to benefit a richer representative worker more than a poor representative worker considered as an individual, since the majority of the workers were from the lower income scale, they, as a group, benefited more from the programme relative to the richer workers as a group. In all regions, except the North, the income distribution within the rural areas improved as a result of the RJCP. In this sense the 1980 RJCP was successful in meeting the major objectives of rural income augmentation and improvement in rural income distribution. Other subsidiary objectives were also fairly successfully met : rural unemployment during the slack season was ostensibly relieved; some unwanted migration was checked; the rural population became more experienced in making their own development planning and its execution.

Nevertheless, the RJCP was not without its defects. One cannot say that the allocative efficiency of this programme was satisfactory, as most of the works done were earth works which had been planned and executed with little technical know-how and were not sufficiently durable. The programme was launched near the end of the slack season, so the job opportunities were not enjoyed for very long before the next planting season began. The wage payment was extremely slow in many areas causing hardship to those very poor workers who had to depend on these wages for their daily food expenses.

Despite all these shortcomings, however, the RJCP can be judged

TABLE 4 *Pre-RJCP and post-RJCP income distributions in rural Thailand*

| Gross Income Class baht '000 | North % Households | North % Income Before | North % Income After | Centre % Households | Centre % Income Before | Centre % Income After | Northeast % Households | Northeast % Income Before | Northeast % Income After | South % Households | South % Income Before | South % Income After | Whole Kingdom % Households | Whole Kingdom % Income Before | Whole Kingdom % Income After |
|---|---|---|---|---|---|---|---|---|---|---|---|---|---|---|---|
| No income | 0.9 | 0.0 | 0.0 | 1.6 | 0.0 | 0.1 | 0.1 | 0.0 | 0.0 | 0.5 | 0.0 | 0.0 | 0.6 | 0.0 | 0.0 |
| Below 2.5 | 6.7 | 0.5 | 0.6 | 3.9 | 0.2 | 0.4 | 3.2 | 0.2 | 0.4 | 2.4 | 0.1 | 0.2 | 4.1 | 0.3 | 0.4 |
| 2.5–4.9 | 12.1 | 2.6 | 2.9 | 9.5 | 1.6 | 1.9 | 11.2 | 2.6 | 3.0 | 8.8 | 1.4 | 1.6 | 10.8 | 2.1 | 2.5 |
| 5.0–7.4 | 12.2 | 4.3 | 4.3 | 9.9 | 2.7 | 3.0 | 13.4 | 5.1 | 5.5 | 7.3 | 1.9 | 2.2 | 11.7 | 3.8 | 4.1 |
| 7.5–9.9 | 9.5 | 4.7 | 4.6 | 10.2 | 3.9 | 4.1 | 14.3 | 7.6 | 7.9 | 6.4 | 2.4 | 2.6 | 11.5 | 5.3 | 5.5 |
| 10.0–12.4 | 8.3 | 5.2 | 5.1 | 6.6 | 3.2 | 3.4 | 11.9 | 8.2 | 8.3 | 7.7 | 3.7 | 3.9 | 9.5 | 5.6 | 5.7 |
| 12.5–14.9 | 7.1 | 5.5 | 5.4 | 7.4 | 4.4 | 4.5 | 8.4 | 7.0 | 7.0 | 9.6 | 5.6 | 5.8 | 7.9 | 5.7 | 5.7 |
| 15.0–17.4 | 6.2 | 5.7 | 5.4 | 4.2 | 3.0 | 3.0 | 7.8 | 7.7 | 7.6 | 7.2 | 5.0 | 5.0 | 6.5 | 5.5 | 5.5 |
| 17.5–19.9 | 5.8 | 6.1 | 6.0 | 4.6 | 3.7 | 3.8 | 5.7 | 6.5 | 6.4 | 8.8 | 7.0 | 7.0 | 5.7 | 5.6 | 5.5 |
| 20.0–22.4 | 5.2 | 6.2 | 5.9 | 4.6 | 4.2 | 4.2 | 3.7 | 4.8 | 4.7 | 5.4 | 4.9 | 4.8 | 4.4 | 4.9 | 4.8 |
| 22.5–24.9 | 4.0 | 5.4 | 5.1 | 4.1 | 4.2 | 4.1 | 3.5 | 5.1 | 4.9 | 3.5 | 3.5 | 3.5 | 3.8 | 4.7 | 4.6 |
| 25.0–27.4 | 2.4 | 3.6 | 3.4 | 4.1 | 4.7 | 4.6 | 2.4 | 3.8 | 3.7 | 4.2 | 4.7 | 4.5 | 3.0 | 4.1 | 4.0 |
| 27.5–29.9 | 2.2 | 3.6 | 3.4 | 3.9 | 4.9 | 4.8 | 2.5 | 4.4 | 4.3 | 3.5 | 4.3 | 4.2 | 2.8 | 4.2 | 4.1 |
| 30.0–32.4 | 2.3 | 4.0 | 3.8 | 2.5 | 3.4 | 3.3 | 1.7 | 3.2 | 3.1 | 2.9 | 3.8 | 3.7 | 2.2 | 3.6 | 3.5 |
| 32.5–34.9 | 1.9 | 3.6 | 3.4 | 2.4 | 3.5 | 3.4 | 1.6 | 3.3 | 3.2 | 2.1 | 3.0 | 2.9 | 1.9 | 3.4 | 3.3 |
| 35.0–37.4 | 1.3 | 2.7 | 2.4 | 1.6 | 2.5 | 2.4 | 1.1 | 2.4 | 2.4 | 2.1 | 3.2 | 3.1 | 1.3 | 2.5 | 2.4 |
| 37.5–39.9 | 1.5 | 3.3 | 3.2 | 1.8 | 3.1 | 2.9 | 1.0 | 2.4 | 2.3 | 1.8 | 3.0 | 2.8 | 1.4 | 2.8 | 2.8 |
| 40.0–44.9 | 1.7 | 4.0 | 3.8 | 3.1 | 5.7 | 5.6 | 1.0 | 2.6 | 2.5 | 3.0 | 5.4 | 5.3 | 1.8 | 4.0 | 3.9 |
| 45.0–49.9 | 1.5 | 4.0 | 3.8 | 2.3 | 4.8 | 4.5 | 1.2 | 3.5 | 3.3 | 2.1 | 4.2 | 4.0 | 1.6 | 4.0 | 3.8 |
| 50.0–54.9 | 1.6 | 4.7 | 4.4 | 2.0 | 4.6 | 4.5 | 0.7 | 2.2 | 2.1 | 1.9 | 4.2 | 4.1 | 1.3 | 3.6 | 3.4 |
| 55.0–59.9 | 0.6 | 1.9 | 1.8 | 1.5 | 3.7 | 3.6 | 0.6 | 2.1 | 2.0 | 1.4 | 3.4 | 3.4 | 0.9 | 2.7 | 2.6 |
| 60.0–69.9 | 1.6 | 2.2 | 5.5 | 2.1 | 5.9 | 5.6 | 0.8 | 3.2 | 3.0 | 1.1 | 3.0 | 2.9 | 1.3 | 4.4 | 4.3 |
| 70.0–79.9 | 0.8 | 3.4 | 3.3 | 0.9 | 2.9 | 2.8 | 0.4 | 1.8 | 1.7 | 1.4 | 4.4 | 4.4 | 0.7 | 2.8 | 2.7 |
| 80.0 and over | 2.7 | 12.8 | 12.6 | 5.2 | 19.2 | 19.5 | 2.0 | 10.3 | 10.5 | 5.0 | 17.9 | 18.1 | 3.3 | 14.4 | 14.9 |
| Total | 100.0 | 100.0 | 100.0 | 100.0 | 100.0 | 100.0 | 100.0 | 100.0 | 100.0 | 100.0 | 100.0 | 100.0 | 100.0 | 100.0 | 100.0 |
| Gini Coefficient | | 0.4687 | 0.4734 | | 0.4797 | 0.4632 | | 0.4377 | 0.4193 | | 0.4393 | 0.4255 | | 0.4690 | 0.4349 |

satisfactory as a short-run measure to alleviate rural poverty and income inequality. In order to improve on the performance of a future RJCP it is recommended that the programme should start earlier, that is as soon as a slack season begins; that the poorer workers be given a better chance to be employed and work for a longer period; that the programme need not always be a nation-wide programme, but concentrate on specific serious poverty areas in order to better utilize limited funds; and that the government makes more conscious effort to increase the technical and administrative capability of rural planners and administrators.

## NOTES

1 As asserted by Meesook (1979) and the World Bank (1980).

2 By the end of June, 1982, three RJCPs would have been completed under the present Prem Government. But only the 1980 (first) RJCP will be analysed here as it is the only programme where a detailed evaluation report is available.

3 See for example, Krongkaew (1981); Meesook (1979); World Bank (1980).

4 Although evaluation of each programme was carried out at the end of the project period, only the evaluations for the 1976 Programme and the 1980 Programme were adequate for serious use. See Poot (1979) for evaluation of 1976 Programme and Krongkaew et al. (1981) for evaluation of 1980 Programme.

5 The number here was smaller than the corresponding number reported in Poot (1979) for the 1976 Programme. In 1976, the man/days of work created were reported at 56.7 million, involving between 3.8 and 5.6 million people employed. These figures were probably too large, due to bias in the selection and size of samples.

6 Luechai et al. (1982) made a similar estimation for the 1981 RJCP for the Northern Region only, and the results were more or less the same as in 1980. Their corresponding estimates are:

1 $$CY_N = \underset{(2.333)}{435.7 + 0.0028\, GY_N}, \; R^2 = 0.01, \; N = 605$$

2 $$CY^*_N = \underset{(6.580)}{346.4 + 15.06\, L_N}, \; R^2 = 0.07, \; N = 605$$

## REFERENCES

Chulasai, Luechai, et al., 'Migration and Rural Job Creation Programme: A Northern Thailand Study', Faculty of Social Science, Chiang Mai University, 1982.

Krongkaew, Medhi, 'The Determination of Poverty Band in Thailand', *The Philippine Economic Journal,* No. 42, vol. 18, No. 4, 1979, pp. 396–417.

Krongkaew, Medhi, *Government and the Income Gap of the People,* Bangkok: Thammasat University Press, 1980 (in Thai).

Krongkaew, Medhi, 'Poverty and Rural Development', in Luechai Chulasai and Mingsan Santikarn (eds.), *Thai Economy : Past and Future,* Chiang Mai : Chiang Mai Book Centre, 1981 (in Thai).

Krongkaew, Medhi, et al., *The Government's Rural Job Creation Project : Evaluation and Analysis,* Bangkok : Thammasat University Press, 1981 (in Thai).

Meesook, Oey Astra, 'Income Inequality in Thailand, 1962/63 and 1968/69', in *Income Distribution, Employment and Economic Development in Southeast and East Asia,* Tokyo, The Japan Economic Research Centre and Manila, The Council for Asian Manpower Studies, July, 1975a, pp. 345–88.

Meesook, Oey Astra, 'Income Distribution in Thailand', Discussion Paper No. 50, Faculty of Economics, Thammasat University, Bangkok, 1975b.
Meesook, Oey Astra, 'Income Consumption and Poverty in Thailand, 1962/63 to 1975/76', World Bank Staff Working Paper No. 364, November, 1979.
Poot, H., 'Evaluation of the Tambon Development Programme in Thailand', Asian Employment Programme Working Paper, ILO-ARTEP, Bangkok, March, 1979.
Wattanavitukul, Somluckrat, 'Income Distribution of Thailand', in Harry T. Oshima and Toshiyuki Mizoguchi (eds), *Income Distribution by Sectors and Overtime in East and Southeast Asian Countries,* Quezon City, The Council for Asian Manpower Studies, January, 1978, pp. 259–89.
World Bank, "Thailand : Income Growth and Poverty Alleviation", a World Bank country study, June, 1980.

## DISCUSSION OPENING – BAMBANG ISMAWAN

I should like to congratulate Dr Medhi Krongkaew for his interesting paper. In it he tries to measure and present some empirical results on a government programme to promote rural development through reduction in rural poverty and improvement in rural income distribution by means of the 'Rural Job Creation Programme'.

It was very encouraging to learn that the Rural Job Creation Programme (RJCP) results show it to be a successful project in meeting the major objectives of rural income augmentation and improvement in rural income distribution. This programme has also helped provide jobs for the rural unemployed and therefore reduced the migration of workers from rural to urban areas. The project also makes the rural population become more experienced in their own development planning of such structures as dams, irrigation facilities and other items of agricultural infrastructure. I have only a small comment on Dr Medhi's paper.

In relation to the theme of this Conference several participants have talked on how to alleviate rural poverty and income inequality. Agrawal has mentioned at least three important factors, namely:

- land ownership and land operation in the rural area;
- equal access to the use of resources in the production process;
- guaranteed marketing of agricultural products.

In several areas land ownership has been the main problem as a source of poverty. Several rural populations are landless but their life depends on the availability of employment in the rural sector.

In his paper Dr Medhi neglected these three factors. It is important to define land ownership and the terms, worker and non-worker, before implementing the Rural Job Creation Programme. If it happens that in the rural area many farmers are landless the RJCP will be only a short-term measure and a temporary tool to alleviate rural poverty and income inequality. Farmers who are landless will be unemployed again when the project is done. If the project builds infrastructural complements to the agricultural production process, as mentioned by Dr Medhi in his paper, landowners, and in particular the larger landowners, will be the ones to benefit. The landless farmer will still suffer and will still be a farm worker. Income inequality becomes wider and wider and poverty will not be alleviated.

If all rural people own land the RJCP will be of benefit to the farmer in the longer run as such infrastructural improvement to agriculture becomes available. With better irrigation and other facilities farming can occupy more than one growing season a year, and, therefore, this will both reduce the labour peak and seasonal unemployment and maybe reduce migration. Therefore a RJCP should be directed towards building infrastructures for a better agronomic condition such as to increase land intensity. RJCP has to be directed first to the area where the project is really needed. I have observed some examples in the Thai experience. Many farmers are landless and most farm land is owned by rich people in urban areas, such as in Bangkok. The farm operator is only a worker and does not own land. This phenomenon will result in a wider gap of income between the poor landless farmer and the rich capitalist owner. The problem may be alleviated through a land reform programme.

Another different example is the small-scale ownership and the lack of farm organization. These farmers are subject to very low prices of agricultural produce during the peak harvest season.

The rich capitalist owner in the city usually is able to buy the product at a very low price. This will cause an even greater income gap between the small farmers and the merchants in the city. One way to eliminate this problem is to introduce co-operation in the marketing of agricultural products.

On the RJCP in particular, I wish to comment that it has been a complaint that some projects (for example dam building) were not done in the time allocated. The reason may be because there was inadequate labour supply due to misinformation on the unemployment figures or because the project was started late and, therefore, it could not be finished before the farmers has to go back to their land. I also wonder whether, given that the scope of the paper is income distribution, the formulae towards the end of the paper are appropriate. It would be more appropriate to compare farm income after and before the project as shown in Table 4. I think there is no reason to regress CY on GY because GY is dependent on CY, even though this will give a similar coefficient. But GY = CY + Income from Non RJCP. This is an identification not a function.

## GENERAL DISCUSSION*–RAPPORTEUR: P.VON BLANCKENBURG

Question and comments from the floor related to agricultural policy aspects in both countries under review: Mexico and Thailand, to methodological aspects of the analyses and to the rural public works programme in Thailand.

In both countries emphasis on rural development in general and

*Papers by Reyes and Krongkaew.

development approaches within the agricultural sector have changed in the periods under observation. It was asked how far these changes were related to changing conditions on world markets and, if government activity had been more consistently balanced, whether this would have influenced income distribution positively in the case of Mexico. Other questions were on the interregional patterns of investment and consumption in Mexico and on the role of migration of workers to the United States.

The speakers agreed that changing emphasis in policies has influenced the course of agricultural growth and also the equity issue considerably. The labour migration to the United States will continue, but it cannot be expected that it will contribute to a decrease in income disparities between families in the places of origin of the migrants. A question as to whether agricultural research, and particularly the research work of CIMMYT in Mexico, had contributed or not to development in Mexico was answered more or less in the negative. The level of adoption of new varieties among peasant farmers seems to be small.

Another question relating to the consistency of the statistical analysis in the Thailand case led to a satisfactory explanation by the author – he denied that inconsistencies existed.

Particular interest from the floor was shown regarding details of the rural job creation project in Thailand. The author admitted that it was difficult to include the poorest rural groups in the programme. The need for emphasis on technologies suited to rain-fed farming under high risk was pointed out in this connection. Although the short-term effect of alleviation of poverty was considerable, the programme may not have a major long-term impact, if methods are not changed. A question whether the programme had spill-over effects, such as increase in food production or non-agricultural activities, was answered in the negative. It was mentioned that not enough money was available for further maintenance of the works completed.

Participants in the discussion included J. N. Barmeda, D. S. R. Belshaw, H. F. Breimyer, C. Gerrara, C. Howe, M. Leupolt, R. L. Meyer, L. Sondath and J. A. Wicks.

JOHN H. SANDERS AND JOHN K. LYNAM*[1]

# *Technological Change and Income Distribution in the Agriculture of Developing Countries: Some Issues and Strategies*

In the 1980s there is an increasing concern with the extent of human misery in both rural and urban areas of most developing countries. Traditional theories about industrial development within dual economies and the role of rural-urban migration were challenged in the 1970s. Even the principal success of the 1960s, the 'Green Revolution', has been under attack for apparent regressive income distribution effects. There is at present interest in focusing developmental efforts on the elimination of rural and urban poverty (see Bell and Duloy, 1974, and the other papers in that volume).

This paper is concerned with the potential of utilizing technological change in agriculture for income distribution objectives. In the first section, the problem of relatively large and absolutely growing rural sectors in most developing countries is set. Various rationales for not being concerned with income distribution in agriculture, when considering technological change, are revalued and some recent results of rural-urban migration research are presented. The second section considers the production of new agricultural technology and complementary strategies to improve the income distribution effect. The conclusions pull together the various policy suggestions.

## BASIC DEMOGRAPHY OF THE RURAL SECTOR IN DEVELOPING COUNTRIES

According to the classic theory of economic development (Fei and Ranis, 1964; Lewis, 1954), there needs to be a transferral of surplus labour from the agricultural to the industrial sector. Higher levels of capital investment foster more rapid rates of industrial development, thereby absorbing more labour from agriculture and increasing the demand for food and other consumer goods.

Since World War II there have been extremely rapid increases of urban populations in most developing countries. 40 to 65 per cent of this urban increase came from rural-urban migration in the 1960s (Todaro, 1976, p.

* Presented, in the absence of the authors, by Brian Hardaker.

10). From 1950 to 1976 the urban population increased by 50 million in Brazil and 27 million in Mexico (Sanders and Lynam, 1981). In both those countries the geometric growth rates of the urban sectors were over 4 per cent during the 1950–80 period. In spite of high rural-urban migration rates, in most developing countries the rural sectors have continued increasing absolutely at 1 to 3 per cent growth rates in the 1970s. In 1970–80 urban growth in Africa continued at a 4.7 per cent rate with a 1.9 per cent increase in rural areas. In Asia and Latin America urban growth had decreased to 3.8 per cent growth rates in this decade but rural growth was still 0.9 per cent. Moreover, the relative size of the rural sector is very large – 30 to 90 per cent of the population in most developing countries. Only in a few of the wealthiest developing countries is this proportion below 30 per cent. With the very large sizes of the rural sectors and their continuing absolute increase over time until the later stages of economic growth, developments within these rural sectors will continue to affect overall growth patterns.

Classical growth theory posits migration as an equilibrating mechanism in sectoral labour allocations, allowing little scope for real increases in urban wages in the initial stages of accumulation of industrial capital. Moreover, technical change in agriculture is critical to classical theory since marketable food surpluses must increase as agricultural labour is released to the industrial sector and since a shift in the terms of trade against agriculture provides further incentives for development of the industrial and tertiary sectors. Technical change in agriculture was thus necessary to relieve the constraints on industrial growth and there was little concern within the theory to consider the impact of technical change on income distribution in the rural sector.

Another rationale for ignoring income distribution within agriculture stems from the consumer surplus, comparative statics analysis of the distribution of benefits from the introduction of new agricultural technology between producers and consumers. Clearly, low price elasticities for food products imply a substantial price decline resulting from increased output, assuming a closed economy with no governmental intervention to support the price. Most of the benefits of the new rice technology in Colombia were received by urban consumers (Scobie and Posada, 1978). Hayami and Herdt (1977) show that small farmers will benefit due to increased subsistence consumption, while large farmers lose money from the introduction of new rice technology. However, this is a special case, for rice in Asia as the marketed surplus varies from 20 to 80 per cent for the two farm sizes and rice comprised 70 to 90 per cent of cereal consumption in different regions of the Philippines (Hayami and Herdt, 1977, pp. 249–50).

Comparative statics analysis has shown that, in the absence of international or interregional trade or government intervention, the principal beneficiaries from technological change in agriculture are consumers and, in most cases, producers' incomes decline. This leads to the familiar treadmill, where the initial innovators benefit and those lagging behind are forced out of the agricultural sector (Cochrane, 1958). The problem with this analysis is the classic problem of the dynamics or time period of adjustment of comparative statics. In the process of reaching this long-run equilibrium with a smaller labour force in the agricultural sector, some farmers will benefit. In the developed countries, particularly at present in Europe, farmers are utilizing their political power to retain larger shares of the benefits of technological change and delay reaching this long-term equilibrium by maintaining high prices, stockpiling agricultural commodities and then dumping them on world markets. In the 1960s and early 1970s PL 480 performed this dumping function for the accumulated stockpiles of American agricultural commodities resulting from the high support prices of the period. In developing countries where the rural population is still relatively large and technical change often occurs within a skewed farm size structure, the rate of adjustment as expressed in rural-urban migration may be too rapid for urban employment and infrastructure to adjust. Governments have also intervened to maintain low urban food prices, causing a further deterioration in the welfare of the rural sector and further migration.

Why should there be a concern with income distribution in the rural sector? An alternative is to ignore the subsistence agricultural sector until it can be absorbed by urban-industrial growth. However, there is evidence that large segments of the population in both rural and urban sectors in most developing countries are suffering from malnutrition (Reutlinger and Selowsky, 1976; Reutlinger and Alderman, 1980). Inadequate nutrition and health investments in the children of the rural poor implies a permanent loss of productive potential and will therefore reduce the returns to future human capital investments in education and on-the-job training (Belli, 1971; Selowsky and Taylor, 1973). If the human capital stock is allowed to deteriorate due to absolute poverty, then an equity issue becomes an efficiency problem.

The traditional solution for rural poverty in developed countries has been rural-urban migration associated with an expanding industrial sector. Most developing countries will need to decrease their birth rates to a considerable degree and in the long run their agricultural sectors will decline substantially. However, at the present time, much of the migration process appears to be a transferral of rural to urban poverty with minimal net gains to society. The principal growth sector with economic development in Latin America has been the unskilled services sector, where average labour productivity was even lower than in the agricultural sector (Sanders and Lynam, 1981; for a literature review on the potential importance of the services sector in developing countries see Baer and Samuelson, 1981). Moreover, several studies have indicated a nutritional decline for the migrating urban poor as compared with the rural poor (see Ward and Sanders, 1980, and the references cited). The high costs to the public sector of the mushrooming slums in the major urban areas of the developing countries are well known (Todaro, 1976).

Developing countries, thus, often have the immediate problem of human capital deterioration in their rural sectors and a lack of policy instruments to change this situation. One immediate policy suggestion is that governments in developing countries avoid all subsidies on labour-substituting innovations. In the absence of technological change substituting for labour, small farmers will have a comparative advantage in the production of many food crops due to the greater availability of seasonal labour on their own farms. Labour-substituting technology would include most mechanization, varieties developed specifically for mechanized production, and herbicides. Public sector subsidies on credit, production, or marketing knowledge rationed to large farmers could have a similar effect of biasing the adoption process towards large farmers. Even after eliminating public subsidies large farmers will still have advantages from being able to pay higher search costs for new information, due to greater potential benefits, from obtaining larger price discounts due to volume purchases, and from being able to take larger risks (Perrin and Winkelmann, 1976; see also Bell and Duloy, 1974, pp. 126ff) However, removing the public subsidies for large farmers (including those on research production) should help small farmers obtain more of the benefits of technological change. Binswanger and Ryan (1977, p. 226) summarized well the income distribution – technical change discussion:

> Taking account of distributional implications among farm size groups in low wage countries thus reinforces the efficiency consideration of concentrating on labour-using the land-saving technical changes while at the same time calling for institutional changes to improve the efficiency of land and labour markets and the access of small farmers to modern input and credit markets.

Efforts to increase farm incomes and improve income distribution within the rural sector and thereby prevent human capital deterioration and reduce rural-urban migration rates appear to be justified. Technical change in agriculture is the key to these efforts but the principal issue remains whether agricultural technology can be designed at the experiment station to reach the low-income rural population.

## PLANNING FOR FUTURE 'GREEN REVOLUTIONS'

In the late 1960s the new dwarf varieties of wheat and rice began their rapid dissemination across Asia. The pessimism about world hunger was temporarily transformed by an optimism about the potential for scientific development to overcome world food deficits if the problems were narrowly defined and the facilities located in developing countries. Eight more international centres were gradually added to IRRI and CIMMYT, thereby including most of the major food components of developing countries. However, by the mid-1970s a disillusionment with the income distribution effects of the dwarf varieties was increasingly reflected in the literature. The principal charcteristic of dwarf varieties was their capacity with irrigation to respond to much higher fertilizer levels without lodging. Hence, the beneficiaries of the technology were those holding the prime lands and able to obtain the increased fertilizer (Ruttan and Binswanger, 1978).

What do the empirical studies of the income distribution effect of the 'Green Revolution' show? Most studies indicate that large farmers adopted faster but small farmers followed with a lag (Perrin and Winkelman, 1976; Ruttan and Binswanger, 1978). Thus, relative income distribution between farm sizes has not worsened though absolute income differences have obviously widened due to the unequal distribution of productive assets. In the Indian 'Green Revolution' there was an increase in both employment and wages. Land rents increased faster than wage rates in the prime production areas since the demand for wheat was fairly elastic nationally and the supply of labour was more elastic than that for land. Moreover, the increased labour demand from the introduction of new varieties encouraged intra-regional migration (Binswanger and Ryan, 1977, p. 229).

An increasingly regressive absolute income distribution between farms and regions in many developing countries has provoked a polarization of the debate on future technology production. Figure 1 is used to put the debate on design of new technologies into perspective.

A________B_____C_________D

| | |
|---|---|
| Irrigated conditions | Farmers' traditional system<br>No water control<br>Low or zero cash inputs<br>Various types of stress<br>Low but stable yields |

FIGURE 1 *Range of environmental conditions toward which the experiment station in a developing country could focus its research activities.*

By breeding new varieties for A, the largest possible gains in rice yield were possible (Jennings, 1964). Moreover, much of the physiological literature on exploiting genetic yield potential under optimum conditions could be utilized. Literature development in the physiology of stress is at present increasing rapidly but suffers from a basic conceptual difficulty; how to specify appropriate levels of the stress variables studied and held constant. The relevant levels of stress will depend upon the environmental conditions for which a new variety is produced and the accompanying input levels. Biological scientists often have a very optimistic view of both. The returns to research depend not only upon the size of the absolute yield differential between farms and the experiment station but also upon the probability of adoption by farmers across the target area. Not all crops will be profitable enough, even with new technology, to move into the prime agricultural areas and to utilize high input levels. Breeding under non-stress conditions appears to be the appropriate strategy for only high value crops (Sanders and Lynam, 1981).

The other extreme of the spectrum is point D, small farmers' input levels and environmental conditions, since most small farmers are located outside the prime land areas. The most fervent critics of the 'Green Revolution' argue that the new varieties should have been selected for the most adverse conditions. These conditions could be marginal rainfall areas, low fertility soils, hillsides, or some combination of the above. Moreover, the critics often argue that the new technologies should not be accompanied by higher inputs than those already utilized by farmers. Finally, if the farmer is producing in association or any other form of multiple cropping, then the new technology should also be produced for this system. D is thus the sociologist's position of introducing the minimum change in the most difficult environmental conditions. The extreme version of D ignores some of the basic biological information about new technology development and underrates farmers. First, one-input changes are unlikely to make much difference to farm yields or income (Sanders and Johnson, 1982). Farmers' systems are biologically complex, hence changing one input, such as density or variety, will often result in other unexpected systems' effects, such as an increase in disease incidence with the higher density or an inability of the new variety to perform under farmers' stress levels or to be acceptable to consumers (Sanders and Lynam, 1982b). Most new agricultural technologies will require a series of changes including some future adaptations to new production systems after adoption. The brown leaf hopper became a problem after the introduction of the first generation of dwarf rices. The second generation rice varieties reflected much more attention to consumer requirements. The most successful innovations have required a series of changes generally involving new varieties, higher input levels, and improved agronomic management. Second, in most regions farmers have already been selecting over long periods of time for adaptation to their stress levels. Without comprehensive changes, new technology is unlikely to improve upon farmers' selection processes.

There is no reason that small farmers will not use higher inputs or even change their systems of production once new technology becomes available. Also, from the perspective of technology development, it is inefficient and will probably be unsuccessful to produce technology for the most adverse conditions (Ruthenberg, 1981). If one objective of agricultural policy is to raise the incomes of small farmers and small farmers are concentrated on hillsides, new technology development can be accompanied by land reform to first get the small farmers down into less inclined and more fertile soils (Sanders and Johnson, 1982). Utilizing agricultural technology as the only instrument to help the rural poor puts an unreasonable burden on both the international and national research centres in developing countries. To the extent that the larger farmers have both most of the better land and greater access to the services necessary for technology adoption to be profitable, it would be almost impossible to prevent larger farmers from being major recipients of the benefits of most new agricultural technologies. Clearly, technology development has to be combined with other instruments to focus its benefits on the rural poor.

If breeding for point D offers little probability of a return on research investment, whereas high returns are assured on the limited prime land areas, one alternative is to increase public and private investment in irrigation and fertilizers, thereby expanding the area of A type environments. In the Punjab, the adoption rate doubled from 30 to 60 per cent when irrigation facilities were extended and improved in the early 1970s (Perrin and Winkelman, 1976, p. 889). Estimates, however, suggest that irrigation investment costs would average $640 (1975 dollars) for each additional ton of food produced per year (Oram, et al., 1979, p. 47). Most countries must weigh these high costs against the potential for increasing rain fed production. For countries outside North Africa and certain Asian countries it appears to be necessary to produce new technology for environments such as B and C.

Developing new technology for intermediate points between A and D will be more difficult than producing for A because yield differentials will be smaller, stress factors will be more important, and returns on input use will be smaller. Characterizing the variability in the target area will be critical to defining an effective research strategy for rain fed crops (Sanders and Lynam, 1982a). Although there will be a wide range of technologies, each particular technology will be more narrowly adapted. Choice between research alternatives will influence the extent to which technology can be directed towards the rural poor. Examples include floury maize for the highlands versus mechanized dent maize for the coast of Ecuador; drought and high temperature tolerant cassava for the Northeast versus long-season cold-tolerant cassava for the South of Brazil; and mechanizable erect-type bush beans versus climbing beans or indeterminate bush beans. Thus, although technology is a blunt instrument for raising the incomes of the rural poor, appropriate technology design can be a component in raising small farmer income as the 'Green Revolution' is extended into rain fed areas.

## CONCLUSIONS

Concern about income distribution within the relatively large and growing rural sectors of most developing countries appears to be a necessary component of development planning due to the efficiency loss resulting from malnutrition and poor health conditions often prevailing there. Stable growth may well depend upon improvements in rural income distributions. Rural-urban migration will undoubtedly play a future role in reducing rural poverty. However, the migration process does not at present appear to be substantially increasing either productivity or welfare of the migrant.[2] Hence, there is increasing interest in improving the conditions of the rural poor before they become the urban poor.

The income distribution effects of new technology can be improved with the following three strategies: removing all public subsidies for research on labour-substituting technological change; eliminating factor subsidies if they are being rationed for large farmers; developing new technology for regions outside the prime areas to be accompanied by low or moderate input levels.

For some regions resource distribution will first have to be modified.

Without land reform, technological change is expected to have only a minimal effect on income distribution in the Andes, where small farmers are concentrated on the hillsides, or in the Brazilian Northeast where small farmers are predominantly in the more marginal rainfall areas. Technological change is not a panacea. Hard choices will be necessary, especially in Latin America, and there will be losers from the development process (Bell and Duloy, 1974, p. 119ff). Moreover, the initial effect from land reform in cultivated areas is expected to be a sharp production decline; hence a comprehensive development policy including new technology, extension, credit, and marketing services will be necessary. This is not a low cost solution.

Attempts to focus technological change and associated agricultural policy to obtain income increases for small farmers will also contribute to an increased understanding of other barriers to achieving this objective. Mechanization research orientated specifically for small farmers could reduce the drudgery of traditional farming systems and help eliminate seasonal labour constraints (Hardin, personal communication, 1982). Developing countries will probably need to increase investment in the human capital formation processs in rural areas, especially to provide minimal public health and education services. However, most improvements in nutrition and health result from individual consumer decisions and therefore require increases in the incomes of the rural poor.

In the 1980s, income distribution is increasingly one of the principal goals of development so that the rural and urban poor in developing countries can become effective participants in these societies. The 'trickle-down' approach to income distribution of earlier years, when industrialization and import substitution were primary goals, has been challenged by the stresses arising from the population and urban explosions in developing countries since World War II. It appears to be possible to do more in the rural sectors of developing countries about income distribution by means of technological change in association with other agricultural policies (see Lynam, et al., 1981).

## NOTES

[1] We are indebted to various scientists at CIAT, especially Peter Jennings, for numerous discussions and critical comments on earlier papers over a five-year period since 1976. We are also indebted to Lowell Hardin for extremely detailed comments on an earlier draft. The authors are responsible for any remaining errors. These views do not necessarily reflect those of CIAT (Centro Internacional de Agricultura Tropical).

[2] A recent review of the migration process summarizing many empirical studies argues that rural migrants take the low wage urban jobs but that their unemployment rates and time periods of job search are lower than those of the urban poor. Hence, there appears to be a churning process with the more marginal urban jobs continually being filled by the new migrants (FAO, 1978, and studies cited). If policy-makers in the developing countries are also concerned with the urban poor, the basic argument here to reduce the rates of rural-urban migration is not affected.

## REFERENCES


Baer, W., and Samuelson, L., 'Towards a Service-Oriented Growth Strategy', *World Development,* Vol. 9, No. 6, 1981.

Bell, C.L.G., and Duloy, H.H., 'Rural Target Groups', in H. Chenery, et al. (eds.), *Redistribution with Growth,* Oxford University Press, London, 1974.

Belli, P., 'The Economic Implications of Malnutrition: The Dismal Science Revisited', *Economic Development and Cultural Change,* Vol. 20, No. 1, October 1971.

Binswanger, H.P., and Ryan, J.G. 'Efficiency and Equity Issues in Ex Ante Allocation of Research Resources', *Indian Journal of Agriculture Economics,* Vol. 32, No. 3, July–September 1977.

Cochrane, W.W., *Farm Prices: Myth and Reality,* University of Minnesota Press, 1958.

Fei, J.C.H., and Ranis, G., *Development of the Labor Surplus Economy: Theory and Policy,* Irwin, Homewood, Illinois, 1964.

Food and Agriculture Organization of the United Nations (FAO), *Economic-Demographic Interactions in Agricultural Development: the Case of Rural-to-Urban Migration,* Rome 1978.

Hayami, Y. and Herdt, R.W., 'Market Price Effects of Technological Change of Income Distribution in Semi-Subsistence Agriculture', *AJAE,* Vol. 59, No. 2, May 1977.

Jennings, P.R., 'Plant Type as a Rice Breeding Objective', *Crop Science,* Vol. 4, No. 1, 1964.

Lewis, W.A., 'Economic Development with Unlimited Supplies of Labour', *The Manchester School of Economic and Social Studies,* Vol. 22, 1954.

Lynam, J.K., Pachico, D., and Posada, R., 'The Socio-Economic Environment in Tropical America', in CIAT staff, *CIAT in the 1980s, a Long-Range Plan for the Centro Internacional da Agricultura Tropical,* Cali, Colombia, November 1981.

Lynam, J.K., and Sanders, J.H., 'An Analytical Basis for Crop Design at the Research Station with Examples from CIAT', mimeo, Centro Internacional de Agricultura Tropical, Cali, Colombia, 1981.

Mellor, J.W., 'Food Price Policy and Income Distribution in Low Income Countries', *Economic Development and Cultural Change,* Vol. 27, No. 1, October 1978.

Oram, P., et al., 'Investment and Input Requirements for Accelerating Food Production in Low-Income Countries by 1990', International Food Policy Research Institute, Research Report 10, Sept. 1979.

Perrin, R., and Winkelmann, D., 'Impediments to Technical Progress of Small Versus Large Farms', *AJAE,* Vol. 58, No. 5, December 1976.

Reutlinger, S., and Alderman, H., 'The Prevalence of Calorie Deficient Diets in Developing Countries', World Bank Working Paper No. 374, Washington, DC, March 1980.

Reutlinger, S., and Selowsky, M., *Malnutrition and Poverty, Magnitude and Policy Options,* Johns Hopkins University Press, 1976.

Ruthenberg, H., *Farming Systems in the Tropics* (3rd ed), Oxford University Press, 1981.

Ruttan, V.W., and Binswanger, H.P., 'Induced Innovation and the Green Revolution', in H.P. Binswanger and V. W. Ruttan (eds), *Induced Innovation Technology, Institutions, and Development,* Johns Hopkins Press, 1978.

Sanders, J.H., and Johnson, D.V., 'Selecting and Evaluating New Technology for Small Farmers in the Colombian Andes', forthcoming, *Mountain Research and Development,* 1982.

Sanders, J.H., and Lynam, J.K., 'New Agricultural Technology and Small Farmers in Latin America', *Food Policy,* Vol. 6, No. 1, February 1981.

Sanders, J.H., and Lynam, J.K., 'Definition of the Relevant Constraints for Research Resource Allocation in Crop Breeding Programs', *Agricultural Administration,* Vol. 9, No. 4, April 1982a.

Sanders, J.H., and Lynam, J.K., 'Evaluation of New Technology on Farms: Methodology and Some Results from Two Crop Programs at CIAT', forthcoming, *Agricultural Systems,* 1982b.

Scobie, G.M., and Posada, R., 'The Impact of Technical Change on Income Distribution: The Case of Rice in Colombia', *AJAE,* Vol. 60, No. 1, 1978.

Selowsky, M., and Taylor, L., 'The Economics of Malnourished Children: An Example of

Disinvestment in Human Capital', *Economic Development and Cultural Change*, Vol. 22, No. 1, October 1973.
Todaro, M.P., *Internal Migration in Developing Countries: A Review of Theory, Evidence, Methodology, and Research Priorities,* International Labour Organization, Geneva, 1976.
Ward, J.O., and Sanders, J.H., 'Nutritional Determinants and Migration in the Brazilian Northeast: A Case Study of Rural and Urban Ceará', *Economic Development and Cultural Change,* Vol. 29, No. 1, October 1980.

## DISCUSSION – RAPPORTEUR: RAMESH SHARMA

Due to the absence of Sanders and Lynam, this paper was presented by Professor J.B. Hardaker. Dr Seiji Sakiur opened the discussion and said that by and large he shared the views expressed in the paper but he had three points to add. First, he noted that the authors had limited their coverage to the rural sector and thus missed completely rural to urban migration which plays an important role in the issues and strategies given in the paper. Secondly, he asked what sort of theoretical assumption underlies their strategy on removal of poverty. Thirdly, he was of the opinion that instead of generalizing a strategy, the authors should have used a separate area focus, for example Asia, Africa and Latin America.

Seven speakers from the floor expressed their comments broadly in four areas; coverage of the paper, labour scarcity, income distribution, and agricultural research. The view was expressed that the paper contained no new evidence or analysis, especially in the area of rural-urban migration, human capital investment and agricultural research. In Brazil the agricultural labour force is going to decline drastically in the future and so labour-productivity, mechanization, power and efficient use of inputs have to be increased. Three points were made on income distribution. The speakers disagreed with the authors that distribution effects of the new modern varieties are ignored by governments. The validity of two of the authors assertions was also questioned: that the new varieties are regressive in income distribution, and that consumer surplus comparative static analysis is a rationale for ignoring distribution effects. On agricultural research, we should try to develop low-fertilizer requiring HYVs. Also raised was the point that one cannot dismiss research for adverse areas purely on grounds of inefficiency and likely lack of success.

Professor Hardaker briefly responded to the queries raised. He agreed with most of the views expressed. But he was not sure that Governments in LDCs had taken serious measures towards equity following the 'green revolution'. For balancing growth and equity considerations, he was of the opinion that it depended upon the social welfare function of a country.

Participants in the discussion included V. Palmer, D. S. Tyagi, D. Hedley, G.O. Hughes, J.P. Hrabovszky, M.G. Chandrakanth and V. Steigerwald.

CSABA CSAKI

# *Limits and Potential of Growth in Agriculture in the CMEA Member Countries – a Quantitative Approach*

The situation and the development possibilities of agriculture in the European member countries of the CMEA, and particularly of the Soviet Union, have often been the subject of discussion in both the Eastern and Western hemispheres. This concern is not surprising, since the European member countries of the CMEA and the Soviet Union can be regarded as countries disposing of about one-fourth of all agricultural resources available in the world. The share of the member countries of the CMEA, including the Soviet Union, amounted in 1980 to 28.7 per cent of wheat, 8.4 per cent of corn, 44.3 per cent of sugar beet and 49.0 per cent of the potatoes produced all over the world. In addition to this, 12.4 per cent of the cattle stock, 17.1 per cent of the pig stock and about 9 per cent of the world's population were held by this group.

In this paper the limits and potential for agricultural growth of the area are discussed, based on the assessment of the present situation and calculations made by using a mathematical model. The basis of our analysis is the *CMEA Agricultural Model* developed at the *Food and Agriculture Programme* of the *International Institute for Applied Systems Analysis* (Laxenburg, Austria)[1] The work summarized in this presentation was supported and initiated by the Food and Agriculture Organization of the United Nations, Rome, Italy.[2] The study covers only the European member countries (Bulgaria, GDR, Poland, Hungary, Rumania, Czechoslovakia), the CMEA and the Soviet Union, including its Asian territories. The aim of the investigation was very clearly a CMEA-level, aggregated analysis. The study of country-specific, region-specific and inter-CMEA problems was not our intention.

## PRINCIPAL SUPPLY AND DEMAND TRENDS IN THE CMEA AREA

The European CMEA countries, excluding the USSR, are situated in the central part of Europe. The natural conditions of agricultural production are generally favourable. The climate is of continental character. The per caput supply of the population with land can also be considered favourable (about 0.7 ha agricultural land per caput). The proportion of arable acreage is particularly high. Possibilities for the increase of agricultural acreage are very restricted, but increasing share of plantations seems to be a general tendency. Agricultural territories amount to 553 million hectares in the Soviet Union (1978), and a significant part of it has a climate inclined to extremes, the climatic conditions being mostly similar to those of the Northern States of the USA and the Canadian prairies. The agricultural territories are relatively northern and only the most southern zones of the Soviet Union have a situation similar to that of San Francisco. The most varied climatic conditions can be encountered in this vast country, and, in addition to the coolness of the climate, the frequent fluctuations in precipitation and the relatively high probability of drought can be pointed out as fundamental characteristics. A significant part of the country's territory is not cultivated at all but in consequence of the unfavourable climatic conditions and of the northern situation, the possibilities of increasing the agricultural acreage and particularly of increasing sowing areas are more or less restricted.

Considerable decreases of agricultural population can be observed during the last two decades in each of the countries. On the other hand, recent years were characterized in CMEA agriculture by large-scale mechanization. The number of tractors and grain-harvesting combines vigorously increased everywhere, although significant differences continue to exist between the individual countries in question. The amount of fertilizer use was also increased (81 kg active ingredients in the Soviet Union, 151 kg in Rumania, 360 kg in the GDR in 1980) and considerable effort was made toward the extension of irrigation and for the improvement

TABLE 1 *Average annual growth of agricultural production in CMEA countries (%)*

| Country | 1966–1970 | 1971–1975 | 1976–1978 | 1976–1978 |
|---|---|---|---|---|
| | Annual growth in the given period on the basis of the previous five years | | | for the whole period from 1961–1965 |
| Bulgaria | 4.7 | 2.3 | 2.8 | 3.3 |
| Czechoslovakia | 3.5 | 2.8 | 2.5 | 2.9 |
| Poland | 3.0 | 3.2 | 1.0 | 2.4 |
| Hungary | 3.0 | 3.5 | 4.1 | 3.5 |
| GDR | 3.7 | 2.1 | 1.9 | 2.6 |
| Rumania | 4.2 | 4.8 | 7.4 | 5.8 |
| USSR | 4.1 | 2.5 | 2.6 | 3.1 |

*Source: Thirty Years of CMEA,* Hungarian Central Statistical Bureau, 1979.

of soils. However, the share of irrigated land is still relatively small (6-10 per cent of the cultivated area). But besides these developments, the level of technical supply in the CMEA agriculture falls behind that of Western Europe and North America.

Agricultural production grew more rapidly in the course of the past decades in the CMEA countries than the world average. The growth of agriculture generally was relatively rapid in the late '60s and early '70s and slowed down at the end of the last decade. Of course, in actual growth there is a considerable country-to-country and commodity-to-commodity variation. For example, between 1961-65 and 1971-75 the gross production of Soviet agriculture increased by 37 per cent, and also the production of the major agricultural products increased at a similar rate. Table 1 summarizes the annual growth of agriculture in the respective countries. The annual growth on a two-decade basis was mainly between 2.5 and 3.5 per cent. The only exception is Rumania, where agriculture developed at a 5.8 per cent annual rate during the past twenty years.

TABLE 2 *Major indicators of grain and meat production (average of 1976-78)*

| Country | Grain production kg/grain cropland | Meat production kg/agricultural land | Grain production kg/caput | Meat production kg/caput |
|---|---|---|---|---|
| Bulgaria | 3425 | 102 | 895 | 69.7 |
| Czechoslovakia | 3802 | 190 | 674 | 89.1 |
| Poland | 2615 | 142 | 594 | 79.5 |
| Hungary | 4077 | 194 | 1162 | 124.6 |
| GDR | 3506 | 276 | 525 | 104.2 |
| Rumania | 3015 | 99 | 889 | 68.4 |
| USSR | 1704 | 24 | 815 | 55.9 |

*Source:* *FAO Production Yearbook,* FAO, 1979.

The rate of increase in animal husbandry generally surpassed that of crop-growing.

Yields in agricultural production generally increased in the region, although showing vigorous dispersion in the diverse countries. The yields of grain crops are relatively similar in Czechoslovakia, the German Democratic Republic, and Hungary and are not very far from the level reached in other developed countries; they are significantly smaller in Rumania and Poland (see Table 2). In comparison with other developed countries, relatively modest yields as well as large fluctuations of yield are ascribed to the impact of the weather characteristic of Soviet agriculture. The fluctuations of grain yields are particularly great here. The annual crop yield might differ from the 5-year average by 30-40 per cent.

TABLE 3 *Share of agriculture and forestry in national income (%)*

| Country | 1950 | 1960 | 1970 | 1975 |
|---|---|---|---|---|
| | % | % | % | % |
| Bulgaria | 42.5 | 32.2 | 22.6 | 21.9 |
| Czechoslovakia | 16.2 | 14.7 | 10.1 | 8.3 |
| Poland | 47.9 | 30.3 | 17.5 | 15.1 |
| Hungary | 47.7 | 29.2 | 16.8 | 16.3 |
| GDR | 28.4 | 16.4 | 11.6 | 10.0 |
| Rumania | 27.3 | 34.9 | 19.1 | 16.6 |
| USSR | 22.2 | 20.7 | 22.0 | 16.8 |

*Source:* *Thirty Years of CMEA,* Hungarian Central Statistical Bureau, 1979.

So far as the structure of agricultural production is concerned, the general tendency is the increasing share of animal husbandry within total production, and this trend definitely will be continued in the future. The share of animal husbandry in the GDR and Czechoslovakia is around 54-56 per cent, and in most other countries higher than 40 per cent or around this level. The structure of crop production has not changed significantly during the past decade. Grain crops and leguminous plants continue to occupy about 60 per cent of total acreage. Within animal husbandry the growth of poultry and pig numbers was the most rapid. Pork production is the most determinant within total meat production. The share of beef shows greater variation and is about 20-30 per cent.

In each CMEA country – including the Soviet Union – agricultural production is performed on farms of different types of ownership and size. Except for Poland, where the majority of the land has remained in the hands of small peasant farmers, most of the land belongs to relatively large-scale state and co-operative farms. Individual farming activity continues, however, to exist, mainly in the form of so-called household farming of co-operative members and in the gardens of people working in the state sector of the economy. The role of the private and household sectors is significant, mainly in meat, vegetable and fruit production. (In some cases 30-40 per cent of the total production is due to these farms.)

In spite of the absolute increase of agricultural production its relative importance within the national economy shows a decreasing tendency in each of the countries of the area until the mid '70s. Since then a slight increase in the share of agriculture in total national income could be observed (see Table 3). Agriculture had the largest share in the production of national income in Bulgaria and Hungary in 1977 and the lowest shares (10.1 and 9.1 per cent) were in the GDR and in Czechoslovakia. The relative role of agriculture decreased also in the Soviet Union. In the period between 1965 and 1975, total national product more than doubled, while agriculture grew by about 1.7 times. The share of agriculture in the total national product of the USSR was 17.2 per cent in 1977.

Food consumption is vigorously increasing in the area and grew to a relatively high level. Regarding total calorie consumption, each CMEA country reached the level of 3,000 calories daily. Comparing the consumption levels of the diverse countries, we can see that consumers' habits express the production potential determined by natural conditions. The inner structure of food consumption is not the most favourable, since the significant part consists of carbohydrates and starch, and the consumption of animal proteins lags behind the desirable level. The development was rather moderate in this respect. First of all, the significant increase in fruit consumption should be pointed out as one of the favourable structural changes, though the consumption of tropical fruits is still rather small. The level of vegetable as well as of milk and dairy product consumption is also relatively high. The meat consumption per caput can still be qualified as relatively small, even at present.

Undoubtedly, the increased incomes of the population played a significant role in the development of food consumption. At present cash availability presents no obstacles to an increase in food consumption per caput. Rising personal incomes and a relatively inadequate supply of manufactured consumer goods have created a situation in some of the countries where the income elasticity of food demand is unusually high. On the other hand, government planners use scientific norms of optimal diet to plan the development in per caput food consumption as well as supply. In this situation, the dynamics of food consumption depend on not only the income, but are also significantly influenced by the supply side.

The European CMEA region as a whole in recent years has had a negative balance of foreign trade in agricultural products. Only Bulgaria, Hungary and Rumania have a considerable positive balance while the agricultural foreign trade balance of the other countries is negative. The share of agriculture within the total foreign trade turnover of the smaller CMEA countries generally shows a decreasing trend and there is a great disparity in its importance among the countries in question. In contrast to this, the agriculture of the Soviet Union takes part to an always increasing extent in the foreign trade of the country and the significance of imports in the satisfaction of consumer demand is ever growing. The increase of the Soviet foreign trade turnover was most dynamic in 1974–75 when compared to the previous year the rate of increase reached 26 and 28 per cent respectively. Even so, however, only a very small part, 3 per cent, of the national income could be realized in the foreign trade turnover. The share of the socialist countries within the foreign trade of the Soviet Union is around 62-64 per cent. Within this increasing foreign trade turnover the share of agricultural products is relatively modest but is also increasing. Foodstuffs and raw materials of the food industry represent an increasing part of global foreign trade turnover (about 15-20 per cent). The share of agriculture within the exports is relatively small, while the share of agricultural produce within the imports increased from 15.9 per cent in 1970 to about 25 per cent in the late 1970s.

As far as the smaller CMEA countries are concerned, grain crops have an outstanding importance in agricultural foreign trade and their import is particularly significant in the GDR, Poland, and Czechoslovakia; but Bulgaria also entered into the group of grain importing countries in 1975. The second in order of importance in imports is fruit, whose quantity most dynamically developed at the same time; it trebled between 1960 and 1975 and the increase of citrus fruit imports had a considerable role in this development. In respect to the exports, grain crops again (in the HPR and the RSR), as well as meat products, vegetables and fruit, had the leading part. The importance of Hungary and of Bulgaria is outstanding in the export of fresh, preserved and canned vegetables and fruit and that of Hungary and Poland in meat export is the most considerable. The general characteristic is that the greater part of the turnover is realized within the framework of the CMEA.

Until the year 1973 the Soviet Union had a net export of wheat but the import share of meat products was also relatively small. In consequence of the unfavourable weather conditions of the years 1972 and 1975 and in recent years, however, the foreign trade of these products has a negative turn and thereby increased the burden that was laid upon the Soviet balance of payment. A large-scale wheat and meat import was also rendered necessary by both the project declared for the improvement of living standards and the disadvantageously developed actual food situation. Concerning the structure of the export and import of the above-specified agricultural and food products, it is characteristic that the *export* of grain is destined for socialist countries, and the main source of *imports* was the United States (recently other countries, for example Argentina, Canada, and Australia, have gained an increasing role as sources of Soviet grain imports), while the major part of the imported meat and meat products has its origin from the capitalist countries and from Hungary. At the end of the 1970s the net grain import of the Soviet Union reached the 14-15 million tonne level annually. CMEA countries were the origin of most of the canned vegetables and about half of the fresh fruit and berries imported. Thus it can generally be established that the role of grains, meat and meat products as well as fresh and canned fruits and vegetables is outstanding within the foreign trade of the Soviet Union. The import of sugar is also considerable, coming almost entirely from Cuba. In recent years cotton was the only agricultural product of which the Soviet Union disposed of a significant surplus.

## GOVERNMENT POLICIES REGARDING GROWTH IN AGRICULTURE

A common feature of agricultural policy in CMEA countries is that to produce the quantity needed for the planned level of personal consumption and industrial demand for agricultural products is the most important overall objective. This general target receives, of course, concrete content depending on specific conditions and the actual economic situation which prevails in the respective country and, in spite of the similarity of the basic objectives, no uniform agricultural policy prevails. The development of industry is put in the centre of the economic policy in each country but, in addition, the increase of agriculture and of food production represents a politically very important task.

The investment policy regarding agriculture is also developed in this context. It is well known that investing activities develop in the CMEA countries according to central plans or in a way determined by them. Thus the scale of agricultural investments or their share within the total of investments gives at a given date expression to the state of economic funds available in the respective country for the implementation of agricultural development. The development of agricultural investments shows a rather varying picture for the region in question regarding both space and time. Agriculture is often allotted considerable financial means surpassing the rate of its contribution to national income, but the reverse example is not infrequent when even the proportionate part of income produced by agriculture does not remain in the sector but it is in part redistributed for the development of industry. If the concrete situation prevailing in recent years is considered, we can establish that the estimation of agriculture was fairly different in various CMEA countries, the role of agriculture within development plans and correspondingly the financial means invested in agriculture were also different.

Regarding the smaller CMEA countries during the last decade, in general the development of agriculture was not the main target. Therefore, the increase of agricultural investments did not surpass the rate of increase of all investments. In some countries (Bulgaria, Rumania) a considerable part of the national income produced in agriculture came to redistribution, that is was used in other national economic branches. The Soviet Union represents a different case, where the development of agriculture was stressed, and during the last two decades, the share of agriculture within all investments highly surpassed the level achieved in other CMEA countries. The fact that in the whole period of the Soviet régime until 1975, a total of 320 thousand million roubles was invested in agriculture, and of this 213 thousand million roubles (that is 66.5 per cent) were invested in the course of the last decade (that is in the period between 1966 and 1975) is more characteristic than anything else of the increasing role of agricultural investment. The redistribution of investment goods to the benefit of the development of agriculture was continued in the Soviet Union in the period 1976–1980. The share of agriculture within all investments was higher than its contribution to the national income (about 30 per cent of all investments were allocated to agriculture and food production).

A very important general characteristic of agricultural policy in the European CMEA countries is the particularly vigorous effort for self-sufficiency. It can be established, in fact, that a fundamental requirement in each country is that domestic demands for all products which can be produced in the respective country should be met to the greatest extent possible from domestic production. It can be observed in each country that the concrete treatment of agriculture and food production depends also upon the state of the balance of payments. In those countries where natural conditions are favourable for agricultural production, the utilization of this sector for augmenting foreign currency receipts figures among the economic political targets. This effort is particularly vigorous in the case of Hungary, Bulgaria and Rumania, where the maximization of foreign currency receipts of the food production sector is one of the most important economic political tasks.

## FUTURE TRENDS IN AGRICULTURAL POLICY

Concerning the details of the expected agricultural policy for the forthcoming years pertinent information is not easily available. Each of the countries in question has certain conceptions about the development of agriculture for a longer term, which includes the period lasting until 1990 and, in some cases, even until 2000. According to the practice of the CMEA countries, however, the Five-Year Plans represent the documents in which those decisions are fixed which are intended to be actually implemented. The present concrete plan period in each country started on January 1 1981. The development of agriculture according to available plan documents will receive more attention in each of the respective countries than previously. Moderate increases (8-10 per cent) in agricultural production are planned in Czechoslovakia and in the GDR. In the Soviet Union the total growth target is 12-14 per cent for the five-year period with the production of 238-243 million tons of grain annually. The targets are the most ambitious in Bulgaria and Rumania, where a 20-25 per cent development of production is aimed at.

Based on conclusions reported at various forums as well as upon the characteristics of the economic situation and on the analysis of the actual result of the current plan period in the respective countries, it is probable that the rate of general economic growth in the European CMEA countries will be more moderate in the forthcoming five years (or very likely in the next ten years) than it has been in the previous periods. The growth rate of agriculture will probably come nearer to the rate of general economic growth, but it will remain at the relatively moderate level of the late 1970s. It is also probable that, as a consequence of problems related to the balance of payments, efforts toward food self-sufficiency will increase and a greater stress will be laid thereby on the development of agriculture.

In connection with slower economic growth, it may be presumed that agricultural investments will increase to a smaller extent than they did so far and it is improbable that the share of agriculture will grow within the total of investments. The increase of grain and meat production will continue to be stressed to the greatest extent within agricultural development. Efforts for the establishment of a production structure better adapted to world market demands will certainly be confirmed in the food-exporting countries, and this will presumably further consolidate the role of the grain economy.

In CMEA countries, so-called direct and indirect policy instruments are used to realize the targets given by the national plan and to manage agricultural production. In general it can be remarked that the application of direct means of economic management is the determinant in the majority of the countries. It is not probably that the basic nature of the government management system will be changed, but serious efforts to improve the efficiency of the system can be expected. It is most likely that economic incentives and indirect means will be applied more intensively to improve the efficiency of the government economic management of agriculture. The further growth of domestic producer and consumer prices of agricultural products seems to be unavoidable. The modification of the low food price policy might have an impact upon consumers' demands, too, and the wider range of price incentives will probably increase the overall efficiency of agricultural production.

The production potential of the so-called 'household farming' of co-operative farm members and industrial workers is far from being utilized in most of the countries. Production can be increased through this channel without government investment. Encouragement of the utilization of these reserves seems to be an economic necessity in the present situation. The increased support of household and individual agricultural production is a new characteristic of agricultural policy in several CMEA countries, including the Soviet Union, but its effect in the increased development of this sector has not shown itself so far. The further support of these activities can definitely be forecast and it is also very probable that the household sector will contribute to the fulfilment of the national target to a larger extent, especially in the forthcoming 5-10 years.

## ALTERNATIVE SCENARIOS OF AGRICULTURAL GROWTH IN CMEA COUNTRIES

To forecast the future development of agriculture in the European CMEA area mathematical modelling was used as a basic methodology. Based on the CMEA model in the food and agriculture model system of the Food and Agriculture Programme of the International Institute for Applied Systems Analysis (Laxenburg, Austria), a mathematical model of the area was constructed. The model is actually a *descriptive, recursive simulation model,* which describes the food and agriculture of the area as a disaggregated part of an economic system closed at the national, as well as the international level.[3] The model, which is eventually a system of interconnected models, is structured according to the major elements of the centrally planned food and agriculture systems.

In the model we assume that the most important long-range government policy objectives as the required growth rate of the overall economy, and private consumption as well as the share of agriculture in total investment, are fixed according to actual data of CMEA countries. Production is modelled by a nonlinear optimization model, consumption and trade are described by a special equilibrium model, government objectives are adjusted by using heuristic routines. The product list of the model conforms to the commodity coverage of AT 2000, but certain commodities are aggregated (food and agricultural commodities in the model: wheat, rice, coarse grains, sugar, vegetables, bananas, citrus fruit, other fruit, vegetable oil, cocoa, coffee, tea, cotton, other non-food products, rubber, other feeds, beef and veal, mutton and lamb, pork, poultry meat, dairy products and eggs). The rest of the economy is represented in the model by one aggregated commodity. The model and its parameters are structured according to the Soviet Union and the smaller CMEA countries, and in practice is run according to two submodels which have identical structures. In the model FAO population and demand projections are used and it is fundamentally based upon data available at FAO.[4]

In the modelling experiment we assume moderate rates of economic growth according to FAO's AT 2000 Normative Medium Scenario. On that basis, two basic scenarios were calculated by the model, namely a *Constant SSR (self-sufficiency ratio) Scenario,* where SSRs of 1975 are kept as minimum requirements in production modules, and a so-called *Free Trade Scenario* where most of the restrictions on self-sufficiency ratios are released. To help to delimit the spectra of production possibilities starting out of the two basic scenarios, several other model versions have been computed, mainly by running the Soviet Union and Eastern European submodel separately. The major questions of these investigations were related to the impact of migration from agriculture; various levels of investment in agriculture; different balance of payment situations; changes in feeding efficiency, and so on.

The two basic scenarios and related calculations give reliable information on the possible lower and upper range of production. First of all, it is necessary to point out that the future course of agricultural development in CMEA countries will largely depend on the national situations. Efforts to satisfy growing consumer food demands and to increase or maintain the level of self-sufficiency can be considered the main driving forces of future growth. Of course, changes in international market conditions might also have some influence. High prices on the world market might represent an additional reason for developing agriculture to save foreign exchange in the importing countries and to utilize export potential in a surplus situation. Low international prices first have an influence on exporting countries, which in this situation might restrain agricultural development and invest more in other areas. However, the CMEA countries' reaction to world market changes will be much more moderate and lagged than that of other developed countries.

Our two basic scenarios are very similar so far as the projected overall growth of agricultural production is concerned. In contrast to the relatively moderate growth of the overall economy, a substantial growth of agricultural production can be projected (2-3 per cent annually). It can be expected that growth of production will be greater than that of domestic demand, parallel to the increase of SSR's of the most important agricultural commodities. This development reflects the fact that very substantial production reserves exist in the area, especially in the Soviet Union. In our opinion, the significant investment allotted to agriculture in recent years will bear fruit in the forthcoming period, and even a moderate food surplus can be forecast by the end of the century. Domestic food demands are forecast according to FAO projections in our scenarios. On the whole, the CMEA region expects a relatively moderate growth of both domestic food demand and consumption. Regarding the total calorie consumption, each CMEA country has already reached a level of 3,000 calories daily. A further increase is not desirable, but the inner structure of consumption will change. During the forthcoming period the structural change of food consumption will be determined by the fast-growing consumer demand for meat and meat products, as well as for fruit and vegetables.

The projected growth of agriculture assumes that the substantial level of investment in agriculture will be maintained. As some of the results of our calculations indicate, agricultural development is closely related to the share of agriculture in total investment. The amount of investment allotted to agriculture determines the improvement of production equipment and physical resources of production in general. We expect about a 13.5 per cent share of agriculture in total investment in the smaller CMEA countries. Model runs with lower figures indicate that, considering the pressure from the consumer side and the need for foreign exchange, lower levels of agricultural investment are not very likely. These results also demonstrate that by increasing agricultural investment, the government can significantly increase agricultural output. In the Soviet Union the share of agriculture will probably fall below the present level, but it will remain relatively high; we expect about 20 per cent, surpassing the contribution of agriculture to total national income. The investigation of the possible levels of agricultural investment indicates that an agricultural share of less than 15 per cent would seriously threaten the realization of major government objectives. Substantial investment in agriculture must also continue in order that the fluctuations in yields and the unfavourable impacts of weather conditions on agriculture be reduced. On the whole, agriculture has to remain at the top of the government preference list.

Labour will still remain a very important factor of agricultural development in the region. Migration from agriculture toward industry and other branches of the national economy will undoubtedly continue. Migration which is not associated with investment to compensate for the departing labour can limit production growth, especially that of labour-intensive products. Our calculations indicate that the estimates of FAO on agricultural population can be considered as one of the possible future trends. For the Soviet Union, the FAO estimates 7.5 per cent of total labour force in agriculture in 2000, and for the other CMEA countries about 15 per cent. Having made calculations with several possible migration levels and after comparison with other developed countries, we have come to the conclusion that migration from agriculture in the Soviet Union will most likely be somewhat less and in other CMEA countries somewhat more than FAO projections. Our projection is a 10 per cent share of agriculture in total working population in 2000, and this is the figure used in the basic scenarios.

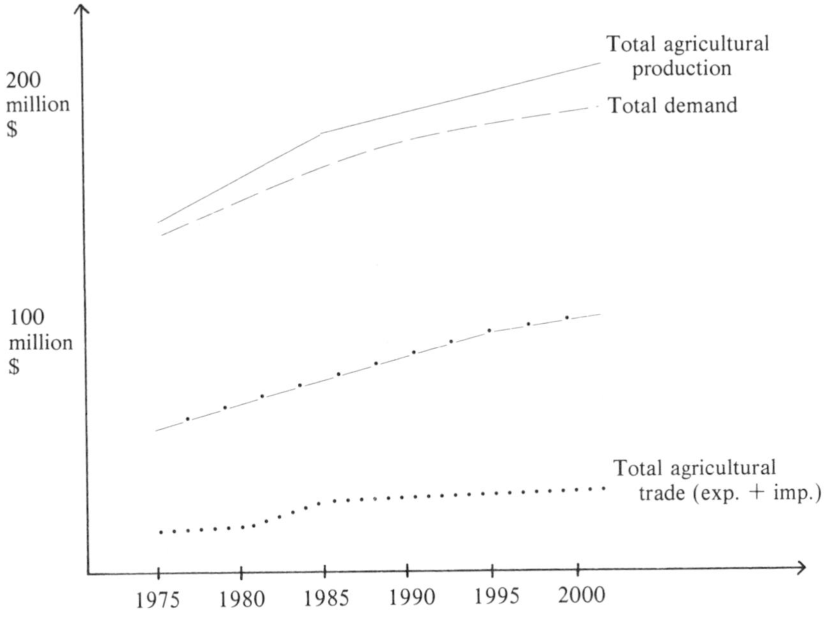


FIGURE 1 *General indicators of Constant SSR Scenario*

## CONSTANT SSR SCENARIO OF AGRICULTURAL DEVELOPMENT

In this scenario the actual SRRs in 1975 of the Soviet Union and the smaller CMEA countries were considered in both submodels as minimum requirements. Analysing the results presented in Table 4 one should remember that upper bounds were not given in the model. Therefore, production growth above the minimum requirements was allowed (see Figure 1). This scenario shows the very considerable agricultural potential of the region. As one can see in Table 4, production of various commodities grows at least parallel to demand or even faster; SSRs, therefore, remain stable or show a continuous increase up to 2000. On the whole the overall food SSR increased. This scenario reflects the realization of the existing long-range policy objectives in CMEA countries aimed at self-sufficiency in food production. The projected food SSR for 2000 is 1.01; practically all cereals are produced domestically, and the substantial surplus of wheat allows an increase in meat production above the projected, relatively moderate level.

Continuing past trends, growth in animal husbandry is faster than that of crop-growing. The substantial meat surplus will most probably be consumed

TABLE 4 *Agricultural output and SSRs of CMEA countries – Constant SSR Scenario*

| | 1975 | | 1990 | | 2000 | |
|---|---|---|---|---|---|---|
| | Total Output | SSR | Total Output | SSR | Total Output | SSR |
| Total cereals[1] | 254369 | 0.93 | 390056 | 10.98 | 437650 | 0.99 |
| Wheat[1] | 108868 | 0.93 | 151725 | 0.98 | 166508 | 1.00 |
| Rice[1] | 2135 | 0.75 | 3837 | 0.79 | 5182 | 0.80 |
| Coarse grain[1] | 143366 | 0.92 | 234494 | 0.97 | 265959 | 0.99 |
| Total meat[1] | 22945 | 1.11 | 33830 | 1.38 | 37505 | 1.32 |
| Beef and veal[1] | 8551 | 0.99 | 13604 | 1.35 | 14744 | 1.32 |
| Mutton and lamb[1] | 1159 | 1.02 | 1845 | 1.49 | 1991 | 1.43 |
| Pork[1] | 10564 | 1.25 | 14357 | 1.49 | 15816 | 1.42 |
| Poultry meat[1] | 2671 | 1.07 | 4024 | 1.12 | 5042 | 1.04 |
| Milk and milk prod.[2] | 129507 | 1.00 | 203398 | 1.13 | 221520 | 1.14 |
| Sugar[1] | 11798 | 0.75 | 16109 | 0.88 | 19268 | 0.95 |
| Vegetable oil[1] | 4937 | 1.11 | 6258 | 1.05 | 7361 | 1.06 |
| Citrus fruits[3] | 135 | 0.11 | 135 | 0.08 | 135 | 0.06 |
| Other fruits[3] | 26753 | 1.09 | 41032 | 1.25 | 45598 | 1.16 |
| Vegetables[3] | 17847 | 0.99 | 24069 | 1.01 | 26740 | 1.02 |
| Cotton[1] | 7662 | 1.00 | 1847 | 1.20 | 12105 | 1.20 |
| Other non-food[3] | 1135 | 0.90 | 2139 | 1.40 | 3104 | 1.74 |
| All agr. comm.[3] | 138890 | 1.00 | 205560 | 1.10 | 230409 | 1.11 |
| Total volume of[3] agr. trade | 7491 | 5.4 | 22249 | 10.8 | 23196 | 10.1 |

[1] in thousand metric tons
[2] in milk equivalent
[3] in million 1972 US $

to a great extent domestically, since the projected 66 kg/caput consumption leaves enough room for further increases and there is no question that consumer demand will also exist for higher quantities. The projected level of grain production, 437 million metric tons, seems to be optimistic, but not totally unrealistic. The SSR in this respect grows continuously and the present grain deficit of the area disappears. The volume of agricultural trade (see Figure 1) grows faster than production, but still remains at a relatively low level (10 per cent of the output). Beside tropical fruit, coffee and citrus fruit, rice, sugar, and tea have SSRs considerably lower than 1. On the other hand, fruit, cotton and most of meat products have a considerably higher SSR than 1.

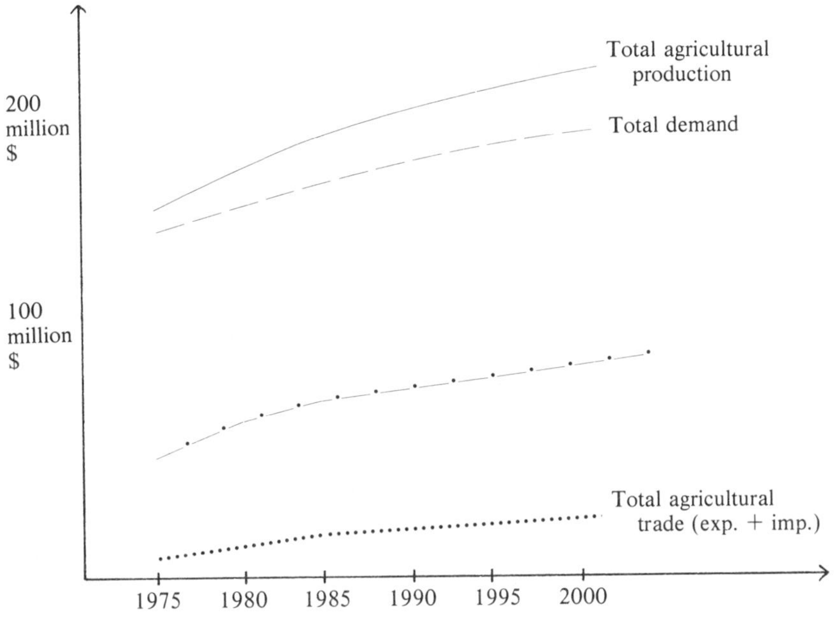


FIGURE 2 *General indicators of Free Trade Sceńario*

## FREE TRADE SCENARIO

This scenario reflects a less constrained production development than that of the Constant SSR Scenario. Constraints on minimal levels of producing various commodities have been removed, and the structural changes and developments were limited only by available resources. As Figure 2 shows, the overall agricultural growth is somewhat higher in this case, but the basic patterns of development are not different than those of the Constant SSR Scenario (see Table 5). Without restriction on the SSRs of the commodities, the relative role of animal husbandry becomes higher than at Constant SSR Scenario (SSR of meat is 1.40). The development of animal husbandry is based partly on imported feeds. The Free Trade Scenario, which releases the restrictions of agricultural production, obviously leads to a faster growth of agricultural trade of the area.

The fastest-growing area of agriculture in this scenario is animal husbandry. Production growth rates lead to substantial increases in the SSRs of animal products, generally to levels greatly in excess of domestic needs. The meat surplus seems to be substantial, even if consumption above the projected level is expected. Meat prodution is partly based on imported

TABLE 5 *Agricultural output and SSRs of CMEA countries – Free Trade Scenario*

| | 1975 | | 1990 | | 2000 | |
|---|---|---|---|---|---|---|
| | Total Output | SSR | Total Output | SSR | Total Output | SSR |
| Total cereals[1] | 254369 | 0.93 | 378740 | 0.93 | 420710 | 0.93 |
| Wheat[1] | 108868 | 0.93 | 147969 | 0.95 | 158439 | 0.94 |
| Rice[1] | 2135 | 0.75 | 1722 | 0.36 | 955 | 0.15 |
| Coarse grain[1] | 143366 | 0.92 | 229049 | 0.93 | 261316 | 0.94 |
| Total meat[1] | 22945 | 1.11 | 35043 | 1.42 | 39998 | 1.40 |
| Beef and veal[1] | 8551 | 0.99 | 14002 | 1.39 | 15581 | 1.39 |
| Mutton and lamb[1] | 1159 | 1.02 | 1895 | 1.53 | 2097 | 1.17 |
| Pork[1] | 10564 | 1.25 | 14974 | 1.55 | 17024 | 1.52 |
| Poultry meat[1] | 2671 | 1.07 | 4173 | 1.16 | 5295 | 1.09 |
| Milk and milk prod.[2] | 129507 | 1.00 | 209886 | 1.15 | 23507 | 1.17 |
| Sugar[1] | 11798 | 0.75 | 14710 | 0.80 | 16968 | 0.84 |
| Vegetable oil[1] | 4937 | 1.11 | 5834 | 0.99 | 6636 | 0.96 |
| Citrus fruits[3] | 135 | 0.11 | 135 | 0.08 | 135 | 0.06 |
| Other fruits[3] | 26753 | 1.09 | 40074 | 1.22 | 44978 | 1.12 |
| Vegetables[3] | 17847 | 0.99 | 22413 | 0.94 | 23455 | 0.89 |
| Cotton[1] | 7662 | 1.00 | 15437 | 1.68 | 20680 | 2.06 |
| Other non-food[3] | 1135 | 0.90 | 2247 | 1.47 | 3374 | 1.89 |
| All agr. comm.[3] | 138890 | 1.00 | 206124 | 1.10 | 232410 | 1.10 |
| Total volume of[3] agr. trade | 7491 | 5.4 | 30794 | 14.9 | 41592 | 17.9 |

[1] in thousand metric tons
[2] in milk equivalent
[3] in million 1972 US$

feeds. By reducing meat surplus, grain self-sufficiency could be reached. In addition to animal products, a surplus can be expected for cotton, other-food and other fruit products. The SSR increases especially for cotton production. On the import side, rice plays the leading role (SSR only 0.15), but there is also a deficit in sugar, vegetables, vegetable oil and tea, and it is obvious that tropical and Mediterranean products must be imported. In the Free Trade Scenario the agricultural trade of the area shows a significant increase. In 2000 agricultural trade (export and import) amounts to 17.9 per cent of output, which does not seem to be a totally unrealistic figure. Obviously, the realization of this trade potential largely depends on to what extent trade restrictions in other countries (for example, meat import restrictions of the EEC) are relaxed.

## FUTURE PERSPECTIVES IN PRODUCTION OF CEREALS

The grain sector, especially the feed grains together with other feeds, form the main bottleneck in agriculture of the CMEA countries at present. Efforts to increase meat production in order to meet fast-growing consumer demands, together with a relatively low level of feed conversion rates, are expressed by the overall negative grain balance of the region. The main reason for excessive feed consumption is a physiologically unbalanced composition of rations, mainly a lack of digestible protein. Significant losses in nutrients and vitamins, caused by the not yet consistently high technical level of harvesting and feeding, but especially by the lack of adequate storage facilities, also exert a negative influence on feeding efficiency. According to OECD estimates, the increase of digestible protein content in one kg of unit feed from the present 85-86 grams to 105-110 grams could in itself be sufficient to improve the feed conversion ratio by 25-30 per cent. This could save about 20-25 million tons of grain in the Soviet Union alone. The region has all the production potential to be self-sufficient in grain production, and the importance of the increase in meat production assures that the investments required to improve feeding efficiency will also be forthcoming. Our scenarios forecast 420-430 million metric tons of grain production for the year 2000. It is most likely that the actual development will follow the line of the Constant SSR Scenario. The domestic food grain needs will definitely be satisfied by domestic production, as well as the feed requirements necessary to produce enough meat to reach the projected level of meat consumption and/or export, but the area might once more become a net exporter of limited quantities of grain. But we should mention that, given the apparently low capital productivity in agriculture, it is highly unlikely that most of the CMEA countries, and especially the Soviet Union, will put more capital into agriculture than is necessary to gain full SSR in grains. Substantial grain import, as in the Free Trade Scenario for the production of meat for export, is not likely to happen, except under a very favourable market situation or if investment levels fall well below expectations.

In our commodity classification protein feeds do not appear as a separate product. The CMEA area has a deficit in this respect. As was referred to above, the relatively low feed conversion rates are partly due to the lack of proteins. Therefore, even though the computed results do not show it, fast increasing demand can be expected for protein feeds in the area. The projected growth of vegetable oil production will cover consumer needs and some surplus might occur. Considering production possibilities and the given natural conditions in the area, the deficit in protein feeds is not likely to disappear until 2000. So far as cereals are concerned, rice has the lowest projected SSR. In the Free Trade Scenario, rice SSR drops continuously and most of the domestic requirement is imported. When irrigation projects and climatic conditions in Soviet Middle Asia are taken into account, the actual trends will probably be closer to the Constant SSR Scenario, where rice SSR is about 0.80. Some rice deficit of the area, about 1 million metric tons of import seems definitely to be a realistic forecast.

## DEVELOPMENT OF ANIMAL HUSBANDRY

Meat production and animal husbandry will be the fastest-growing area within the CMEA agriculture. Both basic scenarios, as well as the related calculation, project considerable growth. The existing meat surplus of the area (SSR 1.11 in 1975) is associated with a moderate level of consumption. The need for foreign exchange in these countries encourages meat exports and limits imports and domestic supply. The production of enough meat for increasing domestic demand is the focus of agricultural policy in the area. This policy assumes the domestic production of feeds as well. One of the most important constraints on future meat production is the growth of domestic feed production.

- Producing meat along the lines of our relatively moderate demand projections seems to be the lower boundary of expected production. In case of unexpected difficulties on the feed side, the import of feeds can be expected, rather than significant meat imports.
- If grain production develops favourably, it will at first result in the increase of domestic meat consumption and only in the case of further opportunities can meat production for export be considered probable.
- Improvement in feeding efficiency can be expected and, if it is accomplished, it can advantageously influence the overall meat production potential.

Along with feed availability, the development of animal husbandry depends on further capital inputs and investments, as well as the availability of the labour force in agriculture. Our computations clearly demonstrate that meat production reacts very sensitively to the level of agricultural investment. Reduction of agricultural investment makes itself felt first in meat production. This is not very surprising and leads to the conclusion that the realization of a meat surplus projected by our two scenarios is rather uncertain when seen from the point of view of present investment trends. Available labour force represents a very important constraint on production growth, but particularly in animal husbandry. Calculation results, even the comparison of the two basic scenarios, indicate that there is serious competition between the labour-extensive and labour-intensive branches of agriculture. Labour can really become a limiting factor during the second half of the projected period. Larger outmigration than that projected by the basic scenarios may result in the fall of production growth in cattle and pig husbandry as well as in fruit production. In place of these activities, a grain surplus and a further increase in poultry production can be expected.

On the whole, the almost 40 million metric tons meat production in 2000 shown in the Free Trade Scenario is almost certainly the upper limit of foreseeable development. Actual growth will more likely follow the Constant SSR Scenario and is expected to be around 33-36 million metric tons. Substantial surpluses of meat will probably not appear on international markets. Export can be expected from the smaller CMEA countries, but not exceeding the level of 4-5 million metric tons, which is double the present export quantity. The internal structure of meat production is not likely to change remarkably. Growth is fastest in poultry production, but beef and mutton and lamb production have almost similar rates of increase. Pork production increases at a somewhat lower rate. SSRs increase in each case, except for poultry, where demand growth exceeds the rate of production development.

## NOTES

[1] The author is grateful to Günther Fischer, Bozena Lopuch and László Zéöld for developing the computer implementation of the CMEA Agricultural Model, to Bonnie Riley for typing and correcting of the related materials, and to Profs. Ferenc Rabár and Kirit Parikh for the support of the whole project.

[2] The analysis made by the CMEA Agricultural Model was used as explanatory and background material in the Agriculture Toward 2000 project of FAO (see Csáki, 1982). The support of Dr. J.P. Hrabovszky and Dr J. O'Hagan of the FAO to this work are also acknowledged.

[3] The Food and Agriculture Model System of IIASA see Keyzer (1980), Fischer and Frohberg (1980), and Csáki (1981).

[4] The detailed description of the model is given in Csáki (1982).

## REFERENCES

Csáki, C. 'A National Policy Model for the Hungarian Food and Agriculture Sector', RR-81-23, International Institute for Applied Systems Analysis, Laxenburg, Austria, 1981.

Csáki, C. 'Limits and Potential in the Further Development of CMEA Agriculture, Research Report, International institute for Applied Systems Analysis, Laxenburg, Austria (forthcoming 1982).

Csepely-Knorr, A. and Szakonyi, L. 'Agricultural Development in the European CMEA Member Countries', Gazdaság, No. 1 (in Hungarian), 1981.

Fischer, G. and K. Frohberg 'Simplified National Models – the Condensed Version of the Food and Agriculture Model System of the International Institute of Applied Systems Analysis', WP-80-56, International Institute for Applied Systems Analysis, Laxenburg, Austria, 1980.

Food and Agriculture Organisation of the United Nations, *Agriculture: Toward 2000,* Proceedings of the 20th Session of the FAO, 10-20 November, 1979, C79-24. Rome, 1979.

Keyzer, M.A., 'An Outline of IIASA's Food and Agriculture Model', WP-80-9, International Institute for Applied Systems Analysis, Laxenburg, Austria, 1980.

Keyzer, M.A., 'Linking National Models of Food and Agriculture: An Introduction', RM-77-2, International Institute for Applied Systems Analysis, Laxenburg, Austria, 1977.

Nagy, J., 'The Present Situation and Future Perspective in the Soviet Agriculture', Agrargazdasagi Kutoto Intezet No. 6 (in Hungarian), 1978.

Nagy, J., and Gabor, J., 'The Present Situation and Future Perspectives in the Agriculture of European CMEA Countries', Agrargazdasagi Kutoto Intezet No. 6 (in Hungarian), 1979.

OECD, *Problems and Perspectives in the Soviet Grain Economy,* Paris 1979.

Popov, T., The General Situation and Main Tendencies of Food and Agricultural Development in the European CMEA Member Countries (1960-1975 and up to 1980)', RM-78-51, International Institute for Applied Systems Analysis, Laxenburg, Austria, 1978.

Sipos, A., 'Agro-industrial Complex of the National Economy and Solution of Food Supply Problems in the CMEA', Gazdálkodás, No. 3 (in Hungarian), 1981.

## DISCUSSION OPENING – HIROYUKI NISHIMURA

Professor Csaki's paper is a fine well-organized work and brings us important information. The author presented an interesting paper concerning agricultural modelling work at the last conference (Csaki, 1981). Since that time I have been looking forward to hearing his results and their interpretation.

With respect to the present paper, I am sure that it has brought us a meaningful suggestion concerning a quantitative approach. I agree that this kind of analytical tool plays a significant role in the planning and management of food and agriculture. However, regarding the interpretation of the study results, I have to confess that I do not have any special knowledge of the CMEA member countries, other than a general knowledge of the theoretical approaches.

Professor Csaki's paper gives a broad picture of how policy can affect the development of agriculture. Although most parts of his presentation are specifically related to CMEA member countries, some of the issues and policies discussed are relevant to the further development of techniques applicable in the planning of other regions.

The paper intends to show the limits and potential of agricultural growth of the area by using a mathematical model. The basis of the analysis is the CMEA Agricultural Model. The model is consistent and comparable with the IIASA's Food and Agriculture model system.

The fundamental characteristics of the IIASA model are: (a) a descriptive character; (b) a recursive simulation technique; (c) linear and non-linear; programming, and econometric methods used in the subsystems.

An aggregated CMEA model was constructed based on the IIASA's model and on experiences resulting from the Hungarian Agricultural Model. The CMEA model is designed to apply to the centrally planned countries. In it, similarly to the general structure and the Hungarian Agricultural Model, the main underlined assumptions are as follows: (a) long-term government objectives are taken as exogenous variables; (b) the central decisions on the production structure of agriculture are transferred directly to producing enterprises. Thus a producer's decision model is not included. The major policy goals in agriculture are to secure an adequate enough consumption level for farm products, which was determined by the national plan.

The important characteristic of agricultural policy in the CMEA countries appears to be the particularly large effort for self-sufficiency. The other characteristic which Professor Csaki observed is the state of the balance of payments.

While care was needed with regard to the underlying assumptions of such large scale models, the approach covered and interpretation of the study results in the paper seem very interesting. It could provide a valuable basis for future research.

## REFERENCE

Csaki, C., 'National Agricultural Sector Models for Centrally Planned Economies', in Johnson, Glenn and Maunder, A.H., *Rural Change,* Proceedings of the 17th International Conference of Agricultural Economists, Gower, 1981, pp. 312–23.

## DISCUSSION – RAPPORTEUR: RAMESH SHARMA

Four participants from the floor commented on the paper by Professor Csaki on three issues: uncertainty aspects, private versus state farms, and pricing assumptions. It was asked whether elements of uncertainty and producer decision models were incorporated in the model. Another speaker asked about trends in production from the private and household sector compared with that of the large state farms, and if these aspects were included in the model. On the free trade scenario of the model, assumptions for pricing in the CMEA countries are important and a question raised was whether these prices relate to world prices or were they centrally planned?

In response Professor Csaki replied that free trade generally means trade within the CMEA countries. He pointed out that as these countries are centrally planned, uncertainty and producer decision models are not considered. The model cannot shed much light on separate production from the private and household sector, but this sector is closely related to the public sector. He reckoned that these models are as useful to CMEA countries as they are for market economies.

Participants in the discussion included J.P. Hrabovszky, M.G. Chandrakanth, J.F. Martin and W. Henrichsmeyer.

# SECTION VI

## *International Aspects of Agricultural Development*

H. E. BUCHHOLZ

# *Domestic or Regional Price-Income Policies for Farmers in Relation to International Trade*

A common feature of agricultural policy and of trade policy is that well established economic principles in both areas are more often violated than in other fields of economic activity. Both policies in the domain of agriculture are closely interrelated and frequently the deviations from economic standards in agricultural policy are the cause for distortions of trade policies for agricultural products. The interdependence of both fields of policy have attracted extensive consideration due to the increased importance that agricultural policy has regained in the process of economic development in many parts of the world, and due to the substantial shifts that throughout the past decades occurred in the direction of international trade flows of agricultural products.

Under the contraints of space and time for presentation given for a paper at this conference it cannot be expected that the agricultural and trade policy problems can be taken up in full detail. Difficulties in coping with this topic are enhanced by the basic differences that exist in the policy approach under different economic systems and at different stages of economic development. The antagonistic poles being represented by market economies and centrally planned economies on the one hand, and by the degree of industrialization and overwhelming reliance on agriculture on the other. Moreover, there exists a large body of literature pertaining to both agricultural and trade policies where theoretical as well as operational aspects have been treated in every possible detail. Finally, problems of both areas of interest have been recurrent themes of contributions to previous conferences of this association such that most participants are well aware of many of the relevant details. The paper, therefore, concentrates on a discussion of policy objectives, characterizes the policy performance of important countries or regions and tries to summarize the impact of growth and equity. This takes into account the basically different position and tasks of the agricultural sector in industrialized and developing countries.

## OBJECTIVES OF PRICE-INCOME POLICIES

Agriculture, as any other economic sector, is required to contribute to economic growth and to make the necessary adjustments to achieve optimal growth. Agricultural policies, therefore, should be designed to facilitate this process by providing guidance for positive adjustment. That is, policies with respect to agriculture need to be considered in relation to broad economic objectives and action taken in the pursuit of agricultural policy objectives have to reconcile the macroeconomic conditions and constraints under which the economy is operating (OECD, 1965). It is widely accepted that optimal recourse allocation throughout all subsectors of an economy is a prerequisite of economic growth and economic welfare. Efficient resource use is a fundamental issue because ultimately the level of efficiency determines what incomes society has available to pursue its objectives. There are, however, basically different views with respect to the type of economic system that is most appropriate to achieve optimum efficiency.

Countries with market economies operate on the basis of liberal doctrine and under a system of decentralized decision-making, that is, the basic decisions are taken by individuals and the market forces help to co-ordinate them. Principally, thus, the interaction of prices, costs, profits and losses should determine what is produced and how the rewards are distributed. Under this perception the pricing mechanism fulfils the basic task of product valuation, resource allocation and distribution of income and does also provide the necessary incentives for dynamic change and growth. Theory suggests that in this way the most efficient resource use and optimal distribution of factor income is to be attained, given that certain assumptions hold.

Protagonists of centrally planned economies hold that the complex economic decisions cannot be left to the vagaries of the market because not only efficient allocation of resources is impossible to achieve in this way but, as a consequence, the distribution of rewards would be inequitable and unjust. Therefore, the production objectives, the methods employed and the distribution of income have to be determined by the central government.

In economic reality neither of the two approaches is practised in all its rigour. Especially in market economies many exemptions from pure economic requirements are made on the basis of equity and social justice considerations and with the objective of counteracting imperfections of the market system in these areas. Agriculture is a case in point. There is hardly any country with completely free markets for agricultural products and perhaps no other group of products for which market policies deviate more strikingly from the principles of the free enterprise system. The specific features of the agricultural sector including its dependence on natural conditions, the fact that food is a fundamental human requirement and the adjustment pressure which dynamic economic growth exerts especially on farm labour create special efficiency problems. In addition, agricultural markets over time have shown considerable price instability with consequential low returns to resources employed in the farm sector. Differential income levels and income distribution have raised concerns about equity within and between farm and non-farm sectors.

In *developed market economies* the questions relating to income levels, income growth and equity for the rapidly declining agricultural populations is at the root of the farm problem. Most of the complex agricultural price/income stabilization and support programmes of industrialized countries focus on the farm income objective with formulations such as:

- to attain a level of real income for farm labour equal to that earned by comparable labour in other sectors of the economy, or
- to offer equality of economic and social opportunity for farm people.

Agricultural price/income stability is also seen as a contribution to general economic stability and frequently it is argued that the rate of change of major economic variables has to be kept within socially acceptable bounds. This is, however, to be achieved with the efficiency objective in mind. The programme objectives, therefore, do not fail to require also:

- to achieve a pattern of production that will make the most efficient use of farm resources in meeting the demands and needs of the consumer.

Finally, food and in particular the regular provision of national food requirements from domestic sources is considered as a matter of national security. It has to be maintained, therefore, even at a cost (Heidhues, 1979).

For the OECD countries the broad objectives which constitute the common framework of agricultural policies have been formulated as follows (OECD, 1975):

- the level and distribution of incomes accruing to farmers;
- the stability, adequacy and safety of the supply of basic farm products to consumers at reasonable prices;
- the productivity and efficiency of farm production and marketing;
- the contribution to balanced regional development and safeguarding the environment;
- the contribution to macroeconomic objectives relating to economic growth, balance of payments, inflation and employment.

These objective are often complemented at the national level by other objectives which reflect the special problems of individual countries. Agriculture is often considered as a major factor contributing to rural infrastructure including non-agricultural needs.

In *centrally planned economies* the decision processes and planning priorities usually are not discussed in public. But it is quite evident that ideologically motivated Marxist objectives have preference over other economic and social objetives. In the area of agricultural policy overriding ideological motivations have led to the collectivized structure of agriculture in these countries. Within this framework the planning objectives in the agricultural sector so far have been uniquely directed towards production and productivity increases.

In the *developing countries* agricultural policy objectives are cast in the equally broad perspective of economic development and thus depend very much on the respective stage of development. In the early stages of take-off, agriculture is the most important sector of the economy and progress in growth and development depends heavily on the performance of agriculture. The overriding goals, therefore, encompass expansion of agricultural output and exports, substitution of imports, accumulation of productive capital and the provision of a pool of labour for sectors other than agriculture. In later stages when sustained growth or semi-industrialization are achieved, policy emphasis should change towards acceleration of growth and increases of productivity. It is at such stages that problems of social equity, which play such a dominant role in the agricultural policy formation of developed countries, are gaining weight. The arising conflicts can become especially severe when food price policies that are no longer consistent with the state of development are pursued further. Interference with agricultural prices for purposes other than agricultural development is characteristic of the agricultural policy situation in many of the developing countries. As specific objectives the following are frequently encountered:

- price intervention in agricultural product markets either to extract from agriculture the capital required for industrial growth or to raise government revenues;
- high cost for agricultural inputs to protect domestic industries;
- provision of low cost food for urban consumers.

Specific income policies for the agricultural population in developing countries are rarely found.

## TRADE POLICY OBJECTIVES

Trade policies comprehend all national and international measures that affect the conditions for commodity exchange among countries. The national attitudes towards international trade largely determine whether trade flows are allowed to move more or less unrestrictedly or not. Within a setting of liberal trade policies it is expected that:

- the expansion of international trade on the basis of economic specialization and division of labour leads to higher levels of welfare in the participating countries;
- co-operative solutions to important international economic and political problems are arrived at (Johnson, 1950).

It has been shown that these general objectives need not be in contradiction to national agricultural price income goals (Johnson, 1950 p. 8).

The liberal trade stance is supported by a considerable body of elaborate theories (Bhagwati, 1981; Chenery, 1961). Based on the principles of comparative advantage and under logical, consistent and rather general assumptions it has been proved many times that there are gains from allowing nations to trade and that restrictions in the free movement of goods ultimately lead to losses of welfare. Empirical evidence, especially in the post-World War II period with high growth rates in the volume of world trade and sustained economic growth, also supports the hypothesis that free trade conditions contribute to economic welfare. This extends also to the developing countries which, on balance, have profited much from favourable trading conditions. The specific advantages of pro trade policies for the development process over and above the expansion of output and subsequent income gains through specialization and improved utilization of resources are to be seen in:

- utilization of scale economies;
- introduction of new products, new technologies, new opportunities for learning and improvement of human capital;
- stimuli and pressures from international competition which can be a major source of motivation.

On the other hand, there are diverging developments. For one thing it is not to be overlooked that actual trade policies of the majority of countries participating in international trade have become more protectionist. At the same time scientists have become more restrained to generalize the policy and welfare implications of their theoretical findings (Corden, 1974; Schuh, 1981). It is recognized that the general proposition always to expect positive gains from trade cannot be upheld in all circumstances. Moreover, the awareness has grown that neoclassical trade theory is preoccupied with problems of allocative efficiency and has more or less neglected questions of distribution and equity (Warley, 1976).

## INTERRELATION OF AGRICULTURAL AND TRADE POLICIES

There is a basic conflict between agricultural price-income policies and liberal trade policies. To the extent that agricultural price policies are designed to maintain certain price levels independently from developments in international markets, interference with international commodity flows becomes unavoidable, that is price support schemes with prices fixed above world market prices cannot work without trade interventions for the respective commodities. With the aim of stabilizing the domestic price level and to prevent repercussions of world market price fluctuations on the domestic market a considerable arsenal of policy instruments is available to bridge the gap between the differing price levels. Domestic markets can become almost completely isolated from price movements on world markets and price competition between domestic and international supplies may become almost eliminated.

Thus, the level of protection has become one of the basic factors in the determination of agricultural production and this in turn determines what possibilities exist for international commodity flows. The methods used to bring about protection in this connection have a decisive influence on the degree of competition as well as on stability in international markets. The way in which protection is granted determines whether foreign competition may or may not exert an influence on the volume and price levels of national agricultural production. In this respect over time a gradual escalation towards higher and more sophisticated forms of protection has taken place. Up to the 1920s import tariffs were the commonly used trade policy instruments. Tariffs basically increase the import value but are rarely prohibitive and do not level out the impact of price fluctuations from external markets. Beginning in the world economic crisis of the 1930s agricultural protection increased in scope and effectiveness. Governments began to introduce a number of other trade regulating instruments, among them import quotas and export subsidies as the most prominent. Later on these were followed by deficiency payments and the famous variable import levies and export restitutions (Bale and Lutz, 1979). This had the primary effect that the chances for arbitrary and discriminatory action became greatly enhanced. Effective protection of any desired degree became a practical reality. Secondly, the possibility of trade protection for export products weakened the political support for a liberal trade policy (Johnson, 1950). The incentives for protection of the agricultural sector in total were considerably increased by the inclusion of export commodities.

While the instruments are available it still makes a difference whether and in which way they are used. A distinction can be made between short-term price stabilization efforts and permanent price support schemes.

Short-term price stabilization aims at eliminating erratic fluctuations of market prices while following more or less the underlying long term price trends. If carried out properly such policies permit farmers to make resource allocation and production decisions according to the long-term market price perspectives. Such price stabilization schemes which make only limited use of subsidies can support farm incomes in periods of depressed international prices and may thus avoid a serious deterioration of existing production and export potentials. The preservation of a country's agricultural potential can be considered as positive with respect to an international division of labour and resource allocation.

The influence of permanent price support measures on trade is more serious, since lasting distortions of allocation and production are to be expected. The experience of countries that have adopted such policies have shown that domestic support prices tend to be fixed above market clearing prices. Therefore, agricultural production is attracting more production resources and the resulting volume of production is higher than otherwise would be the case. Higher production in combination with tight import controls has negative effects on the volume of trade. Moreover, in cases where high domestic price levels have led to high surplus production there is a tendency to dispose of such surpluses on international markets by means of public support. This then leads to trade disturbances to the detriment of other exporters. The result is not necessarily a larger or smaller volume of trade but primarily a problem of distorted competition between domestic and foreign producers. In addition governments have tended to supplement or substitute price policies by more selective aids of a structural, regional or environmental character, which have counteracted more cautious price policies to a considerable extent. More recently proposals to replace price policies by direct income transfers to farmers have come into discussion in order to reduce the supply stimulating effect of price support while maintaining the relative income position of producers. Direct income support measures, however, are likewise hardly production neutral. This is evident in such cases where the payments are linked with the volume of production or with the use of certain factor inputs. But, unless the level of direct income support is restricted to guarantee a bare minimum existence, undesired production and allocation effects result also from schemes where support is extended on a personal basis.

In total, therefore, it can be summarized that as far as the price income policies of developed market economies are concerned these often have the effects of shifting the disequilibria from the factor markets to the product markets. In the absence of supply control measures the combined results often lead to increased instability in international agricultural markets and to distorted competition among the participants in these markets. On the other hand there is little indication that the adjustment problems in the agricultural sector are diminishing. It is known that only under very narrow short term conditions can trade restrictions lead to positive economic effects. In the long run, almost inevitably, protectionist measures will result in losses of economic efficiency. The incentives for structural adjustment are reduced so long as the price distortions are maintained and support prices guarantee higher returns and higher incomes than competing non-protected production. Under the influence of agricultural policy objectives stated earlier many countries evidently are prepared to accept such losses of economic efficiency and there are prospects that such tendencies may, with the advent of slower growth and more constrained labour markets, even become more pronounced.

As a consequence of development strategies prevailing over the last decades the internal agricultural terms of trade in developing countries in many cases turned against agriculture (Johnston, 1970). The domestic agricultural policies of most of these countries were designed to lower the prices of food and agriculture products and to increase the prices of manufactured products. Import and export controls, foreign exchange policies, taxation, direct price and other market control measures, such as restrictions of interregional commodity flows, have been used as instruments for such purposes. The underlying economic rationale was mainly based on the assumptions that:

- small-scale agricultural producers are not very responsive to price incentives and that large-scale farmers would benefit most from higher prices;
- higher food prices would adversely affect the low income urban consumers;
- policies that result in low agricultural prices and increase prices of industrial goods will result in more rapid economic growth and in the end lead to an improved distribution of income.

Nowadays every one of these assumptions has become severely questioned. More and more it became apparent that as a result of such policies the potential of the agricultural production capacity remains underutilized and that lagging agricultural output increasingly constitutes an impediment to overall economic growth. The reduced rate of food supply is the most important reason why, in the long run, low price policies tend to be of limited success in reaching their primary purpose, that is to enable a rapid industrial growth through provision of sufficient low price food, the major wage good in a low income economy (de Haen, 1981). Opportunities to improve developing countries' positions in the export markets cannot be exploited fully because of insufficient supply. Within the agricultural sector, employment may become restricted when price relations are biased against labour intensive products. Finally the desired distributional effects may not work out as expected. For one thing, low prices increase the rural-urban income gap and the benefits from low food prices frequently do not reach the urban poor but serve to increase profits and/or improve the income situation of the middle and higher income groups. By now it is also sufficiently documented that agricultural aggregate output is more responsive to price incentives than sometimes was postulated (Schultz, 1978). Based on such evidence a number of countries have initiated a reorientation of their respective price policies which is leaning more towards efforts to co-ordinate agricultural, trade and development policies.

## POLICY PERFORMANCE

We find today that the problems arising out of increasing agricultural protectionism are at least of as much concern among developed countries as they are affecting the relations between developed and developing countries. The EEC has emerged as a major importing region for agricultural products, whereas the North American countries nowadays are the main suppliers of exports of temperate zone products. The developing countries have a tendency to fall back to their role of suppliers of tropical products. As a rather new phenomenon the central plan countries have appeared as regular customers on the international markets of temperate zone agricultural products.

The Common Agricultural Policy of the EEC is known to be protectionist in character. Its objectives have been pursued primarily through policies of product price maintenance. While trading interests of third countries have not been entirely overlooked, they have been subordinated to the objectives of improving the economic and social position of farmers in the member countries. To this end, community farm prices have been set at levels in general above those prevailing for the same or comparable products on world markets. The predominant use of variable import levies as an instrument of agricultural protection has effectively isolated internal prices from the influence of external supplies. Imports from third countries have thus been forced into a position of residual supplies. As a consequence there has been a tendency within the community to give producers incentives for the increase of production which has resulted in an increase of export surpluses of such products that could not be sold on the internal market at the going market price. The system of protection is, however, not all comprehensive. A number of important import products are not or only minimally protected, among them vegetable oil and protein, certain feed products, agricultural raw materials and tropical products. This has contributed to the strong import position of the EEC in total agricultural trade. In international negotiations the EEC has adopted the position that expansion of agricultural markets must occur within the framework of a regulated international trading régime. Emphasis has been put on stabilization by long term agreements and access to supplies. External attempts to press for changes of the domestic farm support system have been resisted vehemently.

Other Western European countries have similar agricultural structures. The agricultural and trade policy approach, therefore, is not basically different from that of the EEC. The instruments used differ in scope and intensity but not in direction.

In the United States the core of the farm policy has been to find acceptable solutions whereby farm income objectives can be co-ordinated with the necessity to remain competitive on domestic and export markets and to adjust the continuing excess production capacity of her agriculture in order to keep carry-over stocks at manageable levels. Agricultural price stabilization and support efforts are high ranking objectives. The US farm policy is characterized by much formal legislation as is documented in the series of Agricultural Adjustment Acts since the 1930s. Measures of supply control, government purchase and domestic food programmes have been used in different combinations. Farm exports have become an important factor to maintain farm sector income. The United States has favoured liberal trade policies for that part of crop production where the competitive advantages of domestic supplies are particularly favourable, that is especially wheat, feed grains and soya beans. For such products the United States has followed rather aggressive strategies to expand foreign markets. Multilateral liberalization of farm products is considered as an optimum trade strategy with respect to a number of domestic policy objectives including price and income stability, sustaining the balance of payments and minimizing the need for government intervention and budget expenditures. On the other hand, some crop products and the bulk of animal production remained highly protected from international competition. As Johnson (1977, p. 298) has formulated, the US farm and trade policy has continued to be torn between the need to expand exports of some farm products – because otherwise the domestic adjustment problems could be met only by programmes that were too costly to be politically viable – and the unwillingness to reduce significantly its barriers to the imports of several farm products that are produced at a comparative disadvantage.

In exporting countries, such as Canada, Australia and New Zealand, with highly efficient agricultural production the relative importance of agricultural exports is quite large. These countries unanimously strive for better trading conditions on world markets. The dependence on agricultural exports is particularly distinct in Australia and New Zealand since high protection of other industries led to a loss of competitiveness on markets of manufactured products.

Agricultural price income policies in Japan are based on various schemes according to the products concerned. Rice marketing is under direct control of the government. For other crop products the government intervenes in the market to guarantee minimum prices for producers. For some other products deficiency payments are granted. The country has a considerable food import demand and thus has a major interest in access to supplies. Japan is, therefore, in favour of trade arrangements that would result in security of supplies at stable prices. Food security is also the main motivation for the high level protection granted to domestic agricultural production.

Agricultural policies of the USSR and other centrally planned countries as documented in the various recent 5 year plans are striving to increase food production to meet the growing demand for improved diets in these countries. Emphasis is placed on co-ordination of production functions and on improved linkages with supply industries and marketing channels. Food subsidies and investments to increase the production capacity of agriculture take a high percentage of budget appropriations. Recent shortcomings in the production performance gave rise to a number of incentives to encourage private sector production in most of these countries. Trade in agricultural products is used as an instrument to pursue the specific needs of domestic policy objectives (Paarlberg, 1976). However, since centrally planned economics have nearly complete government control over imports and exports, changes in trade flows are not solely a reflection of changes in basic economic variables. There is little participation in multilateral trading arrangements. Long term bilateral contracts are increasingly used to secure imports.

For the large group of developing countries it is difficult to find a common denominator to characterize the national agricultural price-income policies. There are, however, two features that are to be observed rather commonly. One is, and this has been elaborated on already, the fact that real prices received by farmers in developing countries have been substantially lower than prices received by farmers in developed countries. According to Peterson (1979) differences in real farm prices of the order of magnitude of four to five times are common between the most and least favoured nations. Peterson (1979) also states 'the evidence also supports the hypotheses that the long-run aggregate supply elasticity for agriculture is greater than one and that unfavourable farm prices have reduced significantly agricultural output and economic growth in many LDCs'. In contrast to this, there seems to have set in another rather general trend in actual policy performance. The traditional export orientation (plantation crops and so on) of the agricultural sector in LDCs is increasingly supplemented by determined efforts to improve the domestic food situation. The reorientation is not confined to the price policy approach but is pursued in a much broader framework and puts equal emphasis on advances in the material and institutional rural infra-structures. Within the context of development approaches such as Leibenstein's (1957) concept of 'critical minimum effort' growth of farm income is considered an important precondition for the agricultural sector to contribute optimally to overall growth and development. Following such policies, encouraging responses have been observed in countries where agricultural resources are sufficiently available, population growth and density is within acceptable bounds and collective solidarity and social discipline are geared towards national development priorities. There is little indication, on the other hand, that the foreign exchange surpluses of the oil exporting countries are systematically used to expand the agricultural resource base in order to decrease the long term dependence on food imports of these countries. At the other extreme we find a number of low income countries which will have to rely on international support for a long time, no matter what changes in agricultural policies are adopted. In international negotiations the majority of developing countries have rallied behind the requests for a new international economic order (NIEO). In relation to agricultural trade the discussion of the NIEO concentrates on two main issues: (a) the stabilization of commodity markets and (b) the provision of aid.

## ASPECTS OF GROWTH AND EQUITY

The developed countries during the 1950s and 1960s at high levels of GNP have had an extended period of strong overall economic growth which during the 1970s began to level off. The role of the agricultural sector and of particular policies in this process is largely inconclusive because of the many interdependent relationships involved. Looking at the growth rates it can be stated that agricultural growth in these countries was equal and often higher than economic growth. But there remain questions as to whether more positive adjustment could have been achieved by a different use of the given set of agricultural policy instruments that would have allowed for more international competition. The need for further adjustment has not diminished yet, especially in the European countries. With slow economic growth and reduced employment opportunities outside agriculture the conditions for adjustment have become more unfavourable. Expansion of agricultural output, therefore, is likely to attain even more importance as a means to reach the stated farm income objectives.

The growth performance of developing countries in terms of growth rates was likewise high, but the generally lower GNP levels have to be kept in mind. Moreover high population growth rates have caused income growth per caput to come out much more unfavourably. The growth objectives set for the first and second development decades thus in general were not met. But there is also considerable variability among countries. Given the large share of agricultural employment in these countries it is quite obvious that the performance of the agricultural sector has a large and direct influence on the overall growth record. There are countries where over the past 20 years agricultural policies have favourably contributed to integrate the agricultural sector into the overall growth and development process and there are others that have failed in this respect (for examples see World Bank, 1979 and 1981). To a substantial extent misconceptions about agricultural price-income policies have contributed to unsatisfactory growth results. In quite a number of countries the importance of agricultural growth for the development process has been underestimated and agricultural policies have failed to provide the required production incentives.

In spite of widespread agricultural protection in developed countries and frequently inadequate agricultural policies in developing countries, international trade in agricultural products has expanded. But its share in total world trade has declined and its structure and composition have shifted to the disadvantage of developing countries. As suppliers of tropical products the developing countries remain unchallenged. But traditional markets for such products are rather saturated, while the elasticity of supply is high. Consequently, as Lewis (1979) has formulated, for the LDCs as a whole the road to riches does not run in these directions. For markets of competing products in some cases comparative advantage has shifted to highly capitalized forms of production in developed countries (v. Urff, 1979; Houck, 1979). Development in mechanical and biological crop production technology has enhanced the efficiency of developed country suppliers in temperate zone food and feed grains as well as oilseeds. For these products developing countries are running import deficits which are increasing continuously.

With respect to equity, industrialized countries have succeeded in maintaining comparable living standards for the agricultural population but are still beset by large discrepancies in agricultural income distribution. For example, in the United States mounting concentration of agricultural production in relatively few large scale commercial farms (in 1978, 6 per cent of the total number of US producers supplied 53 per cent of total sales) and the consequences for the large number of small farms is becoming a matter of serious concern (Humphries, 1980). Similar trends exist elsewhere. The main problem is that most of the farm policies in operation have an inherent tendency to favour large-scale producers.

In developing countries equity issues extend to include the major part of the total population. In the short run, changes in relative food prices affect directly the relative and absolute real incomes of low-income people. At the same time a high proportion of the population depends on agriculture for employment and income and is, thus, affected by the long-term direction of agricultural price policies. Consequently, there are important trade-offs and conflicts between short-run influences and long-term effects of price policies on the incomes of the rural poor. It is to be observed that over the past decades the living conditions of the rural poor have not improved and may have even deteriorated. An important factor contributing to this development was high population growth; but the impact of agricultural price and income policies was also considerable. There are no easy solutions to the problems of improving the economic situation of the rural poor and opinions about strategies vary widely. Most conceptions are rooted firmly in the belief that by reliance on productivity increase and expansion of production, favourable effects of high overall growth will eventually trickle down and reach the low income strata. To quote Schuh (1980): 'The lot of the world's poor might better be served with investment policies which put more emphasis on efficiency than on equity, especially if that policy focuses on human capital and new production technology.' Others contend that the trickling down is not likely to occur or would take too long and promote approaches to satisfy basic needs directly. Such issues are largely unsolved and require thorough further analysis. As Mellor (1978) has pointed out 'the interrelationships among price, supply of wage goods, pattern of production, and income distribution are so complex, (that) only a general equilibrium analysis can unequivocally determine the various effects of specific food price policies on income distribution'.

In the face of current slow growth and widespread overall economic stagnation which has greatly enhanced the difficulties of further agricultural adjustment, it would not be realistic to simply call for a return to liberalized international trade. Solutions for the multitudinous issues and contradictions of agricultural and trade policies will have to rely very much on international negotiation and specific trade regulations. The direction of such efforts should nevertheless be to achieve again more liberalization of trade.

## REFERENCES


Bale, D. and Lutz, E., 'The Effects of Trade Intervention on International Price Instability', *AJAE,* 61, 1979, p. 512–16.

Bhagwati, J. N., *International Trade: Selected Readings,* Cambridge, Mass. and London, 1982.

Chenery, H. B., 'Comparative Advantage and Development Theory', *AER,* 51, 1961, p. 18–51.

Corden, W. M., *Trade Policy and Economic Welfare,* Oxford, 1974.

de Haen, H., 'Agricultural Price and International Trade Policy', in *Agricultural Adaptation Processes in Newly Industrialized Countries,* Proceedings of an International Seminar in Seoul/Korea, 15-20 Sept. 1980, DSE, Feldafing, and *KREI,* Seoul, 1981, pp. 192–206.

Heidhues, Th., 'The Gains from Trade: An Applied Political Analysis', in J. S. Hillman, and A. Schmitz, (eds), *International Trade and Agriculture: Theory and Policy,* Boulder, 1979.

Houck, J. P., 'Agricultural Trade: Protectionism, Policy and the Tokyo/Geneva Negotiating Round', *AJAE,* 61, 1979, p. 860–73.

Humphries, F. S., 'US Small Farm Policy Scenarios', *AJAE,* 62, 1980, p. 879–88.

Johnson, D. G., *Trade and Agriculture,* New York and London, 1950.

Johnson, D. G., 'Postwar Policies Relating to Trade in Agricultural Products', in L. R. Martin (ed.), *A Survey of Agricultural Economics Literature,* Vol. I, St. Paul, 1977, p. 295–325.

Johnston, B. F., 'Agriculture and Structural Transformation in Developing Countries: A Survey of Research', *The Journal of Economic Literature,* 8, 1970, pp. 369–404.

Leibenstein, H., *Economic Backwardness and Economic Growth,* New York, 1957.

Lewis, W. A., 'Development Strategy in a Limping World Economy', in G. Johnson and A. Maunder (eds.), *Rural Change,* Gower, 1981.

Mellor, J. W., 'Food Price Policy and Income Distribution in Low-Income Countries',

*Economic Development and Cultural Change,* 27 1978, pp. 1–26.
OECD, *Agriculture and Economic Growth:* A Report by a Group of Experts, Paris, 1965.
OECD, *Review of Agricultural Policies:* General Survey, Paris, 1975.
Paarlberg, R. L., 'The Soviet Burden on the World Food System: Challenge and Response', *Food Policy,* 1, 1976, pp. 392–404.
Peterson, W. L., 'International Farm Prices and the Social Cost of Cheap Food Policies', *AJAE,* 61, 1979, p. 12–21.
Schuh, G. E., 'US Agricultural and Trade Policy and Agricultural Development of the LDCs', in R. A. Goldberg, (ed.), *Research in Domestic and International Agribusiness Management,* Vol. 1, Greenwich, Conn., 1980, pp. 119–57.
Schuh, G.E., 'Economics and International Relations: A Conceptual Framework', *AJAE,* 63, 1981, p. 767–78.
Schultz, T. W., *Distortions of Agricultural Incentives,* Bloomington and London, 1978.
v. Urff, W., 'Verstärkte Öffnung der Agrarmärkte', in H. von der Groeben and H. Möller, (eds), *Die agrarwirtschaftliche Integration Europas,* Baden-Baden, 1979, pp. 167–180.
Warley, T.K., 'Agriculture in International Economic Relations', *AJAE,* 58, 1976, p. 820–30.
World Bank, *World Development Report 1979,* Washington, DC, 1979.
World Bank, *World Development Report 1981,* Washington, DC, 1981.

## DISCUSSION OPENING – G. GAETANI-D'ARAGONA

The main points in the very stimulating paper by Professor Buchholz are the two following:

1 A frequent conflict does arise between internal policies to support farm prices and incomes on the one hand and efforts, on the other hand, to implement free international trade for farm products and commodities.
2 On the basis of the performance of agricultural policies, in particular in the less developed countries, Professor Buchholz is extremely concerned about lack of equity between farm and non-farm incomes and among farmers of different areas and locations. Governments of the advanced countries have been relatively successful in defending farm incomes in comparison with the incomes of the industrial and of the service sectors. Their record has, however, been a poorer one so far as equity *among* different farmers is concerned.

We certainly have to agree with Professor Buchholz on the validity and relevance of the above two points. However, while the diagnosis of the situation which has been performed is the right one, the writer of the paper has been extremely vague (or too cautious) in giving us an adequate and comprehensive prognosis. It is a bit like modern medical science which does wonders in recognizing diseases but frequently is not able to cure them. However, we strongly need a valid trade and agricultural policy to improve the overall welfare of the world economy and, at the same time, to provide farmers with a reasonable level of equity.

Some points, therefore, deserve to be further clarified and answered. First of all we have to admit that world wide expansion of a completely free international trade for farm products in every situation and under every condition is not at all the best way to produce overall economic welfare and at the same time achieve incomes equity, given the high short term variability of farm prices and of incomes from the export trade of farm products and the adverse unit and overall terms of trade which prevail in the world markets for agricultural commodities, particularly the tropical ones which are mainly exported by the developing countries.

Recent reports by the international organizations, such as the FAO, do focus on the severe decline in the real prices of most of the agricultural commodities which has been progressively going on in the 20 year period 1960–81. Declines as high as 60 per cent have taken place in the real prices of rubber, tea and of some textile fibres such as jute. If we turn our attention to the realities of international trade we discover that administered markets, not free markets, prevail in the trade of farm products and agricultural commodities. The value of farm exports, which at the present time takes place under administered markets, can be equal to or more than 60 per cent of the overall value of all the exports of farm products. As a matter of fact administered markets intensively regulate the internal and external trade of the farm products of the nine EEC countries, and the trade of the centrally planned economies of Eastern Europe and of South Eastern Asia, and the bilateral medium-term trade and sale arrangements between the main exporting countries of food and feed cereals (the United States, Canada and Australia) and the main importing countries (the USSR and China). Even on empirical grounds it seems to me that valid economic and political reasons exist and have to be credited for the growing expansion of administered markets for internationally traded farm products, both on a worldwide basis and on a regional basis. Arrangements for administered trade on a regional basis are more and more the rule for many large regional areas of the world. One of the reasons for expanding administered markets is, of course, the desire by Governments to defend farming from the short-term instability of farm prices which are by far higher, as we all know, than the variability of industrial prices. While free trade, in the long run, might lead to a better spatial distribution of different crops on the basis of comparative advantages, it is also true, unfortunately, that free trade does not protect farm incomes and export revenues from serious disruptions due to the extreme short term instability of agricultural prices.

However, a second relevant reason for the spread of administered markets is, in my opinion, the absence of any kind of economic and monetary international order after the end of the Bretton Woods monetary system in 1971 at the time of the Nixon administration. Moreover, in recent years the sudden conversion of important central banks to the gospel of monetarism, as evident in the policies of the Federal Reserve Bank in the United States and of the Bank of England, has led to extreme vagaries of real interest rates and of currency exchange rates and also to the monetary induced economic recessions, the 1975 one and the one which started in 1979, the most severe after World War II. A negative consequence of extremely high interest rates has been the very burdensome financial costs which are required to finance adequate stocks of supply for availability purposes in the markets of agricultural commodities. Stocks are also a prerequisite for the performance of commodity agreements between exporting and importing countries. A different situation prevailed in the 1950s and 1960s when adequate stocks of the main agricultural commodities contributed to a great extent to the stabilization of world commodity markets. As we know, the agricultural policy of the EEC has been exposed to severe criticism. However, let us recognize that a stable level of minimum prices which has been given to European farmers from the price policy of the Common Market has defended an important sector of the European economy, the agricultural one, from the disrupting effects on farm incomes of the 1975–6 world recession and of the more severe one which began in 1980 and which is not yet over. A worse happening, by comparison, has negatively affected the export revenues of the less developed countries which export agricultural commodities in the free markets. The slump of prices in the international markets, due to the economic and industrial recession, has severely reduced their incomes by adversely affecting the terms of trade of their exports, particularly of tropical commodities for industrial utilization.

Even if the advanced nations will ever be able in the future to return to some kind of monetary co-operation after the vagaries of interest and exchange rates of recent years, in my opinion, policies have to be implemented to defend farm export revenues from short term instability: such as the Common Fund for eighteen commodities of the UNCTAD agreements of 1980, multilateral commodity agreements relying on buffer stocks and quotas, financial schemes such as the Food Facility of the IMF and the Stabex mechanism which has been in operation between the EEC and the so-called ACP developing countries in order to compensate the export revenues of the latter countries from sudden decline.

Another point, adequate types of Government intervention on the domestic front have to be formulated in order to guarantee an acceptable level of equity not only *between* farm and non-farm incomes but also *among* farmers of different area and location.

On the basis of the experience of the agricultural institutions of the Common Market, a valid approach for the advanced countries might be an agricultural policy which relied less on the rigid support of farm prices and far more on direct income transfers and payments by the Government in favour of marginal farmers. Such a policy would give equity among farmers and would also reduce the damages of excess production of farm crops in the advanced countries, which have been very frequent in the last twenty years in the EEC countries as the result of a rigid support of farm prices at high levels.

JIMMYE S. HILLMAN AND ERIC A. MONKE

# *International Transfer of Agricultural Technology*

## INTRODUCTION

Few would argue with the proposition that technological innovation lies at the heart of successful agricultural development. Yet the transformation of traditional agriculture remains largely incomplete, as more than half of the world's agricultural producers operate under technological constraints that have changed little during the twentieth century. This situation is not a consequence of lack of effort to find new technology – almost all less developed countries (LDCs) have attempted to introduce new intermediate inputs (seeds and fertilizer) or new capital inputs (animal or mechanical devices). Government policies related to land improvement investment, credit availability and controls over importation of inputs such as fertilizer are partly to blame for the slow rate of generation and diffusion of new technology. But more important, market and subsistence orientated farmers alike have shunned new technologies because they offer lower profits or productivity than the traditional technology. Thus the problem of technological change lies primarily with the 'appropriateness' of the new technology for the biological and economic environments of the technology-seeking country.

This essay reviews the substantial literature on agricultural technology transfer, with a focus on the key economic and institutional constraints which account for the stagnation of agricultural technology in LDCs. The principal components of the arguments presented here are drawn from Schultz (1964), Hayami and Ruttan (1971) and Binswanger and Ruttan (1978). The failure of local institutions to develop new technologies has forced a reliance on international sources of both the private and public type. But profit constraints and differences in resource scarcity provide fundamental economic barriers to the development of new technology by foreign private interests, particularly with respect to staple food production. The international research institutes, with the exception of the rice and wheat centres, have also experienced difficulty in the development of widely-adapted and economically efficient technologies. The lack of an effective profit motive or other form of accountability to producers and consumers, and difficulties in the identification of relative resource scarcities of a particular region, again provide a rationale for the failure to develop new technologies. A further difficulty arises because international centres depend primarily on developed countries (DCs) for investment funds. Since DCs see little direct benefit from these investments, high rates of return from successful research do not guarantee increases in financial support. These circumstances imply that the future development of efficient new technologies is likely to require the investment of additional resources at the local level.

## CONCEPTS AND DEFINITIONS

Hazell (1982) provides a useful definition of new technologies:

> If a production function $Y = f(X_1,\ldots,X_n)$ relates the maximum crop yield per acre (Y) attainable with different but permissible combinations of inputs ($X_i$), such as seed, fertilizer and weeding labor, then I shall take the function f() to define a technology. Changes in the combinations of inputs represent movements along the production function, e.g. using more or less fertilizer, and are better described as alternative 'techniques'. However, a change in the quality of seed which leads to a structural shift in the production function, and increases the per acre yield with the same level of inputs, is clearly a 'new technology'.

The distinction by Hazell between techniques and technologies is useful because the barriers to the adoption of each are likely to be different. For example, the availability of credit and fertilizer supplies are likely to have a much greater impact on the level of nitrogen applications per acre than on the variety of seed chosen by the farmer. The introduction of a new technology by local innovation or transfer from outside requires advances in knowledge *and* changed availability of inputs. Schultz (1964) points out that the two elements are inextricably linked. Increased agricultural productivity results from sequential advances in knowledge, changes in the supply of new material inputs, and advances in producers' know-how. Advances in knowledge are differentiated into two categories. One set consists of material things which have come from basic discoveries in the sciences and engineering. The advance in knowledge in this case becomes inextricably associated with the material substance. For example, knowledge with respect to genetic engineering becomes part of the genes. The other set consists of changes in farm practices.

The former set is of principal interest in this paper. This focus is not meant to imply that changes in management practice cannot create increased productivity. Production functions can be modified without introducing new material inputs. Illustrations of this phenomenon are commonplace: changes in rotation, tillage, cultivation practices, seeding rates, irrigation techniques, and the timing of all these.[1] In all cases total resource availabilities are unvaried. Nor are scale economies involved.

Skills, however, become perfected. The key point is that the changes in farm management practices involve improvements in the use of modern technologies. As Schultz has argued, much of the potential for improved management practices within the confines of traditional agricultural technologies has already been exhausted. Thus changes in management practices may be regarded as a second source of productivity increase, but dependent on the initial introduction of a new collection of inputs.

Where can the new input packages and cost-reducing technologies be found? If existing agricultural technologies are not sufficiently productive, then a new technology must be developed locally or transferred from developed countries. If reliance on the international community becomes the principal alternative, a second dichotomy is created by the choice between private, profit-orientated organizations (particularly, multinational corporations – MNCs) and public, internationally-financed sources. The ultimate course followed in the transfer of technology is likely to be a mixture of all alternatives.

## TECHNOLOGY: PROBLEMS IN PRODUCING ONE'S OWN

The theory of induced innovation, introduced by Hayami and Ruttan (1971), focuses on those cases where technologies are produced and diffused indigenously. Factor scarcities or factor prices influence the direction of technical change for the production of a particular commodity. Technical change is directed toward saving the scarce or more expensive factors; that is, saving proportionally more of the scarce factor than of the abundant factor per unit of output measured at constant factor prices. Hayami and Ruttan examined and compared the experiences of Japan and the United States, countries with highly productive agricultural systems which represent the extremes in terms of resource endowment. Japan has little land and much labour, and the United States has abundant land but expensive labour. The agricultural development pattern of the two countries proceeded along radically different paths. Japanese development emphasized yield-increasing innovations, while United States agriculture became increasing land-extensive.

The theory of induced innovation suggests, with some qualifications, that technical change can be treated as endogenous to the development process. The theory has subsequently been elaborated by Binswanger and Ruttan (1978) to develop a theory of induced institutional innovation analogous to the theory of induced technical innovation. While these treatments emphasize economic factors, these researchers remain aware of other forces that could also affect the transfer of technology, such as 'an autonomous thrust toward the accumulation of knowledge', '(natural) constraints on what can be discovered', and 'changes in the evolution of ideas in the general cultures' (Binswanger and Ruttan, p. 4).

The key element of the induced innovation process is the presence of a response by researchers to local resource scarcity and an information dissemination network. Research scientists are aware of local resource constraints and are responsive to these constraints if their salary and job security are somehow dependent on their contributions to the development of new technologies. An extension service or news information service provides a conduit through which producer perceptions about resource scarcity can be transmitted to scientists. This network appears lacking in most LDCs. The LDCs account for only 4 per cent of world agricultural research and development expenditures. A similar pattern persists with respect to expenditures in other research and development (R and D) efforts – only one per cent of global research and development expenditures in health, agriculture, housing and industrial technology are made by developing countries (Paarlberg, 1982). As a result, LDCs lack national agricultural research systems comparable to those which exist in any of the major advanced agricultural countries. Even in the middle-income countries, which have some long-established research institutes, there are inadequate means to keep abreast of advances in the biological sciences, laboratory and field methods and equipment.

It is difficult to explain why, in light of current information about the payoff to knowledge and to investment in physical and institutional infrastructures, developing countries have not moved more rapidly to increase R and D activities. A century ago there were few places in the world where grain yields were significantly greater than one metric ton per hectare. Since then, as shown by Yamada and Ruttan (1975), differences in output per hectare per worker have widened considerably. Differences such as these have not been due to changes in resource endowments; nor, necessarily, to inherent differences in endowments between regions. They have been due principally, instead, to technical and institutional innovation and to investments that have improved the capacity of land and labour to respond to output-increasing opportunities. Additional evidence of the importance of local R and D is provided by Jennings and Cock (1975) in their argument that a technology that is productive in the centre of origin can be more successfully introduced where there is less biological stress on the new cultivar. If the R and D institute is located outside the centre of origin, local development may be rapid, but the transferability of the technology and its impact on productivity will be limited.

Part of the explanation for lagging investment may lie with the constancy of real prices for grains on the international markets over the past two decades. Expanded imports of grain have played an important role in the maintenance of domestic consumer subsidy programmes, as net imports grew by over 100 million metric tons over the past three decades. Technological advances in both the DCs and LDCs have enabled the fulfilment of these increasing demands at constant real prices. This constancy meant that government expenditure on subsidy programmes needed to increase only in so far as domestic income and population increased. Since government revenues are commonly related to these variables, lags in domestic grain production did not provoke the sense of urgency so often necessary to induce changes in government policy.

Investment in agricultural research and development retained a low priority in the allocation of government expenditure.

In addition to lagging investments, a second set of reasons for the absence of local innovation in agricultural technology revolves around the lack of economic incentives for LDC scientists. Rewards in the form of promotion and salary are not necessarily tied to contributions to the development of new technology. Educational institutions of the developed countries (DCs) may also be partially responsible for existing circumstances. As a consequence of low investment in educational facilities, most research scientists necessarily receive their training in DC institutions. They may study with scientists who are responsive to factor scarcity, but the type of factor scarcity in the developed country is likely to be entirely different from that which prevails in the home country. Thus, it is not unusual to find Ph.D. candidates in agricultural sciences from LDCs engaged in the study of biological and production problems which are of no relevance to their home country.[2]

## TECHNOLOGY TRANSFER

Failure to develop new technologies *via* an indigenous process forces a reliance on foreign sources, particularly the developed countries. A number of historical examples suggest that imported technologies can provide benefits to the importing country. Many European practices were directly transferred to the United States in the nineteenth and twentieth centuries. Early Japanese international collaboration with Germany and the Indian-British colonial relationship also proved conducive to the building of national research and extension systems and the spread of technologies (Hanrahan, 1981). A common property of these successful transfers is neutrality of the technology with respect to the factor endowments of the exporting and importing country. For agricultural technology the list of directly transferable technologies is short, due to differences in climate and factor scarcity. Improved seeds and other genetic modifications may be an exception to the above generalization; but even in these cases yield performance is often dependent on a number of complementary inputs, such as fertilizer, irrigation, and land development. For some LDC-LDC transfers, the climatic and factor endowment differences may be less severe problems. But low investment in R and D by the LDCs has done little to expand the shelf of potential new technologies.

Problems arise with the international technology transfer process when the imported technology does not represent a minimum social cost method of production. If the new technology is not a minimum cost method of production only government tax and subsidy policies can sustain it. Otherwise, the new technology will quickly disappear. Producers with traditional technologies will not adopt higher cost/lower profit methods of production, regardless of the vintage of the technology.[3] An illustration of this circumstance involves the attempt to introduce irrigated rice technologies to Liberia and the Ivory Coast (Pearson et al., 1981). Labour is a relatively scarce factor in both countries while land is abundant. Upland rice cultivation is the dominant type of traditional technology. The new Asian technologies, however, are labour intensive and under West African factor prices were less profitable than the traditional technologies. Government subsidy programmes necessary to sustain the new technology were of a limited magnitude in Liberia and of a limited duration in the Ivory Coast. As a result, the new technology was not adopted on a significant scale. In addition to factor price differences, cross-country differences in institutional structures (such as communications networks and equipment repair facilities) or policy objectives of employment and income distribution can result in the imposition of an inappropriate technology.

Where governments are more determined to adopt new technologies, subsidies on input use and protection against imports of the final product can be used to make new technologies more profitable than traditional technologies. A problem arises because technologies appear appropriate from a private perspective but inappropriate from a social perspective. Inefficiency of resource allocation is the result, with negative implications for real income levels. If the new technologies are capital and/or skilled-labour intensive relative to their traditional counterparts, adoption may have a deleterious impact on employment of unskilled labour and income distribution. Gotsch (1971) provides an illustration of these consequences in which adoption of 'Green Revolution' wheat technologies in the Punjab of Pakistan utilized mechanical rather than labour intensive methods of production. One reason for this adoption pattern was the significant subsidization of tractor usage.

If a country relies on the international community for an economically appropriate agricultural technology, it can obtain that technology from either the private sector – particularly the MNCs – or from the bilateral and multilateral public agencies. The potential for development of appropriate technology by MNCs appears greatest for two classes of products: those goods produced in the host country but not in the home country, such as coffee, cocoa, or bananas, and those products or processes which are not traded on international markets and thus must be produced in the host country, such as fresh milk. In the case of export crops, the only alternative technologies are those developed in the host countries, and profit maximization will dictate maximum usage of relatively abundant factors of production. In the case of non-traded products and processes, prices for outputs can increase to cover production costs, and thus positive profits to the MNC are possible from the onset of MNC involvement. Incentives to develop and adapt new technologies are present as well, since the firm will realize additional profit from cost-reducing innovations. Government policies to encourage competition can be utilized to ensure that non-traded goods prices will decline and tax policies can be used to guard against 'excessive' profits by the MNC.

When outputs are traded internationally or produced in the home country, the interest of MNCs in technological innovation and adaptation is likely to be more limited. Grains represent the most prominent outputs of this type. A private firm which utilizes a profitable, capital-intensive technology for production in developed countries, for example, is unlikely to have the incentive to invent labour-intensive technologies for the LDC. Prices for outputs are fixed rather than adjustable to costs of production and thus profits are not guaranteed for introduction of a 'new' technology into the LDC environment. High start-up costs, due in part to a lack of experience and understanding of LDC climatic and soil conditions, will not necessarily be recovered by subsequent increases in efficiency. Further, since these outputs are widely produced, the probability of capturing rents from successful R and D appears limited. Thus socially profitable investments need not result in private profit and investments of private capital in technological innovation will not occur. Government investment in R and D is essential for the realization of these potential gains.

If a LDC cannot obtain an appropriate technology from the private international sector, the public and semi-public sectors represent a final source of new technology. Assistance has been primarily from bilateral programmes, such as the USAID programme and the thirteen international agricultural research institutes (the Consultative Group for International Agricultural Research).[4]

Since World War II many developed countries have extended bilateral agricultural development assistance to low income countries. Notable among these are Belgium, Canada, France, Great Britain, the Netherlands, the United States, and West Germany. The United States has had the largest and most intense involvement in terms of personnel numbers, scope of locally based technology development and transfer, and the number of government institutions involved. One reason for the large US involvement was its own success with the USDA-Land Grant system. President Truman's Point IV statement that 'we now possess the knowledge to alleviate hunger...' implied that the US success story could simply be grafted on to the agricultural systems of the LDCs. Four decades later it is clear that the technology transfer programmes have not met earlier expectations. The AID Project Impact Evaluation Reports provide ample evidence to support this view.[5] The striking feature of these reports is the uniformly limited success that the bilateral assistance programme has had in creating an indigenous, sustainable research-generating and research-diffusing capacity. Substantial numbers of poor farmers have not been able to participate on a sustained basis in the results which the technology allows. Further, policies and institutions of government have not usually changed enough to allow the full benefits of the technology to filter through existing marketing systems.

Considerable analysis has been made of the technological developments of the international research institutes. Evenson and Ruttan (1978) conclude that the programming of most of the centres for research is somewhat misplaced at present, and that not more than half of the new international centres are optimally located to respond to supply and demand linkages for the transfer of knowledge and input materials.

Dalrymple (1978) enumerates several supply and demand factors that have constrained the adoption of high yielding varieties (HYVs) of rice and wheat in developing countries:

> On the supply side, (1) the present HYVs are not suitable for all soil and climate conditions, (2) they require seeds and inputs which are either not available or not fully utilized by every farmer (seed supply is still a problem in many areas), and (3) in some regions there is a strong demand for the longer straw of traditional varieties. On the demand side, (1) consumers may not prefer the HYVs over the traditional varieties, and (2) government price policies may not encourage the production of HYVs. Although increased attention has been given to developing HYVs which meet local tasks and preferences, they still may not meet all consumer requirements.

The induced innovation theory of Hayami and Ruttan allows identification of two problems which hamper the development of locally adapted technologies by international research institutes. First, the linkage between scientist performance and technological innovations may be weaker for the international institutes than for the national research systems. High turnover rates among expatriate research scientists, for example, may hamper the sequential process of problem identification and resolution inherent in the invention of new technology. Second, fundamental conflicts may arise between a crop-specific research focus and the development of technologies suitable for particular resource scarcities. Rice production, for example, occurs under both land-scarce (Asia) and labour-scarce (Africa) conditions. The principal technological advances of the International Rice Research Institute have involved responses to the former rather than the latter constraints. Technological changes in African production methods appear to hinge on mechanical innovations which would increase arable acreage per farm and on the development of improved upland rice production methods. The ability of research institutes to develop these innovations in surroundings of totally different factor proportions remains uncertain. In response to this problem, a dual system of organization employing both disciplinary and problem orientation has been introduced in several of the institutions to prevent an entrenched focus on particular disciplinary or problem sets (Ruttan, in Schultz (ed.) 1964, p. 252).

The difficulties in responding to the diverse environments in which a particular commodity is grown are confounded by the limitations on available investment resources. Numerous programmes of the international centres, such as the development of wheat and rice seed varieties, have demonstrated substantial returns to R and D investments. These rates of return are well above returns to private investment in most economic sectors and in perfect capital markets international research successes would attract increasing amounts of capital investment. While donor countries have responded to some degree to successful research, the allocation of investment remains less than optimal. Where donor countries do not directly experience the benefits of high return investment, high rates of return on R and D will have a limited impact on the resource allocation process. The receipt of investment funds by the international institutes becomes determined by political decisions of donor countries rather than by economic returns. As a result, the international institutes are forced to choose among multiple attractive investments. In the process of investment rationing certain ecological and factor-price environments are necessarily excluded.

## CONCLUSION

Economic development implies the ability to adapt technology to local conditions. Since most developing countries have lagged behind in producing their own new technologies for agricultural production, they have opted for borrowed or imported technology. Private interests, primarily MNCs, have focused efforts on areas where returns from innovation can be captured by the firm, such as export crops or products specific to the host country market. Public agencies have focused on widely traded products, in particular grains and staple starches. Private, public and semi-public attempts to transfer have had their greatest successes with technologies which are neutral with respect to the economic, biological and institutional environment into which they are transferred. Specifically, inputs such as fertilizer and pesticides which can be applied effectively along with farmer knowledge have disturbed the economic equilibrium in traditional societies. Having done so, considerable economic progress has resulted.

In numerous other cases, however, the imported technology has not been cost effective, particularly with respect to small farmers and staple food crops. The tremendous variation in the economic and ecological environments for grain production implies that wide-ranging technological change requires a large number of R and D projects. Given the politically-determined constraints on investment funds from DC donors, local adaptation and the development of appropriate technologies is likely to require an increase in indigenous research and knowledge-disseminating capacity. The focus of domestic investment should exploit regional and commodity complementarities with the efforts of the international research institute. Thus domestic programme design must be predicated on difficult judgements about the future orientation of the international institutes. Research laboratories, experiment stations, and extension organizations in themselves are no guarantee of generating and diffusing appropriate technologies, but they are critically important in linking scientists and institutions to agricultural producers and farming communities. Failure to develop these linkages via changes in national investment policies can only help perpetuate the dominance of traditional technology in agricultural production.

## NOTES

[1]Arizona farmers, for example, at one time applied 6 inches of water per irrigation in daylight hours; they now apply 2 or 3 inches at night, at times after midnight.

[2]These comments are speculative. To our knowledge the importance of initial research orientation for subsequent research performance has not been empirically demonstrated.

[3]This comment is not intended to imply that profitability is the only consideration relevant to the adoption rate of new technologies. Hazell (1982) discusses a number of additional barriers to technology transfer. Nor does the comment imply that cost minimization is the sole criterion for a choice of technology; there are other criteria such as maximization of output and full employment with which a country must contend.

[4]Other international agencies, such as the Food and Agriculture Organization, have also participated in the technology innovation effort.

[5]There have been more than thirty of these specific evaluation reports in the last two years. Examples of these are AID Project Impact Evaluation Reports, No. 2, *Kitale Maize: The Limits of Success,* May 1980; No. 27, *Korean Agricultural Research: The Integration of Research and Extension,* January, 1982; and No. 30, *Guatemala: Development of the Institute of Agricultural Science and Technology (ICTA) and its impact on Agricultural Research and Farm Productivity,* February, 1982.

## REFERENCES

Binswanger, Hans P., Ruttan, Vernon W. et al., *Induced Innovation – Technology, Institutions, and Development,* Johns Hopkins University Press, 1978.

Dalrymple, Dana G., 'Development and Spread of High-Yielding Varieties of Wheat and Rice in the Less-Developed Nations', Foreign Agricultural Economic Report No. 95, Sixth Ed, USDA, Washington, DC, 1978.

Evenson, Robert E., (Ruttan, Vernon W., Comment), 'The Organization of Research to Improve Crops and Annuals in Low-Income Countries', in T.W. Schultz, (ed.) *Distortions of Agricultural Incentives,* Indiana University Press, 1978.

Gotsch, Carl H., 'Technical Change and the Distribution of Income in Rural Areas', *American Journal of Agricultural Economics,* Vol. 54: No. 2, pp. 326–41, 1972.

Hanrahan, Charles E., 'Concentrating AID Assistance on Agricultural Research Technology Development and Institutions', paper prepared for the Joint Research Committee of AID-BIFAD, Washington, DC, 1981.

Hayami, Yujiro and Ruttan, Vernon W., *Agricultural Development; An International Perspective,* Johns Hopkins Press, 1971.

Hazell, Peter B., 'Barriers to Adoption of New Technologies at the Farm Level', paper prepared for a conference on Technological Change and Rural Development in Developing Countries, University of Delaware, 1982.

Jennings, Peter and Cock, James H., 'Centers of Origin of Crops and Their Productivity', *Economic Botany,* Vol. 31: No. 1, pp. 51–4, 1977.

Paarlberg, Robert, 'A Food Security Approach for the 1980s: Righting the Balance', *Agenda 1982,* Overseas Development Council, Washington, DC, pp. 90–3, 1982.

Pearson, S.R., Stryker, J.D. and Humphreys, C.P., *Rice in West Africa,* Stanford University Press, 1981.

Ruttan, Vernon W., in T.W. Schultz, (ed.) *Transforming Traditional Agriculture,* p. 252.

Schultz, Theodore W., *Transforming Traditional Agriculture,* Yale University Press, 1964.

Yamada, Saburo and Ruttan, Vernon W., 'International Comparisons of Productivity in Agriculture', paper presented at National Bureau of Economic Research Conference on Productivity Measurement, Williamsburg, Virginia, 1975.

## GENERAL DISCUSSION* – RAPPORTEUR: ULRICH KOESTER

It was pointed out that Dr Buchholz's evaluation of the effects of national price policies on international trade depended very much on the reference system chosen. It was questioned whether the underlying reference system of the Buchholz paper, namely free trade, was realistic. A preferable system would be where alternative instruments to price policy measures were applied, in order to achieve agriculture's income objectives. However, Dr Buchholz did not agree with this approach. He did not have an optimistic view of the suitability of direct income payments for the purpose of supporting income at a high level. He considered this instrument as supplementary to price policy and to be used in very special circumstances only. Another speaker argued that the statement 'It would not be realistic to simply call for a return to liberalized international trade' did not follow from arguments in the paper. He thought that the performance of developed countries' agricultural policies revealed little success in achieving stated agricultural policy objectives. Hence, he found it logical to argue for a substantial reduction in levels of price protection and for simplification of policies with respect to instruments and their application. Dr Buchholz, in response, felt that there might be some misunderstanding. He was not in disfavour of trade liberalization but saw many obstacles in making progress in this direction.

It was suggested that not only should the impact of restrictions in commodities be evaluated but also restrictions in movement of labour and capital. It was also pointed out that some recent research findings in international trade had been neglected. If uncertainty were taken into consideration, free trade was not the best strategy in order to maximize national welfare. The same held true if a country can affect the terms of trade. It was suggested that the author had overlooked the fact that neoclassicial trade theory does analyse distributional effects of trade policies.

Regarding the Hillman/Monke paper one participant recommended that future research activities with respect to developing new technologies should be based on quantitative models, such as those set up by the International Institute for Applied Systems Analysis. This could help to quantify the consequences of alternative technologies. Another speaker felt that behind the talk about new technology was the assumption that traditional inputs were used optionally in underdeveloped countries. He thought that this was not true. Hence, exclusive emphasis on new technologies was not warranted. It was also suggested that the quality demands of international commodity markets impose constraints upon production technology. It was regretted that many African countries had neglected their agricultural research stations since independence and had looked for other people's technologies, whose resource endowments were different. This opinion was not shared by all participants and it was pointed out that LDCs have been able to generate their own technology but still not

*Papers by Buchholz and Hillman and Monke.

proceed to implement the innovations. Therefore, it was not the agro-biological researcher who should be blamed but the agricultural economist and the agricultural extension specialists. A better education of the farming population should be the aim.

Another participant questioned whether the appropriateness of agricultural economic theory for the social and economic environments of the country should be included in the discussion of technology transfer problems. Another wondered whether the Hillman/Monke statement about labour scarcity in Africa was true. According to his knowledge there was only a shortage of labour in peak seasons and in general there was an abundance of labour. Furthermore, he wanted to know whether the recorded high turnover of expatriate staff in national research institutes was actually higher than that for international research institutes.

Dr Monke responded in his closing statement that the concept of scarcity of labour was a relative concept, labour being considered in relation to land. Therefore, labour was less scarce in Africa than in Asia. Concerning the strategy which developing countries should select, he pointed out that it would be helpful if international institutes had long-range planning. This would help to avoid duplication of international research efforts and would allow individual countries to develop their own research strategy.

Participants in the discussion included S. Tarditi, D. Colman, D. H. Penny, R. Thomsen, K. Parikh, S. H. Destipande, G. Gwyer, M. G. Chandrakanth, Yong Boo Choe and A. Weber.

JOHN W. LONGWORTH

# *Domestic Price-Income Policies for Farmers in Relation to International Trade Policies: Exporting Country*

This paper outlines the general thrust of domestic agricultural price and income policies in Australia and identifies linkages between these policies and Australian trade policy. It also highlights the extent of common interest between Australia and developing nations heavily dependent on the export of agricultural commodities.

The impact of domestic agricultural price and income policies on agricultural trade policies is generally weaker in the case of countries which are net food exporters than for food importing nations. Furthermore, the strength of the interdependence will tend to decrease as the exporter's share of the world market for its products diminishes.[1] Australian agriculture is heavily export orientated but, with some important exceptions, the Australian share of world trade in the relevant commodities is relatively small. Therefore, domestic agricultural price and income policies do not exert a strong influence over agricultural trade policies. On the other hand, and in stark contrast to the situation in most developed countries, the realities of the international market have tended to play an increasingly important role in the development of domestic price and income policies for farmers.

## AUSTRALIA AS AN AGRICULTURAL EXPORTER

In value terms Australia is about the fifth largest agricultural exporter in the world (behind the United States of America, The Netherlands, France and Brazil). Four commodities (wool, wheat, meat and sugar) are responsible for more than 80 per cent of Australia's agricultural export income. These facts and many others about Australia as an exporter of agricultural commodities are discussed by Harris (1982).

Almost all Australian farming industries of any significance (with the notable exception of dairying and fruit growing) have become increasingly dependent on overseas markets during the last two decades. Some of the major agricultural export products and the percentage of output by value exported in recent years are as follows: wool (97 per cent), wheat (83 per cent), mutton (72 per cent), sugar (72 per cent), beef (47 per cent), barley (64 per cent), skim milk powder (74 per cent), and canned (deciduous) fruit (55 per cent).

Despite steady growth in the value of both total output and exports, the Australian agricultural sector has continued to decline in economic importance relative to the rest of the economy. Agriculture now contributes only 6.8 per cent of the Gross Domestic Product and employs only 6.5 per cent of the workforce. Although agricultural exports are still responsible for almost half the nation's total export income, the increase in the export of minerals and energy resources since the late 1960s has substantially reduced the dependence of the Australian economy on the export of rural products. Nevertheless, since trade plays a bigger part in the Australian economy than is the case for most other countries, international trade in agricultural commodities remains of vital concern to the Australian people.

## AGRICULTURAL PRICE-INCOME POLICIES IN AUSTRALIA

There are important constraints which have greatly influenced the development of price and income policies for farmers in Australia. Nevertheless, a remarkable diversity of measures have been tried at different times and in respect to different industries. Over time, there has been a gradual shift in emphasis in regard to both policy goals and policy instruments.

### *Constraints*

The division of powers between the state and federal governments under the Australian Constitution severely limits the scope for effective price-income policies not only for farmers but also for all sectors of the Australian economy. For instance the Constitution assigns control over production to the Australian States thus making nationwide production control an extremely difficult policy instrument to implement. Section 92, which guarantees free trade between the States, is another part of the Constitution which has proven a major obstacle to agricultural policies. As Campbell (1980, pp. 90–2) has pointed out, institutions and procedures have been developed to overcome these Constitutional problems. For example, the Australian Agricultural Council and its Standing Committee were set up in 1934 to facilitate the formal discussion of agricultural policy issues between the federal government and the various state governments. As a result of Section 92, the implementation of a national price or income policy measure requires complementary legislation at both the Federal and State level. In some cases (for example sugar) only one state is involved (Queensland) and reaching agreement is relatively easy. However, when a number of states are required to consider and to pass complementary legislation (for example in the case of wheat), achieving a consensus may be extremely difficult.

Australia is unique among advanced countries in having a significant political party representing farmer interests. The National Country Party (NCP) is the junior member of the two-party coalition which has governed Australia since 1949 (except for the 1972 to 1975 period). The declining economic and demographic importance of the rural sector has not, as yet, substantially reduced the political power of the NCP at the federal level. Nevertheless, the need for State Governments to pass complementary legislation provides opportunities for political point-scoring even when state and federal governments are of the same political persuasion.

Despite the existence of the NCP, political constraints to agricultural price and income policy options have become more important as the farm sector has declined in economic and electoral importance. The increase in the proportion of total output which is exported has reduced the scope for home consumption price (HCP) schemes for many products. As these indirect forms of assistance have lost their effectiveness, direct budgetary measures have begun to assume greater importance. But the political resistance to direct assistance has hardened as Governments attempt to cut-back their outlays. In this context the Australian rural sector has mounted a continuous campaign to educate the public to the costs of indirect assistance to segments of the manufacturing sector by way of tariffs and import quotas. The farmers' arguments have been substantiated by the research of the Industries Assistance Commission (IAC), which has quantified the assistance being given to certain highly protected secondary industries (Quiggin and Stoeckel, 1982). The National Farmers Federation (NFF) has spearheaded the attack on indirect assistance to manufacturing.

The NFF has consistently supported the 'first best' solution, that is reduced protection for secondary industry and a lower exchange rate. However, in their 1982 Budget Submission the NFF tacitly acknowledged political defeat on this front and embraced the 'second best' tariff compensation argument. The essence of this approach is 'protection-all-around' and it dates back to the 1920s when price policies were developed for certain primary industries as a *quid-pro-quo* for the introduction of tariffs for secondary industries (Bridgen et al., 1929). While maintaining pressure for tariff reform, the NFF has now decided to seek direct compensatory policies primarily in the name of national economic efficiency rather than on equity or income distribution grounds. But the political impracticability of achieving significant gains via direct budgetary transfers and the economic realities limiting indirect transfers through HCP schemes, have forced farmer groups to become much more economically sophisticated. Straightforward price-income policies may no longer be the most appropriate way to achieve worthwhile gains for farmers. Nowadays the NFF recognizes that broad sectoral gains can only be achieved through such activities as influencing exchange rate policies and pressuring the Government to continue with its strong anti-inflationary measures.

Technological and geographic constraints also have important influences on the achievement of consensus on policy issues among farmers and the relevant governments. For example, the traditional division between the large-scale specialist producers who advocate 'free-trade' and the smaller-scale mixed farmers who call for 'orderly marketing'. This division is based on differences in technology and geographic conditions (climate and so on) as much as upon size of enterprise. Rapid rates of technological advance, the opening up of large areas of land previously considered marginal cropland in a climatic sense, and the development of large scale irrigation schemes chiefly with private capital, have increased the diversity of Australian farming. Even within the one industry, different farmers in different parts of the country face different problems. It has become increasingly difficult to devise price and income policies which are acceptable to all the relevant farmers. The recent acrimonious debate within the beef cattle industry over beef marketing and price policies is a good example of this kind of constraint on rural policy formulation. These divisions within and between farming industries are another factor inducing the NFF to concentrate on broader sectorally advantageous issues such as exchange rate and inflation policy, rather than specific price-income policies.

*A catalogue of price and income policies*

Despite the constraints, Australia has 'experimented' with a great diversity of measures designed to effect farm prices and incomes. The traditional emphasis has been on 'prices' rather than 'incomes' (Campbell and Fisher, 1982). However, over time the emphasis has shifted towards measures designed to influence incomes directly rather than indirectly via prices.

Unlike the situation in most advanced countries, advocates of farm price and income policies in Australia have always stressed 'stability' rather than 'support' as the primary goal. Naturally enough many of the stabilization schemes have supported farmer returns at levels above what they might otherwise have achieved in some years. But those schemes have also, on occasions, substantially reduced the returns of farmers compared with what could have been achieved if the stabilization scheme had not been operating (Longworth and Knopke, 1982).

Following Lewis (1967), Australian price policies can be classified as to whether they influence farmer returns either by influencing the market supply/demand conditions or by adjusting the market price after it has been determined in a relatively free market.

Supply side policies can be further sub-divided into measures designed to influence the shape and position of the supply curve and instruments which divert supplies once they become available. In the Australian context restrictions on inputs such as water (rice, dried vine fruits) and land (sugar); restrictions on imports (all agricultural commodities with HCP schemes); and marketing quotas (wheat, sugar, tobacco, whole-milk) are examples of measures designed to affect the supply curve. Supplies have been diverted through time using buffer stock arrangements (wool); from one market to another by HCP schemes (wheat, dairy products, sugar, rice, dried vine fruits, eggs); from one purpose to another (whole-milk, sugar, wheat, eggs, peanuts); and from one class of consumer to another (whole-milk).

Measures designed to influence the demand side of the market include mixing regulations (cotton, tobacco, peanuts); restrictions on substitutes (whole-milk, dairy products, sugar); public consumption and foreign aid schemes (whole-milk, wheat, dairy products); and bilateral export contracts (sugar, wheat, beef).

Market prices have been augmented by the operation of buffer funds (wheat, dried vine fruits), deficiency payments (wheat, cotton, dried vine fruit); and direct subsidies (dairy products).

Policy measures designed to affect farmer incomes directly have received more attention in recent years but have not been so numerous. As with price policies, the historical emphasis has been on stability of incomes over time rather than the raising of farm incomes. The year-to-year seasonal and market fluctuations experienced by Australian farmers create extreme variability in farm incomes. Income stabilization measures are often justified on national resource-use-efficiency grounds. For example, it may be in the national interest to assist a major rural export industry such as cattle raising in times of depressed export markets so that private resources are not permanently withdrawn from the beef industry. Another efficiency argument for farm income stabilization springs from the belief that productivity raising investment will be greater with stable rather than unstable incomes.[2] That is, stable farm incomes are likely to create a more modern and hence internationally competitive agricultural sector.

In practice, the major measures designed to stabilize farm incomes operate through (or in conjunction with) the income tax system (for example income averaging for tax purposes, income equalization deposits, and certain special tax concessions for farmers). These measures tend not only to stabilize but also (under certain conditions) to raise the after-tax incomes of farmers. While these forms of income support have been severely criticized by spokesmen for other sectors of the economy, they do not constitute a large transfer of income to the rural sector.

Income stabilization measures which work through the taxation system are of value only to commercial farmers with taxable incomes. Genuinely low income farmers have not received much special attention in Australia. There have been instances of one-shot welfare programmes (such as the cash grants scheme for woolgrowers in 1970/71) but the only long-term policies of assistance to low income farmers have been the various rural reconstruction or adjustment schemes (Longworth, 1978). Rural adjustment assistance to farmers has been justified in national efficiency of resource use terms since it facilitates the restructuring of agriculture. However, rural adjustment schemes also have a modest welfare component in that they provide carry-on finance and rehabilitation and retraining allowances for people forced to adjust out of farming into some other occupation. Poverty-stricken farmers, as with everyone else in the Australian community, also have access to a wide range of pensions and welfare services. Under these circumstances, there may not be any special need on welfare grounds for income support schemes for low income farmers.

*The changing emphasis over time*

The first national agricultural price policy was concerned with marketing arrangements for sugar within Australia after federation in 1901. During the 1920s, as already mentioned, certain agricultural industries were granted assistance as 'compensation' for the growing burden of the tariff (Brigden et al., 1929). In the 1930s farmers saw government guaranteed wheat prices evaporate and the HCP schemes seriously weakened by legal interpretations of Section 92 of the Constitution. War time agricultural price control impressed many farmers who wanted these stable marketing conditions to continue after the war. At the end of the war the Government and farmer leaders were greatly concerned about the possible collapse of agricultural prices. During the 1945 to 1952 period, therefore, the emphasis in agricultural policy debates was on 'down-side' risks. As a result, domestic price policies were developed which emphasized security and stability above all else (for example the wheat industry stabilization scheme).

About the time of the Korean Crisis, there was a major shift in emphasis in Australian rural policies. Increased output became a major policy goal. From the early 1950s to the late 1960s, therefore, Australia introduced a range of measures designed to stimulate productivity and boost agricultural output. These 'golden years' of Australian agriculture were followed by a painful five years between 1968 and 1973 when world markets and seasonal conditions were both far from favourable. During this period rural policymakers were forced to switch their attention from output stimulating measures to stabilization and reconstruction (Edwards and Watson, 1978). The low farm-income problem, so common in advanced industrialized nations, became a major issue in Australia. For the first time, farm *income* stabilization and support, as distinct from *price* stabilization and support, became recognized as the primary goal of rural policies. Traditionally the emphasis had been on price policies but rural adjustment and even direct welfare payments to desperate farmers dominated policy discussions during the depressed 1968 to 1973 period.

The rural depression came to an abrupt end with the commodity boom of the mid-1970s. In addition, the introduction of flexible exchange rates after 1971 and the emergence of mining as a major export sector reduced the traditional concern about the need for greater agricultural exports to maintain balance of payments equilibrium. These economic facts of life plus the change of government for a critical three-year period in the mid-1970s initiated a redirection of rural policy. As a result agriculture has received less and less direct and indirect government assistance.[3] the industry stabilization schemes for dairy produts, wheat and dried vine fruits have all been substantially remodelled. There have been significant moves away from traditional price setting procedures, based on cost of production concepts, to a much greater acceptance of export market realities. In return the Government has agreed to underwrite the new stabilization arrangements for wheat, dairy products and wool. These underwritings provide absolute protection against catastrophic price collapse but under 'normal' conditions should not prove costly to taxpayers.

The emphasis in agricultural policy discussions has now shifted from the narrow domain of price and income policies for individual products or industries to broader issues. The maintenance of international competitiveness is a primary goal. In this regard domestic inflation and exchange rate policies are of vital concern to Australian farmers. As indicated above, changes in Australian international trade and commercial policy in such areas as the exchange rate, tariff reductions, and foreign exchange control, are now seen as crucial to the well-being of Australian farmers.

## AUSTRALIAN AGRICULTURAL TRADE POLICY

Immediately after World War II Australian agricultural trade policy reflected a world-wide concern to avoid a return to the disastrous trading circumstances which prevailed in regard to agricultural commodities for most of the inter-war period. Australia, therefore, strongly supported the idea that agricultural trade issues should be discussed within a multilateral framework such as the General Agreement on Tariffs and Trade (GATT). Unfortunately, agricultural trade issues were considered to be 'special' in many respects and they were not formally considered under GATT until the Kennedy Round in the 1960s. For the first time these negotiations considered the possibility of bargaining across industry sectors. The Kennedy Round failed to make any headway on agricultural trade problems principally because the EEC, Japan and the United States were not prepared to negotiate on domestic protection measures for farmers. One unhealthy outcome of the Kennedy Round as far as agricultural exporting nations were concerned, was the reaffirmation that agricultural trade was 'special'. One common argument was that agricultural trade involved different issues which required different rules. Others felt agricultural trade liberalization required greater effort and was best left until industrial trade had been liberalized. Harris (1980) has argued that the situation was more complex and the GATT has served Australia's interests reasonably well despite the apparent failure of the Kennedy Round.

The Tokyo Round of Multilateral Trade Negotiation (MTN) offered agricultural exporting nations new hope. Not only were these talks concerned with multilateral trade negotiations (including agricultural issues) but also they aimed to rewrite the post-war trade rules.[4] some people felt that multilateral discussions of the Tokyo Round should be used to consolidate discussions taking place in other international forums. This was especially true with respect to food and agricultural trade which had been discussed in UNCTAD, FAO and OECD as well as under GATT, to mention only the major sponsors. Of particular interest to developing countries was the UNCTAD Integrated Programme for Commodities (IPC) covering agricultural commodities, which had become a cornerstone of the New International Economic Order (NIEO) proposals. As explained by Harris (1980; pp. 172–73), at the MTN Australia sought better trading arrangements for world agriculture in general; improved market access for agricultural exports; and the protection of traditional markets. The last point was especially important with regard to the US/Japan negotiations which took place under the MTN (since the United States was pressing Japan for a larger share of the Japenese beef imports at Australia's expense). The achievements of the MTN from Australia's viewpoint were modest but worthwhile and have been summarized by Harris (1980; pp. 174–76).

While emphasizing the need for multilateral negotiations on agricultural trade problems in the widest possible forum, Australia has also pursued bilateral agricultural trade negotiations especially with its major trading partners. These bilateral negotiations have been aimed at improving the competitive trading position of Australia and at gaining access to particular markets.

Australian trade policies stress the need to reduce instability and unpredictability in international markets for agricultural commodities. The convential approach to these problems through multilateral commodity agreements has consistently received strong support from Australia, a signatory to all major post-war agreements covering relevant commodities (for example wheat and sugar). Bilateral agreements have also been negotiated with a view to removing trading uncertainties. Australia has consistently argued that steps to prevent 'collapse and disorder in its main markets' (Harris 1980; p. 174) are of paramount concern, with price stability and market access being of somewhat lesser importance. On the other hand the United States, with its much larger domestic market which can be 'managed' to provide stability for American farmers, has tended to put market access ahead of stability in agricultural trade discussions.

Two recent issues to enter agricultural trade debates have been the need for world food security and the significance of increasing state trading in agricultural products. As one of the world's major exporters of food, Australia has a potentially vital role to play in world food security. Unfortunately, while the principle is an admirable one, no real action has yet been taken on this issue. The major policy proposal so far put forward, namely the concept of a world buffer stock of food grains, has received support from the Australian Prime Minister in international circles. However, no detailed plans have been discussed within Australia as to who should pay for the holding of these stocks. Furthermore, Australian farmers have always been concerned about the price depressing effects on world markets of large carry-over stocks. In the long term, the Australian viewpoint on world food security may be expected to stress the benefits of a properly functioning international market for food commodities rather than a buffer stock approach.

The emergence of state trading has had a number of important effects. The first and most obvious is the impact massive government purchases (or sales) can have on the rather thin residual world market for most agricultural products. The best known example is the Russian 'grain grab' of 1973. In this context state trading creates the potential for greater instability than might otherwise be expected.[5] a second and more subtle and important result of state trading is the ease with which non-price aspects of the transaction can become paramount. Political trade-offs may be linked with grain sales at concessional prices and so forth. State trading also facilitates the use of food as a weapon of international diplomacy. Other than in war time, Australia has not engaged in state trading on a Government-to-Government basis. On the other hand, many of Australia's agricultural products are exported by (or on behalf of) statutory marketing monopolies (for example dairy products, wheat, barley, eggs, sugar). Furthermore overseas sales of wool and meat have come increasingly under the control of statutory corporations. With government corporations dominating the agricultural export scene, Australia has the necessary machinery in place to implement state trading policies if the need arose and if the domestic political climate permitted such a radical step.

## LINKAGES BETWEEN PRICE – INCOME POLICIES FOR FARMERS AND INTERNATIONAL TRADE POLICIES

In economic terms Australia is a small country. In most international commodity markets Australian traders must act as price-takers rather than price-makers. Any exporting country in this position has little scope for manipulating the world price by its trade policies. Therefore, domestic agricultural price and income policies will tend to react to international market conditions rather than vice versa.

There are also some important interrelationships between agricultural trade policies and trade policies in general.

### *Overseas agricultural markets and domestic price-income policies for farmers*

Since Australia is a price-taker on the world markets for most agricultural exports, the price elasticity of demand on these export markets is high (in absolute value) relative to the elasticity on the domestic market. As already mentioned, HCP schemes have been used in Australia both to stabilize and to boost farmer returns by exploiting this opportunity for price discrimination (Lloyd, 1982). It has been argued that these HCP schemes are a form of export 'dumping' and hence contrary to the spirit of GATT. While it is difficult to refute these claims, the extent of the assistance provided to Australian farmers by HCP schemes has never been great and, as pointed out earlier, has diminished over time.

Other trade policies have been developed from time to time in response to overseas marketing conditions which have indirectly influenced the returns of Australian farmers. For example, the voluntary restraint agreements in regard to beef exports to the United States and the meat export market diversification scheme. The buffer-stock, reserve-price scheme for wool may be seen as an economically rational reaction of the Australian wool-growing industry to conditions in the international market for wool. In this case, Australia can exert some market power since

Australian exports dominate the world market for apparel wool. Yet another example, is the recent plan to have the Australian Meat and Livestock Corporation act as a single seller on the Japanese beef market. The aim is to prevent Japanese importers exploiting Australian exporters (and hence beef farmers) who compete vigorously with one another for a share of the Japanese beef import quota.

Export incentive schemes have a long history in Australia. In the 1950s most of the measures introduced to boost agricultural output were really export incentives. More recently the Government has initiated a range of export market development and incentive schemes not specifically designed to assist rural exports. Nevertheless, agricultural exports frequently qualify. These incentives have been the main stumbling block to Australia accepting the new MTN code on export subsidies.

The most important overall link between Australia's international trade and domestic policies with regard to agriculture is that, in both spheres, the risk of international market chaos and hence ruinous prices for Australian farmers is ever present. Therefore, both internationally and domestically, steps have been taken to safeguard the future markets for Australian farm products.

*Australian trade policies in general*

To outsiders Australian trade policies appear inconsistent. The representatives of the export industries (principally, but not only, agriculture and mining) continually argue for freer world trade. At the same time, a significant proportion of Australian manufacturing industry is protected by tariffs and import quotas and the spokesman for these industries vigorously defend their right to protection. In many respects, Australia is a mirror image of most other developed countries. In Europe and in Japan it is the agricultural sector which is 'special' and in need of protection because of low productivity. The political situation and concern about food security in these countries ensures that agriculture remains highly protected in these otherwise internationally competitive industrialized societies. Australia is an industrialized economy in which agriculture has remained highly competitive in international terms but certain segments of secondary industry have not been able to achieve the levels of productivity required to make them internationally competitive (given the historical strength of the Australian dollar). In Australia it is these manufacturing industries which are 'special' in much the same political sense that agriculture has 'special' status in the EEC or Japan.

As already mentioned, the heavily export-orientated farmer groups have vigorously attacked the protectionist aspects of Australian trade policy in regard to certain imports on national efficiency of resource use grounds. Their position has been supported by other exporters and even by the present Government on occasions. Academic economists also appear to have reached an efficiency orientated consensus 'that substantial reductions in protection are highly desirable including a reduction in the dispersion of effective rates' of protection (Quiggin and Stoeckel, 1982). Nevertheless, no policy action has been taken to improve the situation; indeed recent Government decisions have substantially increased assistance for the automobile and footwear, textile and clothing industries. Quiggin and Stoeckel (1982) put forward an explanation based on distributive rather than efficiency arguments as to why this aspect of Australian trade policy has proven so difficult to reform.

The ASEAN nations, in particular, have been highly critical of Australian trade policies with regard to certain manufactured consumer goods. Australian politicians are quick to point out that on a per head of population basis, Australian imports of footwear, textile and clothing are far greater than is the case for the EEC, Japan or even the United States. Nevertheless, protective policies for specific manufacturing industries (footwear, textile, clothing and automobiles in particular) make it more difficult for Australian spokesmen to argue for freer trade for agricultural commodities.

The need for Australia to trade-off gains in the agricultural trade policy area against a reduction in domestic protection for certain manufacturing industries is not new. But, the political and economic climate in Australia has rarely been *less* favourably disposed to such trade-offs than at present.

## FINAL COMMENTS

Despite continuing domestic problems with the levels of protection for certain manufacturing industries, Australian trade policy has consistently stressed the need for freer world trade especially in agricultural commodities. In this respect, Australia is one of the few industrialized nations whose trade policies have the same basic goals as the trade policies of the developing countries heavily dependent on agricultural exports.

Australian farmers are, for the most part, highly efficient and internationally competitive at current exchange rates. Yet the instability and unreliability of international trading conditions for agricultural commodities greatly inhibit agricultural production in Australia. In this regard, the present arrangements for agricultural trade are not only unsatisfactory from the viewpoint of Australian farmers but also a threat to world food security.

## NOTES

1 Net food importing nations sometimes adopt agricultural export policies for certain products which are a direct result of domestic price-income policies (e.g. rice exports from Japan and beef exports from the EEC).

2 Campbell (1958) and others have suggested the opposite, namely that farm investment, on average, could be greater with fluctuating incomes.

3 Full details are available in the *Annual Reports* (and other reports) of the Industries Assistance Commission (IAC). For an up-to-date summary, see Quiggin and Stoeckel (1982).

[4] While the MTN was an international trade negotiation in the GATT tradition, it was not formally a GATT conference.

[5] Similar criticism has been levelled at international commodity agreements, for example, see Johnson (1973 and 1975).

## REFERENCES


Brigden, J. B., et al., *The Australian Tariff:* An Economic Enquiry, Melbourne University Press, 1929.

Campbell, K. O., 'Some Reflections on Agricultural Investment', *Australian Journal of Agricultural Economics,* Vol. 2, No. 2, December, 1958.

Campbell, Keith O., *Australian Agriculture; Reconciling Change and Tradition,* Longman Cheshire, Melbourne, 1980.

Campbell, Keith O. and Fisher, Brian S., *Agricultural Marketing and Prices,* Longman Cheshire, Melbourne, 1982 (forthcoming).

Edwards, G. W. and Watson, A. S., 'Agricultural Policy', in F. H. Gruen, *Surveys of Australian Economics,* Allen and Unwin, Sydney, 1978.

Harris, Stuart, 'Australian Agriculture and World Commodity Trading Arrangements', *Australian Journal of Agricultural Economics,* Vol. 24, No. 3, December, 1980.

Harris, Stuart, 'Agricultural Trade and Its International Trade Policy Context', in Williams, D. B., *Agriculture in the Australian Economy* (Second edn), Sydney University Press, 1982.

Johnson, D. Gale, *World Agriculture in Disarray,* Fontana/Collins (in association with the Trade Policy Research Centre), London, 1973.

Johnson, D. Gale, 'World Agriculture, Commodity Policy and Price Variability', *American Journal of Agricultural Economics,* Vol. 57, No. 5, December, 1975.

Lloyd, A. G., 'Agricultural Price Policy', in Williams, D. B., *Agriculture in the Australian Economy* (Second ed.), Sydney University Press, 1982.

Lewis, J. N., 'Agricultural Price Policies', in Williams, D. B., *Agriculture in the Australian Economy* (First edn), Sydney University Press, 1967.

Longworth, John W., 'Protection or Reconstruction?', in van Dugteren, Theo, *Rural Australia: The Other Nation,* Hodder and Stoughton (for Australian Institute of Political Science), Sydney, 1978.

Longworth, John W. and Knopke, Philip, 'Australian Wheat Policy 1948–79: A Welfare Evaluation', *American Journal of Agricultural Economics,* Vol. 64, No. 4, November, 1982.

Quiggin, J. C. and Stoeckel, A., 'Protection, Income Distribution and the Rural Sector', a paper presented to the 24th Annual Autumn Forum of the Economic Society of Australia and New Zealand, Melbourne, May 1982.

Schuh, Edward G., 'Floating Exchange Rates, International Interdependence and Agricultural Policy', in Johnson, Glen and Maunder, Allen, *Rural Change: The Challenge for Agricultural Economists* (Proceedings of the 17th International Conference of Agricultural Economists), Institute of Agricultural Economics, Oxford (for International Association of Agricultural Economists), Gower, 1981.


## DISCUSSION OPENING – CHAIWAT KONJING

It is a great honour to be the discussion opener of the very important issue of farm policies delivered to this meeting by Professor Longworth.

The paper outlined the general thrusts of the domestic agricultural price and income policies in an exporting country, Australia, the fifth largest exporter of agricultural commodities in the world. The paper also identified the linkages between the domestic price-income policies and the trade policies in Australia and highlighted the extent of common interest between Australia and the developing countries which are dependent on the export of agricultural commodities. On an international basis Australia's agricultural export share falls under the small-country definition, meaning that Australia has little (or no) scope for manipulating the world price by its trade policies or export sales.

Traditionally, the domestic price-income policies for farmers in Australia emphasized over time stabilization of farmers' incomes for many reasons both on efficiency and equity grounds. Measures adopted in income stabilization schemes included those affecting both supply and market demand of commodities. They are, for example, input and import restrictions, marketing quotas, buffer stocks and buffer fund operations, mixing regulations, price discrimination by export monopoly practices and so on. However, these policy measures changed from time to time and from commodity to commodity following changes in political and technological as well as geographical constraints. In particular, a decline in economic and electoral importance, as the economy expands, and an increasing participation in the world market of Australia's farm sector have resulted in a shift in the policy emphasis from traditional price-setting procedures to a much greater acceptance of export market realities. In other words, the recent policy goal of Australia's farm sector is to maintain the nation's competitive position in the international market through more liberalized trade policies, such as exchange rate manipulation, tariff reduction, and the support for freer world trade arrangements.

In practice, however, trade and commercial policies in Australia appeared inconsistent. While advocating competitively free trade in the agricultural sector, a significant proportion of Australian manufacture, particularly the secondary industry, is highly protected by tariffs and import quotas. In addition, the common interest between Australia and the developing countries in supporting international actions for better trade arrangements or freer trade has not been taken seriously by the major world trade partners. Various forms of international trade forums still leave the world trade arrangements with instability and an unreliable trading situation, part of which is attributable to protectionism.

The paper concluded that with existing trade and commercial policies, Australia's farm sector could not be as 'special' as it is in most developed countries; that the instability and unrealiability of international trade in agriculture has prevented Australia from contributing more to world food security; and that the strong political and economic climate which favoured protective policies for some specific manufacturing industries has distorted the need for Australia to trade-off gains in the agricultural trade policy area against a reduction in domestic protection for certain manufacturing industries.

My first comment concerns the technical and economic aspects of the agricultural price and income policy measures. In principle, the stabilization of income could be achieved either through market operation schemes or income compensation schemes. However, neither market operation nor income compensation schemes could relieve the equity problems. In particular, from the small farmer's point of view, these stabilization schemes have been far from desirable. In addition to the technical aspect of the price and income policies, many policy instruments adopted in Australia seem inconsistent with the free trade concept advocated. For example, the establishment of statutory market monopolies and price discrimination practices for some specific commodities not only turned the farm sector towards protectionism but also created equity problems between producers and consumers. My questions relating to the above issue are that if it is not for political reasons what would be appropriate policy options for income stabilization and competitive market objectives? Is protection a necessary condition for growth and equity? If it is, what is its implication for developing countries which have limited resources for protection?

My second comment is directed toward the implications for the developing countries of Australia's farm policy experience. As mentioned in the paper, the strength of the interdependence between the domestic price and income policies and the trade policies decreases as the exporter's share of the world market for its products diminishes. This is also true for Australia. In my view, it is rather a common problem faced by most developing countries from time to time. It has been the farmers in developing countries who cannot do much to solve this problem but simply rely on the principle of comparative advantage. Therefore, the Australian experience in the above problem leaves no guidance for most developing countries, particularly those which are not exporters of agricultural commodities.

My third comment is on the issue of whether or not agriculture should be 'special'. The implication of Professor Longworth's paper is that the developed countries generally favour protection for agriculture for both political and economic reasons. Australia is one among the developed world which could not have agriculture fully 'special'. This argument is controversial since agriculture could be 'special' either directly or indirectly. Keeping in mind that in any country the industrial sector plays an important role as a source of economic growth, it also can be 'special' since growth of the industrial sector brings growth into the agricultural sector sooner or later.

As mentioned in the paper, Australian farm policy is to stabilize farmers' incomes and to have high producer and consumer prices but lower export prices. This policy approach is exactly contrary to that pursued by some exporting countries in the developing world. For example, in Thailand the policy is to have low consumer prices while maintaining a competitive position in international trade. It is interesting to speculate which approach can contribute more to the agricultural sector in regard to growth and equity.

My final comment on Professor Longworth's paper is that the arguments on the advantages and disadvantages of various policy options in many parts of the paper have not been supported by empirical evidence.

ANTÕNIO CORTEZ DE LOBÃO AND FERNANDO BRITO SOARES

# *EEC Price-income Policies and their Effects on North South Relations in European Agriculture*

## NORTH VERSUS SOUTH IN AN ENLARGED EUROPEAN ECONOMIC COMMUNITY (EEC)

The recent integration of Greece and the near future membership of Portugal and Spain in the EEC will profoundly change the present relative economic weight of Northern and Southern regions within the Community. In fact, and even considering that the establishment of a well defined North-South boundary is not an easy task, neither from a theoretical nor a practical viewpoint, it seems unquestionable that the prevailing characteristics of the agricultural sectors of the three new members point towards the reinforcement of the Southern component. While in a nine-member community the South was represented only by Italy (except for its most Northern regions), some regions of Southern France and Corsica, in a twelve-member community the almost entire North-Mediterranean basin and the Iberian peninsula will represent the Southern regions of the Community[1].

Given the difficulty in establishing a well defined North-South boundary within the enlarged EEC we decided to make it in terms of Northern countries and Southern countries, which does not mean that we are not aware of the simplifications involved in not considering North-South dichotomies in some countries. Thus, and in order to pinpoint some of the more important socio-economic differences we consider as Northern countries the Federal Republic of Germany, France, United Kingdom, Netherlands, Belgium, Luxemburg, Denmark and Ireland while Southern countries include Italy, Greece, Portugal and Spain. Based upon this division it is possible to identify a few significant differences between North and South not only regarding the structure of the whole economy but also concerning the agricultural sector.

The analysis of Table 1 reveals that the rate of economic activity, measured by the employment/total population ratio, is higher in the North. In addition the sectoral composition of employment shows a higher percentage of agricultural employment in Southern countries. Moreover, in these countries the contribution of GAP for GDP is relatively higher.

However, and because the aim of this paper is the analysis of the effects

TABLE 1 *Some economic indicators of the enlarged EEC (1977)*

| | EUR 12 | NORTH | SOUTH | | | | |
|---|---|---|---|---|---|---|---|
| | | | Italy | Greece | Portugal | Spain | Total |
| Total population ($10^6$) | 314.3 | 202.6 | 56.6 | 9.3 | 9.2 | 36.6 | 111.7 |
| Employment ($10^6$) | 121.1 | 81.9 | 19.8 | 3.2 | 3.8 | 12.4 | 39.2 |
| Employment/ Total population % | 39 | 40 | 35 | 34 | 41 | 34 | 35 |
| Population in agric. and fisheries ($10^6$) | 13.0 | 5.2 | 3.1 | 0.9 | 1.2 | 2.6 | 7.8 |
| Pop. in agric. and fish. /Employment % | 11 | 6 | 16 | 28 | 32 | 21 | 20 |
| Total area ($10^6$ ha) | 225.4 | 122.5 | 30.1 | 13.2 | 9.2 | 50.5 | 103.0 |
| Agric. area ($10^6$ ha) | 134.5 | 76.1 | 17.5 | 9.2 | 4.1 | 27.6 | 58.4 |
| Agric area/total area % | 60 | 69 | 58 | 69 | 45 | 55 | 57 |
| GDP ($10^6$ EUA - 1975) | 1,219,802.8 | 952,788.5 | 155,382.8 | 16,865.0 | 11,891.5 | 82,875.0 | 267,014.3 |
| GAP ($10^6$ EUA - 1975) | 59,081.4 | 34,112.6 | 12,430.6 | 3,153.8 | 1,759.9 | 7,624.5 | 24,968.8 |
| GAP/GDP % | 4.8 | 3.6 | 8.0 | 18.7 | 14.8 | 9.2 | 9.4 |

*Sources:* The Situation of Agriculture in the Community, Report 1980; Eurostats; UNO Statistical Yearbook.

of price-income policies on North-South relations, one must observe more carefully the structure of agricultural production in the two regions, not only regarding the production volume of different products but also its participation in GAP. From this analysis conclusions can be drawn towards the identification of 'Northern' and 'Southern' products. Thus, the observation of the different product price-policies will allow an evaluation of its effects in both regions.

For that matter, the joint observation of Tables 2 and 3 seems to suggest clearly that cereals, sugar, dairy products, beef, pork, poultry and eggs are 'Northern' products, while wine, olive oil, fruits and vegetables (except for potatoes) can be considered as 'Southern' products.

In the following section the analysis will be restricted to the nine EEC members, before the integration of Greece. This is because of the obvious lack of available compatible data for the three new members of the Community. Thus, Italy is, in our analysis framework, the representative of the Southern component, but the similarities between Italy and the three new members allow for an extension of the conclusions regarding price-income policy effects to the entire South of the enlarged Community.

TABLE 2 *Production of some agricultural products 1976–78 (averages, 1000 metric tons)*

| | EUR 12 | NORTH | | SOUTH | |
|---|---|---|---|---|---|
| | | volume | % | volume | % |
| Cereals (total) | 122,093 | 86,521 | 71 | 35,572 | 29 |
| Sugar | 13,028 | 9,948 | 76 | 3,080 | 24 |
| Olive oil | 1,261 | 1 | 0 | 1,260 | 100 |
| Wine | 17,252 | 7,039 | 41 | 10,213 | 59 |
| Citrus | 6,492 | 28 | 1 | 6,464 | 99 |
| Grapes | 27,650 | 10,570 | 38 | 17,080 | 62 |
| Apples | 7,807 | 4,656 | 60 | 3,151 | 40 |
| Peaches | 2,529 | 489 | 19 | 2,040 | 81 |
| Tomatoes | 10,128 | 1,310 | 13 | 8,818 | 87 |
| Potatoes | 43,082 | 32,331 | 75 | 10,751 | 25 |
| Pork | 9,372 | 7,497 | 80 | 1,875 | 20 |
| Beef | 7,041 | 5,400 | 77 | 1,641 | 23 |
| Poultry | 4,409 | 2,512 | 57 | 1,897 | 43 |
| Eggs | 4,525 | 3,110 | 69 | 1,415 | 31 |
| Cow milk | 108,701 | 91,912 | 85 | 16,789 | 15 |

*Source:* FAO Production Yearbook.

TABLE 3 *Composition of agricultural final production, 1977 (%)*

| | NORTH | Italy | Greece[a)] | Portugal[a)] | Spain |
|---|---|---|---|---|---|
| Meat | 38.0 | 25.9 | 18.0 | 26.0 | 24.6 |
| Vegetables (incl. potatoes) | 8.7 | 15.9 | 12.3 | 11.5 | 18.0 |
| Fruits (incl. citrus) | 3.2 | 9.8 | 4.4 | 10.3 | 9.9 |
| Cereals (incl. rice) | 11.7 | 9.6 | 13.5 | 10.4 | 9.6 |
| Cow milk | 21.2 | 12.5 | 8.2 | 8.9 | 8.6 |
| Eggs | 4.0 | 3.3 | 2.7 | 2.7 | 4.0 |
| Wine | 3.9 | 7.6 | 2.3 | 10.1 | 4.0 |
| Olive oil | 0.0 | 6.5 | 7.6 | 3.6 | 3.2 |
| Other products | 9.3 | 8.9 | 31.0 | 16.6 | 18.1 |
| TOTAL | 100 | 100 | 100 | 100 | 100 |

a) 1976

*Source:* Eurostat; The Situation of Agriculture in the Community, Report 1980.

## PRICE-INCOME POLICIES AND THEIR EFFECTS

*General evaluation of EEC price-income policies*

The Common Agricultural Policy (CAP) of the EEC has been, up to now, almost entirely based upon a set of price-income policies. Nevertheless, it can be said that it represented a major contribution to the building of the Community insofar as it was able to achieve the development of a free-trade system and an effective customs union. In addition, these price-income policies created the mechanisms that ensured, for main agricultural products, a sizable degree of price stability coupled with a high average price-level in comparison with world price-levels. As a consequence, many farmers were able to benefit from these policies with the end result of rapid economic growth of the agricultural sectors, specially until the slow-down of the world economic expansion of the late 1960s.

The inflow of new capital and the introduction of new ideas and technologies allowed for sound productivity gains in EEC agriculture. For the entire Community the average yield of wheat grew from little more than 2,000 kg/ha in 1952 to about 4,500 kg/ha in 1979 and milk production increased from about 3,000 kg/cow/year in 1962 to more than 4,000 kg/cow/year in 1979. Moreover, the improved technologies made possible a rapid output growth resulting in higher levels of Community self-sufficiency. Cereals production reached 116 million tonnes in 1978 (around 77 million in 61/65) and milk production reached 102 million tonnes in 1979 (60 million in 61/65). As to self-sufficiency levels it is nowadays around 100 per cent for cereals (except for corn), potatoes, eggs, meat (except for ovine), wine, etc.; largely exceeds 100 per cent for sugar and dairy products (generating large stocks that are not easy to market); and only for rice, fresh fruits, citrus fruits and fats is the self-sufficiency level below 100 per cent.

On the other hand the creation of employment outside the sector, made possible by the general economic growth, drastically reduced the agricultural population, which in 1970 was only about half of that in 1950. This fact in conjunction with the productivity growth lead to a considerable increase in the farmer's income.

Thus it appears that EEC agricultural price-income policies have contributed positively to achieving the main objectives of the Treaty of Rome, at least on an overall Community level. However if one looks more carefully at regional effects, the picture is not so optimistic.

*Regional effects*

(a) *The increasing gap between developed and less developed regions*
The analysis of the CAP easily shows that its income policy component is almost entirely limited to the results of the price-policy component. This approach shows some important drawbacks. In the first place, the price policy is more beneficial to large producers, thus representing a relative penalty to those whose incomes are in more need for support – the small and very small producers. In the second place, part of the high product prices are transferred into costs, via the utilization of more expensive inputs, instead of incrementing the farmer's income. But the main cause for regional bias in the application of the CAP is perhaps the different degree of guarantee it

TABLE 4 *Percentage of FEOGA guarantee expenditure 1978/80, by products*

(per cent)

| | 1978 | 1979 | 1980 |
|---|---|---|---|
| Northern products | 76 | 76 | 75 |
| Cereals | 13 | 15 | 14 |
| Dairy products | 46 | 43 | 43 |
| Sugar | 10 | 10 | 6 |
| Beef and veal | 7 | 7 | 10 |
| Pork | - | 1 | 1 |
| Eggs and poultry | - | - | 1 |
| Southern products | 7 | 13 | 19 |
| Oils and fats | 4 | 6 | 7 |
| Fruit and vegetable | 1 | 4 | 6 |
| Wine | - | 1 | 3 |
| Tobacco | 2 | 2 | 3 |
| MCA | 10 | 7 | 2 |
| Others | 7 | 4 | 4 |

*Source:* The Situation of Agriculture in the Community, Report 1980

shows for different agricultural products. In this matter the truth is that the products that receive a higher degree of guarantee are cereals, milk and sugar, which account for the bulk of agricultural production in the Northern regions of the EEC. In contrast, typical Mediterranean products, like fruits and vegetables, wine and oils, have a low level of guarantee. This emerges clearly from Table 4. Northern products received around 75 – 77 per cent of FEOGA guarantee expenditures during the 1977, 1979 and 1980 years, while in the same period Southern products only received, respectively, 7, 13 and 19 per cent of those expenditures.

Table 4 deserves an additional observation. In fact, Northern products like pork, eggs and poultry, are assigned low degrees of guarantee. The reason for its Northern location is two-fold. On the one hand, production structures in these regions are better; on the other hand, producers can take advantage of location rents due to the vicinity of main consumption centres.

The regionally biased effects of the CAP were analysed in some recent research ('Les Regions d'Europe', 1981) in which the evolution of farm income was measured by the pattern of Gross Value Added (GVA)/Annual Work Unit (AWU) ratios during the 1968/69 – 1976/77 period.

At the beginning of the period the highest incomes (more than 125 per cent of the GVA/AWU average ratio for the Community as a whole) could be found in the Northern and central regions of the EEC. In contrast, the lowest incomes (less than 75 per cent of the GVA/AWU average ratios, for the entire Community) were found in the Southern and Western regions of the EEC, namely in South-west France and Italy. The growth rate of GVA/AWU during the period under analysis was higher than the average growth rate for the Community in the Northern and Central regions, while for Southern regions it was below the Community average. Summing up the analysis results, it was stated that during the 8 years period 'the ratio between the GVA/AWU average value for the 5 most developed regions and the corresponding value for the 5 less developed regions grew from 6.0 to 6.7' ('Les Regions d'Europe', 1981).

(b) *Allocation of resources and resource flows*

A system of administered prices, like the CAP establishes for some important products, can lead to non-negligible misallocation of resources within the EEC. If prices do not reflect market pressures, resources are channelled to production of goods that have more advantageous prices, easily leading to stock-piling (as happens with some Northern products). But if, in addition, administered prices are set higher than world prices the Community does not allocate resources according to world opportunities, which, given the Community preference principle, ends up by penalizing importing countries (among which are Mediterranean countries).

The most notorious cases of misallocation of resources as a consequence of rigidity in the CAP price policy are dairy products and sugar. Whole milk powder, butter and sugar have guaranteed prices and, as Table 5 shows, Community stocks did not cease to increase during the 1970s. Moreover, the level of guarantee for dairy products and sugar is so high that the areas dedicated to livestock and sugar production range second and third in the

TABLE 5 *Self-sufficiency in dairy products and sugar*

(per cent)

| | | EUR-9 | B–L | Denmark | FRG | France | Ireland | Italy | Neth. | UK |
|---|---|---|---|---|---|---|---|---|---|---|
| Whole milk powder | 1968 | 169 | 219 | 386 | 84 | 169 | 543 | 0 | 347 | 66 |
| | 1977 | 310 | 423 | x | 111 | 409 | x | 0 | 506 | 290 |
| Condensed milk | 1968 | 142 | 115 | 1243 | 93 | 186 | 0 | 93 | 345 | 108 |
| | 1977 | 155 | 25 | 575 | 118 | 165 | 0 | 62 | 310 | 119 |
| Butter | 1968 | 91 | 110 | 332 | 104 | 119 | 198 | 67 | 298 | 10 |
| | 1977 | 111 | 105 | 308 | 135 | 110 | 320 | 61 | 493 | 30 |
| Sugar | 1968 | 82 | 148 | 124 | 89 | 120 | 94 | 94 | 101 | 34 |
| | 1977 | 111 | 190 | 184 | 118 | 171 | 121 | 90 | 146 | 32 |

*Source:* The Situation of Agriculture in the Community, Report 1979

TABLE 6 *Financial relationship with FEOGA (Million £)*

| | | B–L | Denmark | FRG | France | Ireland | Italy | Neth. | UK |
|---|---|---|---|---|---|---|---|---|---|
| Receipts from FEOGA | 1977 | 356 | 454 | 1188 | 1057 | 252 | 406 | 767 | 598 |
| | 1978 | 427 | 545 | 1736 | 1194 | 378 | 516 | 856 | 247 |
| Contributions to FEOGA | 1977 | 368 | 120 | 1657 | 931 | 18 | 480 | 512 | 568 |
| | 1978 | 394 | 137 | 1858 | 1153 | 35 | 860 | 615 | 920 |
| Net position | 1977 | −12 | +334 | −469 | +126 | +234 | −74 | +255 | −470 |
| | 1978 | +33 | +408 | −122 | +41 | +343 | −344 | +241 | −673 |

*Source:* Rollo, J.M.C., and Warwick, K.S., *The CAP and Resource Flows among EEC Member States,* 1978

TABLE 7 *Net effects on trade account (million £)*

| | B–L | Denmark | FRG | France | Ireland | Italy | Neth. | UK |
|---|---|---|---|---|---|---|---|---|
| 1977 | | | | | | | | |
| a) Imp. levies | −12 | +209 | −355 | +463 | +168 | −488 | +545 | −167 |
| b) Export restit. | −41 | +144 | −247 | +318 | +126 | −318 | +361 | −142 |
| 1978 | | | | | | | | |
| a) Imp. levies | −54 | +275 | −434 | +575 | +184 | −588 | +605 | −110 |
| b) Export restit. | −95 | +213 | −282 | +480 | +163 | −442 | +387 | −145 |

*Source:* Rollo and Warwick, *The CAP and Resource Flows.*

TABLE 8 *Effects on balance of payments (£) and agricultural self-sufficiency (%)*

| | Net effect on Balance of Payments per head (central estimate) | | Agricultural self-sufficiency |
|---|---|---|---|
| | 1977 | 1978 | 1976 |
| | £ | £ | % |
| Ireland | +120 | +162 | 210 |
| Denmark | +100 | +128 | 226 |
| Neth. | + 50 | + 54 | 143 |
| France | + 10 | + 11 | 101 |
| B–L | − 4 | − 4 | 96 |
| Italy | − 9 | − 15 | 89 |
| UK | − 11 | − 15 | 62 |
| FRG | − 13 | − 8 | 81 |

*Source:* Rolo and Warwick, *The CAP and Resource Flows.*

Community (cereals area is the largest) and about half of the dairy products producers in the North and Centre regions deliver their production to intervention agencies.

This misallocation of resources has also its reflections in terms of financial relationships between the European Guidance and Guarantee Fund (FEOGA) and each member state as well as in terms of intra-community trade transfers. Regarding the first point Rollo and Warwick

(1978) estimated for 1977 and 1978 the net position of each member state *vis à vis* the FEOGA. The results are presented in Table 6 and they show that Italy (the typically Southern country) is clearly a net loser. The disadvantageous position of the United Kingdom is a direct consequence of it being a net importer of agricultural products, against which, as was said above, the CAP is biased. But the main explanation for the figures in Table 6 is that FEOGA financial resources have been more than 90 per cent allocated to its guarantee section and thus channelled, *via* the guaranteed prices, to the regions where the products that receive a higher degree of support are produced (Northern and Central regions of EEC).

Rollo and Warwick also estimated costs and benefits, measured in terms of import levies and export restitutions and from there the net effects on trade account (see Table 7). Despite some discrepancies in the effects when measured by import levies or by export restitutions, the picture emerging from the Table illustrates the fact that the CAP generates a resource transfer from two periphery countries (Italy and United Kingdom) to Centre countries. Moreover Italy is the main payer.

The same authors went further, computing the net effects on the balance of payments and comparing them with the degree of self-sufficiency of each member state, as shown in Table 8. Here again, it can be concluded that the present price-income policies of the CAP benefits mainly countries of agricultural self-sufficiency, the big losers being periphery countries, specially Italy which can be taken as a proxy for what will eventually happen to new Southern members if the CAP is not reformulated.

## INADEQUACIES OF THE CAP REGARDING SOUTHERN PROBLEMS

Experience has shown that the price-income policies of the CAP have contributed heavily to exhausting the Community budget with actions that have not been able to tackle the problems of Southern regions. In a restricted sense, typical Mediterranean products like olives and olive oil, fruits and vegetables, tomatoes and wine have received a much lesser degree of support, and, in a more general sense, structural and marketing problems have not yet found adequate solutions. As a result the less developed Southern regions have not been able to profit from present price-income policies. In addition, the few incentives awarded to structural change, investment, production reorganization, and so on (as in the case of Directives 159/72, 160/72 and 268/75) are not best suited to the socio-economic conditions of Southern agriculture, and even then have received a very small share of FEOGA expenditures.

Southern regions have thus suffered from a negative attitude of the Community instead of a positive one aiming at the formulation and implementation of integrated regional policies. On the other hand, the policy of high producer prices is passed on to consumers who then are double squeezed as tax payers and as high food price payers. If this situation is less important in growing and affluent economies it is not easily compatible with Southern economies with low income per caput and particularly during periods of economic stagnation. Moreover, and awkward as it may seem, the South (represented by the Italian case) which has the highest percentage of agricultural population and the lowest income per caput within the EEC has been a net contributor to the financing of the CAP.

## NOTE

[1] It should be emphasized that the North-South dichotomy is not the only one possible within the EEC. In a centre-periphery framework the periphery would be represented not only by the regions labelled as South, but also by Ireland and Scotland.

## REFERENCES

*Les Regions d'Europe: Rapport Periodique sur la Situation Économique et Sociale des Regions de la Communauté*, Brussels, Jan. 1981.

Rollo, J.M.C. and Warwick, K.S., *The CAP and Resource Flows among EEC Member States,* Government Economic Service Working Paper No. 27, Ministry of Agriculture, Fisheries and Food, London, Nov. 1978.

## DISCUSSION OPENING – WERNER ZOHINHOEFER

The authors deal with a very interesting problem of high practical importance and actuality: what will be the effects of the EEC's price-income policies with respect to agricultural products for the new member-states, Greece, Portugal and Spain? Their answer to this question is quite pessimistic: 'It can be concluded that the present price-income policies of the CAP benefit mainly countries of agricultural self-sufficiency, the big losers being peripheral countries, especially Italy which can be taken as a proxy for what will eventually happen to the new southern members if the CAP is not reformulated.'

This conclusion, I think, is quite typical of the way the authors argue. Some elements of the statement are to me plausible and convincing. Others are not at all. Having only ten minutes to open the discussion it is quite difficult to do full justice to the paper. I try to do this by concentrating on those major steps in the authors' argument that, in my view, are not really convincing and therefore especially worthy of criticism. The authors' analysis basically rests on three proprositions:

1 Italy is comparable to Spain, Greece and Portugal with respect to the relevant structure of agricultural production.
2 Southern products have been receiving 'a much lesser degree of support' than the so-called Northern products.
3 This divergency in degree of price support 'generates a resource transfer' to the disadvantage of Italy – and the other southern member states in the future.

Let me shortly review these propositions. First, I seriously doubt that Italy is comparable to the new member states for the purpose of this study. On the one hand, with respect to the structure of agricultural production which the authors stress, Italy is also quite similar to France, so that France could also serve as a country of reference. On the other hand, Italy's rate of self-sufficiency in agricultural products is relatively low. This holds true for Northern as well as for Southern products. So even for olive oil Italy is a net importer. In contrast, the new South-European member states have a much higher degree of self-sufficiency in agricultural products in general. At the same time they are not exporters of typical southern products and will increasingly enlarge their exports into other Common Market countries in the future.

All this, I think, makes clear that the similarities between Italy and the three new member states do not allow for an extension of the conclusions regarding price-income policy effects to the entire south of the larger Community. On the contrary, the differences will, in my opinion, be much more significant for the future role the new member states will play in the agricultural sector of the Community.

Let me then turn to the second proposition: Is the degree of support for the Southern products really much lower? The authors back up their contention with the fact that the share of the expenditure of the European Guidance and Guarantee Fund (FEOGA) for price-support is much higher for northern products than it is for southern products. In 1980 the relation was 75:19! Interesting as this empirical fact is, it may be that the result of very different causes. After all, the expenditures behind these figures are a product of two factors: the amount of subsidized production and the subsidy payment per unit of quite a wide range of agricultural products. And what is even more important, to evaluate degrees of guarantee for different products as too low or too high one needs an operational standard to measure what could be considered as comparable degrees of price support for different products. Considerations of this sort, however, are completely neglected by the authors. Therefore the statistical data in question cannot empirically confirm the authors' argument that the degree of guarantee is low for southern as compared to that of northern products.

This result, in turn, has immediate implications for the authors' third proposition. If there is no general divergency in the degree of price guarantee for northern as compared to southern products it cannot generate a resource transfer to the disadvantage of Italy or other countries of Southern Europe. But to be more precise, I should say, only to the extent to which such divergency exists, may we expect a resource transfer to be generated.

Since the paper does not convincingly show this divergency to exist, we should look for different or at least additional reasons to explain the fact that Italy in the agricultural sector of the EEC is no doubt 'clearly a net loser'. In my opinion this fact is clearly related to Italy's relative low degree of self-sufficiency with regard to agricultural products. Being a major net-importer of agricultural goods in the EEC, Italy's net-position *vis à vis* the European

Guidance and Guarantee Fund is bound to be negative – even if there were no divergencies in the levels of price guarantee for different products (however that may be defined). In this respect Italy sits – but for different reasons – in the same boat as the United Kingdom and West Germany (as Table 8 clearly indicates). If this hold true, the economic perspective for the new Southern members of the EEC should be quite different from what the authors of the paper would expect. Since in Spain, Portugal and Greece the degree of self-sufficiency with regard to agricultural products – and particularly to Southern products – is significantly higher than it is in Italy and since at the same time additional production will be stimulated (if the CAP remains what it is), the agricultural sector of the newcomers will probably do much better than the Italians did. One needs to be no prophet to expect indeed that Italy may again – and even more than so far – be on the losers' side. Quite a few well informed observers agree in forecasting that the surplus production of primarily southern agricultural goods, which will come about within the new member states, will strongly aggravate the problem of financing the CAP if it is not modified.

This brings me to my final remarks. Let me in conclusion clarify a few points to prevent misunderstandings. My critical view of major parts of the paper should not be taken to mean that I am defending the traditional CAP. On the contrary, I share the criticisms the authors express with respect to the strong dominance of price policy and the corresponding lack of an effective policy fostering structural adjustments within the concept of a CAP. But it seems important to me to distinguish between distributional effects of the EEC agricultural price policy on the one hand and equity considerations with respect to the question of how to share the financial burden necessary to foster the necessary structural changes in European agriculture, on the other hand. So even if we acknowledge the special adjustment problems of the agricultural sector in Southern countries and the necessity for a transfer of resources in favour of Southern member states within the EEC, increasing the degree of guaranteed prices for southern products, as the authors imply, would certainly contribute more to creating new than to settling old problems. In contrast, an appropriate policy for European agriculture in general and for the Southern countries in particular should – briefly stated – advance along the following lines:

(a) it should (continue to) modify the level of prices and the relative prices for agricultural products so as to gradually approach world market conditions in the long run;
(b) in accordance with this, the expenditure of the European Guidance and Grarantee Fund should further be limited and gradually reduced in favour of a more effective policy fostering structural adjustments in European agriculture;
(c) in addition, it might be necessary that the EEC increases its financial aid for (national) measures to create employment opportunities outside of agriculture in economically weak regions, particularly in Southern member states.

To sum up, the CAP should gradually shift its emphasis from measures of price support to measures aiming at structural effects in order to make for growth by improving the allocation of resources and at the same time to bring about more equity by reducing the income differences among farmers, between farmers and non-farmers and between regions within the larger EEC.

## REFERENCES

Buchholz, H. E., Auswickunzen der Süderweiterung der gemeinschaft auf die gemeinsame Agrarpolitik, *Agrarlewirtschaft,* Vol. 50–1981, p. 197–203.

Schumacher, K.D. and Wöhlken, E., Analyse des charlet ablaufs bei Olivenöd in der EG und den Beitrittslädern, *Agrarwirtschaft;* Vol. 51, 1982, p. 77–85

Strzybny, Xaver, Der Spanische Getreidemarkt, *Berichte über Landwirtschaft,* Vol. 51, 1982, p. 140–149

Wiss Beirat beim Bundesminsterium für Ernährung, Landwirtschaft und Forsten: EG – *Erweitering – Agrarpolilische Probleme einer Erweiterung der EG (Gutachten),* Mühster-Hiltrup, 1980.

## GENERAL DISCUSSION* – RAPPORTEUR: ROSEMARY FENNELL

Discussion on the Longworth paper was mostly concerned with conflicts between the interests of various groups – for instance the conflict between those who sought free-trade conditions for Australian agricultural products and those who demanded protection for industry at home or, on the wider front, the conflict between industralized nations which tend to have a pro-farm bias in their agricultural policies (not true of Australia) and the developing countries which have an urban policy bias. Other issues raised were the impact on Australian agriculture of policies pursued in other exporting countries, the extent of the switch in destination of Australian agricultural exports away from Europe towards the Pacific area, and the effect of the sharp fluctuations in the fortunes of the farm sector in Australia on capital – in particular on the level of land values and rents.

There was considerable disagreement among the participants over the validity of certain statements contained in the de Lobãs and Soares papers. These centred particularly on the relative degree of support for northern and southern type products (and the reasons for the difference in treatment); the suitability of using Italian experience of the CAP as a guide to the likely impact of membership of Greece, Spain and Portugal; and on the interpretation of the data quoted in the paper on the foreign exchange effects of the CAP.

Concerning the relative degree of support for northern and southern type products, the participants also disagreed among themselves as to the correct interpretation of the situation. One view put forward was that the relative

*Papers by Longworth and Labão and Soares.

support was consistent with the rate of self-sufficiency for the various products and also with the contribution of the products to final agricultural output. In contrast, it was contended that the very nature of the instruments of policy themselves (which differ from commodity to commodity) created totally different levels of support.

The authors had drawn attention in their paper to the adverse impact of the CAP in some regions but the point was made in discussion that the CAP was not the only cause of regional income disparities and that the Community had introduced some policy measures to counteract such regional inbalances. it was better to try to improve regional specialization in agriculture than to increase the levels of price support. The authors had omitted to make any references to the resource cost implications of the level of support, concentrating solely on the access-frontier transfer, nor did they take into account the possibility of a positive supply response in the new member states which could lead to a resource transfer to them from northern Europe. Finally, the point was made that it was inappropriate of the authors to single out certain groups of producers as being responsible for the production of surpluses of certain products – all producers of surplus commodities were culpable.

Participants in the discussion included R. Bohall, M. Petit, C. Haebler, B. F. Stanton, S. Tarditi, C. Capstick, D. Bergmann and D. Parlberg.

CHRISTOPHER D. GERRARD

# *Government-controlled Food Grain Markets, External Trade in Food Grains and Agricultural Development: the Case of Four Countries in East Africa*

## INTRODUCTION

Governments pursue two major kinds of policies that affect agricultural production and incomes. First, they control the domestic prices of agricultural commodities, which cause *movements along* agricultural supply curves. Second, they invest in agricultural research, education, and transportation systems, which *shift* agricultural supply curves over time. The first will be called 'commodity' policies and the second, 'development' policies. Positive policies of either type can increase agricultural production and, given input prices, agricultural incomes, but the means of achieving such increases, as Ricardo (1970 [1821], p. 79) pointed out more than 160 years ago, greatly affect the overall rate of economic development in less developed countries. This paper examines these two types of policies in the case of four countries in East Africa.

Kenya, Malawi, Tanzania, and Zambia are all former British colonies that became independent between 1961 and 1964. Owing to their common geographical and historical legacy, they have similar economic and institutional structures, including their governments' interventions in domestic food grain markets. All have been blessed with stable government since independence and considerable continuity in economic policy. The four countries are an economic laboratory for studying the impact of agricultural commodity and development policies.

Between 1964 and 1978 – which excludes the effects of the most recent drought to hit the region, beginning in 1979 – real GDP grew faster in Kenya and Malawi than in Tanzania and Zambia (see Table 1.) Real GDP per caput also grew faster in Kenya and Malawi. But a more striking difference between the two groups of countries is that while real private consumption per caput grew in Kenya and Malawi, it actually *declined* in Tanzania and Zambia. Not only did real GDP per caput grow more slowly in Tanzania and Zambia, but also government consumption grew more quickly than in Kenya and Malawi.

In all four countries, real growth in GDP has been associated with a declining share of agricultural production (see Table 2). But in Kenya and

TABLE 1 *Annual rates of growth in GDP, 1964 to 1978*
(per cent)

| | Kenya | Malawi | Tanzania | Zambia |
|---|---|---|---|---|
| Real GDP | 6.4 | 6.2 | 5.0 | 4.0 |
| Population | 3.5 | 2.6 | 2.7 | 3.1 |
| Real GDP per caput | 2.8 | 3.4 | 2.2 | 0.9 |
| Real private consumption per caput | 1.4 | 2.1 | −1.2 | −3.3 |

*Note:* All annual rates of growth in Tables 1 and 2 have been calculated by ordinary least squares from the equation, $Y_t = (1+r)^t Y_o$, estimated in logarithmic form.

*Source:* IMF, International Financial Statistics, 1981 Yearbook.

Malawi, domestic food grain production per caput has declined slightly, while export crop production has increased significantly. In Tanzania and Zambia, domestic food grain production per caput has increased slightly, while export crop production has declined significantly.

TABLE 2 *Annual rates of growth in domestic agricultural production per caput, 1964 to 1978*
(per cent)

| | Kenya | Malawi | Tanzania | Zambia |
|---|---|---|---|---|
| Real GDP per caput | 2.8** | 3.4** | 2.2** | 0.9* |
| Major food grains | −0.6 | −1.0 | 1.5 | 1.8* |
| Major export crops | 3.2** | 4.1** | −4.2** | −6.2** |
| Major food grains and export crops | 1.4** | 1.9** | −2.4** | 0.03 |

*Note:* * indicates significant at the 5 per cent level and ** at the 1 per cent level.

*Source:* USDA, ESCS, 'Indices of agricultural production in Africa and the Near East', Statistical bulletins 556 and 623.

The main thesis of this paper can now be stated briefly. These trends are not accidental but are the result of government commodity and development policies. All four countries have controlled domestic food grain prices at levels that have maintained a relative degree of domestic self-sufficiency in food grain production over time. Hence, the rate of growth of food grain production per caput has been significantly different from zero for only one country, Zambia. In Kenya and Malawi, domestic self-sufficiency has been maintained by development policies that have successfully shifted agricultural supply curves to the right, so that domestic food grain prices have declined relative to world prices and export crop production has expanded. In Tanzania and Zambia, domestic self-sufficiency has been maintained more by movements along agricultural supply curves, so that domestic food grain prices have increased relative to world prices and export crop production has declined. The different ways of maintaining self-sufficiency have translated into higher rates of economic growth in Kenya and Malawi than in Tanzania and Zambia.

## GOVERNMENT INTERVENTIONS IN DOMESTIC FOOD GRAIN MARKETS

Maize is the staple grain throughout East Africa. It is consumed in both rural and urban areas and produced wherever rainfall is sufficient. Notwithstanding the lingering influence of British policies that encouraged European settlement on large farms, domestic production comes primarily from small African farmers who cultivate small plots of land – generally less than 8 hectares. The typical small farmer grows food crops, such as maize and beans, and cash crops. For some, food crops are a cash crop, but for most, the cash crops are for export, such as coffee, tea, cotton, tobacco, and groundnuts, depending on the country.

Maize has not always been the staple. Before 1900 it was almost unknown in East Africa. Sorghums and millets were predominant and these are still grown by small farmers in drier areas where moisture is insufficient for maize.

Wheat is the next most important grain in terms of consumption, except in Tanzania. For wheat, large farms predominate, producing virtually 100 per cent of the crop in Kenya and 90 per cent in Tanzania. Malawi and Zambia do not produce much wheat, because it is a temperate crop that only grows successfully at altitudes above 1,800 metres in East Africa.

Rice is the least important grain, except in Tanzania which has a large upland rice crop. Kenya and Malawi grow rice under irrigation and Malawi has recently become a net exporter.

All four governments systematically control the domestic prices of food grains at both the producer and consumer levels. They enforce official prices through marketing boards that are statutory monopolies for food grains that enter national markets (that is, that are not consumed in close proximity to their production), and for international trade. The boards draw down stocks and/or import grain when domestic production is too low to meet the demand at the ruling prices, and they accumulate stocks and/or export when production is high. Government subsidies cover any losses incurred by the boards due to their fixed-price margins. In spite of the logistical difficulties in enforcing official prices, the controls have been effective. The present author has successfully estimated domestic supply and demand equations for food grains for all four countries as functions of official prices.[1] The quantity of food grains produced in East Africa depends directly on the level of government prices.

## GOVERNMENT PRICE OBJECTIVES FOR FOOD GRAINS

The ideology of the four governments differs in many ways but in this respect their policies are uniform. The declared objective of all four governments is to achieve domestic self-sufficiency in those food grain crops for which significant domestic capacity exists. This permeates development plans, agricultural sector strategies and public discussions of food price policy. The most concise statement of government policies in this regard is found in FAO (1976). The political pressures for self-sufficiency are strong. In 1980, when Kenya was forced to import maize for the first time in nine years, the Minister of Agriculture was made the public scapegoat for this national failure and demoted to become Minister of Culture (Kwitny, 1980).

Of course, governments can say one thing and do another. To test the hypothesis that the governments set domestic prices in order to maintain domestic self-sufficiency, the author has estimated food grain models for the four countries in the eight cases where significant domestic production capacity exists – maize, wheat, and rice in Kenya and Tanzania, and maize in Malawi and Zambia.[2] Because a free-market model is clearly inappropriate, the models contain government price-setting, stock-adjustment, and net import demand equations in addition to domestic demand and supply equations.

The governments' main instrument of control is the annual determination of producer prices. From their public statements, the four governments apparently associate a welfare cost with dependency on external trade, either as an importer or an exporter. They desire to meet their own food grain requirements from domestic production at the lowest possible price to consumers in order to insulate themselves from demand and supply shocks transmitted from abroad. The world price, however, is the opportunity cost of grain to the country as a whole, and for a small country in international trade, there are also welfare costs when domestic prices diverge from world prices. The government must consider these costs as well, which will be larger, the greater the gap between world and domestic prices, and the more important the crop to domestic consumption.

It is postulated that each government has a long-run target producer price for each food grain, $PP_t$, and that it sets these prices in order to *minimize* the following welfare losses:

$$W(PP_t) = a\,(PP_t - SSP_t)^2 + b\,(PP_t - WP_t)^2,$$

where $SSP_t$ is the self-sufficiency price, $WP_t$ is the world price, and $a$ and $b$ are non-negative government behavioural parameters to be estimated. The $SSP_t$ is the producer price that would clear domestic markets under autarchy in an average year. It is the intersection of the domestic supply and demand equations at the producer level with zero random disturbances, with real private consumption expenditure (the income shifter in the demand equation) equal to its trend value, with consumer food grain prices at the government-controlled margin over producer prices, and with domestic producer prices of export crops also at their government-controlled level.

The government's welfare function implies that welfare losses occur when domestic producer prices diverge from either the self-sufficiency or the world price. Unless $SSP_t$ equals $WP_t$, the government must trade off one type of loss against the other. At one extreme, if $b = 0$ and $PP_t = SSP_t$, then the government can be said to be pursuing a policy of *absolute* self-sufficiency, or autarchy. At the other extreme, if $a = 0$ and $PP_t = WP_t$, then it is pursuing a policy of 'free trade', albeit with government price controls. In the intermediate range, say, with a greater than u and $PP_t$ closer to $SSP_t$ than to $WP_t$, the government can be said to be pursing a policy of *relative* self-sufficiency.

TABLE 3 *Estimates of government behavioural parameters*

| Commodity | Maize | | Wheat | | Rice | |
|---|---|---|---|---|---|---|
| | $\hat{a}$ | $\hat{b}$ | $\hat{a}$ | $\hat{b}$ | $\hat{a}$ | $\hat{b}$ |
| Kenya | 0.047 | 0.407** | 0.602** | 0.206** | 1.042** | −0.150 |
| Malawi | 0.444** | 0.118** | - | - | - | - |
| Tanzania | 0.665** | 0.528** | 1.057** | −0.347 | 0.779** | 0.071 |
| Zambia | 0.898** | 0.108** | - | - | - | - |

*Note:* ** indicates significant at the 1 per cent level on a one-tailed test

It is not possible to report the complete econometric results of the eight models here, but the estimates of a and b are presented in Table 3. This first test supports the hypothesis that governments have been pursuing a policy of relative self-sufficiency. In every case but maize in Kenya, $\hat{a}$ is the correct sign, significant, and larger than $\hat{b}$, which is the correct sign and significant only in the four maize models and for wheat in Kenya. In addition, in Kenya and Tanzania, the more important the commodity to domestic consumption of food grains, the more significant is $\hat{b}$. (Maize is most important in both countries, followed by wheat and rice in Kenya, but rice and wheat in Tanzania.) This is not considered a coincidence. The governments understand that the more important the crop to domestic consumption, the greater the costs of maintaining domestic prices that diverge from world prices.

A second test of the self-sufficiency hypothesis comes from direct comparisons of $PP_t$, $SSP_t$, and $WP_t$, which are presented in Table 4. Again, producer prices relate more closely on the whole to self-sufficiency prices than to world prices. There are a couple of inconsistencies – Kenya and

Tanzania, for example, have taxed rice production to an extent that has endangered self-sufficiency – but the following general pattern emerges. In relation to world prices, converted at official (over-valued) exchange rates, governments subsidize high-cost food grain production such as wheat in Kenya and Tanzania, and tax low-cost production, in each case moving in the direction of self-sufficiency. This explains why none of the countries has historically been a major exporter or a major importer of food grains that can be produced domestically, although net imports have fluctuated, sometimes dramatically, from year to year. Notice, however, that domestic prices relative to world prices, $PP_t/WP_t$, have been declining over time in

TABLE 4 *Comparison of government-controlled producer prices*

| Commodity | Ratio | Mean | Linear trend |
|---|---|---|---|
| Kenya, 1964 to 1978 | | | |
| Maize | $PP_t/SSP_t$ | 1.151 | 0.007 |
| Wheat | $PP_t/SSP_t$ | 1.073 | −0.016** |
| Rice | $PP_t/SSP_t$ | 0.912 | −0.006 |
| Maize | $PP_t/WP_t$ | 0.869 | −0.026** |
| Wheat | $PP_t/WP_t$ | 1.077 | −0.012 |
| Rice | $PP_t/WP_t$ | 0.645 | −0.004 |
| Major export crops | $PP_t/WP_t$ | 0.953 | 0.001 |
| Malawi, 1965 to 1978 | | | |
| Maize | $PP_t/SSP_t$ | 1.023 | −0.032** |
| Maize | $PP_t/WP_t$ | 0.504 | −0.017** |
| Major export crops | $PP_t/WP_t$ | 0.508 | −0.023** |
| Tanzania, 1964 to 1977 | | | |
| Maize | $PP_t/SSP_t$ | 0.946 | 0.018* |
| Wheat | $PP_t/SSP_t$ | 0.8363 | 0.0001 |
| Rice | $PP_t/SSP_t$ | 0.881 | −0.001 |
| Maize | $PP_t/WP_t$ | 0.760 | 0.023** |
| Wheat | $PP_t/WP_t$ | 1.152 | 0.015 |
| Rice | $PP_t/WP_t$ | 0.638 | 0.010 |
| Major export crops | $PP_t/WP_t$ | 0.683 | −0.024** |
| Zambia, 1965 to 1978 | | | |
| Maize | $PP_t/SSP_t$ | 1.0039 | −0.0002 |
| Maize | $PP_t/WP_t$ | 1.022 | 0.005 |
| Major export crops | $PP_t/WP_t$ | 0.892 | −0.023** |

*Notes:*

1 World prices of food grains are export prices, f.o.b. gulf ports US for maize and wheat, and f.o.b. Bangkok, Thailand, for rice, converted to domestic currency at official exchange rates.

2 Producer prices of food grains are long-run target prices after the effects of short-run influences on prices such as government-held grain stocks and foreign exchange reserves have been eliminated.

3 The ratio, $PP_t/WP_t$, for export crops is an average of export prices, weighted by the quantities of the various export crops produced.

Kenya and Malawi, while increasing in Tanzania and Zambia, in order to maintain domestic self-sufficiency.

Table 4 also shows producer prices of export crops in relation to world prices. Again at official exchange rates, taxes on export crop production have been about 5 per cent in Kenya, 11 per cent in Zambia, 32 per cent in Tanzania, and 49 per cent in Malawi.[3] Kenya stands out as the country with the lowest and most stable rate of taxation. In the other three countries, the rate of taxation has been increasing significantly by more than 2 percentage points per annum.

TABLE 5 *Actual and simulated net exports of food grains, thousand metric tons, 1964 to 1978 average*

| | | Kenya | Malawi | Tanzania | Zambia |
|---|---|---|---|---|---|
| Maize: | Actual | 71 | 17 | −17 | 43 |
| | Simulated | 500 | 600 | 120 | 360 |
| Wheat: | Actual | 7 | - | −37 | - |
| | Simulated | −45 | - | −90 | - |
| Rice: | Actual | −1 | - | −23 | - |
| | Simulated | 8 | - | 80 | - |

Government commodity policies have significantly affected external trade in food grains. In Table 5, the author has simulated external trade assuming that domestic prices of food grains and export crops were at world prices, and that governments neither subsidized nor taxed consumers of food grains through the consumer-producer price margin.[4] These calculations are not definitive because they are based on extrapolations of supply and demand curves outside the range of the data, particularly for Malawi, but they are suggestive. If governments had not been pursuing their policy of relative self-sufficiency, all four countries could have been net exporters of maize, while Kenya and Tanzania would have been net importers of wheat and net exporters of rice.

## AGRICULTURAL DEVELOPMENT POLICIES

This section now examines the four governments' agricultural development policies. Owing to the nature of the questions addressed, the results of this section are less definitive, and more suggestive of areas for future research.

British agricultural development policy was fairly uniform throughout these four East African colonies. Before World War II, the colonial governments directed most attention to British settler agriculture. After the War, they finally began to pay some attention to the small African farmers. The major problem was thought to be that rapidly growing populations using the traditional slash-and-burn system of cultivation were creating problems of soil depletion. Efforts to correct this spawned a large number of administrative ordinances that attempted to govern cultivation practices. When these measures failed to improve the situation, policy shifted in the mid-1950s towards increasing the intensity of land use in the high-potential areas (typically those of higher-altitude) by consolidating land-holdings, by distributing improved seeds and fertilizers, by concentrating extension advice on 'progressive farmers', and by introducing cash crops. These measures produced a truly dramatic upsurge in agricultural production in the late 1950s and early 1960s in all four countries. They also brought about considerable inequalities in the level of development between different regions of each country (in the case of Kenya, see Heyer, 1975).

Notwithstanding land transfer programmes like the Million-Acre Settlement Scheme in Kenya, the most striking feature of post-independence agricultural development policies in Kenya and Malawi has been their essential continuity with colonial policies (Harbeson, 1973, p. 78 and Chanock, 1977, p. 407). They have continued to emphasize small farm production, individual land tenure, and expanded services to the rural areas. They have developed technologies appropriate to small farms, promoted them through their agricultural extension services, and extended transportation systems that link products with markets. British policy had created a rural middle-class that took over the reins of power when Kenya and Malawi became independent. This class, which had benefited from British development policies before independence, continued them afterwards.

In Tanzania and Zambia on the other hand, in line with their commitment to socialism, governments have attempted to change the organization of agricultural production. This policy has advanced furthest in Tanzania with the *Ujamaa* villagization scheme which relocated scattered small farmers in villages where, in principle, the government could more readily provide services that would improve the technology of rural life, and combine individual plots into large fields where 'more efficient' large-scale cultivation practices could be applied. In practice, according to the noted French agronomist, Rene Dumont, many villages are too large, are located long distances from the fields, and are contributing to rapid soil depletion (Africa Research Bulletin, 1980, p. 5739). Programmes such as *Ujamaa,* the National Maize Production Programme, and the 'farming as a matter of life and death' campaign have suffered from poor organization and lack of trained personnel, and have disrupted the activities of the agricultural research stations and the agricultural extension service.

Zambia has experimented with co-operative farms and Rural Reconstruction Centres – both attempts at large-scale farming. When the latter could only produce maize at four times the unit cost on small farms, President Kaunda announced Operation Food Production in June 1980, a programme to build two state farms of 20,000 hectares in each of Zambia's nine provinces (Africa Research Bulletin, 1980, p. 5556). The farms are to be highly-mechanized, financed by foreign donors, and managed by skilled ex-patriate personnel. Clearly, the government has no confidence in its own small farmers to achieve rates of growth of output like those in Kenya and Malawi.

These policies have influenced the rates of growth of agricultural production in the four countries, as shown in Table 2 above. They have also affected the domestic cost of producing food grains relative to world prices over time. The author has simulated these domestic costs, $DP_t$, as the intersection of the domestic supply and demand curves, assuming that domestic prices of export crops equalled world prices and that consumers were neither subsidized nor taxed through the consumer-producer price margin.[5] The simulations in Table 6 show the impact of agricultural development on domestic costs of production in relation to world prices. They more accurately measure trends in domestic costs than a simple comparison of population growth, real consumption growth per caput, the expenditure elasticity in the demand equation, and the time trend in the supply equation.

The results are consistent with previous observations. All four countries are low-cost producers of maize (even at official exchange rates). But the domestic cost of producing maize has been declining only in Kenya, and significantly so. Of the other three countries, it has been increasing the least in Malawi, increasing somewhat more in Zambia, and increasing significantly in Tanzania. Government development policies have been more favourable to domestic production in Kenya and Malawi than in Tanzania and Zambia. Given the self-sufficiency objective in all four countries, it is not surprising to recall from Table 4 that producer prices of maize have been declining *vis-à-vis* export crops in Kenya, increasing the least in Malawi, somewhat more in Zambia, and the most in Tanzania.

## CONCLUSIONS

In their work on the Asian rice economies, Timmer and Falcon (1975) demonstrated the importance of government-controlled domestic prices of grain in explaining international trade in rice. This paper continues in their footsteps with regard to four maize economies of East Africa.

In East Africa also, governments pursue commodity policies that affect agricultural production and incomes and external trade in food grains. They control domestic prices at levels that amount to a substantial indirect tax on agricultural production, even at official exchange rates and even more so at realistic ones. While agricultural economists have long recognized that governments control domestic agricultural prices, it is time to stop studying agricultural development as if they did not. Looking only at the growth rates of food grain production in Table 2, for instance, one might have erroneously concluded from the superior rates in Tanzania and Zambia that the domestic cost of producing food grains has been declining in these two countries relative to Kenya and Malawi. Government food grain policies are orientated towards urban consumers. Their purpose is to reduce domestic prices of food grains to the minimum level consistent with domestic self-sufficiency. Government commodity policies are also part and parcel of the general development Strategy in all four countries, which can be characterized as import substitution industrialization.

TABLE 6 *Comparison between domestic costs of production and world prices of food grains over time*

| Country | Commodity | $DP_t/WP_t$ | |
|---|---|---|---|
| | | Mean | Linear trend |
| Kenya, 1964–78 | Maize | 0.724 | −0.028** |
| | Wheat | 1.121 | 0.008 |
| | Rice | 0.776 | −0.002 |
| Malawi, 1967–76 | Maize | 0.765 | 0.005 |
| Tanzania, 1964–77 | Maize | 0.899 | 0.019* |
| | Wheat | 1.513 | 0.013 |
| | Rice | 0.732 | 0.013 |
| Zambia, 1965–78 | Maize | 0.754 | 0.011 |

In spite of taxes on agricultural production, Kenya and Malawi have achieved impressive annual rates of growth in agricultural production exceeding 4.5 per cent in total and 1.5 per cent per caput since independence, which have permitted a relative decline in domestic food grain prices. This successful experience suggests, first, that agricultural land resources do not yet limit agricultural production in East Africa, since Kenya and Malawi already support the most intensive use of land. It suggests, second, that small African farmers do respond to opportunities to improve their productivity if appropriate technologies are developed and made available, since Kenya and Malawi have based their agricultural development strategies on the small farms. These results are consistent with T.W. Schultz's well-known views expressed in *Transforming Traditional Agriculture* in 1964. With little doubt, this successful experience has contributed significantly to overall economic development in these two countries.

Tanzania and Zambia have been less successful in promoting agricultural development. Domestic self-sufficiency in food grain production has been maintained at the expense of export crop production, by raising domestic prices of food grains relative to those of export crops. The comparisons between the two groups of countries suggest that this has impeded overall economic growth in Tanzania and Zambia. These two countries appear to be experiencing a classical Ricardian bottleneck to economic growth as food prices rise in consequence of population growth more rapid than technological advance in agriculture.

## NOTES

[1] The supply and demand equations are conventional. The former are Nerlove partial adjustment models with two supply shifters: an index of the producer price of export crops, and a time trend as a proxy for technological change. Demand is a function of consumer prices and private consumption expenditure. All nominal variables are deflated, by the consumer price index in the demand equations, and by the domestic price of fertilizer in the supply equations, see Gerrard, 1981.

[2] Malawi is now a net exporter of rice, but this model could not be estimated due to a lack of consumer price data. The other models, which are the same for each food grain, resemble Abbott's (1979) model, except that Abbott proceeded to estimate reduced form equations – net import demand as a function of the exogenous variables – for a total of thirty-three countries, as opposed to structural equations for four countries, done by the author.

[3] Accurate calculations of the degree of overvaluation are hard to find. But *Pick's Currency Yearbook, 1976–77* reports that the average black market premium for the Kenya Shilling was 32 per cent in 1971 and 31 per cent in 1976; for the Malawi Kwacha, 63 per cent in 1971 and 114 per cent in 1976; for the Tanzania Shilling, 62 per cent in 1971 and 207 per cent in 1976; and for the Zambia Kwacha, 49 per cent in 1971 and 191 per cent in 1976. The over-valued exchange rate represents a substantial tax on the export sector of each country and the degree of taxation has been increasing over time in every country but Kenya.

[4] The author's best estimate is that Zambia subsidizes the consumer-producer margin by about 45 per cent, Malawi taxes it by about 55 per cent, and Kenya and Tanzania are intermediate.

[5] This is not the same as $SSP_t$, which is conditional on *actual* export prices that prevailed during the period and *actual* subsidies or taxes on the consumer-producer price margin.

## REFERENCES

Abbot, P.C., 'Modeling International Grain Trade with Government Controlled Markets', *Amer. J. Agr. Econ.,* Vol. LXII, No. 1, 1979.

*Africa Research Bulletin: Economic, Financial, and Technical Series,* Vol. XVII, Africa Research Ltd, Exeter, England, 1980.

Chanock, M., 'Agricultural Change and Continuity in Malawi', in R. Palmer and N. Parsons, *The Roots of Rural Poverty in Central and Southern Africa,* University of California Press, Berkeley, 1977.

Food and Agricultural Organization of the United Nations, *National Grain Policies: 1975,* Rome, 1976.

Gerrard, C.D., *Economic Development, Government-Controlled Markets, and External Trade in Food Grains: The Case of Four Countries in East Africa,* Ph.D. Dissertation, University of Minnesota, 1981.

Harbeson, J.W., *Nation-Building in Kenya: The Role of Land Reform,* Northwestern University Press, Evanston, 1973.

Heyer, J., 'The Origins of Regional Inequalities in Smallholder Agriculture in Kenya', *East African Journal of Rural Development,* Vol. VIII, 1975.

Kwitny, J., 'Kenya Is Comfortable, Stable, and Optimistic, But Severe Tests Loom', *Wall Street Journal,* 27 October 1980, p.1.

Ricardo, D., *On the Principles of Political Economy and Taxation,* 3rd ed, Cambridge, Royal Economic Society, 1970 [1821].

Schultz, T.W., *Transforming Traditional Agriculture,* Yale University Press, 1964.

Timmer, C. P. and Falcon W. P., 'The Impact of Price on Rice Trade in Asia', in G.S. Tolley and P. Zadrozny, *Trade, Agriculture, and Development,* Ballinger, Cambridge, Mass., 1975.

## DISCUSSION OPENING – M. L. A. de SWARDT

It seems to me that what the paper is saying is that Kenya and Malawi, with their policies of 'improving' and intensifying agriculture within the existing system and at the same time promoting export crop production, have succeeded in shifting their agricultural supply curves and in maintaining food self-sufficiency. Tanzania and Zambia, on the other hand, who have tried to 'transform' their agricultural sectors and concentrated on state farms and centrally-run co-operatives and who have stressed food self-sufficiency at the expense of export crops, have only succeeded in achieving food self-sufficiency by moving up the supply curve by maintaining high producer prices for food crops at the expense of export crops which have been heavily taxed. This has been said in a different way by a number of different writers (Lele; Jansen) but never quite in this way and not so closely examined. It is good to have the empirical research analysed so as to highlight the differences and give substance to the arguments.

However, I have the following queries:

1 Has the author run his regressions with the period broken up, taking say 1962–72 or 1964–70 and 1970–78? It is my understanding that in both Tanzania and Zambia agricultural commodity prices – including those for food crops – were kept low in order to extract a surplus from agriculture (Tanzania) or to keep the influential urban workers happy (Zambia). It would therefore be a more recent phenomenon that food crop prices have been increased to increase food supply. If this is the case then (for Tanzania anyway) it may be the high export taxes that account for declining export crops and increasing food crops, or it may even be the result of the 'development' policies which in these two countries have tended to ignore or discourage export crop production. On the other hand, if prices for the earlier period were relatively more favourable to food crops than export crops then the given interpretation stands. Or perhaps reversal has been so great in the latter period that it has overridden the effects of the earlier.

2 I am not happy with SSP, the self-sufficiency producer price, and would like some detail on how it is derived. Another thing the author does not mention in taking world price at f.o.b., US gulf or Thailand – has he made any allowance for transport differentials? That is would not it have been better to use a border price and producer costs to estimate welfare losses of pricing policy rather than to use current government price setting to measure the effects of that price fixing?

3 Can he give details of his estimates of consumer-producer margin subsidies and taxes? I am interested to find out how he went about his calculations here.

4 There appears to me to be an inconsistency in Table 3. Using government behavioural estimates the long-run target producer price for wheat was below the world price (for wheat in Tanzania, b was 0.347) whereas in Table 4 it comes out positive at 1.152 and is used as an

example to show that Tanzania subsidizes wheat (the high-cost grain). I do not know whether they do or not but I do know that real wheat prices have declined by approximately 20 per cent since 1972.

5 If the author has simulated net food exports, has he taken cross-price effects with other crops (particularly other export crops) into account in his supply models? Or does he not consider land, labour, management or whatever, to be a constraint on total possible agricultural output from these countries?

Food self-sufficiency is a major goal for most developing countries. The mechanism by which it is achieved differs from country to country with varying degrees of success. The Zambian and Tanzanian attempts to shift production along the supply curve has been dependent on heavy government intervention in the market along the following lines:

(a) control of producer prices;
(b) control of input costs;
(c) by definition, therefore, government controlled margins.

If the farmers do not perceive this margin as adequate in real terms they simply will not produce for sale. The discouragement of export crops, be they food grain or non-food grain, carries a high cost. The active discouragement of farmers from producing export crops by the use of pricing, explicitly denies the country access to agriculturally earned foreign exchange. All too often these developing countries have no manufacturing base and therefore this curtailment of exports reduces the external purchasing power of the country dramatically. The Tanzanian example currently bears this out where one of the principal sources of foreign exchange is aid money, either in the form of expatriate salaries or in project money itself.

It must also be noted that this paper only deals with data up to 1978. This seems to be a key period for Africa and one wonders why. Zambia has been on the market twice since then for maize, both times in the order of 300,000 tonnes, which is approximately equal to half its marketed volume. On each occasion there have been severe payment difficulties. Does food self-sufficiency only imply local production of food, or does it also contain an element of substitutability between export crops and local food grains? Had Zambia maintained its cotton and tobacco production programmes, the country might not have found itself in quite the foreign exchange difficulties it does now, despite the problem in copper production. More important, the natural complementarity between these crops and maize would have ensured that farmers continued to produce at least their subsistence food requirements.

Farmers will respond to price; if the real margins were good enough sufficient maize would be produced even now. Zimbabwe, faced with having to import maize in 1979 (some 90,000 tonnes) put sufficient incentive into the price, which produced a three-year stockpile. Similarly during UDI when Australian wheat supplies were cut off, an incentive produced a wheat stockpile that lasted three years.

An important consideration in countries that have had their economies deteriorate as far as those of Zambia and Tanzania is the purchasing power of money. If there is nothing to buy then money becomes worthless. The important issues then appear to be:

1 A healthy export programme, whether agricultural or manufacturing based.
2 Foodcrops need to find their own competitive niche. The history of maize in Africa shows it be highly complementary to other cash crops.
3 Subsidies ought to be spent on technological means that effectively move the supply curve to the right.
4 Small-scale farmers are very sensitive to price movements and are smart enough to grow a food crop if the margin is right.
5 Where government is in control of both inputs and outputs it is in the unique position of determining the margin to growers.
6 A grower will not produce by decree. He must identify his own labour and the returns to his own labour. The moment he loses the clear definition of his inputs and is forced to operate at the lowest common denominator he is not interested and begins to subsist.

KIRIT S. PARIKH

# *Analysis of National and International Agricultural Policies for Sustainable Growth and Equity and Stability in an International Setting**

## INTRODUCTION

Food problems – efficient production or procurement of food and the appropriate distribution of food among members of family and society – are endemic problems of mankind. Yet the nature and dimensions of these problems have been changing over time. As economic systems have developed specialization has increased and this has led to increased interdependencies of rural and urban areas, of agricultural and nonagricultural sectors, and of nations. The importance of public policies in resolving these problems has grown with this growing interdependence of nations, reflected in increasing volumes of food trade, and this requires that the exploration of national policy alternatives be carried out in the context of international trade, aid and capital flows.

The objective of the Food Agriculture Programme (FAP) of the International Institute for Applied Systems Analysis (IIASA) is to find national and international policies that would help ensure adequate food for all in a sustainable way (Parikh and Rabar, 1981). Our primary emphasis is on policies with a five to twenty years perspective. But we recognize that the policy options available to individual nations are significantly affected by the policies of other nations. Policies have to be evaluated in the context of the objectives of national governments. Growth, equity, stability and sustainability may in general be considered to be the objectives of the governments' economic policies. Specific policy instruments, even policies relating to primarily agricultural issues, affect these objectives differently. This can be seen in Table 1 which summarizes the possible impacts of some important policies on those objectives in a large developing country such as India. Thus to evaluate policies we need to determine quantitatively the impact of policies on various objectives. This can be done satisfactorily only with a policy analysis model system. The model system we have

* The paper describes the work of many people who constitute the FAP Network, to all of whom the credit for its substance goes. In writing this I have benefited from the help and comments of Gunther Fischer, Klaus Frohberg and Douglas Maxwell.

constructed consists of price endogenous, descriptive, general equilibrium national policy models of 23 selected countries, or groups of countries, covering 80 per cent of the world's agricultural production, consumption, and trade, which explicitly incorporate governmental policies and which are linked through trade, aid and capital flow. The models are to be used in a year by year simulation mode. The FAP of IIASA has been working on this task since 1977 with the help of a large network of collaborating institutions around the world.

TABLE 1 *Some effects on objectives of various policy instruments*

| Policy instrument | Objective | | | |
|---|---|---|---|---|
| | Growth | Equity | Stability | Sustainability |
| Investment level | ↑ | ↑↓ | ↓ | |
| Income tax | ? | ↑? | | |
| Indirect tax | ↑ | ↓ | ↓ | |
| Irrigation | ↑ | ↓ | ↑ | ↓ |
| High yield varieties | ↑ | ↓ | ↓? | ↓ |
| Fertilizers | ↑ | ↑↓ | | ↓ |
| Mechanization | ↑? | ↓ | | |
| Land ceiling and redistribution | ↑↓ | ↑ | | ↑↓ |
| Tenancy reforms | ↑ | ↑ | | ↑?↓ |
| Public food distribution | ↓ | ↑ | ↑ | ↑ |
| Procurement of food grains | ↓ | ↑ | | |
| Buffer stock operation | ↓? | | ↑ | ↑ |
| Food aid | ↑↓? | ↑ | ↑ | ↓ |

↑ Further objective.
↓ Adverse effect on objective.
? Questionable effect.

*Source:* Parikh, 1977.

Our model system differs from many past global models (FAO, 1971; Japanese MAFF, 1974; Takayama, et al., 1976; Rojko and Schwartz, 1976, and Lundborg, 1981) in that we distinguish nations. MOIRA (Linnemann, et al., 1977) distinguishes nations but only has one commodity and a restricted set of government policies.

Policy in our national models is directed to understanding structural change in terms of composition of output in agriculture and non-agriculture, of rural to urban populations and of changing comparative advantage of the nation. The linked system permits policy analysis within an environment in which countries adapt their policies to each others' actions. The general equilibrium methodology at both the national and international level provides a rigorous tool to account for the interactions between different actors – producers, consumers, governments – and ensures balance not only at the commodity but also at the financial level of each of the actors. Government policies are restricted to specific instruments whose effectiveness is thus judged in the context of behavioural responses of economic agents.

The paper is organized as follows: in the next section the structure of a typical national model and their international linkages are described. A number of policy applications are then briefly presented. Finally our approach to incorporating objectives of long-term sustainability is indicated.

## A TYPICAL NATIONAL POLICY MODEL OF THE FOOD AND AGRICULTURE PROGRAMME

The basic elements of the model system of the FAP are the national policy models. A national model has to reflect the specific problems of interest to that particular nation. Thus the national models differ in their structure and in their descriptions of government policies. The model system of the FAP permits linking of such diverse models but requires that the models meet a few conditions. They have to have a common sector classification at the international trade level, nine agricultural and one nonagricultural sectors, and some fairly reasonable additional technical requirements. For example, net exports have to be independent of absolute level of world prices and continuous functions of them. Even though the national models differ from each other, the broad structure is common to most models. Each model covers the whole economy and together they cover the whole world. Thus there are no infinite sources or sinks in the system to absorb policy impacts and mask feedback and other secondary effects. Food supply and demand are distinguished by various income groups. A typical model is shown in Figure 1.

Past prices and government policies affect production decisions. The domestic production in the n sectors of the economy,[2] $y_1, y_2, \ldots, y_n$, is determined by each of the various income groups – represented by superscript j. Thus for group j, its share of the national product is given by the vector $y^j_1, y^j_2, y^j_3, \ldots, y^j_n$. The income this share amounts to is determined by the price that these products command. For example, a farmer who has grown two tons of wheat and one ton of rice would have an income of twice the price of a ton of wheat plus the price of a ton of rice, minus the cost of producing wheat and rice. The matrix $[y^j_i]^0$ thus describes the initial entitlements of the different products for the various groups. Government policies may redistribue these entitlements to $[y^j_i]$.

Given these entitlements and world prices, the $j = 1, \ldots, J$ income groups trade among themselves under the influence of government policies, which include national market policies, (price, bufferstock, trade) public

FIGURE 1 *A typical national model*

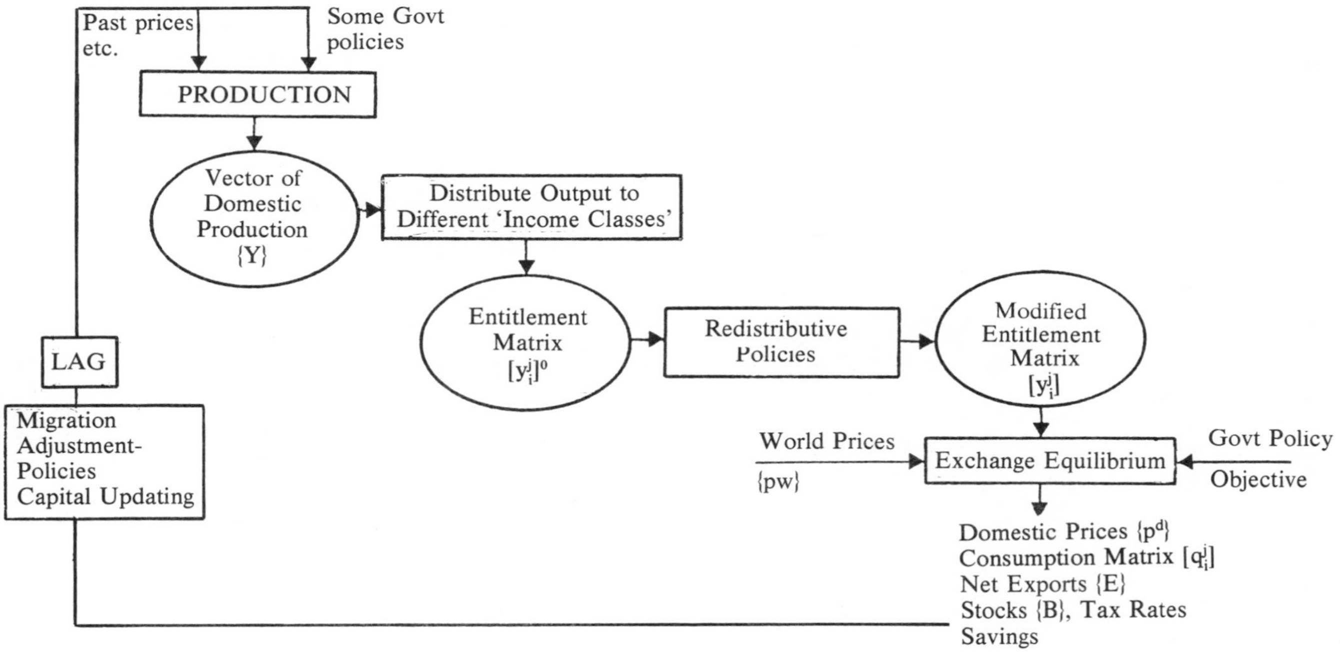


*Source:* Parikh and Rabar, 1981.

finance policies (balance of payments, public demand, direct tax) and international market and finance policies (agreements on price, bufferstock, trade, financing). The resulting exchange equilibrium determines the domestic prices, net exports, tax rates, and the consumption patterns of different income groups whose demand behaviour is characterized by a linear expenditure system and which clears the markets and meets the balance of trade constraint.

## THE INTERNATIONAL LINKAGE

The net exports of all the countries are thus calculated for a given set of world prices and market clearance is checked for each commodity. The world prices are revised and the new domestic equilibria giving new net exports are calculated once again for all countries. This process is repeated until the world markets are cleared in all commodities. It may be noted that at each stage of the interaction the domestic markets are in equilibrium. The procedure is shown schematically in Figure 2. It may be noted that any international agency – such as a bufferstock agency – can be represented as a country and the effectiveness of its policies can be evaluated within a framework in which country policies react to the policies of the agency.

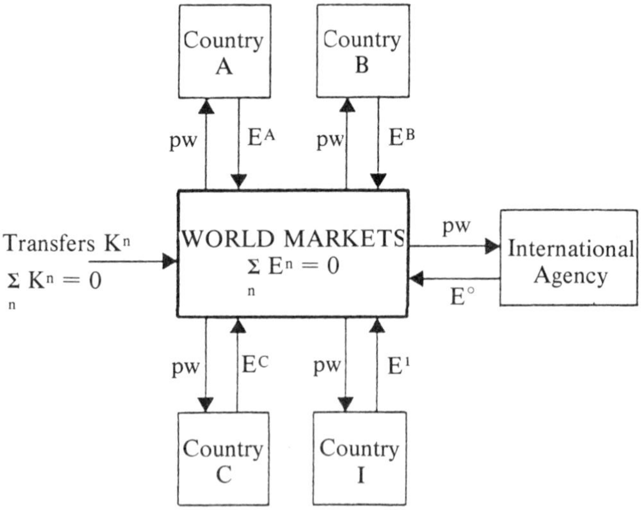


FIGURE 2 *International linkage*

*Source:* Parikh and Rabar, 1981

This process yields international prices as influenced by government policies. The outcome of this process is examined by governments who may change their policies for the next period.

Since we go through these steps period by period, we have a dynamic simulation that we use for a five-to fifteen-year period to predict the consequences of various policies, not only for individual countries but also for the entire system.

The approach of the FAP model system described briefly above is certainly ambitious but if the policy issues raised here are to be adequately explored, we believe that such a level of complexity is inescapable.

## IMPLEMENTATION – A NETWORK APPROACH

The countries selected and the status of the models are shown in Table 2. As can be seen, most of the detailed models are being developed with the help of collaborating institutions. The collaborating institutions bring knowledge of specific countries and through their expertise are able to make national models more realistic. Moreover, they provide contact with national decision makers, help disseminate findings and ensure that the work of the FAP will find real-life applications. The development of the methodology of linking the country models together, as well as the methodology of the computation of domestic equilibrium under the influence of government policies, was begun at IIASA and continued at the Centre of World Food Studies in Amsterdam, by M. Keyzer (1981).

TABLE 2 *Status of detailed national agricultural policy models, April 1982*

| Some policy analysis made | Nearly ready | Well underway | Scheduled to start |
|---|---|---|---|
| *Hungary | *EEC | *Egypt | Australia |
| CMEA | Kenya | *Poland | New Zealand |
| *India | *US | *Japan | *Mexico |
| Brazil | *Finland | *Canada | Nigeria |
| *Sweden | | China | Pakistan |
| *Austria | | | Argentina |
| *Thailand[a] | | *Bangladesh[a] | *Indonesia[a] |

* Built with the help of collaborating institutions

[a] Co-ordinated by Centre for World Food Studies, Amsterdam

The FAP group also developed a number of detailed country models (Parikh, Narayana, 1981; Csaki, 1981), as well as a simplified system (Fischer, Frohberg, 1980) consisting of models of all the selected countries based on a data bank (Sichra, 1981) organized by IIASA around data obtained from international organizations. The simplified system of models demonstrated the feasibility of linking various national models, and established the computational efficiency of the algorithms developed. The simplified national models were further developed with the help of specialists from various countries into an intermediate version of models which constitute a system called the *basic linked system.*

## SCOPE OF ANALYSIS

Some of the more important policy questions that can be explored with the *basic linked system* and the detailed models are listed below:

*National policies*

For growth:

- What is the impact of price policies on production and consumption?
- What are the impacts of fertilizer prices, irrigation and 'modernization' on production, food prices and consumption?
- How does agricultural growth affect employment and migration patterns?

For equity:

- Does a price increase in the cities benefit the farmers?
- Is it better to ration food or to issue food stamps for public food distribution programmes?
- What role can a food-for-work programme play in relieving rural poverty?
- How do changes in landholding patterns and in tenancy structure affect production and consumption?

For stability:

- Is price stabilization desirable for consumers?
- What is an appropriate national bufferstock policy to stabilize prices?
- How can stable incomes for farmers be ensured? What are the costs and benefits of alternative schemes of deficiency payments and set-asides?

For self-sufficiency:

- How to realize an appropriate agricultural self-sufficiency level?
- Should food aid be sought? What are effective ways of utilizing food aid?
- What are appropriate trade policies of trade quotas, tariffs, and export incentives?

*International policies*

- What are the consequences of adoption of large-scale programmes for alcohol/energy plantations by energy-deficient countries with food surpluses?

What is the most effective way to operate an international bufferstock agency that tries to ensure that prices for specific commodities either remain at a given level or remain within a prescribed range?
What would be the economic consequences of an agreement to keep world market prices at given levels by adjusting internal prices, either for all nations or for a subset of nations?
What would be the size of a bufferstock to withstand a shock such as might result from a series of crop failures?
What levels of international food transfers are required to banish hunger within a prescribed time limit?

## EXAMPLES OF POLICY ANALYSIS

In a short paper one can only present a few selected examples of such analysis which give a flavour of the kind of analysis that is possible:

*If only the rich countries ate less and exported more*
What impact would it have on the hungry people of the poor countries if the rich countries were to eat less and export more, thereby lowering world prices and allowing the poor countries to import more than they do now?

This was explored by F. Rabar (1981). It was assumed that a hypothetical country enters the market with the firm intention of selling thirty million tons of wheat each year, at any price, to help poor importers. A series of adjustments start as soon as the first thirty million tons appear on the market. The international market response is immediate. Argentina, Australia, Canada, the US, Mexico and India reduce their export of wheat, and Austria, Japan, Brazil, Egypt, New Zealand, the EEC, Thailand, Kenya, Pakistan, Nigeria and the rest of the world increase their imports. The CMEA countries, China and Indonesia show no reaction. Yet the quantity is too high to be completely absorbed at prevailing prices. The wheat price drops and it stays depressed for the next ten years.

The second-level adjustment on the part of the exporting countries, after reducing their exports, is to reduce their production as well. This happens with different time lags, different speeds and different intensities. This is, though, the general response of all the exporters.

The second-level adjustment on the part of the importers, after increasing their imports and their home demand, is the reduction of their home supply. In other words, they substitute their home production with cheap imports. Of course, they reallocate their production capacities to other products: because of these substitutions the consumption of wheat increases only marginally and hungry people do not eat much more.

A slight improvement in the nourishment of the population can be observed in some developing countries, but not all. The real advantage seems to be in the beef market. In almost all countries there is an upward shift in feed consumption: either wheat is directly used as feed or producers substitute wheat with coarse grain production. Bovine production and export figures in the exporting countries and imports in the importing countries go up and for some years after the shock an upswing in the beef market is created, until prices and production begin to adjust.

After all these adjustments we may ask the question: where are the additional thirty million tons of wheat, put on the market by an imaginary country? The answer is that it was absorbed in the system. Almost none of it reached the hungry people of the countries represented.

*Growth or redistribution, or both*

Per caput food production has grown in India at an annual rate of 1 per cent over 1950–80 and yet the percentage of rural population below poverty line with insufficient food has remained more or less constant. To test the effectiveness of redressing poverty and malnutrition what we call a 'free food programme', in which the government annually distributes freely to everyone 75 kg of food-grains, the model of India was used by Parikh and Narayana (1981).

The questions that arise are the following:

What would be the impact on poverty, on consumption and on income distribution?

What would be the impact on government budget, its budgetary surplus and public investment, and consequently the impact on the growth rate of the economy?

What would be the impact on domestic market prices of foodgrains and their impact on supply?

The simulation is carried out up to 1990 – where the policy changes are introduced in 1977. Four scenarios are generated to explore the issues. To eliminate the problem of domestic supply disturbances, we ensure in all scenarios the same prices to farmers – that is, the same incentives – through complete domestic price stabilization. The food distributed freely is purchased by the government on the market and is financed by reducing public investment which affects economic growth. The results of the runs are shown in Table 3. The two base scenarios of high and low growth are generated through change in savings rate.

TABLE 3 *Indian agricultural model results: annual growth rates 1971–90*

(per cent)

| | High growth | | Low growth | |
|---|---|---|---|---|
| | Base | Free food | Base | Free food |
| Real GDP | 5.40 | 4.77 | 4.60 | 3.86 |
| GDP agriculture | 2.59 | 2.59 | 2.59 | 2.59 |
| GDP non-agriculture | 6.95 | 6.07 | 5.78 | 4.70 |

Between the base and the free food scenarios a fall in growth rate of real GDP of about 0.7 per cent per year is observed. A major impact of the programme is in the distribution of consumption. Under the free food programme the number of people in absolute poverty drops to around 10 million in 1977 from its 1976 level of more than 160 million people in the rural areas. When we compare the two base scenarios we see no change in poverty levels. So growth alone is not enough to reduce poverty. It is clear that such a free food programme can be very effective in reducing poverty. Its cost is lowered growth. A reduction of 0.8 per cent in growth rate from the low and high growth base rates of 4.6 and 5.4 seems quite acceptable to us. But a reduction from an average annual growth rate of 3.5 per cent, as achieved by India over the past three decades, may not be so obviously acceptable. The growth rates in our base cases are higher than actual because of our assumption of reduced capital/output ratios in the non-agriculture sector. Thus, if growth is stepped up, redistribution becomes easier but it is still necessary to redress poverty.

*What if climate changes were to reduce yields of some foodgrains in the United States*

Climate changes such as disturbance of the ozone layer may reduce rates at which yields of soyabeans, maize and wheat increase in the United States. Such changes affect acreage allocations in the United States, its exports and world prices. The impact would be global. This was explored with our US model (Abkin, 1981) linked to our *basic linked system.*

The yields of soyabeans, maize and wheat grow by 1.83, 1.68, 2.06 per cent per year, respectively, in the base run. We assumed that climate disturbances would lower these rates to 0.93, 1.54 and 1.61, respectively, from 1982 onwards. The effects were predictable but the magnitudes somewhat surprising. Though the US yields in 1990 were lowered by 8.3, 0.82 and 4.1 per cent for soyabeans, maize and wheat, respectively, their US outputs reduce by 6.75, 1.87 and 2.56 per cent only, and the world production changes even less. It is interesting to note that the area under maize increases whereas areas under soyabeans and wheat decrease. The world prices of soyabeans are higher in all years from 1982 to 1990 but the prices of maize and wheat are lower in some years though higher in most years. The meat prices are also higher. These adjustments in production structures in the United States and the world somewhat soften the impact of such changes. The above runs can also be interpreted to show what would happen if the rates of technical progress were to slow down in soyabean, maize and wheat yields in the United States.

*What if the United States were to raise the price of its grain exports*

A bill proposed to the US Congress would raise the price of exported wheat and maize to 'the cost of prodution' – a technical US agricultural term that is calculated on a generous basis. What would be the consequence of such a bill on prices, production and farmers' incomes? This will be explored with the help of our US model (Abkin, 1981) linked ot our *basic linked system.*

One expects that:

- — The US prices would rise to the 'cost of production'.
- — The world price would rise to the US price less transportation differentials. This would happen because the price rise is low enough and the US is an important enough supplier so that the US would still export.
- — There would be large acreage restrictions on US production of maize and wheat.
- — The acreage restrictions and higher prices could affect farmers' incomes either way
- — The effects on coarse grains exports from the United States would be slightly moderated by substitution to other feedgrains.
- — Non-US production of wheat and coarse grains would increase. The extent of this is the main key to whether US farmers would be helped or hurt.
- — The United States would expand its production of other agricultural commodities, especially, perhaps, rice.
- — As the model is now set up the US price of meats would rise, reducing consumption.

Without linkage to models of other countries provided by our basic linked system, it would have been difficult to explore this issue. Runs made with the US model in a stand-along mode would fail to show the effects outside the United States where exporting nations, or those nearly ready to export, would be helped while importers would be hurt. But more importantly, the impact of the world on the United States would have to be captured by an export demand function. Even when reasonable estimates of these are available, changes in them, due to policy adjustments of other countries consequent to US policy changes, would be hard to capture in such an unlinked run.

## ENSURING LONG TERM SUSTAINABILITY

From a longer term perspective of thirty years, the increasing demand for food from the growing population of the world which is also becoming richer, questions of the availability of resources to produce adequate food, the efficiency of techniques and environmental consequences come to the fore. Land would have to be cultivated much more intensively. What is the sustainable production of the world? How do we sustain it and what are the policy options needed now?

For this purpose we use a physical crop production model developed on agronomic principles which define yield functions given soil, climate and genetic information. This is further extended to give associated environmental effects of cultivation when additional information on cultural practices are provided. The environmental effects in turn are fed back to modify soil characteristics and future yield functions. Thus we can explore interactions of technology, resources, environment and economics, and summarize the outcome for a given crop in a region as shown in Figure 3.

FIGURE 3 *Summarizing technology, economics and environmental interactions*

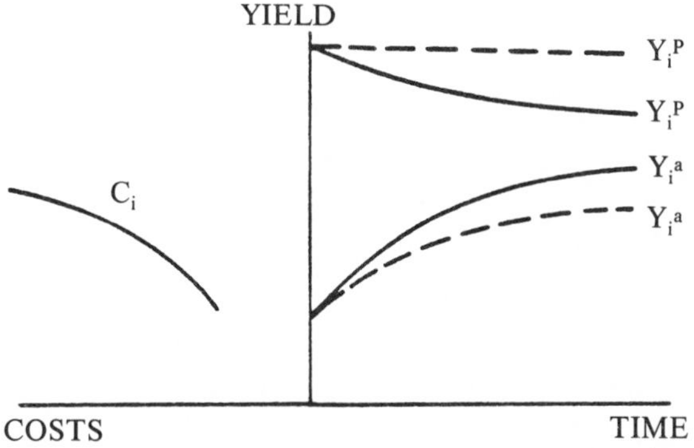


$Y_i^a$..........Actual yield (when farmers maximize profits) with technology set i

$Y_i^P$..........Potential yield (when inputs are free) associated with $Y_i^a$

One can define sustainability in many ways such as $Y^P(t) \geq Y^P(t\text{-}1)$ or $Y^P(T) \geq Y^P(0)$. The former ensures monotonic increase in potential yield, but the latter only insists that it be restored by the end of the planning period. To bring considerations of sustainability into medium term policy analysis we visualize the connections shown in Figure 4.

FIGURE 4 *Bringing sustainability into medium-term policy*

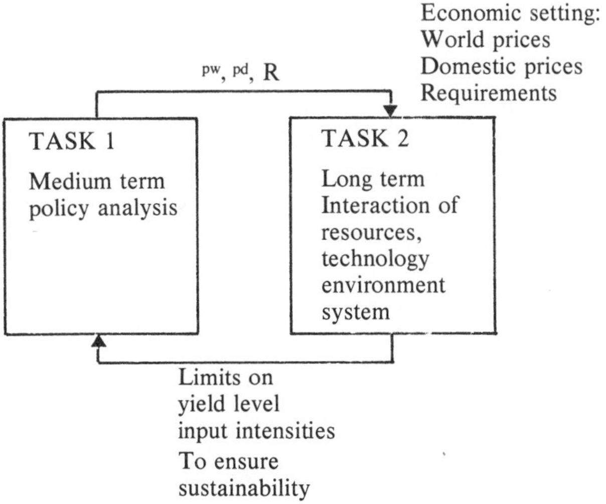

The findings of Task 1 will provide a starting point for the scenarios of Task 2, providing a realistic basis for long-term investigations. The findings of Task 2 might modify the representations of permissible intensities of technologies in Task 1. Present policies and actions may have to be constrained to keep open options for technological transformations in later decades.

## REFERENCES

Abkin, M.H., 'The Basic US Model for the IIASA/FAP Global System of Food and Agriculture Models: Domestic Utilization and Prices', WP-81-38, International Institute for Applied Systems Analysis, Laxenburg, Austria: 1981.

Csaki, C., 'National Policy Model for the Hungarian Food and Agriculture Sector', RR-81-23, International Institute for Applied Systems Analysis, Laxenburg, Austria, 1981

FAO, Food and Agriculture Organization of the United Nations, 'A World Price Equilibrium Model', Projections Research Paper No. 3, CCP/WP3, Rome, 1971.

Fischer, G. and Frohberg, K., 'Simplified National Models: The Condensed Version of the Food and Agriculture Model Systems of the International Institute for Applied Systems Analysis', WP-80-56, International Institute for Applied Systems Analysis, Laxenburg, Austria, 1980.

Japanese Ministry of Agriculture and Forestry, 'Outline of the World Food Model and the Projections of the Agricultural Products for 1980-85', Tokyo, 1974.

Keyzer, M. A., 'The International Linkage of Open Exchange Economies', (Doctoral Dissertation), Free University of Amsterdam, 1981.

Linnemann, H., J de Hoogh, Keyzer, M. A., and van Heemst, H.D.J., MOIRA: Food for a Growing Population', CP-77-1, International Institute for Applied Systems Analysis, Laxenburg, Austria, and North Holland Publishing Company, Amsterdam, in the Series *Contributions to Economic Analysis,* Number 124, 1979.

Lundborg, P., 'Trade Policy and Development: Income Distribution Effects in the Less Developed Countries of the US and EEC Policies for Agricultural Commodities' (Doctoral Dissertation), Department of Economics, University of Gothenburg, 1981.

Parikh, K.S., 'A Framework for an Agricultural Policy Model for India', RM-77-59, International Institute for Applied Systems Analysis, Laxenburg, Austria, 1977.

Parikh, K.S., and Rabar, F., 'Food Problems and Policies: Present and Future, Local and Global – Food for all in a Sustainable World: The IIASA FAP Program', SR-81-2; International Institute for Applied Systems Analysis, Laxenburg, Austria, 1981.

Parikh, K.S. and Narayana, N.S.S., 'An Agricultural Policy Model for India – An Illustrative Exploration of a Right-to-Food Program – Food for all in a Sustainable World: The IIASA FAP Program', SR-81-2, International Institute for Applied Systems Analysis, Laxenburg Austria, 1981.

Rabar, F., 'Policy Insights from the Basic Linked System – Food for all in a Sustainable World: The IIASA FAP Program', SR-81-2, International Institute for Applied Systems Analysis, Laxenburg, Austria, 1981.

Rojko, A.L. and Schwartz, M.W., 'Modeling the World Grain-Oilseeds-Livestock Economy to Assess World Food Prospects', *Agricultural Economics Research* 26, pp. 89–98, 1976.

Sichra, U., 'The FAP Data Bank – Food for all in a Sustainable World: The IIASA FAP Program', SR-81-2, International Institute for Applied Systems Analysis, Laxenburg, Austria, 1981.

Takayama, T. and Hashimoto, H., 'Dynamic Market-Oriented World Food Projections and Planning Models and their Empirical Results for the 1970-1974 World Food Situation', World Food Projections Report No. 2, Department of Agricultural Economics, University of Illinois, 1976.

## DISCUSSION OPENING – DOUGLAS D. HEDLEY

It is with considerable pleasure that I respond today to Kirit Parikh's paper. First, the Department of Agriculture in Canada has had a very close association with the FAP at IIASA for some time and we are keenly interested in the Phase II work outlined in the paper. Second, I am particularly pleased to be returning 'home' for these meetings.

The task facing IIASA in modelling a high proportion of world agricultural production and consumption on an individual country basis is awesome. In almost every case, the country models are based on a history of previous models, and some are directly linked to larger models in the individual country. In the case of Canada, the Canadian component in IIASA has a much longer companion model, the Farm and Regional Model, which is used continuously and heavily in both forecasting and assessment of policy alternatives for agriculture.

Some reflection on the growth of modelling over time is worthwhile. As the quantitative techniques emerged during and after World War II, there was an explosion of effort to use these new techniques in the practical world of problem solving. Computer hardware and software lagged behind in applying many of the multi-equation techniques and the highly iterative processes that the theoreticians generated, until at least the late 1960s. During the 1970s computer technology advanced to the point that the cost of relatively sophisticated modelling became easily within the reach of many organizations, national, international, private and public. At the same time, however, the economic shocks of the 1970s began to show up, particularly energy and cereal grain prices and more recently interest rates. While models have not been able to forecast these events, creating considerable scepticism regarding their use, models have been very helpful in exploring the impacts and longer-run implications of these fundamental changes in the domestic and international economic structure.

The conclusion I draw from this review is that while Dr Parikh has presented to us a number of policy issues he wishes to explore, one must recognize that the conclusions drawn are representative of the economic structure embedded in the model. In almost every case, these models reflect the historical or existing economic structures of individual countries. The results of any policy scenario are conditioned by that economic structure. As events unfold in the 1980s further significant adjustments in world economic structure are likely to occur, possibly invalidating the conclusions IIASA may draw in Phase II. The result is that any exercise such as FAP is a continuing process and not one that can be turned on and off. The argument I am building here is that the FAP at IIASA should have a continuing role with a long term commitment at some international organization. By the late 1970s, funding of large models had largely stabilized, replacing the surges of interest and disinterest in modelling efforts. It is important to maintain this stability throughout the 1980s.

Let me turn now to the issues raised by Dr Parikh in the policy analyses he proposes for examination by the FAP model. The approach used by Dr

Parikh relies heavily on exploration of policy issues within individual countries and then tracing the international impacts of these policy actions to other countries. At the outset, I want to express a major concern with the apparent sequence of events and efforts in the work of FAP. Model development is being undertaken in Phase I of the work with policy identification and analysis of policy issues and alternatives following in a subsequent phase of the work. Model development appears to have been conducted with only an informal and largely implicit understanding by the modellers of the issues and problems to be explored. Dr Parikh is only now identifying a lengthy list of issues both national and international in his paper. This is certainly not a fatal flaw in the work of IIASA. It could however lead to the need to redevelop some components of the overall linked model system to add specific policy instruments or economic relationships which were not earlier identified. This iterative process of model development and redevelopment to incorporate new components is well-known and recognized in the large-scale models designed for continuing use in forecasting and policy analyses. From a pragmatic point of view, it may indeed have been impossible to fully define a set of policy issues robust enough to have withstood the changing economic environment during the period of model development.

In reviewing the list of policy concerns proposed in Dr Parikh's paper it is difficult in the time allocated to me here to examine each. I want to comment on one significant issue in economic development which appears to be missing, and to explore, as well, one included in the set of international policies.

An emerging concern over recent years involves the complex set of relationships involving commodity prices, interest rates, private and institutional credit and changing debt maturities and the impacts these variables have on foreign exchange earnings, capital generation within a country and debt servicing in many countries. First, the rapid increase in interest rates since 1979 has added substantially to the debt service burden in the Third World. Second, shorter debt maturities, primarily from private credit institutions, have increased the proportion of debt falling due in each year thereby increasing the vulnerability of many countries to the vagaries of credit markets. Third, a large number of developing countries have over the past two decades moved towards private credit markets and away from the international institutional credit of the IMF, IBRD and regional development banks. The significant expansion of credit from private sources during the last decade particularly is unlikely to continue as strongly in the 1980s. The implication of this is to add to the vulnerability of many countries in debt services. Finally, as I review commodity prices generally, the coincidence of low prices across many diverse sectors is cause for concern. The base metals, ones such as phosphates, the industrial or plantation crops in agriculture – tea, coffee, cocoa, rubber, palm oil, sugar – and cereal prices, all appear to be simultaneously low. The implication is very heavy pressure on foreign exchange earnings, adding to the debt servicing problems and deeply affecting capital formation, capital rationing between and within countries and sectoral growth rates.

If these four factors I have outlined persist for any extended period of time, levels of trade and capital development and growth processes in much of the Third World could be significantly affected for the remainder of the 1980s. It should be noted that the poorest nations of the Third World are likely to bear the least immediate impact of these events; the NICs will be most affected, possibly pushing many back towards international institutions for assistance. In Figure 1 of Dr Parikh's paper I cannot readily identify the model components to acceptably address this issue. Figure 2 is suggestive but insufficient detail exists to provide assurance that the linked system can either.

Let me now turn to an issue which Dr Parikh does raise in his paper – international buffer stocks. I doubt that the political will or the economic rationale for international buffer stocks exists today of the type commonly proposed. Valdes and Siamwalla at IFPRI have identified a range of sources of insecurity in food supplies. Many of the sources of insecurity lie completely outside the agricultural sector and do not necessarily manifest themselves in domestic or international prices and supplies. It would seem more valuable to use the taxonomy of Valdes and Siamwalla or some other comparable set of food insecurity sources and begin to address individually these issues. Certainly the broad issue of nutritional adequacy in diets is very important but I cannot visualize an international buffer stock as a means to deal with a myriad of concerns in this area. I cannot judge from Dr Parikh's presentation if the models he describes have the detail sufficient to deal with the individual issues.

My final comment on Dr Parikh's presentation has to do with the concerns of this conference – growth and equity. Table 1 gives equity as one of the objectives of agricultural policy, yet in the description of the models in Figures 1 and 2 there is little indication of how this objective is dealt with in the models. My concern stems from the relationships shown in Table 1. Growth and equity objectives are viewed as incompatible for high yielding varieties, contrary to the results of Professor Hayami noted earlier in the conference. Several other cases in Table 1 can be cited as questionable. If these relationships in Table 1 are taken as *a priori* in development of the model, then the model results may indeed be questionable. Possibly, Dr Parikh needs to re-work Table 1 substantially and to explore more thoroughly the conditions under which his proposed relationships may hold. Certainly a country by country review would seem to be needed.

In closing, I want to applaud the work of Dr Parikh and his team at IIASA for the leadership and skill they have brought to their work. All of us look forward to Phase II of the FAP work and the insights which their work can bring to the processes and policies in international agricultural development.

## GENERAL DISCUSSION – RAPPORTEUR: ZULKIFLY HJ. MUSTAPHA

*Papers by Gerrard and Parikh*

The questions and comments from the floor were generally in line with those raised by the openers of the discussion.

On Dr Gerrard's paper, the general discussion centred basically around pricing policy relating to the choice of producer prices as against world prices in food grain production and marketing towards self-sufficiency policy and the effects of such pricing policy. This was particularly raised as producer prices normally discount possible opportunity costs as well as other charges including transport and handling costs, and that if these costs were taken into account, and they should be in a pricing policy, there would be a different result. Other comments involved the analysis of government price behaviour in the context of the real grain market structure, changes in the inter-sectoral terms of trade as a result of such pricing policy, the relationship between British colonial policy and the prevailing agricultural development policy in East Africa, and the desire to achieve other goals (for example, fiscal goals) from that of self-sufficiency alone.

In his response to the general and technical comments raised by the opener as well as from the floor, Dr Gerrard explained that there exist some shortcomings and deficiencies in the analysis. He admitted to the fact that the governments in the four selected countries in East Africa in their producer pricing policy obviously have other goals apart from that of self-sufficiency alone, and that the paper did not elaborate appropriately and adequately on the evolution of agricultural development policy in the selected East African countries in relation to former British colonial policy. He also agreed on the prevailing diversity in the food grain market structure. At the same time, he claimed that the application of world prices instead of producer prices would create problems and other related issues pertaining to the choice of appropriate border prices, particularly in view of the effects associated with producer margins, the country's status as an exporter or importer, and their overall implications on the food grain self-sufficiency policy. In summation, he indicated that the producer prices used in the analysis were the official government prices, that is the prices received by the farmers on delivery of their produce to the marketing board.

So far as Dr Parikh's paper was concerned, the discussion was mainly on the applicability of the policy analysis model formulated by the FAP of IIASA. Comments and questions raised were on discrepancies in data presentation, the extension of the model to include economic policies over time, and the relationships between sectors, in particular the indigenous sector to the general economy.

In reply, he indicated that the model had implicitly considered sectoral relationships in the economy as economic policies were normally taken in the context of various objectives of national governments. The model incorporated both national and international economic policies for growth, equity, stability and self-sufficiency. Although some variables, for example inflationary cycles, were not accounted for by the model, others were taken care of through the international trade equilibrium mechanism and other internal and external policies. Policy variables such as allocation of funds between activities and capital injection into a sector can also be incorporated into the model. He further indicated that the model has been applicable, citing the case of India, to analyse and evaluate the impact of policies on various objectives, though there were difficulties, as an example, to determine the magnitude of benefits and the beneficiaries of policy objectives. In the light of the dynamic economic situation, he agreed that the model should be continuous over time so as to consider further developments in economic policies.

Participants in the discussion included Joachim von Braun, Susumu Hondai, D. Belshaw, W. Henrichsmeyer and I. Carruthers.

GLENN L. JOHNSON

# *Synoptic View**

We are at the end of a full, productive conference ably orchestrated by Professor Ohkawa. I have read and/or listened to most of the papers presented. They are credits to their authors and collectively are a tribute to Professor Ohkawa's leadership and skill in suggesting topics and selecting speakers.

We are also at the end of a delightful stay in Jakarta where we have all benefited from the hard work and conscientious efforts of Dr Birowo and others on the national organizing committee. In these ten days we have been together in Jakarta we have learned much from each other. Equally important is that we have come to appreciate each other's points of view and backgrounds. We have also learned about Indonesia and its people as we have lived here.

At each IAAE conference I conclude anew that it really takes ten days of professional exchanges, social events and, above all, personal conversation really to begin to know each other. I, for one, have long hoped that we will never get so pressured by work, time restrictions and lack of money that we cannot spend ten days together every three years. I believe sincerely that the world is improved because we know each other better and that Leonard Elmhirst and our early leaders were correct about the need to know each other. It seems to me that those of us who are too busy to stay for the full ten days should simply come late or leave early without insisting that those who can stay be deprived of this important opportunity.

I recall with great pleasure the opportunity I had to spend sixteen or seventeen days with a whole new community of scholars in Finland at my first IAAE meeting. The friends and congenial relationships I developed there are still some of the most valued I have attained in my career as an

* This is a 'synoptic view' of all the papers presented at the Eighteenth Conference of the International Association of Agricultural Economists which met in Jakarta, Indonesia, 24 August – 2 September, 1982. Names are used to refer to papers presented by various speakers at the conference. Such references should be adequate in a proceedings volume which will contain most of the papers and will be accompanied by a 'contributed papers' volume, *(IAAE Occasional Papers No. 3)* containing the remaining papers.

agricultural economist. It was important that I had enough time to get really acquainted with such people as Nils Westermarck, Wilfred Cave, Edgar Thomas, Wat Thomas, John Raeburn, Arthur Jones, Finn Reisigg, and A. Eskeland to name only a few.

The synoptic view which I am to present was probably instituted to force Presidents Elect to do their homework. Though I have, indeed, tried to do my homework, I must apologize in advance for the many errors of omission (as well as commission) I will inevitably make. The number, complexity and overall excellence of the papers are such that it is beyond my ability to do them justice in the time available.

In order to be of most help, I believe I should deal with the Elmhirst Lecture, the Presidential Address and the Indonesian presentation, first, and then with the plenary, invited and contributed papers as they have developed our theme of growth and equity.

I turn now to Keith Campbell's Elmhirst Lecture which is not, and was not, intended to be within our theme. As we are interested in what the outstanding individuals we select as Elmhirst Lecturers have to say on a subject of interest to them, we do not expect them to conform to our theme.

## THE ELMHIRST LECTURE

Keith Campbell gave us an independent, penetrating, critical paper on our responsibilities and opportunities in connection with the *World Conservation Strategy* report. That report was commissioned by the World Wildlife Fund and the UN Environmental Programme. It was produced by the International Union for Conservation and Natural Resources. After commending the report for not being antigrowth, Campbell stressed its 'exaggerations, quasi-facts and economic disorientations'. He feels we should be challenged by the report's reliance on the 'environmental movement's disregard for facts and economic principles'. Campbell expressed his concern that ecology, once a respectable science, has become a kind of religion. He also regretted that transfiguration (over recent decades) of land economists into resource economists who now, in his view, mainly dispute about externalities, shadow prices and discount rates for future benefits.

Campbell's main concern is that we have ignored the environmental movement rather than been challenged by its shortcomings. He feels we should participate in setting priorities with respect to conservation policy, address the economics of land uses (only one of which is for farming), deal with the anti-technology bias present in the *World Conservation Strategy* report, and do a better job of bringing the powerful tools of economics to bear on issues involving pollution, endangered species and genetic diversity.

In his conclusions, Campbell recognizes that there are important environmental issues in obtaining indispensable agricultural growth in the next twenty-five years but feels that we cannot abandon the policy arena to 'urban-based environmentalists or the scientifically illiterate'. A later paper by John Mellor underlined Campbell's view that 'ecological diversions' have interfered with agriculturally based development strategies.

## THE PRESIDENTIAL ADDRESS

Our President, Theodor Dams, challenged us in his presidential address to strengthen the IAAE as an insitution. He wants us to be innovative while conserving our valuable inheritance from our predecessors by maintaining the right of all our members to express themselves and participate in our activities as individuals regardless of national origin and the vagaries of international political conflicts and ideologies. I note that he who uses force to restrict the individuality of another, automatically sets a precedent for his own repression.

Innovation, Dams indicated, is also needed on the human side of agricultural economics and in analyzing the linkages between the farm and non-farm sectors. He implied a need to deal innovatively with the interrelation among the political, social and economic systems within which farming takes place in all of their 'spiritual, moral and social dimensions'. His comments on rural poverty anticipated those to come later in the programme from Nural Islam. We must, he said, design strategies for farm production and development which will benefit the poor masses without reliance on prohibitively expensive but ineffective 'poverty oriented programmes'.

Dams also stressed the need at our conference for individual respect, an atmosphere of goodwill, the exchange of knowledge and the stimulation of mind, emotion and friendship. The members of our conference have not disappointed Professor Dams – we have taken his advice and we and our discussion groups have profited from it. As Professor Dams hoped, I feel as if I have spent ten highly productive days with family and friends.

## THE INDONESIAN PRESENTATION

We all rejoiced as our Indonesian colleagues made their presentation last Friday. After experiencing their kindness and generosity in looking after us, we had another pleasant experience that Friday. We experienced the goodness of seeing a substantial amount of rather newly created human capital functioning in a highly effective manner. We benefited from their analyses, data and explanations about this diverse country; a country so large that it would extend from San Francisco across North America well into the Atlantic Ocean. The book they generated is an important output of the IAAE. It joins that of Judith Heyer on Kenya, at the Nairobi conference, as one of the notable achievements of our Association.

## GROWTH AND EQUITY – THEIR MEANING

I turn now to our theme 'Growth and Equity'. In putting together this synoptic view of our conference, I have been impressed with the different meanings attached to the phrase 'trade-offs between growth and equity'. Further examination of the papers indicated wide differences in the meanings attached to the words 'equity' and 'growth'. The English word 'equity' has to do with justified or justifiable distributions of rights and privileges among people. An equitable distribution need not give everyone the same rights and privileges but it must be justified in some sense – legally, morally, by custom, by practicality or on some other basis.

By contrast, the English word 'equality', when applied to the distribution of rights, privileges, incomes, property and so on, deals with how equally they are distributed among people.

At this conference and the planning of this conference, the word 'equity' has been misinterpreted by most of us, including me, as meaning equality. As I became aware of this in preparing my synoptic comments, I checked with people competent in the French, German, Spanish, Portuguese, Chinese and Russian languages for corresponding terms. In French, I find *égalité* and *équité* – in Spanish *equidad* and *igualdad.* In Portuguese the corresponding words are *eqüidade* and *igualdade.* I find little consensus among my German colleagues. One possible pair of words is *equitat* and *equalitat,* but Professor Dams says those words are not correct. In Chinese I find *shang dung* and *gong ping.* Of the two words given to me by a Professor of Russian using the Latin alphabet, Victor Nazarenko says that one is wrong and that the other is not even a word! This small linguistic excursion underscores the difficulties we have in communicating with each other about 'equity'.

We also have problems with the word 'growth'. This word was sometimes used at this conference to mean the increase in output and sometimes an increase in resources with which to produce output. Typically we are not very specific about what it is we want to attain with growth. Despite the difficulties we have experienced with different meanings for the words growth and equity, I am pleased that we have been able to carry on very useful discussions about growth and equity. This success, however, does not absolve us from responsibility for clarifying our language and concepts.

Before leaving Michigan to come here, I experimented with various diagrams to use in clarifying our discussion. During this conference, I further developed these diagrams in discussions with a number of you. My diagrams which deal with equality, equity and growth are rather similar to those used by Tarditi in opening the discussion of Hayami's paper dealing with trade-offs between growth and equity. Tarditi's use of his diagrams encouraged me to use my own. I hope my diagrams will help provide the kind of perspective you should expect of a synoptic presentation.

In my diagrams, growth is viewed as the creation of increased capacity to attain all the conditions, situations and things which people (as individuals and as members of societies) find valuable. Equality is but one of the

DIAGRAM 1

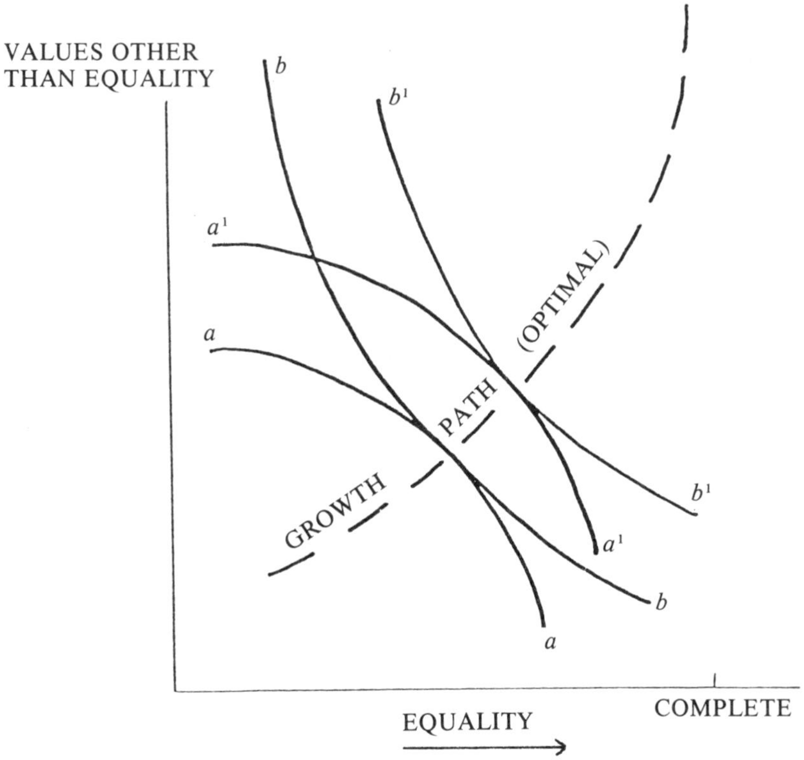


conditions we value. In Diagram 1, equality is on the horizontal axis. At the right end of the horizontal axis is complete or perfect equality. On the vertical axis we find all other values. The capacity of a society can be used to attain various combinations of equality and other values. Using Diagram 1, we can envisage the trade-offs between attaining equality and other values. In this connection, two relationships can be considered: first, there are 'possibilities lines' such as aa or $a^1 a^1$ which show all combinations of equality and other values which are attainable with a given amount of capacity and, second, there are social indifference curves such as bb or $b^1 b^1$ between equality and other values. However, there is still a third kind of trade-off between equality and other values. This trade-off involves growth.

Growth consists of increased capacity to attain desirable conditions, situations and things, one of which is equality. The increase in capacity represented by the difference between aa and $a^1 a^1$ is growth. Such growth makes it possible to move to the higher social indifference curve $b^1 b^1$ from *bb*.

The dashed line in Diagram 1 can be interpreted as an *optimal growth path* or *trajectory*. It indicates the 'best' proportions between attainment of equality and other values. Upward movements along this trajectory involve the attainment of both growth and equality. This important relationship is much different than the trade-offs along a possibilities line. Once growth and equality are so viewed, it becomes difficult to conceive of diagrams with growth on one axis and equality on the other. Some of our authors have discussed the relationship between growth and equality along such trajectories while others have discussed trade-offs along opportunities lines in some sort of growth/equity diagram of questionable consistency.

DIAGRAM 2

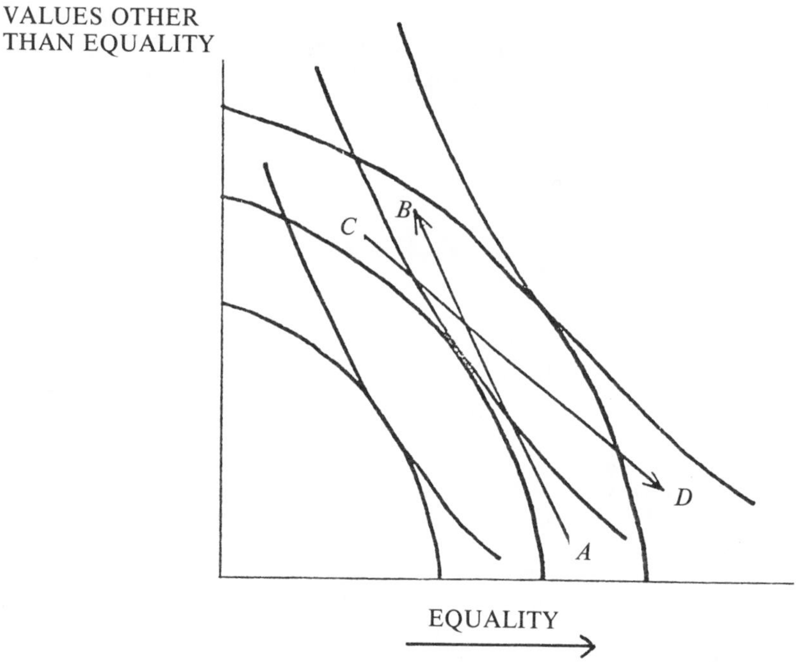


We can also envisage non-optimal growth trajectories such as those indicated in Diagram 2. The line from point *A* to point *B* illustrates a non-optimal growth trajectory which attains other values while giving up equality. The line from point *C* to point *D* illustrates another non-optimal growth trajectory which gives up attainment of other values in order to attain equality. Obviously, we cannot expect a market involving uncoerced exchanges to find an optimal trajectory calling for coerced redistributions. A 'political market place' wherein government responds to political processes by forcibly redistributing rights and privileges can be conceived of but not without the difficulty of dealing with existing distributions of political power. In a sense, the degrees of equality or inequality found along an *optimal* growth trajectory are *justified* socially and economically by the social indifference curves. The degrees of equality along the optimal growth trajectory *can be regarded as equitable.* This gives us a definition of equity which is very different from that implied by most of our papers. The relationships between equity and growth cannot be as fully presented and explained in diagrams with growth on one axis and equity on the other.

It must be stressed that diagrams such as these reflect many conceptual and empirical difficulties not the least of which is their gross oversimplification and, even, misrepresentation of the complex phenomena they purport to represent. More attention will be given to these difficulties later. Nonetheless, papers presented at this conference, such as those by Hayami, Rousser and others, have used some of these concepts with success while still other papers can be fruitfully interpreted in terms of this diagram. Some of our papers deal with the shapes of the possibilities lines. Others deal with the nature of the growth paths or trajectories while still others deal with problems encountered in measuring equality and growth. Few, if any, touch on the nature of social indifference curves. In the section which follows, I will use these concepts and such diagrams to interpret the contents of various papers.

## THE PLENARY, INVITED AND CONTRIBUTED PAPERS

I will first summarize the world agricultural situation with respect to growth and equity as revealed in various papers presented to us. Following this, I will take up various conceptual and empirical problems considered in other papers.

### *The world agricultural situation*

At our conference, the world agricultural situation was ably summarized in the first third or so of Nural Islam's paper. He stressed the increased production of agriculture in the developed countries, the encouraging productivity of Asian agriculture and the unfortunate situation in Africa where unbridled population growth outpaces agricultural production. Looking to the future, Islam stressed the immensity of the production task ahead for world agriculture and the critical nature of prospective poverty levels, both rural and urban.

Significantly, I believe that no paper reflected an antigrowth attitude. Further, none reflected the serious conviction that the food needs of expanding populations could be solved by feasible redistributions of present levels of agricultural production.

Gustav Ranis's excellent paper on growth and equity dealt with growth through time – with a growth trajectory. He analyzed the success of the Province of Taiwan, China, and the lesser success of Colombia in attaining equality as well as other values by giving the rural poor the opportunity to produce for both domestic and export markets. In effect, he argued that such a trajectory attained much growth with considerable additional equality. By contrast, strategies of countries seeking industrial without agricultural development have generated less growth and less equality.

Van der Meer's very useful and quite empirical paper on experiences in the developed countries dealt with the growth trajectories of Western European, Oceanic and North American countries. He noted differences among countries in rates of growth from the year 1818 to date. In general, rates of agricultural growth per caput have been little better than GDP growth per worker. Farmers, he found, have suffered recurrent crises when demand for farm products has lagged behind supply. Over the years he finds that vanguard farmers and consumers have been the main beneficiaries of agricultural growth in the market economies. Van der Meer deplores off-farm migration as more disadvantageous than I do. I should point out that I am a landless, off-farm migrant myself – my wife is a land-owning, off-farm migrant. Neither of us regret our migration and we think that goes for most of our fellow off-farm migrants. Three or four sentences in van der Meer's paper about stagnation of US agriculture since 1973 are not quite consistent with the 1981 bumper US crop, the fact that my wife's entire 1981 grain crop sits unsold in government storage and that 10 per cent of her 1982 acreage is idle under a production control programme, the even bigger crop predicted for 1982 and the 20 per cent reduction in US wheat acreage presently requested for 1983. Van der Meer's closing remarks about farm sizes appear very appropriate. In the countries he covered, large but still family operated farms have not lost their comparative advantage to corporate farms employing large numbers of labourers.

Nils Westermarck's paper complements the van der Meer paper. Westermarck concentrates on the question of whether there has been a widening disparity between the incomes of poor and well-to-do farmers in Finland, Belgium, Austria, West Germany, Switzerland, Norway and Japan. In effect, he disaggregates the equality axis of our diagram. Reports from four of these countries indicate that in the decades since World War II, 'technological development' and, I add, the operation of the market, have widened the gap. Public measures have not been adequate to prevent the widening. In Switzerland, partly in Norway and perhaps also in Belgium, government actions to support small farmers and farmers in remote regions have been adequate to narrow the gap.

With respect to Africa, Dharam Ghai finds little of a growth trajectory to discuss. Failure of African countries to invest in land maintenance or improvement, lack of human capital investment, policy failures to provide incentives, adverse weather, and military and social unrest have combined to hold increases in agricultural output near the increases in the rapidly growing populations of Africa. Ghai finds that 'a great majority of the rural population in a large number of African countries must have suffered declines in their real incomes in the 1970s', a conclusion consistent with the high rate of rural migration to African urban slums. These findings for Africa are consistent with Gustav Ranis' analysis of the disadvantages of not including agricultural development in a growth trajectory.

In Southern and Southeast Asia, the first version of V.S. Vyas' paper described an 'all pervasive picture of buoyant agriculture with only a few notable exceptions' but with 'very little impact on the extent of poverty'. His paper describes a near vertical growth trajectory with little increase in equality. He finds that the high yielding varieties (HYV) did not increase equality despite their labour intensity. This, he found, was because of firstly, population increases and secondly, a lack of knowledge of the new HYVs on the part of the poor and their inadequate access to the inputs necessary to produce the HYVs. In effect, he agrees with the papers by Sanders and Lynam and by Antle that it is too much to expect technological change to redistribute ownership of income producing resources. Such expectations place too heavy a burden on the technologists. Vyas argues that in addition to getting more production with HYVs, the trajectory of growth needs to be modified by institutional changes and investments in human capital to attain more equality. In so arguing he adds a valuable dimension to the Ranis argument. In addition to providing incentives for farmers to produce, Vyas sees the need for redistributions along possibilities lines in order to get to a more optimal growth trajectory for attaining equality as well as other values. Similarly, John Mellor's paper noted that the strategy he and Bruce Johnston advocated in the early 1960s recognized land reform as a possible precondition for agricultural growth. Land reform can be viewed as a movement along a possibilities line to a more optimal growth trajectory.

With respect to Japan, Yamada reports an historical analysis (1885 to 1979) of the growth trajectory of the Japanese economy and its agricultural sector. His conclusions for three periods are too detailed and extensive for succinct summarization. Following a dual economy approach, he analyses how development and policy adjustments have kept ratios of output per worker high in both real and nominal terms while attaining favourable ratios between non-farm/farm household incomes per caput. His conclusions draw on the Japanese experience to indicate how development may proceed in contemporary developing countries. He, as well as Mellor and Khan, stresses the importance of 'family farming units' for production and welfare.

The Sugai/Teixeira paper on Brazil indicates a near vertical growth trajectory of questionable optimality. They report little diminution in relative poverty but perhaps some progress on absolute poverty. Former small disadvantaged subsistence farmers, small tenant farmers, share croppers and squatters (without benefit of human capital investments) have migrated to urban slums despite resettlement schemes, agribusiness employment promotion and new crop development programmes. Children from medium-sized owner-operated farms near urban centres received better educations and have migrated to better urban opportunities. A small group of large livestock farmers has participated in the integration of production and processing to offset production losses. Large commercial crop farmers producing mainly export crops are benefiting from agricultural credits and governmental emphasis on exports. The authors conclude that Brazil will have to change its policies if it wants to get on a less vertical perhaps more optimal growth trajectory which will attain more equality.

Reyes' paper on regional income inequality in Mexico also disaggregates the equality dimension of Diagram 1. It deals with the growth trajectory of a country 'grown out of revolution and committed to equality'; however, since 1940, output per worker has increased threefold while productivity and income differentials have widened both between rural and urban dwellers and within the rural sector. The growth trajectory has been upward to the left, largely because of exploding populations and regional differentials in government investments which have favoured non-agricultural development and, within agriculture, the more productive regions. Reyes also cites corruption as a contributing factor.

Csaba Csaki discussed growth trajectories for socialized Eastern European countries. He indicates that those countries of the region which have invested in agriculture and have provided incentives for agricultural production have grown more rapidly than those which have not, after taking into account differences in soil and climates. Csaki did not deal with the social, legal and political inequalities in centrally controlled countries. Neither did Nazarenko in his paper. At a later point, I will consider such inequalities.

In his paper which questions whether there is or is not a trade-off between growth and equity, Hayami was not always clear as to whether he was considering trade-offs along different growth trajectories *or* along possibilities lines. Because of this vagueness, there is the danger that his paper may be interpreted as indicating that there is a great deal of complementarity between the attainment of growth and equality along opportunities lines when, for the most part, he was considering growth trajectories involving the attainment through growth of both equality and other values. Hayami's main contribution was the important points he made about growth trajectories. Those points were: (a) technological advance is essential for attaining the necessary increases in production (growth), (b) technological advance is not necessarily a source of inequality, and (c) population increases cancel out the effects of improved technology on income per caput and make it difficult to attain equality and growth. He agrees with Vyas in seeing the need to supplement HYVs with institutional change but goes farther. He sees HYVs as promotive of induced institutional change, though I would question the adequacy, in some instances, of such induced changes. He calls for dialectical interactions between technological and institutional innovation to avoid the Ricardian trap while recognizing the possibility of the malinteractions Andrews and de Janvry stress as having resulted in stagnation and inequality for Argentinian agriculture.

The Johnston/Clark paper maintained a clearer distinction between possibilities lines and growth trajectories than did Hayami's. They saw the need for reforms along possibilities lines in order to get on better growth trajectories. Verbally, Johnston, and the opener, Brandes, noted the danger that attempts to move along a possibilities line may destroy considerable physical and human capital and, thus, cause negative growth. (See Diagram 4 and discussion thereof later in this paper.)

Kahn's paper contained excellent discussion of the possibilities of carrying out land reforms in Asia. The reforms in Japan, the Taiwan area and South Korea were carried out largely by occupying powers without additional destruction of productive capacity. He is not optimistic about the possibility for further such reforms in Asia.

*Conceptual and empirical difficulties*

Earlier in this presentation, I recognized the conceptual and empirical difficulties inherent in dealing with growth, and the trade-offs between the attainment of equality versus other values. With some misgivings I implied that our concepts were clear enough and our data good enough for us to discuss trade-offs and alternative growth paths. It is now appropriate to consider the papers and authors addressing themselves to some additional conceptual and empirical difficulties encountered in dealing with growth and equity.

We have already seen that a diagram with equality on the horizontal axis and all other values on the vertical axis has been useful in interpreting the contributions of several speakers. At this conference several papers have dealt with the measurement of equality. The 'Gini ratio' measures the degree of equality or inequality in a system. The proportion of people living in absolute poverty (however defined) is another measure of inequality as is the income level which includes the bottom, say, 40 per cent of a population.

The Bhalla/Leiserson paper addressed itself to the question of how to measure income equality. They considered the advantages of per caput versus per household data. Of particular value is their review of research and literature on (a) the relativistic nature of poverty and (b) difficulties involved in defining absolute poverty. They note that studies of 'Gini ratios' or of the incomes of the bottom 40 per cent do not identify the regional or occupational locations of the poor. They believe it is often easier and more desirable to affect incomes for specifically identified groups than for all of the poor in a country. Relative to this point, Johnston and Clark note that while some poverty battles can be won by piecemeal action, attaining the basic goal of overcoming poverty requires strategic and, hence, overall thought and actions. A number of other papers dealt with or pointed out the need to consider regions, subsectors, villages and individual families. Among such papers not already mentioned are those by J. Y. Lee, Tyers and colleagues, the Veemans, de Melo, Sabbarano, Lingard/Wicks, da Silva/Raza, Kada, I. J. Singh, Peters/Maunder and several more. These papers disaggregated aspects of the equality dimension of our diagrams to add much realism. Their contribution was in avoiding the problem of aggregating different kinds of equality. Their weakness was that we still need some aggregation to evaluate the more macro arguments of Mellor, Johnston/Clark, Ranis, and Kahn. These aggregation problems may be a partial explanation of the unfortunate tendency of development assistance agencies to fluctuate faddishly between local (micro) and central (macro) planning without attaining an appropriate balance between the two.

In addition to income equality, there are legal, political and social equality, not to mention equality in the security of one's personal rights, whether those rights are guaranteed or threatened by military and police forces. The equality axis of our figures is also an aggregation of such equalities and inequalities. Aggregation requires a common denominator among the value of such equalities. Utility appears inadequate. Whether or not knowledge of such a common denominator can exist is questionable.

Frederic Sargent's paper states 'we assume that equity is a public value or goal co-equal with productivity and efficiency'. In addition to raising the problem of whether equity means equality, discussed earlier, this statement raises the problem of measuring attainment of the aggregate of values other than equality. Productivity has to do with attaining both equality and values other than equality. How do you weigh different products together into an overall measure of output? With market prices? If you do, the weights become functions of changing incomes and income demand elasticities, in which case the meaning of the vertical axis of our diagram becomes a function of the variable on the horizontal axis – that is, the meaning of 'values other than equality' becomes a function of the level of equality! This calls into question the whole of Diagram 1. This difficulty would be even greater if growth were on one axis and equality on the other. Perhaps this conceptual and empirical problem can be avoided by using intrinsic instead of exchange values as weights but that requires objective research on values. As indicated in my Nairobi IAAE paper and in Volume 3-2/3 of the *European Review of Agricultural Economics* (pp. 207–34), I personally believe such research is possible.

For modest redistributions we can probably make do with weights based on exchange values but for major redistributions so drastic that real tests of power are required to make them, such as considered by Khan, Johnston, and Brandes, quantifying the vertical axis requires a common denominator valid across such intrinsic values as loss of life, starvation, participation, alienation, clothing, public infrastructures, and national security. Brandes took the position that we must make judgements about such important values. I agree and would stress my conviction that such judgements can be based on experience and logic. I regard value judgements as quite similar to the factual judgements reached in the so-called hard sciences which, incidentally, I view as simpler and easier than the social sciences.

In acquiring knowledge of intrinsic values, experience and logic are supplemented by insight and empathy. Empathy seems to be a prerequisite for communication of all knowledge, positive or valuational. In particular, it is a prerequisite for understanding the badnesses of injustice and inequality and the goodnesses of justice and equality.

While Diagram 1 can be used to gain considerable insight, I have also called it into question in connection with my discussion of power. Shifting conceptually from exchange values which are functions of power distributions to intrinsic values which are less dependent on power distributions represents a conceptual improvement. However, we must also note that the configurations of possibilities lines are likely, in many cases, to be a function of which growth trajectory is followed. This is part of the institutional, technological and human dynamics of growth trajectories to be discussed later. Technological change orientated to the needs of small farmers produces a different set of opportunities lines through time than technological change orientated to the needs of large-scale farmers. The same is true for institutional change and human development activities.

A related conceptual problem involves power. Power comes from ownership of income producing, political, social, religious, civic and military rights and privileges. Power is the source of both equality and inequality, as power is used to maintain the equalities and inequalities which distinguish equity from inequity. In playing such roles power creates conceptual difficulties for measuring both axes of our diagrams. Even if intrinsic as contrasted to exchange values are used in aggregating values, imperfections in knowledge of those values make it necessary to employ power (a) in decision rules in order to resolve redistributive conflicts; (b) as weights in measuring attainment of values other than equality and (c) as a means of avoiding chaos and indecisiveness which diminish productivity.

Part of the difficulty is that attainment of equality involves redistribution of power, yet true power cannot be forcibly redistributed. To the extent that power can be redistributed it is less than power. But to the extent that power is redistributed, the meaning of the vertical axis of our Diagram 1 changes along with the shapes of the opportunities and social indifference curves as power can be used to constrain the shapes of effective social indifference lines. Imperfect knowledge about power leads to tests of power – wars, political and social conflicts and civic and religious disorders. Such conflicts are often destructive of rights being defended or redistributed. Though conflicts are typically destructive, they are not always effective in redistributing power. The important destructive conflicts are between groups with much to lose. Those who have nothing to lose have little with which to fight. Those with much to lose have the power to be destructive.

DIAGRAM 3

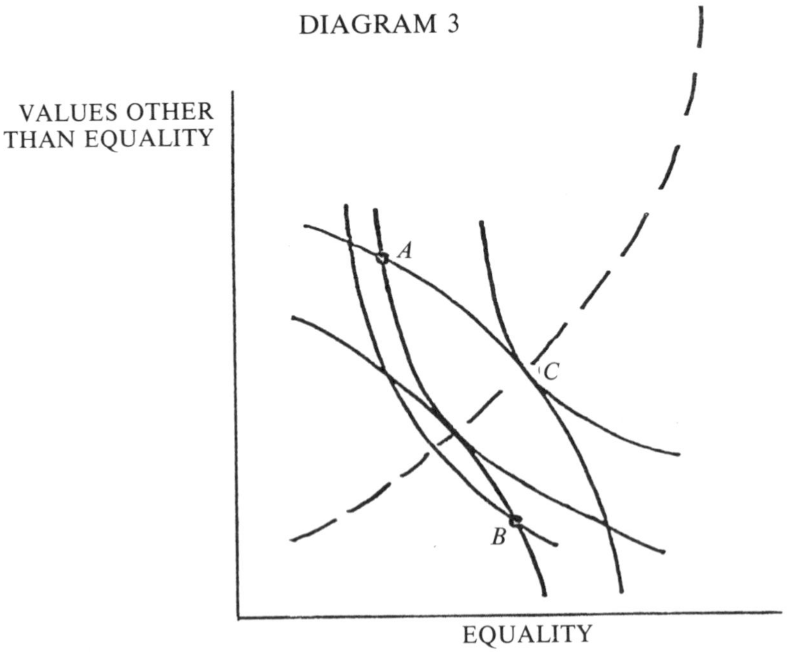

Brandes and Johnston discussed the consequences of destructive redistributions. Our diagrams can be modified to examine such consequences. Diagram 3 is such a modification. In trying to get more equality from point *A* through a destructive test of power, a society may encounter negative growth by shifting to a lower possibilities line and lower indifference curve on a trajectory to point *B* from point *A* with *B* being below the optimal trajectory. Without destruction it could go to point *C* on a higher indifference curve.

Kahn's very interesting paper indicated that the initial land reform in the continental provinces of China was probably regarded by policy-makers as suboptimal. At least they subsequently changed away from rather equal small holdings to large communes. Now, China is again searching for the optimal trajectory by redistributing certain agricultural rights and privileges more equally from the large communes to individuals.

In general, this conference has given less attention to political, social, and civil inequalities than to the inequalities in income which result from unequal ownership of income producing rights and privileges. This was previously noted with respect to the Nazarenko and Csaki papers. Equitable distributions are justified or justifiable distributions, equal or not. Except for justifying distributions as being equitable because they are on relatively optimal aggregate trajectories, as was implied by Mellor, Ranis, and Johnston and Clark, this conference has not dealt with how much of the many forms of equality or inequality is or is not justified.

DIAGRAM 4

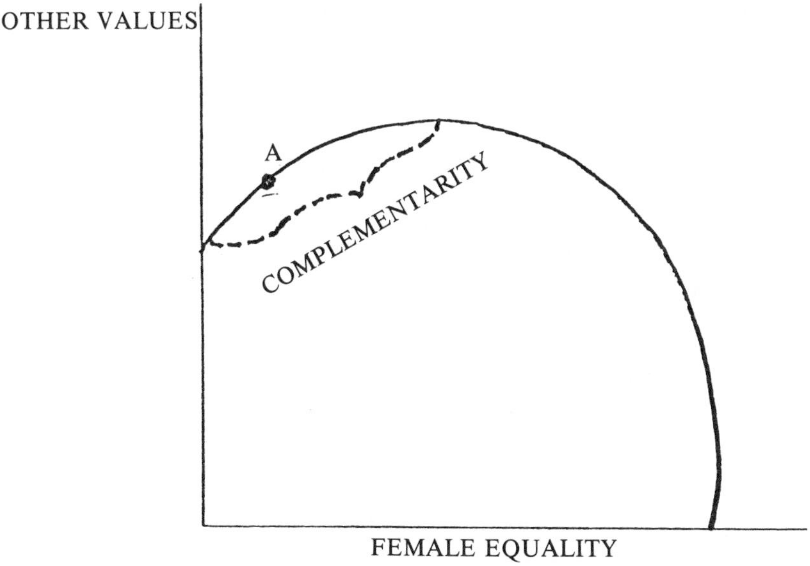

Abe Weisblat helped facilitate the organization of an excellent session on the role of women in agriculture which is related to the inequalities almost universally experienced by women. Our unfinished business reveals the need for more attention to legal, social and political as well as income inequalities, including especially those experienced by women. I, for one, am quite convinced there is a high degree of complementarity along the possibilities line between equality for females and the other values. See Diagram 4 which implies that more equality for women and more attainment of other values may be possible from point $A$ through reforms to grant more equality for females. Other diagrams similar to Diagram 4 could be used to envisage the trade-offs and complementarities between various values including those between the values of two different forms of equality such as legal and income equality, *ceteris paribus.*

Income, civil rights, police and military protection (and oppression) and religious freedom are not distributed equally among countries, within countries, between farm and non-farm sectors, among regions within farm sectors, in societies as a whole and among racial and sexual groups within societies. Income inequalities between farm and non-farm sectors have been discussed by van der Meer for the developed countries, Sugai from Brazil, Reyes from Mexico, and Ghai from East Africa.

The OPEC countries have recently exercized new-found power to reallocate income to themselves from both developed and less developed countries with little regard to how such redistributions have both increased and decreased certain international inequalities. This example indicates something about the realities of power. This redistribution was possible as it was not opposed by power distributions capable of preventing it. Still other redistributions are obviously infeasible as opposing distributions of power are either invincible or at least capable of extracting prohibitive costs. Part but not all of what justifies unequal distributions of the ownership of income producing, civil, religious, military and other rights and privileges is the power of the existing distributions themselves. However, there is the surprising long-run power of knowledge of the intrinsic value of equality and of the value of other conditions, situations and things which can be attained in the process of growth. We have done little with the concept and reality of power at this conference. One lesson which can be learned from what we have and have not done in this respect is that the study of equity and power goes beyond economics to political science, military science, sociology, law and philosophy.

There is also the very important dynamics of growth trajectory which I mentioned earlier. This topic has not been entirely neglected at our conference. In addition to accumulation of physical capital, the three prime movers along growth trajectories are (a) technological change, (b) institutional change, and (c) improvements in the quality and, in some instances, the quantity of people (investments in human capital). The technological dynamics of growth trajectories have been explained and indeed defended by Hayami, Mellor, Sanders and Lynam, Byerlee and others. Hillman and

Monke place 'technology at the heart of the development process'. On the other hand, Johnston, Brandes, Vyas and others including Mellor, recognized the importance of policies, institutional changes and reforms but are justifiably cautious about lending support for the conclusion that destructive redistributions are needed.

Other authors went further into the institutional dynamics of the growth trajectory. We had papers by Petit, Sargent, Andrews and de Janvry, and Bromley and Verma (among others) some of which deal fruitfully with this topic. There are, of course, the previously mentioned problems of measurement, aggregation, changing power distributions and of whether knowledge of instrinsic values is possible which are particularly troublesome in dealing with the institutional dynamics of growth trajectories. In my view, the papers on institutional change and, particularly, the latter group of more venturesome papers were important in offsetting a tendency at this conference to neglect the institutional dynamics of growth trajectories. So often the problem is to find institutional changes to obtain more equality along existing possibilities lines without becoming involved in destructive redistributions and negative growth shifts to lower possibilities lines.

The human change element of growth trajectories has also been relatively neglected at our conference. A number of speakers have addressed themselves to the need to control increases in the numbers of people – equality among nations in willingness and ability to control population is an important aspect of the human dynamics of growth trajectories. Reyes, Hayami, and Sugai dealt with the adverse effect of high rates of population increase. However, changes in the quality of people through education may be even more fundamental than controlling numbers. Without scientists a country remains dependent on foreign technologies. Similar dependencies result from shortages of entrepreneurs, government administrators, doctors and, indeed, the teachers so important in the indigenous generation of human capital. Though the Sugai/Teixeira, Antle, Pudasaini and some other papers have stressed the role of education and extension work in improving the human agent, I have the general impression that we have not given as much attention to human capital formation as T.W. Schultz, our first Elmhirst lecturer, would desire.

I believe we need to expand our thinking to try to understand how the opportunities lines and indifference curves of Diagram 1 depend on firstly, which growth trajectory is followed and, secondly, the emphasis placed on technological, institutional and human change and on physical capital accumulation.

Growth trajectories and equity are profoundly and fundamentally affected by the international trading and financial relationships among countries. Important papers on this were given by Buchholz, Hillman and Monke, Longworth, and de Lobáo and Soares. These papers could provide the basis for developing a theme on international trade and financial relationships as they affect agriculture either for an IAAE main conference or for an inter-conference seminar.

## CONCLUSION

Let me close by recalling our President's stress in his address on the spiritual, moral and social dimensions of our work.

Reinhold Niebuhr, a prominent Christian theologian, has argued that the fruits of a person's life are his senses of

charity,
proportion,
justice

As most religions of the world are concerned with these same values, I think it is appropriate to stress them here. The theme of our conference has been growth and equity. Equity involves Niebuhr's senses of charity and justice. Many economists subsume the laws of dimishing productivity and of diminishing marginal utility under the single law of variable proportions. Thus, production, consumption and welfare economics are (collectively) concerned with proportion, charity and justice.

Our concerns about growth at this conference have been tempered by our concerns about the relationship of growth to equity – we sought the proper *proportionate* relationship between growth and equity. I believe the fruits of this conference include an improved sense, on our parts, of charity, proportion, and justice. If this is so, I believe it is because our two leaders, Professors Dams and Ohkawa, have provided us with a programme which has strengthened these senses. I thank them for what was referred to in the Presidential Address as 'moral and social leadership' in studying the 'political, social and economic systems' in which agriculture exists.

# Index